LISTENING TO HELOISE

THE NEW MIDDLE AGES

BONNIE WHEELER

Series Editor

The New Middle Ages presents transdisciplinary studies of medieval cultures. It includes both scholarly monographs and essay collections.

PUBLISHED BY ST. MARTIN'S PRESS:

Women in the Medieval Islamic World: Power, Patronage, and Piety
edited by Gavin R. G. Hambly

The Ethics of Nature in the Middle Ages: On Boccaccio's Poetaphysics
by Gregory B. Stone

Presence and Presentation: Women in the Chinese Literati Tradition
by Sherry J. Mou

The Lost Love Letters of Heloise and Abelard: Perceptions of Dialogue in Twelfth-Century France
by Constant J. Mews

Understanding Scholastic Thought with Foucault
by Philipp W. Rosemann

Constructions of Widowhood and Virginity in the Middle Ages
edited by Cindy L. Carlson and Angela Jane Weisl

For Her Good Estate: Elizabeth de Burgh (1295–1360)
by Frances Underhill

Motherhood and Mothering in Anglo-Saxon England
by Mary Dockray-Miller

Listening to Heloise: The Voice of a Twelfth-Century Woman
edited by Bonnie Wheeler

LISTENING TO HELOISE

THE VOICE OF A TWELFTH-CENTURY WOMAN

Edited by Bonnie Wheeler

St. Martin's Press
New York

LISTENING TO HELOISE

 For information, address St. Martin's Press, 175 Fifth Avenue, New York, N.Y. 10010.

ISBN 0-312-21354-9

Library of Congress Cataloging-in-Publication Data
Listening to Heloise:the voice of a twelfth-century woman/
edited by Bonnie Wheeler.
p. cm.—(The new Middle Ages)
Includes bibliographical references and index.
ISBN 0-312-21354-9
1. Héloïse, 1101–1164. I. Wheeler, Bonnie, 1944-.
II. Series.
BX4705.H463L57 2000
271'.97—dc21 [B]99–27776
CIP

Design by Letra Libre, Inc.

First Edition: April 2000
10 9 8 7 6 5 4 3 2 1

Dedicated to the memory of
John F. Benton

CONTENTS

SERIES EDITOR'S FOREWORD

The New Middle Ages contributes to medieval cultural studies through its scholarly monographs and essay collections. This series speaks in a contemporary idiom about specific but diverse practices, expressions, and ideologies in the Middle Ages; it aims especially to recuperate the histories of medieval women. *Listening to Heloise: The Voice of a Twelfth-Century Woman* is the fourteenth book in the series and the first collection of scholarly essays to be dedicated exclusively to the figure of Heloise, one of the most prominent and highly regarded monastic women of the twelfth century. The essays gathered here interrogate Heloise's place in the intellectual, monastic, erotic, and cultural tumult of her time. Hers is a story of both vast opportunity and equally complete confinement, since she came of age at a moment when it was still possible for a brilliant young woman to receive an education comparable to that of her male counterparts, a prospect that disappeared in the course of her own lifetime. These essays seek to distance the traditional view of Heloise from the lens of Abelard, and in so doing, to listen with untrammeled ears to a Heloise who has previously been eclipsed by Abelard. Here Heloise as writer, lover, and thinker occupies our full attention.

Bonnie Wheeler
Southern Methodist University

ACKNOWLEDGMENTS

The contributors to this volume have been exceptional collaborators, reading and commenting on drafts of each other's chapters and patiently enduring my requests for revisions. Linda Georgianna's "Any Corner of Heaven: Heloise's Critique of Monasticism" first appeared in *Mediaeval Studies* 49 (1987): 221–53 and is reprinted here in revised form with permission of the editors. I am grateful to the anonymous readers of St. Martin's Press for very pointed and useful critiques. Mary Martin McLaughlin has shared portions of her forthcoming book on Heloise, including the precise information on Heloise that we append to Monfrin's generally accepted chronology of the lives of Abelard and Heloise. With characteristic generosity and scholarly clarity, Professor McLaughlin has corrected my errors as she has taught me about Heloise. I am grateful to Dean Narayan Bhat of Dedman College, to the Department of English, and to the Medieval Studies Program of Southern Methodist University for providing aid for student assistants. Amy Golden and Louisa Benton were very helpful in this role, and Matthew Ervin's exemplary work can be seen in the bibliography. Many colleagues, especially John Carmi Parsons, have given aid, but none more so than Jeremy duQuesnay Adams, helper in all things, who has encouraged and abetted this project at every step.

CHRONOLOGY

Heloise and Peter Abelard

1079 Birth of Abelard at Le Pallet in Brittany (Loire-Atlantique), son of Lucia and Berengar.

1101? Birth of Heloise, daughter of Hersende, niece of Canon Fulbert of Notre Dame, Paris; perhaps related through both parents (although her father is unidentified) to a cadet branch of the Montmorency and other noble families of the Paris region.

1113–17 Abelard dominant in the world of the Paris schools.

1116? Heloise brought from Argenteuil to the home of her uncle Fulbert in the clerical quarter of the Île-de-la-Cité in Paris.

1116–17? Exchange of love letters of Heloise and Abelard. Secret love affair, followed by public scandal. The birth of their son, Astralabe; clandestine marriage. Heloise sent by Abelard to Argenteuil. Fulbert's vengeance: Abelard's castration.

1118/19 Heloise and Abelard take religious vows, she at Argenteuil, he at Saint-Denis.

1122 Abelard's views on St. Dionysius provoke a scandal at Saint-Denis; death of Abbot Adam, who was succeeded by Suger. Abelard, released from Saint-Denis, establishes an oratory dedicated to the Holy Trinity.

1122–27 Abelard resumes teaching at his oratory near Quincey in Champagne, now rededicated to the Paraclete.

1129 Abbot Suger of Saint-Denis appropriates abbey of Argenteuil where Heloise was prioress and expels its nuns. Abelard invites Heloise and the nuns loyal to her to the Paraclete, where they establish a new community.

1130–34 Establishment of the collaboration of Heloise and Abelard at the Paraclete. Composition of much of the Paraclete "corpus," which is largely completed by 1136/37. (For amplification, see Mary Martin McLaughlin, *Heloise and the Paraclete: A Twelfth-Century Quest,* forthcoming).

1131 (November 28) Innocent II: Letter confirming the prioress Heloise and her nuns in possession of the Paraclete, the earliest dated reference to her.

1131–32? Abelard writes his *Historia calamitatum,* in part to prepare the way for his departure from Saint-Gildas, which was probably final by 1133 at latest.

1142 (April 21) Abelard dies at the Cluniac priory of Saint-Marcel-sur-Saône.

1142? Founding of Sainte-Madeleine-de-Traînel, first of the Paraclete's dependencies.

1143/44? Peter the Venerable announces Abelard's death in letter of consolation to Heloise.

1144? (November 16) Abbot Peter delivers Abelard's body to Heloise for burial at the Paraclete.
Heloise's solicits Peter's aid in finding a prebend for her and Abelard's son, Astralabe.

1147 Heloise receives papal letter confirming possessions acquired by the Paraclete since its foundation.

1147/51? Founding of the Paraclete's second dependency, the abbey of La Pommeraye.

1153–63 Founding of the final four dependencies: Laval (c. 1153); Noëfort (bef. 1157); Saint-Flavit (bef. 1157); Boran or Saint-Martin-aux-Nonnettes (by 1163).

1163/64? (May 16) Heloise's death at the Paraclete, where she was buried in a crypt before the altar of the "Petit-Moustier."

ABBREVIATIONS

The following is our standard citation format for the *Historia calamitatum* and the *Epistulae:*

HC, ed. Monfrin 00, Hicks 00, Muckle 00 (Radice 00)
Ep. 2, *Ep.* 4, *Ep.* 6 for Heloise's three letters (numbered 1, 3, 5 by Radice)

No full scholarly edition of all the works of Abelard or Heloise yet exists, and even the numbering of their letters remains a source of confusion. Here we follow numbering established by André Duchesne in the 1616 edition of the *Opera Omnia* reprinted in PL 178:113–314, with *Ep.* 1 being the *Historia calamitatum,* and *Ep.* 2, 4, and 6 being the three letters of Heloise. Betty Radice follows Muckle in identifying Heloise's letters as 1, 3 and 5 in her translation of the correspondence, *The Letters of Abelard and Heloise.* The *Historia calamitatum* is referred to here by the pages of the Monfrin, Hicks, and Muckle editions; in notes, it is referred to as *HC.* The letters of Heloise are cited by the editions of Muckle and Hicks (as well as of Monfrin in the case of *Ep.* 2 and 4), with page references to the Radice translation.

CCCM	Corpus Christianorum: Continuatio Mediaevalis (Turnhout: Typographi Brepols Editores Pontificii, 1966-).
CCSL	Corpus Christianorum, Series Latina (Turnhout: Typographi Brepols, 1953-).
	Colloque *Pierre Abélard-Pierre le Vénérable.* Colloques internationaux du Centre national de la recherche scientifique 546 (Paris: CNRS, 1975).
Constable	Peter the Venerable, *The Letters of Peter the Venerable,* 2 vols., ed. Giles Constable, Harvard Historical Studies 78 (Cambridge, MA: Harvard University Press, 1967).
CSEL	Corpus scriptorum ecclesiasticorum Latinorum (Vienna-Leipzig: Hoelder-Pichler-Tempsky *for* Academia Litterarum Caesareae Vindobonensis [vols. 1–70], Academia Scientiarum Austriaca [vols. 71-], 1866-).
Ep. 2	Heloise, *Epistula* 2: "I. (Heloisae suae ad ipsum deprecatoria)," in "The Personal Letters Between Abelard and Heloise," ed. J. T. Muckle, C. S. B., *Mediaeval Studies* 15 (1953): 47–94, specifically: 68–73. "Appendice: I. Heloyse sue ad ipsum deprecatoria," in [Peter] Abelard, *Historia calamitatum, texte critique avec une introduction,* ed. J. Monfrin, Bibliothèque des Textes Philosophiques (Paris: J. Vrin, 1959, 1967), pp. 111–17. "II. Heloyse sue ad ipsum deprecatoria," in *La vie et les epistres, Pierres Abaelart et Heloys sa fame, Traduction du XIIIe siècle attribuée à Jean de*

Meun, avec une nouvelle édition des texts latins d'aprés le ms. Troyes. Bib. mun. 802. [Only one volume has yet been published]. *Tome I: Introduction, textes,* ed. Eric Hicks, Nouvelle Bibliothèque du Moyen Âge 16 (Paris: Champion-Slatkine, 1991), pp. 45–53.

Ep. 3 — Peter Abelard, *Epistula* 3:
"II. (Rescriptum ipsius ad ipsam)," in "The Personal Letters Between Abelard and Heloise," ed. Muckle, *Mediaeval Studies* 15 (1953): 47–94, specifically: 73–77.
"III. Heloise, dilectissime sorori sue in Christo," in *La vie et les epistres, Pierres Abaelart et Heloys sa fame,* ed. Hicks, pp. 54–60.

Ep. 4 — Heloise, *Epistula* 4:
"III. (Rescriptum ipsius ad ipsum)," in "The Personal Letters Between Abelard and Heloise," ed. Muckle, *Mediaeval Studies* 15 (1953): 47–94, specifically: 77–82.
"Appendice: II. Rescriptum ipsius ad ipsum," in [Peter] Abelard, *Historia calamitatum,* ed. Monfrin, pp. 117–24.
"IV. Unico suo post Christum," in *La vie et les epistres, Pierres Abaelart et Heloys sa fame,* ed. Hicks, pp. 60–69

Ep. 5 — Peter Abelard, *Epistula* 5:
"IV. (Ipse rursus ad ipsam)," in "The Personal Letters Between Abelard and Heloise," ed. Muckle, *Mediaeval Studies* 15 (1953): 47–94, specifically: 82–94.
"V. Sponse Christi, servus ejusdem," in *La vie et les epistres, Pierres Abaelart et Heloys sa fame* ed. Hicks, pp. 70–87.

Ep. 6 — Heloise, *Epistula* 6:
"V. (Item eadem ad eundem)," in "The Personal Letters Between Abelard and Heloise," ed. Muckle, *Mediaeval Studies* 15 (1953): 47–94, specifically: 94. (Text of introductory section only—this incomplete text is not cited unless expressly stated in the reference.)
"V. (Item eadem ad eundem)," in "The Letter of Heloise on the Religious Life and Abelard's First Reply," ed. J. T. Muckle, C. S. B., *Mediaeval Studies* 17 (1955): 240–81, specifically: 241–53 (full text).
"VI. Suo specialiter, sua singulariter," in *La vie et les epistres, Pierres Abaelart et Heloys sa fame,* ed. Hicks, pp. 87–106.

Ep. 7 — Peter Abelard, *Epistula* 7:
"VI. (Rescriptum ad ipsam de auctoritate vel dignitate ordinis sanctimonialium)," in "The Letter of Heloise on the Religious Life and Abelard's First Reply," ed. J. T. Muckle, C. S. B., *Mediaeval Studies* 17 (1955): 240–81, specifically: 253–81.
"VII. De ordine sanctimonialium," in *La vie et les epistres, Pierres Abaelart et Heloys sa fame,* ed. Hicks, pp. 107–147.

Ep. 8 — Peter Abelard, *Epistula* 8:
"VII. Institutio seu Regula Sanctimonialium," in "Abelard's Rulefor Religious Women," ed. T. P. McLaughlin, C. S. B., *Mediaeval Studies* 18 (1956): 241–92, specifically: 242–92.

HC — Peter Abelard, *Historia calamitatum:*
"(Abaelardi ad amicum suum consolatoria <Epistola>)" in "Abelard's Letter of Consolation to a Friend, (*Historia calamitatum*),"

	ed. J. T. Muckle, C. S. B., *Mediaeval Studies* 12(1950): 163–213, specifically: 175–211.
	"Historia calamitatum," in Abelard, *Historia calamitatum,* ed. Monfrin, pp. 63–109.
	"I. Abaelardi ad amicum suum consolatoria," in *La vie et les epistres, Pierres Abaelart et Heloys sa fame,* ed. Hicks, pp. 3–44.
Könsgen	[Anonymous], *Epistolae duorum amantium: Briefe Abaelards und Heloises?* ed. Ewald Könsgen, Mittellateinische Studien und Texte 8 (Leiden: E. J. Brill, 1974).
MGH SS	Monumenta Germaniae Historica, Scriptorum [Series], ed. [vols. 1–12, 16–23] Georg Heinrich Pertz, Societas Aperiendis Fontibus Rerum Germanicarum Medii Aevi, 32 vols. (Hanover: Impensis Bibliopolii Aulici Hahniani, 1826–1934)
PL	Patrologiae cursus completus, series Latina, ed. Jacques-Paul Migne, 221 vols. (Paris: Garnier, 1844-).
Problemata	Heloise, *Problemata Heloissae* in PL 178.677–730.
Radice	Peter Abelard and Heloise, *The Letters of Abelard and Heloise,* trans. Betty Radice (Harmondsworth: Penguin, 1974).
SBO	Bernard of Clairvaux, *Sancti Bernardi Opera,* ed. Jean Leclercq, Charles H. Talbot, and H. M. Rochais, 8 vols. (Rome: Editiones Cistercienses, 1957–75).
Trier	*Petrus Abaelardus (1079–1142): Person, Werk und Wirkung,* ed. Rudolf Thomas et al., Trierer Theologische Studien 38 (Trier: Paulines-Verlag, 1980).
Women Writers	Peter Dronke, *Women Writers of the Middle Ages. A Critical Study of Texts from Perpetua (†203) to Marguerite Porete (†1310)* (Cambridge: Cambridge University Press, 1984).

INTRODUCTION

LISTENING TO HELOISE

Bonnie Wheeler

> By a kind of holy portent . . . God has specially marked you out for heaven by calling you Heloise, derived from his own name of Elohim.
>
> —Abelard, *Epistle 4*

> Niemand liest oder hat je gelesen wie Du.
> [No one reads or has ever read as you do]
>
> —Hannah Arendt to Martin Heidegger, June 18, 1972

There are many "stories" of Heloise: the literary prodigy, passionate lover, reluctant bride, submissive wife, and adept abbess. Heloise is a model of the French public female intellectual, the first and one of a very few such figures before modern times. Great and learned women abounded in the Middle Ages, but not many others had what in later times would constitute the equivalent of a university education—an education denied women until the modern moment. Heloise's narrative comes to us in part in her own voice. She is one of history's most expressive writers; her letters glow with the supple, playful erudition that marks the twelfth century's vivid embrace of high Latinity. Stories of Heloise inevitably detail her intimate intellectual collaboration with Peter Abelard, her tutor, lover, husband, and fellow monastic. The *frisson* of their intensely passionate engagement often makes it difficult to distinguish the teacher from the taught, the dancer from the dance.

This volume locates Heloise in the volatile culture of twelfth century northern France in which she was a notable figure until her death in the mid–1160s. She came of age in the culturally liminal early decades of the twelfth century. Her story is one of closure as well as possibility: When Heloise was young, a woman might hope to be taught by the great masters of philosophy, and she might even dream of being counted in their number. By the time the institutional structures of the University of Paris were forged in the early thirteenth century, women had been thoroughly excluded from its formal institutional life. Even in her youth, however, Heloise was a *rara avis* whose fame for learning preceded her. Unlike most women for millennia before (and for nearly a millennium after), she claimed an identity of her own in addition to that provided by her familial and social networks. She was "supreme in her abundant literacy": Heloise was known for what she knew.

What do we know about Heloise before we begin to read this volume? We are less certain now than we used to be about many "facts" of Heloise's narrative. We do not, for instance, know the year of her birth. Most historians assume that she was born around 1100, but recently there has been speculation about an earlier birth date. Was she teenage, or might she have been in her late twenties when she met Abelard? Is it reasonable to imagine that Heloise might have left Argenteuil in her late twenties? Heloise's family origins are also, to some degree, a matter of speculation. We know she came from a family of aristocratic status and resources, and we can pinpoint the precise places in which she spent most of her life. We know from the Paraclete obituary that her mother's name was Hersinde; her uncle, the well-connected Fulbert, canon of the cathedral of Notre Dame in Paris, is listed in the same necrology. However, we do not know for certain who her father was. Was she illegitimate? Fulbert acted as her guardian; he brought his niece from Argenteuil to Paris where she was tutored by Abelard. Although there is no proof that Heloise was illegitimate, some have tried to assess her rank in late eleventh- and early twelfth-century northern French society partly on the basis of what social historians conclude about the treatment of illegitimate children in various social strata. In recent years we also have learned a great deal about the career opportunities available to educated women with or without patriarchal patrons, with or without monastic vows. Solid analysis has been done about the content and methods of Heloise's education and hence about her early years in the convent of Argenteuil, but we do not yet know whether she was expected from childhood to enter monastic life.

Heloise, as Mary Martin McLaughlin points out in chapter 1, is a woman already accruing significant power as a monastic ruler at the Paraclete when she receives a letter from Pope Innocent II and moves "into the light of history" on November 28, 1131. Around this same time, perhaps as late as 1132, Abelard arrogates her story as he folds it into his own coruscating autobiographical letter of complaint known as the *Historia calamitatum*. This letter was not addressed to her, but it provoked her intense response. We hear that response in the so-called Personal Letters (Betty Radice's well-known but problematic division) that she subsequently addressed to Abelard and in her later letters on religious life. This traditional listing and sequencing of Heloise's recorded writings should also include the love letters that Abelard reports exchanging with her at the time that they first knew each other. Constant J. Mews argues that we are able to identify excerpts of those letters of 1116/17 in a fifteenth-century manuscript copied by Johannes de Vepria that provides our earliest image of Heloise.

What do these current chapters establish about their subject? This collection focuses on Heloise as a compelling intellectual figure and a daring writer. As the first collection devoted to Heloise's life and writing, this volume is hardly comprehensive—it is an opening salvo. Each of these chapters, mostly by literary scholars, focuses a slightly different facet of Heloise's world and discourse. Mary Martin McLaughlin grounds our considerations with an authoritative historical overview of Heloise's career as a monastic ruler both during Abelard's lifetime and for the two decades after his death. Here we see Heloise absorbed in the major work of her independent adulthood: securing and expanding the Paraclete.

The rest of the volume then turns to the issues provoked by Heloise's literary *oeuvre.* Although the "authenticity controversy"—the scholarly debate about whether the historical Abelard and Heloise wrote the highly stylized correspondence traditionally attributed to them—does not drive contemporary analysis, it has been an irrepressible element of any conversation about the two. The long gap between their lifetimes and the earliest extant copy of their correspondence inevitably teases the imagination. The consistent artfulness that enthralls the reader has often troubled the historian. Heloise's elegantly composed letters, read in sequence with Abelard's replies, shape the divergent narratives of their romance as well as those of their public lives into a remarkable aesthetic achievement. In chapter 2, John Marenbon—historian of philosophy and author of the recent study *The Philosophy of Peter Abelard*—nails the authenticity controversy into a well-crafted coffin and tries to bury it (and its adherents) in the graveyard of mortally flawed arguments. Marenbon insists that clear thinking coupled with a respect for evidence requires scholars to acknowledge Heloise's authorship of her letters. Although Marenbon's premises go against the grain of postmodern inquiries and will provoke controversy, most of the scholars in this volume find themselves in agreement with his conclusion that the correspondence is the authentic work of Abelard and Heloise.

Constant J. Mews, like Marenbon, is an intellectual historian who has written widely on Abelard. In chapter 3, Mews presents the core of his study of the de Vepria fragments, usually called the *Epistulae duorum amantium,* arguing that these early letter-excerpts reveal a very different picture of the early flowering of the romance of Abelard and Heloise from that presented in the *Historia calamitatum.* Mews demonstrates Heloise's fluency as a collaborator in philosophic debates, especially about matters of ethics and love, as well as her control of complex letter-writing conventions. These innovative arguments are then tested in chapter 4 by historian of rhetoric John O. Ward and student of *dictamen* Neville Chiavaroli, who comb Mews's evidence to test its relevance to twelfth-century rhetorical practices. Ward's intricate analysis builds a formidable case for the general acceptance of Heloise's participation in the *Epistulae duorum amantium.* Ward argues that these early letter excerpts deepen our understanding of her biography, temperament, and cultural context as he asks, for example, just what sort of relationship Heloise might have had in mind when she proposed the famous *meretrix-non imperatrix* solution to their predicament as lovers. Could she, as Ward notes, perhaps have meant a familiar form of clerical concubinage, with its quasi legal guarantees? Such relations were never formally sanctioned by ecclesiastical authorities, but these widespread and traditional long-term arrangements generally were acknowledged even in canonical sources before reformers set out to purge the church and the canon law of "Nicolaitism" and to forbid any form of clerical marriage. Ward's notion that Heloise may have been suggesting a durable liaison gives us an alternative reading to the dominant romanticized "story" in which Heloise is cast as an implausibly farsighted precursor of an eighteenth-century or 1920s adherent of "free love." His analysis strengthens the boldness of Heloise's hyperbolic *meretrix* in that often-quoted and easily distorted rhyming formula.

Ward argues that Heloise's early writing demonstrates the keen grasp and explicit use of classical literature and rhetorical conventions that mark her later writing; particular aspects of her artful control are demonstrated in subsequent chapters by literary analysts. In chapter 5, Katarina Wilson and Glenda McLeod show how Heloise's subtle persistence finally achieves Abelard's rhetorical if not ethical conversion. In chapter 6, Phyllis R. Brown and John C. Peiffer II explore some ways in which Heloise refracts her own subjectivity through her response to pagan classical works, especially Ovid's *Heroides,* "to explore potential new identities, not imagined by classical authors, that she and Abelard might assume." In chapter 7, Jane Chance furthers this argument in her analysis of Heloise's inversion of Abelard's presentation of himself as mythological hero. Chance argues that Heloise "substitutes a Boethian manning of the hero as Christian." These chapters focus on the complex dialectical energy of the Abelard–Heloise correspondence, exposing differing facets of the ethical, emotional, rhetorical, and intellectual processes by which Heloise educates Abelard. In each case, the authors note the moral clarity and intellectual motility that mark Heloise's writing as she masters the master.

These initial chapters demonstrate Heloise's imaginative and intellectual control of philosophical and rhetorical traditions. The central chapters then follow the trajectory mapped by Linda Georgianna when she examined Heloise's spiritual self-understanding within monastic traditions. Georgianna's 1987 article is updated here in chapter 8. This chapter, along with chapter 9 by Peggy McCracken, chapter 10 by Donna Alfano Bussell, and chapter 11 by Morgan Powell, probes Heloise's third letter (*Ep.* 6). Chapters 8, 10, and 11 explore Heloise's sense of the urgent need to reform monastic life and principles to accommodate new communities of religious women. What did Heloise see as the nature of needed reforms (Georgianna, Powell)? What did she view as the requirements and standards for initiation into monastic life, or the nature of that passage (Bussell)? How does she theorize issues of difference, especially in relation to bodily practices (McCracken) and gender (McCracken, Powell)? How does she write both within and to a religious community (Powell)? Chapter 12 by Alcuin Blamires and chapter 13 by Brian Patrick McGuire are linked by a concern common to most contributors to this volume: How did Heloise bring Abelard to recast his notion of consolation? How did she interpret the Benedictine Rule and traditions, especially in regard to such issues as consolation (Blamires, McGuire, Georgianna) and friendship (McGuire)? Powell explores a neglected internal hermeneutic of Heloise's letters, attempting to listen to Heloise with the ears of her monastic daughters. In Powell's essay, Heloise is heard as only one voice in a performance constructed for the monastic audience of the Paraclete, possibly, but not necessarily, by Heloise herself. Her life becomes a text that gives birth to a community identity. Her physical maternity is addressed in chapter 14 by Juanita Feros Ruys, who shows that, even as a mother who separated from her child, Heloise inhabited, expressed, and even defended maternity. In her obituary, the nuns of the Paraclete recollect her as their brilliant mother: "mater nostre religionis Heloisa, prima abbatissa, documentis et religionis clarissima, spem bonam ejus nobis vita donante, feliciter migravit ad Dominum." This epideictic recognition of Heloise's practical and spiritual maternity is the first record of her historical reception. Chapter 15 by Deborah Fraioli concludes the volume with an example of the modern cultural reception accorded Heloise, in this case by the ironic, magisterial encyclopedist Pierre Bayle. As this example suggests, Heloise was and remains a touchstone for the problematic reception of vibrant intellectual women.

By considering Heloise as a thinker and writer, and especially as an individual separate from Abelard, this collection also indicates how much more there was to Heloise's life than Abelard could have imagined. Heloise was, after all, a great institution builder long after Abelard's death, and her full story as an abbess has yet to be told.

Historically informed biographies of Heloise are needed; happily, one is forthcoming in this book series from Mary Martin McLaughlin.

The current volume whets our appetite for further knowledge of Heloise in her context. In the realm of social history, one hopes for a closer, more time-sensitive consideration of her putative social contexts and origins: "minor aristocracy" is inadequate and anachronistic as a categorical label. Good comparisons can be made by considering Robert Bautier's work on Abelard and John Benton's on Suger. In the realm of politics and diplomacy, historians might consider Heloise's possible adult alignments with aristocratic networks whose often overlapping boundaries and interaction must be seen as the ground for any comprehensible analysis of contemporary power structures. In the orbit of the Capetian court, the Montmorency and Garlande factions—sometimes allied and sometimes in conflict, but always competing—merit a look. The meticulous prosopographies of Bautier and Benton have shown the way here; their researches may help us map the track of Heloise's careful exercise of diplomatic initiative as abbess of the Paraclete and perhaps illumine her earlier involvement with Abelard. The sympathy of key members of the Champagne-Blois-Chartres dynasty, self-evidently crucial to Abelard's foundation of the Paraclete and to its continuing security under Heloise and her successors, deserves exploration along the paths that have been expertly charted by Michel Bur. More speculatively, is it possible to find documentary evidence for any interaction between Abelard's kinsmen and Heloise? When she was abbess, did she distance herself from them thoroughly, or did some residual connection survive?

In this vein, is there nothing more we can discover about Astralabe, for whose eventual benefice, as we know, Heloise lobbied Peter the Venerable? Further work might reveal alignments with yet other politically active members of the Cluniac party as well as with the often-contrarian Cistercian faction and the dense family network of Bernard of Clairvaux, locally important on either side of the Champenois-Burgundian border. Châtillon-sur-Seine and Montbard, the two foci of Bernard's inherited familial influence, were not far distant from the Paraclete and its properties. The report of Bernard's lack of hostility to Heloise and of her use of Cistercian reforms at her monastery are clues too blatant to ignore.

There is far more to be gleaned about Heloise's intellectual stances: Where do we locate her in the thought patterns of her moment? What were her historical ideas? What was her knowledge of, and interest in, church history? Peter the Venerable's description of her as the Miriam, Deborah, and Penthesilea of her age is clearly a double-edged compliment. How would Heloise have credited his comparison of her to Deborah, an exemplary Jewish religious leader, indeed a Judge of Israel, responsible for forty years of peace with the Philistines but also to Penthesilea the Amazon queen? Did the abbot of Cluny celebrate her defiance of convention in her daring earlier life and in her later life as esteemed abbess, or was he praising her for exchanging that defiance for monastic submission?

There is a need for further study of Heloise's other writings that focus not only on her subjectivity but also on the "cosmography," as George Steiner says in another context, "of the thinking heart." What does it suggest in psychic terms that Heloise cultivates the language of humility and celebrates the position of victim? What might close semiotic scrutiny of the *Letters* and the *Epistulae duorum amantium* show us about her perceptions of the makeup and movement of the will and the psyche: *cor, anima/animus, mens, intentio, opus/operatio, peccatum/vitium,* and so on. Her use of these terms might usefully be compared with their uses by Abelard, Bernard, and Hildegard—and, of course, the likely master source, Augustine. Historians of literary romance might look particularly at ways Heloise connects sexual and spiritual desire with renunciation and suffering. Furthermore, as Peter the Venerable says, Heloise provided "public instruction" for her monastic community: what then was her pedagogical philosophy? The *Problemata Heloissae* is a very rich source, little explored in this collection, for consideration of her theoretical as well as pragmatic discussion of the spiritual and intellectual formation of women in religious communities. In this respect Heloise might usefully be contrasted with Abelard and compared with Jerome. Mary Martin McLaughlin elsewhere demonstrates that Jerome's Marcella was the model, but the whole range of Jerome's commentaries on the education of women (in, for example, his letter to Paula on the education of Eustochium) might provoke our curiosity.

This volume amplifies our understanding of Heloise's magisterial accomplishments as the products of an original and probing mind. Her philosophic and religious ideas are marked by brilliant insight and wide intellectual range. Furthermore, she lived her ideas about the morally profound and philosophically alert life: she understood, embodied, and furthered Abelard's doctrine of intentionalism. As these chapters collectively demonstrate, the totality of her commitment to Abelard—she was his comforter, his own paraclete—did not cloud the clarity, integrity, and palpable passion with which she pursued the work of her monastic life. The study of Heloise is strengthened by analyses found in this volume that map the rich, allusive processes of her writing. As we delve into Heloise's words, we begin to understand more deeply her intellectual collaboration with Abelard. He taught popes, princes, historians, and philosophers, but she was his best student. She was also his best and most subtle teacher. That new "story" of Heloise is one reinforced in this volume. It is elegantly stated in the Schaffhausen epitaphs—Heloise was Peter Abelard's equal in feelings, deeds, and intellectual skill: *Ilia suo Petro par sensu, moribus, arte.*

CHAPTER 1

HELOISE THE ABBESS: THE EXPANSION OF THE PARACLETE

Mary Martin McLaughlin

A survey of the innovative monastic program of Heloise and Abelard introduces a closer study of her governance of the Paraclete in its social and economic setting.

God has granted such grace in every one's eyes to that sister of mine who rules over the others that the bishops love her as a daughter, the abbots as a sister, the laity as a mother . . . and all alike marvel at her piety, her prudence and the incomparable sweetness of her patience in all things.

—Abelard, *Historia calamitatum*

If Heloise seems at last on the very verge of liberation from her long imprisonment in the "authenticity debate," in current scholarship the first abbess of the Paraclete has, it seems, not yet fully escaped the constraints of the correspondence.[1] There are, however, at least two passages in the early letters that reveal more clearly the larger aims of her collaboration with Abelard at the Paraclete and the intentions of the new project on which they had embarked. Heloise guides us in this direction in her first letter, when she reminded Abelard of the "many important works the fathers have written to instruct, encourage, and console holy women" and reproached him for his failure to offer her and her nuns similar consolation.[2] Pursuing this theme at length in his second letter to her and offering the consolation she sought, Abelard urged his "inseparable companion" to "see and understand how the Lord has fished us up from the depths of this most perilous sea by the dragnets of his mercy . . . as if he were preserving us for some noble purposes, . . . as if he were offended and aggrieved because these talents of learning that he entrusted to us were not being used for the honor of his name."[3]

When he wrote these words, Abelard and Heloise were perhaps already launched on a truly innovative enterprise, the body of works that is at once the outcome and the record of their collaboration in the creation of a new community. In important respects both like and unlike the "works of the fathers," theirs was as a whole an achievement unparalleled in the monastic literature of the twelfth century. It would give the Paraclete texts that no other women's community of their time could boast. Their talents produced not only an "institute" or "rule" for nuns, along with the letters that preceded it,[4] but also the hymns, sermons, treatises, and a second dialogue, the *Problemata,* which completed a distinctive and coherent monastic program. Embracing virtually every aspect of life at the Paraclete, from its daily routine to its scriptural studies, this extraordinarily personal program gave shape to a "feminized" version of the "textual community" that is, as concept and reality, perceptively examined in Brian Stock's recent study.[5] In this community and the texts of its founders, the influences of two particularly innovative movements of the twelfth century, the ideas of an "intellectual renascence" and the ideals of an "evangelical awakening" came together directly, to achieve their most original contemporary embodiment.[6]

If Abelard's contribution to this program was by far the larger quantitatively, Heloise's role in its inspiration and direction was also critically important. As it is portrayed in the works themselves, her share in their production was an active one, moving from simple requests to quite detailed proposals, explaining what she wanted and why she wanted it. This is true even of the texts ascribed wholly to Abelard. In the preface to his first series of hymns, for example, he attributes to her the extensive and detailed argument justifying this undertaking.[7]

In responding to another of her requests, this time for a commentary on the early chapters of Genesis, Abelard emphasized her insistence, and his mock resistance, in the words of St. Paul. These need not, perhaps, be taken literally to convey an essential truth about the exigency of her initiatives: "I have given way to vanity; it was you who drove me to it."[8] Similarly, it was at her request that he assembled a collection of sermons intended, it seems, for refectory reading rather than for actual preaching. His compositions for the Paraclete itself were probably a careful selection from the sermons now included in a mixed printed collection, a selection that marked the unfolding of sacred history from the Annunciation through Pentecost.

It is, however, in her third letter and her *Problemata* that we meet Heloise at her most active in the role that dominates her share in the creation of the Paraclete program. As Heloise the "questioner," the maker of "just requests," she was, it seems, the first woman of her time to speak to the larger issues of the expanding religious life of women. The first also to raise the question of the "authority" for this life, she would examine in detail and in the perspectives of women's differences from men the problems now posed more acutely by the vigor and diversity of their responses to the religious movements of their time.[9] Among its great abbesses, Petronilla of Fontevraud, Hildegard of Bingen, and Herrad of Hohenbourg, Heloise was alone in raising critical, often original, and even prescient questions concerning why and how women should live this life. With these questions she initiated in the correspondence and in other works for the Paraclete a major testament to the quests that made the "following of Christ" central to what has been called the "reformation of the twelfth century."[10]

For her role as abbess, too, she might seem uniquely qualified, especially by her learning, but also by its combination with her experience of the traditional monastic life in her early years and, later, in the decade after her return to Argenteuil. Indeed, judging by her placement there as a child and her uncle's remarkable, and fateful, concern for her education, it is not unlikely that she was intended from the first for the vocation and office in which she was to spend more than half of her life.

But the singularities of this life should not blind us to her share in another kind of female experience, that of the growing multitude of women who seemed often, in her own critical view, to be found among those "rushing without sufficient discretion to the monastic life."[11] Whether women were drawn by religious fervor or driven by social pressures—among these a growing population and adverse changes in dowry and inheritance practices—their numbers, in the thousands, would far outrun the places available in existing communities. To meet the needs of these women and their families, as the currents of monastic reform and social change moved more rapidly in the early twelfth century, new foundations like the Paraclete multiplied in impressive, even astonishing numbers. In contrast with the preceding century, which saw only forty-six new communities of women in various parts of France, by the end of the twelfth century there would be some three hundred. This meant, Bruce Venarde concludes, that there were at least as many new foundations for women in France in this one century as in the five preceding centuries combined.[12]

Not only women rejected by their husbands, but women fleeing from them, or from marriage itself, swelled the numbers of those taking refuge or finding new opportunities in the monastic life.[13] Though Heloise argued the case against it with exceptional learning, opposition to marriage and remarriage was far from uncommon among twelfth-century women, even if it was more rarely acted upon with the determination of a Christina of Markyate.[14] Representing more than simply resistance or opposition to marriage itself, however, in this context Heloise belonged to a perhaps larger, more diverse company of women, the concubines and wives of priests and other clerics, whose uncertain status was increasingly threatened by reforming popes and their supporters. Having yielded against her better judgment to the marriage that was her and Abelard's undoing, Heloise entered the married state at a time when the "long Indian summer" of clerical marriage was turning sharply colder.[15] The more aggressive drive against this practice would add the women involved to the diverse groups seeking refuge or a new way of life during this time.

Just as Heloise shared with a multitude of her female contemporaries the kinds of experience that might lead to the monastic life, so too her Paraclete would mirror the other changes touched on here, the monastic expansion of the time, the social and economic forces that impelled it, and the opportunities for diversity and experiment it fostered. It is as ruler of the Paraclete, after all, that Heloise herself moved into the light of history for the first time and on the same day, November 28, 1131, in a letter of Pope Innocent II.[16] When she arrived with her companions in the "forested and half-settled" countryside northwest of Troyes, she faced the hard beginnings of most new communities. Material support was evidently a pressing need for a prioress, as she was then, who would soon make more exigent requests to meet the spiritual demands of her new foundation. Even as these were being answered, however, her neighbors may already have foreseen, and contributed to, the Paraclete's future prosperity.

Heloise can hardly have been established at the Paraclete for much longer than two years when Abelard was moved to the words of praise quoted in the epigraph. She would only have begun to assume the challenging roles of "model" and "teacher" that would be hers in implementing their ambitious program for the new community. But she was already well launched, it seems successfully, on the still more demanding tasks of abbess and administrator, confronting the complex realities that shaped the life of her abbey and its social environment.

During the thirty-five years of her abbacy, the last twenty and more without Abelard's collaboration, hers was clearly the real authority and responsibility for the governance of the Paraclete, for its spiritual reputation and the recruitment of its nuns, for its well-being and success. Her sense of the demands imposed by these obligations is suggested by one particularly revealing question among her *Problemata:* she asked how we are to reconcile Christ's injunction to take no thought for the morrow with St. Paul's counsel about "exercising authority with anxious care."[17] What made the Paraclete successful, it appears, was precisely the careful exercise of authority by this "prudent" abbess whose practical accomplishments were manifest in the high regard and material advancement she won for her community. At first with Abelard's help, but largely through her own energies and administrative gifts—and the response these evoked in prospective benefactors—Heloise gradually achieved the considerable prosperity reflected in the charters of her middle and later years.

Although the surviving evidence does not let us follow the earlier stages of growth in detail, its outcome is summed up in a papal letter of 1147.[18] The longest document in the cartulary for her time, this very specific inventory of the Paraclete's possessions gives us a measure not only of Heloise's achievement but of her administrative acumen, her concern for the enumeration of every donation, no matter how small. In less than two decades after its foundation, she had acquired for her community, through the benefactions of clerics and lay people, goods and properties ranging in character and value from an annual gift of twenty hens to mills and ovens, tithes and tolls, and extensive forests, fields, and vineyards scattered through more than sixty villages, chiefly in southwestern Champagne and neighboring regions. Including eventually at least ten granges or compact centers of agricultural exploitation, these acquisitions were augmented by further donations during her later years, to remain throughout the medieval centuries a most substantial portion of the Paraclete's endowment.[19]

Yet even this brief survey of its possessions may seem rather more impressive than the reality. Although this abbey enjoyed the favor of popes and kings as well as the patronage of the counts and countesses of Blois-Champagne, its chief benefactors were members of local castellan and knightly families.[20] During this period families of the lower aristocracy were, in general, most active in the founding and support of new communities of women. Modest donations and bequests also came to Heloise's community from those lower in the social scale, the holding of the wife of Payen the saddler, for example, and vineyards from Gaucher the mason, along with houses from other ordinary men and women.[21] As historian Sir Richard Southern has observed, for the Paraclete and for other new foundations of the time, their endowments consisted not of the lavish grants of earlier centuries but largely of "clippings" from the estates of donors and the tithes and churches dispersed through these holdings.[22] Such often fragmented and scattered properties must have imposed on Heloise, as on others in her situation, a heavy and distracting burden of administration, intruding on the monastic peace and contemplation so important to Abelard's ideal.[23]

In this as in other ways, the price of success was inextricable involvement in the social and economic structures of local society and the constant pressure of its needs and practices. From the beginning, for instance, and despite Abelard's hostility to this practice, the Paraclete had accepted from both lay and ecclesiastical donors gifts of church tithes and became in considerable measure economically dependent on them.[24] The effort to secure these and other possessions led inevitably to the conflicts and litigation he also deplored. This is not to suggest that Heloise was a litigious abbess, like her determined successor, Melisende, or her still more formidable contemporary, Abbess Petronilla of Fontevraud, who engaged for more than a decade in a fierce and ultimately successful battle with Bishop Ulger of Angers over the rights to important bridges and tolls.[25] On the contrary, Heloise seems to have maintained the most amicable relations with local ecclesiastical authorities, enjoying the friendship and patronage most particularly of the archbishops of Sens and the bishops of Troyes as well as the good will of local priests and clerics.[26]

Although the surviving records of her abbacy offer no evidence of disputes with secular lords, there is testimony to the kinds of conflicts that were most likely to arise when two monastic communities shared portions of the same properties or income. Such was the case in the three conflicts of which there is evidence from her time. Two of these involved prolonged disputes over tithes with the male abbeys of Saint-Pierre in Troyes and Saint-Jacques in Provins.[27] The third dispute is more important because it reveals most clearly the Paraclete's economic environment and the kind of competition the abbey faced; this episode also suggests what Heloise may have learned in various relations with her closest monastic neighbor. This was the Cistercian abbey of Vauluisant, with which she was engaged for some years in conflicts over the use and the boundaries of certain properties, chiefly those lying between the two abbeys, in which both had an interest. Both houses had been founded at the same time, in the late 1120s, and both had received donations from members of many of the same local families.

Often involving quite elaborate arrangements for the exchange and division of properties, the agreement of 1144 between the two abbeys was intended to resolve their differences by defining boundaries, arranging for the common use of certain forests, and enabling each to consolidate its holdings.[28] The particular significance of this agreement, confirming an apparent pact of friendship between the two abbeys, is that it shows Heloise in a close encounter with the local representative of the great monastic land developers and managers of the twelfth century. The Cistercians dominated the "phenomenal proliferation" of monastic houses in the heavily wooded and sparsely settled land of the bailliage of Troyes during the half century between 1115, when Clairvaux was founded, and the founding of Sellières in 1168.[29] Five abbeys appeared during Heloise's lifetime, and their numerous granges dotted the entire region. Far from renouncing the kind of property from which most other monasteries derived their income, as we used to believe, Cistercians monks, we now know, "were always involved in the various activities that characterized the evolving economy of the twelfth century."[30] With their concentration on properties organized granges worked by a corps of lay brothers, the Cistercians offered their contemporaries a model of efficient land management, "one of the masterpieces of medieval planning."[31]

Illustrating some important principles of this economic model, the settlement of the issues in dispute between the Paraclete and Vauluisant sought to provide specifically for such divisions and exchanges of property that, wherever possible, the holdings of each abbey might be contiguous or otherwise in keeping with its needs. Vauluisant, for example, ceded to the Paraclete all of the woods the monks possessed in the region of Pouy while retaining the arable land. It was agreed also that if either abbey should in future receive gifts of property in an area ceded to the other, such gifts would be added to the properties already ceded.

Although consolidation seems to have been a major goal of the agreement, retention by each abbey of some control of divided properties often apparently played a part in these arrangements. The special importance of forests in these divisions is underscored by recent studies noting the involvement of Vauluisant, beginning about 1140, in the mining and forging of iron, which required generous supplies of wood.[32] Pointing up also the place of grazing animals and pasturage in the monastic economy, Vauluisant, for example, ceded to the Paraclete a part of another forest, with the reservation that the woods could be cut only enough to allow the passage of carts and that the Paraclete might not pasture its pigs there without permission from Vauluisant, which retained possession of the acorns.[33] There is no evidence that these somewhat complicated arrangements caused difficulty during Heloise's lifetime, but they may well have led to the conflicts that apparently became endemic by the century's end.[34]

The settlement of the Paraclete's dispute with Vauluisant took place at Traînel, in the presence of Lord Anseau, the mediator and a principal donor to both abbeys, and members of his family as well as Heloise herself and the abbot of Vauluisant. Traînel, already the site of her first daughter house, was here a scene of the kind of "conflict resolution" that lets us glimpse the small world of friends, neighbors, and local rivals that was the setting of the Paraclete and its abbess. Like members of similar communities, female and male, she and her nuns played their essential roles in sustaining a social fabric whose fragilities often demanded such repairs. A half century later a lady of the family of Traînel, perhaps a granddaughter-in-law of Lord Anseau, presided over still another settlement of this ongoing dispute between the Paraclete and its Cistercian rival.

Since, economically speaking, communities of women were often at a disadvantage both in the competition for donations and in the management of their properties, there was clearly much to be learned from the Cistercians. Indeed, anyone dealing with them needed a good head for business, and we may suspect that Heloise's managerial acumen was honed by association with her Cistercian neighbors. Whether she learned the lesson of consolidation from them or not, the practice is evident in what we know of her management of property. Although, as the confirmation charter demonstrates, the Paraclete controlled property in more than eighty places, its holdings were much more compact than those of Fontevraud. With one exception, all of the Paraclete properties in 1147 were within twenty miles of the mother house; "a vast majority were within ten miles in a region reaching north from the Paraclete across the Seine and south and east toward Troyes."[35] Although both the Paraclete and Fontevraud were most fortunate in the managerial talents of their abbesses, Fontevraud is highly exceptional, especially for a community of women, in the survival of an extraordinary number of its early records; more than two hundred charters from its first two decades, 1100 to 1120, are extant.[36]

Already reflected or foreshadowed in Heloise's arrangements with Vauluisant is the organization of the Paraclete properties in granges or centers of exploitation, near or on which several of the daughter houses were situated. The territory lying around and between the Paraclete and Vauluisant encompassed at least five of the Paraclete granges.[37] Another essential feature of the Cistercian model was the use of lay brothers as a highly disciplined workforce. From this, too, Heloise may have learned something about the management of the brothers who provided much manual labor for her community.

Like other monasteries of women not affiliated with a male house or order, the Paraclete was served by one or more chaplains—clerics, it seems, more often than monks—who performed necessary religious functions.[38] The group of lay brothers supplying manual labor naturally outnumbered the chaplains, though we cannot say how numerous these *conversi* or *fratres* were in Heloise's time. In 1156 she was granted permission to bury deceased lay brothers in the nuns' cemetery, since they had no burial ground of their own.[39] This fact suggests that at that time their number was not very large; no doubt both chaplains and lay brothers became more numerous with the expansion of the Paraclete. There is, however, no evidence at all to support the view that in the twelfth century these men constituted a distinctive entity or community, either of the kind that Abelard had envisaged in his wishfully inspired plan for a "double monastery" or of the kind that formed part of the institutional structure of Fontevraud, though the lay brothers were subordinated to the abbess of the Paraclete or the prioresses at the dependencies.[40] With its lay brothers and lay sisters subject to the authority of the abbess, the organization of the Paraclete had, it seems, developed along lines close to those followed by similar autonomous houses as well as female abbeys associated with the Cistercian order.[41]

If the Paraclete was involved in relations both competitive and amicable with male abbeys in its region, especially with Vauluisant, as the first community of women in the countryside northwest of Troyes, it had the field very much to itself in these early decades. Its dominance of this region of western Champagne may, in fact, help to explain the paucity of Cistercian abbeys of women and Premonstratensian houses there in the twelfth century.[42] From the start the fortunes of the Paraclete had been closely and favorably bound up in its relationships with neighboring families belonging to the "old aristocracy" of the region. Among the most generous of its early benefactors, an important patron of local monasteries, Lord Anseau I of Traînel was directly engaged in the establishment of the first Paraclete dependency, Sainte-Madeleine-de-Traînel; other near neighbors were the castellan family of Nogent, one of whose members had donated the land on which Abelard's original oratory had been built.[43] Approving the donations of their knightly fiefholders, these castellan lords and others continued to provide support and protection to a community that amply answered their own social and religious needs. It was evidently a relationship of great mutual advantage; Heloise was a good neighbor to her noble friends after their deaths as well as during their lifetimes, even going so far as to obtain papal permission to provide burial places in the community's cemetery for those under interdict, if this penalty had not been incurred for their own crimes.[44]

Satisfying a more urgent need of these families, the Paraclete offered an honorable and dignified life to those of their female members for whom the alternative of marriage was not available, convenient, desirable, or desired. Among women in this period, as we have learned, many others besides Heloise showed signs of resistance to marriage or remarriage.[45] During these years the growing appeal of the Paraclete, and its inescapable ties with its noble benefactors, clearly forced its abbess to confront further challenges to the ideals she shared with Abelard and to her own administrative prudence. Along with the gifts there came in increasing numbers the kinswomen of the givers; in at least eighteen cases up to 1147, donations were made specifically in behalf of daughters, sisters, nieces, and in one instance, a mother, who became nuns of the Paraclete.[46] In some cases, too, the benefactions were accompanied by the benefactors themselves; we find a number of women at this time and later making donations in their own right for their reception at the Paraclete, or in behalf of daughters and nieces.[47]

Coming as children or young girls or as widows and as wives separated from their husbands (as converted or rejected wives), in all of their diversities of age, talents, and commitment to the monastic life, some of these prospective nuns were no doubt drawn by genuine vocations for this life; others, perhaps more numerous, came to suit family strategies rather than their own wishes. We know nothing at all, in fact, about most of these women as individuals, let alone their motives; we know only their names and family connections in some cases, like those of Abelard's nieces, Agnes and Agatha, and Hersende and another Heloise, and Ermelina, an early recruit who became a nun in 1133, bringing with her half of the mill at Crevecoeur, some vineyards, and other properties.[48] But we may imagine that, along with other motives, many of them responded to the magnetism of Heloise herself—some drawn by the high standards of learning and spirituality she strove to maintain, others taking a special comfort in the example and achievement of an abbess who, perhaps like some of them, had entered the monastic life less than willingly.

If the needs and strategies of noble families supplied the Paraclete with most of its recruits, the family connections of these women posed another problem, the threat of aristocratic domination, which had particularly troubled Abelard. Indeed, his anxieties about the influence of "these people with their easy confidence in their birth" had led him to enjoin the nuns of the Paraclete never, if it could possibly be avoided, to choose an abbess from a noble family, especially one whose proximity and power might be damaging to the community.[49] He was quite right to be anxious about a kind of social dominance that was the nearly inescapable fate of Benedictine monasticism, whether male or female, but he was exceedingly unrealistic in entertaining the notion that this influence could be avoided in a twelfth-century environment. For Heloise, the founding of La Pommeraye, her second daughter house, may well have been a troubling case in point.

Domination on either side, however, is hardly the word to describe her relations with her social world. The charters of her abbacy show her a sturdy, if usually conciliatory, defender of the interests of her abbey. Yet it is also clear that she was no more able than the rulers of similar communities, however innovative their beginnings or exalted their ideals, to escape the demands arising from the social needs and changes that had, in fact, fostered the proliferation of new foundations like the Paraclete. Its remarkable growth during the 1140s and 1150s meant that during these decades Heloise came to preside over a small "order" or congregation and at its center a community larger and apparently more distinguished than its neighbors, filled with the daughters of noble families and facing the problems of an expansion that Abelard could hardly have foreseen and would almost certainly have deplored.

Six daughter houses sprang up between the early 1140s when Sainte-Madeleine-de-Traînel was founded as a colony of nuns from the Paraclete—and, perhaps significantly, dedicated to the patron of penitent sinners—and the early 1160s, when the last priory is mentioned in the charters.[50] Beginning with the first foundation, groups of nuns were sent out from the mother abbey to each of its dependencies: La Pommeraye, about 1147; Laval, Saint-Flavit, and Noëfort in the 1150s; the most distant, Boran, or Saint-Martin-aux-Nonnettes, north of Senlis in the valley of the Oise, a former abbey, became a priory of the Paraclete sometime before 1163, perhaps in the late 1150s.[51]

A noteworthy reflection of the appeal of the monastic life to women during these years, this rapid and at the same time circumscribed expansion raises questions about the particular social and religious forces that propelled a growth so intensive and so soon completed. Given the increasing numbers of women's houses in this and other parts of Champagne, perhaps it amply met the current and continuing needs of women and their families in the region to which it was largely confined; four of the six dependencies lay within a radius of twenty-five or thirty miles of the Paraclete.[52] Their proximity to the mother house also suggests that they may have served as outlets for the growing numbers of women at the Paraclete itself. Perhaps, too, the strains this expansion imposed on the human and material resources of the mother house may have discouraged the further extension of its congregation. Such strains are suggested by the tone of the Paraclete statutes.[53] In a time of rapid economic change, even her abbey's relative prosperity may have seemed precarious to an abbess whose recollections of its early poverty were apparently vivid. With characteristic foresight, Heloise may have anticipated the approaching end of the golden age of monastic expansion in this region, an end that was evidently reached in the decades after her death.[54] For all of these reasons, probably, the congregation over which Heloise presided remained a small one, nothing so large or so highly centralized as the order over which the abbess of Fontevraud exercised a supreme authority.[55]

Although the relations between the Paraclete and its five priories are not fully or explicitly defined in the early charters, Heloise and her community evidently reserved the right to appoint and remove the prioresses; in other ways, too, these dependencies were more completely subject to the Paraclete than was her second and most distinguished daughter, the abbey of La Pommeraye.[56] Reflecting aristocratic influence at the most exalted level, its foundation seems to have been a joint venture of Heloise and the dowager Countess Mathilde of Champagne, the widow of Abelard's benefactor, Count Thibaut, and in her own view the badly treated mother of the young Count Henry.[57] Built on land belonging to the Paraclete and ceded by Heloise to her friend, the new foundation enjoyed the patronage of the countess, who spent her last years, died, and was buried there.[58] Probably because of this high connection, La Pommeraye was the only dependency to be raised to the status of an abbey.

From the outset there was thus a special and potentially troublesome tie between the Paraclete and this daughter house. No doubt with Heloise's approval, its first abbess, Gertrude, "a noble and honorable woman," had been chosen from the nuns of the Paraclete.[59] But future abbesses were to be elected unanimously from among its own nuns, if a suitable person could be found. If not, La Pommeraye was to receive an abbess from the Paraclete alone and from no other monastery or order; nor was this abbey to hold and follow the customs of any order other than the Paraclete.[60]

Although subordinated to the mother house, La Pommeraye enjoyed the distinctive status reflected also in the rights of mutual visitation existing between the two abbeys. Twice a year the abbess of La Pommeraye was to visit the Paraclete "for instruction in the order." Similarly the abbess of the Paraclete was to visit the daughter abbey twice yearly, to correct whatever might need correction and to deal with other affairs pertaining to the order. In recognition of her superior position and authority, she was to take her place in the chapter of La Pommeraye *tanquam magistra*. These rights of mutual visitation evidently did not extend to the priories, where visitation seems to have come from the Paraclete only; there is no evidence of an annual general chapter, which was the custom at Fontevraud and some female abbeys affiliated with Cîteaux.[61]

Confirmed in her lifetime, these arrangements demonstrate Heloise's concern to secure the authority of the abbess of the Paraclete and at the same time to recognize the special status of La Pommeraye. There is certainly nothing in the early records to support the mid-thirteenth-century claims of the daughter houses to participate "by ancient right" in the election of the abbess of the Paraclete.[62] Nor are there evident signs of the particular tensions between the mother house and La Pommeraye that may have played a part in this later conflict. The provisions worked out so carefully in Heloise's time seem designed to avoid potential difficulties between the two abbeys. But these provisions also underscore the changes that made the years around 1147 a watershed in Heloise's abbacy, a time when she confronted more sharply than in earlier years the need to resolve the discrepancies between the ideals she shared with Abelard and the realities of monastic development.

If the material expansion precisely detailed in the confirmation charter of 1147 had demanded some compromise, so, it seems, had the high patronage of La Pommeraye. Yet these issues pertained to what Heloise might well have regarded as nonessentials, not to the heart of the monastic life. The nature of her collaboration with Abelard, however, makes it more surprising, perhaps disconcerting, to learn that she may have been responsible for another kind of departure from their monastic program, one that touched the inner life of her community very directly. It concerned the liturgical program that was one of its most distinctive features, embodying Abelard's large and highly original collection of hymns, along with his other contributions to the office of the Paraclete.

It is beyond question that by the late thirteenth century, from which our earliest version of this office dates, the signs of Cistercian influence were noteworthy.[63] But we cannot be sure that all of these changes were the work of Heloise, though it is quite possible that the Paraclete's adoption of some pre-1147 Cistercian hymn texts occurred in her time, perhaps in her community's earliest years. The borrowing also extended to the adoption of the Cistercian calendar, although the Paraclete retained the special commemorations of its antecedent calendar and those added later. Again, if it would go beyond the evidence to lay all of this "Cistercianizing" at Heloise's door, we may agree with Chrysogonus Waddell that these changes reflect a freedom of spirit in accord with Paraclete practice as we meet it also in the collection of statutes that may with reasonable confidence be attributed to her.[64]

Whenever they may have occurred, these liturgical changes did not prevent the Paraclete from retaining a great deal of its Abelardian originality, including many features reflecting the distinctive ideas and ideals of the founders. Their own and their abbey's "feminism" was still exhibited in the commemorations of female saints given marked prominence in the calendar. To those whose commemorations were shared with the Cistercians, the Paraclete added, along with St. Ursula and her 11,000 companions, ten others, among them the Frankish saints Radegund and Aldegund, who were added to the early Christian Thecla and Eugenia, the transvestite "monk" and later "abbot" who enjoyed a special cult in this community.[65] Of Abelard's large repertory of hymns, about two-thirds were retained. Close study of the later liturgical books shows that his contribution by way of special offices, antiphons, and responsories was considerably more important than has hitherto been suspected.[66] So persistent, indeed, was his influence that even after the reform of the Paraclete office, much of his personal achievement managed to survive, though often in fragmented form.

One reason why such liturgical changes might have been thought necessary lies in the very originality, and the incompleteness, of the Abelardian program. Some of his hymns are idiosyncratically bold in their imagery, among them one, to be sung every Thursday at Lauds, that joins the physical and the spiritual in a fashion perhaps more startling to modern than to medieval sensibilities.[67] "Just as the body fills with manly power," it ends, "Love consummates our wills with virtue's power." Often brilliantly imaginative and poetic, his hymns are "virtuoso pieces"; as Waddell remarks, in a monastic liturgy "a steady diet of Abelard's astonishing feats of composition would be a bit like dining on chocolate mousse six times a week."[68] Liturgically speaking, what was needed was something more neutral, lending itself more easily to constant repetition. But whether or not the processes of stocktaking and change that occurred in the late 1140s also affected the Paraclete liturgy, there emerged in these years strong, perhaps pressing, reasons for tempering what was most idiosyncratic in the life of the Paraclete.

By 1147 Abelard himself had been dead for five years; the return of his body to the Paraclete, in 1144 or later, would have driven home to Heloise the finality of his departure and her sole responsibility for the future of her community and its dependen cies. She would also have received from Peter the Venerable, Abelard's friend and protector, the greatly desired letter of absolution for Abelard, which was hung above his tomb. But even this, along with his "confession of faith" addressed to her, perhaps their last communication, could hardly erase the adverse public effects of his condemnation at Sens in 1140, which had been confirmed by a decree of Pope Innocent II, imposing perpetual silence on Abelard as a condemned heretic.[69] These harsh decisions had been preceded by attacks more directly pertinent to the monastic concerns of the "abbot without responsibility" portrayed by Bernard of Clairvaux, who also described him as "Peter the dragon," attacking the faith of St. Peter.[70]

Not only the damage to his reputation in these years, but the expansion of the Paraclete beginning after his death and the task of adapting its unique program to changing times and the life of the daughter houses would have encouraged some modification, some "normalizing," of its more exotic features. Bringing us back, with Heloise, to the texts and the program with which we began, this task appears more insistent as her attention became more sharply focused on the inner world of her abbey and its daughter houses, on the shaping, and reshaping, of communal life. With their emphasis on the scriptural inquiries of her *Problemata,* these concerns reveal more directly the spiritual guide and teacher, and always the questioner, displaying the independence and critical judgment that we meet in this account of Heloise the abbess. No longer solely the woman of her first two letters, she is here also the "prudent" ruler and administrator, always mindful of the place and functions of her community in its larger world, acutely aware of its human and material realities. Even in this more public aspect of her life, we perceive the woman mourned by her community as the "mother of our religious life . . . distinguished for her learning and monastic devotion," and admired in her lifetime by Peter the Venerable as "this Deborah of ours . . ." this "leader and teacher."[71]

Notes

Except for its introductory pages, this chapter is based substantially on a chapter in my forthcoming book, *Heloise and the Paraclete: A Twelfth-Century Quest* (The New Middle Ages Series, St. Martin's Press, forthcoming).

1. Among the last doubters regarding Heloise's authorship of the letters attributed to her was the late Georges Duby; see *Women of the Twelfth Century,* vol. 1, trans. Jean Birrell. For recent arguments in favor of authenticity, see the following: Barbara Newman,

"Authority, Authenticity, and the Repression of Heloise," in *From Virile Woman to WomanChrist; Studies in Medieval Religion and Literature,* pp. 46–75; Eric Hicks, *La vie et les epistres Pierres Abaelart et Heloys sa fame; traduction du XIIIe siècle attribuée à Jean de Meun, Avec une nouvelle édition des texts latins d'après le MS Troyes, Bibl. Mun. 802,* Introduction, especially p. xvii, xxiv, xxv; John Marenbon, *The Philosophy of Peter Abelard,* pp. 82–93, and see also his chapter 2 in this collection.

2. *Ep.* 2, ed. Muckle 70, Monfrin 113, ll. 114–17.
3. *Ep.* 5, ed. Muckle 88–90 passim, Hicks 79–82.
4. I include here Letter 9, "On studies," Edmé Renno Smits, ed., *Peter Abelard, Letters IX-XIV,* pp. 219–39. Lacking the customary attributes of the epistolary genre and designated *sermo* in the only manuscript (Paris, Bibliothèque nationale, MS lat. 14511, fol. 18r), this text is not, in my opinion, a separate letter but originally the last section of *Ep.* 8, which ends abruptly with a passage from which this text follows in unbroken continuity.
5. Brian Stock, *Listening for the Text: On the Uses of the Past,* especially pp. 22–24; pp. 150–57; p. 188, n. 31.
6. Jacques Verger, "Abélard et les milieux sociaux de son temps," *Abélard et son temps,* pp. 109, 125–28.
7. Waddell, *Hymns Collections,* II, Praef., pp. 5–9.
8. *Expositio in Hexaemeron,* Praef.: PL 178:714.
9. *Ep. 6,* ed. Muckle 242–53, Hicks 87–106.
10. On the "following of Christ," see Giles Constable, "The Ideal of the Imitation of Christ," in his *Three Studies in Medieval Religious and Social Thought,* pp. 143–218. See also his magisterial *The Reformation of the Twelfth Century,* especially chapters 4, 5, and 7.
11. *Ep. 6,* ed. Muckle 246, Hicks 96, ll. 254–58.
12. Bruce L. Venarde, *Women's Monasticism and Medieval Society: Nunneries in France and England, 890 - 1215,* pp. 11–16.
13. Christopher Brooke, *The Medieval Idea of Marriage,* pp. 89–92 and passim.
14. C. H. Talbot, ed., *The Life of Christina of Markyate,* new enlarged edition.
15. Brooke, *The Medieval Idea of Marriage,* especially pp. 78–92; for the quoted phrase, p. 84.
16. For the pope's letter, see *Cartulaire,* no. 1, pp. 1–3; the original of this charter is in the Bibliothèque municipale, Chalons-sur-Marne (pièce 31). There is a copy in the Archives de l'Aube (24 H 1).
17. *Problemata Heloissae* XVIII, PL 178: 707bd. For the epigraph, see *HC,* ed. Muckle 205–206, Monfrin 100, ll. 1326–328.
18. *Cartulaire,* no. 6, pp. 7–14 (Eugene III: 1 November 1147), which lists the properties acquired up to that time, mentioning a number, but by no means all, of their donors. A great many of these earlier donations were among those lying within his diocese, which were confirmed by Bishop Garnier of Troyes in 1194 (no. 83, pp. 95–105); here more donors are identified, along with many witnesses to the charters confirmed in this important document.
19. For later papal letters of confirmation, see *Cartulaire,* no. 7, pp. 14–16 (Anastasius IV, 1153); nos. 9, 10. pp. 17–21 (Adrian IV, 1157); nos. 12, 13, pp. 22–23 (Alexander III, 1163). See also no. 14, pp. 25–27 (Alexander III, 1164; La Pommeraye).
20. In 1135 the Paraclete had received a royal exemption from all customary taxes (*Cartulaire,* no. 46, p. 64). Charters reflecting the patronage of the counts and countesses of Blois-Champagne are no. 52, pp. 70–71 (1146); no. 55, pp. 71–73 (1147 or later); no. 58, pp. 77–78 (1160).
21. *Cartulaire,* no. 6, p. 12.
22. Richard W. Southern, *Western Society and the Church in the Middle Ages,* pp. 232–33. For more penetrating analysis, see Venarde, *Women's Monasticism,* pp. 52–88. The Paraclete is among the twenty-six female monasteries studied in Penelope Johnson's *Equal in*

Monastic Profession: Religious Women in Medieval France, see especially pp. 222–24, and on La Pommeraye, pp. 199–202.

23. For Abelard's admonitions regarding the dangers of monastic overexpansion, excessive hospitality, and the burdens of administration in general, see *Ep.* 8 (7), pp. 284–85.
24. On his opposition to the acceptance of tithes and involvement in litigation, see Sermon XXXIII (PL 178:588); cf. Giles Constable, *Monastic Tithes from Their Origins to the Twelfth Century,* p. 144 and passim.
25. This struggle over material interests is described by Jean-Marc Bienvenu, "Le conflit entre Ulger, évêque d'Angers et Petronille de Chemillé, abbesse de Fontevrault."
26. For relations with the archbishops of Sens, see *Cartulaire,* no. 47, pp. 64–65 (1136); no. 48, pp. 65–66 (1142 or later); no. 53, pp. 71–73 (1143 - 1147); no. 54, pp. 73–74; no. 60, pp. 79–80 (1142 - 1168). Another charter (no. 50, p. 69) records a grant of tithes from the bishop of Troyes in 1145.
27. *Cartulaire,* no. 56, pp. 75–76, records the settlements with mutual concessions, of the Paraclete's dispute with the abbey of Saint-Pierre in Troyes (1155); a similar dispute with the abbey of Saint-Jacques, Provins, was settled in 1162 (no. 59, pp. 78–79).
28. *Cartulaire,* no. 49, pp. 66–69, records this agreement between the two abbeys, which was made first in the Paraclete priory, Sainte-Madeleine-de-Traînel, in the presence of Lord Anseau of Traînel. It was later confirmed by the entire chapter of the Paraclete, and signed and sealed by the abbess and the abbot of Vauluisant; there is a copy in the cartulary of Vauluisant, Paris, Bibliothèque nationale, MS lat. 9901, fol. 48rv.
29. Theodore Evergates, *Feudal Society in the Bailliage of Troyes under the Counts of Champagne, 1152–1284,* pp. 7–9, table 1 and map 3. On the role of the Cistercian houses in the forest of Othe, southwest of Troyes, in clearing land, supplying wood for village construction, and exploiting iron deposits, see Heinrich Rubner, *Untersuchungen zur Forstverfassung des mittelalterlichen Frankreich,* pp. 26–35; cf. Evergates, *Feudal Society in the Bailliage of Troyes,* p. 213, n. 11.
30. That the Cistercians from the beginning readily accepted the kinds of property that their early legislation forbade has been demonstrated most persuasively by the recent studies of Constance Hoffman Berman, *Medieval Agriculture, the Southern French Countryside, and the Early Cistercians: A Study of Forty-Three Monasteries,* and Constance B. Bouchard, "Cistercian Ideals Versus Reality: 1134 Reconsidered," p. 217. See also her *Holy Entrepreneurs: Cistercians, Knights, and Economic Exchange in Twelfth-Century Burgundy.*
31. See Southern, *Western Society and the Church,* pp. 252–67, and for excellent discussion of the operation of Cistercian granges and the advantages of *conversi* labor, see Berman, *Medieval Agriculture,* pp. 61–93, especially pp. 69–70; pp. 78–79.
32. On Vauluisant and iron-mining, see Denis Cailleaux, "Les religieux et le travail de fer en Pays d'Othe," pp. 183–87. I am grateful to Sharan Newman for this reference.
33. *Cartulaire,* no. 49, pp. 67–69.
34. Recording the judgment of a dispute between the Paraclete and Vauluisant by the Lady Ermancia of Traînel, a document of 1196 reports as common knowledge that there had long been discord between the two abbeys regarding certain lands and forests. At the command of the pope and in the presence of the archbishop of Sens, Ermancia decreed that Vauluisant should cede to the Paraclete whatever the nuns had claimed and the nuns in turn should give up to Vauluisant whatever land and forests they held on the road of Bagnaux (*Cartulaire,* no. 91, pp. 113–14). That this settlement was not final is evident in two apparently somewhat later (early thirteenth-century) references to continuing disputes in the cartulary of Vauluisant (Paris, Bibliothèque nationale, MS lat. 9901: A.f. 11r; B, ff. 29v–30r). I thank Bruce Venarde for examining and transcribing these charters for me.
35. On Heloise's managerial skills, see Venarde, *Women's Monasticism,* pp. 120–24. See also his study of her and her contemporaries, especially Petronilla of Fontevraud, "*Praesidentes negotiis:* Abbesses as Managers in Twelfth-Century France."

36. On the early records of Fontevraud, see Venarde, *Women's Monasticism,* pp. 118–19. In sharp contrast, only a few more than thirty charters survive from Heloise's time, but Fontevraud could claim nothing to compare with the Paraclete's texts.
37. *Cartulaire,* introduction, pp. XI-XII. According to Lalore, there were ten of these granges by the end of the twelfth century, and I have been able to identify all but one or two of them. Several of the dependencies were situated in close proximity to these centers of cultivation.
38. In the charters of Heloise's time only the agreement with Vauluisant refers to a priest as witness for the Paraclete; "Erardus, presbyter" was possibly one of its chaplains. Not until 1179 does a document specifically mention its clerics as witnesses for the Paraclete (*Cartulaire,* no. 66, p. 85). Only one other charter of this century, a letter of 1182, is witnessed by three chaplains, along with several nuns (no. 69, p. 87). In the early thirteenth century, a letter of Pope Innocent III refers to the "chaplains" and "lay brothers" (no. 22, p. 39).
39. *Cartulaire,* no. 8, pp. 16–17 (February 13, 1156); the original of this bull is in the Archives municipales, Metz. Here designated *fratres,* the lay brothers performing manual labor are clearly meant. Cf. *Statutes,* p. 11, no. 7, where they are called both *conversi* and *fratres.* The reference of another document, the agreement between the Paraclete and Saint-Pierre, Troyes (*Cartulaire,* no. 56, p. 75) to *monachi* pertains to Saint-Pierre itself and not to the Paraclete, as Pascale Bourgain mistakenly thought ("Héloise," *Abélard en son temps,* p. 222).
40. Micheline Pontenay de Fontette, *Les religieuses à l'âge classique de droit canonique: recherches sur les structures juridiques des branches féminines des Ordres,* pp. 77–80.
41. Pontenay de Fontette, *Les religieuses,* pp. 50–51.
42. Regarding Premonstratensian communities, it is noteworthy that there was never a house of Norbertine sisters in the diocese of Troyes, though such "parthenons" existed in adjacent dioceses: Avigny in the diocese of Châlons and Fossemore, just south of Sens, both founded c. 1140.
43. *Cartulaire,* no. 48, pp. 65–66. Regarding Milo of Nogent, see no. 52, pp. 70–71 (1146). The first donor mentioned specifically in the later (1194) confirmation of Bishop Garnier of Troyes was Simon of Nogent, who gave fields from his alods, on one of which Abelard's oratory itself was built (*Cartulaire,* no. 83, p. 95). Among donors named in twelfth-century charters are the families of Nogent, Quincey, Traînel, Barbuise, Ferreux, Marigny, Rouilly, Courgivaux, and Courcimain. For several of these families, see Evergates, *Feudal Society in the Bailliage of Troyes,* Appendix, pp. 103–104 (Traînel); p. 186 (Marigny); pp. 189–90 (Nogent-sur-Seine); pp. 195–96 (Quincey). See also Alphonse Roserot, *Dictionnaire de la Champagne méridionale,* pp. 86–87 (Barbuise); 579 (Ferreux); 861–86 (Marigny); 1032–1033 (Nogent).
44. *Cartulaire,* no. 11, p. 21 (dated November 25, 1156–58). Lalore published this bull from the fourteenth-century cartulary; no original or copy exists in the Archives de l'Aube. The Pierpont Morgan Library in New York acquired in 1979 an unsigned twelfth-century copy, which shows several verbal differences from the version in the cartulary.
45. Another adverse development besides those already discussed was the heavy drain on the supply of potential husbands resulting from the diaspora of young men from the European heartlands, as crusaders, conquerors, and settlers on and beyond the periphery of western Christendom: see Robert Bartlett, *The Making of Europe: Conquest, Colonization and Cultural Change, 950–1350,* passim.
46. I have identified these donations by comparing the evidence of the papal confirmation of 1147 with that contained in the charter of Bishop Garnier of Troyes, 1194 (*Cartulaire,* no. 83, pp. 99–105), in which more donors and witnesses in earlier charters are named.
47. Some twenty gifts from women are noted in the confirmation charter of 1147, although by no means all of these are associated with nuns of the Paraclete (above, n. 18).

Bishop Garnier's charter records some eighty gifts of property in his diocese, of which a good many were originally made before 1147, Of these, nine were specified as direct donations by women. To this evidence may be added that of the papal confirmations of 1153 (*Cartulaire,* no. 7, p. 15), which records two donations by women not specifically mentioned elsewhere, and 1182 (no. 15, pp. 28–29), which mentions by name four female donors not noted elsewhere. For donations made by women to La Pommeraye, which was founded and endowed by a woman, see below, n. 58.

48. For Ermelina, see *Cartulaire,* no. 43, pp. 62–63 (1133). Lacking the kind of personal evidence we have concerning Heloise, we can only speculate about the role of "choice" (limited as it often was) and the motives or reasons for becoming a nun of the Paraclete. In these matters much depended on local and regional circumstances and, more often, it seems, on the needs of families than the wishes of individuals. Judging by what we know of the girls and women who became nuns of the Paraclete in the early decades of the new foundation, they belonged for the most part to families of the "middle" or lower aristocracy, who were its principal supporters (cf. n. 43). Many female members of local families would have had sisters, aunts, cousins, and even mothers in the Paraclete and its daughter houses, dominant in this region. Regarding the appeal of Heloise herself, probably more powerful than any other, Penelope Johnson notes the popularity of the name in Champagne for both lay women and nuns a generation after the death of the great abbess (*Equal in Monastic Profession,* p. 234).
49. For Abelard's opposition to noble influence and feudal entanglements, see *Ep.* 8 (7), pp. 253–54; pp. 283–84; PL 178, Sermon XXXIII, 587d, 588b, 590ad.
50. On the founding of Sainte-Madeleine in 1142 or later, see *Cartulaire,* no. 48, pp. 65–66.
51. Regarding the sending of nuns to the dependencies, see *Statutes,* p. 9, no. II. In order of foundation, after Sainte-Madeleine, they were: La Pommeraye, ca. 1147 (*Cartulaire,* no. 53, pp. 71–73); Laval (Seine-et-Marne), ca. 1153 (no. 7, p. 13); Noëfort (Seine-et-Marne), before 1157 (no. 9, p. 17); Saint-Flavit (Aube), before 1157 (ibid.); Boran or Saint-Martin-aux-Nonnettes (Oise), by 1163 (n. 12, p. 22). Although Boran is first mentioned in this papal confirmation, it could have been incorporated sometime between 1157 and 1163 or possibly earlier; see Philippe Racinet, "L'implantation monastique dans la basse vallée de l'Oise au Moyen Age," p. 11; the author suggests, without giving his evidence, that Saint-Martin-de-Boran became a dependency in the *second* quarter of the century, rather than in the commonly accepted late 1150s or early 1160s.
52. The four were Sainte-Madeleine, La Pommeraye, Laval, and Saint-Flavit. The other two priories were considerably farther from the Paraclete: Noëfort in the diocese of Meaux and Boran near Senlis.
53. See *Statutes,* pp. IX-XI, especially nos. III, IV, VII. Although there is no precise evidence of numbers at the Paraclete in Heloise's time, by the very late twelfth century Abbess Melisende was obliged to appeal for papal permission to limit to sixty the number of choirnuns, on the grounds that the demands of its neighbors for places were overburdening the abbey's resources (*Cartulaire,* no. 23, pp. 33–34). Similar limitations were imposed on the dependencies early in the next century, in the case of Sainte-Madeleine-de-Traînel, to twenty-five (no. 25, p. 41).
54. Evergates, *Feudal Society in the Bailliage of Troyes,* p. 8.
55. At Petronilla's death in 1149, the order of Fontevraud numbered some fifty priories; on its growth, see Venarde, *Women's Monasticism,* pp. 60–64. For its organization and the power of its abbess, see Pontenay de Fontette, *Les religieuses,* pp. 72–73.
56. *Cartulaire,* no. 6, p. 13, dated 1147, referring to the two earliest foundations, Sainte-Madeleine and La Pommeraye. The "subjection" of its dependencies to the Paraclete was confirmed in a papal letter of 1157 (no. 10, p. 18), in which these two and three others are mentioned. In the thirteenth century and very likely earlier, the consent of the Paraclete was required for the sale, exchange, or donation of property by the

priories (no. 193, p. 180; no. 217, p. 198). Largely because most of these communities were moved elsewhere during the seventeenth century, few of their medieval records seem to have survived. Most significant is the fifteenth-century cartulary, *terrier* and *censier* of the priory of Noëfort, containing some charters from earlier centuries (Paris, Bibliothèque nationale, MS fr. 19835).

57. In a letter of about 1152 Bernard of Clairvaux consoled the countess in her extreme distress over the continuing bad behavior of her eldest son, Henry, who had just succeeded his father as count of Champagne. For a translation of this letter, see *Feudal Society in Medieval France: Documents from the County of Champagne,* ed. and trans. Theodore Evergates, pp. 107–108.
58. A charter of the archbishop of Sens, dated between 1143 and 1147, confirms a grant of land to the Paraclete "in the place called La Pommeraye," by the knight Baudouin of Clus (Clos) fontaine, from the lands he had from his wife, Anne (*Cartulaire,* no. 54, pp. 73–74). For Heloise's concession of the land to the countess of Blois, see no. 54, pp. 71–73; there is a copy of this charter in Paris, Bibliothèque nationale, MS Baluze 46, fols. 43–44. For the foundation charter of La Pommeraye, see *Cartulaire générale de l'Yonne,* ed. Maximilien Quantin, 1, 493–99. The possessions of this abbey, clearly the largest and most generously endowed of the Paraclete's dependencies, are listed in the papal charter of 1157 (pp. 18–20); they included two donations from women acting independently and three more by women acting jointly with a husband, father, or son (pp. 19–20).
59. *Cartulaire,* no. 53, pp. 71–72. For a translation, see Evergates, *Documents,* pp. 62–63.
60. *Cartulaire,* p. 72. In a letter of Pope Alexander III, 21 March 1164, addressed to Abbess Amelina of La Pommeraye and confirming its possessions, the "agreement" between her abbey and the Paraclete is also confirmed (no. 14, pp. 25–26).
61. Pontenay de Fontette, *Les religieuses,* pp. 37–42 (Tart and its filiation); p. 73 (Fontevraud).
62. *Cartulaire,* no. 26, pp. 42–43; a letter of Pope Innocent IV.
63. See Chrysogonus Waddell, "St. Bernard and the Cistercian Office at the Abbey of the Paraclete." Waddell's earlier conclusions regarding Heloise's role in the "Cistercianizing" of the Paraclete office are somewhat modified in his more recent studies (see his conclusion, *Hymns,* especially pp. 84–85). The Mass books in use at the Paraclete seem to have been quite independent of Cistercian usage.
64. See *Hymn Collections,* I, especially p. 85.
65. See Waddell, *The Paraclete Ordinary and the Paraclete Breviary,* I, p. 335, for St. Eugenia and her cult. See also *Ep.* 7 (6), p. 281, where Abelard stresses the example of this female "transvestite" who, after living for some time as a monk, was elected abbot, or "provost," of her community. On the theme in general and St. Eugenia in particular, see also John Anson, "The Female Transvestite in Early Monasticism: The Origin and Development of a Motif," especially pp. 12, 20–29.
66. Chrysogonus Waddell, "Peter Abelard as Creator of Liturgical Texts," pp. 267–86.
67. Waddell, *Hymn Collections,* II, 36 (Feria IV: In laudibus matutinis, III). Cf. Colin Morris, *The Papal Monarchy: The Western Church from 1050 to 1250,* pp. 368–69; the translation is his.
68. Waddell, "St. Bernard and the Cistercian Office," pp. 107–108, noting that many of the Abelardian hymns dropped from the Paraclete office belonged to the ferial day cycle in which extensive repetition was involved.
69. Constable, *The Letters of Peter the Venerable,* Letter 167; 1, pp. 400–401. See p. 401 for Heloise's reference to this letter of absolution. Regarding the time, Peter's visit may have been in 1144, but it could have taken place later, between 1146 and 1148. For Abelard's letter, see Charles S. F. Burnett, "'Confessio fidei ad Heloissam:' Abelard's Last Letter to

Heloise? A Discussion and Critical Edition of the Latin and Medieval French Version," pp. 147–55. For Pope Innocent's decree, see PL 179, Ep. 447: 517ad.

70. Ep. 330, (*Sancti Bernardi Opera,* eds. J. Leclercq and H. Rochait, 8, 266–68). Perhaps in earlier years in Paris Abelard had been a teacher of Pope Anacletus (Pietro Pierleone; d. 1138); he had certainly taught two cardinals (and future popes) who defended him at Sens: Guy of Città di Castello (Pope Celestine II) and Hyacinth Bobo (Pope Celestine III).

71. Peter referred to her as *ductrix et magistra* in Letter 168 (Constable, *The Letters of Peter the Venerable,* 1, p. 401); cf. Letter 115 (1, pp. 303–304). For the obituary, see *Recueil des historiens de la France. Obituaires de la province de Sens, IV. Diocèses de Meaux et de Troyes,* dir. Auguste Longnon (Paris, 1923).

CHAPTER 2

AUTHENTICITY REVISITED

John Marenbon

This chapter assesses the attitudes toward evidence and argument in the debate over the authenticity of the Abelard–Heloise correspondence during the last twenty-five years, including the impact of feminism on the discussion.

In 1974, the distinguished literary historian Peter von Moos published a book called *Mittelalterforschung und Ideologie* (Medieval Research and Ideology). It might seem, at first, an odd title for a book discussing the authenticity of the love letters of Abelard and Heloise, especially for one taken up entirely by a survey of previous scholarly controversy. But von Moos's work is no ordinary history of scholarship. He makes clear from the start that his main concern is not about whether the Letters are authentic or not. He is interested, rather, in the controversy itself, because it enables him to make a general point about the history of scholarship that has important implications for how medieval scholars understand and go about their work. For nearly two centuries—from 1616, when they were first printed, until early in the nineteenth century—the Letters of Abelard and Heloise were widely read, translated, and imitated, with no suggestion that they were not genuine. Questioning their authenticity was part of the move to make history a properly scientific discipline, which by going back to the sources and scrutinizing them, no longer regarding them as at once "strange" and yet "distanceless," provides an objective, demythologized account of the past.[1] Von Moos's main point is that such historical objectivity is an illusion: behind "'objective data,' 'assured facts,' and 'better readings,' there is played out a conflict between views of the world. . . ."[2] Historians cannot take a purely objective, unideological standpoint, for there is none. But they can, argues Von Moos, scrutinize their own and others' acknowledged or concealed ideologies. His book aims to begin this task, taking for its material one of the longest-running controversies in medieval scholarship.

This chapter continues the task von Moos began, and I, too, hope a general moral emerges from my particular observations, although not the same moral as his. I shall begin chronologically where von Moos stopped. He covered a span of 170 years; I shall have just 25. But they have been crowded years for specialists in this field, and an important new element has entered the discussion that makes my task particularly relevant for a volume that focuses not on Abelard but on Heloise. Much of the most recent writing about the love letters has been by scholars working from a variety of feminist perspectives (as this present volume indeed illustrates). Their contributions have given a new twist to the underlying ideological debate, which I shall look at later. Before that I will very briefly sketch out the main lines of the historical and philological debate, as they were in 1974 when von Moos wrote and as they have developed since then, and examine the ideological conflict before the major impact of feminist scholarship.[3]

The Recent Controversy: An Outline

Doubts about the Letters' authenticity had been raised in the nineteenth century, but it was not until 1913 that a sustained case was made, when in a series of articles the German scholar Bernhard Schmeidler suggested that the whole correspondence—the *Historia,* the Letters signed by Abelard *and* those supposedly by Heloise—was the work of Abelard himself.[4] Schmeidler based his view on discrepancies between the *Historia* and the Letters, the stylistic homogeneity of the whole collection, and the existence of precedents for fictional letters. Later writers who have taken the same view (most emphatically D. W. Robertson) have been led to it also by the surmise that the thoughts and feelings expressed by Heloise in her Letters cannot have been those of a medieval abbess. If Heloise's Letters are Abelard's fiction, they have argued, then it becomes possible to read them without anachronistic romanticism, as carefully contrived revelations of human weaknesses; and to see the climax of the whole dossier in the two final Letters, which provide a history of female monasticism and a Rule for the Paraclete.[5] The case *for* authenticity was eloquently argued, however, by the historian of philosophy Etienne Gilson in his very widely read *Héloïse et Abélard* (1938), where he managed to explain away many of Schmeidler's supposed discrepancies and other evidence.[6] Influential historians such as Sir Richard Southern had followed Gilson's view, but when von Moos wrote his survey in the early 1970s, no consensus had been reached among historians for or against authenticity.[7]

In the last two decades, the controversy has taken a new turn. Until the early 1970s, almost all those who doubted the authenticity of Heloise's Letters—and certainly everyone whose arguments were taken seriously—considered that, if she did not write them, Abelard did. Then the American medieval historian John Benton advanced the thesis that all the Letters, Abelard's and Heloise's, and the *Historia calamitatum,* are forgeries, the work of two different forgers—a "twelfth-century epistolary 'novelist' and a 'thirteenth-century institutional scoundrel'"—who were able to draw on some authentic material.[8] Benton brought as his evidence the fact that the earliest manuscript of the material is from the mid-thirteenth century; various features of the *Historia* and Letters that he claimed would be anachronistic if they had been composed in the twelfth century; and much information, and speculation, about the institutional history of the Paraclete in the thirteenth century. It is surprising that this ingenious, but extraordinary, construction commanded as much credence as it did. But in 1979 Benton carefully took down the house of cards he had built up, explaining why he could no longer accept his earlier arguments.[9] Not long after he had done so, however, a fresh and even wilder hypothesis of forgery was propounded by the Belgian scholar Hubert Silvestre.[10] Silvestre takes as his clue the fact that Abelard and Heloise are mentioned as lovers in Jean de Meun's continuation of the *Roman de la Rose* and that, probably, it was Jean de Meun who translated the *Historia* and the Letters into French. According to Silvestre, Jean was not just a translator but also a forger of genius, who made up the Latin text of the *Historia* and the Letters. His reason for doing so, Silvestre argues, was to advocate the idea that clerics should be allowed concubines and to do this most powerfully by putting the arguments—Heloise's arguments against marriage—into the mouth of a woman. Silvestre also found his own list of historical and textual discrepancies to bolster his case.

Meanwhile, other scholars continued to propose the older view that the Letters were a literary fiction, composed entirely by Abelard. Chrysogonus Waddell, an expert on the liturgy of the Paraclete, argued for it, as did Benton, once he had abandoned his forgery theory; so, at times and with qualifications, did von Moos.[11] The position also seemed to receive support from the study of *cursus* (the rhythmical pattern of sentence endings) which suggested that the letters do date from the twelfth century but could well be by the same author.[12]

The strongest case, however, made by recent scholars is that for the oldest view: that the *Historia* and Letters are authentic and that the Letters preserve, perhaps with minor changes, a genuine epistolary exchange between Abelard and Heloise. David Luscombe, an expert on Abelard and his influences, has been energetic in following up the various discrepancies detected by one or another advocate of inauthenticity and showing that they are illusory.[13] Peter Dronke has argued for the genuineness of the correspondence in three ways. First, he has shown that Silvestre's theory about Jean de Meun's authorship must be wrong, since Jean's French translation clearly misunderstands the Latin texts, which, according to Silvestre, Jean himself forged.[14] Second, he has shown up the falsity of the assumption, made by Robertson and von Moos, that only a Christian reading of the Letters, as the story of a sinful life followed by conversion, would have been possible for medieval readers. On the contrary, medieval responses both to the Letters themselves and earlier to stories of the affair between Abelard and Heloise often were sympathetically romantic, in just the way that "historical" critics denounce as a modern anachronism.[15] Third, Dronke has looked in detail at the question of *cursus* and found some evidence here also to support the view that Heloise did write the letters attributed to her.[16]

To me, Dronke's and Luscombe's arguments are convincing, and they can be supported with further evidence and argument. I have tried to set out the case in *The Philosophy of Peter Abelard*.[17] The focus of this chapter is different: not the question of authenticity itself, but the ideological debate surrounding it—and it is to that I now turn.

The Ideological Conflict

What ideologies underlie the different positions taken by these (and other) scholars? My answer to this question is surprisingly simple. Just one ideological distinction counts: between those scholars who respect evidence and the burdens of argument based on it and those who do not.[18] This distinction cuts right across the more obvious division between upholders and deniers of the Letters' authenticity. Hubert Silvestre and Peter Dronke jostle side by side in the first group, as do John Benton and David Luscombe. The second group is equally various.

It is important to emphasize that, when I say of some scholars that they respect evidence and the burdens of evidence-based argument, this by no means implies that their arguments are convincing. For example, I unhesitatingly count Silvestre among this group. Although his position is almost certainly unsustainable (the very brief account of it earlier will have hinted as much), no one has been more diligent than he in searching out evidence—internal evidence of supposed inconsistencies in the Letters, external evidence from other accounts of Heloise and Abelard and of the practices of their time—and arguing from it. No matter that, on scrutiny, Silvestre's arguments fail: the important point is that he provides this evidence for scrutiny, and he argues from it step by step. Nor, when I describe some scholars as respecting evidence and argument, is this to suggest that they do their work from a neutral standpoint—as if this were possible—uninfluenced by presuppositions and prejudices linked to their wider view of the world. Here again Silvestre provides a very clear example. His prejudices are rather touchingly patent. First, there is a Francophone Belgian scholar's dislike of France and wish to debunk French culture. As he writes (in his fullest statement of his position, which, hardly by accident, he chose to write not in French but German): "The love story of Abelard and Heloise is an integral part of the cultural heritage of France and represents to a certain point an element in the collective consciousness of that country."[19] Second, and more important, Silvestre presents himself almost as a caricature of the scientific scholar stripping away the "novelistic accretions" from a story that, he thinks, all too many modern writers, following the footsteps of Petrarch, Villon, and Pope, have told with "touching naiveté."[20] Silvestre defines himself by contrast with such scholars. At the end of his article, he quotes the romantic musings that Heloise's wrongly-supposed handwriting inspired in a learned archivist a century ago—"imagination, spontaneity, playfulness, grace . . . combined with a little sweet tyranny and considerable self-satisfaction." How powerful, he remarks, is the myth that can draw from an old piece of parchment so tremulous a lyric: against it, he fears, "the arguments of historical criticism will always remain powerless."[21] It is easy for anyone familiar with postmodern debates to turn the tables on Silvestre and remark his own simplistic attitude to interpretation and his lack of self-awareness in presenting himself as the lone fighter for historical truth in a world too easily lured by romantic fiction. Nonetheless, there can be no doubt about Silvestre's commitment to argument and evidence.

What is true of a scholar given to extremes, such as Silvestre, is even more obviously true of better-balanced writers. Take, for instance, Silvestre's strongest opponent, Peter Dronke. Dronke's forte is literary criticism of a highly personal, imaginative kind, which works not by argument so much as evocation. Much of his treatment of Heloise's Letters is given over to this type of reading. But Dronke does not imagine that his skill at such interpretation can in itself establish what he wants to assume as its basis: that Heloise really wrote the letters attributed to her. Nor, for a moment, does he suggest that the question of authenticity is irrelevant. Rather, as the résumé I have provided indicates, Dronke meets the arguments against authenticity with counter-arguments that are clearly relevant and considerable (and, in my view, persuasive). Yet Dronke, no more than any scholar, writes from a neutral standpoint. Throughout his work he strives to develop a view of medieval literature as complex, open to religious doubt, often subtle and accommodating in its treatment of sexuality and emotion.[22] Anyone who knew the rest of Dronke's writings but not those on Abelard and Heloise could guess that he would want to argue that Heloise really did write the letters attributed to her. In this sense, Dronke's position is rooted in an overall view of medieval literature and, more widely, in a certain view of the world. Yet this in no way should be seen as undermining his commitment, like Silvestre's, to argument and evidence. Nor should it detract from the power of his arguments, which should be judged on their own merits. The same point could, of course, be made with regard to many other scholars.

What about those writers who fall on the other side of the central ideological division I have made and who fail to respect evidence and the burdens of argument? They fall into two groups. Some show their failure to respect evidence and the burdens of argument positively, by presenting a view on the question of authenticity without evidence and argument of the sort that could reasonably support it. Others show this failure negatively, by refusing to take a stand at all on the question of authenticity, although their projects require them to do so.

To begin with the positive group. It includes, of course, both scholars who support and those who attack the Letters' authenticity. I do not put scholars in it simply because the considerations they adduce for or against authenticity are unpersuasive, but because they are not of the sort that could reasonably be held as grounds for belief in the position which these scholars use them to uphold. In practice, this criterion is clearer and simpler than it may seem in theory. Take, for instance, the essay by the literary critic Deborah Fraioli that appeared in the prestigious *Monumenta Germaniae Historica* volumes on *Forgeries in the Middle Ages.*[23] Fraioli begins by arguing that Jerome intended his *Adversus Jovinianum* [*Against Jovinian*] as a satire. Its "disingenuous prose" and "irrelevancies," the "illogical and absurd aspects" of its argumentation are not, she says, marks of the low level of Jerome's polemics but devices to undercut what is ostensibly said—for instance, that even among pagans virginity is virtuous. The *Adversus Jovinianum,* she argues, provides the context within which the *Historia calamitatum* can be recognized as a satire. Once "certain citations" are "set back in their original contexts," Abelard and Heloise "become ludicrous caricatures of pride, ignorance, impertinence and lust." Fraioli then proceeds to set a handful of citations from the *Historia* back in their contexts.[24] For instance, a rather distant parallel in structure between a rhetorical question asked by Heloise and one posed by Paul in 2 Corinthians is argued to imply, ironically, that Heloise is an unbeliever—and that *this* would be a genuinely good reason for Abelard not to marry her.[25] And the use of Jerome's *Adversus Jovinianum* is itself ironic, she claims, because it places the Christian and pagan arguments against marriage side by side (as a literal reading of the text would do), without acknowledging their incompatibility (which is the basis for Fraioli's own satiric reading of it).[26] From such considerations, Fraioli feels entitled to conclude that the level of ridicule of Abelard and Heloise is so high "the possibility of their having anything to do with the authorship of these texts becomes too remote, in my opinion, to be entertained even as a possibility."[27] Fraioli thinks that, by making these observations, she has solved the authorship question. The *Historia* and the Letters were written by a "third party" hostile to the couple, and she ends by congratulating herself on having removed "from Abelard and Heloise themselves, the ridicule that will continue to follow them as long as they remain the reputed authors of these letters."[28]

There are two main objections to Fraioli's procedure. First, each of the elements of the argument she assembles is far too weak to support the structure she builds, so that by the end she has entered a science fiction world where Abelard and Heloise can be saved from a public ridicule they have never in fact been given only by rejecting the authenticity of the Letters. Second, Fraioli bases a claim about authorship on a type of evidence that, even if it were better than it in fact is, *could* not be strong enough to establish her case. Judgments claiming satiric intent for authors of the distant past must always be treated with great caution, unless they can be backed up with unambiguous evidence from outside the supposedly satirical framework. In any case, even if all Fraioli's dubious ironical and satirical interpretations are accepted, the question of authorship still remains open, since it is possible—although Fraioli cavalierly dismisses the possibility—that Abelard and Heloise were ridiculing themselves.[29] As this final point especially makes clear, nothing in these observations is intended to question Fraioli's abilities as a literary critic. The problem is, rather, that no amount of literary critical skill could make arguments of the sort she gives yield a conclusion about who actually wrote, or did not write, the letters.[30]

Is it best, then, for literary critics and any other scholars who wish to use the Letters for their work without entering into the historical intricacies of the authenticity debate simply to profess no view of their own about the authorship? There are two quite different ways in which this might be done. A scholar might choose to rely on the authority of others, accepting the conclusions of those who have come to one or another position about authenticity without claiming to have sifted all the arguments and evidence for herself. Or a scholar might profess genuine agnosticism: she has no view about who wrote the Letters. The first of these approaches is unobjectionable. It would be ridiculous to require all scholars always to sift the evidence and arguments for themselves. Even on disputed matters, we often must appeal to the authority of others; so long as the appeal is clear and open, we cannot be faulted (although we might turn out to have been unwise!).[31]

Genuine agnosticism is a different matter. It is compatible with some types of scholarly work on the Letters: for instance, with study of their language and rhetoric, their genre, or their classical and biblical allusions. But agnosticism should not be an option for those who are proposing to *interpret* the Letters in a way that deserves to engage our interest. To uphold agnosticism in this context is a failure of respect for evidence and argument.

Such a failure is illustrated by the comments Paul Zumthor, the medievalist and literary theorist, made about Heloise and Abelard back in 1958. At this stage, his view about the authenticity of the Letters was firm (and unargued). Heloise, he commented, "is present in her entirety in her letters, passionate and incoherent—her heart's cries leave no room for error."[32] By 1979, when he introduced his widely read French translation of the Letters, his views had changed. He very briefly summarizes the positions that have been held about the Letters' authorship and then declares that he will not attempt what is useless, "to go back to the event." "We have," he continues, "a story to read, to savor and, if we are so minded, to judge; there is nothing more, despite what lingering romantic habits of mind might lead us to look for there." "It matters little," he continues, "whether it is a fictional narrative or an autobiographical account. The text carries its own meaning, engendered in the utopic place where there resound in it the echoes of a world (that of the twelfth, the thirteenth century) against which it constructs itself by making itself like it."[33] Zumthor then announces that he will henceforth italicize "Abelard" and "Heloise" to make it clear that he is not claiming to speak about the real Abelard or Heloise. After which, he continues to write about the life and love of the italicized couple exactly as he might have done twenty years before, when their names were still in roman print and Heloise's passionate heart assured the authenticity of her Letters. Zumthor's subterfuge lies not merely in writing some sentences that sound impressive but mean perhaps very little at all but in drawing a contrast between just reading the story and the romantic habits of mind that lead us to look for more than a story. Just to read the story, as the *Historia* and Letters tell it, of Abelard and Heloise (italicized or roman) is precisely to regard the Letters as genuine (at least for the purposes of interpretation), because that is how the plain story they offer presents itself. Zumthor is asking his readers to accept the very romantic presuppositions he has sneeringly cast off. He wants to keep a good story—and his theoretical sophistication. There is no room for such encumbrances as considerations of how a medieval writer or audience might have regarded the Letters. The twelfth century, the thirteenth—what does it matter to him?

A different sort of agnosticism is practiced by one of the best known modern French medievalists Georges Duby in his elegant essay on Heloise. It is what might be called "pretended agnosticism."[34] Duby appears, in fact, to have been persuaded by a view that has much in common with the one Benton advanced in 1970s (and retracted in the 1980s): that the Letters as they survive are compiled from mid-twelfth-century material, by a writer with didactic and institutional ends in view. Accordingly, he begins his essay with an account of Heloise based on sources other than the Letters. Then he gives a summary of the story the Letters tell and goes on to bring out their supposed moral. They are to be read as a story of conversion, a work in defense of good marriage that sets up a role model for women, and even men, by showing how Heloise overcame her innate feminine sensuality. There would be nothing at fault *methodologically* with such an interpretation, if Duby presented it plainly as based on accepting this or that theory of the Letters as inauthentic. Rather, he pretends agnosticism: he "will not enter into the controversy."[35] With an appearance of fair-mindedness, he declares at one point: "Let us grant that Heloise did indeed write her three letters—which I personally doubt to be the case."[36] Duby then goes on to remark that, even so, it would be wrong to think of the Letters as private confidences; they were, rather, public documents. This is an important point, but it does not, as it is supposed to do in the rhetorical structure of Duby's exposition, bridge the gap between acceptance and rejection of Heloise's authorship. If the correspondence is authentic, then it is extraordinarily difficult to see how Duby's interpretation can be retained. By pretending an agnosticism that he does not actually follow, Duby gives the impression that his interpretation will not be affected should historians discover (as indeed they had discovered even before he published his piece!) good evidence to support the authenticity of the correspondence. Respect for evidence would demand a greater openness to being shown wrong.

Another sort of agnosticism is the self-conscious, somewhat tortured agnosticism—ultimately abandoned—of the scholar who, more than any other, has devoted himself to thinking about the authenticity of the Letters and the theoretical problems linked to this question: Peter von Moos. In the early 1970s, when he wrote *Mittelalterforschung und Ideologiekritik,* von Moos had the following attitude to the question of authorship: he himself was less interested in finding an answer than in investigating the play of ideologies revealed by its historiography. But he believed that the question was one that in principle might be answered, although no satisfactory solution had yet been found. In seeking for it, scholars needed to become self-conscious and reflective about their own ideologies and to avoid the "inner-literary pseudo-history" that a narrowly specialized literary approach tends to bring, in favor of a sociological approach, which draws together, in an interpretative circle, an understanding of texts and that of the reality from which they derive.[37] Yet very soon after he published this book, von Moos seems, at least in part, to have abandoned his own principles. Impressed—overimpressed—by Benton's arguments in favor of forgery, yet not fully convinced by them, he appears to have given up any hope the problem of authenticity might be solved and sought a way of putting it aside. In his article "The Silence of Heloise," he remarks that

> although everyone says that the *Historia* and *Letters* are a unique masterpiece of world literature, where are the historians and literary sociologists who have genuinely concerned themselves with them? They have left the stage to a legion of historian-biographers who have, so to speak, monopolized research on Heloise. As a result, interest has been in "everything other than the text," as the French poet Charles Péguy said against the positivists."[38]

Von Moos proposes, by contrast, to study the text "as the visible effect of an unknown cause." After all, he adds, the "reality of the author," when transmitted in writing, "loses its brute autonomy and takes on the value of a sign." Von Moos is not, however, trying to cut all links between the text and the world outside but merely the special links traditionally thought to hold between a text and whoever wrote it. A text, he says, is "an integral part of a communication which cannot be understood outside the social context inextricably formed by the author, the reader and the book at a precise place and time."[39] Yet despite this inextricability, he suggests that we can, given our ignorance about the author, concentrate on the other two points of this triangle: a set of readers and a certain milieu. Von Moos takes these as being, respectively, some of the presumed medieval readers of the Letters and the monastic milieu in which the collection took the shape it has in the manuscripts. Often, though, in his practice, von Moos writes as if even such tenuous historical links are unnecessary. He is inclined to assume the Letters' inauthenticity, so that he can treat them as a single, unified composition and use his formidable skills as a literary critic and historian to reveal the interconnections within the Letters and *Historia,* between them and Abelard's theological work, and with a multitude of classical sources.

Von Moos, however, has implicitly come to see that such agnosticism is unsatisfactory. By 1980 he was advancing a somewhat strange hypothesis about the question of authorship itself, according to which Abelard and Heloise were indeed *both* authors of the Letters, but not as genuine correspondents; rather, they wrote them together as a collaborative composition.[40] In his (so far as I know) latest pronouncement on the subject, an article in a collection on forgery published in 1988, von Moos has moved even more definitely away from agnosticism. The Letters and *Historia,* he now claims, are definitely from the twelfth century and are *definitely* the work of a single author. The question that remains unsolved is whether they are a literary fiction (presumably Abelard's own) or a forgery.[41] I think that von Moos is wrong in his judgment, since the evidence points definitely toward authenticity. But I also think that von Moos, who has thought more carefully than anyone about the theoretical questions linked to the debate, is completely right to have seen that the positions he took immediately after he first wrote on the subject are unsatisfactory; that interesting discussion of the *Historia* and Letters requires the scholar to take a position about their composition and authorship.

My argument against agnosticism may seem too sweeping. Does it not simply exclude a purely literary approach? By what right can critics be prevented from merely reading and interpreting the texts, as they stand? Of course, there is no such right. Let literary critics interpret the texts as they will (although even they must acknowledge that in doing so they are bringing to bear all sorts of assumptions that are in fact linked to a presumed historical origin of the text—for instance, that the language they are written in is in fact Latin, that "Paris" refers to the place of that name in France, and so on). But they must convince their readers that their discussions are worth reading in the terms to which they lay claim: as purely literary readings of the texts. And why should we be interested in an exercise that can claim be to be no more than a display of the modern critic's ingenuity, since it renounces any claim to illuminate what someone, or more than one person, wrote at some time or times? If critics have something of their own to say, which they might do using any text or no text at all, let them be open about this. I suspect, though, that the main interest for almost every reader, medieval historian or nonspecialist alike, who comes to the *Historia* and Letters is linked to the fact that they were written in the Middle Ages and that, authentic or not, they help us to understand this remote past.

Feminist Scholarship and the Authenticity Debate

When, over the last two decades, scholars began to look at the Middle Ages from a feminist perspectives, the figure of Heloise could not but loom large. If Heloise wrote the Letters in her name, then—however interpreted—they are not merely one of the most remarkable pieces of writing by a medieval woman but a rich source for investigating many of the central themes in feminist scholarship: women and the body, women and language, women's use (and subversion) of male rhetoric. *If* Heloise wrote them—feminist scholars could no more ignore the authenticity controversy than they could Heloise herself, especially since it is only in the last few years that the weight of opinion among Abelard specialists has started clearly to favor authenticity, and this change has yet to filter through completely to the wider circle of medievalists.

Feminist scholars have reacted in four main ways to this troublesome "if." Some have simply accepted the authenticity of the Letters on others' authority—a perfectly acceptable procedure, which requires no more comment.[42] Some have adopted agnosticism. Some have entered the debate and tried to resolve it in favor of authenticity using (I shall claim, misusing) specifically feminist arguments. Finally, some have used the new contexts and emphases provided by feminist history to change the direction and nature of the authenticity debate.

The literary critic Peggy Kamuf, in her *Fictions of Feminine Desire: Disclosure of Heloise,* relegates discussion of the Letters' authenticity to a footnote. After mentioning just three scholars, two of whom wrote before World War II, she breezily remarks that "It cannot, of course, be a question of deciding the issue," and she quotes, mistranslating, Zumthor's remark about utopic spaces.[43] Another literary critic Glenda McLeod, in her article on self-definition in Heloise's Letters, opines that "we cannot prove their complete authenticity" but also that "we have no compelling reason to doubt that the letters are" by Abelard and Heloise. From this she concludes that the prudent course is "to turn from investigations of authenticity to look at the letters themselves"; doing which, she claims, "at the very least . . . sheds light on one of the 'two opposing and irreducible psycho-dynamisms' that dominate the letters."[44] In chapter 5 of this volume (co-authored with Katharina Wilson), McLeod keeps the same position: "Whether Heloise and Abelard wrote these Letters does not affect the argument that they evince a tense and highly fluent debate between well-matched opponents engaged in a sophisticated game of one-upmanship. . . ." Certainly, so far as the mere detection of rhetorical strategies is concerned, this remark is just. Whatever view is taken about authenticity, Wilson's and McLeod's searching out of these strategies remains valuable. But as soon as the critic engages in interpreting the strategies, the question of authenticity becomes important. There is a world of difference in how we understand a real game and a game that has been staged (which is what the "sophisticated game of one-upmanship" would be, were the Letters not authentic). And, in fact, despite their professed agnosticism, Kamuf, McLeod, and Wilson go on to treat the *Historia* and the Letters exactly as if they had vindicated—or accepted a vindication of—their authenticity. The *Historia* and Letters are a rich source for the study of women in medieval life, whether Heloise's contributions are authentic or not. But the evidence they bring is very different in each case. The particular interpretations Kamuf and Wilson/McLeod advance are plausible only given that the Heloise Letters are really hers. In short, their agnosticism seems to be like the "pretended agnosticism" of Duby.

The two articles on the Letters by French literary critic Claire Nouvet, one in French, one in English, show what turns out to be a rather different sort of agnosticism.[45] In the French article, it seems as if Nouvet, too, is a "pretended agnostic." She begins by declaring that her intention "is not to contribute to an historical debate which clearly seems as if it must remain unresolvable, but rather to read the history which is inscribed beneath these names" and goes on to explain that the names "Abelard" and "Heloise" must be taken to refer to the body of Letters attributed to each, not to their historical bodies.[46] Yet she then continues quite as if there were no problem about authenticity and "Abelard" and "Heloise" had their normal reference. But her English article, published in the same year, suggests that, for Nouvet, the contrast between real (human) bodies and the body of a text is much more than an incidental conceit. The article proceeds until the last paragraph as if there were no problem of authenticity and the Letters were written, as professed, by Abelard and Heloise. Nouvet provides a complicated analysis of the discussion about what Heloise and Abelard are to call each other: what name is Heloise to be given? Suddenly, as the essay is about to close, Heloise herself disappears from the discussion and we are referred to "the text written under the name of 'Heloise.'"[47] "Written under the name of 'Heloise' as if 'she' had indeed written it, this text," says Nouvet, "might name her better than any proper name could ever do. . . . 'Heloise,' in other words, names a text."[48] Nouvet thus gives the impression that, somehow, her discussion moves on a textual level to which considerations of historical authorship are irrelevant. This impression, though, is misleading. Whatever the merits of her analysis of naming and "the economy of sacrifice," its implications are quite different depending on whether it is taken to be a pattern of thought and rhetoric that emerged during a real exchange between two people, Abelard and Heloise, or a pattern within a work that is the product, or adaptation, of a single writer.[49]

An example of the third reaction of feminist scholars to the authenticity problem is an essay that has, rightly, been widely praised and, in all respects except that which I shall discuss, is a well-argued and widely informed study. In "Authority, Authenticity and the Repression of Heloise," the respected literary historian and critic Barbara Newman writes perceptively about these topics as they figure in Heloise's discussions, but she spends more than half of her article on the question of authorship.[50] She is an out-and-out defender of the Letters' authenticity. She draws, sensibly, on some of the best recent presentations of this position and adds in passing some acute remarks of her own. Yet there is something awry about her overall approach. Her strategy is double-edged. First, she goes through the most celebrated opponents of authenticity, showing that in each case these men—and those she cites are all male scholars—have shown a prejudice against women. They have tried to assert their authority and repress Heloise by denying her claims as an author. As a result, Newman argues, their practice has illustrated the very concerns about authority and repression of the female voice Heloise herself raises. Newman's thesis is elegant, and Robertson, Silvestre, and Benton are easy targets, since they are unselfconsciously prejudiced against women. But what about their arguments? A person's beliefs may be founded on prejudice, wholly or partly, but still be true. Newman sees no need to engage with the arguments against the view she favors; it is enough, she feels, to dismiss those who have propounded them. The other side of her strategy is to try to show the psychological impossibility that Abelard could have written the Letters attributed to Heloise. Newman recognizes that some question the strength of psychological arguments, but she responds by observing that "these scholars' appeals to abjure psychology allow their own psychological assumptions to go unchallenged, especially on the subject of gender"[51]—a point that is probably true but does not provide a vindication for psychological arguments. Those that Newman goes on to develop illustrate well why skepticism about this form of argument is necessary, all the more because she is a skillful and persuasive reader. The certainty that she claims about what was psychologically impossible for Abelard is simply not to be had, especially since the one set of documents that might give an insight into Abelard's character are precisely those—the *Historia* and the Letters—the interpretation (and authorship) of which are in dispute. Indeed, what Newman claims as psychological impossibilities have been cited by others as good ways of explaining why Abelard would have written the Letters attributed to Heloise: for example, the lavish praise of Abelard put into Heloise's mouth.[52]

The two examples I shall give of the fourth feminist reaction to the authenticity debate may seem, at first sight, strange: one is the English historian M.T. Clanchy's recent biography of Abelard, the other is chapter 3 in this volume by Constant Mews.[53] Their apparent unsuitability could not be more striking, since they both seem to sidestep the debate over authenticity rather than contribute to it, and neither is obviously a work of *feminist* scholarship. Yet these appearances are deceptive, and as a conclusion to this whole discussion I shall try to show how they do in fact affect the debate on authenticity, why (and in what sense) they should be considered feminist, and how they meet burdens of argument from evidence better than the other feminist writings discussed in this section.

Clanchy does not, indeed, enter into the detail of the authenticity debate, remarking in his preface that he is convinced by the case David Luscombe and Peter Dronke make for authenticity.[54] Yet, in fact, Clanchy's biography makes a large implicit contribution to making the case for authenticity absolutely firm, by showing the plausibility of both the Letters' composition (as a real correspondence) and of what they describe. Moreover, Clanchy shows that, if we look at the evidence carefully, without assuming Abelard's intellectual dominance, it seems that, in many respects, it was Heloise whose ideas were the bolder and whom Abelard copied.[55] One does not need to accept all the features of Clanchy's sometimes slightly shaky edifice to see the persuasiveness and importance of his argument.

Similarly, one can recognize the importance of Mews's discussion of Heloise, whether one accepts the contention that we have not only the well-known Letters, written in the 1130s, but a very full record of an earlier correspondence between Abelard and Heloise, while they were still lovers. Like Clanchy, Mews sees the relationship between the two as an intellectual relationship, even at that stage—and one in which Heloise was by no means the docile pupil. The wider study that Mews has also published will do even more to bring new material and new knowledge about women in the twelfth-century to bear on Heloise. Both Clanchy and Mews have, therefore, done more for the authenticity debate than they would have achieved had they merely addressed the questions in which it has traditionally been framed and added a new analysis or fresh evidence. They have raised new questions to be considered; they have changed the very terms of the debate.

The change they have effected also explains why their contributions should be thought of as feminist, since their new approach is based on insights derived from feminism. Feminist scholarship comes in many varieties and is linked to many different theoretical approaches. Much of it, however, stems from the perception that, until recently, women were pushed into the background by political, social, and intellectual historians. Even when, as in the case of Heloise, a female writer could hardly be simply ignored, the tendency was to view her in subordination to Abelard, as his adoring pupil, submissive wife, and intellectual follower. The once popular idea that Abelard himself was the author of Heloise's Letters may have owed some of its popularity to the fact that it takes this subordination to an extreme. Clanchy and Mews have learned—from the theoretical positions of feminism and, more importantly, from the historical research on medieval women carried out under its impetus—to challenge this picture.

They have mounted the challenge by producing evidence and arguments to support claims about various past states of affairs. These claims are ones that are falsifiable by the discovery of new evidence that definitely contradicts them or by flaws in the arguments on which they rest. There is a contrast to be drawn between Mews and Clanchy on the one hand and the other feminist scholars examined here. The aspect of Mews's and Clanchy's work that relates to (and transforms) the authenticity debate is fully open to counter-argument, new evidence, and reevaluation of evidence; the claims made in it are fully explicit and are open to being rejected (as some of them surely will be). By contrast, the treatment of the authenticity debate in the other feminist discussions is, I have argued, not fully open to counter-argument and to rejection in the face of new or reevaluated evidence.

Does this judgment mean that these other feminist scholars have produced bad scholarship? No, because in many ways their work is fine. But it does, arguably, imply that their discussions are flawed in a particular respect—that is, insofar as they concern the debate on authenticity. Only arguably, however: there is a higher-level objection to my position. Some feminists would reject the idea that there are ways of establishing, at least with a high degree of probability, the truth about states of affairs in the distant past. They would argue that what count as acceptable methods of argument and choices of evidence reflect the preconceptions and interests of particular groups and that therefore the views I have stated about the burdens of argument and evidence and truth about the past are fanciful. An attitude of scholarly neutrality in the search for truth is deceptive, they would say; and, some might add, feminist scholars do better to promote the cause of feminism through their work than to pursue an objectivity toward evidence that, even if it were attainable, could serve no good purpose. It would go far beyond the range of this chapter to explain why I would reject this view, which so many find so powerful and appealing.

Notes

1. Peter von Moos, *Mittelalterforschung und Ideologiekritik. Der Gelehrtenstreit um Héloise,* pp. 21–22.
2. Von Moos, *Mittelalterforschung,* p. 18.
3. I present a very brief sketch of the controversy. For a fuller account, see John Marenbon, *The Philosophy of Peter Abelard,* pp. 82–90.
4. Bernhard Schmeidler, "Der Briefwechsel zwischen Abälard und Heloise eine Falschung?," "Der Briefwechsel zwischen Abälard und Heloise als eine literarische Fiktion Abälards," "Der Briefwechsel zwischen Abaelard und Heloise dennoch eine literarische Fiktion Abaelards," "Abaelard und Heloise: eine geschichtlich-psychologische Studie."
5. D.W. Robertson, Jr. *Abelard and Heloise.*
6. Étienne Gilson, *Héloïse et Abélard,* 1938.
7. Richard W. Southern, "The Letters of Abelard and Heloise" (edn: Oxford, 1970), pp. 86–104.
8. John Benton, "Fraud, Fiction and Borrowing in the Correspondence of Abelard and Heloise," in Colloque pp. 469–511.
9. John Benton, "A Reconsideration of the Authenticity of the Correspondence of Abelard and Heloise," in Trier 1980, pp. 41–52.
10. Hubert Silvestre, "Die Liebesgeschichte zwischen Abaelard und Heloise: der Anteil des Romans" in *Fälschungen im Mittelalter* 5, MGH Schriften, 33.5, pp. 121–65.
11. Chrysogonus Waddell, *The Paraclete Statutes: Institutiones nostrae: Introduction, Edition, Commentary,* pp. 48–50.
12. Tore Janson, "Schools of Cursus in the Twelfth Century and the *Letters* of Heloise and Abelard," *Retorica e poetica tra i secoli XII e XIV.* pp. 171–200.
13. David E. Luscombe, "From Paris to the Paraclete: The Correspondence of Abelard and Heloise."
14. Peter Dronke, "Heloise, Abelard, and Some Recent Discussions," in his *Intellectuals and Poets in Medieval Europe,* pp. 245–342, at pp. 323–42.
15. Peter Dronke, *Abelard and Heloise in Medieval Testimonies,* rep. 1992, pp. 247–94.
16. Peter Dronke, "Heloise, Abelard," especially pp. 333–42.
17. Marenbon, *The Philosophy of Peter Abelard,* pp. 90–93.
18. It might be objected that this distinction is not ideological at all, but methodological. But if by ideology one means a set of ideas (in the broadest sense: arguments, positions, aims) by reference to which a person's actions and beliefs can be explained, even though the person might not have envisaged or accepted this explanation, then the distinction I make is, clearly, ideological as well as methodological. I realize, however, that most of those who favor ideological explanations will not be convinced by my distinction because it leaves little room for ideological explanations of the sort usually given. But this, of course, is precisely my point.
19. Silvestre, "Liebesgeschichte," p. 164. All translations from articles written in languages other than English are my own.
20. Silvestre, "Liebesgeschichte," p. 123.
21. Silvestre, "Liebesgeschichte," p. 165.
22. See the collection of Peter Dronke's main contributions to the authenticity debate in the section "Heloise With and Without Abelard" of Dronke's *Intellectuals and Poets,* pp.

245–342. See also Peter Dronke, *Women Writers,* pp. 107–39, and the book as a whole to see Dronke's overall approach.

23. Deborah Fraioli, "The importance of satire in Jerome's Adversus Jovinianum as an Argument against the authenticity of the Historia calamitatum," pp. 167–99.
24. Fraioli, "The Importance of Satire," p. 185.
25. Fraioli, "The Importance of Satire," pp. 193–94.
26. Fraioli, "The Importance of Satire," pp. 189–90.
27. Fraioli, "The Importance of Satire," p. 185.
28. Fraioli, "The Importance of Satire," p. 200.
29. See M.T. Clanchy, *Abelard: A Medieval Life,* p. 145.
30. In the section entitled "Feminist Scholarship and the Authenticity Debate" I will make a similar point about an article, admirable in many respects, by Barbara Newman, which takes the opposite view about authenticity.
31. This is done by M.T. Clanchy in his new biography, although he also adds an important new element to the whole discussion, which I discuss later.
32. Paul Zumthor, "Héloïse et Abélard," p. 314.
33. Paul Zumthor, ed. and trans., *Abélard et Héloïse: Correspondance,* p. 11–12.
34. Georges Duby, *Dames du XIIe siècle* 1, p. 73–110.
35. Duby, *Dames du XIIe siècle,* p. 91.
36. Duby, *Dames du XIIe siècle,* p. 92.
37. Von Moos, *Mittelalterforschung,* p. 127.
38. Peter von Moos, "Le Silence d'Héloïse et les ideologies modernes," pp. 425–68, at pp. 433–34; revised as "Die Bekehrung Heloises." My references are to the French version.
39. von Moos, "Le Silence d'Héloïse."
40. Peter von Moos, "*Post festum:* Was kommt nach der Authentizitätsdebatte über die Briefe Abaelards und Heloises," pp. 75–100.
41. Peter von Moos, "Heloise und Abaelard," pp. 150–61.
42. Two examples are: Martin Irvine, "Heloise and the Gendering of the Literate Subject," pp. 87–114; and Nancy F. Partner, "No Sex, No Gender," pp. 433–39. (On Partner's chosen authority, Barbara Newman, see below).
43. Peggy Kamuf, *Fictions of Feminine Desire: Disclosures of Heloise,* p. 149, n. 1.
44. Glenda McLeod, " 'Wholly Guilty, Wholly Innocent': Self-Definition in Héloïse's Letters to Abélard," pp. 64–86, at p. 64.
45. Claire Nouvet, "La castration d'Abélard: impasse et substitution" and "The Discourse of the 'Whore': An Economy of Sacrifice."
46. Nouvet, "La castration," p. 259.
47. Nouvet, "The Discourse," p. 772.
48. Nouvet, "The Discourse," pp. 772–73.
49. A similar, obfuscatory agnosticism is adopted by Jean-Charles Huchet in "La voix d'Héloïse." He prefaces his discussion with the remark that (p. 272): "For us, the text will be more important than its supposed author: Heloise and Abelard will remain the convenient signifieds of a written expression which is divided and turned-back on itself, which has no non-textual referent, and which sees in femininity the splendid game of writing which makes fun of sexual difference."
50. Barbara Newman, "Authority, Authenticity, and the Repression of Heloise," reprinted in *From Virile Woman to WomanChrist: Studies in Medieval Religion and Literature.* My references are to this reprinted edition.
51. Newman, "Authority, Authenticity," p. 53.
52. Newman, "Authority, Authenticity," p. 60. See Marenbon, *The Philosophy of Peter Abelard,* p. 87, n. 21.
53. Clanchy, *A Medieval Life.* Constant J. Mews, *The Love Letters of Abelard and Heloise: Perceptions of Dialogue in Twelfth-Century France,* and his chapter 3 in this volume.

54. Clanchy, *A Medieval Life,* p. xi.
55. Peter Dronke, however, deserves the credit for being the person who first began the new approach to Heloise, especially in his chapter on Heloise in *Women Writers.* See also Marenbon, *The Philosophy of Peter Abelard.*

CHAPTER 3

PHILOSOPHICAL THEMES IN THE *EPISTOLAE DUORUM AMANTIUM*: THE FIRST LETTERS OF HELOISE AND ABELARD

Constant J. Mews

This chapter considers the early relationship of Heloise and Abelard as a literary and philosophical relationship through the testimony of the Epistolae duorum amantium, *argued to be a record of their early letters.*

> When you sought me out for shameless pleasures, you showered me with incessant letters, you placed your Heloise on the lips of everyone through frequent song: I resounded through every market-place, each house. But how much more rightly might you now arouse me in God, as then you aroused me in lust! Consider, I beg you, what you owe me; listen to what I demand; and so I finish a long letter with a brief conclusion: Farewell, my only one.1

The exchange of letters between Heloise and Abelard has long fascinated readers as one of the great accounts of a love affair in medieval literature. Yet the question has often been asked whether a woman in religious life could really have written such an open letter to the man who was once her teacher at Notre-Dame.[2] None of the songs that Heloise says Abelard wrote in her honor have ever been conclusively identified (although educated guesses have been made about at least one poem in the *Carmina burana*).[3] Even less critical attention has been given to those "incessant letters" that she recalls at the end of her initial response to reading the *Historia calamitatum*. She was appalled that Abelard should have neglected her so brutally after entering the religious life while at the same time sharing the story of his life so openly with a unnamed friend, identified simply as "beloved brother in Christ, dearest companion from the religious life."[4] Abelard talks about Heloise as once the focus of his debauchery in the past and now his revered sister at the Paraclete but never addresses her in person (unless the *amicus* is a fiction by which he seeks to speak to her indirectly). He structures his narrative around contrast between worldly *amor* and the true consolation offered "to those who love God" (Romans 8.28: *diligentibus Deum*) by the Holy

Spirit. Heloise asks Abelard to resume an epistolary dialogue with her in which he offers as much *consolatio* to her as to his male friend. Her famous three letters to Abelard make sense only in relation to this earlier exchange of letters, to which she attaches great importance even though Abelard dismisses them as no longer relevant.

Heloise tends to be remembered as a paragon of selfless love for Abelard rather than as a student of philosophy. Yet the issues that she seeks to discuss with Abelard have profound ethical significance. Heloise insists in her first letter that he had not represented her views fully in reporting their discussion of love and marriage and her conviction that true *amor* was not driven by any desire for material reward. Her famous assertion that she would rather be called Abelard's prostitute than the Empress of Caesar employs a rhyming antithesis [*meretrix/imperatrix*] to emphasize a traditional philosophical ideal, that true friendship is not driven by any external reward, here applied to the friendship of a man and a woman. Her sentence that the word "friend" [*amica*], even "concubine" or "whore" [*concubine vel scorti*], was sweeter to her than the word "wife" [*uxor*] creates a deliberate literary shock to convey her argument that she was not interested in any material reward from her friendship.[5] The common translation of *amica* as "mistress" in this sentence misleadingly implies that she wanted to offer him sexual favors. Her argument, however, is that the friendship that she wanted, defined both by *amor* and *amicitia,* was not driven by any desire for material advantage or worldly reputation.[6] She calls God as her witness to the purity of her love.

The suddenness with which Heloise launches into an elaborate discussion of love after a silence of over fifteen years becomes much more comprehensible if she had already exchanged letters with him about the idea of love in the past. She sees no antithesis between *amor* [love by passion or inclination] and the *dilectio* [love by conscious choice] that he now offers her, but laments that his *dilectio* does not take into account her specific situation.[7] Heloise saw Abelard as having turned away from ideals about *amor* that she thought they had once shared. The major aspect of *amor* that Abelard recalls in the *Historia calamitatum* is the distraction it provided from truly philosophical inquiry, so as to emphasize his theme that God's consoling love (the Holy Spirit or Paraclete) had indeed come to his aid after carnal passion had proven itself empty. For all his enthusiasm to embrace pagan philosophy as consistent with Christian wisdom, he maintained a traditional view of *amor* as base passion in the *Historia calamitatum*. The model of friendship that he puts forward in that narrative is predicated on an assumption that he had transcended his sexual identity. Heloise wanted to resume within a religious context that more personal epistolary dialogue such as they had once shared in the past.

Abelard himself refers to this earlier exchange of letters with Heloise in such a way as to imply that they were simply a pretext by which he could seduce her: "I believed that she would consent all the more easily to me, the more I knew that she both possessed and loved knowledge of letters, and that even when separated, we could be present to each other through intermediary messages and that it was more daring to write about many things than to discuss them; thus we could always enjoy delightful conversations.[8] Abelard does not dwell on these written communications with Heloise but rather portrays their early relationship as one of unadulterated passion and sexual union. His account has exercised a powerful influence on the way their affair has been remembered, as more to do with sex than with philosophical discussion.

The image of the young Heloise as an impressionable teenager infatuated with her teacher has been reinforced since the seventeenth century by frequently asserted claims that she was about seventeen years old at the time of their affair (probably 1116/17). As M.T. Clanchy points out in his recent biography of Abelard, there is simply no documentary evidence for the claim that she was born around the year 1100.[9] The word *adolescentula* by which Abelard refers to her does not mean adolescent in the modern sense, but someone between the age of fifteen and twenty-eight. Abelard describes himself in the *Historia calamitatum* as an *adolescentulus* when he started to teach at Melun (probably about 1102, when he was twenty-three).[10] Peter the Venerable's comment to Heloise that he admired her for her learning even before she became a nun, coupled with Abelard's comment that she already enjoyed a great reputation for learning in the kingdom, suggests that she is more likely to have been in her early twenties when she met Abelard. It is quite possible that she had already developed her reputation for letters at Argenteuil (where she had been raised and educated) and that she came to Notre-Dame of her own will, because Abelard was teaching there.[11] Abelard consistently minimizes any initiative that she may have taken in developing their relationship.

Consequently little attention has been given to the character of her exchanges with Abelard during 1116/17. It has always been assumed that these messages have disappeared. Scholarly preoccupation with the issue of whether Heloise wrote the famous letters attributed to her (the authenticity of which has been challenged more often than that of the *Historia calamitatum*) has tended to divert attention from these early letters that the two apparently exchanged. Yet the final sentences of Heloise's first letter to Abelard leave little doubt about the importance that she attached to them. Her three famous letters to Abelard constitute part of her attempt to resume a dialogue to which she attached great importance.

One way to gain an idea of the sort of letters Heloise could have exchanged with Abelard is to look more closely at the *Epistolae duorum amantium,* a collection of over one hundred love letters and poems preserved as an exchange between a famous teacher and his brilliant young female student, edited by Ewald Könsgen in 1974 from a manuscript copied at Clairvaux in the late fifteenth century by Johannes de Vepria (or Jean de Vepria, to use the French form of his name).[12] This transcription, which does not always copy letters in their entirety, is now preserved in the Bibliothèque municipale of Troyes as MS 1452, fols. 159–167v. Könsgen established that Johannes de Vepria was a meticulous scribe who devoted his life to copying rare and unusual texts, both secular and religious, in the library of Clairvaux with great accuracy. From a close study of the vocabulary of these letters he argued that the transcription was a record of a genuine correspondence between two people from the first half of the twelfth century "very like Abelard and Heloise."[13] He noted a few obvious parallels between these lovers and that couple, such as the woman's admiration for the man's gifts in both poetry and philosophy, very similar to remarks made by Heloise about Abelard's gifts.[14] In letter 49 the woman comments on his greatness and reputation as a teacher, "to whom French pigheadedness rightly yields and for whom the haughtiness of the whole world rises in respect" [cui jure cedit francigena cervicositas et simul assurgit tocius mundi superciliositas]. This phrase suggests that her teacher is an outsider to France, understood in the twelfth century as the royal domain or the modern Île-de-France. In letter *50,* he addresses her as "the only student of philosophy among all the young women of our age, the only one on whom Fortune has completely bestowed all the gifts of the manifold virtues . . ." [Soli inter omnes etatis nostre puellas philosophie discipule, soli in qam omnes virtutum multiplicium dotes integre Fortuna conclusit . . .]. He praises her as so skillful in arguing about the laws of friendship that "you seem not to have read Cicero, but to have taught him instead." This is clearly a very gifted young woman. In letter *22,* the teacher exclaims that he directed his words to others, his intention to her, and often stumbled in his words because his thought was not in them, just as Abelard comments in the *Historia calamitatum.*[15] Könsgen did not engage in a detailed comparison of the ideas of the teacher and his student about love or in any more detailed comparison with known writings of Abelard and Heloise, a task that would have entailed issues far beyond the scope of a critical edition. Johannes de Vepria endeavored to identify the two parties in the correspondence as Woman and Man—*M[ulier]* and *V[ir]*—but did not always determine who was speaking or indeed whether there was a break between two letters. This suggests that the manuscript from which he was copying recorded a continuous exchange without clear demarcation between one letter and the next. A comment in letter *14* about the man wanting to hold on to her tablets longer, if he could, implies that she sent him messages on wax tablets and that he replied on the same tablet, carried by a messenger [*nuncius*] mentioned in letter *37.* One of the two parties must have kept a parchment copy both of the original message sent on a wax tablet and the reply received. A similar phenomenon of a teacher engaging in a verse dialogue with a female student is preserved in a twelfth-century manuscript from Regensburg.[16] All medieval students were required to use wax tablets to communicate with their teachers.[17] The Regensburg exchange seems to record an exercise in verse composition initiated by the teacher with a female student. It turns into an elaborate literary negotiation about the conduct of a relationship eventually terminated by the young woman concerned. One can always argue that these exchanges from Troyes and Regensburg are invented dialogues, as has sometimes been claimed for the famous Abelard–Heloise letters. The other possibility is that Johannes de Vepria came across a record of a genuine epistolary exchange, maintained (and perhaps subsequently edited) by the woman as a record of her dialogue with her teacher.

These letters attracted little critical attention in the two decades after their initial publication in 1974. One reason for this neglect may be related to the renewal in the 1970s and early 1980s of sometimes vitriolic debate about the authenticity of the letters of Heloise. As prominent an historian as Georges Duby asserted that all twelfth-century writing about love, including the letters of Heloise, was a male invention.[18] In a climate of sharp polarization between advocates of their authenticity and those who argued that they were simply textual inventions, few scholars risked sticking their necks out for some anonymous letters that might have even less claim to authenticity than the better-known letters of Heloise.

One of the few scholars to comment on the love letters was Peter Dronke, who devoted a couple of pages to them, both in a lecture published in 1976 and again in his book on medieval women writers, first published in 1984.[19] Interpreting them as representative of a tradition of literary exchanges in the early twelfth century, Dronke doubted that they were by Abelard and Heloise on the grounds that they seemed to present an idealistic relationship, very different from the explicitly sexual union described in the *Historia calamitatum.* He noted that in one letter (84), the woman exploits Pauline phrases to exclaim that "you have manfully fought the good fight, but you have not yet received the prize" to justify his suggestion that the letters "had not yet led—or perhaps would never lead—to physical fulfillment." The love letters were translated into Italian by Graziella Ballanti in 1988, but without any more than a brief summary of Könsgen's introduction.[20] In 1996 Étienne Wolff provided a regrettably incomplete translation of these letters in an anthology of various medieval texts about love, but again with very little critical analysis.[21] Wolff repeated Dronke's argument that their idealizing professions of love seemed different from the sensual indulgence recalled both by Abelard and Heloise. In a recent history of medieval French literature, Jean Charles Payen confidently asserted that these letters constitute an epistolary novel perhaps written by a male disciple of Abelard but offered no argument to substantiate his thesis, which runs diametrically against that put forward by Könsgen.[22]

Whatever its origin, Johannes de Vepria's transcription of sixty-five letters from a famous teacher and forty-eight from his female student, not all copied in their entirety, constitutes an extraordinary record. A number of features enable us to date these letters to the twelfth century. Könsgen pointed out that whereas Ovid is enthusiastically alluded to throughout the correspondence, there is no trace of any classical author discovered after the twelfth century. He also identified allusions to the poetry of Marbod of Rennes (c. 1035–1123).[23] The style of rhyming prose used in the woman's letters was much practiced within monastic circles between the tenth and twelfth centuries.[24] The man's letters are more influenced by a classicizing tendency to avoid excessive rhyme in prose.

Intimate Greetings in the Early Twelfth Century

The elaborate formulae of greeting in these letters serves to confirm a date in the first half of the twelfth century for the exchange. In epistolary convention going back to classical antiquity, it was customary for a person of higher rank to address someone of lesser status with the formula: "X, to Y: *salutem.*" A polite letter from an inferior to a superior or between two friends of equal rank followed the formula "To Y, X: *salutem.*" In an incisive survey of letter salutations in the medieval period, Carol Lanham has shown that the practice of finding elaborate variations on *salutem* first develops in a significant way in the late eleventh century.[25] The letters of Ivo of Chartres (1040–1116), St. Anselm (1033–1108), and St. Bernard of Clairvaux (1090–1153) all illustrate the way letter writers singled out intimate friends from other individuals by constructing more intimate forms of greeting. Mostly these are to other men, but sometimes they are to other women.[26] Count Stephen of Blois writes to his wife, Adela, from Nicaea in 1097 reporting the progress of the first Crusade: "Stephanus comes Adelae comitissae, dulcissimae amicae, uxori suae, quicquid mens sua melius aut benignius excogitare potest"[27] [Count Stephen to countess Adela, sweetest friend, his wife: whatever is better or more gracious than the mind can think]. This greeting is of particular interest in relation to the Abelard–Heloise letters as it shows how Stephen saw no inconsistency between addressing Adela as both wife [*uxor*] and friend [*amica*] in personal terms while respecting the convention that as her superior he put his name before hers (a convention that Heloise accuses Abelard of not observing in his first letter to her). Elsewhere Stephen addresses Adela as "your love" [*dilectioni tuae*] and as "dearest" [*carissima*].[28] While no letter written by Adela survives, poetry dedicated to her by Baudri of Bourgueil leaves no doubt that she was an unusually well educated noblewomen, fully conversant with classical and religious literature.[29] Whatever the pressure put on aristocratic women to marry for dynastic reasons, salutations like those composed by Count Stephen of Blois to Adela remind us that such marriages did not preclude expressions of personal affection.

In the love letters, the greetings provide an opportunity for both parties to elaborate at length on what makes the identity of the other person so special. For the most part they expand upon the polite formula: "To Y, X: greeting." The opening salutation of the woman's first letter is constructed from rhyming phrases that allude to the Song of Songs (4:10). Instead of identifying her lover by name, she describes him as her love: "Amori suo precordiali, omnibus aromatibus dulcius redolenti, corde et corpore sua: arescentibus floribus tue juventutis, viriditatem eterne felicitatis" [To her heartfelt love, more sweetly scented than any spice, She who is his in heart and body: the freshness of eternal happiness (even) as the flowers fade of your youth]. The man's first reply (*2*) does not employ her imagery or rhyming phrases but rather defines her uniqueness and singularity in being a comfort for his tired mind: "Singulari gaudio et lassate mentis unico solamini, ille, cuius vita sine te mors est, quid amplius quam seipsum, quantum corpore et anima valet" [To the singular joy and only solace of a tired mind, he whose life without you is death: what more than himself in so far as he is able in body and soul]. For most of the correspondence, the two lovers seek to outdo each other in the way they define their relationship. Even in these first two greetings, however, key differences between the letters of the man and the woman can be glimpsed, suggesting that the two individuals already have distinct literary identities. The difference in prose style is only one of many features that, as Könsgen pointed out, make it exceedingly unlikely that the letters could have been written by one person.[30]

In these letters, the woman is much more likely than the man to employ scriptural imagery. The word *cor* [heart] occurs thirty-one times in her letters, compared to only thirteen times in his letters (even though there are more letters from him than from her). By contrast *unicus* [unique] is a word that he uses in many letters, including the last message from him to carry a greeting: *2, 31, 37, 47, 63, 75, 89, 99, 110.* She uses *unicus* only twice, the first time in direct imitation of her teacher's farewell in the previous letter, "Farewell, my only rest" [*Vale . . . unica quies mea*]. It occurs at the end of a short letter (48), worth quoting in its entirety as an example of her literary gift. As in letter 18, *Par pari . . .* ["An equal to an equal . . .], she reverses the traditional epistolary order of an inferior addressing a superior. Her little poem in letter 48 is not copied as verse in the manuscript: "Amans amanti amoris viriditatem. / Nemo debet vivere / nec in bono crescere, / qui nescit diligere / et amores regere. Quid pluribus opus est verbis? Igne amoris tui succensa te diligere volo per secula. Vale, unica salus mea et solum in mundo, quod amem" [From lover to lover: the freshness of love. / No one ought to live / or grow in good, / who does not know how to love / and rule their desires. / What need is there for more words? Aflame with the fire of desire for you, I want to love you forever. Farewell, my only well-being and all that I love in the world]. Her theme in this letter, written after a particularly passionate message from the man (*47*) about having a sleepless night because he thinks of her all the time, is that loving [*diligere*] involves ruling the passions [*amores*]. At the same time, she sees no inconsistency between being on fire with love [*amor*] and loving [*diligere*] by conscious choice. She introduces *unicus* at the end of her letter to demonstrate that she is responding to his letter and is not rejecting him. The only other time she uses *unicus* is in a technical phrase about understanding all men as individuals (88: *omnes homines capiendos in unicos*).

A related word that he uses in his first letter to her but that she never employs as a term of endearment is *singularis,* occurring four times in his letters to emphasize the importance he attaches to "singularity" (*2, 4, 54, 56*). The only time she uses *singu-*

laris is within a sentence (23) employing a consciously scholastic definition of the well-constructed statement as one in which one thinks of "the qualities of individual parts." She prefers *specialis* to signify that which is important to her. In letter 21 she employs philosophical vocabulary not easily translated into English to identify her beloved both in his special and his general or essential nature: "To her beloved, special from the experience of the reality itself: the being that she is" [Dilecto suo speciali, et ex ipsius experimento rei: esse quod est]. While *esse* could refer to the sender, it seems more likely that she is offering him her own being. In previous letters she had offered him herself (5, 11), just as he had offered himself in his first letter (*2*), but now she wants to offer him that which she is, identifying him as someone who she knows from experience is special.[31] Her greeting suggests that she wants to engage in philosophical debate with him. While her effort might not get high marks from a logician to whom "special" can apply to different members of a species, her greeting manifests a desire (albeit very unformed) to express a distinct philosophical position.

The woman articulates her desire to absorb philosophical art from early in the correspondence. In letter 5 she begs God, giver of all art and *ingenium,* that she be endowed with "the skill of the art of philosophy, in order that I may greet you in writing, most beloved, according to my will" [philosophie artis impleat pericia, quo te possim, dilectissime, ita salutare scriptis ad consensum mee voluntatis]. Perhaps in response to criticism made of her efforts in letter 21, she complains at length in letter 23 about her inability to address him as she sought in terms of an internal soliloquy between her spirit [*animus*] and her capacity [*ingenium*]. This leads up to her major observation in letter 23, that although she has profited so much from the riches of her philosophy, she is still not completely happy: "the greatest joys have flowed and flow to me from the riches of your philosophy, but, to speak frankly, they make me less than completely happy in this matter" [Scio quidem et fateor ex philosophie tue diviciis maximam michi fluxisse et fluere copiam gaudiorum, sed, ut inoffense loquar, minorem tamen quam que me faciat in ea re perfecte beatam]. She is still dissatisfied by his often rather brief protestations of love, which do not evoke the philosophical seriousness that she wants to apply to an understanding of their relationship. As if aware that she is wanting more from their exchange, he engages in letter *24* in discussion of the nature of love, in response to a question she apparently was accustomed to ask him (although not in any of the previous letters copied by Johannes de Vepria). Even by letter 49, however, she feels that she is still not fully satisfied by his letters, much as she yearns for them. In the exchange she is always the partner who wishes to experiment further in the articulation of her ideas.

Unusual Words in the Woman's Love Letters

One of the many intriguing features of the woman's vocabulary in the second half of the exchange is her propensity to play with unusual words, often turning a familiar adjective into an abstract concept. The word she uses to describe the arrogance of the whole world, *superciliositas* (49) derives from *supercilium,* or brow [above the eye], just as *cervicositas* derives from *cervicosus,* stiff-necked. She also likes making up unusual adjectives from verbs by adding an *ibilis: inepotabilis* (86), 'unquenchable' from the verb *epoto,* drink up; *innexibilis* (94), 'bindable' from *innecto,* bind; *dulcifer* (98), 'sweetness-bearing' from *dulcia fero.*

Of particular interest for determining the authorship of the love letters is the word *scibilitas,* which she uses in the opening of letter 53: "De favo sapiencie si michi stillaret guttula scibilitatis, aliqua olenti nectare cum omni mentis conamine alme dilectioni tue litterarum notulis conarer depingere. Ergo in omni latinitate non est sermo inventus qui aperte loquatur erga te quam sit animus meus intentus, quia deo teste cum sublimi et precipua dilectione te diligo" [If any droplet of knowability could drop down to me from the honeycomb of wisdom, I would try with every effort of my mind to portray in the jottings of my letter various things with a fragrant nectar for your nourishing love. But throughout all Latinity, no phrase has yet been found which speaks clearly about how intent on you is my spirit, for God is my witness that I love you with a sublime and exceptional love]. The only author prior to the thirteenth century whom I have found to use *scibilitas* is Peter Abelard. In his *Dialectica,* composed before the *Logica 'Ingredientibus'* (c. 1118–20) and quite possibly in large part before he became a monk at Saint-Denis, Abelard explains that forms can be applied to what is formed through their *nomina.*[32] Sometimes two forms could be applied to a single adjective, as in the case of *scibilis* [knowable]: "For as 'knowable' can be said to be 'knowable by knowledge,' thus also 'knowable' can well be said to be 'knowable by knowability' and indeed more properly, since this is the proper form of 'knowable,' as it clearly happens according to Plato that it can have two relatives, or perhaps more."[33] Abelard's point is that 'knowable' [*scibilis*] can apply to something known and to an ideal form of 'knowability.'[34] He repeats the idea that *scibilitas* is the power of knowing [*potentiam sciendi*] by which something becomes knowable when he resolves an apparent contradiction between Porphyry and Aristotle on the relation between knowledge and what is knowable in his gloss on the *Categories.*[35]

In letter 53 the woman combines *scibilitas* with a vivid image of nectar dripping from the honeycomb of his wisdom (an allusion to Song of Songs 4.11), a poetic rendering of precisely the same relation between the potential for knowing and what was known as interested Abelard. Her use of *scibilitas* must invite the question whether she is Abelard's most famous pupil. Heloise's fascination with creating new words and new combinations of words was singled out as a distinctive feature of her command of Latin by Hugh Metel (d. c. 1150), writing probably not long after Abelard's death in 1142: "Your reputation, flying through the void, has resounded to us; resounding worthily from you, it has roared on us. It has informed us that you have surpassed the female sex. How? By composition, by versifying, by joining new words, making known words new, and what is more excellent than everything, you have overcome womanly weakness and have hardened into virile strength.[36] The creation of neologisms is a characteristic feature of twelfth-century scholastic prose. The woman's use of *scibilitas* within a letter about the limitations of Latinity to articulate what is in her spirit [*animus*] gives vivid expression to a wider contemporary desire among the intellectually adventurous to go beyond the traditional boundaries of Latin expression.

The Greetings in the Monastic Letters of Heloise and Abelard

There are other parallels between the vocabulary of the love letters and that of Heloise and Abelard. The woman and the man have different ways of identifying the individuality of the other person. The contrast between the teacher's preference for *singularis* and his student's fondness for *specialis* illuminates Heloise's greeting in her third letter to Abelard: "*Suo specialiter, sua singulariter.*"[37] While the sense of this greeting was obscured by the erroneous reading of *Suo* as *Domino* in the 1616 edition and subsequent translations, its true meaning is certainly "To him who is hers specially, she who is his singularly." Heloise is reminding him of the difference between the epithet *singularis* that Abelard used of her and the epithet *specialis* that she used of him. When both St. Bernard and Hato of Troyes (Heloise's own bishop) combine *singulariter* and *specialiter* in one sentence, they treat them as synonyms.[38] Heloise was aware of the contrast between the two terms, both of which referred to the intimacy she wished to recover. The close correspondence between the vocabulary of the love letters and that of Heloise's greeting must itself constitute important evidence for considering the love letters to have been written by Abelard and Heloise.

The greeting *suo specialiter, sua singulariter* makes sense only as part of a larger dialogue played out in the greetings of Heloise and Abelard's response to them. In the *Historia calamitatum* (which does not open in the manner of a conventional letter), Abelard had addressed his narrative not to Heloise but to an unidentified male friend, who serves as a focal point by which Abelard can tell the story of his life. In that account Heloise is initially the focus of his lust and then becomes the saintly leader of a community of nuns, but she is never someone whom he addresses directly. Heloise opens her first letter to him in the most general way possible, befitting a nun writing to an abbot, but then moves toward a more individual form of address: "To her Lord or rather father, to her husband or rather brother, his servant or rather daughter, his wife or rather sister, to Abelard, Heloise" [Domino suo immo patri, conjugi suo immo fratri, ancilla sua immo filia, ipsius uxor immo soror, Abaelardo Heloysa]. Aware of the formality by which she ought to address Abelard, she intimates her desire to communicate with him as an individual writing to an individual. Particularly unusual is the absence of any synonym for *salutem*. The intimate tone of the letter is conveyed in its first sentences, in which she addresses him as *dilectissime* and then *unice* [only one]. The very last line of this letter, *Vale unice,* itself functions as the climax to her greeting. Having opened by addressing Abelard in the most formal terms possible, she concludes by employing a term of endearment that he had at one time used so often of her in his letters in the past.

Abelard replies to her salutation by picking up its closing terms, but rephrases them into a deliberately formal expression of the religious character of his love for her: "To Heloise, his beloved sister in Christ, Abelard, her brother in him" [Heloise, dilectissime sorori sue in Christo, Abaelardus, frater ejus in ipso].[39] Like her, he breaks with convention in not offering a synonym for *salutem*. The final metrical farewell of his first reply to Heloise itself recalls the elaborate farewells in the love letters, but now extended to take into account her new situation: "Live, fare well, and may your sisters live and fare well. May you all live, but, I beg, remember me to Christ" [Vive, vale, vivantque tue valeantque sorores. / Vivite, sed Christo, queso, mei memores].[40]

In her second letter to Abelard, Heloise makes a point of showing how she recognizes his identity within Christ, but employs the term *unicus* with which she had concluded her first letter: "To her only one after Christ, his only one in Christ" [Unico suo post Christum, unica sua in Christo].[41] She does not conclude this second letter with any formula of farewell. In his second reply Abelard returns to a studied formality, identifying her only in general terms: "To the bride of Christ, the servant of the same" [*Sponse Christi, servus ejusdem*].[42] He hammers home this theme in his farewell: "Fare well in Christ, bride of Christ, fare well in Christ and live in Christ. Amen" [Vale in Christo, sponsa Christi, in Christo vale, et Christo vive. Amen].[43] In her third greeting Heloise returns to the theme of individuality by invoking the two different epithets that they had used of each other, *specialis* and *singularis.* Her final farewell has an astonishing coolness: "Speak to us and we shall listen. Fare well" [Loquere tu nobis, et audiemus. Vale].[44] She was unable to make Abelard acknowledge her individuality in the way that he had done so often in the love letters.

The Discussion of Love in the Love Letters

Scibilitas and the *singularis / specialis* contrast are not the only words in the love letters that parallel the known vocabulary of Abelard and Heloise. In letter *24,* after the woman has complained that his letters make her less than completely happy, her teacher opens up a philosophical discussion in response to her frequent question to him: what is love? His answer is revealing not so much for its originality as for betraying a distinctive interpretation of Cicero's *De amicitia,* influenced by the concerns of a logician more than of a thinker about ethics:

> Soles a me querere dulcis anima mea quid amor sit, nec per ignoranciam excusare me possum, quasi scilicet de re incognita sim consultus, cum ita me idem amor imperio suo subiecerit, ut non extranea res, sed multum familiaris et domestica, immo intestina videatur: Est igitur amor, vis quedam anime non per se existens nec seipsa contenta, sed semper cum quodam appetitu et desiderio se in alterum transfundens, et cum altero idem effici volens, ut de duabus diversis voluntatibus unum quid indifferentur efficiatur. . . .
>
> Scias quia, licet res universalis sit amor, ita tamen in angustum contractus est, ut audacter affirmem eum in nobis solummodo regnare, in me scilicet et in te domicilium suum fecisse. Nos enim duo amorem integrum, invigilatum, sincerum habemus, quia nichil est dulce, nichil quietum alteri, nisi quod in commune proficit; eque annuimus, eque negamus, idem per omnia sapimus. Quod inde facile probari potest, quia tu sepe meas cogitaciones anticipas; quod ego scribere concipio, tu prevenis et, si bene memini, tu illud idem de te dixisti
>
> [You often ask me, my sweet soul, what love is—and I cannot excuse myself on grounds of ignorance, as if I had been asked about a subject unfamiliar to me. For that very love has brought me under its own command in such a way that it seems not to be external but very familiar and personal, even visceral. Love is therefore a particular force of the soul, existing not for itself nor content by itself, but always pouring itself into another with a certain hunger and desire, wanting to become one with the other so that from two diverse wills, one is produced without difference. . . .
>
> Know that even if love is a universal thing, it has nevertheless been condensed into so confined a place that I would boldly assert that it reigns in us alone—that is, it has made its very home in me and in you. For the two of us have a love which is pure, tended and sincere, because nothing is sweet or carefree for the other unless it has a common benefits. We concede equally, we decline equally, we feel the same about everything. This can be easily shown by the way that you often anticipate my thoughts: what I think about writing, you write first, and, if I remember well, you said the same thing about yourself. Farewell, and regard me with unfading love, just as I do you].

The teacher's definition of *amor* provides a rare opportunity for us to hear him adopt a pedagogic voice. His definition relies on a fairly literal paraphrase of Cicero's comments on friendship, with a few significant modifications. In his *De amicitia,* Cicero had commented that just as it is characteristic of all living creatures to love themselves and seek out others of their kind, so it is a human characteristic for a man to love himself and seek out another "whose spirit he mixes with his own, so that it makes almost one thing out of two." A friend is thus an *alter idem,* another self.[45] Elsewhere Cicero speaks of the force of friendship making one mind out of several.[46] He also suggests that *amor* and *amicitia* both derive from love that does not seek any self-advantage.[47] The teacher agrees that there is a union between two wills but changes Cicero's definition slightly to explain that it makes two wills the same "not differently." He had used *indifferenter* in a previous letter (*16*) when offering his beloved affection, "the more enduring as the well-being of each of us is made a shared affair without difference" [quo in unius nostrum salute res communis indifferenter agitur].

The idea that two individuals can be the same *indifferenter,* as distinct from being the same in essence, is precisely the position that Abelard says in the *Historia calamitatum* that he forced William of Champeaux to accept in a public disputation in around 1109, when Abelard was teaching at Sainte-Geneviève and William was still at Saint-Victor.[48] William of Champeaux subsequently applied this terminology of two individuals being the same in being not different in discussion of the Trinity.[49] The position was not in itself profoundly original. Boethius himself had commented that *indifferentia* was the cause of unity in the case of the divine Trinity, as Roscelin reminded Abelard.[50] In 1109 the young Abelard was still much influenced by Roscelin's emphasis on the separateness of individuals belonging to the same species or genus and had not yet formulated the more sophisticated analysis of universals presented in the *Logica 'Ingredientibus'* and '*Nostrorum petitioni.'* He was perceived by his critics as simply one of those "modern dialecticians" who rejected the real existence of universals, to echo the claim of St. Anselm.

The usage of *indifferenter* in letters *16* and *24* is illuminated by fuller discussion of the term in the *Sententie secundum magistrum Petrum,* preserved in a manuscript (Orléans, Bibliothèque municipale 266) that records the opinions of various masters active in Paris in the years 1109 to 1113. When discussing the meaning of "who" in the phrase *mulier que dampnavit, salvavit* [the woman who has damned (us), has saved (us)], Abelard explains that "who" does not refer to the same person as Eve but to the female sex in general. He explains that when the phrase "Socrates is a man" is defined as "Socrates is that which he is," *id quod* refers without difference [*indifferentur*] both to the person and nature of Socrates.[51] Abelard picks up the problem again in his commentary on Aristotle's *Periermeneias,* certainly written after he had become a monk at Saint-Denis, c. 1117"" . . . just as when it is said 'through woman came death, through the same one life' and 'woman who has damned [us], has redeemed [us],' we apply pronouns indifferently, not personally, as if one said "the woman has damned and the same one, that is the thing which is her sex has redeemed [us]," namely similarly, so that it is said according to the non-difference of sex rather than according to the identity of person"[52] He is arguing that Eve and Mary are not different in so much as they are both women, even though they are not the same person. Abelard's use of "non-difference" as a concept is not echoed in discussions of the phrase offered by his contemporaries.[53] Unlike William of Champeaux, he refuses to identify identity through nondifference as a *res,* or thing.[54] When Abelard comments on the phrase "a woman damned the world and the same one saved it" in his *Christian Theology* (c. 1122), he explains identity in terms not of "womanly nature" as in the *Sententie* but of definition.[55] Yet even if he is here moving away from an essentialist understanding of "woman," he still legitimizes traditional assumptions about Eve and Mary by finding a logically acceptable interpretation for the phrase.

A further sign of the teacher's philosophical position is provided by his changing Cicero's definition of friendship as "a thing contracted" [*contracta res est et adducta in angustum*] into "a universal thing contracted" [*res universalis . . . in angustum contractus*]. The teacher does so to argue that love is a universal thing that exists only between himself and his beloved.[56] The modification allows him to slip in the thought that no true universal substance exists other than their love. By implication, all other objects in the world are separate individuals, not sharing any universal thing in common. In all his mature discussions of universals, written after he had become a monk at Saint-Denis, Abelard avoided any description of a universal as a *res,* or thing. Yet he does once refer to a *res universalis* in his *Dialectica,* a treatise certainly earlier than the *Logica 'Ingredientibus'* and very likely composed at least in part before he became a monk.[57]

The woman responds to her teacher's definition of love with her own thoughts in letter 25. She also draws on Cicero's *De amicitia* but is concerned much more with discussing its specifically ethical dimension, as distinct from the issue of identity and difference in which he is interested. Less convinced that true love already exists between them, she speaks more of love as an ideal always to be reached. She reminds him that if their love dissolved, it would not have been true love. Her synthesis draws on both Ciceronian and Christian ideas about love to create a distinct position. Where Cicero had considered complete *caritas* to exist only between two people or a few people, she considers *caritas* to be a Christian duty that should be shown to all. She describes intimate love not as *caritas* but as *dilectio,* and uses *specialis* to refer to that love which is not general without making any claims about the uniqueness or singularity of the focus of love. Roman philosophers, like Cicero, considered the ideal of friendship, or *amicitia,* as a male ideal quite different from a relationship between a man and a woman, based on emotion.

The woman employs *amor* and *dilectio* in almost equal frequency in her letters. (*Dilectio* occurs thirty-nine times in her letters as quoted by Johannes de Vepria, compared to ten times in his, even though her letters are fewer in number; *amor* occurs in fifty-two times in her letters, forty-seven times in his.) Whereas her teacher prefers traditional Ovidian vocabulary about love as an escape from reason, she develops the notion of *amor* as an ideal. For all his effort in letter *24* to define *amor* according to Cicero's definition of friendship, the dominant notion of *amor* that he employs is that of emotion, uninfluenced by Christian literature. She combines Ovidian ideas of love as passion, Ciceronian ideals of friendship, and Christian ideals of *dilectio,* interpreted as a special kind of *caritas.* In letter 49 she relates Cicero's theme that true friendship does not seek pleasure or profit to the *dilectio* she seeks to develop with her beloved: "Nam qui ob divicias vel volumptates sese diligere videntur, eorum nullomodo diuturnam arbitror amiciciam, cum res ipse propter quas diligunt, nullam videantur diuturnitatem habere. Quo fit, diviciis vel voluptate deficientibus eorum eciam deficiat simul et dilectio qui non propter se res, sed se propter res dilexerunt" [For I do not consider the friendship of those who seem to love each other for riches and pleasures to be durable at all, since the very things on which they base their love seem to have no durability. Consequently, when their riches or pleasure run out, so too at the same time love may fail, since they loved these things not because of each other but each other because of these things]. Ideas such as these lead her teacher to observe in letter *50* that she discusses the laws of friendship with such subtlety that "you seem not to have read them in Tully, but to have given precepts to Tully." His comment is in many ways fully accurate. She transforms Cicero's ideals of *amicitia* with Christian vocabulary of *dilectio.* This letter *50* provides the first occasion on which he speaks of their love as *dilectio.* In letter 82, she exclaims "If I owned whatever Caesar possessed, such riches would be as nothing to me."These ideas are not totally original to Heloise. Similar sentiments can be seen in the poetry of Marbod of Rennes and an anonymous *puella* to whom some love poems are attributed.[58] The protestation about preferring to be Abelard's *meretrix* rather than Caesar's *imperatrix* was a more poetically dramatic assertion of the same ideal.

The woman's love letters defend precisely the Ciceronian position that Gilson pointed out as central to Heloise's argument about love (although Gilson was incorrect in thinking of it as a purely pagan position).[59] Heloise's protestations about loving him for himself alone, "*te pure, non tua concupiscens,*" so often construed as evidence of her loving disposition, articulate carefully considered ideas about the character of true love, which transform Roman ideals of friendship into a reflection about the relationship between a man and woman rather than just between men. In the *Historia calamitatum* Abelard attributes to Heloise many exempla from classical antiquity, culled from Jerome's *Against Jovinian,* that demonstrate the incompatibility of marriage and the philosophical vocation. He had already quoted a number of these passages at greater length in the *Theologia christiana,* written not long after 1121.[60] As the woman alludes to a number of passages from Jerome's correspondence in her love letters, it may be that Heloise did draw on Jerome when arguing against marriage, as Abelard insists. It is not impossible that his own familiarity with Jerome had been prompted by the researches of Heloise.[61] We simply cannot tell if she delivered her arguments against marriage in writing to Abelard from Brittany before he returned to Paris to make her his wife. Even if Heloise had inspired those passages of Jerome in praise of the chastity of the ancient philosophers in the *Theologia christiana,* Abelard had not absorbed for himself the full significance of her arguments about selfless love. Like Abelard, Heloise is committed to the study of philosophy, as formulated by the ancient authors, but her major interest is in ethics rather than logic. She accuses him of not doing justice to her arguments about preferring love to marriage. Her early ethical concerns about the nature of love subsequently developed into a range of other spheres. Subsequently she applied those concerns to a discussion of how to observe the religious life and the meaning of many difficult passages in scripture. Elements of her thinking about love as not pursuing any other end than God himself surface in Abelard's definition of *caritas* in the *Theologia 'Scholarium,'* drafted in the 1130s. His discussion here occurs within a different context, however, from those of an intimate debate between a teacher and his student.

The Evolution of the Relationship

The relationship undergoes a major crisis midway in the exchange, culminating in her making the decision in letter 60 that their relationship should cease. Something had happened to prompt his admission in letter *59* that: "I am guilty, who have forced you to sin" [Ego nocens sum, qui te peccare coegi]. His language is allusive, shaped by assumptions about sin (a concept never mentioned in her letters), but it seems that he felt remorseful about pushing her into a sexual relationship. The first major crisis occurs when she asks in letter 60 that their writing should cease, a request presumably related to his confession of guilt in *59* that he had forced her to sin.

After this point in the exchange, she starts to experiment with metrical poetry, expressing her emotions in an even more controlled way than in her prose. Her poems articulate ideas that she has already raised in prose. After a long phase in which the lovers seem reconciled to each other, her tone changes dramatically in letter 94, in it she accuses him of not being a true friend, after he sends a note lamenting that *amor* and *pudor* were pulling in different directions. She accuses him of changing his behavior. He protests his constancy, but in *101* repeats his argument that they ought to be more cautious, to quiet rumors that were spreading. By letter *106* he exclaims "I bear the price of foolishness because I have not known how to keep that good as I ought" [Ego precium ob stulticiam fero, quia bonum illud, quod retinere, sicut decuit, nescivi . . .]. The final letters in the exchange do not flow smoothly from one to another, as if the extracts copied by Johannes de Vepria represent only fragments from a much fuller dialogue.

Her attitude changes once more in her last major letter (112), the only one in which she greets her beloved formally as her teacher. She reports that she is "carried away by great exultation of mind" and recalls how in the past she was "taken up into the third heaven" by his letters. She is confident that in the future "the mountaintops will bow down before you." She on the other hand can find no words to express her joy that "I am reaching the haven of your love secure and not ungrateful" [quod portum tue dilectionis secura nec ingrata optineo]. Inexplicably this letter is followed by a short note from her, carrying a brief judgment from Johannes de Vepria that it comes "from another [letter]": "Uni est amor et dilectio, ibi semper fervet exercicium. Jam fessa sum, tibi respondere nequeo, quod dulcia pro gravibus accipis ac per hoc animum meum contristaris. Vale" [Where there is passion and love, there always rages effort. Now I am tired, I cannot reply to you because you are taking sweet things as burdensome and in doing so you sadden my spirit. Farewell]. Her lament parodies the Maundy Thursday hymn, *Ubi caritas et amor, Deus ibi est.* She is finding that it far from easy to combine those ideals of *amor* and *dilectio* that she wanted to link. Her beloved was treating what she thought were sweet things as troublesome. This note is followed by the final letter in the exchange, a lament from her teacher about how he had been "conquered" by *amor,* seduced by her external beauty. His perspective on love here is shaped not by Ciceronian ideals of *amicitia* or her ideals of true love but by a traditional Ovidian theme that love is a passion by which a man succumbs to the charms of a woman. His claim in letter *24* that their love was the only universal thing carries little weight in the face of the chasm in attitudes toward love evident in these final letters of the exchange.

The contrast in attitudes of the teacher and student toward love is very similar to that which divides Abelard from Heloise. Coupled with other parallels between the vocabulary of the love letters and that of early logical writings of Abelard, this similarity must constitute strong circumstantial evidence in favor of identifying the *Epistolae duorum amantium* as an incomplete copy of the lost letters of Heloise and Abelard, exchanged at the time of their affair in 1116/17. If this exchange is an epistolary novel, it is a dialogue of astonishing brilliance. These letters document a student's desire to acquire mastery of philosophy, above all in relation to ethics. In the *Historia calamitatum* Abelard was eager to show that he had transcended what he considered to be the one major blemish on his career, his seduction of Heloise. She took the opportunity of reading his account (perhaps deliberately written with the idea that it should also be read by Heloise) to urge Abelard to enter again into a more intimate epistolary dialogue such as she had once enjoyed at Notre-Dame. Although initially reluctant to make that step, Abelard did evolve in his willingness to participate in the life of the Paraclete, as the unfolding of his correspondence makes clear. Yet Abelard always remained committed to academic and monastic values, profoundly patriarchal in character. There were limits to the extent to which an educated man was prepared to go in his dialogue with a woman. In those early years of their relationship, Abelard had difficulty in providing Heloise with the kind of philosophical dialogue that she sought. Those early difficulties never fully disappeared.

Notes

This chapter, originally delivered in Paris at the conference "Les échanges intellectuelles au XIIe siècle," organized by the Centre Nationale de Recherche Scientifique (CNRS), summarizes certain key features of my argument in *The Lost Love Letters of Heloise and Abelard: Perceptions of Dialogue in Twelfth-Century France* (St. Martin's Press, 1999).

1. *Ep.* 2, ed. Monfrin 117, Hicks 53, Muckle 73 (Radice 118): "Cum me ad turpes olim voluptates expeteres, crebris me epistolis visitabas, frequenti carmine tuam in ore omnium Heloysam ponebas; me platee omnes, me domus singule resonabant. Quanto autem rectius me nunc in Deum, quam tunc in libidinem excitares? Perpende, obsecro, que debes; attende que postulo. Et longam epistolam brevi fine concludo: vale, unice." My translation differs slightly from that of Radice. Heloise's allusion to her being proclaimed in all marketplaces and houses may be a rhetorical allusion to Song of Songs 3.2.
2. Peter von Moos discusses the history of the questioning of the letters of Heloise since the early nineteenth century in *Mittelalterforschung und Ideologiekritik. Der Gelehrtenstreit um Héloïse.*
3. P. G. Walsh discusses a number of scholarly suggestions about *Hebet sidus,* no. 169 in the *Carmina Burana, Love Lyrics from the Carmina Burana,* pp. 192–95.
4. Abelard addresses this friend in *HC* as "dilectissime frater in Christo et ex divina conversatione familiarissime comes" ed. Monfrin 107, Hicks 43, Muckle 210 (rendering *divina* as *diutina*). Radice 104, does not translate *ex divina conversatione.*
5. *Ep.* 2, ed. Monfrin 114, Muckle 71, Hicks 49 (Radice 113, translating *amica* as mistress); see also when Abelard quotes Heloise in *HC,* ed. Monfrin 78, Hicks 17, Muckle 189 (Radice 74, again translating it as mistress): "Addebat denique . . . et quam sibi carius existeret mihique honestius amicam dici quam uxorem . . ."
6. Martin Irvine emphasizes her desire to link *amicitia* and *amor* in "Heloise and the Gendering of the Literate Subject," pp. 87–114, especially pp. 101–103.
7. *Ep.* 2, ed. Monfrin 116, Hicks 52, Muckle 73 (Radice 117): "Utinam, dilecte, tua de me dilectio minus confideret, ut sollicitior esset!"
8. *HC,* ed. Monfrin 71, Hicks 10, Muckle 183 (Radice 66): "Tanto autem facilius mihi puellam consensuram credidi, quanto amplius eam litterarum scientiam et habere et diligere noveram; nosque etaim absentes scriptis internuntiis invicem liceret presentare et pleraque audacius scribere quam colloqui, et sic semper jocundis interesse colloquiis."
9. M. T. Clanchy, *Abelard. A Medieval Life,* pp. 173–74; Radice (p. 66 and n. 1) translates *adolescentula* as "young girl" and remarks that "it can be assumed that she was about seventeen at this time."
10. *HC,* ed. Monfrin 64, Hicks 4, Muckle 176 (Radice 59).
11. *Ep.* 115, ed. Constable, p. 303 (Radice 277); *HC,* ed. Monfrin 79, Hicks 17 (Radice 74): "ubi ipsa olim puellula educata fuerat atque erudita." Radice translates *puellula* as small girl, although this could simply mean younger than *puella* (a term used by Baudri of Bourgueil of nuns at Le Ronceray with whom he exchanged poetry). If Heloise is to

be identified with one of the two nuns called *Helvidis monacha* mentioned as nuns of Argenteuil in the funeral roll of Matilda (d. 6 July 1113), first abbess of Sainte-Trinité, Caen, then Heloise went to Notre-Dame either at about the same time or shortly after Abelard had acquired his position at the school of Notre-Dame (probably late 1113); ed. Leopold Delisle, *Rouleaux des morts du IXe au XVe siècles,* no. 184, p. 262 (misleadingly confused with Queen Mathilda, d. 1083). Only one *Helvidis* is mentioned in the Argenteuil contribution for Vital of Savigny (d. Sept. 16, 1122); Delisle, *Rouleaux des morts* no. 41, p. 299. This is not itself certain, as Heloise was not officially a professed nun in 1113.

12. Könsgen. References are given to the numbers of the letters (not the page numbers) assigned by Könsgen, those from the man being cited in italics. The translations from the love letters that follow are by Neville Chiavaroli and myself, as provided in *The Lost Love Letters.*
13. Könsgen, pp. 97–103.
14. Letter 112: "Jam philosophie laribus nutritus, poeticum fontem ebibisti." Cf. *Ep.* 2, ed. Monfrin 115, Hicks 51, Muckle 68 (Radice 115).
15. Letter 22: "Ad alios verba, ad te intencionem dirigo. Sepe in verbis cado, quid cogitacio mea ab eis extraneis est." Cf. *HC,* ed. Monfrin 73, Hicks 12, Muckle 184 (Radice 68).
16. Peter Dronke, ed. and trans., *Medieval Latin and the Rise of the European Love Lyric,* 2 vols., 2nd ed., 2:422–47.
17. Pseudo-Boèce, *De disciplina scolarum* 4.1, p. 110.
18. Georges Duby, *Dames du XIIe siècle. I. Héloïse, Aliénor, Iseut et quelques autres,* pp. 73–110; *Women of the Twelfth Century,* trans. Jean Birrell (edn: Cambridge, 1997), pp. 42–65. Duby had mentioned his doubts about the authenticity of Heloise in *Que sait-on de l'amour en France au XIIe siècle* and *Mâle moyen âge. De l'amour et autres essais,* p. 45, p. 120; Duby, *Love and Marriage in the Middle Ages,* trans. Jane Dunnett, p. 31, p. 96.
19. Peter Dronke, *Abelard and Heloise in Medieval Testimonies,* pp. 24–26, repr. in Dronke, *Intellectuals and Poets in Medieval Europe,* pp. 270–72; *Women Writers,* pp. 94–95.
20. Graziella Ballanti, trans., *Un Epistolario d'Amore del XII secolo (Abelardo e Eloisa?).*
21. Étienne Wolff, trans., *La Lettre d'amour au moyen âge: Boncompagno da Signa, La Roue de Venus; Baudri de Bourgueil, Poésies; Manuscrit de Tegernsee, Lettres d'amours; Manuscrit de Troyes, Lettres de deux amants (Héloïse et Abélard?),* pp. 117–51.
22. Jean Charles Payen, *Histoire de la littérature française. Le Moyen Age,* revised edition, p. 58.
23. Könsgen, pp. 93–97.
24. Karl Polheim, *Die lateinische Reimprosa,* p. 362.
25. Carol Dana Lanham, *Salutatio Formulas in Latin Letters to 1200: Syntax, Style, and Theory,* especially pp. 7–12.
26. E.g., Jean Leclercq, ed. and trans., *Yves de Chartres. Correspondance,* no. 5, p. 14: "Ivo, Dei gratia Carnotensium humilis episcopus, Adelae nobili comitissae: recta in Christo sapere (Ivo, by the grace of God humble bishop of Chartres to Adela, noble Countess: may you taste right things in Christ)." SBO, *Ep.* 116: "Dilectae in Christo filiae suae Ermengardi, quondam eximiae comitissae, nunc humili Christi ancillae, Bernardus, abbas Claraevallis: pium sanctae dilectionis affectum [To his beloved daughter in Christ, Ermengard, formerly a distinguished countess, now a humble maidservant of Christ, Bernard, abbot of Clairvaux: the pious disposition of holy love]."
27. Heinrich Hagenmeyer, ed., *Epistulae et chartae ad historiam primi belli sacri spectantes. Die Kreuzzugsbriefe aus den Jahren 1088–1100,* no. 4, p. 138. I am indebted to John Pryor for drawing this letter to my attention.
28. Hagemayer, ed., *Epistulae et chartae,* no. 10, p. 149: "Credas certissime, carissima quod nuntius iste, quem dilectioni tuae misi . . ." This letter, perhaps like the earlier one of Stephen, was written down by "my chaplain, Alexander" according to an addendum (p.

152) written in the same style as the rest of the letter. As Hagenmayer remarks (p. 54), there seems no reason to doubt that Stephen himself wrote these letters.

29. Gerald Bond discusses a range of authors who address Adela (including Stephen, whose letter he translates in part on p. 133) in *The Loving Subject: Desire, Eloquence, and Power in Romanesque France,* pp. 129–57.
30. Könsgen provides an invaluable comparative list of images used by the man and the woman of each other and themselves on pp. 68–71; cf. n. 23 above.
31. John O. Ward has pointed out to me that the phrase *esse quod est* is used by Anselm of Canterburyin his *De Veritate,* but it is not clear whether this is in the same sense, *Anselmi Opera Omnia,* ed. Franciscus Salesius Schmitt, 1:178.
32. I argue that the *Dialectica* is earlier than the *Logica 'Ingredientibus'* in "On Dating the Works of Peter Abelard": 73–134; I am now inclined to accept John Marenbon's argument in *The Philosophy of Peter Abelard,* pp. 40–45, that the *Dialectica* was composed before 1117.
34. Abelard, *Dialectica,* ed. Lambert Marie De Rijk, 2nd ed., p. 85.
34. Marenbon, *The Philosophy of Peter Abelard,* pp. 138–49.
35. The debate relates to *sensus* and *sensibile,* but Abelard extends this to that between *scientia* and *scibile;* Abelard, *Logica 'Ingredientibus,'* in Bernhard Geyer, ed., *Peter Abaelards Philosophische Schriften,* p. 214: "Nam quicquid scitur, scientia scitur et quicquid potest sciri, scientia potest sciri. Sed si bene sensum Porphyrii attendamus iuxta verba Boethii, non est Aristoteli contrarius, cum ait scibile non prius esse scientia. Scientiam enim aliter accepit quam Aristoteles, ipsam videlicet scibilitatem quae facit scibile . . . Cum enim dixit 'scientia in natura,' tantundem valuit, quantum si dixisset potentiam sciendi, quae est scibilitas, qua quidem potentia scibile prius non est, ideoque Porphyrius ad scibilitatem minus quam ad scientiam scibile referri iudicat, non tamen ideo veri relativum esse astruebat."
36. Hugo Metellus, *Ep.* 16, in *Sacrae Antiquitatis Monumenta,* ed. Charles-Louis Hugo, 2:348–49: "Helvidi Abbatissae Venerabilis Paracleti: Fama sonans per inane volans apud nos sonuit, quae digna sonitu de vobis, nobis intonuit. Foemineum enim sexum vos excessisse nobis notificavit. Quomodo? Dictando, versificando, nova junctura, nota verba novando, et quod excellentius omnibus est his, muliebrem mollitiem exuperasti, et in virile robur indurasti."
37. *Ep.* 6, ed. Muckle 241, Hicks 88. Radice (p. 159) is misled by the faulty reading of *Domino* for *Suo* given in the 1616 edition, reprinted in PL 178:213A, to translate the greeting as: "God's own in species, his own as individual." Linda Georgianna discusses the various interpretations and translations of this greeting in chapter 8 in this volume.
38. Bernard, *Sermo* 23, SBO 1:138: "Sine mora aperitur ei, tamquam domesticae, tamquam carissimae, tamquam specialiter dilectae et singulariter gratae." [It is opened to him without delay, as if to an intimate, as if to a dearest, as if to one specially beloved and singularly pleasing.] Hato of Troyes, bishop responsible for the Paraclete and thus personally familiar with Heloise, writes to Peter the Venerable in March 1138, *Ep.* 71, ed. Constable, 1:205: "Salutat uos Odo archidiaconus nepos meus, tam specialiter uester, quam singulariter noster [My nephew, archdeacon Odo, as much specially yours as particularly ours, greets you]. Was Hato inspired by Heloise's third letter?
39. *Ep.* 3, ed. Hicks 54, Muckle 69 (Radice 119).
40. *Ep.* 3, ed. Hicks 60, Muckle 73 (Radice 126).
41. *Ep.* 4, ed. Monfrin 117, Hicks 61, Muckle 77 (Radice 127).
42. *Ep.* 5, ed. Hicks 70, Muckle 82 (Radice 137).
43. *Ep.* 5, ed. Hicks 87, Muckle 94 (Radice 156).
44. *Ep.* 6, ed. Hicks 106, Muckle 253 (Radice 179).
45. Cicero, *Laelius* [*De amicitia*], 80–81; *On the Good Life,* trans. Michael Grant, pp. 216–17: "est enim is, qui est tamquam alter idem. Quod si hoc apparet in bestiis . . . deinde ut

requirant atque appetant ad quas se applicent eiusdem generis animantis, idque faciant cum desiderio et cum quadam similitudine amoris humani, quanto id magis in homine fit natura qui et se ipse diligit, et alterum anquirit, cuius animum ita cum suo miscet, ut efficiat paene unum ex duobus." I have modified Grant's translation slightly.

46. *Laelius* 92 (Grant, pp. 221–22): "Nam cum amicitiaeis sit in eo, ut unus quasi animus fiat ex pluribus."
47. *Laelius* 100 (Grant, pp. 225–26): "ex quo ardescit sive amor sive amicitia. Utrumque enim dictum est ab amando; amare autem nihil est alius nisi eum ipsum diligere quem ames, nulla indigentia, nulla utilitate quaesita."
48. *HC,* ed. Monfrin 65, Hicks 5, Muckle 178 (Radice 60).
49. William of Champeaux, *Sententiae,* vol. 5, pp. 192–94.
50. Boethius, *De trinitate* 1, quoted by Roscelin, *Epistola ad Abaelardum,* ed. Joseph Reiners, in *Der Nominalismus in der Frhhscholastik. Ein Beitrag zur Geschichte der Universalienfrage im Mittelalter,* Bd 8.5, pp. 63–80 at 71: "Huius unitatis causa est indifferentia."
51. Lorenzo Minio-Paluello, ed., *Sententie* xxiv, *Twelfth Century Logic. Texts and Studies II. Abaelardiana Inedita,* p. 118: "Cum vero dicimus hoc 'mulier que dampnavit salvavit,' non circa eandem personam sed circa naturam sexus muliebris . . . [xxvii] Similiter, cum in ista argumentatione dicimus hanc enuntiationem 'Socrates est homo' enuntiare 'Socratem esse id quod ipse est,' istud 'id' non secundum personam discrete proferimus, sed indifferenter tam secundum naturam quam secundum personam illud accipimus."
52. Abelard, *Logica 'Ingredientibus',* ed. Geyer, p. 397: "sicut et cum dicitur: 'per mulierem intravit mors, per eandem vita' vel 'mulier quae damnavit, ipsa salvavit,' scilicet similiter, ut videlicet eadem secundum indifferentiam sexus, non secundum identitatem personae dicatur."
53. C. H. Kneepkens discusses Abelard's interpretation at length, alongside that of his contemporaries in an invaluable study, presenting all the relevant texts, "'Mulier Quae Damnavit, Salvavit': A Note on the Early Development of the relatio simplex," pp. 1–25.
54. Abelard, *Logica 'Ingredientibus',* ed. Geyer, pp. 13–14: "Cum autem omnes res ita diversas ab invicem esse velint, ut nulla earum cum alia vel eandem essentialiter materiam vel eandem essentialiter formam participet, universale tamen rerum adhuc retinentes idem non essentialiter quidem, sed indifferenter ea quae discreta sunt, appellant, veluti singulos homines in seipsis discretos idem esse in homine dicunt, id est non differre in natura humanitatis, et eosdem quos singulares dicunt secundum discretionem, universales dicunt secundum indifferentiam et similitudinis convenientiam." Cf. *Logica 'Nostrorum petitioni sociorum,'* ed. Geyer, p. 518.
55. Abelard, *Theologia christiana* 3.144, ed. Eligius-Marie Buytaert, CCCM 12: 250.
56. *Laelius* 20 (Grant, p. 187): "Quanta autem vis amicitiae sit ex hoc intellegi maxime potest, quod ex infinita societate generis humani, quam conciliavit ipsa natura, ita contracta res est et adducta in augustum, ut omnis caritas aut inter duos aut inter paucos iungeretur."
57. Marbod of Rennes, *Rescriptum ad amicam,* ed. Bulst, "Liebesbriefgedichte Marbods," p. 185.
58. Abelard, *Dialectica,* ed. De Rijk, p. 186: "Nam universalis rei quantitas in diffusione sua per inferiora consistit."
59. Étienne Gilson, *Héloïse et Abélard,* 3rd ed., pp. 77–78.
60. *HC,* ed. Monfrin 75–78, Hicks 14–17, Muckle 186–89 (Radice 71–74), alluding to passages in *Theologia christiana* 2.38, 67, 96–97, 101, ed. Buytaert, CCCM 12:148, 159–60, 173–74, 177. On the evolution of Abelard's knowledge of Jerome, see Mews, "Un lecteur de Jérôme au douzième siècle," pp. 31–44.
61. Könsgen (p. 83) notes possible allusions to Jerome in the woman's letters 25, 27, 45, 49, 69.

CHAPTER 4

THE YOUNG HELOISE AND LATIN RHETORIC: SOME PRELIMINARY COMMENTS ON THE "LOST" LOVE LETTERS AND THEIR SIGNIFICANCE

John O. Ward and Neville Chiavaroli[1]

Assuming that the "epistolae duorum amantium" are indeed the letters of Abelard and Heloise, this essay argues that studies in the trivium *meant for Heloise a passport to an intellectually fulfilling life involving sex and children but not marriage, a package that Abelard could not comprehend.*

In chapter 3 of this volume and in his book *The Lost Love Letters of Heloise and Abelard: The Perception of Dialogue in Twelfth-Century France,* the historian Constant Mews has effected a revolution in our study of the "real" Heloise. The identification he has made between the "epistulae duorum amantium" published by Ewald Könsgen in 1974[2] and the letters exchanged by Abelard and Heloise at the height of their passion[3] is the greatest challenge to students of Heloise since Jean de Meun put the letters later edited by J. Monfrin, J. T. Muckle, Eric Hicks, and others into vernacular circulation. If Mews is right, historians now have a unique opportunity to peer more securely than ever before into the deep obscurity of the "real" Heloise. Indeed, in the case of these "lost" *litterae,* some acceptable model of "reality" is the simplest way to explain a collection of texts that would otherwise be an insuperable puzzle.[4] As one reads slowly through them again in Könsgen's edition, it becomes more and more difficult to explain them in the terms usually appealed to by proponents of inauthenticity. They are neither uniform nor uniformly elegant for stylistic or didactic purposes of the period. The manuscript from which Johannes de Vepria made his extraordinary extracts clearly saw no scholastic or didactic usage, and it is clear from his own choice of extract that although initially interested in *salutatio* formulas and other possibly useful turns of phrase, he soon became caught up in the storyline revealed by the letters themselves.[5] So it is with us, and this chapter is an attempt to explore the next stage in our discussion of these *litterae,* once we have accepted, as I think we must, the case Mews presents for their "authenticity" as a set of extracts made in the fifteenth century from a now-lost manuscript copy made perhaps by Heloise herself of an exchange between herself and Abelard, originally committed to wax tablets in the second decade of the twelfth century. The manuscript, which would have kept alive for Heloise the emotional dimensions of her only passionate love affair, in the end must have seemed to serve little purpose; perhaps she gave it to her friend Bernard of Clairvaux, who placed it in the library at Clairvaux, where it lay for three centuries until Johannes de Vepria chose to look through it as a candidate for extracting and, perhaps, disposal.[6]

Mews has chosen to draw a line between these *litterae,* "as a ('real') record of her [Heloise's] dialogue with her teacher [Abelard]," and a comparable "Regensburg exchange, an exercise in verse composition by the teacher but taken up by a female student, turned into an elaborate literary negotiation about the conduct of a relationship that was eventually terminated by the young woman concerned."[7] The Regensburg verses, along with others that may be placed alongside them,[8] no doubt assisted immeasurably the practice of working out emotional relationships in writing.[9] It is important to remember that our first practitioners of sophisticated literary writing in the Middle Ages are exactly those who suffered from many constraints upon their ability to mix face to face with those selected for the literary exercise of amorous epistolary "play."[10] Nevertheless, the Regensburg verses display exactly that uniformity and didactic suitability that led not only to their preservation but set them apart from the de Vepria collection.[11] In some senses they "legitimate" the practice evident in the originals from which the de Vepria collection has been drawn: the letter is a trace of the writer, the bed will reveal all, the exchanges are written on (wax) tablets and conveyed by messengers, devotion matches absence, from time to time some hesitation as to what to write is displayed and a measure of uncertainty as to the real attitude of the writer is expressed; responses are deemed inadequate and excuses for not writing are feigned; there is a perceived need for restraint, and threats from rumor, jealousy, and popular disclosure are ever-present.[12] The presiding deity of rhetoric, Mercury,[13] clearly provides the discourse in which those who do not and indeed cannot consummate their "real" relationships—despite the stated fact that love [*dilectio*] "consists not in words but in gracious deeds" [non constat verbis . . . sed benefactis][14]—can sublimate and play while learning and acquiring facility in the essential learned language of the time and its equally essential canon of precedents in classical literature (works by Ovid and Lucan as well as Cicero's *De amicitia* for example).

Mews draws a fundamental distinction between the literary text that is indicative of (at most) a relationship of actual/real-life, or imagined, *amicitia* based on the rhetorical triad of *ars, imitatio,* and *exercitatio*[15] and the text that is indicative of a relationship of actual/real-life *amicitia* but reinforced by the actual/real-life "*amor* the bed reveals"[16]—the "green sofa and the excitement" so to speak.[17] It is not simply a matter of collapsing all relationships of the second sort into the first, because even the second sort of relationship has to be situated in a context of literacy ("*littera*-cy"): the de Vepria *litterae* excerpts are an arena for self-development in relatively systematic thought and expression, a pioneering translation of evolving real-life emotions into "*littera*-cy" form, and the product must not be confused with the "set-piece" rhetoric of the schools/*scriptoria,* later to be codified into the *artes poetriae.* It is not that real-life situations do not underline or give relevance to the latter form of composition, or that "*littera*-cy" generated by passionately held convictions does not have much rhetorical art;[18] rather it is a question of balance: how much art, how much real life enmeshed with that art?[19]

The striking feature of the de Vepria *litterae* excerpts is their unshowiness, their "*littera*-cy" rather than their "literariness." At times their language is so minimal, so idiomatic, in comparison with their freight of meaning, that it is hard to imagine their use for any would-be *dictator,* or collector of fine prose/verse.[20] This circumstance, combined with the other arguments for "authenticity" expertly assembled by Mews, is the initial challenge to scholars, who must now work slowly through the collection, building up a picture of the real-life relationship represented and integrating it into the established picture indicated well enough lately by, among others, M. T. Clanchy and John Marenbon.[21]

Mews comments particularly on the *salutatio* formulae in the de Vepria excerpts, and this is indeed an intriguing feature that, it seems, first attracted the attention of Johannes de Vepria. The *salutationes* here are pioneering in their prosiness,[22] as Catullus' verse was pioneering in a different way, in its development "of a new kind of poetry."[23] Implicit in Mews's discussion is the fact that this very "prosiness" preserves more of the real-life relationship than would be the case in more polished literary or poetic efforts. The general absence in the de Vepria excerpts of any dominant dictaminal flavor or pattern as far as the body of each *littera* is concerned can only reinforce this view, even if it raises important questions about the kind of "dictamen" or "composition" that was taught in the second decade of the twelfth century in Paris, for these excerpts seem to have functioned for Heloise (and possibly for Abelard) in the way that John of Salisbury records Bernard of Chartres' *declinationes/collationes*—and indeed his grammatical teaching in general—to have functioned.[24] Evenings were devoted to recalling, putting into practice the lessons of the day (exposition and imitation of selected classical Latin writers), the aim of the whole being to acquire facility in expressing thought in the best classical manner (prose and verse), without resorting to plagiarism and the borrowing of wholesale "patches" [*panni*]. Although the lost love-letters from which the de Vepria excerpts are drawn were in part necessitated by distances that separated the writers, it also seems plausible that they were part of a *collatio*-type practice whereby texts read and issues discussed together could be rehearsed and aired. There are indications that Cicero's *De amicitia* was thus read and discussed, together with Ovid's poetry and much scripture;[25] it seems that philosophical terminology also formed part of the day's debate.[26] Some of the verse in the collection is sufficiently jejune as to suggest *collatio*-type practice.[27] The didactic reality that lies behind the de Vepria excerpts can be of much interest only in so important a transitional and so ill-documented an age.

Mews is also concerned with the ideas and vocabulary of the letters, partly to support his views about authenticity but partly also to rehabilitate Heloise as a (moral) philosopher. Indeed, the picture of Heloise that emerges coincides strikingly with that found by the historian C. Stephen Jaeger, in his recent *The Envy of Angels: Cathedral Schools and Social Ideals in Medieval Europe 950–1200,*[28] to be characteristic of the "preliterate," oral, charismatic age of cathedral-school learning that flourished down to the end of the eleventh century and was extinguished by the very literate, scholastic attitudes that Mews documents as first coming to the fore in Abelard's own writings after about 1120.[29] Jaeger's ideas, indeed, may help us flesh out the *in tempore* context for the de Vepria excerpts.

If we subject to renewed study the Ovidian humanism of the second half of the eleventh century and the first decade or so of the twelfth, the period may be considered a liminal one, between the literary world of the courtier-bishop that stressed morals, ethics, language, and learning for life and the scholastic, post-Abelardian world, nostalgic for the lost oral charisma of the prescholastic age and enmeshed in a form of textual literacy that placed learning and philosophy within a systematic procedural world that, while not without oral features, lay beyond the reach of court and society in general. This divorce between life and learning was eventually, in the mature university age of the thirteenth century, to deal a fatal blow to the Ovidian and Ciceronian humanism of the earlier age. That Jean de Meun had to take up the cudgel for this kind of humanism, in the vernacular, or that the compiler of the Benediktbeuern manuscript of the *Carmina Burana* had to use primarily twelfth-century materials, is indicative.[30]

Brian Stock puts the transition from the "oral" to the "literate" in the period thus:

> If we take as our point of departure the admittedly arbitrary date of the year 1000 A.D., then it is arguable that there were both oral and written traditions operating simultaneously in European culture, sometimes working together, sometimes working in separate spheres of thought and action. However, from about the second half of the eleventh century, a widespread transformation began to take place. Oral traditions did not simply decline, although that happened to some degree as the force of the written word became progressively stronger. Instead, they realigned themselves so as to be able to function in relation to a reference system based upon texts. . . . The spoken and the written were therefore drawn into closer interdependence than they had been at any time since the end of the ancient world.[31]

The literary texts that derive from this transitional period do not inform as we expect such texts to. Jaeger speaks of the "silence that enfolds most of the life of the cathedral schools prior to the 12th century": " . . . something was going on at the early cathedral schools that is not transmitted clearly by the sources or set in intelligible structures by current frames of explanation." Whether monastic or secular, the educational culture of the eleventh century is "a charismatic culture. It cannot be assessed by weighing and measuring its documentation, which by its very nature it tends not to produce." "Education becomes [in the eleventh century] a process of transmitting personal qualities through the charismatic effect of a well-disciplined, well-'composed' teacher." There is an emphasis on the etiquette of behavior, on the court as the theatre of activities, on oral, face-to-face, culture; on *conversatio, mores.* The discipline of manners is linked to eloquent speech, and classical models function to open up new ways of thinking about important contemporary issues (for example in Alcuin's pioneering use of the *De inventione* in his *Dialogus de rhetorica,* written some two centuries prior to the year 1000).[32] There are looser links between letters and conduct in ecclesiastical education, but cathedral-school education produced "men who would work well at court and in the episcopate and serve the *utilitas ecclesie et rei publicae.*" Dignity, gravity, and eloquence are the qualities Fulbert of Chartres himself displays; they are not characteristics of the texts he discusses. It is the person of the teacher, not the nature of the text, that is persuasive.[33] We are in a milieu in which the ruling *disciplina* is the *cultus virtutum:* the formation of character, the cult of personality, the courtier-philosopher, elegance of manners, friendship. "Teaching by example became the dominant pastoral duty in the new houses of canons regular that burgeoned after the second half of the eleventh century." "The schools nourished an ideal of amiability, charm, good humour, mutual love and respect in the shared life of student and teacher. Administrative service was the context in which these 'virtues' became effective." "Monastic writers became the policemen of virtue." Onulf of Speyer rejected rhetoric in favor of *mores.* Poetry became the "end point and fulfillment of studies." Orpheus and the skill of poetry transforms "an entire society from savage inhumanity to courteous sociability," much as the *quidam vir magnus et eloquens* transformed humankind from savagery to civilization in the *De inventione* proem, a key text for the eleventh century.[34]

From the second quarter of the twelfth century onward, literate modes of thought gained important ground. The cultural consequences were considerable. "Texts [argues Jaeger] represent the rigidifying of thought, which develops in the living dialogue through assertion, challenge, and response. Writing everything down mummifies thought and threatens the death of the mind." "By the early twelfth century, the 'discipline of manners' has been largely displaced at the schools and replaced by definitions and systematising, frameworks of argumentation and harmonising of inconsistencies." The world of Bernard of Chartres and his evening *declinationes* and *collationes* was passing. "The humanists of the 12th century wrote out of nostalgia, not out of the vaulting self-confidence of an age of Renaissance. Their works are shoring to stave off the inevitable collapse of a culture passing out of existence." By the twelfth century "[m]agisterial authority ha[d] shifted away from men and into texts."[35]

Gerald Bond's recent *The Loving Subject: Desire, Eloquence, and Power in Romanesque France* is also pertinent here. During the period from about 1075 to 1125, a new discourse of *amor/amicitia* developed, laced with antique literary exemplary forms, to accommodate a new urge to reflect on the self in fictive and semifictive forms. Whether in the form of wax tablets or booklets, much of this discourse has been preserved to this day,[36] and in many cases the motive seems to have been the prospect of literary fame and social distinction.[37] Within this discourse, the fictive form or "persona" and the "real" person behind the form are elided into the one, often to the detriment of the latter.[38] Protestations of rustic inexpertise, an incipient exploration of systematic dictaminal form, an urge toward preservation of text and hence literary survival, and a fascination with the implications of Ciceronian friendship theory (*amor/amicitia*),[39] the *fedus amicitiae,*[40] and the centrality of the epistolary genre,[41] for the spicing of lived relationships that could not partake physically of such intimacy characterize the early (monastic) phase of the literacy development Bond discusses.[42] It requires no great imaginative leap to see much of this as underlying the various phases of correspondence between Abelard and Heloise, toward the end of the period of which Bond writes. By the end of Bond's period, the constraints of the monastic world are being lifted and practitioners of the *studium litterarum* are gathering to share in the ferment of early cathedral-school teaching that characterized the Paris of the first three decades of the twelfth century.[43]

These quotations and suggestions from both Jaeger and Bond, strung together inadequately thus, are not meant to be more than an informal, impressionistic sketch into which we are invited to place the figure of Heloise as revealed in the de Vepria excerpts. The oral/charismatic/ethics-oriented cultural world of the prescholastic age in Europe underwent massive strains toward the end of the eleventh century, as paradigm after paradigm was subjected to new pressures and found wanting: the conventional priesthood of the "old world," with its married clergy or clerical concubinage and lay patronage buckled in the crises of the *pataria* and the Investitures Controversy; apocalyptic tensions and changing conceptions of evil, guilt, and penance eventually produced the crusading movement and a more sharply defined image of the witch;

notions of the devil and sin were subjected to new analysis; the wandering preachers who preached apocalypticism toward the end of the century and their critics developed at the turn of the twelfth century the full-blown image of the heresiarch; and a fervor of new research and new methodological concepts were worked out for the *artes* and the theological truths they were thought to illuminate.[44]

Women came to share in these developments. While the prescholastic courtier-culture could boast only an exceptional woman, Hrotsvit of Gandersheim, the late eleventh century saw a startling rise in the visibility of women who demanded an educational and literary culture in which they could participate.[45] Contemporaries were amazed at the ability with which an intellectual like Robert of Arbrissel could draw women from a variety of backgrounds—whether aristocratic families or brothels—into his orbit.[46] Robert's successors, Tanchelm and Henry of Le Mans, also developed a special relationship with women.[47] A tantalizing fragment suggests that the wives and daughters of the charismatic scholar Manegaldus (Manegold of Lautenbach) participated as teachers in the scriptural (and artistic?) studies of the time,[48] perhaps as *magistrae* among the canonesses (like the later Tengswich,[49] who challenged the authority of Hildegard of Bingen). Bond's discussion of "changes in the conception of the private secular self that took place in French elite culture around the turn of the twelfth century" has already been mentioned.[50] The geographical focus of this culture is French, but the ruling language idiom is Latin interlarded with classical, particularly Ovidian, overtones. Women play an important role, both *in tempore,* it seems, and as literary images. Heloise, by way of her initial education at the monastery of Argenteuil,[51] must have been put into contact with such a cultural phenomenon, interlarded as it was with ethical themes drawn from Cicero (especially the *De amicitia*), St. Jerome, the scriptures, and comparable texts.[52]

At the climax of this poetic, ethical, oral-charismatic cultural phase in Western history, we are invited by the de Vepria collection and by the narrative of the *Historia calamitatum* to picture a young woman, late teens, mid-twenties perhaps, *non infima in facie,* making her way to the same foyer of schools, teachers, and clashing ideas that drew Abelard from remoter Brittany, the same that educated Robert of Arbrissel. Who knows what Heloise's intentions must have been, whose support/advice she relied upon, what domestic tragedies may have had a bearing on her decision to take up residence with her adulatory uncle (and guardian) Fulbert in the cloister or cathedral close of Nôtre-Dame-de-Paris on the Île-de-la-Cité in Paris.[53] What myriad of unrecorded, stray, personal contacts, textual fragments, and images were to join with the rude tenements, hay-strewn "streets," underpopulated (by our standards) meadows and pastures, oddly grand temples to God, occasional lay forts and residences, in founding a young woman's postmonastic *vita nuova* in Paris?[54] That Heloise had her own ambitions and contacts within this small-scale and intense intellectual urban environment we can infer from the trouble they seem to have caused her correspondent in the de Vepria collection. It is attractive to see her as someone whose intelligence and linguistic skills had opened up a crucial literary world to explore and plumb for moral and ethical guidance in life.[55] Heloise may have been different from Abelard in that her cultural ambitions were probably moral and behavioral rather than textual and procedural. She perhaps did not see her gender, her sexuality, as the looming obstacle that it ultimately became; it was precisely this situation that ushered her into a much more intense phase in the quest for ethical guidance and behavioral relevance from the immense store of literature and learning that was agitating the age in a unique manner.

Heloise's particular disappointment, increasingly apparent in the de Vepria collection, seems to have centered around her partner's inability to sense the continuum between life, love, lust, body, gender, learning, and literature with which she seems to have started her academic life. She, who wanted to see the ingredients of this continuum as all part of the same package, is confronted with a partner who can only categorize and place things in separate boxes: Heloise as wife, or nun, or scholar, or student, or mother; Heloise as his partner, or someone else's, or God's or Christ's.[56] Whatever the great project was that drew her to the intellectual foyer of Paris in the early twelfth century, it came unstuck; the intellectual partnership with Abelard, extraordinarily illuminated in both sets of correspondence that have come down to us, died—or was conventualized—at least twice, and Heloise, was left without child, without partner, without the varying and electrifying personal and intellectual contacts and opportunities of the open world of dusty, littered pathways, bridges, and schools that she was forced to abandon when Abelard conventualized her (at Argenteuil).

With the demise of Heloise's great project comes also the deaththroes of the oral ethical/intellectual vitality that marked the prescholastic age. A world recognizable to us is born, a world in which women are marginalized or banished from an intellectual milieu that is increasingly patriarchal, increasingly textual. If we accept Mews's reconstruction of Heloise, we have restored to us not only a set of lost love letters but a lost chapter in the complicated *longue durée* of letters, life, and learning, a chapter that can only reinforce our ability to discern difference within that shell of sameness that stems from our inevitable tendency to background the cultural preoccupations of our own day.

The "Lost" Love Letters and the *Historia calamitatum*

In pursuing the image of Heloise in the de Vepria collection and that presented to us by Abelard in hindsight mode in his *Historia calamitatum,* with its vantage point of a thoroughgoing apologetic program, we notice an intriguing gap opening up. To explain what drew him to Heloise in the first place, Abelard alleges *carnales illecebras, immunditia, superbia, luxuria,* etc. on his own part—"in huius itaque adolescentule amorem totus inflammatus" as he admits he became, and a desire on the part of Fulbert, "qui eam . . . in omnem qua poterat scientiam litterarum promoveri studuerat," "ut amplius semper in doctrinam proficeret [Heloissa] litteratoriam."[57] Even if this were the truth, we are left with the problem of Heloise's motives. Was she alone in being a woman in the Paris scholastic milieu, or was she motivated by much the same urges that drew other would-be *scholares* to Paris? Accustomed as we are to view her as exceptional and tragic, we may have occluded the dimensions of the liminal environment of the time, an environment in which, perhaps, gender barriers may have been relaxed. Was there already a gender divide in the schools of Paris, with Abelard in the schools, and Heloise at home "guarded" by her uncle, or was Heloise shopping around this early supermarket of learning more or less as her companion males were?[58] The former seems to be what Abelard himself implies: in his famous phrases he tells us that there was a young female (adolescent) with a great reputation for her abundant knowledge of literature who lived with an uncle keen to advance her learning in letters. He felt she *could be got* to agree to his advances [*mihi consensuram*] *because* she had a desire for and loved learning and literature. His first idea seems to have been some sort of exchange of letters [*jocundis colloquiis*][59] but what actually occurred was in accordance with another, or parallel, *proposal,* to set up an *occasionem* [arrangement] that might be appropriate [*familiarem*] for "domestica et cotidiana conversatione," to write to her and thus to initiate an exchange of letters. He creates the impression that Heloise was at home with Fulbert and that some casual contact was needed to set up some familiarity and that he could "draw her into an agreement for a relationship with him" only by "domestica et cotidiana conversatione"—this with a young woman with a national [*in toto regno*] reputation for her literary skills! It requires the intervention of friends (of Fulbert's) and an agreement with Fulbert himself before Abelard's plot could come to fruition and the protected and vulnerable girl be "seduced," as it were.[60] Clearly, although Fulbert's house, with Heloise in it, was near to the schools Abelard frequented, contact could be made only via Fulbert and by Abelard moving into his house.

There are some difficulties with this story as Abelard presents it. We are told, for example, that he had not hitherto mixed scholarship with the company of noble women, nor had he talked much with lay women, and he had certainly not frequented prostitutes.[61] Yet he also tells us that Heloise was well known in "France" (i.e., the area around the Île-de-la-Cité) for her learning—and Peter the Venerable later corroborates this, saying that in his youth he "used to hear of a woman, not yet despatched from the entrapments of the secular world, who gave maximum attention to the study of literary knowledge and secular wisdom—a very rare thing—and could not be dissuaded from so useful a proposal [*propositum*] of instruction in the arts."[62] How could such a reputation be consonant with the picture of a vulnerable teenager sitting at home in the guardianship of her uncle, and what does Peter mean by referring to learning the arts as a "useful proposal"? Should we infer that Heloise had a larger vocational purpose in seeking fluency in the major language of communication of the day?[63] How many other women so sought to advance their vocational prospects at the time? On the other hand, if Heloise *were* but one of a number of females studying in the schools of Paris at the time, would she have drawn the attention of Abelard and Peter the Venerable and caused them to remark her learning and gender? We must recall the extremely small-scale nature of the "Paris" academic world at the time: "Abelard had ample opportunity to encounter Heloise in the course of his comings and goings. He may well have passed the girl while surrounded by a throng of students debating earnestly, for he often taught in the open air, like Aristotle himself; or on his way to class; or on a feast-day, when masters and students mingled in the overcrowded cathedral."[64] It is time to look again at the general context for Heloise's early life and studies.

The view that Fulbert himself entrusted Heloise to Argenteuil as a *puellula* for the purposes of education is unfounded.[65] If, as seems possible, even probable, Heloise was of local subaristocratic stock[66] from the region around Paris, a placement at Argenteuil would have conformed to a widespread pattern recently elucidated by the historians Penelope D. Johnson[67] and Bruce L. Venarde.[68] From the latter's graph it seems that the number of foundations and refoundations of monasteries for women increased massively in the period from about 1100 to 1175 (the lifetime of Heloise), reaching a peak of nearly seventy new houses per decade in France and England, about four times the previous peak around A.D. 640 to 720 (of about seventeen houses per decade).[69] The later peak was never to be attained again (despite a peak of some forty houses per decade between 1175 and 1275). In what Venarde calls his "central tier"—"the archdioceses of Reims, Rouen, Sens, Tours, and Lyon and the dioceses of Metz, Toul, and Verdun"—the phenomenon is most advanced: between 1101 and 1150, some 111 new foundations are recorded, compared with thirty-one for the northern tier (which peaked later, between 1151 and 1200, at eighty-seven houses) and sixty-six for the southern tier (at its peak).[70] "The appearance of new nunneries . . . was not simply a result of population expansion" argues Venarde.[71] Nor was it "simply a reflection or imitation of male-centered reform monasticism."[72] The generating circumstances, in fact,[73] touch upon aristocratic patronage and eremitical fever,[74] but "the initiative of men and women of the lower nobility . . . were key instigators of the multiplication of nunneries."[75] From just such a family, we may suppose, Heloise derived her origins, and it seems most natural to suppose that she was sent to Argenteuil—a seventh-century foundation, but one renewed about A.D. 1000 by royal favor, the Queen Mother Adelaide playing a key role[76]—by her parents or, if her father was by then deceased, by her mother, just as Guibert of Nogent's mother, herself by then a nun at—or near—Saint-Germer-de-Fly, entrusted her son to that local monastery.[77] Abelard, although he is keen to mention his own relatives in far-off Brittany and takes Heloise there to have their child,[78] seems unaware of any of her relatives living within a day's ride of Paris, which supports the possibility that her father had died or left the family and the mother retired to a local monastery by the time of Heloise's affair with Abelard.[79]

The custom of one or both parents of aristocratic or subaristocratic stock in this period taking their daughter as a very young girl [*puellula* or *parvula*] to a female monastic foundation to be raised until old enough to take vows is well attested;[80] not uncommonly, such girls often married later in life.[81] Parental motives varied: to preserve an inheritance, to create a spiritual link thought to be of benefit to a local family's social and spiritual standing, to provide for a girl with a handicap, to avoid the crippling expense of a dowry, because the support of a family's children was beyond the parents' means, because a girl wished to remain a virgin or feared unwanted male advances, or was orphaned, or else that the girls in question might receive "a better schooling than they could obtain in the world."[82] Social mobility, too, was a factor: "the urge for upward social mobility made monastic institutions seem particularly attractive and enhanced the appeal of professing in a house where one would associate with daughters, wives, and widows of the nobility. This was particularly true for women from the lower knightly and bourgeois families, which in the central middle ages were aspiring to better things."[83] Some nunneries, indeed, seem to have operated almost as a kind of "family house."[84]

We do not know at what age Heloise entered Argenteuil, nor what degree of personal choice was involved. Nevertheless, it is important to see her "oblation" as part of a widespread social trend of the time; in the same way, her later entry into the same monastery as a married woman was equally precedented.[85] Indeed, the image of Heloise "farewelling the world" and entering a strictly cloistered nunnery may be misplaced.[86] Similarly, the image of notorious moral laxity in many nunneries of the time may be exaggerated.[87] Our understanding of the monastic world Heloise entered (twice) needs to be carefully etched in: women in early twelfth-century convents may have enjoyed a curious combination of spiritual asceticism and worldliness that puzzles us today with our notion of a strict opposition between "the world" and "the cloister."[88] Heloise's position in a nunnery such as Argenteuil cannot have been as untypical or as isolating as readers of her later correspondence may imagine. Indeed, the notion of Heloise as "unsuited" to monastic claustration as it was then envisaged is an odd one. What she may have grieved was the loss of her son and of a life of intellectual, social, and sexual concubinage with a learned and challenging cleric in exciting times; the kind of clerical concubinage Heloise may have aspired to was rapidly becoming out of date in the wake of the Gregorian reform movement, but this is easier to see with hindsight. Presumably the attraction of this kind of lifestyle led her to abandon Argenteuil and live in Paris with her uncle, where she might have thought to advance in some way an already firm command of the Latin language.[89] To see her as Fulbert's pawn in both her original placement at Argenteuil and in her later departure from it may well be to impose an unnecessarily patriarchal frame on things.[90]

Thus Heloise, exceptional both in her learning and her gender, may have frequented the Parisian schools of her day—Peter the Venerable, as we have seen, speaks of the combination of learning and femininity as if it was something one would normally expect to be "dispatched from the world!" Abelard seemingly unused to consorting with noble or lay women, was seduced by Heloise's appearance and reputation into devising a scheme whereby he would have unique access to her.[91] He thus fell in love with her apparently before any actual sign from her that she was of similar heart.

A gloss on the *De inventione,* representing either the lectures of William of Champeaux or similar teaching at Laon in connection with the activities of masters Ralph and Anselm of that school, seems to hint that in some circles, at least, the seduction of Heloise was punishable because she was a nun.[92] It seems unthinkable that Abelard deliberately obscured Heloise's situation before his relationship with her—and in any case Peter the Venerable explicitly says that Heloise at the time was "not yet dispatched from secular ties"—but the reference only serves to underline the obscurity of Heloise's early status and studies at Paris.[93] What light do the "lost" love letters throw on this?

Appendices A and B present a detailed reading of the de Vepria collection on the assumption that they do represent the wax-tablet exchanges between Heloise and Abelard around 1116 to 1118. Nevertheless, while stressing that only a careful personal inspection of these *litterae* excerpts in the context of the *Historia calamitatum* can provide the reader with a basis for assessing their authenticity, one group of excerpts may serve to illustrate the integration proposed here.[94]

Letter 84 (M) is a highly significant remnant of a letter that raises the question of the kind of mutual relationship Heloise envisaged for herself and Abelard at the mature phase of their relationship. In letter 76 (M) we saw Heloise describe herself as "certe sodalitatis amica." In letter 84, in a crescendo of her musical prose, and after a dense *salutatio* offering her beloved "gaudium cum salute" and "gaudium . . . per evum," she goes back to the beginning of their relationship [? post mutuam nostre visionis allocucionisque noticiam] and, reversing the implication of *HC* M 290, claims that *she* chose Abelard from thousands [*teque solum elegi ex milibus*][95] in order to make a *pignus,* which, when achieved, would enable her to end her cares for the future. This could be an extraordinary statement, for it can mean that Heloise was (perhaps) an orphan (or person deprived of a father?) and without the normal aristocratic ways of securing a stable marital arrangement in life (dowry?), and, with her intellectual interests, perhaps indisposed to the normal marital patterns of her class. These were her "cares," and the way she chose to resolve them was, in an exact reversal of the pattern Abelard alludes to when *he* claims that he chose to seduce Heloise to solve *his* problems, to form a *pignus* with a man of her choice and suitable to her ambitions, penchants, and talents.[96] The word "pignus" is a curious one to use, as it quite normally in classical Latin referred to "children as the guarantee of the reality of a marriage."[97] What relationship was there in Heloise's mind between *pignus* and *conubium?* We are required to believe from the *Historia calamitatum* that Heloise was at the time adamantly opposed to marriage and the bringing up of children—although it is not unlikely that her own and even Abelard's views on these matters underwent changes later in life, as Juanita Ruys seeks to show in chapter 14 in this volume. The possibility of clerical concubinage at this time has been canvassed and rejected as an adequate answer to the question of what Heloise wanted out of her relationship with Abelard.[98] Whether concubinage was any more acceptable to the life of a cleric and a philosopher in the second decade of the twelfth century in Paris, it does seem valid to claim that Heloise

> played ideals of aloof and dignified scholarship against the riot and indignity of a household because she feared the deindividualization of a woman in marriage. As she saw it, a wife can only be a sexual distraction, a mother and a domestic worker, and never a lover, a friend or a fellow-scholar. . . .
>
> What Heloise really wants from Abelard, as becomes entirely clear from her letters, is an intellectual and emotional communion—"unitas mentium," to use Egbert's phrase. Such relationships are not founded upon obligation, and she is prepared to waive her rights over Abelard's means and his household in order to ensure that their relationship remains pre-eminently a disinterested one. In parallel with the popes, theologians and lawyers who taught that marriage was essentially and sacramentally a consensual matter even at the expense of destablilizing it in practice, Heloise insisted that only the purity of her motives could justify her relationship with Abelard, even if that obliged her to sacrifice her own security within it.[99]

Such a statement is consonant with the picture that emerges from letter 84, and from, for example, the odd slip in gender from *Quis* to *Quae/Que* evident in most manuscripts of the *Historia calamitatum* at M 475. Indeed, Heloise in letter 84 goes on to say that Abelard was as natural a habitat for her as shady groves were for birds, streams for fish, mountains for stags.[100] She then shifts gear oddly and writes: "hactenus mecum mansisti [Abelard], mecum viriliter bonum certamen certasti, sed nondum bravium accepisti." This is the passage that the historian Peter Dronke[101] uses, perhaps influenced by the appearance of the word *bravium* in the *Carmina Burana,* to argue that the relationship between M and V was not consummated, while that between Heloise and Abelard was.[102] This is hard to follow, and unnecessary. The *certamen* could just as easily be the bed (as it was in marital encomiastic literature), and in any case it is clear that *bravium* is not to be so lightly interpreted.[103] Both *certamen* and *bravium* in the scriptural references cited by Könsgen mean the good fight of the faithful and the reward is heavenly.[104] Ascetic overtones are clear. In secular usage, however, the word *bravium* or *brabe[i]um* means the prize won in athletic games.[105] The passage that would have followed the word *bravium* in letter 84 has been omitted by the medieval editor. We can only suppose that in Heloise's eyes the word meant fulfillment of the relationship she had in mind, in the way she wanted it fulfilled. It is time, she says, to move on from the master/pupil relationship to a fuller relationship: that "prologum, quem composuisti michi [the prologue (for our life together), which you composed for me, . . . I will repay] cum graciarum actione [cf. *actio HC* M 390], cum amoris servitute"—with the *Charites,* or Graces, or young and beautiful attendants upon Venus, who were in antiquity worshipped in the same temple as the nine Muses.

The *salutatio* of Abelard's reply (#85 [V]) proposes a unity between himself and Heloise that is broken only by the notion of his greeting "the best part of his body considered in a divided sense" (i.e., her). There follows a paragraph in which *he* laments *his* failure to supply words to match *her* deeds [*beneficium*].[106] Words such as 'segnities'[107] and 'pre nimia mentis alienatione' hint at the kind of quasi-estrangement that might have followed their agreement to disagree on the issue of marriage, and the last sentence [ignis noster . . . vincat] can not only be taken appropriately with *HC* M 564–66 but alludes to letter 84 [in which: *certamen* = #85: *concertacio*].

With Heloise's letter 86 (M) we have the kind of letter that might have matched that phase in the couple's lives referred to in *HC* M 383–390. Indeed, the *salutatio* may be close to the *cum summa exultatione* of *HC* M 392–93: "to the bottomless fount of sweetness, that part of his soul which has been individuated [an allusion to the *salutatio* of letter 85] gives him the possibility that after the worries of Martha and the fecundity of Leah, he will possess the best part of Mary."[108] What can this refer to other than that Heloise expects a period of time as mother and housewife, but, following that, a continuation of her life (with Abelard) as an intellectual? What follows could easily be taken as an exultant, passionate prologue of affection that would have preceded the communication of her pregnancy, had not the medieval editor effected an omission at this point. After the omission, we have a heartfelt wish expressed for something "si salva gracia dei posset fieri": "before God none can lie, and with him as my witness there is nothing on earth I would desire more [than to bear your child]. Your *affectus* ["desire," "fondness," "disposition to love me"—always her word][109] makes me fat [= pregnant?], but your love [*amor*] can never fill me (compare the comparable use of 'implet' in Ovid's *Metamorphoses* XI.265). My salvation/welfare [*salus*] is your life, you are all I desire, my every good thing. Farewell half of my heart and the burning fire of complete happiness and love."

Letter 87 (V), a competent effort in elegiacs, offers the *amor* that letter 86 says will never "fill" Heloise (however much "*affectus*" "fattens" her). It is based on nice plays on the shortness and length of time balanced against the brevity of the lovers' moments together:

> The year that has passed, since first love bound us together has been both brief and long: when I think back over the beauty (of which I can never have enough) of your form, and that goodness which is so characteristic of you, it seems I have had but an hour of familiarity with you [in Classical Latin *notitia* can imply carnal knowledge][110]—though each thought of you [*nova cura* = Ovid, *Amores* 1.9.43: *formosae cura puellae*] is a fresh one to my longing—and when I think back how rare have been those moments of contact between us, countless years run by me, for each day without you seems like thirty years [a generation?].[111]

Thus Abelard commemorates for Heloise the first anniversary of their mutual love, perhaps during those painful days of separation following the birth of Astrolabe and the secret marriage (*HC* M 564–66). Certainly such a supposition fits the feeling expressed in letter 87: ll. 23ff. that the new year of their relationship will require a new path, a path in which "*amor*" will not be wounded by anything "*amarus*": their recent bitter recriminations and differences must be replaced by a new constraint on Abelard's part [ad nutus domine me cohibebo mee], and nothing "*amarus*" must wound any further Heloise's soft body [corpus . . . tenerum]. Alluding perhaps to *HC* M 355:

carmina . . . amatoria, Abelard says that there should be no "*carmina dura*" [songs lamenting a lover's intransigence, Ovid, *Amores* 1.9.19: *durae limen amicae?*], that he should be forgiven the wounding things he wrote to her in the past (l. 33).[112] In a rare moment of genuine regret, he wishes that he could retract what he had said: when he calls to mind his *dilecta*'s tears [*lacrimas* = *HC* M 554: *lacrimans*], he cannot hold back his own: "you should accept it when someone confesses his errors, accept it and do not recall other grounds for blame; accept it, for I pray that you do, O dearest, with unceasing tears: I will beg it even on bended knees." A hint at Heloise's fears may be contained in the last couplet, coming after this extended plea: "may the day that dawns for me be my last if there is any woman I would place before you."

Such a poetic apology may well be a generalized exercise between invented/fictive *personae,* or it may be what Abelard himself, compelled to correspond with Heloise because of their decision to live separately and conceal the marriage he forced upon her, and deeply ruing the precipitous course of the past year, chose to set down in the literary form they had come to love to devise for each other.[113]

The end of the correspondence is signaled by two letters, both by Heloise, and each in their way terminal. Letter 112 (M) is a strange and forced composition, which can only be taken as an attempt by Heloise to reformulate their epistolary relationship in terms appropriate to monastic "censorship" and monastic friendship: her letter is addressed in formal but relatively neutral terms to "the most noble and learned master," whose condescending act of correspondence [*nobilitas* writing to *parvitas*] produces ecstasy and elevation to the "third heaven" (a biblical reference) in the writer.[114] Appropriate reference to the recipient's philosophic and poetic studies is matched with an equally appropriate reference to the writer's new vocation [sitire deum et illi adherere soli necessarium est omni viventi], and the letter ends with a curiously wordy and formal attempt to place their relationship in terms that might have seemed uncontroversial to a monastic superior. Is Heloise now trying to set up a situation for correspondence closer to that which obtained between Baudri of Bourgeuil and Constance of Le Ronceray?[115] This latter correspondence had its wax tablets,[116] its year-long relationship,[117] its hyperbole,[118] its reading and re-reading of *litterae,*[119] its "*foedus amoris,*"[120] its "*verus amor,*" "*immemor,*"[121] and related language of emotional attachment. It is a far cry from the de Vepria fragments, embedded dramatically as they seem to be in the traumas and processes of urban life outside the monastery, but it may have represented to the tortured Heloise some appropriate formula for the changed future that lay ahead for her relationship with her (former?) husband. As such, it may not have lasted long, for letter 112a seems to say that there cannot be love without exercise of it: "I am tired now, I cannot reply to you, because you take amiss what I write in good faith, and by doing this you make my mind sad. Farewell." It is a portentous fragment,[122] and an appropriate one to end the collection—though someone (Heloise?) actually has rounded the assemblage out with a pretty piece (#113 [V]), presumably by Abelard, celebrating his falling for Heloise (and hence, perhaps, from period I in Appendix C). It contains some characteristic touches: Abelard has never been "conquered" before (*HC* M 70–71), Heloise's *forma, genus,*[123] *mores, honores* fill the streets of Paris;[124] it is only Heloise who gives Abelard his Latin eloquence [*facundum me sola facis*]. The physical passion hinted at in ll. 11–12 match *HC* M 332–46 and the "hindrances" to consummation [fortuna pudorque . . . et populi murmura] are appropriate to the conditions under which the couple fell into physical passion. It is a far more pleasant "end piece" than letter 112a would have been.

Certainly, by 1129[125] when Heloise and her companions, ejected from Argenteuil, went to the Paraclete, Abelard was frequently in his former wife's presence again, and remained so on and off until his removal to Paris and the composition of the *Historia calamitatum* (ca. 1132), which seems to have so aroused Heloise.[126] The celebrated letters that followed Heloise's reaction indicate a considerable break in their correspondence prior to the *Historia calamitatum,* and prior to about 1129, after which correspondence would have seemed less crucial in light of Abelard's frequent presence at the Paraclete.[127] Those letters numbered 87–113 that date from the period following Heloise's removal to Argenteuil must come from the earlier years. What seems to have aroused Heloise when she received the *Historia calamitatum* was not so much that she had had neither news of nor visits from Abelard in the years from about 1118 to 1132, but rather the fact that this self-conscious correspondence, this time with another, aroused in her the vivid and nostalgic memory of their earlier correspondence, and she felt Abelard's epistolary loyalty should be to her, not to a nameless friend. Hence her request for a resumption of the correspondence.[128] Indeed, we may imagine Heloise in her early days at Argenteuil, reading and rereading their earlier correspondence,[129] as she waited for the visits [letter 110: quam iocunda michi sit . . . persone tue presencia], which Abelard himself later admitted he paid to her at Argenteuil in those early days,[130] visits that, as he admits, involved renewed sexual encounters with his wife.

Whether the de Vepria collection can bear the "interpretations" hinted at here and in appendices A and B is more important than the actual details of the interpretations. Acceptance of Mews's proposition opens the letters up to *some* process of identification with established texts and fixed points in the reconstructed lives of the two lovers. We have above, and in appendices A and B, simply made an essay in this direction, and, though a close fit between the de Vepria collection and the later letters is disappointingly difficult to establish, and although there are other collections of similar letters also from the twelfth century,[131] we believe that there is enough of a fit to support Mews's view of the matter. In time we may come to know more.

Heloise and the *Trivium*

In discussions of the lives and learning of Abelard and Heloise, notions of rhetoric are often vaguely expressed. In his recent *Abelard: A Medieval Life,* for example, the historian M.T. Clanchy speaks of "the rhetoric of the classical authors (Virgil, Cicero, Ovid, and so on),"[132] of Abelard and Heloise as "trained in Latin rhetoric," for whom "writing anything down made the author adopt a particular literary stance and speak with an artificial voice,"[133] and of "the rhetoric of letter-writing (the *ars dictaminis* or 'art of dictation')," which he says "was taught along with Latin in the classroom."[134] Such vague and inaccurate blurrings of reality will not do if we wish to understand what elements of the *trivium* were current in Abelard's day, what he learned and taught, what Heloise learned (and where), how these aspects differed—if they did—from what was elsewhere and otherwise taught and learned.[135]

"Rhetoric" in the sense of (Latin) "composition," that is, style and (vaguely) sentence and paragraph structure, was certainly acquired from reading the classical, late classical, and patristic *auctores* intensively (John of Salisbury's depiction of the teaching of grammar by Bernard of Chartres in *Metalogicon* 1.24 remains canonical here).[136] It was reinforced by continuous and sensitive readings of the scriptures themselves. Such training inculcated not only the Latin periodic sentence, the singsong rhymed prose of the monasteries, and an acquaintance with the *colores* or figures of speech and thought taught in the fourth book of the *Ad Herennium* and brought into recent focus by Marbod of Rennes' pioneering *De ornamentis verborum,* but it also equipped the student with a thousand snatches of past prose to weave into (but not to substitute for) his own compositions.[137] This acquaintance would have come to the student under the heading of "grammar" rather than rhetoric—a circumstance brought home to us by the initial lack of interest in the *Ad Herennium* in early studies in the art of rhetoric and by the impoverished nature of those early commentaries on book IV of the *Ad Herennium* when interest in that text did, finally, manifest itself.[138] As Clanchy stresses, the training in discourse imparted by such instruction was important to contemporaries of Abelard and Heloise "because it was the only way they knew to give their thoughts lasting shape."[139] At its most advanced level, such training inculcated a level of Latin rhetorical and poetic skill that enabled a blurring of the lines that divided fictive creation from reality, desire from eloquence, and permitted "literary exchange" to "become the ultimate object of all drives, sexual as well as religious."[140] As Marbod of Rennes himself wrote, "you who want to write . . . should strive to reproduce gender, age, emotion, and social status as they are distinct in reality."[141] Thus it is not unreasonable to suppose that when Abelard and Heloise decided to set up their early literary correspondence, their aim was "to be penfriends and have fun, like Lady Constance and Baudri of Bourgeuil,"[142] that is, to rehearse and practice their literary capacities in the "learned language," much as the author of the *Ad Herennium* advised when he asserted that skill in all the parts of rhetoric can be obtained "arte, imitatione, exercitatione,"[143] that is by knowing the rules of the art, by imitating the best authors (and the rules), and by frequent practice. If the result was a blurring of fiction and reality that has bedeviled the modern student ever since, the credit should go to those masters of literary composition in the half century that divides the birth of Abelard from the writing of the *Historia calamitatum,* the masters who believed "that the material world (including discourse) contained powers which could be extracted for human use through *studium,*" who brought "the mutual reinforcement between *ars* ("training") and *natura* ("native ability") in the theories of Pseudo-Cicero [the *Ad Herennium*] and Horace . . . [to] . . . a new level of abstraction," who, finally, achieved "the mastery of the Ciceronian ornamentation of discourse, . . . a synthesis rather than a simple digest, of rhetorical theories and the educational systems built around them," a synthesis founded on "the well-known idealization of the civic self in the figure of the orator, which found its most permanent form in the complex articulation of an elite-educational system founded on the [Graeco-Roman] *ars rhetorica.*"[144]

Rhetoric in the sense of the doctrines expounded (for example) in the *De inventione* of Cicero (and to a lesser extent in the parallel *Ad Herennium*), however, was a different matter. Now we are unsure as to the exact motivation for the intense study of what seems to be a thoroughly outmoded system of Greco-Roman rhetorical theory in Abelard's day,[145] a study that was to reach a magnificent climax in the *Ad Herennium* commentary of a certain Magister Alanus,[146] but the evidence is clear that this learned system of ancient theory was as zealously studied in Abelard's day as the poetical and compositional theories so stunningly illustrated by Baudri of Bourgeuil and Marbod of Rennes. The system was learned directly from the Greco-Roman technical texts themselves, in particular the Greek-influenced *De inventione* of Cicero and the somewhat more Romanized and almost contemporary anonymous work known as the *Rhetorica ad Herennium,* together with some lesser texts from the collection known as the *rhetores latini minores.*[147] Such we know from—at least—the famous collections of texts known as the *Heptateuchon* of Thierry of Chartres.[148] We can be fairly sure that Abelard had studied at least parts of this theoretical curriculum very carefully,[149] although whether by the time of his initial exchange of *litterae* with Heloise (A.D. 1116/1117) or not is unclear.[150]

What is clear, for Abelard and his contemporaries, is the absorption of rhetoric into dialectic. William of Champeaux's lectures on rhetoric were, in fact, dialectical in orientation,[151] and even in a work such as the *Metalogicon* of John of Salisbury, aimed it seems at the elite in the world, references to rhetoric rarely intrude upon the dialectical or grammatical subject matter of the book[152]: dialectic, the art of discussing the different subject matters of the *artes,* matters of general significance in life and topics subject to probability-oriented rather than certainty-oriented reasoning, was the legacy of the schools to the intelligent society of Abelard's day.

What therefore can we say of contemporary studies of the *trivium* and its role in the de Vepria collection? What *in tempore* reality, in this regard, do these epistolary texts mask, preserve, enrich, and transform? The arsenal of trivial texts and readings that informed the learning experience underlying the wax tablets on which these two people, *mulier* and *vir,* Heloise and Abelard impressed their versions of it seems to have been required to function in a white[153] heat that at once outmodes and surpasses the intellectual world of the Loire monasteries.[154] We are puzzled by the absence of any set curriculum in the readings and studies that produced the de Vepria collection, and by the distance between what appears to have fueled the *litterae* and the ever-present disputation in dialectic that seemed to have dominated the schools during Abelard's early teaching days in Paris.[155] We have Ovid but no Priscian, the *De amicitia* but not the *De inventione,*[156] *salutatio* formulas, and *Reimprosa* but little else from the developing dictaminal curriculum of the day. We find snippets of rational philosophy and an intensified ransacking of patristic and classical ethical literature for guidance on the more complicated aspects of life (should a man marry, can one philosophize and "carnalize"?) but little to help us answer fundamental questions. What drew Abelard and Heloise together initially? What were her motives? Where else, with whom, and in what manner had she been pursuing her postmonastic career and literary studies? Was she seeking an acquaintance with dictaminal skills, and if so, with what ultimate career in mind? Was she conscious of the prevailing theory and practice of learned *amicitia,* seeking to place herself in its midst, rather like—and more successfully than—the more aspiring of her Italian Renaissance successors?[157]

We can only guess at the answers to these questions. The Könsgen source annotations[158] and list of proverbial expressions[159] reveal a pattern of reading consistent with the idea of private tutorship in grammar and the auctores, together with wide-ranging discussions of contemporary moral issues based on readings in scriptures and patristic writings. From an initial glance at Könsgen's extensive and careful annotations,[160] the major works likely to have been read or seemingly reflected would appear to be:

Baudri of Bourgeuil:	*Carmina.*
Bible:	Acts, Apocalypse, Song of Songs, 1 Corinthians, 2 Corinthians, Daniel, Deuteronomy, Ecclesiasticus, Ephesians, Esther, Exodus, Ezekiel, Genesis, Hebrews, Isaiah,

	Job, Joel, Joshua, John, Jonah, Judges, Judith, 3 Kings, Luke, Matthew, Proverbs, Psalms, Romans, Ruth, 1 Thessalonians, 1 Timothy, 2 Timothy, Wisdom.
Boethius:	*Consolatio, De arithmetica.*
Cicero:	*De amicitia, Epistulae, De officiis, Tusculanae disputationes.*
Claudian:	*In Rufinum.*
Ennodius:	*Opuscula.*
Gregory the Great:	*Homiliae in evangelium, Cura pastoralis.*
Horace:	*Carmina, Epistulae, Saturae.*
Isidore:	*Etymologiae.*
Jerome:	*Epistulae.*
Juvenal	
Lucan:	*Pharsalia.*
Marbod of Rennes:	*Carmina amatoria.*
Ovid:	*Ars amatoria, Epistulae, Fasti, Heroides, Metamorphoses, Pontica, Remedium Amores, Tristia.*
Persius:	*Saturae.*
Plautus:	*Stichus.*
Pliny:	*Historia naturalis.*
Prudentius:	*Apotheosis.*
Statius:	*Thebias, Silvae.*
Terence:	*Andria, Eunuchus, Heauton Timorumenos, Hecyra.*
Vergil:	*Ecloga, Georgica, Aeneis.*

There is little that is exceptional here, but the interweaving of the texts with the processes of life and its dilemmas must be considered unique in the annals of humanism.

If we look closely at one of the pieces in the de Vepria collection, we shall see how a distinctive pattern arises out of mutual textual readings. Letter 45 has one of the longest, if not the longest, *salutationes* in the collection, a litany of isocolon [*conpar, Ad Her.* 4.20.27], homoeoptoton [*similiter cadens, Ad Her.* 4.20.28], and asyndeton [*dissolutum, Ad Her.* 4.30.41] based on allusions to the Bible and Ovid.[161] The biblical overtones continue to provide the fabric of the richly balanced [voluntatem . . . effectus/per litteras . . . per corporalem . . . presenciam/spiritu et mente . . . corpus stolidum et inutile/fortuna deposuit . . . consolacio . . . restituit (etc.)] and rhyming [discedente . . . mente/patrie . . . inutile/abscencia . . . sciencia . . . secreta (etc.)] prose. Heloise's ability to work phrases from the Bible into her own literary construction is suddenly balanced by a series of secular allusions (unfortunately truncated by the medieval editor): "I [Heloise] cannot deny you [Abelard] any more than could Byblis her Cauno, Oenone her Paris, Briseis her Achilles." We are suddenly thrust into the "real life of the schoolroom," but when we refresh our memory of Heloise's allusions, there is a chilling "reality" about the fictions of the classical schoolroom. The Byblis of Ovid's *Metamorphoses* IX.453ff. has used the *eloquentia* of the wax tablet [563–64: plena . . . cera manum, 570: *tabella,* 586: *tabellis,* etc.] to propose a love to Byblos (her brother) that was as passionate as it was forbidden; it is a reminder that Heloise, especially in Fulbert's household, was a kind of sister to Abelard, but one unable to restrain her passionate erotic emotions, emotions she too committed to wax tablets. As in letter 84, there is a hint that Heloise initiated the relationship, and although Abelard's initial reception of such "overtures" was warm, he ultimately claimed, as Byblis claimed of Cauno's response to her own passions [623–24: non hoc . . . Deo, sed victa libidine], that he was drawn by lust rather than love.[162] Oenone, too, in Ovid's *Heroides* (V.79ff.), draws a contrast between the rustic love that bound Paris to her before he entered upon the paths of fame, glory, and tribulation that took him from the flocks of Mt. Ida to the palaces of Priam and Troy and his later aristocratic loves. Briseis, also, in *Her.* III.75ff., draws a contrast between her own humble love service and Achilles' aristocratic expectations (71ff.), although in the case of *Her.* III, the fiction would suggest that Fulbert had other, more aristocratic marital plans (*Her.* III.20) for Heloise (whose former attachments [Argenteuil? a former betrothed?], like Briseis' former brothers and husband, lost in the Trojan wars, were abandoned in circumstances beyond her control), which she would have resisted out of loyalty to Abelard, who would then be pictured as Achilles, refusing to play ball with Agamemnon/Fulbert (that is, refusing to proceed with Fulbert's plans for the educational enrichment of his ward [*HC* M 321–22], just as Achilles refused to go along with his expected role in the battles against Troy until Briseis were restored to him). Yet the fiction of *Her.* III is more complicated: Achilles is portrayed (ll. 22 and 25) as sluggish in his claim to have Briseis restored, even opposed: Briseis (portrayed in the Latin *Iliad* as "well-proportioned in her figure, amiable in her manners and fascinating in her looks")[163] portrays herself as a pawn in the negotiations between Agamemnon and the Greek leaders, and sees suspicions in regard to her having succumbed in bed to Agamemnon as the obstacle impeding Achilles' reclaiming of her.[164] The notion of Heloise/Briseis as a pawn in the hands of males (Fulbert, Abelard/Achilles, Agamemnon) joins with that of jealousy on the part of the male,[165] and a relationship (Briseis and Achilles) based on the passion of the female, and without much to do with formal marital ties, to form an appealing combination.

Even the parting touch, the reference to Terence's *Heauton Timorumenos*[166] or "The Self-tormenter,"[167] is suggestive. Heloise refers to the pleasure Antiphila (the girl) received when Clinia was restored to her, not the other way around, even though the context demands that Heloise give *gaudia* to Abelard. In the *Heauton Timorumenos* Clinia (the male) is described as falling in love with "filiam . . . virginem" and treating her almost as a wife—"prope ut pro uxore haberet."[168] It is made clear in the play that Antiphila [Heloise] is a simple, natural girl, with none of the contrived arts of the society female.[169] It is stated further that in the case of girls like Antiphila [Heloise] *formae* match *mores,* that Antiphila [Heloise] is a perfect match of *ingenium* and *oratio,* and that she has only to want to pass her time with a particular man whose *mos* resembles most her own, and the man is devoted to her at once, with the happy outcome that both are truly bound together and no calamity can befall their *amor.*[170] Antiphila [Heloise] replies to this estimation of her talents and prospects with the humble sentence: "nescio alias: mequidem semper scio fecisse sedulo, ut ex illius commodo meum compararem commodum": "I'm not sure about the rest, but I have certainly always done my best to see that my interests are his." Her beloved, Clinia, then claims that only Antiphila has brought him back "in patriam," linking up with the "patrie" and "ne tardas venire" of letter 45.

There is an intriguing play between various realities, textual and otherwise, in letter 45, and a pointedness about the classical literary allusions that suggests an intelligent, well-stocked mind. Our modern ignorance of the conditions for such writing should not lead us to trivialize it by placing it in the category either of the lifeless school exercise or in the category of the true-to-life narrative *relatio.* There is an intriguing space somewhere between these two poles in which we must place such curious attempts to work out a troubled but tolerably "real" relationship in a discourse selected because of its rich tradition, its availability, and its capacity to permit exploration and resolution of conflict. In terms of the present enquiry, we need to note the way in which such "real life" concerns guided and animated not only curriculum reading of the *auctores* in grammar in the monastery, under a tutor, and perhaps also (if vestigially) in the developing cathedral school studies of the day, but also motivated the *collationes* or *imitationes* that followed such reading in the account left to us of Bernard of Chartres' grammatical teaching, in the pages of John of Salisbury's *Metalogicon*.

The hints at some knowledge of dialectical terms and ethical problems debated in the schools have been already touched upon, but the relationship between the de Vepria collection and the teaching of technical rhetoric requires further comment. Important developments were taking place in Paris and the surrounding schools during the lifetimes of Abelard and Heloise as far as the teaching of technical rhetoric, that is, the rhetorical doctrines of the Roman republican treatises, Cicero's *De inventione,* and the (anonymous) *Rhetorica ad Herennium,* was concerned.[171] While Abelard seems to have been involved in these developments,[172] there is little trace of them in the de Vepria collection (though Heloise is not unfamiliar with the *De inventione*).[173] What we find in the earlier collection is an emphasis on compositional, grammatical, ethical humanism, with an evident concern for the developing niceties of dictaminal etiquette, such as, for example, in the elaborate *salutationes.*

Although letter practice doubtless preceded letter theory,[174] dictaminal rules and dictaminal model letter collections were very much in vogue by the time that Heloise and Abelard responded to a growing contemporary fascination with Cicero's *De amicitia* and the examination and "publication" of personal emotional experiences and fell themselves into epistolary dialogue in the middle years of the second decade of the twelfth century.[175] Not only were the Italian rule books beginning to penetrate north of the Alps, but contemporaries were already putting together outstanding collections of actual letters for later use as models, as is clear from the remarks of I. S. Robinson on the literature of the investiture controversy and its preservation in primarily German dictaminal collections made during the half century following the outbreak of the controversy itself: "it was the preoccupation with the *clausula* and the rhyming prose in the twelfth century German schools which ensured the survival of many polemical works."[176] Although, according to Constable,[177] the *ars dictaminis* "of the *dictatores,* especially at Bologna, . . . was hardly felt north of the Alps before 1150," "many of its constitutive elements had been developed much earlier," for example, "the fourfold division so characteristic of its method—*exordium . . . narratio . . . petitio . . . conclusio.*"[178] An initial glance at the dictaminal elements present in the de Vepria collection suggests the dimensions of the relationship between epistolary practice in the period and the formulated rules that were to become dominant in the schools by the second half of the twelfth century.

The very preservation of his collection clearly reflects de Vepria's interest in *dictamen* rather than love letters per se. The accompanying texts contained in the manuscript which preserves them is abundant evidence of the primary concern of the copyist: Cassiodorus' *Varie,* collected letters of Sidonius Apollinaris, Ennodius, Cyprian, Transmundus, and John of Limoges and model letters of Carolus Virulus. (The two exceptions are William of Malmesbury's *Gesta regum Anglorum* and Cicero's *De officiis*).[179]

But if their survival reflects late fifteenth-century interest in Latin composition, the letters themselves obviously reflect the concerns of the correspondents, although the main themes discernible are possibly sharpened by the selectivity of their transcriber. One of these concerns the very medium they were employing: the letter, its composition, nature, and role in their relationship. The heightened sensitivity of the writers toward the letter as a genre is a valuable witness to the importance of epistolary composition at a time when and in an area where the manuals of the *ars dictaminis* were just beginning to emerge from the Italian schools.[180]

Although the de Vepria collection predates the circulation of such manuals in France, it nevertheless reflects many of the characteristics that would become stock features of dictaminal literature of the twelfth and thirteenth centuries. This is so even at a terminological level, with the words *dictamen/dictare* and their derivatives occurring in several places: *novus dictandi fervor* (#33); *quid dictem?* (#66); *ut tales litteras dictare queam; qua dictaminis dulcedine te alloquar, dilectissime?;* and *in ipso doloris cursu dictavi—et utinam non dictassem* (both in #75).[181] In all these occurrences, the term is used in the sense that will become standard in subsequent manuals: formal, artistic, prose Latin composition. That is, the term *dictamen/dictare* comes to connote the entire mental and physical process involved in literary composition, not just the restricted sense of the English word "dictation."[182]

The collection also shows a predilection for the general maxims or proverbs that, as part of the *captatio benevolentia* or *exordium* of the letter, would become a standard feature of many of the theoretical texts.[183] This interest is especially prominent in the early thirteenth-century manual entitled *Candelabrum* by Bene da Firenze, where 168 such *sententie* are gathered and arranged in alphabetical order.[184]

The close link between epistolary practice and rhetorical teaching also can be discerned in the de Vepria letters. In letter 23, for instance, which has already been noted for its rhetorical elements, the woman[185] relates her inner debate over how she should compose a letter of thanks to her teacher/lover. The recourse to the form of the *controversia* is obvious, and she seems to draw attention to it herself when she resumes the letter in her own voice: *hac hortaminis et dehortaminis alternacione suspensam* [suspended between this alternating encouragement and discouragement," or, less literally, "caught between these pros and cons].[186] Significantly, the internal debate is not whether she should write back but whether she is capable of doing so appropriately; that is, "appropriately" with respect to the conventions of the *littere graciarum*. Indeed, the description of the required method of writing such a letter reads like a textbook prescription: "For anyone who assumes to praise anything at all must ultimately divide it into parts and with the utmost care weigh the qualities of each individual part, honouring each one according to its merit with a suitable tribute of praise; otherwise he harms the object of praise whoever [. . .] lessens its elegance with an excessive description."[187] While we are not aware of parallels in twelfth-century dictaminal texts, an early thirteenth-century dictaminal collection, the *Boncompagnus* of Boncompagno da Signa, provides a comparable compositional method. As part of his model letters, the author provides several paired examples of *suasiones* and *dissuasiones* that might be used to argue opposite points of view with respect to certain topics: ecclesiastical elections, the merits of the various religious orders, and the choice of marriage partner. An example of the latter is: "An argument-for based on commendation of character, physical beauty, and nobility" and "An argument-against based on unfit character, physical deformity, and humble birth." Such paired models form the outline for potential debates and reveal the rhetorico-legal basis of much of dictaminal literature.[188]

Another feature of the correspondence that exemplifies a specific dictaminal precept is its anonymity—nowhere do the writers' names appear. This of course may be a result of editorial censuring on the part of de Vepria, but the most obvious site for names, the salutations, appear by and large intact.[189] More likely, then, the discretion was on the part of the correspondents themselves, eager to conceal their identities should their tablets end up in the wrong hands. We get a sense of this concern in letter 69 when the woman writes: "Let not jealous eyes read these verses, I ask: / I do not want hearts full of guile to know them."[190] Similarly, in letter 101 the man makes a virtue of necessity by suggesting that such caution is both inherently and circumstantially advisable: "If you care to note, I am now speaking to you more cautiously, and approaching you more cautiously; shame tempers love, modesty checks love, lest it collapse in its boundlessness. This way we can fulfil our sweet desires and gradually diminish the report which has arisen about us."[191] Such discretion would eventually be held up as a basic principle of writing love letters, as the following passage from Boncompagno's treatise on the subject reveals: "And it should be noted that both women and men, whatever their order or condition, should obscure the salutation of love-letters of this kind in such a way that if the letter should come into the hands of others, they would not be easily recognised."[192] What we have instead of names in the salutations are periphrastic phrases describing the particular qualities of the writer and addressee: "to her heart's love" (#1), "from her only one" (#4). Such periphrastic phrases derive from the epithets that regularly accompanied the names of the salutation formulas. Common practice throughout medieval letter writing, such epithets generally exalted the addressee while humbling the writer, and they quickly became a standard feature of the dictaminal manuals. Boncompagno would even dedicate a small treatise to listing all the terms that could suitably describe people of various ranks and offices.[193]

The primary dictaminal interest of the de Vepria collection, however, lies in its salutations. This holds not only for de Vepria himself, who began his transcription by focusing on them before being drawn into copying out substantial parts of the actual letters, but to the correspondents themselves. Their salutations are frequently the subject of discussion in their letters. They are varied, often elaborate and interactive, and at times quite innovative. They reveal not only an abiding concern with epistolary form but constitute an important means of relating through "epistolary play." Above all, they reflect the important role attributed to the letter in their relationship.

The anatomy of the medieval letter salutation has been thoroughly described by Lanham.[194] Its three components are the *intitulatio* [sender's name and/or attributes], the *inscriptio* [recipient's name and/or attributes], and the *salutatio* proper [the actual greeting]. Each element has its own grammatical case—dative for the addressee, nominative for the sender, and accusative for the greeting—which is dependent on an elided verb (normally "to send," "offer," or "wish").[195] Obviously important from a practical perspective (who is writing to whom?), the salutation was possibly more important from the point of view of protocol (what is the respective rank and importance of the correspondents?). Accordingly, definitive rules governed both the attributes of the correspondents and the relative positions of their names, as the following prescription from one of the earliest surviving manuals reveals: "If an inferior should write to a superior, the higher person is placed first, the lower next. If a superior to an inferior, the same applies. If an equal to an equal, either of the two can be placed first or second, according to the writer's preference. Moreover, the salutation should represent the person and the rank through different qualities, there being one for superiors, one for inferiors, and another when we greet equals."[196] Any deviation from these conventions inevitably carried significative force. A salutation was denied, for example, enemies or infidel. Curiously, it also could be denied a superior through the conceit of humility and reverence.[197] But whatever the motivation, such divergence from standard salutatory practice was instantly recognized and noted.

The writers in the de Vepria correspondence reveal themselves to be acutely aware of the importance of the salutation, not only in terms of getting it right but also making sure it reflects their feelings for the other. The woman is especially sensitive to this. In letter 5, for example, she writes: "May the Bestower of every art and the most bountiful Giver of human talent fill the depths of my breast with the skill of the art of philosophy, in order that I may greet you in writing, most beloved, in accordance with my will."[198] Her wish is surprisingly specific—not for eloquence in general but for the dictaminal ability to greet appropriately. In other letters, she is troubled and frustrated by her inability to do so: "For a long time, and with a blazing struggle of heart and body, I have considered how I should address you, my graceful jewel, but the difficulty of expected failure has so far defied the intention of my feeling."[199] In the end, she decided to extend the metaphor of fire to the salutation and resort to a rhetorical topos for the greeting in order to resolve her predicament: "To one deserving to be embraced with the ardor of a special love, from the fire of love for you: may you gather as many greetings as flowers which perfume the delightful season."[200] Such protestations of inadequacy are manifestly rhetorical. Elsewhere, for instance, she negotiates the "salutation block" just as elegantly and ingeniously: "I send you the salutation which I would like sent to me. / I know of nothing more salutary than this."[201] And the salutation of letter 45, which Peter Dronke singled out for particular attention, demonstrates beyond doubt that the woman had a firm grasp of both the conventions and poetic potential of the salutation: "To her house of cedar, from the ivory statue on which the whole house rests: the whiteness of snow, gleam of the moon, radiance of the sun, splendour of stars, perfume of roses, beauty of lilies, softness of balm, fertility of the earth, serenity of the sky, and whatever sweetness is embraced in their circumference."[202]

Being the most regulated part of the letter, the salutation clearly provided the best opportunity to "bounce off" those principles and to play with the conventions of epistolary style. The necessity for allusive identifications in letters of love thus had a twofold function: first, it concealed the identities of the correspondents (unfortunately from posterity as well as from contemporary readers); and second, it provided an opportunity for imaginative and affectionate circumlocutions and metaphors that constituted a lover's code. At their most elemental, admittedly, such phrases can be somewhat trite: "To her heart's love, more sweetly scented than any spice" (#1), "From one whose life without you is death" (#2), "To one who is sweeter every day, loved now as much as possible, and always to be loved more than everything, From her only one" (#4). But as the writers warm to the task and the challenge, their allusions become more imaginative and elaborate: "To the sweetest protector of her soul, planted at the root of her caring love, from one in whose love you are firmly established and in whose honeyed taste of love you are well founded" (#23, woman); and, in response to her imagery, "To the soul, brighter and dearer to me than anything the earth has produced, from the flesh, which that same soul causes to breathe and move" (#24, man). In so doing, the salutation is instilled with much more meaning than a simple formulaic structure; it comes to symbolize the writers' intellectual and emotional engagement with each other, it heightens the excitement of their epistolary relationship (what if someone should "crack the code?"), and it teasingly challenges the other to do better. In other words, it becomes part of the lovers' game.

The inclusion of a greeting, in the form of a verbal offering or benevolent wish for the other, was a fundamental part of the salutation. Its omission was always pointed, and usually implied disfavor or ostracism, as many *dictatores* expressly remarked.[203] However, in correspondence between lovers, such transgressions, while noted, seem to have acquired a different meaning. In letter 95, for example, the woman's failure to offer a greeting as part of the salutation triggers the following response from the man: "To half my heart and part of my soul. I send what I am: yours, as long as I live. Farewell, even though you sent no greeting to me."[204] The man's own greeting, however, would have revealed that the reproach was good-natured. Perhaps with this in mind, a few letters later (#109) the woman teasingly suggests that a formal greeting is not necessary since they can readily meet—and then she provides one: "Since each of us is presently able to come into the sight of the other, my letter does not need a greeting. Nevertheless I want you to be well, clothed with the grace of the virtues, covered with the jewels of wisdom, endowed with integrity of character, and decorated with the adornment of complete composure."[205] And in one letter the man employs *salve,* the characteristic term of the salutation, in the closing formula: "Farewell, and make sure that you compare no mortal with me, for I will tenaciously persist with the same intention toward you. Greetings, my most beloved, and keep me in your memory as forever yours."[206] The novelty does not go unnoticed, and with an epistolary wink, the woman replies in her own salutation: "Greetings to you too, most beloved, worthy of every delight!"[207]

The salutations of the de Vepria correspondence are noteworthy for their variation. Lanham has identified three main types of greeting formula used in medieval correspondence: (1) an accusative phrase containing a wish/hope or a promise/pledge; (2) *quicquid* phrases: as in letter 18: *quidquid amans amanti* [sc. *mittit, optat,* etc.]; (3) and infinitive phrases, as in letter 9: *sic pugnare ut vincat, sic currere ut comprehendat.*[208] All three types occur regularly in the correspondence, with the woman clearly favoring the accusative phrase, while the man uses all three types more or less equally. More important, the writers show a preference for a particular type of greeting in certain phases of their correspondence.[209] While such responsiveness and sensitivity to the other's lead might be expected on a thematic level, it is remarkable to find it on a formal one.[210] Again, it suggests that these writers were extraordinarily sensitive to the form and conventions of the letter and that it constituted a common interest and concern, both at an explicit level and an unspoken formal one.

Some letters omit a reference to the writer/sender altogether. It is a device employed by both writers, initially by the woman (letters 3, 5, 9, 25, and 27), before the man takes up the lead at letter 28 and thereafter employs it regularly. Only near the end, however, does he call attention to the artifice:

> My sun and my serene day, my light, greetings.
> You are my sweetness, without you nothing is sweet.
> If you should ask who sends words so sweet to you:
> He who is yours does so, whose life you remain,
> Whose drink has been tears with you away,
> Whose food has been mixed with grief and sighs.[211]

The absence of the sender's attributes from its usual place—immediately before the greeting—would have been as conspicuous as the omission of a greeting. The man thus plays the epistolary equivalent of the lover's game of "guess who?" teasingly asking his recipient to guess his identity, before alluding to it for her. The fact that she would have known from the start from whom the wax tablet had come is beside the point, for pretending is all part of the game.

Some letters even lack a salutation altogether, a flagrant impropriety in any other epistolary situation.[212] Letter 13 from the woman is the first one to lack a salutation, although the ellipses in Könsgen's text suggest that either he or de Vepria thought that it had been lost. However, as the letter reveals, the omission was intentional and strategic: "Since the grateful benevolence of my mind, of its own accord and out of duty always bound to you, could not send all the greetings which it wished, it remains silent over the many, lest by listing some it might seem to offend them all."[213] While the man makes no direct reference to her innovation, the fact that his own reply also lacks a salutation (the first of his letters to do so) suggests that he had noted it and acknowledged it through imitation. This will set the pattern whereby the omission of the salutation by one is often imitated by the other (usually the man, as in letters 13–14, 29–30, 32–33, and 66–67), as if the harmony of their relationship is measured by the formal harmony of their correspondence.

On the other hand, several letters consist of the salutation alone (letters 15, 65, 70, 97, and 99 by the man; 81, 92, and 95 by the woman). Such contentless letters may also be readily interpreted as a further part of the lover's game, ways of displaying affection and eliciting charming responses, such as: "Indeed your words are few, but I made them many by re-reading them often. Nor do I measure how much you say, but rather how fertile is the heart from which it comes. Farewell, sweetest."[214] At times, the salutation also is used to signify estrangement, mock or otherwise. This is made more poignant by a combination of linguistic and formal features. One of the man's letters begins by adopting an unprecedented deferential tone: "To his reverend lady, from her humble servant: his devoted service."[215] Then, in a thoroughly scholastic manner, he provides a gloss of his own salutation, explaining the cool formality of his greeting: "For this is how I must now address your ladyship: no longer saying 'you,' but 'Madam,' not 'sweet' nor 'dear' but 'lady,' because I am not as familiar as before and your ladyship is too much a stranger to me."[216] Since this tone lasts just one letter, it is probably just part of the lovers' game rather than a sign of an actual breach; it is a subtle and highbrow way of saying "I haven't heard from you for a long time."[217]

Arguably the most important principle of medieval dictaminal theory, however, one whose transgression was at least as provocative as omitting a greeting, was the order of names/attributes in the salutation.[218] The five salutations, all by the woman, in which she places her own attribute before the man's, contrary to her usual practice and the conventional social order, therefore carry special meaning. These are:

From an equal to an equal . . . [#18: *Par pari*]
From a lover to a lover . . . [#48 and #84: *Amans amanti*]
From beloved to beloved . . . [#62: *Dilecta dilecto*]
From faithful to faithful . . . [#100: *Fidelis fideli*]

The convention that the woman is breaking here is not a social one, however, since whenever the man writes to the woman, he always places her first. Evidently, in the case of letters between lovers, different rules applied.[219] Given that another of the medieval letter writer's overriding concerns (apart from observing salutation etiquette) was the "capturing of goodwill" [*captatio benevolentie*], to which a special part of the letter was assigned, the placing of the lover's name/attributes first is perhaps not so surprising when seen as a gesture of deference and ingratiation.

Thus the woman contravenes a specific convention of love-letters in placing her own name first. It is significant that she uses the same word to describe him as she does herself, but on its own this apparently does not justify the rearrangement; on the one occasion that the man applies the same attribute to himself as to her (#68: *Dulcissime dulcissimus* ["Sweetest to sweetest"]), he retains the conventional order between lovers. Rather, in the woman's hands, the device is used to make a point of their parity. While the use of the same attribute might temper to some extent the impact of the innovation and its implication of precedence, these salutations remain striking assertions of the equality of their relationship, rendered through lexical, syntactic, and formal means. Indeed, the very words that herald the innovation—*par pari*—suggest an allusion to the precept of Adalbertus cited earlier, as if the woman is subtly pointing out that since they *are* equals, she can happily choose the order *iuxta placitum scriptoris.*

On the whole, the woman appears most aware of and imaginative in her use of the salutations, even though she also most often expresses her own sense of compositional inadequacy. In letter 49, for instance, she claims: "It is very rash of me to send studied phrases to you . . . ; unless I knew the unfailing friendship of true love to be implanted in you, I would not presume to send you inelegant letters of such unrefined style."[220] Elsewhere: "If a droplet of knowability had trickled down to me from the honeycomb of wisdom, I would try with every effort of my mind to portray in the jottings of my letter various things with a fragrant nectar for your nourishing love."[221] Coming after her description of herself as *tocius expers pericie* [devoid of every skill] in the salutation, such claims of incompetence begin to sound distinctly rhetorical. The man, on the other hand, comes close to such self-doubts only once, in letter 75, when he writes: "Therefore who am I or what quality is there in me that I could compose such a letter which would prove me worthy of your golden breast, your ivory arms, your milk-white neck?"[222] But this comes only after he has made similar disclaimers for Cicero and Ovid, so that such a protest seems more literary posturing than genuine complaint. In general, he simply shares with her a sense of frustration over the inadequacy of words and a letter to convey one's true feelings.[223]

Yet the letter—and its composition—remained a crucial part of their relationship, even, perhaps especially, when that relationship was threatened. Letter 58 heralds a major (although temporary, it turns out) rift between the two, and the subsequent letters reveal the extent of their falling out:

> [Woman]: Take your complaints away from me, I will not hear your words any more. For where I expected many good things to be of benefit to me, there emerged instead tearful sighs of the heart.
>
> [Man]: Certainly if anyone examined your words more thoroughly, he would find them to be not those of a lover but of one seeking estrangement. Nowhere in them do I detect a tender heart, but rather I perceive a cruel breast and one impregnable to love.[224]

Despite such inflammatory words, the woman somehow manages to avoid responding in kind. Instead, she steers their letters toward the subject of composition and her claims of incompetence, although it is difficult not to detect an underlying sarcasm: "If such cleverness of expression were within me that I could respond prudently to your words, I would reply to you however gracefully I could with a willing spirit. But nevertheless, although I am not capable of doing so satisfactorily, I shall reply as best I can and within the limits of my small learning."[225] The man accepts her lead and, adopting the tone of the teacher, initially provides a critique of her letter, before succumbing to the language of the lover eager for reconciliation: "The letter which you sent had a logical and orderly arrangement, and it contained mature judgements. Certainly I have never seen anything more fittingly set out. God willing, I shall keep aside for you, sweetest, many very sweet and joyful hours."[226] Significantly, the pedagogical dimension of their relationship proves to be a point of stability amid the emotional turmoil, for only following its reestablishment is emotional harmony restored. Such a central role for the letter is suggestive of a relationship founded initially on training in Latin composition and evidently one in which the well-composed letter could also play a reconciliatory role.

The strategy of using the conventions and implications of the salutation to go succinctly and subtly beyond its conventional formality finds a striking parallel in the canonical letters of Heloise to Abelard. In her famous first letter to him after reading the *Historia calamitatum,* Heloise reestablished their correspondence with the following salutation: "To her master, or rather her father, husband, or rather brother; (from) his handmaid, or rather his daughter, wife, or rather sister; to Abelard, Heloise."[227] With these words she evocatively and succinctly captured the memories evoked by renewed contact with her former lover. Abelard's salutation in reply—"To Heloise, his dearly beloved sister in Christ, (from) Abelard her brother in Christ"—makes it clear that he prefers to avoid the issue of their past and to focus on their current relationship. His letter provokes what initially appears to be a rather pedantic response from Heloise: "I am surprised, my only love, that contrary to custom in letter-writing and, indeed, to the natural order, you have thought fit to put my name before yours in the greeting which heads your letter, so that we have woman before man, wife before husband, handmaid before master, nun before monk, deaconess before priest and abbess before abbot."[228] But is Heloise here really indulging in point-scoring over epistolary correctness? The picture we have of her from the rest of her correspondence with Abelard suggests otherwise, as do the forgoing observations on the epistolary skill and sensitivity of the de Vepria correspondents. Is it not more likely that Heloise, inevitably recalling their earlier love letters where each writer would have routinely placed the other's name first, was stung by the inappropriateness of Abelard's readoption of that practice? The more sympathetic interpretation would be to see Heloise's objection as a cry of the heart evoked by the bittersweet reminder of their former relationship, perhaps too as a cutting remark that sprang from anger, and certainly a provocative challenge to Abelard to confront their past openly.[229]

A final topic in the area of dictaminal/*trivium* studies is the use of *cursus* patterns. Peter Dronke has argued that Heloise's known letters make use of a peculiar *cursus* pattern linked with that of the contemporary Italian dictaminal expert Albertus Samaritanus[230]: "a preponderance of [*cursus*] 'tardus' over 'velox' [which] is extremely unusual in medieval Latin rhythmic prose."[231] This view has not gained much acceptance from those skilled in the area.[232] Nevertheless, in view of the fact that "the *cursus* was not invented by the *dictatores* but was widely practiced in Europe for several centuries before formal descriptions of its rules began to appear in the French *artes dictandi* of the late twelfth century,"[233] it is worth asking what *cursus* patterns are evident in the de Vepria collection. The following is a brief sampling.

We start with the contention of Tore Janson "that in the period we are studying, when Latin was no one's mother tongue, and its users had several languages and prosodies, it was hardly possible for anyone to grasp the principles of [accentual] *cursus* only by reading or listening to Latin texts. One had to be taught before one could produce *cursus,* or even recognise it in the Latin of others."[234] With this in mind we have analyzed the sentence-end *cursus* patterns[235] of letters 22 (V), 23 (M), 24 (V), 25 (M), 49 (M), and 50 (V) in the de Vepria collection. Every sentence-end has been coded thus:

1 = monosyllable
2 = bisyllable, always paroxytone ('p')
pp = (trisyllabic) proparoxytone

All other words in the selected sentence endings have been codified as 'p' or 'pp' followed by the number of syllables in the word. This is a variant of Janson's own method. We have accepted as formally 'velox' the following terminations:

pp p4
pp p5
pp pp5

We have accepted as 'tardus' *clausulae* the following combinations:

p4 pp4
2 pp4
2 pp5
pp pp
pp 4pp
pp 4pp
pp pp4

We have accepted as 'planus' *clausulae* the following combinations:

2 p3
2 p4
p5
pp 2
p3 p3

If these words are found in the selected sentence endings, they are described as "actual" *cursus* endings. If, on the other hand, we pay regard only to terminal rhythm and not to the syllabic content of the final words of the selected sentence endings, then we accept as "virtual" *cursus* endings the following rhythms[236]:

'velox':–""''–' or–""""–' or–"""–" (where–is a stressed syllable and ' an unstressed one)
'tardus':–"–" or–""'–"
'planus':–"–' or–""'–'

The sample covers a total of thirty-eight sentence endings for "vir" and seventy-three for "mulier." Sixty-eight percent of sentence endings for *both* "vir" *and* "mulier" do *not* conform to "actual" *cursus* patterns as defined above. Of those that do conform, we find 21 percent of the total of sentence endings for the man are 'planus', 2.6 percent 'velox', and 7.9 percent 'tardus'. For the woman 15 percent are 'planus', 4.1 percent 'velox', and 12.3 percent 'tardus'. If we take into account only the basic rhythmic patterns, then 34.2 percent of the sentence endings for the man do not conform to *cursus* rhythms, but only 23.3 percent of the woman's sentence endings do not conform. Of those that do conform, 42.1 percent of the total sentence endings for V are 'planus', 5.3 percent 'velox', and 18.5 percent 'tardus', contrasting with 39.8 percent of sentence endings for M as 'planus', 12.13 percent 'velox', and 24.7 percent 'tardus'.[237]

Thus, 68 percent of sentence endings for both writers do not conform to the actual *cursus* patterns taught in twelfth-century and later textbooks, with Abelard showing a preference for 'planus', then 'tardus', then 'velox' patterns, and Heloise showing a reduced preference for 'planus' and a greater interest in 'velox' and 'tardus' endings. If we consider basic sentence-ending rhythms, without regard to word-syllable length, Heloise's nonconforming sentence endings drop to an interesting low of 23.3 percent as against 34.2 percent for Abelard, with both writers displaying again a preference for 'planus' endings, then 'tardus', then 'velox', but with Heloise again showing much greater interest than Abelard in 'velox' and 'tardus' with less interest (by a small percentage) in 'planus' endings.

Our initial conclusion, then, is that neither party in the de Vepria letters has consciously learned or sought to imitate the formulaic *cursus* pattern endings of twelfth- and thirteenth-century dictaminal manuals—a circumstance that may be seen as an argument for the spontaneity and authenticity of the letters in question—but that the woman displays a greater "unconscious" absorption of and sensitivity to the approved patterns than the man, and was more receptive to all types of endings than he was. This conclusion confirms an impression we have that Heloise expresses herself naturally and fully in prose and is less adept at "distinguishing" genres and generating compositions that illustrate the different requirements of nonrhythmic prose, rhythmic prose, verse using classical meters, and accentual verse, whereas Abelard is prosaic in prose, less interested in rhythmic prose, good at verse using classical meters, and a positive genius at accentual verse. Again, Abelard is the "compartmentalized" mind, Heloise the integrated person. Such comparisons do not take into account a careful study of all the verse Heloise might be said to have written, but sum up our current impressions.

Further, the de Vepria collection reveals how the nature and conventions of the letter were an ever-present and conscious backdrop to the amatory relationship. These conventions constituted not only a stylistic goal to be aspired toward for its own sake but a framework against which variations inevitably carried meaning. The salutation was especially suited to this role, for its formulaic nature allowed it to convey its meaning structurally as well as linguistically. Through variation, imitation, and innovation of their salutations, the lovers could implicitly acknowledge and celebrate their shared literary culture, confirm their mutual understanding, and engage in amorous play. Far from being solely a formulaic, ornamental part of the letter, then, the medieval salutation in many ways constituted a barometer of the amorous epistolary relationship.

This of course presumes a heightened awareness of the form and symbolism of the letter, one conceivably produced in a pedagogical context and/or scholastic environment. Heloise's correspondence clearly displays such awareness. The woman of the de Vepria collection shows a similar sensitivity, along with a dictaminal creativity and prodigiousness not incompatible with Heloise's. In many ways, her male correspondent shows similar affinities with the picture of Abelard that emerges from his letters to Heloise, although these could conceivably stem from the pedagogical role they share. Nevertheless, the common preoccupation with and sensitivity toward epistolary form displayed by both couples constitutes further evidence that the de Vepria correspondence may represent the early letters of Abelard and Heloise.

The major emphasis of Heloise's prose style and literary leanings, in fact, have been well emphasized by Dronke himself in several publications[238] and conform to what we know of Latin stylistic developments in the later part of the eleventh century and the early twelfth.[239] The de Vepria collection strengthens and reinforces this knowledge and, if Mews's view of authorship is accepted, provides new raw materials for a more precise estimation of the state of Heloise's literary expertise at the time of her meeting with Abelard. If, as letter 87 indicates, most of the de Vepria collection was written during a single year, it is clear that Heloise must have brought most of her skills to the relationship rather than learned them during it. We have to imagine, therefore, a much more mature and equally balanced relationship, with Heloise demonstrating, perhaps, fuller acquaintance with and interest in prose style and the grammatical *auctores* and Abelard a more professional knowledge of the arts of the *trivium* as taught in the cathedral schools of his day, and with a greater degree of sophistication and expertise in the writing of poetry. While such conclusions are no more than many have long suspected or asserted, it is fascinating to see the pattern of linguistic skills displayed by teacher and pupil in action some fifteen or more years before writing the materials on which estimates of Heloise's literary and intellectual attainments have hitherto been based.

Conclusion: Heloise the Arts Student, or Heloise the Anomaly?

We are compelled, we believe, to see Heloise not as the surviving member of a larger class of females attending the proto-university cathedral schools of Paris more or less on the same terms as males but as a *rara avis,* a young woman attracted to the environment of the city's schools by exceptional circumstances, circumstances not unrelated to her obvious literary talents but not a direct consequence of them. Once there she seems to have become renowned for her literary talents, but without formally enrolling as a student in any one of the masters' schools that were available at the time. She must have been, as it were, "partially" in circulation, but not so fully as to make opportunities for acquaintance easy for Abelard. Nevertheless, some chance opportunities to see her would not have been unexpected, and, as he tells us, "hanc igitur, omnibus circunspectis que amantes allicere solent, commodiorem censui in amorem mihi copulare."[240] He goes on, in famous lines, to say he felt her love for and knowledge of letters [*litterarum scientiam*] would facilitate his conquest. Once in communication with

Heloise, however, Abelard found that sex and genuine intellectual exchange and partnership were hard to keep apart, and the result seems to have been not unlike that envisaged in a recent film for the early seventeenth-century female painter Artemisia, and her older, skilled artist-lover, Agostino Tasso, whom Artemisia's father had engaged to "teach her."[241] Heloise's attempt to sort out her own emotions, the relationship between letters and love, between Abelard and the rest of her life, are vividly recalled in the de Vepria collection, but we are forced to conclude that what Abelard and Heloise taught each other or learned from each other belonged in the main to a world that was passing, the world of the Loire monastic verse friendship ambience. Transferred though this clearly was to the much more dynamic environment of the early twelfth-century Paris schools, fused with a genuine and relatively unrestricted physical relationship, and translated (for the most part) into prose of a unique and varying pattern, it is nevertheless observable that Heloise does not seem to have shared in the intellectual activities of the schools in her district. While not excluded from discussions with Abelard on various terms and positions that must have fallen within the fields of rational and moral philosophy, their mutual reading and "exercises" clearly fell more within the field of "grammar," sensitive reading and imitation of the prescribed *auctores,* exploration of the literary dimensions of *amicitia* as an alternative to *nuptiae* as a foundation for a sexual relationship, of *amor* as "a creative and complex natural force expressed in the sweetness of lovers' intimacy."[242] In all these respects the de Vepria collection does not so much change our picture of Heloise and Abelard in the second decade of the twelfth century, as sharpen it immensely and reveal its tragic poignancies, the shortcomings of the male and the infinite flexibility and optimism of the female, laying all the while a much firmer basis of understanding of the later, more celebrated letter collection and its vain but moving demand for a resumption of the dialogue that has been preserved for us in the "lost" letter collection.

APPENDIX A

A DETAILED READING OF THE "LOST" LOVE LETTERS AND THE *HISTORIA CALAMITATUM*

The following analysis of the way that the "lost" love letters (letters 1 to 83) might fit into the known biographical details of Heloise and Abelard will seem an odd appendix to a chapter devoted to the young Heloise's Latin rhetoric. Yet much of the sense of Heloise's Latin studies at this point in her life can be gained only from a close study of these "lost" letters. Since their authenticity can become clear only after readers have pondered Mews's book on the subject, it seems preferable to take any reader through the letters, avoiding the translations and commentary Mews provides. In this way we allow the place of letters to emerge from the involvements of life rather than break the letters down into systematized categories, as E. Le Roy Ladurie has done for his source in *Montaillou: Cathars and Catholics in a French Village 1294–1324,* trans. B. Bray (New York: Penguin Books, 1980), a method that has destroyed in large part the individuality of the characters with which he deals. Such a procedure should only be attempted when all of Heloise's prose and poetry is available for consideration and close study. For the moment then, the place of the *trivium* in life and letters for men and women at Paris in the second decade of the twelfth century AD, must be left to filter through to the reader's mind, as the human relationship between Abelard and Heloise unfolds *in litteris.*

It is clear that the de Vepria collection contains only some of the letters exchanged by Abelard and Heloise at different times, and most have been expurgated and deprived of unequivocal references to events of their lives. Thus it is difficult to make comparisons with the extant letter collection of Heloise and Abelard: these latter are longer, complete, and specific in their reference to detail, and both writers were clearly more skilled at the longer epistolary form in the 1130s than they were twenty years earlier.[243]

The de Vepria correspondence[244] opens—if the order of extracts has anything to do with the chronological order of composition[245]—with the *mulier* emphasizing a kind of profound religious friendship within the orbit of devotion to Christ (#3 [M])[246] of the sort that must have been devised to link Baudri with his female correspondents,[247] and with the *vir* presenting a kind of lassitude (#2 [V])[248] that sits well with the statement in the *Historia calamitatum* that just prior to his affair with Heloise, Abelard was gripped with a "mundana tranquillitas" that "vigorem enervat animi."[249] Heloise (accepting her identification with the *mulier*) alludes to the invigorating effect of her friendship when she offers her addressee, whose youth is fading,[250] the bloom of eternal happiness (#1 [M]) and seeks, for her own part, *tota ars, ingenium,* and *peritia philosophie,* in the belief that this will enable her to greet Abelard (accepting his identification with *vir*) in writing ["scriptis"] "ad consensum mee voluntatis" (the latter phrase tallying with the "ad consensum traherem" of *HC* M 303). Curiously, however, if we see these exchanges as opening the correspondence indicated in *HC* M 298—and letter 9 with its "litteris iuxta preceptum tuum intercurrentibus precordialis inter nos firmetur amicicia" confirms the impression—Heloise sees "peritia philosophie" to be a prerequisite and not a consequence of the new acquaintance, and looks to heaven for it, not to Abelard himself. Indeed, she is often otherwise preoccupied (#11: "quia ocium in scribendo non habeo"; #17: "quod tu tarda distulisti"; and #22: "et tu tamen ita differs") and has acquired without Abelard a good knowledge of Latin

Reimprosa,[251] mastery of a number of classical, scriptural, and patristic texts, elementary knowledge of the liberal arts[252] and a penchant for novel or unusual expressions or strings of words (#18: "sub immarcido liliorum candore"; #21: "inextinguibilis . . . superabilis . . . insanabilis . . . medicabilis"; #25: "assiduitas familiaritatem, familiaritas fiduciam, fiducia negligenciam, negligencia fastidium peperit"; #49: "rose immarcessibili"; #53: "guttula scibilitatis"; #62: "presentialiter"; #86: "inepotabili"; #94: "innexibilis"; etc.). Despite professions of disciplinary subordination (#5, 23, 25, 49, 53, 62, 76, etc.),[253] Heloise often hints at the equality of her intellectual position and the value of what she writes[254]; Abelard accepts this estimation of herself (#18–19, 24, 50, etc.). In letter 98 Heloise actually refers to Abelard as "the novice" [Tyroni et amantium dulcissimo] and herself as "fundamentum stabilis amicicie"![255]

In letter 3 [M] Heloise provides a *salutatio* mentioning her most pure love for Abelard, who is worthy of the most intimate loyalty, because of the state of true affection [*dilectionis*] between them and the secret of dear trust. The mention of secret is appropriate at this stage of their relationship.[256] Heloise places much emphasis upon God as the mediator between them, on Christ who as king of kings will save Abelard for the sweetest of eternities, on Him who rules everything on earth. These hints at Heloise's already existing religious feelings perhaps help supply a want in the picture of her provided by D. M. Stone in 1989.[257]

Letter 4 (V) asserts that Heloise is daily sweeter to Abelard and is now particularly cherished and is in all things to be cherished; Abelard offers Heloise the same unchangeable constancy of sincere trust that she offered in letter 3. Abelard calls Heloise a most brilliant star, his most noble sweetness and his only consolation, his health/welfare. The "nunc quam maxime" may refer to some new (sexual?) stage in their relationship.

In letter 5 (M) Heloise calls Abelard her joyous hope and offers her trust, herself with all devotion as long as she is living. She asks that the dispenser of all art and human talent fill the interior of her breast with the skilled knowledge of philosophy necessary for her to greet Abelard, her most cherished, in writings as much as she wants. This seems to fit the relationship at this stage, based on mutual learning and mutual writing, with Heloise aspiring to an appropriate amount of learning for the purposes of writing appropriately to the teacher.[258] This letter has been copied completely by Johannes de Vepria, despite its apparent lack of literary flourish.

Abelard replies with letter 6 (V), continuing the star image of letter 4, saying that he has recently delighted in Heloise's rays (a sexual reference?) and hoping she will remain in cloudless splendor. He calls her his sweetest mistress [*domina*], who instructs [*precepisti*], presumably in love, or the art of love-letter writing, or perhaps even in the idea of commencing such a correspondence, because the next phrase says "or, to speak more truly, since the most ardent flame of love compels [him]," her beloved cannot contain himself but must in place of his presence, greet her by means of a letter [*litterarum officio*]. He says he cannot refrain from writing to her in place of his presence because she instructs him, or, better, the ardent flame of love commands him. His *valedictio* is rhythmic but not rhyming, though we have the repetition of *mea/mea*. The *valedictio* also contains a neat idea: I am never awake without finding you located in my mind. The letter has a certain prosiness (the two *quins*, the "ut verius dicam" [cf. also #16 (V) for this phrase]). It has been copied by de Vepria completely. It falls presumably within the period during which Abelard and Heloise lived in Fulbert's house following the "oscula quam sententie" of *HC* M 337, either as a quasi-literary exchange or something thrust into the hands of the go-between to explain a day away at the schools during which Abelard is unable to provide a "lesson" for Heloise.

Letter 7 (M) introduces an odd note of caution [*hucusque dilecto*], despite which Abelard is "semper diligendo." Heloise offers rather prosy greetings (but with her whole "re et affectu"), joy [*gaudia* has a sexual overtone in Ovid, *Her.* XVI.319],[259] and the progress/profit/convalescence [*profectum*] of all usefulness and uprightness. The *valedictio* is emotional in that "vale" is repeated; there is more stress on God [*regnum dei*]. The *salutatio* of letter 9 (M) is full of set biblical phrases, implying that Abelard has a sort of biblical importance for Heloise. She goes on to say that she greatly desires that a very deep friendship should develop between them nourished by letters as their go-betweens. This is in accordance with his "preceptum" (whereas in letter 6 he says it is her "preceptum"). All this is accompanied by a longed-for anticipation of the actual sight of Abelard. This suggests that the two are some way apart or not actually able to meet as often as Heloise would like, a situation difficult to square with Abelard's residence in Fulbert's house. (Is the letter out of place, or did Abelard from time to time leave Paris or stay elsewhere for periods of days?) Heloise's *salutatio* in letter 11 (M) is nicely expanded and conveys the notion of herself as the most trusted of all. The only sentence de Vepria has copied from the body of the letter expresses in rhythmic and rhymed prose her complete love, beyond any contrived concealment [*ulla secreti machinacio*].[260] *HC* M 363 "paucos . . . decipere" may also refer to their need to "keep up pretences." Again Heloise calls upon God to be her witness. This is an element absent from Abelard's letters. If genuine, it would suggest that Heloise began as the more religiously committed of the two, a circumstance appropriate for someone who grew up in a convent and was the niece of a canon, living with him. To some extent their later career reverses these positions.

In letter 13 (M; de Vepria omits the *salutatio*), Heloise uses the technical terms *benivolencia* and *officio* to say that Abelard has won her goodwill, and her *officium* is to be submissive/beholden to him.[261] She cannot give as many *salutes* as she would like but does not want to specify those she does not send because to do so might somehow prejudice those she does send. This is a difficult sentiment to make out and recalls (although not in language) Catullus' playing with the number of *basia* that must be exchanged by himself and his lover (e.g., Catullus, poems 5 and 7). Heloise then implies that she does write, again and again, repetitively because he and she are, as it were, the same person.[262] So it is like talking to oneself. In him she lives, yet in that she lives in him she dies in herself (says her *valedictio*). These complicated ideas seem worthy for their message rather than their elegant style—de Vepria could hardly be copying them for the latter aspect.

De Vepria copies the whole of letter 14 (V), a little letter that sets out the epistolary situation, perhaps as it existed during Abelard's and Heloise's joint residence in Fulbert's house[263]: they are exchanging wax tablets. As each one arrives the interlocutor is expected to read it and add a reply; but it seems that it must be done while the courier waits, for he says that he would write more if only he could hang on to the tablets a little longer; he then reveals this to be only a conceit by saying that even if he had all the time in the world for writing and did nothing else, he would never run out of material owing to her great honesty and merit as he sees them. Again it seems unlikely that de Vepria copied this letter out for its style. Equally unlikely is it that we have here but an imitation of the classical love and wax tablets theme (as, e.g., in Ovid, *Amores* 1.11 and 12). The usages in the de Vepria excerpt collection seem so individual as to suggest the actual use of wax tablets, not a reading of their use in past times. This is, indeed, the conclusion of all modern students of the wax tablet in the Middle Ages,[264] and the conclusion suggested by such passages as that in which Guibert of Nogent states that when forced to prepare his *Hexameron* commentary "in secret" [*clam*], he did not entrust the composition and writing to wax tablets (as would presumably have been the case had he been composing in the normal manner) but rather put what he had to write by way of commentary without alteration straight on to the parchment.[265]

Letter 15 (V) is another wax tablet two-liner. The allusion seems indeed to be to Ovid, *Her.* XXVI.320, where Paris speaks of Helen sleeping alone without him, and opines that if they were to share *communia gaudia,* then it would truly be as bright as day in the middle of the night for him. *Candidus* thus stands for a brilliant sexual night.[266] So Abelard wishes Heloise such a night and with him. It is a wish that would certainly be appropriate in a house where their relationship is expected to be strictly intellectual.

The *salutatio* of letter 16 (V) contains a technical term familiar to Abelard.[267] Here he seems to be adopting realist terminology; he asserts that he and Heloise share a commonality (the seal[268] and its imprint) because although they are distinct, they are similar in their lack of difference. (The realist would say the lack of difference concerns their humanity, whereas for lovers it is their common troth—and here Abelard emphasizes the notion of being "totus in te" as is often found in their exchanges [cf. #6, 7, etc.].) As if taking up the cue from letter 8, he now accuses her of forgetting the man who is her very soul (i.e., himself), using the language of the Roman love poets (*immemor,*[269] *oblita,*[270] *dura*[271]), although he still claims, with his prosy "ut verius dicam" (cf. also letter 6) to be one with her ("totus in te," etc.). We have here either the required lover's tiff or some genuine slight, loss of contact or diversion, put interestingly but not very elegantly.

In letter 12 (V) Abelard offers a kind of courtly love service (according to the *amoris regula*) and feels that this is rewarded by Heloise's deeds as well as by her words. This emphasis is picked up again strongly in letter 22 (V), where Abelard writes that a divorce has developed between the words he addresses to others and the meaning [*intentio*] that is always reserved for Heloise. He alludes to the same circumstance in *Historia calamitatum* (M 348ff.). What is it that Heloise "does" to earn Abelard's gratitude here? Despite Dronke's opinion,[272] it seems possible to equate letter 22, with its hint at the poem often ascribed to Abelard, *Hebet sydus*[273] (#22: "sine te [h]ebes"), and *HC* M 347ff. "nocturnas amori vigilias et diurnas studio . . . carmina . . . amatoria, non philosophie secreta," to suggest that under cover of some "secreti machinacio" (#11), many a white night (#15) is being passed. Heloise herself later referred to frequent letters and frequent *carmina* accompanying "turpes voluptates" at this time.[274]

It is clear from a letter such as 23 (M) and Heloise's own remarks that Heloise is either attending the schools as freely as Abelard or has acquired very considerable literacy from them prior to Abelard's onslaught.[275] "Me platee omnes, me domus singule resonabant": would not Heloise also have trod those streets and passed those houses in the course of her studies? "Cum me ad turpes olim voluptates expeteres": Abelard and Heloise go about their studies and business with Heloise under Abelard's *magisterium,* except for those moments when Abelard might be free and was "teaching" Heloise, and any other moments when he "sought her out" [expeteres] for sex.[276]

Letter 23 (M) is a set-piece demonstration of dictaminal competence: it is a combination of rhymed *isocola,*[277] apostrophe,[278] *amplificatio/chiasmus*[279] ["liberalis benignitas et benigna liberalitas"], and *exercitatio* in the demonstrative or epideictic oratorical *genus:* the exercise is to praise Abelard by way of a *controversia* or *altercatio,* or presentation of competing *persuasiones* [*hortamen/dehortamen*],[280] and Heloise reveals an acquaintance with the technographic rhetorical literature.[281] The didactic fiction here blends life and learning: assume the task is to praise Abelard in a letter, assume a contrast between *copia dicendi* and *sublimia* on one hand and *defectus ingenii* on the other; assume that the student comes to the master for the nectar of his eloquent tongue (#23: "suavi oris . . . nectare") and assume that beyond the words of the exercise (#23: "Quid pluribus opus est verbis?") lies the urgency behind the instruction, the "dilectio/amor" before the eyes of God (#23: "Deo teste") that binds the couple in their novel and presumably still officially secret relationship. This letter and its response (#24 [V]) reveal both the scope and seriousness of the exercises and instruction that surrounded the core of their relationship and the amount of current scholastic learning that marked Heloise's approach to life.

Abelard's response (#24 [V]) compliments Heloise ("litterarum tuarum copiosa . . . ubertas") and reveals that much of their scholarly dialogue must have been on the very subject of their relationship and the relationship between themselves and the *amicitia* of which Cicero spoke and which was so much in the air among monks and clerics of the day. In their relationship they are equals, all trace of master/student disappears: "eque annuimus, eque negamus, idem per omnia sapimus." When one writes, the other thinks the same things. There is a similitude between their *mores* and their *studia* (#25).

In this latter *littera* (#25 [M]), written it seems away from Paris ("ast nunc, tui presencia dum careo, cantibus volucrum, viriditate nemorum permota amore tuo langueo")[282] Heloise presents a considered reflection on "verus amor" as perceived "naturali intuitu" (although the reading of Cicero's *De amicitia* lies behind the reflections).[283] Their relationship must now take on new intensity: hitherto it has been but a simulation of love, a matter of "soothing and simple words" [verba mollia et plana]: the "veri amoris officia" require an eternity that even life cannot fulfill. There must always be a shortfall in what a friend can do and does for a friend, just as "in te salutandi officio" there is a shortfall between "velle"[284] and "sufficientia." In language that seems an unlikely candidate for scholastic dictaminal imitation, and which while lamenting the physical separation of the lovers expresses an appropriateness about the preservation of desire and longing that absence promotes (and presence kills), Heloise refers to Abelard's initiation of their relationship: "indeed, it was with great enthusiasm that you began to want me ["me appetere"—"to try to get access to me"] when the friendship between us was born, and it was with an increased enthusiasm that you strove to increase and to make permanent our affection," but things did not go smoothly and you made your happiness and your bitterness mine. But you (Heloise addresses Abelard) should not have tried to complete what was perfect: it is one thing to complete what we have begun, quite another to try to increase what is complete.[285] You see, we display complete charity [*integra caritas*] toward all, but that does not mean we love [*diligimus*] everyone in the same way: that which is general to all becomes special when directed toward certain people in particular: it is one thing to be invited to court to advise a ruler [*princeps*], quite another to be drawn to love someone. (Heloise uses the words "ad amorem trahi," as Abelard had said "ad consensum traherem" [*HC* M 304].)

Where is this thought train going? Why did de Vepria choose to copy it out? Although nicely patterned, the drift is obscure and hardly useful for *imitatio*. The climax of obscurity is reached with the sentence "and so I do not owe you so much thanks because you didn't turn me away, but because you took me up with open hand": there is a difference between being actually welcomed ("drawn to love") and merely received ("to give advice," Abelard in the analogy being the prince). Heloise is thanking Abelard for treating her as special rather than general. So there is a difference between genuine and continuous love, and mere "verba mollia et plana": to love Abelard is general, to forget him is special. That is to say, to require words all the time is to distrust: their relationship has gone beyond this and if Abelard cannot trust Heloise without continual reinforcement, his love is not "verus."

The point of the letter steals in with suddenness: "tam fideli amice rarus[286] esse noli": Abelard has been "distant" on some pretext or other and has not provided "colloquium et presencia secundum velle meum," that is, has not sought her out in person.[287] In his response—if letter 26 (V) is a response—Abelard admits that he does not yet "know" Heloise "interius" and calls upon her sweet breast [*pectus*], her complete charm [*integra venustate*], and her juice-filled body [*corpus succi plenissimum*] to reveal its secrets.

The *litterae* that follow suggest a gamut of situations[288]: the jealousy and tittle-tattle of the envious (#28 [V])[289]; apparently bleak moments when Heloise seeing all her ambitions, hopes, relationships going astray, is reliant on Abelard alone but hints that this is even more hopeless a plight than that of Ovid's wife as her husband went into exile: Heloise cannot even utter the sad words that marked the ancient occasion[290]; illness and light snowfalls (#32 [M]); renewed zeal for composition (#33 [V]: "novus dictandi fervor") and meetings—*colloquia*—that suggest a still covert relationship and some measure of living at different addresses or in distinctly different parts of a largish establishment (#34 [M]); minor differences (#35 [V] in which the classical opposition between the *vir/homo durus* and the *sermo mollis . . . suavis* of the woman is mentioned[291]; and letter 36 [V] in which a degree of estrangement is associated with the use of the term *domina* and the replacement of the "tu" by the "vos"; hints of sexual frustration (#37 [V] "Interroga nuncium quid egi, postquam litteras perscripsi . . ." and letter 38a [V] "tangere sic pectus iam gestio temet anhelus"). Exchanges of verse (one with a Catullan hint) suggest the practical dictaminal range of the *exercitia* set up between the two, and one short letter seems to say that the teacher has on the occasion in question no particular "praeceptum" for composition: the student should just write something, a couple of words at least (#41 [V]).[292]

This last four-line *littera* (copied intact by de Vepria [why?]), so simple and didactic as it may seem, is followed by three more from Abelard (#42–44 [V]) that suggest an interruption to the literary exchange and a distancing on the part of Heloise. The way flashes of classical texts glitter behind the prose of these *litterae*[293] suggests not that they are composed as dictaminal models but that the vicissitudes of life are fusing with the processes of learning, a unique feature of the humanism of this transitional moment in Western history.[294]

Letter 45 (M) and 49 (M)–50 (V) demonstrate this. Letter 45 seems to refer to a departure of Abelard from "France" (not recorded here in the *Historia calamitatum* but compare "nec aliud relictum fuit patrie" with the word "repatriare" at *HC* M 156) and laments the relationship thus ruptured both lyrically (in the *salutatio*) and learnedly (in the allusions found in the remaining body of the letter). By this time their physical relationship has reduced the role of letters (cf. also # 46 [V]–48 [M]), but, as the *Historia calamitatum* indicates, even the news of Heloise's pregnancy was conveyed to Abelard in writing (M 393).

Letter 49 is another great excursus on the nature of the friendship/love that unites the pair.[295] Its significance is perhaps indicated by the fact that although three pages in length, it is copied by de Vepria without apparent deletions. This essay on the nature of friendship begins conventionally by pointing out the distinction between friendship based on probity, virtue, and deep love and that based on expectation of riches or pleasures. After an arresting *salutatio* in which "she" [*illa*], describing Abelard, in ecclesiastical Latin, as "an unwithering rose" and "the blooming flower of blessedness," [offers him] a *chiasmus* "florendo crescere et crescendo florere," Heloise points out that her love for Abelard is based on a "quite different agreement" [pacto longe tibi alio]: "sola excellentissima virtus," not a "sitis habendi" compelled her to love Abelard. Much of the argument here is faithfully echoed later by Heloise in her response to the *Historia calamitatum*.[296] The theme is suddenly interrupted by a dense ten-line sentence that invokes in spell-binding detail the deeply tangled nature of their extraordinary relationship: a young woman known throughout "France" for her learning (*HC* M 288), locked into an emotional and physical relationship with the same kingdom's greatest master ["cui jure cedit francigena cervicositas"], confesses that the relationship has no future other than in an uneven correspondence and that, even thus, she cannot attain the heights of her partner/teacher's fame and eloquence. The letter contains mixed themes and emotions. Protestation of an urge to pursue learning with Abelard without regard to career or fortune mix with a profound understanding of the new processes surrounding the acquisition of "florid eloquence" (the ingestion to the point of habit of devoted attentions to every detail and every setting forth [*dispositio*] of the arts),[297] with the realization that she herself lacks that capacity for comprehensive detail and that even if she were perfected to her fingernails in such matters, such crafted skill in the arts would be no match for the virtues, the moral charisma of her partner in life. The contrast between oral, ethical charisma and the new craft of the *artes* suggests again that confrontation between eleventh-century and twelfth-century humanism hinted at by Jaeger.

Thus Heloise confesses—in language that recalls a rather more routine letter that Stephen of Blois sent his wife, Adela—that it is great temerity for her "to send words to you in the manner of a letter,"[298] for it is not good enough to "floridum eloquencie vultum depingere" as if it were worthy of the sight of so great a master, for someone whose talents *were* "honed to a pitch"[299] and whose ingestion of the system of the *artes* has been perfected by long habit and close attention. At this point Heloise shifts key enigmatically—"much less to me (she goes on, the dative matching *conspectui* immediately preceding and *cuique* four lines previously) who seems scarcely ready for such insubstantial/fickle/unreliable/inconstant things, things which certainly do not savour of gnawed fingernails, or thumped desks." We are abruptly informed that it is not so much Abelard's greatness that shames such eloquence (of which Heloise is incapable) but the shameful nature of the composition. To explicate this Heloise has given us the clue: Persius, *Sat.* 1.106, where the poet is deploring the verse of the day and, by implication, the corrupt, hedonistic morals that produce it.[300] The inference we derive from line 106 is that real "quality" verse should derive from gnawing of the fingernails and thumping of the desk: the poets of Persius' day engage in no such hard work. Heloise, however, is telling Abelard, and us, that even if someone were to produce their best composition [*floridum eloquencie vultum*], she herself would consider it trite and deceptive. Eloquence is a false indicator of truth, and it is rash to write letters to Abelard because the better they were, the less truthful they would be, the less they would involve genuine fingernail-gnawing and desk-thumping. There is even a sort of irony. The "honed-to-a-pitch" writer has "omnis dispositio artium" transformed into habit by diligent and long-standing attention, but Heloise is not so "arranged" [*vix videor disposita*]: for her, fingernail-gnawing and desk-thumping betoken a real person facing real moral dilemmas, not a consummate poet of the day producing "spumosum et cortice pingui,/ut ramale vetus vegrandi subere coctum."[301]

Part of the ambiguity of Heloise's prose at this point is created by the word *michi* ["nedum michi"], which seems to be a dative of indirect object but may well be a dative of agent, implying not a parallelism with "tanti magistri . . . conspectui" but with "cuique litteratissimo" read in another way: "it is not good enough even for a most polished person to produce eloquence, let alone for me to do so. . . ." The latter rendition fits in with the theme that Heloise is incapable of the literary capacities she aspires to, whereas the former opens up a much darker theme, that eloquence is a (male) fraud. She immediately goes on to stress Abelard as a man of virtue and moral integrity to whom proud France and the arrogant world would yield;[302] she then switches to the literary theme: whoever might have prepared himself [or whatever speech/document might have been composed], whoever might have thought himself to be a by-word for learning, at once he would judge himself to be tongueless and mute [when confronted by so morally charismatic a figure as Abelard]. There is even a usage from Jerome's letters[303] to hint at Abelard's literary *persona*.[304]

The letter continues with an odd usage of 'credula' used of a thing rather than a person. We are brought to mind of Ovid's "credula res amor est" from *Heroides* 6.21. The context is suggestive. Jason, having made Hypsipyle pregnant, has been slow to correspond with her once he departed in search of the Golden Fleece, and rumors of his infidelity have reached the Lemnian maiden. Yet, she says, if one is in love, one will always believe in the best outcome and discredit the rumors. So she continues to hope that Jason will be faithful to the marriage vows he made her. A comparable context of a possibly unfaithful lover in Ovid sees the same phrase used in the opposite sense: that love makes us disbelieve the truth.[305] Heloise, perhaps with these competing, self-undermining contexts in mind says that Abelard's kindness ["benignitas"] will always seem credible to her (or will seem misplaced), because she believes that underlying it, sewn into it as it were, is (or should be) the undying friendship of love ["dilectionis indefectam amiciciam"]. That is why she can send him unpolished letters, rude in style, because they say the moral truth to someone of great virtue, better than polished eloquence from someone whose eloquence may exceed their morals (or because *litterae* and truth are in any case incompatible).

In dark and opaque phrases the letter goes on to hint that this "indefective caritatis dulcedinis . . . stimulus" which drives Heloise to love Abelard may well be lacking in his case, and, if she had her way, there would be much cause for her to write her (unpolished) letters (because she would believe Abelard's *benignitas*): she would write only to him, if her estimation of his "dilectionis indefecta amicicia" (= *mea res?*) truly warranted it, and then, it would be her delight never to have a holiday from writing—though he might not reply because (a) his "dilectionis indefecta amicicia" may be wanting, (b) her letters might strike him as unworthy from a literary point of view because he was a great scholar, or (c) her letters might strike him as unworthy from a literary point of view because they were actually too "florid" (and a man such as Abelard is too lofty even for the most florid eloquence). Whatever we make of these criss-crossing threads and the (intentionally?) inadequate language in which they are expressed (she herself calls it "sermone impexo,"[306] and we are indeed led to wonder how such enigmatic language could be of any use in the dictaminal schoolroom), the resolution is clearer: "when I am in my most withdrawn mode," she seems to say, in her singsong Latin, "and grow weak with a longing for my friends, you [Abelard] would assuage my grief a great deal if you were to use a fuller style [of writing]."

From what follows, it seems Heloise has received only a "salutationis compendium" [summary greeting], which she will read and reread as if it were his angel, and she will kiss it in place of him, for, she says, nothing gives her greater delight than to speak to him, or to hear him speaking, or to write to him. A bundle of possibilities float before us: having yielded her body to him, and still being constrained to secrecy, she is dependent on his initiative to continue the relationship that she obviously found thrilling; yet he, sidetracked by any male shortcoming (solidarity with his studies and male contacts, postcoital nonchalance, etc.) is less than forthcoming. Yet, she finishes, he must have some inkling of how she feels and will one day see it all in its full truth, as the primacy of moral values: genuine emotion, love and friendship rather than books and pretty phrases (the desire to master which may have led her, or her uncle, to engage Abelard as tutor in the first place).

It is a complicated letter, too complicated in our view to be the product of some forger of dictaminal materials. She terms it an *exclamacio,* a technical term of classical rhetoric used to indicate an exceptional full-voice outburst (*Ad Her.* 3.12.22), or a mode of speaking suitable to *distributio,* which Caplan translates as "The Broken Tone of Debate": "oratio frequens cum raris et brevibus intervallis, acri vociferatione" (*Ad Her.* 3.13.24): "The Broken Tone of Debate is punctuated repeatedly with short, intermittent pauses, and is vociferated sharply."[307] Quintilian advises that only exclamations "simulata et arte composita" are properly called figures of speech ["*schemata,*" Quintilian, *De institutione oratoria* 9.2.27]. To one familiar with these citations, Heloise would be drawing attention not only to the exceptional nature of her outburst but to its artistry: a perplexing combination. She might even have followed up Quintilian's reference at the same place to "licentia" in "Cornificius," and if she took that to indicate (as modern editors do) the *Ad Her.* 4.36.48, she would have found there *licentia* described as a figure of speech ["frankness"]: "when, talking before those to whom we owe reverence or fear, we yet exercise our right to speak out, because we seem justified in reprehending them or persons dear to them, for some fault."[308] However justified all this may seem by the context, philology forbids us to imagine that Heloise was an early believer in the "Cornifician" authorship of the *Ad Herennium!*[309]

Nevertheless, the line in which the word *exclamacio* appears is an odd one. The word is contrasted with *racio,* which is used in the *Ad Herennium* (and in other rhetorical treatises) to express the second part of "absolutissima et perfectissima . . . argumentatio," "the proof of the reason of the most complete and perfect argument" (*Ad Her.* 2.18.28; Caplan, p. 107). In Heloise's sentence, the *racio* is elaborated as the "method by which our [an odd objective genitive] love can be held fast," and it is "paid as a due," "restored," "recited, represented or reproduced by imitation," "given in return," "interpreted/translated," or "administered" [as in the administration of justice], or whatever meaning we are meant to attach to the Latin word *reddo, reddere.* Perhaps the meaning of "restored" or "given in return" is intended, for what follows is a neat three-line piece of hexametric verse composition in praise of Abelard, no doubt intended by Heloise to "repay" him for what he had taught her. The *racio* would then be: letters [*litterae, litterae humaniores*] drew us together, letters must maintain our friendship, but only such letters as are accompanied by "dilectionis indefecta amicicia."

One cannot insist on all or indeed on any of these complex of interpretations. Who knows what Heloise meant by letter 49? Who knows whether letter 49 had anything to do with her? Nevertheless, we would argue that all the overtones and twists of thought to which we have drawn attention are possible, that the letter is too complicated and ill-expressed to serve as a dictaminal model (especially for the tastes of the twelfth century), and that the *in tempore* situation that a little imagination may construct for us is both poignant in itself and appealing to our late twentieth-century sense of "reality."

The *salutatio* of Abelard's "reply" (#50 [V]) stuns us with its appropriateness: "To the only [female] disciple of philosophy among all the girls [*puellas*] of our age, to the only one, upon whom Fortune has fastened completely all the endowments of the numerous virtues, to the only pretty ('speciose' cf. letter 960 [disciple of philosophy], to the only charming/obliging ('graciose') [disciple of philosophy] . . ." recalls *HC* M ll. 284–95 closely enough to encourage us to believe that it is Abelard writing to Heloise, but not closely enough to suggest a "forger" wishing to make capital out of the resemblance. De Vepria has displayed less patience with Abelard's reply than he had displayed toward Heloise's letter, for he cuts passages out of it. Enough remains, however, to convince us that Heloise's letter succeeded in shaking Abelard out of whatever complacency had produced letter 49. Not only does he echo her account of friendship, appropriately larded with reference to Cicero's *De amicitia*—in the reading of which Abelard admits Heloise holds first place—but he also matches her phraseology (#49: "pacto . . . alio"; #50: "alio pacto") and tells us that he "chose her among thousands" for her "many virtues"! This arrogant anticipation of *HC* M 289 differs only in that whereas now he claims to have "chosen" Heloise for her virtues, later (in the *Historia calamitatum*) he claims he "chose" her for her "not unattractive looks and knowledge of letters": no wonder Heloise was annoyed with the *Historia calamitatum!*

Heloise's sentiments in letter 49 inspire Abelard to a lyrical assertion of his dependence upon the *puella* as "omnium miserarum . . . lenimen": his decision to seek the company of girls (*HC* M 252ff.) came at a favorable moment in his life (*HC* M 241ff.), but the general narrative of the *Historia calamitatum* provides enough to justify his use of "omnium miserarum" in letter 50. What follows throws fascinating light on the initiation of their relationship. Whereas the *Historia calamitatum* ascribes the relationship to Abelard's lust and initiative, or to Fulbert's ambitions, letter 50 admits that it was some "good opinion of me," perhaps, "that made you deign to call me to your notice." In a rare moment of humility, Abelard now admits that Heloise is actually his superior: "ingenium tuum, facundia tua ultra etatem et sexum tuum iam virile in robur se incipit extendere": "your talent, your eloquence goes beyond your years and your sex: it now begins to endow you with manly strength; (even where I seem to have the edge, [he goes on] it is you who really outstrip me)." The final paragraph of the letter seems a heartfelt response to the main allegation leveled in letter 49, that Abelard has failed to appreciate the nature of Heloise's affection for him. In an impassioned outbreak he claims he is not a blockhead at all and knows "ubi verus amor sit et quis me ex corde diligat." He may even make an allusion to the same Persian satire that Heloise used.[310] In a later letter he is prepared to admit a religious basis for their affection (#52 [V]). This is the first letter in which Abelard has used the word *dilectio* (common hitherto in Heloise's letters). One suspects that Abelard learned as much about life from Heloise as she claims she learned of bookish wisdom from him.

It is clear from letter 53 (M) that the two are still kept apart, by distance, preoccupation, or the need for secrecy. Its *salutatio* suggests a consciousness of Abelard's physical (sexual?) form and Heloise's statement that she lacks "peritia," while it may refer to her usual posture of literary inadequacy, seems from the context to refer to his greater physical (sexual?) abilities. Certainly this letter seems to indicate that their physical and emotional relationship has far exceeded her ability—even if some small drop of knowledge had derived from his teaching—to "paint in *sermo,* with the marks of letters," her love. The use of *depingere* recalls letter 49.

Letter 54 (V) refers to the literary exercise of *ecphrasis* or the literary commendation of set topics, and to the use of arguments in (legal) advocacy.[311] Both, Abelard claims, are no longer necessary in praise of love since now Heloise has learned/been taught (? "quia in rebus abundantes sumus") how to see it in its nonverbal nakedness. But still, the writer claims, the "edax malorum hominum invidia" requires continued use of the *littera* as a means of communication. It is difficult but not impossible to square this with Abelard's presence in Fulbert's house and the loveplay that he claims they indulged in there: the phrase in letter 54: "nos pro libito nostro iungi non patitur" seems to imply a date before the "[p]rimum domo una conjungimur, postmodum animo" of *HC* M 332–33, which in turn suggests that in the *Historia calamitatum* Abelard has telescoped the stages in their relationship indicated by *HC* M 296–303.[312] Nevertheless, as indicated above, the supposition of consummated sexual relations *before* Abelard's move into Fulbert's house is possibly unwarranted by the language of the *Historia calamitatum*.

The ensuing letters indicate a maintenance of this agitated but satisfying state of mutual affection (#55 [M] and 56 [V]) but #57 (M) indicates a breach in their "familiaris confabulacio":[313]

Abelard is no longer able to supply his "presencia ad libitum meum" and letter 58 (M) actually refers to Abelard's withdrawal of the "privilege of love" from Heloise. Letter 59 (V) supplies a telling comment from Abelard: "causa necessaria" keeps him away from Heloise, and it was wrong of him to force her into sin. Letter 60 (M) is movingly appropriate: the "pact" of letters 49 and 50 is broken, Heloise does not hear Abelard's words (because they do not speak truthfully of "dilectionis indefecta amicicia"); his "sapiencia et scientia" deceived her (Abelard himself says why—*HC* M 294–96), so "pereat scriptura."

There seems in this letter such little art and such desperate recourse to Latin (rhymed) prose as the only medium of intelligent epistolary communication that the reader is challenged to place it within the known framework of the Abelard-Heloise affair, that is, in the narrative presented in the *Historia calamitatum*. This is difficult to do and letter 61 (V) (which may, in fact, be two letters conflated, the "mulier" portion beginning at "Non sunt hec dicta amici . . .")[314] does not help for Abelard claims he does not know what "peccatum" on his part has alienated Heloise (although in #59 he seems to know well enough).[315] He refers again to Heloise's role in solacing his trials and tribulations (cf. #50). Clearly a severe rupture has occurred in their relationship, which does not match anything in the *Historia calamitatum* before events such as Heloise's pregnancy (which might, one would have thought, figure in the Könsgen correspondence, unless de Vepria or an earlier editor has excised all matters that might easily have led to the identification of the correspondents).

In letter 62 (M) Heloise, with a perfunctory *salutatio,* assumes again the *persona* of an only roughly literate person ["sermonum facecia . . . modulo scienciole"] and cautions her lover to avoid danger (to himself) and scandal (to her). Despite the breach of *fedus*[316] in letter 60 she can refer again to some "arrangement" [quoque pacto—cf. #49 and 50] by which he can discuss with her "presentialiter" the things which he had entrusted to letters. Their letters must have contained "amaras atque flebiles descriptiones"[317] and matters that, she, Heloise, thinks run the risk of driving Abelard to tears. It is difficult to believe that Heloise can be referring to her pregnancy—concerning which she wrote to Abelard, according to the *HC* M 392–93, "cum summa exultatione"—and we are left only with the possibility that the tribulations associated with *HC* M 379ff. are being referred to. It is possible that Abelard "took fright" when their affair became known, causing Heloise to write letter 60. At any rate, the matter is not sufficiently serious to prevent her from exhorting him to press the wax on more auspicious topics.

The letters that follow seem to preserve aspects of the above relationships, but not necessarily in the chronological order that we seem to have detected in the previous letters,[318] and ensuing letters continue the fragments of the story.[319] In some senses letter 75 is a set piece, using an inverted version of the 'inexpressibility' or 'outdoing' topos discussed by Ernst Curtius.[320] The context could easily be a demonstration by Abelard of "how to do it," using an alleged improvident *promissio* or *vox nimium preceps et temeraria* in their real or fictive love relationship. At any rate it seems a "curriculum" effort, mentioning Ovid for his "metrum" and Tullius for his "facundia," alluding to Vergil, *Aeneid* VI.129 along with other passages from Vergil, Ovid, and Horace (*Ars poetica*).[321] The context is a stock one: the lover "dictates," causes to be written, "in ipso doloris cursu," something he wishes he had not so set to writing ("et utinam non dictassem"), something that seems to have to do with the growing old of their relationship (? "non michi vetus res"). Yet there are hints that this is discourse adapted to the anguish of reality: he describes himself as "tanta sciencia plenus," "labiis circumcisus." The latter phrase seems to contrast with the phrase "incircumcisis . . . labiis" used in letter 23 and biblical in inspiration (Exodus 6.12, 30) to express verbal artlessness.

Yet here the implication seems to be that the speaker/writer is too skilled in words,[322] and too unskilled in their effect ["noli verba, sed facta consulere"], one who needs advice on how to "sapienter amare"(note the contrast between "tanta sciencia plenus" and "sapienter amare.") The allusion to public opinion ["et fame nostre sollerter consulemus"] suggests an ill-considered remark about their relationship to a third party, some word of which has gotten back to Heloise. In her "reply" Heloise makes a complicated transition from their didactic or "school" relationship to a genuine or "adult" relationship: she confesses that without his "magisterialis institucionis . . . sollercia" she would have been like (to adopt a phrase of Vergil's) "a lazy herd."[323] But now the literary rivalry between them should cease and they should become *sodales.* There are two enriching literary allusions here. The first is to the last line of Vergil's *Eclogue* III, which alerts us to the nature of the "contest" Heloise thinks should cease. *Eclogue* III records a poetic context between two unfriendly shepherds, Menalcas and Damoetas [Damon], and the last line, cited by Heloise, is an agricultural metaphor to the effect that the streams of poetry should now cease. What follows in letter 76 deepens the sentiment: the heavy and legalistic "decrevit hoc mea intencio" is advanced to end an "alterna contencio," that is, litigation rather than poetic rivalry. The reference to Statius *Thebaid* 1.411–12 "mox ut iactis sermonibus irae intumuere satis" [when flung taunts had swelled their anger to the pitch],[324] with the addition of the word *dire* to intensify *ire,* completes a sudden transition from the didactic and the bucolic, to the blood-torn and the real. Letter 77 (V) seems to accept the new challenge, admittedly (and this seems to contradict the spirit of letter 76) in language borrowed from the Roman comedians ["ut ergo operas demus, tu es ego et ego sum tu"].[325] Letter 77 (V) could, of course, come from any stage in the couple's relationship, as could letters 80 (V) and 83 (M). Letter 81 (M), however, with its reference to the malevolence, perhaps, of those who had enforced the "separatio" referred to at *HC* M 380,[326] and its elaborate *salutatio* referring to Abelard's skill as a lover, to (again) Heloise's incapacity to thank him adequately, and assigning praises to all who serve him [because he should be served by all?] and all beauty [because it excites him?], seems to suggest an earlier period in the relationship. Letter 78 (V), from a slightly later period, seems to suggest that when one has reached the stage of *sodalitas,* writing is unnecessary.

Letter 79 (M), a difficult, contemplative, and biblically influenced letter, seems redolent of the dangers that prompted Abelard to send Heloise back to Argenteuil[327]: "unde vehementer ille commotus crebris eam contumeliis afficiebat."[328] The meaning of the two dense paragraphs "si grande . . ." and "ego tamdiu . . ." is hard to make out. Heloise draws a parallel between the application of *labor* and *studium* to achieve an external manifestation of some internal intention [*intencio* picks up the same word in letter 76][329] and notes a tendency "deficere, cum ad votum, quod cupit, non potest pervenire." The second paragraph applies this sentiment to a task being faced by Heloise herself, a task in which the expectation of *defectus* weakens the "intencionem mei affectus." The task so confronting Heloise is the task of addressing/appealing to/seeking help from Abelard, conscious as she is of the *beneficia* he has bestowed upon her and the *grates* she owes him for these. What is her rather formally expressed purpose here? Perhaps the key lies in some words from the *Historia calamitatum:* "moxque occulte divisim abscessimus, nec nos ulterius nisi raro latenterque vidimus, dissimulantes plurimum quod egeramus . . . quod cum ego cognovissem" of *HC* M 564–66 and 573: at this point in their relationship Heloise may certainly have felt that there were dangers, that calling upon Abelard for further intervention was difficult, that she had no wish to offend him further,[330] and that *dolor,* now that she was separated both from Abelard and Astrolabe, was to succeed *amor* (*HC* M 555–57).

Letter 82 (M) seems written in that grief of resignation to which Abelard refers in the *Historia calamitatum.*[331] Somehow—this is more a matter of what is in the reader's mind than of anything Heloise or the writer of letter 82 may have intended—*pyra* (#82.12) and *late* (#82.13) call to mind two of the most poignant moments in Vergilian verse, the one Dido's abandonment by Aeneas, the other Orpheus' grief at the loss of Eurydice[332]: Heloise imagines first the stones that Deucalion placed on the earth to repopulate the world after the flood: once thrown down they liquefied into life, those thrown by Deucalion becoming men, those thrown by Pyrrha becoming women. When the (funeral) pyre (of Abelard and Heloise's life and loves) is likewise liquefied having been placed on the stones (this time paving stones), love vanishes with the burned bodies. The *longa tempora* of the Sibyl is an ironical wish, for the Sibyl refused to grant her lover (Apollo) requitement and grew old and haggard because she forgot to ask for health and beauty when she asked of him that she live for as many years as there were grains of sand in her hand. So, too, the wish that Abelard live the long life of Nestor is ironical, for

Nestor's long life was spent in the contentment of his family.[333] It is not difficult to imagine Heloise penning such verses as letter 82 in the discontent and resignation that followed her failure to convince Abelard that they should live together openly as *sodales* rather than secretly as *conubiales.* Whatever their lack of poetic merit may be, these lines reveal a well-stocked literary mind and a sharp sense of occasion: the single line of prose at the end relies on a neat inversion: instead of love binding, in this case it constricts, as it prevents Heloise from agreeing with Abelard's view of their relationship.

APPENDIX B

A DETAILED READING OF THE "LOST" LOVE LETTERS 88 TO 111 AND THE *HISTORIA CALAMITATUM*

The remainder of the Könsgen collection (#88–113) is a mixture of the generalized, the exemplary poetic (#113 [V] for example, an appropriate end piece, with its memorable, if Ovidian, "facundum me sola facis" and the line "urbi te nostre conspicuam faciunt," to which Heloise seems later to refer),[334] and those that bear a tinge of nostalgia and regret that may date them to the years following Heloise's removal to Argenteuil, and possibly even after she took the veil there, that is, between about 1118–1120 and 1129.

Letters 88 (M) to 93 (V) seem, however, to suggest the moments of separation and difficulty occasioned by the couple's decision to conceal their marriage and live apart (*HC* M 563–71). Letter 88 (M) begins with a curiously heavy biblically influenced *salutatio* in which Heloise likens herself to a "very well built and consummately finished house" [domus superedificata atque optime consummata][335]—based on the foundation that is Abelard's love for her—providing (for her builder)[336] a neighborly congeniality and stability for their *fedus.*[337] The Pauline analogy here—if Heloise intended it—is complicated, in that for St. Paul he himself, the wise builder, with the grace of God, laid the foundation, while another built upon it, using gold, silver, precious stones, wood, hay, straw: "unusquisque autem videat quomodo superaedificet . . . Dei aedificatio estis . . . templum Dei estis"[338]: both the foundation and the subsequent building are the work of Heloise, and Abelard, like God, is the helper, and Heloise is Abelard's helper: "Dei enim sumus adiutores."[339] It is hard to escape the inference that Heloise is her own finished product, and a *domus* rather than an *aedes* or *templum,* the first term implying a measure of homely human comfort perhaps lacking in the two last terms, which seem required by the Pauline context. In a conscious allusion not only to Vergil but also to her own previous statement (#84 [M]) that Abelard is her own natural habitat, Heloise alludes to the difficulties and labor involved in writing back to him, but claims her ready will enables her to triumph over the obstacles. Hovering in the background and summoned by the learned allusions is the male's lament to the woods and groves for his lost mistress.[340] With a rather purposeful and complicated reference (by implication) to Abelard's physical excellence ["corpus . . . bene politum"], Heloise seems to allude to being apart from him, having him present to her mind waking and sleeping, wanting to be "fida, stabilis, immutabilis et non flexibilis," despite the *fallacia* that seems now to govern their relationship (cf. later in letter 88: "plus absconditur," "oculis corporeis a me non videaris, tamen ab intentione mentis non labescis,"[341] "si caute cineribus sepelitur" and *HC* M 564–66: "occulte divisim . . . raro [cf. letter 88: "raro quendam"] latenterque . . . dissimulantes"), despite the "iniuria" done her by Abelard (cf. #87.42: "nec culpe sis memor ulterius"; *HC* M 552–53, perhaps too 559: "parvulo nostro sorori mee commendato"; or even 573: "transmisi eam ad abbatiam"?). In an odd phrase, Heloise states her adherence to their new, hidden, postmarital relationship: "even if all men were made into "unique ones," nothing would force or drive me from you." Use of the term "unicos" represents Heloise's deliberate allusion to Abelard's favored way of addressing her. Only once has she used the term in these letters, and then not with reference directly to Abelard, but to the "unica salus mea" that he represents for her.[342] Here she seems to be ironically turning the term ["even if you were to me, in spades, what you say I am to you . . ."], just as in her *salutatio* to one of the later, well-known letters, she also plays ironically with the term in an ostentatious way.[343]

In his reply (#89 [V]) Abelard picks up (in his *salutatio*) Heloise's use of 'unicus' and (in the four lines of letter proper) the contrast between will or intent and action ["verba" and "mittentis voluntatem"] referred to in her letter, matching it with other contrasts—*inopia/copia* (from Ovid's *Metamorphoses*), *dubitando/faciendo, erumpere/se invicem officiunt.* His *valedictio* "gemma tocius Gallie" recalls (for us) the "in toto regno" of *HC* M 288 and (for her) the "gemme sue" of letter 22 (V).

Heloise's response (#90 [M]) adopts an evocative floral metaphor that picks up again letter 84 [(M): "nemorum umbrosa diligunt volucres"] and ends with the *color adnominatio* ["augmentum . . . incrementum"].[344] Her letter is notable in its explicit reference to the painful conditions that prevent adequate contact and even correspondence, and her phrases "me impediunt cure"[345] and "pre nimio dolore" seem to refer to the "crebris eam contumeliis afficiebat" of *HC* M 571–72.

The group of letters that follow (#91 [V], 92 [M], and 93 [V]) continue an elaborate play that seems to have begun with letter 22 (V). There Abelard was the moon and Heloise the sun, with this difference, that as the moon approaches the sun, it becomes obscured, while as Abelard approaches Heloise, he glows. Away from Heloise, Abelard becomes "fuscum et pallidum": the moon is obscured upon approaching the sun, Abelard is obscured when away from his Heloise. All this renders the *salutatio* of letter 91 (V) a little startling, for there Heloise is herself addressed as a "most splendid moon" which drives away all the shadows, a moon whose "splendor" should always "fulgere" ["shine, gleam, glitter," etc.]. This letter refers again to the *cure* that give Heloise anguish and represent all the more powerful an argument of her *fides,* and the conclusion couples in an interesting way "pectus" and "ambirem," rather as do Lucan[346] and Ovid,[347] and puts forward the proposition that were Abelard present with Heloise, he would "give shape again to [her] happiness" [leticiam tibi integre reformarem].

In her own response (#92 [M]) Heloise furthers the play on light, the moon, and the sun. Picking up Abelard's statement (#22) that without her, he has no *lumen,* Heloise addresses him as "lumini clarissimo," immediately complicating the epithet by reference to the solstice, when the sun is at its brightest: Abelard is now the sun (as Heloise in letter 91 is the moon), but the allusion to letter 22 is maintained by her choice of the words "fuscis tenebrarum," a direct reference, perhaps to the "tenebris" and "fuscum" of letter 22, where Heloise is *sol* (as she is again in letter 108 [V])[348] and Abelard *luna.* The *salutatio* of letter 92 then places Heloise as the recipient of the rays of both sun *and* moon, in the course of which we have an allusion—for those who know the poem and there is no evidence that Heloise or Abelard did—to Catullus' poem 8: the line (3, 8) "fulsere quondam candidi tibi soles" is echoed in the words selected for letters 91 and 92—"semper fulgere . . . solsticio . . . semper candoris . . . tu sol . . . candescere . . . fulgere"—though Abelard is not yet farewelling his mistress, as Catullus is in poem 8. Pain, yet, is on his mind, as letter 93 (V) refers again to the shadows ["tenebris"] penetrated by Heloise's "splendid light" and laments in language that recalls the later *Historia calamitatum* to us his own[349] luckless plight, being drawn in different directions by both *amor*[350] and *pudor.*[351]

In a sudden, virtuoso display of isolated language and language seemingly redolent of Prudentius and the Song of Songs, Heloise (in #94 [M]), as the *luna plena,*[352] offers the "innexibilis[353] amoris delicia" to [her?] first quality "spice, multiplied one-hundred-fold in the desert air, with the seed of sweetness."[354] The body of the letter, however, forms a sharp contrast: with an Ovidian flourish, Heloise dismisses Abelard as a fair-weather friend, following her contempt up with an even more pointed letter (#95 [M]), prosy and colloquial in tone, in which, using a nautical metaphor, she contrasts herself, unmoved by the winds, with Abelard as a ship in danger of sinking and without "the anchor of true fidelity." She offers this Abelard whatever is appropriate to his infidelity, stressing again that *she* chose to "affix *him* firmly to her heart, before all" yet found him in the end unresponsive. To those familiar with Penelope's lament to Ulysses

(Ovid, *Her.* 1.10) there is an evocative bonus here: as is clear from the *Historia calamitatum* narrative at this point, Heloise is living apart from Abelard.[355] So Penelope has been abandoned by Ulysses, who is "slow of return"[356]; Penelope is "deserto . . . lecto . . . frigida," and the "pendula tela" hangs lifelessly in her "viduas manus." It is a powerful reinforcement of her mood and recalls no doubt their reading together of the classical *auctores,* just as it reinforces the fusion between life and art that is so characteristic an aspect of what Bond has called "the revolution in twelfth-century secular lyric."[357] As its master architect Marbod of Rennes puts it, "ars simulat verum mutatque vocabula rerum": the recipient is urged: "me non ex libris, sed totis dilige fibris."[358] In his "reply" (#96 [V]) Abelard, using the "estuans" of the famous *cri-de-cœur* of the "archpoet," wishes his "speciosa"[359] all that his physical passion for her might yield "iugiter." Again, the *suavissima dulcedo* of Heloise is likened to the "sol quotidie novus."[360] The reference to Heloise as a "martyr" must refer either to her confinement at Argenteuil or to the suffering she was at the putative time of the previous letters enduring for Abelard and his version of their relationship.[361]

Letter 98 (M) has an elaborate *salutatio,* which proved of some interest to Johannes de Vepria, but the rest of the letter has been crucially pruned. The letter opens with the arresting word "Tyroni." The associations deriving from a momentary equation between Heloise herself and Tyro "a beautiful nymph . . . [who], removed from her father's house by her uncle . . . exposed [her two sons] to conceal her incontinence from the world [and who, sometime after her love affair with Neptune/the river Enipeus] married her uncle . . ."[362] are, of course, quickly banished when we realize that Heloise is addressing Abelard as a "tiro" in love, a novice, a beginner, a young soldier. She offers herself as the "fundamentum stabilis amicicie" and, referring to his expressions in letters 22 [*fusca nescire*] and 96 [*ardentius estuare*], exhorts him to remain passionate about her. The excised portion must have contained something very specific, because the only remaining line of the letter breathes a quite contrary spirit of broken dejection, in which the writer says that her *vota* ["marriage vows," "wishes" in the matter now lost?] have profited her nothing; both she and "hers" (the "vota," her "proles"?) are now cheap to him, and he puts up with the *delectacio* (her "proles"?) of the joy they had together, but *iratus.* The apparent response, referring as it does to the "amoris leges" and to Heloise as one who has *scientia* of them, seems hardly adequate and may be a generalized note from any period of the relationship (#99 [V]), as indeed may be the case with letter 100 (M), with its interesting periphrasis ("nodum, qui nunquam denodatur" for letter 94 *innexibilis*). An appropriate response from the man comes only with letter 101 (V): picking up the "mando, quod sum: tibi sum, dum vivo" of 97 and the "idem, qui fuerat" of 99, Abelard asserts: "ego sum, qui fui," but this time he elaborates in language that strongly suggests the period after their clandestine marriage when they are living apart (*HC* M 496–502). He speaks to Heloise "cautius," he approaches her "cautius"; *pudor/verecundia* constrains *amor,*[363] lest *amor in immensum proruat.* Such restraint, he argues, will permit both fluency/abundance [*copia*][364] as far as their *vota* are concerned, and some attenuation of the *fama* that is developing around them and that will eventually undo them, Abelard physically, Heloise emotionally. Abelard is arguing that only by continued discretion and secrecy can they enjoy their relationship, in word and in deed. One is reminded forcefully of *HC* M 566–69: "avunculus autem ipsius atque domestici ejus, ignominie sue solatium querentes, initum matrimonium divulgare et fidem mihi super hoc datam vilare ceperunt."

Heloise's "reply" (#102 [M]) picks up notes from earlier letters (the unchanging stability of her love from letter 98, the notion of "intention" from letter 88 [but this time "cordis" rather than "mentis"]) and offers a simple (in concept) but rich and rhythmic (in expression) assertion of commitment ["quod preciossimum habeo, tibi do, scilicet meipsam"], but the slightly cautious *valedictio* ["nec me per te ledat"] hints at Abelard's continued capacity to fall short of the image of devotion roundly proffered in letter 102. Abelard's "rejoinder," a prosy statement of facts (livened only by the "repetition" of "semper . . . nunquam . . . nunquam" and the ornate *salutatio,* with its picturesque notion of Heloise exceeding all the pigments/colors in aroma and savor, and the perplexing "blanda novitate"),[365] promises a visit ["tibi familiariter intimabo"]—perhaps the sort of visit referred to in the later correspondence, after Heloise's removal to Argenteuil.[366]

Letter 104 (M) seems to hope for Abelard some greatness from his "regimen scholarum/magisterium"[367] ["ut dignitas tua ineffabili gloria renovetur," "et adipiscaris quandoque coronam immortalitatis eterne"]. Heloise's emotional attachment to Abelard grows within her and forces her to maintain contact by writing. Echoing his phraseology ["superanti" and "nunquam . . . labascit" from letter 103] she states movingly that she can only grieve for someone loved "tenere . . . interne" but whom she cannot see: recalling, perhaps, the coupling of "turtur amice" and "dole" in *Amores* 2.6.12 (#104: "doleo . . . doloris . . . in modo turturis"), Heloise rams together images from previous letters: for one who will never slip "ab intencione mentis" (cf. #88) and who cannot be physically experienced, only an eternal "pignus amoris"[368] will serve (#60, 69.12, and 84).

Letter 105 (V) responds prosily, but 106 (V) seems to reflect some kind of a growing apart (perhaps produced by their different situations "te quidem Parisius scolis presidente et me ad imperium tuum Argenteoli cum sanctimonialibus conversante"), a growing apart that stimulates Abelard to intense regret and a sense of finality about their relationship, a finality matched by the fragments of a Boethian visitation (#107 [M]) in which Heloise seems to liken herself to the late Roman philosopher in prison, as she focuses her *animus* from "multa" to "singula," and attempts to harness "spiritus sancti gratia" against "saecularibus calliditatibus."[369]

Notes

1. Neville Chiavaroli has been responsible primarily for the comments on dictaminal practice at notes 181–229, John O. Ward for the rest. However each has reviewed the work of the other. The present text is a slightly abridged version of the original, without the epigraphs, and with much material relegated to appendices. It also lacks an 'Appendix C' that presented a detailed chronology of the lives of Heloise and Abelard from the *Historia calamitatum* and other sources, with indications of the possible places occupied by the de Vepria letters. J. O. Ward wishes to express his thanks to the members of the Sydney University Medieval Latin Reading Group: John Scott, Deirdre Stone, Alison Waters, and Sharon Davidson with whom he had the valued opportunity of reading through the letters during 1998. On one occasion the group had the pleasure of Constant Mews's company, and Ward would like to express his profound thanks to Mews, whose generous invitation to read his *The Lost Love Letters of Heloise and Abelard: Perceptions of Dialogue in Twelfth-Century France,* with Neville Chiavaroli, in first draft was responsible for arousing his interest in the present subject. J. O. Ward would also like to acknowledge the help and stimulation that he has received, in all phases of the present topic, from Juanita Ruys.
2. Könsgen. We generally cite this collection in what follows as the de Vepria collection.
3. *HC,* ed. Monfrin 71: ll. 296–99; ca. AD 1116–17: "nosque etiam absentes scriptis internuntiis invicem liceret presentare et pleraque audacius scribere quam colloqui, et sic semper jocundis interesse colloquiis"; ed. Hicks xii and 10 (ll. 265–67); "crebris me epistolis vistabas": Heloise, "Appendice: I. Heloyse sue ad ipsum deprecatoria," in *HC* ed. Monfrin, 117 l. 270.
4. It is difficult to credit Neil Cartlidge's remark that the de Vepria collection "is a purely literary collection, its impression of temporal development being simply the impression given by patterns in the sequence—just as in Elizabethan sonnet-sequences" as anything more than a hasty and ill-formed judgement (*Medieval Marriage: Literary Approaches, 1100–1300,* p. 60, n. 142). According to Graziella Ballanti, ed. *Anonimo: un epistolario d'amore del XII secolo (Abelardo e Eloisa?),* p. 23: "la maggior parte dei critici sono con-

vinto . . . che quelle di Troyes sono vere lettere, e non letterarie finzioni." Könsgen, pp. 80 and 83 for the same view.

5. The manuscript is an advanced resource book for dictaminal and epistolary purposes: Könsgen, pp. ix-xiv.
6. These matters are all examined with great skill and sympathy in Mews, *The Lost Love Letters.*
7. Peter Dronke, ed. and trans., *Medieval Latin and the Rise of the European Love-Lyric,* 2nd ed., 2 vols.: 1, *Problems and Interpretations* and 2, *Medieval Latin Love-Poetry,* vol. 2: pp. 422–47 and commented on in vol. 1: pp. 221–29 and in *Women Writers,* pp. 91–92.
8. Gerald A. Bond, *The Loving Subject: Desire, Eloquence, and Power in Romanesque France; Women Writers,* chapter 4; Mews, *The Lost Love Letters.* The collection edited and discussed by Therese Latzke, "Die Carmina erotica der Ripollsammlung," pp. 138–201, also requires close attention in this context. Cf. also Latzke's "Zum 'Iudicium de calumnia molendini Brisesarte' und zu den vier Nonnenepisteln des Hilarius," pp. 73–96.
9. The verses envisage love between (male) master and (female) pupil. (Dronke, *Medieval Latin,* p. 424)
10. Dronke, *Medieval Latin,* pp. 422–23: "iam pergito lusum" [let love's play go on]; "ludos ymenei" [the sports of wedded love]; "nimium deludis amores" [you make sport of constant love]. In the Regensburg collection the context seems monastic—'frater/sorores' and from the Liège region ["nec habet te Legia natum"]. Dronke, *Medieval Latin,* pp. 430, 433.
11. The Regensburg verses no doubt have a didactic origin: "corrige versiculos tibi quos presento, magister" [correct the brief verses I am sending you, master]. Dronke, *Medieval Latin,* p. 424. Cf. also pp. 430–34.
12. Dronke, *Medieval Latin,* pp. 425–27, 429, 435–42.
13. Dronke, *Medieval Latin,* pp. 426, 441–42.
14. For Mercury: Dronke, *Medieval Latin,* p. 443.
15. *Rhetorica ad Herennium* 1.2.3, Marx *ed. min.* p. 3.
16. "Quod celat pectus modo, tunc retegit tibi lectus," Dronke, *Medieval Latin,* vol. 2: p. 426.
17. Frank McCourt, *Angela's Ashes: A Memoir,* p. 324.
18. Cf. I. S. Robinson, "The *colores rhetorici* in the Investiture Contest," *Traditio* 32 (1976): 210–38, on the investiture controversy *epistolae* and the *colores.*
19. As Ballanti maintains, all love letters of the time involved art; those who wrote them were "sempre persone 'di scuola,' non puramente di cultura." *Anonimo,* p. 13.
20. "Sono in massima parte, veri *billets doux,* come potrebbero scambiarsi due amanti che pur essendo vicini non fossero liberi di comunicare apertamente; non sono elaborati, ma immediati, con tuttto la forza e i limiti del primo impulso." Ballanti, *Anonimo,* p. 29.
21. John Marenbon, *The Philosophy of Peter Abelard,* especially pp. 82ff. and 298ff.; M. T. Clanchy, *Abelard: A Medieval Life;* and, of course, Mews, *The Lost Letters.* See Ballanti: "Bisogna dunque estendere alle *Lettere di Troyes* la stessa considerazione che vale per l'*Epistolario:* che siamo in presenza di un documento prezioso, interessante e rivelatore di un'epoca, di un tipo di cultura e costume, a di una speciale situazione scolastica, che sono quelli del tempo di vita di Eloisa e Abelardo; e che non è un grave errore leggere quelle lettere 'come se' fossero loro, pur dubitando che lo siano." *Anonimo,* pp. 18–19.
22. The topicality of the *salutationes,* nevertheless, is indicated by, among other things, the place they occupy in the nearly contemporary *Codex Udalrici:* see Robinson, "The *colores rhetorici,*" p. 210.
23. Kenneth Quinn, *The Catullan Revolution,* p. 24.
24. John of Salisbury, *Metalogicon* 1.24, most recently in *Ioannis Saresberiensis Metalogicon,* ed. J. B. Hall.
25. For an initial indication see Könsgen's source citations, and below.

26. For philosophical terminology, see Könsgen, p. 9 litt. 21: "et ex ipsius experimento rei esse, quod est . . . equipolenter": see R. W. Southern, "Lanfranc of Bec and Berengar of Tours," pp. 42–43; Anselm, *De veritate*, "magister 'ad quid facta est affirmatio?' Discipulus 'ad significandum esse quod est,'" and the recurring uses of the phrase *esse quod est* in what follows. On *equipollenter* see *De veritate*, pp. 41–43 "aequipollentia" and "per aequipollentias propositionum."
27. "Et quia in toto preexercitamine erudiendorum nichil utilius est . . . humilitas," PL 199.856A; Clement Charles Julian Webb, *Ioannis Saresberiensis Episcopi Carnotensis, Metalogicon Libri IIII*, p. 57; D. D. McGarry, trans., *The Metalogicon of John of Salisbury: A Twelfth-Century Defence of the Verbal and Logical Arts of the Trivium*, p. 70: "A further feature of Bernard's method . . ."
28. C. Stephen Jaeger, *The Envy of Angels: Cathedral Schools and Social Ideals in Medieval Europe 950–1200*.
29. Mews, "Orality, Literacy, and Authority in the Twelfth-Century Schools," p. 480.
30. J. O. Ward, "Rhetoric in the Faculty of Arts at the Universities of Paris and Oxford in the Middle Ages: A Summary of the Evidence," especially pp. 229–31; Winthrop Wetherbee, *Platonism and Poetry in the Twelfth Century*, chapters 6 and 7.
31. Brian Stock, "Literacy and Society in the Twelfth Century" in *The Spirit of the Court*, p. 1; a fuller text is to be found in his "Medieval Literacy, Linguistic Theory, and Social Organization."
32. Halm #16; Howell (J. O. Ward, *Ciceronian Rhetoric in Treatise, Scholion and Commentary Typologie des Sources du Moyen Âge Occidental* 58, p. 34). All relevant references are in Ward at this page.
33. Cf. picture of Fulbert teaching in MS Chartres Bibl. Mun. nouv. acq. 4, edited and discussed by René Merlet and l'Abbé Clerval in their: *Un Manuscrit Chartrain du XIe Siècle: Fulbert, Évêque de Chartres, Martyrologie à l'usage de l'église de Chartres; Fulbert et sa Cathédrale; Nécrologie du Chapitre Nôtre-Dame de Chartres; chartes et pièces liturgiques*, Société Archéologique d'Eure-et-Loir (Chartres, 1893), color plate opposite p. 227. No longer extant in the manuscript when Merlet and Clerval studied it were illustrations of Fulbert visiting the poor and succoring the sick.
34. See Cicero, *De inventione* 1.1 *et seqq.*; J. O. Ward, "*Artificiosa Eloquentia*" J. O. Ward, ed., *Ciceronian Rhetoric*, I, pp. 44ff., 48; C. Stephen Jaeger, *The Origins of Courtliness: Civilizing Trends and the Formation of Courtly Ideals, 939–1210*, especially chap. 6.
35. References to Jaeger, *The Envy of Angels*, throughout the preceding paragraphs are: pp. 2, 4, 6, 9, 11, 48, 62, 66, 79, 106, 110, 131, 137, 141, 147, and 218. On the general significance of the modern literacy/orality debate in the period, see: Peter Biller and Anne Hudson, eds., *Heresy and Literacy, 1000–1530;* Guy Lobrichon, "The Chiaroscuro of Heresy: Early Eleventh-Century Aquitaine as Seen from Auxerre," pp. 80–103; R. I. Moore, trans., "Literacy and the Making of Heresy ca. 1000-ca. 1150" in *Heresy and Literacy*, pp. 19–37, also available in *Debating the Middle Ages: Issues and Readings*, pp. 363–75; Edward Peters, *The Magician, the Witch and the Law*, especially chap. 2; Brian Stock, *The Implications of Literacy: Written Language and Models of Interpretation in the Eleventh and Twelfth Centuries*, chap. 5 and pp. 104–106 and 115–17; Stock, "Literacy and Society in the Twelfth Century"; J. O. Ward, "The First Crusade as Disaster: Apocalypticism and the Genesis of the Crusading Movement," pp. 253–92.
36. Bond, *The Loving Subject*, pp. 4–5. Whether the wax tablet, carried between correspondents by trusted servants (of the sort whose disloyalty resulted in Abelard's castration: "quodam mihi serviente per pecuniam corrupto" *HC* Monfrin ll. 83–84), was less "public" (in the sense discussed by Bond, *The Loving Subject*, pp. 47–48) than the letter on parchment is an interesting point for the subject of this chapter. For the carriage and delivery of letters in Abelard's day, see Constable, *The Letters of Peter the Venerable*, vol. 2: pp. 23ff.

37. For motives, see Bond, *The Loving Subject,* pp. 37–38, and cf. the somewhat later example of Stephen of Rouen: J. O. Ward, "Quintilian and the Rhetorical Revolution of the Middle Ages," p. 253ff.
38. Bond, *The Loving Subject,* pp. 7–8.
39. On *amor/amicitia,* see R. W. Southern, *Scholastic Humanism and the Unification of Europe,* vol. 1, pp. 28ff. and, especially, Brian Patrick McGuire, *Friendship and Community: The Monastic Experience 350–1250,* chap. 5.
40. For the *fedus amicitiae,* see Catullus, poem 109: "aeternum hoc sanctae foedus amicitiae" in *C. Valerii Catulli Carmina,* ed. R. A. B. Mynors, p. 102. On *foedus/amor* in Baudri of Bourgeuil's poetry, see Gerald A. Bond, "'Iocus Amoris': The Poetry of Baudri of Bourgeuil and the Formation of the Ovidian Subculture," pp. 172–74. For "matrimonii foedera" see *Ep.* 2, ed. Muckle 71, and for "sordida foedera carnis" see Aurelius Clemens Prudentius, *Apotheosis* [*On the divinity of Christ*], 2 vols., vol. 1: p. 186, l. 910.
41. For the centrality of the epistolary genre, see in addition to Bond's remarks and those of I. S. Robinson, "The *colores rhetorici,*" pp. 210ff., L. Merlet, "Lettres d'Ives de Chartres et d'autres personnages de son temps," *Bibliothèque de l'École des Chartes,* and note the remark of Southern, *Scholastic Humanism,* p. 164 n. 2.
42. On the early monastic phase of the developments under consideration, see Bond, *The Loving Subject,* pp. 45–49. It interesting to note that the concept of monastic "otium" discussed by Bond, "'Iocus Amoris,'" pp. 156–58, approaches the notion of Ciceronian and humanist *otium* so crucial for the cultural productivity of both the Roman Republican and the Italian Renaissance periods: see John F. Tinkler, "Renaissance Humanism and the *genera eloquentiae,*" pp. 286ff., and Brian Vickers, "Leisure and Idleness in the Renaissance: The Ambivalence of *otium.*"
43. *HC,* ed. Monfrin l. 20.
44. Thoughts on these developments and some references will be found in J. O. Ward, "Magic and Rhetoric from Antiquity to the Renaissance: Some Ruminations"; Ward, "Rhetoric, Truth, and Literacy in the Renaissance of the Twelfth Century," pp. 126–57; Ward, "The First Crusade as Disaster"; as well as his "From Marginal Gloss to *catena* Commentary: The Eleventh-Century Origins of a Rhetorical Teaching Tradition in the Medieval West."
45. Dronke, *Women Writers,* chap. 3; E. Bos, "Patterns of Male-Female Religious Friendships and Their Influence on the Construction of the Literary Identities of Medieval Women," pp. 326–36; J. O. Ward, "After Rome: Medieval Epic," pp. 285ff.
46. R. Howard Bloch, *Medieval Misogyny and the Invention of Western Romantic Love,* pp. 178–84; Bruce L. Venarde, *Women's Monasticism and Medieval Society: Nunneries in France and England, 890–1215,* index *sv.* "Robert of Arbrissel;" J. M. B. Porter, "Preaching of the First Crusade? Robert of Arbrissel after the Council of Clermont."
47. R. I. Moore, *The Origins of European Dissent,* 2nd ed., pp. 63–105; R. I. Moore, ed., *The Birth of Popular Heresy,* pp. 27–38; Brenda Bolton, *The Medieval Reformation,* chap. 5; Jacqueline Smith, "Robert of Arbrissel: *Procurator mulierum,*" pp. 175–84; J. Dalarun, "Robert D'Arbrissel et les femmes," and the same author's *L'impossible sainteté: la vie retrouvée de Robert d'Arbrissel (1045–1116) fondateur de Fontevraud.*
48. "His temporibus florere coepit in Theutonica terra Manegaldus philosophus divinis et saecularibus litteris ultra coetaneos suos eruditus. Uxor quoque eius et filiae religione florentes multam in scripturis habuere notitiam, et discipulos proprios filiae eius praedictae docebant." Max Manitius, *Geschichte der lateinischen Literatur des Mittelalter,* vol. 3, p. 178. The (slightly fuller) original text may be consulted in E. Martène and U. Durand, eds., *Veterum Scriptorum et Monumentorum Historicorum, Dogmaticorum, Moralium amplissima Collectio,* vol. 5, col. 1169. For *scriptura* see Jaeger, *The Envy of Angels,* p. 68; and for *notitia* see Stock, *The Implications of Literacy,* p. 245; also PL 148.1417, 152.1316B, 156.525C, and 669D, confirming that the phrase "in scripturis habere notitiam" means

to have a knowledge of the scriptures. From the other personages mentioned in the immediate context, it is apparent that the original entry in the chronicle (cols. 1160–1174 "Chronicon Richardi Pictavensis monachi Cluniacensis" covering the years 754 to 1153) concentrates on the dates 1060 (death of Henry I of France), 1024 (death of Henry II of Germany), 1049 (death of Odilo, Abbot of Cluny), 995/96–1030 or 1058–1086 or 1086–1126 (rule of "William, duke of Aquitaine," either William V, VIII or, less likely, IX), 1054 (death of Leo IX), and 1073 (death of Alexander II). Col. 1171 mentions the floruit of "Anselmus philosophus." J. O. Ward would like to thank Constant Mews here for profitable discussions on the likely implications of the passage. Manegold's teaching is mentioned in a letter of the early twelfth century. (Southern, *Scholastic Humanism,* p. 202). Richard, a monk who may have spent time at Cluny, was probably an approximate contemporary of Heloise and Peter the Venerable. For his chronicle see Elie Berger, "Notice sur divers manuscrits de la bibliothèque Vaticane: Richard le Poitevin, moine de Cluny, historien et poëte," pp. 43–138. Berger has for *uxor quoque et filiae* "filii (*lege:* 'filiae') . . ." (p. 99) and thinks that Richard, who dedicated his chronicle to Peter the Venerable and seems to have put together the earliest versions in the 1140s and 1150s, got his "sèches indications" on Berengar of Tours from "des annales monastiques": "pour les faits antérieurs [to his own day] il parait avoir eu sous les yeux quelque chronique monastique, rédigée en Poitou, et sans doute dans l'une des maisons qui appartenaient à l'ordre de Cluny" (p. 97). It seems that the manuscript used by Martène and Durand for their excerpts goes back ultimately to the first redaction of Richard's chronicle (pp. 56–57). On the dedication to Peter the Venerable: see Constable, vol. 2: pp. 38–39. Richard seems to have felt that the reference to Manegold's wives and daughters was not odd enough to require any special explanatory comment from him. Nevertheless, all trace of their activity has dropped from the record. Richard's list of great teachers includes Hildebert of Tours (Lavardin), Gilbert the Universal, Alberic of Rheims, Pierre de Saintes, Hugh of St. Victor and Abelard.

49. For Tengswich, see J. L. Baird and Radd K. Ehrman, trans., *The Letters of Hildegard of Bingen,* vol. 1: pp. 127–30. See also J. O. Ward, "Women and Latin Rhetoric from Hrotsvit to Hildegard."
50. Bond, *The Loving Subject,* p. 1. See also Dronke, *Women Writers,* chapters 4–5, and D. M. Stone, "Heloise: *la très sage abbesse* of the Paraclete," p. 26.
51. Enid McLeod, *Héloïse: A Biography,* 1938 edn., book 1.
52. See Stone, "Heloise: *la très sage abbesse,*" pp. 26–28, for a sensitive discussion.
53. Clanchy, *A Medieval Life,* map 2 on p. xvi.
54. Régine Pernoud, *Heloise and Abelard,* 1973 edn., pp. 47–48, gives a vivid picture of the "academic" quarter of Paris in Heloise's youth: The Paris "cathedral close, like those of Wells and Salisbury, with a cluster of small houses, provid[ed] accommodation for the members of the chapter. About forty of these houses stood at the eastern extremity of the Île-de-la-Cité. They may have been walled off from the rest of the town, for the area had always enjoyed a considerable measure of autonomy: officers of the crown were not allowed to set foot in it. . . . Thus, the tip of the Île-de-la-Cité was the home of a small, self-sufficient ecclesiastical colony, containing churches and chapels, cloisters and schoolhouses, gardens and private residences—including the house of Canon Fulbert. According to legend, it stood close to the corner of the Rue des Chantres and of the present Quai aux Fleurs." Abelard's "school" at the time of his first affair with Heloise was very close to Fulbert's house. Pernoud, *Heloise and Abelard,* p. 52.
55. See Pernoud, *Heloise and Abelard,* pp. 47 and 53.
56. "The erotic will always dance between people who teach and learn, and our attempts to manage its shocking charge are often flat-footed, literal, destructive, rigid with fear and the need to control. For good or ill, Eros is always two steps ahead of us, exploding the constraints of dogma, turning back on us our carefully worked out *positions* and

lines, showing us that the world is richer and scarier and more fluid and many-fold than we dare to think." Helen Garner, *The First Stone: Some Questions About Sex and Power,* p. 161. It is tempting to imagine that Heloise would have realized this "truth," even if Abelard did not.

57. Monfrin pp. 71–72. Hereafter for citations from the letters of Abelard and Heloise, cite "M" for Monfrin's edition of the *Historia calamitatum.*
58. Cf. Brooke cited in Clanchy, *A Medieval Life,* p. 155.
59. *HC* Monfrin ll. 296–99; for the implications of the term *colloquium,* see Bond, *The Loving Subject,* p. 53. Abelard's approach to the subject of initiating a relationship with Heloise suggests a mature woman rather than the teenager of tradition.
60. 'ipsius' *HC,* ed. Monfrin l. 304.
61. *HC,* ed. Monfrin ll. 272–75. Some contemporaries, of course, had other ideas about Abelard's relations with prostitutes and loose women. For Fulk of Deuil's allegations, see Mews, *Peter Abelard,* p. 45 [37], and Clanchy, *A Medieval Life,* index *sv.* "Fulk of Deuil."
62. *HC,* ed. Monfrin l. 288: "puellam . . . in toto regno nominatissimam." "Audiebam tunc temporis, mulierem licet necdum saeculi nexibus expeditam, litteratoriae scientiae quod perrarum est, et studio licet saecularis sapientiae, summam operam dare, nec mundi voluptatibus, nugis, vel deliciis, ab hoc utili discendarum artium proposito retrahi posse" (Constable, vol. 1: pp. 115 and 303). According to Constable, "[t]his, one of the most famous of all Peter the Venerable's letters . . . may not have been written before 1144" (vol. 2: p. 177). Mews posits (*Abelard,* p. 12[4] n. 14; Clanchy, *A Medieval Life,* pp. 173–74, 369, n. 4, and elaborated in Mews, *The Lost Letters*) that Heloise was about the age of Peter the Venerable (i.e., in his/her early twenties at the time of the exchange of the letters excerpted by Johannes de Vepria). This view requires a different understanding of the relationship between Heloise and Abelard, which must have been much more mature than is commonly believed, even if it does raise new questions about the pattern of Heloise's life between her return from Argenteuil and her meeting with Abelard. Peter the Venerable grew up and was educated in Burgundy. See Constable, vol. 2: pp. 257ff.
63. Pernoud, *Heloise and Abelard,* p. 53: "She [Heloise] herself was committed to a life of scholarship." See Bond, *The Loving Subject,* p. 110, on Guibert of Nogent's devotion to letters in youth ("solis litteris intentus") for the attainment of high status and wealth ("culminum opumque assecutiones").
64. Pernoud, *Heloise and Abelard,* p. 48.
65. E. McLeod, *Héloïse,* p. 12.
66. Cf. #113: l. 29 'genus,' Könsgen, p. 63.
67. Penelope D. Johnson, *Equal in Monastic Profession: Religious Women in Medieval France.*
68. Venarde, *Women's Monasticism.*
69. Venarde, *Women's Monasticism,* p. 8.
70. Venarde, *Women's Monasticism,* p. 10.
71. Venarde, *Women's Monasticism,* p. 9.
72. Venarde, *Women's Monasticism,* p. 14.
73. Examined in Venarde, *Women's Monasticism,* chapters 3 and 4.
74. Cf., for example, the patronage of Robert of Arbrissel. Ibid., pp. 57ff.
75. Ibid., p. 55; "was" seems to be required by the syntax of the sentence rather than 'were'.
76. Venarde, *Women's Monasticism,* pp. 43–44.
77. Guibert of Nogent, *Self and Society in Medieval France: The 'Memoirs' of Abbot Guibert of Nogent (1064?–c. 1125),* ed. John F. Benton, trans. C. C. Swinton Bland, p. 16. Heloise's mother, Hersindis, Hersende (E. McLeod, *Héloïse,* pp. 9, 12), has the same name as that of "a forceful noblewoman [who] made a major donation to [a priory] . . . in Périgord in 1010": Johnson, *Equal in Monastic Profession,* p. 21.
78. According to Pernoud, illegitimate children were brought up in the father's family *Heloise and Abelard,* p. 63.

79. Abelard's own mother retired to a monastery. "Thirty-five per cent of the nuns entering Ronceray before 1100 were widows or married women." Mary Skinner, "Benedictine Life for Women in Central France, 850–1100: A Feminist Revival," pp. 87–113, p. 98. Pernoud assumes that Heloise's parents directed her education at Argenteuil and her remove to Paris to live with Fulbert, not Fulbert himself. See Pernoud, *Heloise and Abelard,* pp. 32, 47, 53.
80. Johnson, *Equal in Monastic Profession,* pp. 15–16, 18–27.
81. Cf. the case of Ermengaud of Anjou, the recipient of a 'sermo' from Robert of Arbrissel (Bond, *The Loving Subject,* pp. 138–39).
82. Shulamith Shahar, *The Fourth Estate: A History of Women in the Middle Ages,* p. 8, cited in Johnson, *Equal in Monastic Profession,* p. 33. Cf. Shahar, *The Fourth Estate,* chap. 3 in general. On nunneries as places of expectation for a schooling and literacy for daughters, see Johnson, *Equal in Monastic Profession,* pp. 144–47 (including consideration of a poem allegedly written by Heloise—see Mews, *The Lost Letters*). Constant Mews, in *The Lost Love Letters,* refers to the case of Vital of Mortain, who, according to Marbod of Rennes, enabled a girl to obtain an education that otherwise would have been unavailable because of the expense involved (Marbod, *Ep.* 4, PL 171.1474AB). See also Skinner, "Benedictine Life for Women," p. 98.
83. Johnson, *Equal in Monastic Profession,* p. 28.
84. Johnson, *Equal in Monastic Profession,* p. 29.
85. Johnson, *Equal in Monastic Profession,* pp. 31–32.
86. Johnson, *Equal in Monastic Profession,* pp. 150–163; cf. also Michel Parisse, *Les Nonnes au Moyen Âge,* pp. 182ff.
87. Johnson, *Equal in Monastic Profession,* pp. 112–130; Parisse, *Les Nonnes au Moyen Âge,* pp. 240ff.
88. The "worldliness" of Argenteuil during Heloise's time there is stressed by Thomas Waldman, "Abbot Suger and the nuns of Argenteuil," citing Matthew of Albano and by Lindy Grant ("Abelard and Heloise used the nunnery like a hotel"): references at Lindy Grant, *Abbot Suger of St. Denis: Church and State in Early Twelfth-Century France,* pp. 190–93.
89. Pernoud, *Heloise and Abelard,* pp. 47 and 53.
90. On this subject, see also: Eileen Edna Power, *Medieval Women,* chap. 5, for an older view, emphasizing the limited number and aristocratic nature of nunneries (in England) but mentioning education as a motive for entering the female foundations (p. 91); Henrietta Leyser, *Medieval Women: A Social History of Women in England 450–1500,* pt. 4: pp. 189ff., again restricted to England, but revising Power, especially on the number of nunneries (pp. 190ff.); patterns of growth and patronage of women's monastic foundations in England are also investigated by Sally Thompson in her *Women Religious: The Founding of English Nunneries After the Norman Conquest;* some remarks on the continental scene will be found in Edith Ennen, *The Medieval Woman,* pp. 122–37, and in Herbert Grundmann, *Religious Movements in the Middle Age.* See also Ernest William McDonnell, *The Beguines and Beghards in Medieval Culture, with Special Emphasis on the Belgian Scene,* and Ward and Bussey, eds., *Worshipping Women.* Parisse surveys the topic "par le biais de la noblesse et de l'histoire germanique, parce que je voulais comprendre l'originalité que représentent les chapitres de dames nobles, et les raisons de leur opposition aux abbayes bénédictines traditionelles." *Les Nonnes au Moyen Âge,* p. 9. For our period, Parisse writes (p. 63): "Le plus souvent, le monastère féminin est conçu comme une maison d'accueil pour les jeunes filles non mariées et les veuves qui renoncent à d'autres noces. C'est une affaire de famille, de société, moins souvent de religion." He stresses "un élitisme [social] certain dans la vie monastique féminine," pp. 131–34 and cf. pp. 208ff. On the female monastics of our period, see Michelle Pontenay de Fontette, *Les religieuses à l'âge classique du droit canon: recherches sur les structures juridiques des branches*

féminines des Ordres. Ward would like to acknowledge the generous assistance of Deirdre Stone on this topic.

91. According to Pernoud, *Heloise and Abelard,* p. 49, Heloise was "beautiful."
92. All references found in Ward, *Ciceronian Rhetoric.* Here, *Ciceronian Rhetoric* p. 30, Dickey 1968, p. 15: "noli iacere cum monialibus quia ex huiusmodi negotio evenit hoc nuper quod quidam testes amisit." Castration was the punishment meted out to the Count of Nantes (Dronke, *Abelard and Heloise in Medieval Testimonies,* pp. 19 and 45–46 and reprinted in *Intellectuals and Poets in Medieval Europe,* pp. 247–94); Fredborg 1976b (Ward *Ciceronian Rhetoric* p. 30) and Ward 1978 (Ward *Ciceronian Rhetoric* p. 38) p. 47 n. 60.
93. *HC,* ed. Monfrin 573ff.
94. For the letters down to #84 see Appendix A below. Citations in the following notes assume a reading of the notes to Appendix A.
95. As Könsgen notes (47 n. 6) the phrase is taken from the Song of Songs; the *sponsa* speaking.
96. Cf. the comments at n. 345 below.
97. P. G. W. Glare, ed., *Oxford Latin Dictionary,* p. 1379; Propertius 4.11.12: "famae pignora tanta meae," 73: "communia pignora"; *Res Gestae Divi Augusti,* ed. and trans. Frederick W. Shipley, p. 396. In Baudri of Bourgeuil the "security or pledge [*pignus*] for this contract [between the poet and Galo] is the letter-poem itself": Bond, *The Loving Subject,* p. 65.
98. Cartlidge, *Medieval Marriage,* p. 65 (citing Luscombe).
99. Cartlidge, *Medieval Marriage,* p. 66.
100. See Skinner, "Benedictine Life for Women," p. 102.
101. Dronke, *Women Writers,* p. 95. For Dronke's general (negative) discussion of the authenticity of these letters, see his *Medieval Testimonies,* pp. 24–26.
102. "certatim pro bravio curramus in amore." "Veris leta facies," [Anonymous], *Carmina Burana* 1.2 *Text: Die Liebeslieder,* p. 138, where the word 'bravium' seems to imply "a state of true love," that is, mutual acceptance and loving devotion expressed equally by both parties in the couple: love, in this sense, crowns/rewards those who seek it.
103. For example, in *Menander Rhetor* (*Menander Rhetor,* p. 149), advice for the "bedroom speech"—*kateunastikos.*
104. Könsgen, p. 47, nn. 8–9.
105. C. T. Lewis and C. Short, *A Latin Dictionary,* p. 248.
106. Cf. his #61 and her #53 for the interchangeability of this idea.
107. Cf. Ovid, *Amores* 1.9.41 'segnis,' where the word seems to imply neglect of 'amor.'
108. The failure to mention Rachel and our recall of the identification of "Mary" with Mary Magdalene that is found in many sources adds a twist to a commonplace in patristic, medieval and especially monastic literature: Giles Constable, *Three Studies in Medieval Religious and Social Thought: The Interpretation of Mary and Martha, the Ideal of the Imitation of Christ, and the Orders of Society,* pp. 16, 27, 51, 73–74, and 87. A characteristic monastic reference to the two pairs of biblical figures will be found in R. E. Pepin, ed., *Scorn for the World: Bernard of Cluny's "De contemptu mundi": The Latin Text with English Translation and an Introduction,* pp. 22–23. See Ballanti, *Anonimo,* p. 33 of #86: "Forse, è l'eco della maternità di Eloisa. . . ."
109. See Könsgen, p. 113, providing nine references, all the woman's. In *Ep.* 2, ed. Monfrin 116: l. 212, Muckle 72 (Radice 115) Heloise sets up a contrast between the outcome of some alleged wrong act and the intention behind it in the mind of the doer, using for the latter "efficientis affectus." Perhaps the contrast between *affectus* and *amor* is intended to be the particular intention that inspires a particular act (*affectus,* in this context to make love?) as contrasted with a general disposition to love someone (*amor*)? Certainly #23 seems to use the word *affectus* in this localized sense. In #76 the word seems to mean "my great desire for you at this particular moment," and in #79 we find

the actual phrase "intencionem mei affectus"—the "intention that my desire for you promotes at this particular moment." This is the sense in which Heloise uses the word in *Ep.* 2, ed. Muckle 72 (Radice 115): "non enim rei effectus sed efficientis affectus in crimine est." Abelard uses the word in the sense of conscious choice or favor (versus "animal coercion") in his *Carmen ad Astralabium:* Josepha Marie Annaïs Rubingh-Bosscher, *Peter Abelard, Carmen ad Astralabium, A Critical Edition,* p. 113: l. 124. Juanita Ruys and J. O. Ward are currently engaged in a complete annotated translation of this *Carmen* and the *planctus Abelardi.*

110. J. N. Adams, *The Latin Sexual Vocabulary,* p. 190.
111. This is a paraphrase of the lines in question.
112. Abelard knew of Ovid's songs—*HC* Monfrin l. 390 = Ovid, *Amores* 1.9.39–40.
113. See for the letters that follow Appendix B below. Citations in the footnotes below assume a reading of the footnotes to Appendix B.
114. There is a sad irony in the use of these words "summa . . . exultacione": *HC* Monfrin ll. 392–93.
115. Bond, *The Loving Subject,* pp. 170–193.
116. Bond, *The Loving Subject,* p. 188: l. 103.
117. Cf. Bond, *The Loving Subject,* p. 184: l. 62 with #87.
118. Cf. Bond, *The Loving Subject,* p. 182: l. 29 with #50.
119. Cf. Bond, *The Loving Subject,* p. 182: l. 6 with p. 172: l. 51.
120. Bond, *The Loving Subject,* p. 172.
121. Bond, *The Loving Subject,* pp. 170–172.
122. Mews observes that de Vepria has "effectively silenced the woman's voice" by cutting out all that preceded the fragment preserved. *The Lost Love Letters.*
123. Does this settle the question of Heloise's social class?
124. *HC* ed. Monfrin 117 ll. 271–72.
125. Clanchy, *A Medieval Life,* p. 239.
126. Clanchy, *A Medieval Life,* p. 125.
127. *Ep.* 2–5, ed. Monfrin 111–125, Muckle 47–94 (Radice), in particular.
128. Radice 110–111 and 116; it is not hard to jump from such lines as "solus quippe es qui me contristare, qui me letificare seu consolari valeas" (*Ep.* 2, ed. Monfrin 114: ll. 133–35, Muckle 70 [Radice 113]) to the de Vepria collection.
129. Rather as Abelard himself claims to have done, #110 [V] "quotiens tuas litteras incipio, tanta interius suavitate perfundor, ut litteram, quam legi, sepe cogar repetere, quia attencionem michi magnitudo aufert leticie."
130. *Ep.* 5, ed. Muckle 88 (Radice 146).
131. Fully and interestingly surveyed in Mews, *The Lost Love Letters.*
132. Clanchy, *A Medieval Life,* p. 14.
133. Clanchy, *A Medieval Life,* p. 16.
134. Clanchy, *A Medieval Life,* p. 16.
135. 'Ars dictaminis' does not mean 'art of dictation,' nor—in its sense as the art of epistolography—can it be shown to have been taught "along with Latin in the classroom" of Abelard's day.
136. See Clanchy, *A Medieval Life,* pp. 50ff. and 58ff.
137. Bond, *The Loving Subject,* p. 85: "If I consider this booklet a crafted text of its own age rather than a degenerate rhetoric from Antiquity, its significance becomes clearer. It is the first high medieval rhetoric for poets, and displays a strong interest in 'translating' the study into the terms of its own age. . . ." Such a view, satisfying as it is to medievalists, works against the implications of Brian Vickers's *In Defence of Rhetoric,* chap. 4.
138. For example, in the *Ad Herennium* commentary beginning "Etsi Cum Tullius" attached in many manuscripts to the more authoritative and exhaustive *De inventione* commentary known as "In primis": Fredborg (1976b) as cited in Ward *Ciceronian Rhetoric,* p. 32.

139. Clanchy, *A Medieval Life,* p. 52.
140. Bond, *The Loving Subject,* p. 53.
141. Bond, *The Loving Subject,* p. 86.
142. Clanchy, *A Medieval Life,* p. 56.
143. *Ad Her.* 1.2.3.
144. Bond, *The Loving Subject,* pp. 86–87.
145. See Ward 1972a in Ward *Ciceronian Rhetoric,* p. 48.
146. MS London, BL Harley 6324. See Ward *Ciceronian Rhetoric* pp. 29 [Caplan 1970] and 369 [index *sv.* 'London B. L. MS Harley 6324']).
147. ed. C. Halm (as cited in Ward *Ciceronian Rhetoric* p. 34).
148. Ward *Ciceronian Rhetoric* index *sv.* '*Heptateuchon*'.
149. Ward *Ciceronian Rhetoric* index *sv.* 'Peter Abelard'.
150. Outlined in Constant Mews, *Abelard;* Clanchy, *A Medieval Life,* pp. 24, 120, and 204; and Hicks xi-xv.
151. Ward *Ciceronian Rhetoric* pp. 108–109.
152. John of Salisbury, *Metalogicon* 2.9, trans. McGarry, pp. 93–95 and 3.10, pp. 190–201, etc.
153. Cf. Pernoud's description of the later correspondence: "the white-hot correspondence which has survived the passage of the centuries" (*Heloise and Abelard,* p. 55).
154. There is much that is suggestive here in Bond, *The Loving Subject,* pp. 64–69. Not only are Abelard and Heloise exactly the social types identified by Bond as participants in the new Ovidian humanism—people with less established social networks of power—but they represent and perhaps aim at exactly the audience Bond envisages for the writings of such as Baudri of Bourgeuil—"the teachers and especially the students and pupils of the cathedral and monastic schools." Further, their correspondence illustrates well "the collapse of character and author associated with the emergence of the complete literary persona."
155. Pernoud, *Heloise and Abelard,* p. 11; cf. *HC* Monfrin ll. 25, 28–30, 59, 65, 69, 81, 84, 92, etc.: despite reference to "litteratoria disciplina," "studium litterarum/philosophie," 'rethorica' and similar phrases in the early lines of the *HC,* the universal (no pun intended) preoccupation seems to have been what passed for 'dialectical' disputation.
156. Despite Abelard's interest in that text, and despite the role alleged for the text by some in the later letter collection—see chapter 5 by Wilson and MacLeod in this volume.
157. See: Margaret H. King and Albert Rabil Jr., *Her Immaculate Hand: Selected Works By and About the Women Humanists of Quattrocento Italy;* Albert Rabil Jr., *Laura Cereta: Quattrocento Humanist;* Diana Robin, trans., *Laura Cereta: Collected Letters of a Renaissance Feminist.*
158. Könsgen, pp. 3ff. (foot of page).
159. 'Anhang 6,' pp. 67–68. See also Ian Thomson and Louis Perraud, eds. and trans., *Ten Latin Schooltexts of the Later Middle Ages: Translated Selections.*
160. Elsewhere in this chapter we suggest a few possible additions to Könsgen's annotations.
161. See Könsgen's annotations p. 23.
162. *Ep.* 5, ed. Muckle 88 (Radice 146–48).
163. Dares Phrygius as reported in J. Lemprière, *Classical Dictionary,* p. 121.
164. Cf. Heloise in #60 "nosti quoque, si tantum dignaris, quod nunquam fuit erga te duplici animo nec esse volo."
165. It is sometimes insisted that Abelard's decision to place Heloise back at Argenteuil after their marriage was in part motivated by an unwillingness to leave her in society where she could have the sexual relations that he himself could not. Juanita Ruys supplies the following references: Marjorie Muir Worthington, *The Immortal Lovers: Héloise and Abélard,* p. 57; Elizabeth Hamilton, *Héloïse,* pp. 49–50; D.W. Robertson, Jr., *Abelard and Heloise,* p. 58; Radice 22–23 and her "The French Scholar-Lover: Heloise," p. 94; Glenda McLeod, "'Wholly Guilty, Wholly Innocent': Self-Definition

in Héloise's Letters to Abélard," pp. 68, 84 n. 17; Linda S. Kauffman, *Discourses of Desire: Gender, Genre and Epistolary Fictions.*

166. Terence, *Hauton Timorumenos,* ed. Alfred Fleckeisen, pp. 51ff.
167. Terence, *Terence, The Comedies,* trans. Betty Radice, pp. 93ff.
168. Terence, *Hauton Timorumenos,* ed. Fleckenstein, p. 56: *ll.* 97–98.
169. Terence, *Hauton Timorumenos,* ed. Fleckenstein, p. 65: *ll.* 286–91.
170. Terence, *Hauton Timorumenos,* ed. Fleckenstein, p. 69: *ll.* 382–95 (Terence, *Terence, The Comedies,* trans. Radice, p. 118).
171. See Ward *Ciceronian Rhetoric* pp. 134ff.; Ward, "From Marginal Gloss"; Ward, "Women and Latin Rhetoric from Hrotsvit to Hildegard" in *Women and the Rhetorical Tradition,* eds. Christine Sutherland and Rebecca Sutcliffe; Ward, "The *Catena* Commentaries on the Rhetoric of Cicero."
172. Ward *Ciceronian Rhetoric* pp. 108ff.
173. *Ep.* 2, ed. Monfrin 115: *ll.* 169ff., Muckle 71 (Radice 114).
174. Giles Constable, "Letters and Letter-Collections," p. 31.
175. Constable, "Letters and Letter-Collections," pp. 32–33.
176. Robinson, "The *colores rhetorici,*" p. 215.
177. Constable, vol. 2: p. 31; Constable, "Letters and Letter-Collections," p. 35.
178. Bond, *The Loving Subject,* p. 45.
179. See Könsgen, pp. ix-xiv.
180. According to the *Repertorium der Artes dictandi des Mittelalters (Von den Anfängen bis um 1200)* of Franz Josef Worstbrock, Monika Klaes, and Jutta Lütten (vol. 1, Münsteresche Mittelalter-Schriften 66; Munich, 1992, p. 183), only a handful of such *artes dictandi* had been produced by that stage: Alberic of Montecassino's works, Adalbert of Samaria's *Praecepta dictaminum,* Hugh of Bologna's *Rationes dictandi prosaice* and Henry Francigena's *Aurea gemma.* These were all products of the Italian schools; the first surviving dictaminal text produced in France is the anonymous *Aurea gemma Gallica,* which Worstbrock et al. assign most likely to Tours around 1154.
181. The term is used by Heloise in a later letter, *Ep.* 2, ed. Muckle 73 (Radice 115): "you left many love-songs and verses which won wide popularity for the charm of their words and tunes [*prae nimia suavitate tam dictaminis quam cantus*] and kept your name continually on everyone's lips," a suggestive echo of the woman's words to her lover in #69.
182. The term, though current in late Latin, seems to have gained particular currency from the eleventh century on, to judge from its occurrences in the *Patrologia latina.*
183. Their occurrences are conveniently identified and listed by Könsgen, pp. 67–68.
184. Gian Carlo Alessio, ed., *Bene Florentini Candelabrum,* pp. 274–86.
185. Since here we are stressing the "formal," dictaminal elements of the de Vepria correspondence, we will revert to a more neutral position with respect to the correspondents' identities.
186. According to the *Oxford Classical Dictionary,* 'declamation,' the main pedagogical technique for rhetorical training, consisted of two main forms: the *controversia* ("a speech in character on one side of a fictional law case") and the *suasoria* ("a deliberative speech advising a course of action") Simon Hornblower and Antony Spawforth, eds., 3rd edn., p. 436. See also Carol Dana Lanham's article "Freshman Composition in the Early Middle Ages: Epistolography and Rhetoric Before the *Ars Dictaminis,*" where she explores the link between such schoolroom rhetorical exercises (*progymnasmata*) and the development of the *ars dictaminis.*
187. "Quippe qui rem quamlibet assumit laudare, debet tandem in partes distribuere singularumque partium qualitates summa cautione pensare et quamque secundum dignitatem congrue laudis celebritate conorare. Alioquin rei laudande iniuriam facit, qui [. . .] eleganciam enormi narracione deterit." All translations from Latin in this section

of the paper are by N. Chiavaroli unless otherwise indicated. Translations of the de Vepria letters are essentially those of *The Lost Love Letters* by Mews and Chiavaroli. Chiavaroli would also like to register his thanks to Mews, with whom many of the ideas in this section were discussed during the collaborative translation of the text.

188. Boncompagno da Signa, *Boncompagnus* 6.2.7: "Suasio de commendatione morum et pulchritudine corporea et nobilitate"; 6.2.8: Dissuasio propter morum ineptitudinem, deformitatem persone atque ignobilitatem." The text of the *Boncompagnus* has been extracted and partially edited by many scholars in succession but is only now being edited as a whole, by Steven M. Wight. His edition-in-progress may be found on the Internet at www.loop.com/~swight, from which the above letter rubrics are taken.
189. Ballanti (*Anonimo,* p. 9) thinks de Vepria himself rendered the letters anonymous, but Könsgen (p. 76) feels that even for him they were anonymous.
190. "Hos, rogo, ne versus oculus legat invidiosus / Hosque sciant nolo pectora plena dolo."
191. "Cautius modo te alloquor, si notare vis, cautius aggredior, pudor se amori contemperat, amorem verecundia cohibet, ne in immensum proruat, ut et nostris dulcibus votis copiam demus et famam, que de nobis orta est, paulatim attenuemus."
192. "Et est notandum, quod tam mulieres quam viri, cuiuscumque sint ordinis vel conditionis, debent epistole titulum in huiusmodi lasciviis taliter occultare, quod si littere ad aliquorum manus pervenerint, nequeant de facili cognosci": *Rota Veneris,* ed. Paolo Garbini (Rome: Salerno Editrice, 1996), p. 36—[this edition is based on that of Friedrich Baethgen].
193. The *Corona,* identified by Emil J. Polak in his *Medieval and Renaissance Letter Treatises and Form Letters. A Census of Manuscripts Found in Part of Western Europe, Japan, and the United States of America,* Davis Medieval Texts and Studies 9, and edited by Franco-Lucio Schiavetto, "Un'opera sconosciuta di Boncompagno."
194. In Carol Dana Lanham's study *'Salutatio' Formulas in Latin Letters to 1200: Syntax, Style and Theory,* especially pp. 7–8.
195. These are the usual cases, although as Lanham discusses (*'Salutatio' Formulas,* pp. 106ff.), they were occasionally challenged by some *dictatores.* Throughout this chapter, the term 'salutation' (or *salutatio*) will refer to the entire three-part structure, while the English term 'greeting' will be used specifically for the third part only.
196. "Si minor scripserit maiori, maior persona preponitur, minor subsequitur. Si maior minori, eadem semper precedit. Si par pari utralibet potest preponi et subponi iuxta placitum scriptoris. Salutatio vero diversa qualitate personam et ordinem designet, aliter enim superiorem, aliter inferiorem, aliter salutamus equalem" (Adalabertus Samaritanus, *Praecepta Dictaminum* 1.8–13). I have adopted the attested variant *designet* for Schmale's *designat.*
197. See Lanham, *'Salutatio' Formulas,* pp. 114–16.
198. "Tocius artis largitor et humani ingenii largissimus dator mei pectoris interna philosophie artis impleat pericia, quo te possim, dilectissime, ita salutare scriptis ad consensum mee voluntatis."
199. "Ego tamdiu tractavi cordis et corporis flagranti nisu, qualiter te, o gemma decora, apellarem, sed intencionem mei affectus hucusque distulit difficultas suspecti defectus" (#79). Cf. also #90 by the woman: " . . . pre nimio dolore cordis vix proferam aliqua verba salutacionis" [I can barely find any words of greeting because of the great grief in my heart].
200. "Merito specialis dilectionis amplectendo amore incendium tui amoris, quot ameno tempore redolent flores, tot percipere salutes." For the rhetorical 'quot-tot' topos, see Könsgen, p. 79.
201. "Quam michimet vellem mitti, tibi mitto salutem. / Nescio, quod magis hac esse salubre queat" (#82). I take the *salubre* of the second line to be a deliberate echo of *salutem,* playing on its two meanings of 'salutation' and 'well-being,' and possibly also its third as

'divine salvation'. Obviously, no English translation can hope to do justice to such density of meaning.

202. "Cedrine domui sue eburnea statua, supra quam domus innititur tota, nivis albedinem, lune fulgorem, solis candorem, stellarum splendorem, rosarum odorem, lilii pulchritudinem balsamique suavitatem, terre fertilitatem, celi serenitatem et quicquid in eorum dulcedinis comprehenditur ambitu." The translation is Dronke's, although I have removed the word 'from' at the beginning of the greeting, presumably a typographical error (*Women Writers,* p. 95).

203. For example, Guido Fava, in his *Summa dictaminis:* 62—Que persone non debent salutari and 63—Quando salutatio in epistola non ponatur . . . , ed. Augusto Gaudenzi in *Il Propugnatore* 23 ns. 3 (1890): 1.287–338. In his early treatise, the *Palma,* Boncompagno was evidently more interested in typology than protocol: "For I myself once obtained from the lord pope Celestine a letter, stamped with the apostolic bull, in which the same Pope completely denied a greeting to the Florentine consuls and the entire populace. Yet it was a letter and a complete one too, since it had a heading; that is, the name of the sender and recipient were placed at the beginning." [Nam ego ipse a domino papa Celestino unam epistolam impetravi apostolica bulla impressam, in qua idem papa consulibus Florentinis et toti populo salutationem penitus denegavit. Verumtamen epistola fuit et perfecta, quia titulum habebat id est nomen mittentis et recipientis erat in principio positum], Carl Sutter, *Aus Leben und Schriften des Magisters Boncompagno: ein Beitrag zur Italienischen Kulturgeschicte im Dreizehnten Jahrhundert,* pp. 105–27 [109].

204. "Cordi dimidio, parti anime mando, quod sum: tibi sum, dum vivo. Vale, quamvis nullum miseris michi salve." This occurs in letter 97 and may imply an error in sequencing.

205. "Quia uterque nostrum alter alterius conspectui modo in momento presentari valet, littere nostre salutacione non indigent. Cupio te tamen esse salvum, virtutum decore indutum, sophie gemmis circumtectum, morum honestate preditum, omnisque composicionis ornatu decoratum."

206. "Vale et, ut neminem mortalium michi compares, diligenter observa, quia ego in eadem circa te intencione tenaciter perseverabo. Salve, dilectissima, et me semper tuum in memoria habe!" (#72).

207. "Salve et tu, dilectissime, omni dulcedine digne!" (#73).

208. Lanham, *'Salutatio' Formulas,* pp. 9–12.

209. Accusative phrases: #1–16, 42–61, and 76–90; 'Whatever' phrases: #18–28, 55–56, 62–63, and 68–75; and Infinitive phrases: #6–10, 31–37, 44–54, 91–93, and 98–104.

210. As in the sequence of letters from #91 to #94, where the writers play with the imagery and symbolism of the sun and moon, light and darkness.

211. "Sol meus atque serena dies mea, lux mea, salve. / Tu mea dulcedo, te sine dulce nichil. / Si queris, quis verba tibi tam dulcia mittat: / Vita manes cuius, hoc facit ille tuus, / Cui potus lacrime te discedente fuere, / Cui dolor et gemitus mixta fuere cibus" (#108).

212. Assuming, of course, that they have not been omitted by the copyist without signaling. But given his particular focus on them, this would appear unlikely, and as Könsgen shows (pp. xxviii-xxx), de Vepria was careful to indicate where he elided text.

213. "Grata mentis mee benivolencia, pro se et officio suo tibi semper obnoxia, cum omnes quas vellet salutes expedire non potuit, permultas et iam siluit, ne plures enumerando offendere sibi videretur universas."

214. "Pauca quidem verba tua sunt, sed ea plura feci sepe relegendo, nec ego penso, quantum dicas, sed de quam fecundo corde procedat, quod dicis. Vale, dulcissima" (#19, in its entirety). The *dictatores* were often concerned with such questions as whether letters of this kind could be considered legitimate. Boncompagno, for example, thought they should, claiming in the *Palma* that while such letters might be termed 'incomplete,' they still constituted letters, in support of which he adduces a letter of Yvo of Chartres, com-

plete with episcopal seal (Carl Sutter, *Aus Leben und Schriften des Magisters Boncompagno,* p. 109).

215. "Reverende domine sue humilis servus eius devotum servitium" (#36).

216. "Sic enim vos appellare iam michi opus est, ut non dicam tu, sed vos, non dulcis, non cara, sed domina, quia non sum familiaris ut antea et vos michi nimis estis extranea."

217. A later use of the formal plural by the woman, on the other hand, appears more significant (#58). It is followed by several letters that suggest that a genuine rift had occurred. See also Appendix A below.

218. See the quotation from Adalbertus Samaritanus above.

219. Whenever Boncompagno furnished sample salutations in his *Rota Veneris,* he regularly had his correspondents place the other first (Boncompagno, *Rota Veneris,* ed. Garbini, pp. 30–35).

220. "Magne temeritatis est litteratorie tibi verba dirigere . . . ; nisi scirem vere dilectionis indefectam amiciciam tibi insitam esse, impolitas tam rudis stili litteras non tibi mittere presumerem."

221. "De favo sapiencie si michi stillaret guttula scibilitatis, aliqua olenti nectare cum omni mentis conamine alme dilectioni tue litterarum notulis conarer depingere" (#53).

222. "Quis ergo sum ego aut que in me facultas, ut tales litteras dictare queam, que me aureo sinu tuo, eburneis brachiis tuis, lactea cervice tua dignum exhibeant?"

223. This sense of the ineffability of love and the inadequacy of the letter to convey it has been identified as a major theme in love letters, especially as part of the discourse of the female correspondents. See Kauffman, *Discourses of Desire,* p. 254, who claims that "amorous discourses are always critiques of language, for the alphabet of the body has to be replaced with what is considered an inadequate system of signs: words."

224. "Clamor tuus recedat a me, verba tua ultra non audiam. Nam unde michi profutura multa speravi bona, inde lacrimabilia cordis creverunt suspiria" (#60). "Certe, quisquis verba tua diligencius consulit, reperiet ea non esse amantis, sed discidium querentis; nusquam in eis cor molle respicio, sed pectus durum et amori inexpugnabile adverto" (#61).

225. "Si inesset michi tanta sermonum facecia, ut verbis tuis prudenter respondere valerem, quantocunque decentius possem, libenti animo tibi responderem. At tamen, licet satisfacere non valeam, pro posse et modulo scienciole mee respondeo" (#62).

226. "In litteris, quas misisti, mature fuerunt sentencie, racionalis et ordinata composicio; nunquam certe aptius vidi dispositas. Ego, dulcissima, multas horas deo volente tibi prestabo dulcissimas et letissimas" (#63).

227. *Ep.* 2, ed. Muckle 68 (Radice 109).

228. *Ep.* 4, ed. Muckle 77 (Radice 127).

229. Yet Abelard will again avoid the subtext and respond to Heloise's complaint on a superficial level only: the pre-placing of her name was appropriate, he retorts, for once she became a nun, she also became the bride of Christ, and thus, ipso facto, his superior. It is not dissimilar to the man's adoption of a pedagogical tone seen earlier; in both cases, the male correspondents seem to have missed the point. See Juanita Ruys, "Role-Playing in the *Letters* of Heloise and Abelard: Readings of the Correspondence Between Heloise and Abelard," p. 53ff.

230. Dronke, "Heloise's *Problemata* and *Letters:* Some Questions of Form and Content" in Trier pp. 53–73, [p. 56]; Stone, "Heloise: *la très sage abbesse,*" p. 26. According to Constable "the *ars dictaminis* and formulary of Albert of Samaria, the earliest of the known Bolognese *dictatores* [to be used in France], appear in conjunction with a group of French letters of about 1130/50 and with the letter collection of Prior Peter of St. John at Sens, who died about 1146" (Constable, vol. 2: p. 32). It is highly unlikely, therefore, that such materials were being taught or were available for imitation in the Paris of the years A.D. 1116 to 1118.

231. Dronke, "Heloise's *Problemata,*" p. 55.

232. Neither Martin Camargo nor Constant Mews, who have been kind enough to communicate their views orally to us, are prepared to support Dronke's arguments in regard to the relationship between Heloise's *cursus* patterns, as evident in the known letters, and Adalbert of Samaria's *Precepta dictaminum.*
233. Martin Camargo, *Ars Dictaminis, Ars Dictandi,* p. 26.
234. Tore Janson, *Prose Rhythm in Medieval Latin from the 9th to the 13th Century,* p. 35.
235. Excluding 'Vale'.
236. The selection of *cursus* patterns has been taken, by no exhaustive search, from Janson, *Prose Rhythm;* Giovanni Cremaschi, *Guida allo studio del latino medievale,* pp. 110–111; N. Denholm-Young, "The *cursus* in England," in his *Collected Papers,* pp. 42ff.; Terence Tunberg, "Prose Styles and *cursus,*" pp. 111ff.; and Paget Toynbee, *Dantis Alagherii Epistolae: The Letters of Dante, Emended Text with Introduction, Translation, Notes and Indices, and Appendix on the Cursus,* 2nd edn., pp. 224–47, and other basic textbooks. The provisional nature of the method adopted will, we think, be justified by the conclusions reached. We have ignored, for this exercise, the *cursus medius,* the *cursus trispondaicus,* apparently a French specialty (Camargo, *Ars Dictaminis,* p. 26), and some other less common cadences dealt with from time to time in the manuals.
237. This latter exercise requires for 'V' in two instances a monosyllable to be taken unstressed with the previous word to make '2 + pp,' and, for 'M,' on one occasion, a monosyllable needs to be assmilated to a previous 'p3' making a 'pp4'.
238. *Women Writers* and "Heloise's *Problemata.*" In *Women Writers,* pp. 110–136, Dronke stresses Heloise's verbal artistry; preference for *cursus tardus* and *velox;* careful letter-structure; balanced sentence structure ("tanto . . . quanto"); rhyming antitheses; word play; symmetrical questions and parellelisms; "rhetorical and poetic shaping" (p. 126); "rhymes, rhythmic symmetries and cadences" (p. 127); and "parallelistic rhymed prose, heightened prose, laden with rhymes" (p. 135).
239. See the remarks of Terence Tunberg in *Medieval Latin,* pp. 112–13: the leading authors of the eleventh and twelfth centuries, many of them monks, "emphasized symmetry and parallelism in the structure of their ample sentences through the use of such devices as *isocolon . . . , anaphora . . . ,* and end rhyme. In many cases, especially by the mid-twelfth century, the harmony of formal prose is enhanced by the practice of ending sentences and clauses with accentual rhythms, or *cursus. . . .*" Classicism (involving, among other things, avoidance of [monastic] parallelism of sound and structure, and cultivation of a more periodic style), and, in the more dictaminal texts, what might be called 'manneristic' writing is progressively evident. See, further, J. O. Ward, in *Classical Rhetoric and Medieval Historiography,* pp. 133–35.
240. *HC,* ed. Monfrin ll. 288–90.
241. *Artemisia* (1997), directed by Agnes Merlet and starring Michel Serrault and Valentina Cervi, et al. For the "facts" of the matter, as far as they can be obtained, see Germaine Greer, *The Obstacle Race: The Fortunes of Women Painters and Their Work,* ch. 10. It is worth noting that Artemisia in the filmed reconstruction is about the age that used to be assumed for Heloise (mid-teens). In the film Camille Claudel, the "heroine" (noted perfunctorily in Ionel Jianu, *Rodin,* pp. 65, 123–24) also shares a sense of disillusion, blunting of artistic talent by another (male), a sense of imprisonment/confinement by and for the convenience of males, with Heloise.
242. Bond, *The Loving Subject,* p. 62.
243. It might not be impossible to render the longer letters more similar to the de Vepria collection by the deletion of certain paragraphs. For example, if we were to delete from *Ep.* 2, ed. Muckle 68–73 the following material: p. 68 between "Erant memini . . ." and " . . . consummasti" and "Per ipsum . . . participes habeas"; p. 69 "Deo autem . . . complexa sum," "non matrimonii foedera . . . imperatrix," "Duo autem fateor . . . accendit

invidiam," "Dic unum si vales . . . Deo mancipasti," "Memento, obsecro . . . inchoaverim principio," and "Cum me ad turpes . . . excitares?"

244. The following review is designed simply to develop at close range the idea that 'V' = Abelard and 'M' = Heloise. Since Constant Mews's book on the de Vepria collection is accompanied by a translation no systematic attempt has been made here to convey any exact idea of the contents of each letter.
245. See Bond, *The Loving Subject,* p. 61 in regard to the manuscript and chronological order of Baudri of Bourgeuil's letter-poems.
246. We cite the de Vepria correspondence by the number of each letter assigned in Könsgen's text, followed by 'V' to indicate that the man, here considered to be Abelard, is speaking, 'M' to indicate that the woman, here considered to be Heloise, is speaking.
247. Bond, *The Loving Subject,* and Dronke, *Women Writers.*
248. Abelard claims to have a tired mind of which Heloise is the sole solace; there is no reference to Abelard's "youth" (which one might expect in a 'set-piece' letter).
249. *HC,* ed. Monfrin l. 252.
250. The curious tartness of this reference (which contradicts *HC,* ed. Monfrin l. 292) may be expunged by inferring that the "viriditatem" is to last as long as life, but the positioning of the elements in the *salutatio* does not seem to support this interpretation: "to her heartfelt love, to the one sweetly redolent of every aroma, [she] with her heart and body, with the flowers of your youth becoming exhausted/fading/pining away [Lucan/Vulgate], [offers] the bloom of eternal happiness."
251. E. Norden, *Die antike Kunstprosa vom VI J/h v.Chr. bis in die Zeit der Renaissance,* vol. 2: pp. 760–63.
252. Könsgen, p. 9: #21 ("et ex ipsius experimento rei esse, quod est . . . equipolenter") and #13 ('benivolencia' and 'officio' represent concepts that would have been met with early in an acquaintance with the *auctores* in rhetoric: *Ad Her.* 1.2.2, 1.4.6, etc.).
253. See Bond, *The Loving Subject,* p. 88 for such pretensions (in a male) as an artistic pretence.
254. On the notion of men and women living equally and freed of sexual passion at the time see Mary Skinner, "Benedictine Life for Women," p. 102.
255. The context is doubtless amatory: cf. Ovid, *Ars Amatoria* 3.566.
256. Perhaps when Abelard was living in Fulbert's house, since his presence there did not in itself abrogate the need for wax tablets: exercises set would still have to be completed and the fiction of their apparent relationship could always be used as a code for their real relationship: the wax tablet exchanges could easily therefore function as both *exercitia* and as communication. It seems unlikely that the intimate relationship already reflected in these letters could be earlier.
257. D. M. Stone, "Heloise: *la très sage abbesse,*" p. 21: "the present paper [. . .] has a [. . .] modest aim—to view the monastic experience of Heloise in terms of some virtues dear to the heart of monasticism [. . .] chastity, poverty, obedience and silence." Stone claims that "we have no evidence that the source of her [Heloise's monastic] practice [of these virtues] lay in Christian spirituality" (p. 24) and feels that Heloise's exceptional learning (Latin, Greek, and Hebrew) derived from her time at Argenteuil (p. 26). Rejecting the argument that the nuns at Argenteuil before their expulsion at the hands of Abbot Suger behaved in an 'immoral' manner (pp. 23–24), she asks: "might it have been a rather too close acquaintance with worldly literature that gave Suger the opportunity for criticism of the nuns?" (p. 26). After a look at Abelard's *Ep.* 9 and the *Problemata Heloissae,* she concludes that "we see a monastic influence on Heloise's love of learning [. . .] more clearly than we can see a monastic influence on her practice of the virtues."
258. When Abelard is resident inside Fulbert's house.

259. As commonly in classical love poetry (J. N. Adams, *The Latin Sexual Vocabulary,* pp. 197–98).
260. Cf. *Ep.* 2, ed. Muckle 68: "falsorum machinationem accessisti."
261. *Ad Her.* 1.2.2, 1.4.6, etc.
262. An idea much circulated in what Bond calls "Romanesque France," *The Loving Subject,* p. 49.
263. How many rooms did Fulbert's house boast? Did it have a kind of separate area or "apartment" that a teacher of the rank of Abelard might have used as his quarters? And would this have been some noticeable distance from where Fulbert's niece slept? Régine Pernoud has Abelard longing "for the curfew, for the dying away of noise within the unlit house, for the moment when he could safely steal along the corridor and up the stairs to the door which led to paradise" (*Heloise and Abelard,* p. 58)!
264. See Bond, *The Loving Subject,* p. 54 (or his "'Iocus amoris,'" pp. 175–76) for a recent statement of the position here.
265. "opuscula enim mea haec et alia nullis impressa tabulis dictando et scribendo, scribenda etiam pariter commentando immutabiliter paginis inferebam" (Guibert of Nogent to be found in: Guibert de Nogent, *Guibert de Nogent, Autobiographie,* p. 144; Guibert, *A Monk's Confession: The Memoirs of Guibert of Nogent,* trans. P. J. Archambault, p. 63; and *Self and Society in Medieval France,* p. 91.
266. The use of 'candidus' or a variant is nevertheless a commonplace of 'erotic' poetry; cf. "candore gulae," "candentes dentes," "crura candidiora nive," "papilla nive," "candore Dianam," "candor inest Veneri," etc., in Therese Latzke, "Die Carmina erotica der Ripollsammlung," pp. 183–84.
267. *HC,* ed. Muckle 16; *HC,* ed. Monfrin l. 91.
268. Abelard had, I am informed by Juanita Ruys, a double-sided seal, which is referred to at the end of Roscellin's letter to Abelard.
269. Catullus, poems 30.1; 64.58, 123, 249; etc.
270. Catullus, poem 83.3, etc.
271. Catullus, poem 8.11; Tibullus 2.6.28, K. Quinn, *Latin Explorations: Critical Studies in Roman Literature* (London: Routledge, 1963), p. 133, etc.
272. *Women Writers,* pp. 94–95.
273. [Anonymous], *Carmina Burana* 1:2 *Text: Die Liebeslieder,* #169: p. 285. Cf. also the "sed michi sydus hebet" of #20.2 (Könsgen, p. 9).
274. M 117: ll. 269ff., *Ep.* 2, ed. Muckle 73; for *voluptas* as sexual pleasure see Adams, *Sexual Vocabulary,* pp. 197–98.
275. M 117: ll. 269ff.
276. M 318; all students were normally required to register with a master, the only real guarantee of existence and progress through a very informal arrangement of study possibilities. For this practice in later times, see Hilde de Ridder-Symoens, ed., *Universities in the Middle Ages,* vol. 1 of *A History of the University in Europe,* p. 157. Robert de Sorbonne put the matter this way in 1215: "nullus sit scolaris Parisius, qui certum magistrum non habeat" (*Chartularium Universitatis Parisiensis,* eds. H. Denifle and E. Châtelain vol. 1: p. 79). While it cannot be argued that thirteenth-century practices date back to Abelard's day, it is reasonable to assume that some informal equivalent of the practice later known as "registration" existed and that what Fulbert is doing is ensuring that Abelard would be Heloise's *magister.* Abelard himself, in the *HC,* refers to his *magisterium* (Monfrin 33), his aspiration "ad scolarum regimen" (Monfrin 46), his "scolarum nostrarum tirocinio" ([Monfrin 58] and cf. Könsgen, #98, "Tyroni"), to William of Champeaux as his *preceptor* (Monfrin 71); he uses the phrase "publicas scolas exercere" (Monfrin 80), describes the position of leading teacher in an art as "me dialectice studium regente" ([Monfrin 108–109] and see "in scolis . . . preminere" [Monfrin

226–27]), speaks of "succeeding to the schools" (Monfrin 105), "adhering to our master" (Monfrin 103), "hastening to our teaching [*doctrinam*]" (Monfrin 104), and "retiring from teaching" [*a regimine scolarum cessare* (Monfrin 141)]. To 'give a lecture' is to assume the role of *expositor* and to proceed *ad lectionem* (Monfrin 203–204), with a second and third lecture being described as "ad secundum et terciam lectionem concurrere," the *auditores* then busily occupying themselves with making copies of the previously heard lecture(s) ("de transcribendis glosis" [Monfrin 218–20]). Apparently a successful lecturer would be asked to formally gloss a text in accordance with the tenor of his lectures ("me secundum hunc nostre lectionis tenorem ad glosandum compellerent [auditores]" [Monfrin 216]). Quite how this latter was achieved is not made clear, whether through further lectures, or some form of formal 'publication' alongside or beyond lectures. When Anselm of Laon "forbade me to exercise further in the place where he held the *magisterium* the work of glossing that I had begun" [mihi interdixit inceptum glosandi opus in loco magisterii sui amplius exercere (Monfrin 232–33)]—work, we remember that had been undertaken because Abelard felt he needed no further *magisterium* "ad expositiones sanctorum intelligendas" (Monfrin 195)—it seems, from the excuses Anselm alleged, and the reaction of the *scolares* when they heard about the ban, that a fairly informal practice prevailed. Abelard must have provided his "opus glosandi" in the form of aural lecturing, more or less supplementary or alternative to the lectures of the teacher who "held the *magisterium*".

277. *Ad Her.* 4.20.28.
278. *Ad Her.* 4.15.22.
279. Richard A. Lanham, *A Handlist of Rhetorical Terms,* 2nd edn., p. 33.
280. Cf. Isidore of Seville, "De rhetorica," ed. Halm 520.3–4: "aliae exhortativae, cum ad sententiam provocamus . . . aliae dehortativae, cum a contrario vitio peccatoque reducimus."
281. *De inv.* 2.59.177, 2.53.159, etc.
282. Did Heloise ever 'visit' the coutryside around Paris? Or return to Argenteuil? Or visit her mother (McLeod pp. 9, 12), if she was still alive, or some other relative?
283. Cf. Könsgen n. to #25.
284. John Marenbon, *The Philosophy of Peter Abelard,* pp. 258ff. on "*voluntas* and its cognate verb *velle.*"
285. Cf. *HC,* ed. Monfrin l. 1290; *Luke* 14.30.
286. See meaning no. 4 in the OLD, p. 1575: col. a.
287. Könsgen, p. 16: "colloquio et presencia." See *HC,* ed. Monfrin l. 299: "jocundis . . . colloquiis."
288. Many of these letters are little more than a line or two, copied without deletions by Johannes de Vepria. They are thus indeed suggestive of a series of actual wax tablet exchanges.
289. See *HC,* ed. Monfrin l. 363.
290. #29 (M): Ovid, *Tristia* 1.3.80 reading *verba* not *dicta.*
291. Cf. also Jakob Werner, *Beiträge zur Kunde der lateinischen Literatur des Mittelalters,* 2nd edn., #116: pp. 45–46 (reference courtesy of Mews, *The Lost Love Letters*).
292. #38b: l. 6 = the opening of Catullus, poem 76.
293. E.g., #29: Terence, *Andria* 1.1.134 and Ovid, *Tristia* 1.3.80 or the "si fas est" of #43 (see Catullus, poem 51); #42: "amiciam ad calculum" and the same phrase in #50.
294. This was the moment when "writing, desire and self begin to merge" (Bond, *The Loving Subject,* p. 62).
295. For background see Marenbon, *Philosophy,* chap. 13 "Virtue, love and merit" and *Excursus* II pp. 298ff. "Love, selflessness and Heloise."
296. *Ep.* 2, ed. Monfrin 114–15, Muckle 71 (Radice 114).
297. *Ad Her.* 1.2.3: 'dispositio est ordo et distributio rerum, quae demonstrat quid quibus locis sit conlocandum.'

298. "litteratorie tibi verba dirigere"; compare Stephen of Blois's "litteratorie tibi mandare," (epistle 1). The two letters from Stephen to Adela are in *Epistulae et chartae ad historiam primi belli sacri spectantes,* ed. H. Hagenmeyer, letters IV (pp. 138–40) and X (pp. 149–52). I thank my colleague John Pryor for bringing these letters to my attention in the present context. See now his Stephen of Blois: Sensitive New-Age Crusader, or Victim of History" *Arts: The Journal of the Sydney University Arts Association* 20 (1998): 267–74. The *salutationes* of the letters should also be compared with those found in the de Vepria collection. See Bond, *The Loving Subject,* chap. 5 for Adela.
299. "ad unguem": Horace, *Sat.* 1.5.32, used of Fonteius Capito, "a man of great abilities and elegant manners sent by Anthony to settle his political disputes with Augustus" (John Lemprière, *Classical Dictionary,* p. 138).
300. Persius helps Thierry of Chartres make a personal point at the outset of his lectures on the *De inventione* (*The Latin Rhetorical Commentaries by Thierry of Chartres,* ed. K. M. Fredborg, p. 49).
301. Persius, *Sat.* 1.96–97.
302. Using *conduplicatio* (*Ad Her.* 4.28.38, Bond, *The Loving Subject,* p. 74) and a variety of other *colores.*
303. *sciolus:* Jerome, *Letters* 48.18, 58.5, and 125.16 (Lewis and Short, *A Latin Dictionary,* 1933, p. 1644, col. b; Könsgen, p. 26, n. 7).
304. See Mews as on p. 75 [67] of his *Peter Abelard.*
305. Ovid, *Met.* 7.826.
306. Könsgen, p. 28; Lewis and Short, but not the OLD, give Tacitus, *Or.* 20, as the only comparable classical usage of this word.
307. H. [Cicero], *Ad Herennium De ratione dicendi (Rhetorica ad Herennium),* p. 197.
308. Caplan, p. 349.
309. John O. Ward, "Quintilian and the Rhetorical Revolution of the Middle Ages."
310. Könsgen, p. 29 n. 9: Abelard seems to express the sentiment of Persius, *Sat.* 1.47, but with the phraseology of Pliny, *Nat. Hist.* 11.159 or Cicero, *Nat. Deor.* 1.101.
311. C. S. Baldwin, *Medieval Rhetoric and Poetic (to 1400) Interpreted from Representative Works,* p. 17ff.
312. "nosque etiam absentes scriptis internuntiis invicem liceret presentare et pleraque audacius scribere quam colloqui, et sic semper jocundis interesse colloquiis . . . In huius itaque adolescentule amorem totus inflamatus occasionem quesivi qua eam mihi domestica et cotidiana conversatione familiarem efficerem et facilius ad consensum traherem."
313. Cf. *HC,* ed. Monfrin l. 302: "familiarem."
314. The gender of "benivolus . . . qui . . . querit . . . qui . . . expectaverit . . . locuta . . . anima mea" is difficult for either hypothesis.
315. Some members of Sydney University Medieval Latin Reading Group were not unduly worried by any implied contradiction here between #61 and #59: the latter might refer to sexual transgression, the former to some larger neglect in a relationship.
316. Bond, *The Loving Subject,* pp. 45 and 65. According to Bond "the word was also used from Ovid on to imply sexual union."
317. Letter 62, Könsgen, p. 62.
318. Letter 63 (V) seems to be the teacher's compliments for exercises well completed, with the promise of long lessons appropriate to the spirit of *HC,* ed. Monfrin l. 319: "ut quotiens mihi a scolis reverso vaccaret"; #66 (M) is a tyro verse composition of the sort Heloise might have written early in their relationship, to demonstrate competence in work assigned; and #69 (M) looks like a poetic form of #60: some phrases pick up earlier expressions (#69: "eius sermonis credula" and #49: "sit michi credula benignitas"; #69: "pignus fidei" = #60: "rumpi fedus"; #69: "cur tam raro venit" = #62: "si vincula . . . ," #49, 54, etc); others touch upon ideas common to the Roman love poets

(e.g., #69: *ll.* 15–16 = Catullus, poems 5.2–3, 11; 7.11–12) and the whole is in the form of what the author of the *Ad Herennium* calls "conformatio" (4.53.66)—used elsewhere by Heloise (#23). Just when we have convinced ourselves that #69 is a set piece we read on and the twist of pace perplexes us: Heloise is experimenting with different sweetnesses of composition [*dictamen*] in an attempt to communicate with Abelard. Her mind wanders off into obscure analogies: Abelard is at the centre of every kind of love for her, as the heart itself is seated in the midst of the [body's] blood; just so Abelard is at the center of all kinds of *dictamen,* but it is beyond the 'valency' of her mind to find the key; words become darts piercing the heart, Abelard himself becomes part of the heart: she addresses that part of her heart and wonders why it can have broken loose from the seal, the tenacious anchor of love. There is a sudden shift to the garb of mourning ("Idcirco cultrix cineris . . .") and the letter ends with Heloise confronting Abelard and his miseries (#50 and 61) with her miseries.

319. Letter 73 (M) seems unrelated to the ebb and flow of personal problems, a piece of school poetic *ecphrasis,* perhaps as "set" by Abelard, or as thought appropriate by Heloise in view of her reading in the classical poetic *auctores* (cf. the use of the word *undisonus,* l. 12). Letter 71 (M) seems to express a disturbed resignation, an acceptance of Abelard's instructions (in handling the looming crisis of *HC,* ed. Monfrin l. 379ff.?), another reference to her "inornatas litteras," an inability to concentrate on her studies and a wish to be with, speak with him, despite the bitterness that poisons her mind. Her *valedictio* puns bitterly on the *salutatio* of his #67. The *salutatio* of #72 (V) picks up the discontents of #59 and 61 and the prose portion of #69 (M); it seems to be adjusting *amicitia/amor* theory (Bond, *The Loving Subject,* p. 50, etc.) to practice: Abelard has recovered some intimacy ("receptus in graciam") lost by earlier "peccata" (#61). Letter 74 (V) is in a similar vein, without a *salutatio,* and apparently overwhelmed by consciousness of an *iniuria* done Heloise by her partner's "stupid and thoughtless hastiness." While he elsewhere thanks Heloise for her deeds (as distinct from words, cf. #22), Abelard now applies the same distinction to reverse effect: "what I said was only words, *nichil significans.*" Abelard apparently uttered a *vox cassa* against Heloise and he refers to it again in #75, which decries again the emptiness of words and the vainness of a certain "promise" in writing made by Abelard, a promise that has not come down to us in the extant correspondence.

320. Ernst Robert Curtius, *European Literature and the Latin Middle Ages,* pp. 159–65, and cf. #50: "ut non Tullium legisse, sed ipsi Tullio precepta dedisse videaris."

321. Parodied in Ovid's *Ars amatoria* 1.453, p. 112: "this is the kind of parody which involves mocking one's own pretensions."

322. The balance of citation in Lewis and Short and OLD for *circumcisus* (and the word is often found in a rhetorical context) suggests that it means 'trimmed and polished'.

323. Vergil, *Georgics* IV.168.

324. *Statius with an English translation* vol. 1: p. 371.

325. To Könsgen's annotation (p. 44 n. 7) add Terence, *Phormio* 267.

326. Not the malevolence of those ("avunculus autem ipsius atque domestici ejus" [*HC,* ed. Monfrin ll. 566–67]) who wished to bring them together!

327. *HC,* ed. Monfrin ll. 562–66: the period after the clandestine wedding ceremony during which the couple were living apart. Heloise living—and arguing—with Fulbert.

328. *HC,* ed. Monfrin ll. 570–572: the letter refers retrospectively to the redoubling of Abelard's *honor,* had the two of them been permitted to live together to the end (presumably adding her literary fame to his scholastic fame); "now" she goes on, "I choose rather to be cut off by the peril of death, than by sweet life to be deprived of the joy [*gaudium,* used in #2, 7, etc. and in the classical love poets, with sexual undertones] that comes from the sight of you." The reference to *amica* in the *salutatio* of #76 and in *HC,* ed. Monfrin ll. 547–48, to "quantum leticie et exultacionis" in #78 and to "cum summa exultatione" in *HC,* ed.

Monfrin ll. 392–93, to "honor . . . geminasse" in #78 and "honestius" in *HC,* ed. Monfrin l. 547 (etc.) suggests this moment in their lives.

329. On "Act, intention and consent" in Abelard see Marenbon, *Philosophy,* chap. 11.
330. *HC,* ed. Monfrin l. 553: "nec me sustineret offendere" and cf. the implications of M 637–38.
331. *HC,* ed. Monfrin ll. 545–578: "si quicquid Caesar . . ." is picked by M 548 and M p. 114.160 (*Ep.* 2, ed. Muckle 71), M 541 matches M p. 115.170 (*Ep.* 2, ed. Muckle p. 71), *gaudia* (#82.6) is picked by *gaudia* (*HC,* ed. Monfrin l. 551), *dolor et luctus* (#82.7) is picked by *dolor* in *HC,* ed. Monfrin l. 556, Abelard's rueful ascription of prophetic powers to Heloise in *HC,* ed. Monfrin l. 558 is ironically preceded by Heloise's ascription of prophetic powers to Abelard in #82.14 (although he is enjoined in a further irony, to live prophetically as a woman, a Sybil).
332. Vergil, *Aeneid* IV.494 and *Georgic* IV.515.
333. "After the Trojan War, Nestor retired to Greece, where he enjoyed, in the bosom of his family, the peace and tranquillity which were due to his wisdom, his services, and his old age. . . . From that circumstance, therefore, it was usual among the Greeks and the Latins, when they wished a long and happy life to their friends, to wish them to see the years of Nestor" (Lemprière, *Classical Dictionary,* p. 439).
334. *Ep.* 2, ed. Muckle 71–72 (Radice 115).
335. For the biblical foundations of the language here see Könsgen's annotation *ad loc.* Cf. also " . . . tu post Deum solus es fundator, solus hujus oratorii constructor, solus hujus congregationis edifficator. Nichil hic super alienum edificasti fundamentum" M p. 113: *ll.* 77–79 (*Ep.* 2, ed. Muckle 69).
336. Abelard, the "sapiens architectus" of 1 Cor. 3.10.
337. See poem #60 above.
338. 1 Cor. 3.10, 9, 16.
339. 1 Cor. 3.9.
340. Vergil, *Eclogue* X.8–11, and cf. the way in which, elsewhere in Vergil, a forest echoes the laments of a singing, poetic lover who has lost his wife (*Georgic* IV.510).
341. The references in #88 to will and intention ("voluntarius. . . . intencione mentis") recall passages from *Peter Abelard's* [later] *Ethics,* ed. and trans. D. E. Luscombe, p. 32 and p. 140 *sv.* "intention." Cf. also "verba" and "mittentis voluntatem" in #89.
342. #48 and see Könsgen, p. 136 *sv.* "*unicus.*"
343. M p. 117: "Unico suo post Christum unica sua in Christo." See Juanita Feros Ruys, "Role-Playing in the *Letters* of Abelard and Heloise," p. 53ff.
344. *paronomasia, Ad Her.* 4.21.29, eight types.
345. See #87.6 for a nuance in this word that Abelard would have been expected to grasp, and the use of the word in Vergil, *Aeneid* IV.1 and 5 (on which R. G. Austin comments: "possibly *cura* here has a wider sense than in line 1, implying her [Dido's] general 'worry' at her situation" [*P. Vergili Maronis Aeneidos Liber Quartus,* pp. 26–27); cf. also Vergil, *Aenied* X.217 and Abelard, *Carmen ad Astrolabium,* l. 201.
346. Lucan, *Phars.* 8.67.
347. Ovid, *Met.* 2.355.
348. This poem, placed late in the collection, is a generalized statement about parting and return (compare "te discedente" in line 5 with the same phrase in #45), though the reference to "pudor et metus" suggests the period of the relationship after the clandestine marriage.
349. Taking "nobis . . . rapiunt" as the 'royal plural' rather than as referring to both Abelard *and* Heloise, which, of course, it might.
350. *HC,* ed. Monfrin l. 333: "amori penitus vaccabamus."
351. *HC,* ed. Monfrin l. 402: (Fulbert's *pudor*) and 624: (Abelard's *pudor*). Cf. *Carmina Burana,* "in trutina mentis dubia fluctuant contraria lascivus amor et pudicitia" cited in Köns-

gen, p. 54 n. 1. Cf. also Therese Latzke, "Die Carmina erotica der Ripollsammlung," p. 164.

352. Juanita Ruys informs me that this expression often implies pregnancy in such texts as the *Gesta Romanorum*.
353. Not in R. E. Latham, *Revised Medieval Latin Wordlist from British and Irish Sources;* Alexander Souter, *A Glossary of Later Latin to 600 A.D.;* Leo F. Stelten, *Dictionary of Ecclesiastical Latin;* Lewis and Short; or OLD.
354. Song of Songs 3.6: "per desertum . . . ex aromatibus," etc. Also: Prudentius, *Liber Cathemerinon* 5.89 in *Prudentius,* ed. and trans. Thomson, vol. 1: p. 42: l. 89: "cui ieuna eremi saxa loquacibus" "at thy command the barren rocks of the desert gush with babbling springs"; also: *The Last Poets of Imperial Rome,* trans. Harold Isbell, pp. 139 and 175.
355. Period after the clandestine wedding ceremony, living apart, Heloise living with Fulbert and arguing with him.
356. Ovid, *Heroides and Amores,* in *Ovid in Six Volumes,* 1986 p. 11.
357. Bond, *The Loving Subject,* p. 98.
358. Bond, *The Loving Subject,* p. 240, n. 64.
359. Again the image is taken from the Song of Songs.
360. Compare the phrase *novus est* with the *Carmina Burana,* lines: "Oh, Oh, Oh! / totus floreo, / iam amore virginali, / totus ardeo, / novus, novus amor / est, quo pereo" (W. Meyers, A. Hilka, O. Schumann, *Carmina Burana* I, Text, 2 'Die Liebeslieder', Heidelberg: Winter 1971 (2nd edn.), p. 298 (poem #179).
361. Period after the clandestine wedding ceremony, living apart, Heloise living with Fulbert and arguing with him.
362. John Lemprière, *Classical Dictionary,* p. 701.
363. See again the extract "in trutina" from the *Carmina Burana* cited in Könsgen, p. 54, n. 1.
364. *Ad Her.* 1.1.1: *copia dicendi,* a standard phrase for 'eloquence'.
365. 'agreeable' / 'ingratiating' / 'fawning' / 'deceptive' / 'being different' / 'newness' / 'unexpectedness' (?)
366. *Ep.* 5, ed. Muckle 88 (Radice 146); and for Heloise's reference, *Ep.* 4, ed. Monfrin 120, Muckle 79 (Radice 130). See also #109–111, which seem to imply such visits or their prospect.
367. *HC,* ed. Monfrin l. 114, 141 for these terms, and Radice 130/M p. 120: ll. 111–13, for Abelard "presiding over the schools" while Heloise was at Argenteuil.
368. Astrolabe?
369. M p. 120: ll. 111–13.

CHAPTER 5

TEXTUAL STRATEGIES IN THE ABELARD/HELOISE CORRESPONDENCE

Katharina Wilson and Glenda McLeod

The letters, viewed in the light of assumed parity, tell the story of Abelard's rhetorical if not ethical conversion.

When readers have not been plagued with the question of the authenticity of the famous correspondence between Abelard and Heloise, often they have focused on the question of Heloise's conversion.[1] Do the letters illustrate a transformation in the heroine—spiritual, psychological, or rhetorical—or do they not? In fact, when seen as a rhetorical exercise, the correspondence frequently has been reduced to a didactic demonstration of such a conversion: a triumph of (male) intellect over (female) flesh.[2] The explosively sensual passages in Heloise's letters are then explained away as mere rhetorical devices meant to brighten the argumentative contrast or raise the argumentative stakes between the combatants. Other commentators have argued differently, of course, maintaining that the Heloise of the letters did not repent and that in fact the correspondence reveals a portrait of a stubborn woman determined to remain true to her own feelings and experiences, even if those are considered sinful.[3]

We suggest that a small shift in the question may be appropriate. By making Heloise's conversion the issue, one categorically assumes that the Abelard of the correspondence controls the debate, that *her* presentation (not his) is (or is not) being perfected and changed. Despite overwhelming evidence to the contrary concerning the real Abelard and Heloise,[4] rarely have the letters themselves been examined in the light of the moral or even intellectual parity that such attributions recommend.[5] In fact, many readers have missed what the correspondents did not: although throughout the *Historia calamitatum* Abelard insists on his conversion and salvation, precious little in his attitude or tribulations has changed. We argue that once the letters are viewed in the light of assumed parity, they indeed tell the story of a conversion, but the conversion is Abelard's, not Heloise's, and it is a rhetorical rather than ethical one.

In making this argument, we intend neither to affirm nor to deny the correspondence's authenticity through rhetorical strategies. Whether Heloise and Abelard wrote these letters does not affect the argument that they evince a tense and highly fluent debate between well-matched opponents engaged in a sophisticated game of one-upmanship, a game in which "Heloise" upstages and successfully masters the master "Abelard" by outperforming him in the very genres and on the very terms he chooses in the *Historia calamitatum*. When we ascribe motivational intentions, however, we side with the emerging consensus headed by Peter Dronke and simply accept the authenticity of the letters on others' authority rather than maintain our previous stance of agnosticism. Looking closely at the rhetorical strategies and attempting to ascribe motivational significance to them, we find ourselves in increasing accord with Dronke's argument.[6]

The Heloise of the correspondence effects such a coup by calling on the techniques of academic disputation, techniques once central to her original relationship with a man who is now "her master, or rather father, husband or rather brother."[7] She wins this debate and (metaphorically) achieves her status as a *magistra* because, like any ambitious young academic, she applies to her argument the same sources and often the same methodologies as her teacher but does so more accurately and persuasively.[8] Her response is studded with intricate analogies and contrasts—to Abelard's *Historia calamitatum* and his letters as well as to various *auctoritates*—which, although often manifested in rich, multifarious, and intertwining patterns, largely enact two controlling strategies: drawing parallels in her story to the two principal crises that Abelard identifies in his own in the *Historia calamitatum* and inverting (and subverting) in her self-representation the earlier one by Abelard in the same book.

Central to both strategies is a single, important change in the key values of that book, a change in the posture of humility essential to the confession that both seek to make. Where Abelard had argued in the *Historia calamitatum,* "I am great, innocent and unjustly maligned," she argues in the letters, "I am sinful, low, unjustly elevated and praised." Heloise thus assumes a more humble stance than Abelard does, but she also adopts a brazenly feminine role that risks—and often has excited—misinterpretation. Literary and historical critics' interidentification of Heloise's image not only with femininity but also with sexual femininity has long obscured obvious contrasts between that image and its assumption as a rhetorical stance within a confession. After all, it is her "image" and not her intellect, her imagination, or her use of that image that has called up all the scrutiny, beginning with Jean de Meung.[9] The risk, however, frees the writer to raise implicit but pointed questions about many issues: Abelard's victimization, his alleged conversion, and the representations of himself and the historical Heloise in the *Historia calamitatum*.[10] Indeed, the image becomes integral to the disputation for a key element in Heloise's rhetorical posturing is her assumption of a series of different feminine *figurae* that act not in isolation but instead imply, respond to, and interact with various male positions in such a way as to transvalue and reconstruct both themselves and the images of the other.[11] As the reader moves from the *Historia calamitatum* to the letters, he or she also moves from the single, gendered representation of the former to the organic and interacting representations found in the last stages of the latter. While the pictures of the correspondents are most fully realized only by *Ep.* 5, this process of refraction is suggested as early as the famous and oft-glossed superscription of Heloise's opening salutation, which points in its profusion of roles to the male and female models of Ovid's *Heroides,* particularly Jason and Medea. Like Jason, Abelard has become master, father, husband, and brother to a Heloise who, like Medea, has given up everything to follow a man who has repudiated her. Unlike

Medea, however, whose story Heloise refracts, Heloise plans not revenge but reconciliation and conversion. She will effect this change by assuming a posture of greater humility than Abelard as an invitation to rewrite both the account of their relationships and their self-presentations.

Such refractions were not unheard of in medieval literature. One following a very similar pattern to the one we are suggesting for Heloise occurs in an account of Eve and Adam found in an extremely popular text of the pseudepigrapha. In the *Vita Adae et Evae,* the couple, expelled from Eden and looking in vain for food, are driven to despair until Eve asks Adam to slay her. Since she alone sinned, she says, perhaps her death will reconcile Adam and God. Adam responds to this humility by abandoning his despair, renewing his relationship with Eve, and avowing he can never slay the flesh of his flesh.[12] The trick of speaking from the humbler level in the Heloise letters functions in the same way: as a bid (paradoxically) to bring Abelard and Heloise to a level of parity. Indeed, Heloise herself describes the nature of this transvaluation when in speaking of her youth to Abelard she notes, "I believed that the more I humbled myself on your account, the more gratitude I should win from you."[13] Such an interaction can be traced throughout the first five letters of the correspondence until it reaches a point of equity at *Ep.* 5.

In our comments we will limit ourselves to the first five letters, even though it is now clear that the Personal Letters and Letters of Direction are rhetorically and thematically connected.[14] We believe that the argument (or at least the initial debate) ends with Letter 5; with Letter 6 the collaboration begins. The Letters of Direction thus mark not only a generic transformation but also a change from a relationship between unequals to one between peers. In a subsequent study, we will seek to expand the inquiry to include the latter epistles.

In Heloise's first letter, she places her opening gambit. While several things about the *Historia calamitatum* disturb her deeply, two are especially worrisome: Abelard's presentation of her arguments against marriage (and by consequence his portrait of their love and themselves) and his failure to fulfill the generic expectations aroused by the promise of a consolation (and by consequence his failure to depict a genuine conversion). Both objections are presented as rhetorical issues. The first irritation may well seem understandable to a modern reader since the Heloise of the *Historia calamitatum* seems to merit little attention. Like the lady of troubadour verse, she provides the occasion for Abelard's inner crisis and evolution but reveals little of her own development and motivations in the narration of these events. His presentation of her arguments against marriage, for example, involves not the quality of *her* love but the danger to *his* reputation. *Ep.* 2 treats this difference. Heloise's concern with the second failure—to console—comes in *Ep.* 3, where she provides the model of a true consolation for Abelard.

The two problems are not unconnected within the posture of the *Historia calamitatum*'s Abelard and the ethical frame of the medieval text. The failure to console has much the same roots as the failure to love: pride or an overzealous devotion to self. On Heloise's side, the rhetorical picture is more nuanced and cannily drawn. Her recognition of the seriousness of Abelard's failed consolation—it throws doubt on both his conversion and his love—and her attempt to redress this problem at all costs effectively project a portrait of a selfless love compared to Abelard's portrait of self-absorption. Heloise's rhetorical stance thus acquires an integrity that Abelard's lacks in the *Historia calamitatum* where he claims to have undergone a conversion. Where his arrogance challenges his self-identifications with Christ and the early Fathers, she "proves" through better rhetorical management that she is who she says she is: a woman whose love for him is spiritually chaste, absolutely genuine, and so boundless as to necessitate self-obliteration for the beloved's good.[15] As the epistles move forward, Heloise points persuasively to contradictions between Abelard's words, narratives, and analysis of his spiritual state, thus accomplishing the equivalent of a rhetorical double take by providing both a true consolation for him and a convincing defense of *her* love and character. Like Abelard, she distinguishes between reality and reputation, an inner and an outer truth. However, her self-representation not only inverts his—she disclaims an excellent reputation; he disclaims a poor one—but it also accords more closely to the spiritual desiderata of humility and unsparing self-scrutiny.

Heloise's self-presentation does, however, evolve in response to Abelard's: it develops through an exploration of two crises in her past life chosen to parallel Abelard's own. Early on in the *Historia calamitatum,* Abelard claims to have been "totally enslaved" [cum igitur totus in superbia atque luxuria laborarem] to two sins: pride and lechery.[16] For his lechery, God castrated him; for his pride, he was forced to burn the book "of which . . . [he] was so proud" [illius libri quo maxime gloriabar] after the trial for heresy at Soissons.[17] Abelard admits that he was punished for lechery when guilty, but he maintains he was innocent when he was punished for pride—an odd claim since throughout the description of the trial at Soissons Abelard's intellectual arrogance if not his heresy is apparent.[18]

In her letters, Heloise presents two parallel crises in her life but with an inverted analysis of guilt. The first (corresponding to Abelard's lust) involves the catastrophe of marrying Abelard and, like all wives, bringing her husband to ruin. The second (corresponding to Abelard's pride) involves her hypocrisy (for leading an apparently pious life while remaining subject to carnal sin) as well as her pride (for refusing to bend to God's will). To the sin of lechery, she, unlike Abelard, pleads guilty now but innocent when punished; however, she acquits herself of the charge of pride in the past while admitting to a continuing struggle with it in her life as a nun. In both cases, the authors are attempting to explode a "myth": a negative or positive appearance versus an oppositional reality. In the medieval sense, however, Abelard's is clearly the larger error because it assumes spiritual perfection, persists, and goes unacknowledged, the first step to a true penance and conversion.

Evidence for this persistence can be found in a series of flattering poses Abelard assumes throughout the *Historia calamitatum:* there he comports himself as a victorious warrior, a matchless scholar, and a pious monk whose virtues far exceed those of his fellow monks and charges.[19] He compares himself explicitly to many saintly figures, including and especially Job (the traditional *figura* of the *planctus* genre), St. Jerome, and Christ Himself.[20] He appears more often as a just man unjustly harassed than as a sinner justly punished. Despite his claims of conversion and salvation, he thus gives little evidence of change in his attitudes, behaviors, or difficulties. He is still arrogant, willful, and argumentative; and just like the student who once challenged Anselm of Laon, he is still having difficulties with his colleagues. If anything, these difficulties have worsened, since now they threaten his life as well as his career.

In contrast, Heloise, universally respected and praised, adopts a posture of abject humility. She presents herself as sinful, wretched, the most lost of women, a soul too frightened of losing everything to fight for a crown in heaven. She accuses herself of impiety and grievous sin. While all may admire her, her case is far more serious than his because she is inwardly stained while Abelard, outwardly mutilated, claims to have lost his reservations about a concomitant inner wound.[21] Abelard thus compares himself with Christ, while Heloise compares herself to such famous sinners as Eve and Delilah.[22] Of course, such *exempla* are part of the stratagems used in the war of words between the two; however, Heloise deploys her forces more cunningly. Both sets of *exempla* invite contrasts as well as comparisons between themselves and the writers, but in Heloise's case, unlike Abelard's, the contrasts work to her rhetorical benefit. Unlike Eve (the seducer), *she* was seduced: systematically, rationally, and in cold blood. Unlike Delilah, who killed her lover, *she* tried to save Abelard by dissuading him from the destructive path of matrimony. In the contest between Heloise's humility and Abelard's arrogance, of which this contrasting use of *exempla* is but one instance, Heloise proves the more effective rhetorician. Indeed, in *De inventione,* a source for both Abelard and Heloise, Cicero had recommended that the speaker win the goodwill of his or her audience by praising his or her services without arrogance (as Heloise does in speaking of her services to Abelard; as Abelard does not in speaking of his teaching of the monks) or by speaking of his or her disabilities, needs, loneliness, and misfortunes (as Heloise does more effectively than Abelard because of her greater humility).[23]

Heloise also follows Cicero's advice that the basis of a defense or prosecution lies in identifying the issue under discussion.[24] In *Ep.* 2 she centers on her past and her love for Abelard, but the real issue is not so much marriage as a placement of priorities: does one value the external event or the internal motive? Summarily noting "you kept silent about most of my arguments for preferring love to wedlock, freedom to chains" [exponere non es . . . amorem coniugio libertatem vinculo praeferebam], Heloise answers his opening claim to have been enslaved by lust by presenting the charge she will investigate.[25] Ostensibly she is investigating her culpability in marrying Abelard, an act that endangers his promotability. Her opposition to this act was presented earlier in the *Historia calamitatum* as a pragmatic decision clothed in philosophic arguments and prompted by both her altruism and her total erotic and intellectual devotion to Abelard. As Heloise presents her case now, however, other issues emerge. Most prominently, we see the first opposition between an Abelard obsessed with external glories and an Heloise focused on inner truths.

Wisely she erects a defense based on motive, another instance of her adherence to Ciceronian principles.[26] Like Abelard at Soissons, she will argue that she intended no wrong; her love, unlike his, was not lust. In the *Historia calamitatum,* Abelard had presented two reasons for Heloise's strong opposition to the marriage: "the risk involved and the disgrace to myself" [pro periculo quam pro dedecore meo].[27] Yet in his presentation of her arguments, he clearly is obsessed by the latter: he spends most of his discussion and quotes all of his authorities—St. Jerome, Theophrastus, Socrates, St. Paul—when speaking of the disgrace, a parallel to his ongoing concern with a glorious reputation.

Heloise responds by claiming her dissuasion was based on other terms, terms both internal and unselfish: the preferability of a love freely given to one exacted by contract. She defends her love by her lack of interest in her reputation. Indeed, she wanted to gratify "not my own pleasures and wishes . . . but yours" [non denique meas voluptates aut voluntates sed tuas].[28] She "never sought anything" [Nihil . . . requisivi] in Abelard but himself.[29] Even after the marriage her "perfect love . . . [kept] the ties of marriage unbroken not so much through bodily continence as chastity of spirit"[ut perfecta dilectio illaesa custodiat matrimonii foedera non tam corporum continentia quam animorum pudicitia].[30] In her presentation, Heloise is at pains to answer the charge of "enslavement": a love freely given is no enslavement at all. If Abelard is still concerned with nonfundamentals (such as other men's opinions), she was concerned only with the true merit of the man before her.

To support her argument, and of course attack Abelard's, Heloise also musters an array of authorities carefully chosen to refute his. In the *Historia calamitatum,* for example, Abelard attributes to Heloise the assertion that "great philosophers of the past have despised the world . . . and have denied themselves every pleasure so as to find peace in the arms of philosophy alone" [Unde et insignes olim philosophi mundum maxime contempnentes, nec tam relinquentes seculum quam fugientes, omnes sibi voluptates interdixerunt ut in unius philosophie requiescerent amplexibus].[31] He supports this notion with a quotation from Seneca, who advised his friend in *Epistulae ad Lucilium:* "We must resist all other occupations, not merely dispose of them but reject them" [Resistendum est occupationibus nec explicande sunt, sed submovende].[32] Heloise strongly objects in *Ep.* 2. She had *not* argued, as Seneca had, for separation from the world or herself. Therefore, when she asks for a continuing connection with Abelard through letters, she quotes the very same source, the *Epistulae ad Lucilium,* to show how much comfort can be derived from "the one way in which . . . [the writer] can make . . . [his] presence felt" [uno modo potes te mihi ostendis].[33]

In like manner, when Abelard uses the example of Socrates' marriage as "a warning" [exemplo ejus cautiores efficerentur][34] against wedded bliss, he appears to be cautioning against wives like Xanthippe, who once poured out an "endless stream of invective . . . [and] dirty water" [infinita convitia . . . aqua profusus immunda] on poor Socrates' head.[35] In Heloise's letters, the argument against marriage presents no such denigration of wives; in fact, her letter contains an example that, although probably drawn from Cicero's *De inventione,* is correctly attributed to the dialogue of Socrates' pupil, Aeschines Socraticus.[36] In this passage, the learned woman Aspasia expounds the true basis for a chaste marriage as the belief that "there is no better man nor worthier woman on earth" [ut neque vir melior neque femina in terris electior sit] than one's spouse.[37] By applying these "saintly words" [sancta profecto haec] to her own love of Abelard,[38] Heloise asserts her innocence, opposing an example from Socrates' life (which, again, relates external accidents) to one from his pupil's writings (which, again, concerns internal verities). True love, she argues, is based only on merit, not reputation: it was because of his merit that she loved him, because of his merit that she would rather be called his whore [*meretrix*] than the wife of Augustus Caesar,[39] because of his merit that she is willing to "continue up to the present moment in complete obedience" to his will [cum omnia propter te compleverim nunc in tuo maxime perseverans obsequio].[40] Abelard had presented an Heloise worried about his physical survival and his reputation; Heloise responds with the picture of a woman whose every movement is a judgment of what lies behind those actions and reputations.

She thus draws a parallel between Abelard's trial at Soissons and the presentation of her views on marriage in the *Historia calamitatum.* As Abelard's writings were unjustly represented at Soissons, so her arguments against marriage have been unjustly presented in his book and for precisely the same reason—an obdurate refusal to consider the accused's intentions, the inner thoughts and motives behind the deed. In speaking of this betrayal, however, Heloise also composes a narrative of self-invention that refracts Abelard's experience at Soissons in important ways. She suggests a clear faith in her innocence. Where Abelard had complained that "the words 'Our enemies are judges'" [et inimici nostri sunt judices] were fulfilled in himself at Soissons,[41] Heloise *invites* her enemy to judge her when she tells Abelard in regard to her intention, "you alone who have known it can judge. I submit all to your scrutiny, yield to your testimony in all things" [solus qui expertus es iudicare potes. Tuo examini cuncta committo, tuo per omnia cedo testimonio].[42] On the other hand, she is also unwilling to rest in a posture of sanctity or abused innocence as does Abelard when speaking of Soissons, lamenting the verdict because of "the purity of my intentions and love of our Faith" [tam patentem violentiam sincera intentio amorque fidei nostre].[43] Heloise is more exacting: "Wholly guilty though I am, I am also, as you know, wholly innocent. It is not the deed but the intention of the doer which makes the crime" [Quae plurimum nocens, plurimum ut nosti sum innocens. Non enim rei effectus sed efficientis affectus in crimine est].[44]

Both were betrayed in these crises, but the portraits they present of themselves in this betrayal follow a pattern: Abelard focuses on a public trial at which one sees his absolute innocence and the judges' iniquities. Heloise focuses on an inner judgment that seesaws between condemnation and acquittal of herself. Abelard's posture is static, Heloise's volatile. Where Abelard sees himself at Soissons as Susanna,[45] a woman falsely accused of adultery by men who were guilty of that very sin, Heloise focuses on Abelard's judgment of her, accusing him of thinking of her as Lot's wife, who broke her promise by not trusting in the Lord and by looking back at Sodom and Gomorrah. It is not the marriage or the entry into religious life that fills her with "grief and shame" ["minus te de me confidere" and "*dolui* atque *erubui*"] but this "lack of trust."[46] Her choice of words echoes Abelard's assertion that the unwarranted burning of his books made him suffer "grief and indignation . . . shame") [*dolore . . . erubescentia*].[47] In his case, however, he suffers from his loss of reputation rather than a loss of trust, another celebration of external over internal concerns.

When Heloise closes, she invites a response. She wants "some word of comfort" [consolationem] from him.[48] This word also implies a rhetorical conversion since such a sign would mean (as the Latin implies) a correction of his failed consolation. She has defined her terms: against an Abelard obsessed with the things of this world, she has posed an Heloise who puts her trust in inner merit. The challenge—and the invitation to retract and change—could not be clearer.

Abelard's own response in *Ep.* 3 often has been seen as an evasion of the points Heloise's first letter raises, an attempt to turn her from a discussion of their physical love to a discussion of their present avocation. In asking for her prayers, however, Abelard recognizes the strengths of many of Heloise's arguments even if other readers have not, for he bases his request on a long discussion of wives and women that essentially rewrites many of the implications of his antimarriage arguments in the *Historia calamitatum*. Clearly, these examples also apply to Heloise, whom he praises in the letter's opening. He may have understood her concern for him as well as for herself, for many of the examples he cites deal with wives who saved their husbands. Most significantly, these examples (unlike those in the *Historia calamitatum*, where the misogynist examples often are drawn from classical sources) come from the Bible.

The best illustration of this process is found in the first example Abelard gives, the story of Jeptha who foolishly vowed to sacrifice to God the first thing he saw when he came home and so was compelled to sacrifice his daughter. This story was a favorite of Abelard's; he later composed a verse lament of Jeptha for the Paraclete. Here the story ostensibly is applied to the "lords of the earth" [principes terreni], but the comparison clearly extends to Abelard as well; for in refusing to break his promise to Fulbert to wed Heloise, Abelard, like these lords, proved "obstinate rather than just" [obstinati magis quam iusti] and feared to "appear untruthful if . . . [he] change[d] a pronouncement . . . which lacked foresight" [mendaces si edictum suum mutent vel quod minus provide statuerunt non impleant].[49] Likewise, Jeptha's foolish vow cost his daughter her life in the same way that Abelard's foolish promise to wed led Heloise to follow his command and, in her own words, "destroy" [me ipsam . . . perdere] herself.[50] Thus Abelard accords Heloise some points: he *was* interested in external niceties, he could be stiff-necked, she did suffer in the marriage.

In other examples, Abelard builds on this concession by comparing Heloise and himself to various biblical couples. He implies that while she is like Abigail, the wife of Nabal the Carmelite, he is Nabal; for just as Nabal rebelled against David, so Abelard has rebelled against the Lord. Now Abelard hopes that Heloise will intercede and turn the Lord's wrath away as Abigail did with David. In so doing, Abelard thus presents a heightened fear for his spiritual as well as his physical well-being. Whereas in the *Historia calamitatum* Abelard presents himself as saved, he now assumes a more humble and uncertain stance in regard to his salvation. Numerous examples of women for whom the miracle of resurrection was performed—the mothers of Elijah and Elisha, Mary and Martha, and the widow at the city of Nain—also underline this new emphasis on the spirit. Abelard hopes that Heloise and her sisters can intercede with God not only for his safety but also for his spiritual salvation, which the word "resurrection" invokes. Moreover, he continues to concede to Heloise a posture that in many ways inverts the position of the wicked wife in the *Historia calamitatum.* He refers to the good wife described by Proverbs and Ecclesiasticus and applies her model to Heloise. He also explicitly compares her to Clovis's wife, who converted her husband to Christ and saved his soul.

Yet if, in the first part of the letter, Abelard bends, modifies his depiction of their relationship in the *Historia calamitatum,* and hints at a recognition of misplaced priorities in his earlier presentations, in the final passages, his posture remains stiff and self-congratulatory, and the examples themselves do nothing to change the relationship to one of parity: distance is maintained by inferiority even if Abelard claims the humbler position for himself, a rhetorical posturing modeled partially on Heloise's stance and used, as in her case, to gain mastery of the discourse. However, the posture is not completely realized, nor is he entirely successful in reversing his valuation of outer over inner worth. In beseeching burial at the Paraclete, Abelard compares himself implicitly to Christ (an identification also found in the *Historia calamitatum*).[51] He concerns himself not only with his guilt and spiritual salvation but also with his physical safety, including a prayer to be said for that by Heloise and her convent. Finally, he ends by reproving Heloise for the error he has just committed, calling her "overanxious" about the danger to his body and telling her to have as "chief concern the salvation of my soul" [nimia sollicitudine laboratis, tunc praecipue de salute animae sollicitae].[52]

Such a response leaves largely unresolved the issues of Abelard's pride, their mutual love, and his continuing despair over the possibility of his death, with which much of letter is taken up. In *Ep.* 4, therefore, Heloise tries another tactic, issuing a fiery self-indictment that refracts aspects of Abelard's powerful treatment of his castration, just as her investigation of their marriage corresponds to his description of the trial at Soissons. In the *Historia calamitatum,* Abelard had judged himself at fault only in the past and in regard to lechery; Heloise now confesses herself still subject to carnal sins and arrogant in her inability to subordinate her wishes to God's demands. In doing so, she implicitly attacks Abelard's position: he has failed to confess to the magnitude of his sin and to trace current patterns of sin in his own life. In the *Historia calamitatum,* Abelard had presented himself as separated from his past arrogance: physically mutilated but spiritually whole. Now Heloise presents herself as inextricably involved with her past: physically whole but spiritually mutilated. Speaking in this voice, she is most bothered by her failure to repent, a failure to love God that also stems from pride. In *Ep.* 4, then, Heloise challenges Abelard on the issue of pride, his most grievous sin, and to do so, she is willing to subject herself or the representation of herself to a scathing and dramatic analysis.

This letter provides the model of the true consolation that Abelard's own letters had not given. In the literary genre of the *consolatio,* an ancient one even in the twelfth century, the core rhetorical strategy was "the articulation of certain philosophical *topoi* and the enumeration of consoling *exempla* of greater tragedies than those experienced by the recipient."[53] In the original *Historia calamitatum,* Abelard had made himself this *exemplum,* evoking his despondency at his lost reputation, his failed plans, and his deteriorating circumstances. But Heloise undercuts this stance by revealing flaws in its presentation. In contrast, she offers a more appropriate—or at least more Christian—consolation by showing that if he has told the truth, then in comparison with her problems, his trials really are what he called those of the unknown recipient of the *Historia calamitatum,* "nothing or only slight, and [therefore] . . . easier to bear" [in comparatione mearum tuas aut nullas aut modicas temptationes . . . et tolerabilius feras].[54] He may complain of having lost his reputation, but he boasts of maintaining his spiritual integrity. If so, he fares better than the Heloise who presents herself, the chief *exemplum* of her consolation, as openly admired but secretly and spectacularly flawed. In the game of one-upmanship, she trumps her opponent once again by assuming a more complete and abject posture of humility that reveals and attacks the arrogance characterizing Abelard's postures in the *Historia calamitatum* and *Ep.* 3.

She also offers Abelard a more complete consolation than his own by modeling a more searching confession than his. In the *Historia calamitatum,* Abelard had based his consolation on a *confessio peccatorum,* designed to demonstrate the author's sense of his own sinfulness. Heloise's confession is more sweeping than his, however: she sees nothing in herself of which she can be proud. In her first letter, she had defended her love of him by defining herself in respect to this love as outwardly wanton but inwardly chaste. In *Ep.* 4, she accuses herself as the bride of Christ who is externally chaste but inwardly wanton and untrue. In the confessional, she thus assumes the role of a humble petitioner who honestly admits the full scope of her sin and accepts no easy absolution.

She begins by asserting her inferiority and denying Abelard's praise, two rhetorical gestures whose counterparts are largely absent from Abelard's *Historia calamitatum.* They function, of course and rather indirectly, as a means of controlling the discourse. Unlike Abelard's humility in *Ep.* 3, her postures are unmitigated and uncompromised; therefore, they are more powerful. She protests that he continues to dwell on his death and, in provoking thoughts of death, has once more shown a lamentable self-concern and despair, both of which belie his claims of salvation. To prove her points she calls upon his own sources, once again quoting Seneca's *Epistulae ad Lucilium,* which

Abelard uses in the *Historia calamitatum* to bolster Heloise's arguments against marriage.[55] She warns him that it is not necessary " . . . 'to summon evil'" [mala arcessere].[56] She implicitly speaks not only of herself and her community but also of Abelard himself when she warns that a "heart . . . preoccupied with anxieties genuinely cannot find peace, nor can a mind preoccupied with anxieties devote itself to God" [confectus moerore animus quietus non est, nec Deo sincere potest vacare mens perturbationibus occupata].[57] Her crowning injunction to " . . .'hope on in . . . fear'" [sperare timenti][58] is Christian in sentiment but derived from Lucan's *Pharsalia,* a significant source in the correspondence. While Heloise herself uses Lucan only this once, Abelard quotes from the work twice in the *Historia calamitatum,* the first time to dismiss arrogantly and rather unfairly his old teacher, Anselm of Laon, who is characterized as the "shadow of a noble name" [magni nominis umbra];[59] the second time to embellish the depiction of an Heloise who fears she has ruined her husband. He notes that upon entering the monastery after his castration, she recited Cornelia's words from the *Pharsalia* at the death of her husband Pompey:

> O noble husband,
> Too great for me to wed, was it my fate
> To bend that lofty head? What prompted me
> To marry you and bring about your fall?
> Now claim your due, and see me gladly pay . . .
>
> [O maxime conjux!
> O thalmis indigne meis, hoc juris habebat
> In tantum fortuna capud? Cur impia nupsi
> Si miserum factura fui? Nunc accipe penas
> Sed quas sponte luam][60]

In both instances, Abelard presents himself in flattering poses, once at the expense of his teacher, then at the expense of his wife. Fittingly, then, Heloise uses the same source to supply her most apt description of the stance Abelard has failed to adopt—to "hope on" (and avoid despair) but "in fear" (and hence avoid pride).

Heloise exemplifies this stance in her ensuing confession. She begins by considering the consequences of their fall, how "the laws of equity in our case were reversed" [in nobis aequitatis iura pariter sunt perversa].[61] The word "equity," or *aequitatis,* sets up an important echo, for Abelard also used the word "equity" [*equitatem*] when he recalled reproaching God for deserting him at Soissons;[62] and spiritual blindness marks Abelard's description of his self-presentation in Soissons. Although he had acknowledged earlier that the trial was punishment for his past arrogance, he gives no consideration for that sin at all when speaking of Soissons.[63] Instead, he confirms most compellingly his misplacement of priorities, his emphasis on outer reputation at the expense of inner merit. He compares the earlier physical harm to the trial's harm to his reputation and notes that he wept "much more for the injury to my reputation than for the damage to my body" because he feels he "had brought upon myself the damage to my body" while the trial at Soissons had come upon him only "because of the purity of my intention and love of our Faith" [Parvam illam ducebam proditionem in comparatione hujus injurie, et longe amplius fame quam corporis detrimentum plangebam, cum ad illam ex aliqua culpa devenerim, ad hanc me tam patentem violentiam sincera intentio amorque fidei nostre induxissent].[64] In contrast, as Heloise explores and exploits her guilt fully, in reference to both her marriage and her later religious life, she does not spare her reputation in the search for her inner flaws. In this she presents him with a salutary example and a direct inversion: Abelard at Soissons, she at the Paraclete; his concern for reputation, hers for spiritual wholeness.

Unlike Abelard, who seems particularly, even comically, vulnerable on this point, Heloise opens with disinclination to believe the praise of others. In *Ep.* 3, Abelard had quoted Proverbs, Ecclesiastes, and I Corinthians in his discussion of the good wife, a role assigned Heloise; she now opposes them with a discussion of the wicked wife supported by biblical citations from Proverbs and Ecclesiastes. Comparing herself to such traditional *exempla* as Delilah, Eve, and the wives of Solomon and Job, she handles her sources with an admirable dexterity. As with Abelard's customary use of *exempla,* the underlying contrasts are often more interesting than the surface similarities, but these contrasts do not work against her arguments as they do so often in Abelard's case. Although she ostensibly identifies with the bad wife, the circumstances of the *exempla* make the husband's situation equally applicable to her own, another instance of the letters' ongoing program of transvaluing and refracting male and female *figurae.* Like Samson she "was driven . . . to destroy" herself [se . . . cum ruina hostium opprimeret].[65] Like Adam, she was seduced from joy by her helpmate. Like Solomon, she is driven to abandon "the worship of God" [divino cultu derelicto].[66] Finally, like Job, with whom she, like Abelard, often identifies herself, she is fighting her "last and hardest battle" against her spouse [in uxore novissimam et gravissiam sustinuit pugnam].[67] The laws of equity have been indeed reversed.

This significant subtext does not, however, fully exonerate her, as she is at pains to show. Like these men she also finds that she is not "wholly free of guilt" [me penitus immunem ab huius reatu sceleris esse non sinunt].[68] She confesses to her lechery and says, "I yielded long before to the pleasures of carnal desires and merited then what I weep for now" [Quod videlicet diu ante carnalium illecebrarum voluptatibus serviens, ipsa tunc merui quod nunc plector].[69] Unlike Abelard, she does not attempt to justify or gloss her error, nor is she willing to claim complete innocence with regard to God as she had proven herself willing to do with regard to Abelard. Unlike Abelard, she confesses that "an evil beginning must be expected to come to a bad end" [et malis initiis perversus imputandus est exitus] and so suggests a link between current difficulties and past sins.[70] She is addressing thus Abelard's problem as well as her own when she makes the famous confession that even "during the celebration of the Mass, when our prayers should be purer, lewd visions of those pleasures take such a hold upon my unhappy soul that my thoughts are on their wantonness instead of on prayers. I should be groaning over the sins I have committed, but I can only sigh for what I have lost" [Inter ipsa missarum solemnia, ubi purior esse debet oratio, obscena earum voluptatum phantasmata ita sibi penitus miserrimam captivant animam ut turpitudinibus illis magis quam orationi vacem. Quae cum ingemiscere debeam de commissis, suspiro potius de amissis].[71] One cannot help but remember Abelard's history, filled with sighs for his many losses—for his burned book, for his missing students, for his abandoned Paraclete, for his destroyed opportunities, for his lost reputation—and too empty of groans for his sins.

Against the matter of reputation (perhaps Abelard's clearest misplacement of priorities), Heloise vents her most scathing attack. Unlike Abelard, she does not spare *her* reputation as she accuses herself of rank hypocrisy for leading an apparently pious life while remaining subject to carnal love. She emphasizes the legitimacy of this confession by prefacing her remarks with a discussion of its bitterness of spirit, a bitterness that, although appropriate to repentance, is all too rare, as she proves with a quotation from St. Ambrose.[72] This discussion takes aim at the ending of the *Historia calamitatum* where Abelard's concern for his reputation is reflected in his use of citations not to accuse himself in humility of spirit but to justify and exalt himself as one of the saved.[73] Often her quotations come from the same books of the Bible he uses. Where he quotes Romans 8.28 to show he is one of the redeemed, Heloise quotes Romans 7.24 to express her unworthiness.[74] He quotes Psalms 52 to show God's championship of his cause; Heloise quotes Psalms 8.28 to refer to a God who "searches our hearts and loins" [qui cordis et renum probator est] and can find nothing to praise in her.[75] Later she explicitly corrects Abelard's use of authorities when she quotes Ecclesiastes' warning that wise words should be "'sharp as goads, like nails driven home'" [quasi clavi in altum defixi], not to praise and justify, as Abelard has used them.[76] She begs him to cease his praise of her lest he "acquire the base stigma of being a flatterer or the charge of telling lies, or the breath of my vanity blows away any merit . . . in me to praise" [mendacii crimen incurras . . . in me suspicaris bonum, ipsum laudatum vanitatis aura ventilet].[77] Implicitly, he stands in danger of doing himself this very disservice.

In her closing rejection of his praise, she quotes 2 Corinthians 12.9—"Power comes to its full strength in weakness" [Nam virtus in infirmitate perficitur]—and 2 Timothy 2.5—"He cannot win a crown unless he has kept the rules" [Non coronabitur nisi qui legitime certaverit].[78] The warning not to use these words to praise her underlines her point: his misappropriated posture of humility flaws his argument and his analysis of their lives. Indeed, if he follows her earlier prescriptions, neither will he take these words as praise for himself but as sharp yet good advice to "pierce through" [pungere] the wounds of his failings. Finally she invites him to imitate her humility and "not seek a crown of victory" [Non quaero coronam victoriae]; rather it should be "sufficient . . . to avoid danger" [Satis est . . . periculum vitare].[79] If, like her, he can be satisfied in "whatever corner of heaven God" [angulo coeli Deus] shall place him, he will find an end to his troubles, which he has said often have sprung of envy; for here is a place where nobody "will envy . . . and what each has will suffice" [invidebat . . . quod habebunt suffecerit.][80] She closes by calling on the "weight of authority" [ex auctoritate] to support her plea.[81] In doing so she quotes one of Abelard's favorite sources against him, the Father whose arguments against marriage she had left untouched in *Ep.* 2. If he truly wishes to be like St. Jerome, Abelard should "confess . . . [his] weakness" [Fateor imbecillitatem] and abandon his view of himself as a victorious soldier (a metaphor that permeates the *Historia calamitatum*).[82] Instead he will not " . . . wish to fight in hope of victory . . . [lest he] lose the battle" [nolo spe victoriae pugnare ne perdam aliquando victoriam].[83] If Heloise's first letter teaches Abelard how to be gracious when falsely accused, the second teaches how to be humble both in confession and in ambition. In this letter, then, she adapts the strategy the correspondence attributes to Abelard as her teacher. In the *Historia calamitatum,* Abelard confesses he had once struck her with blows that "were prompted by love and tender feeling rather than anger and irritation, and were sweeter than any balm could be" [amor, non furor, gratia, non ira, que omnium ungentorum suavitatem transcenderent].[84] Now it is she who is the teacher and who uses the same approach (but on herself as well as her pupil) as she entreats him not to dismiss her advice a second time.

If one judges by Abelard's *Ep.* 5, these efforts did not go unnoticed. There he yields to many of Heloise's objections directly and, perhaps most important, responds to her rhetorical posture by imitating it. The arrogant and self-centered tone of much of the *Historia calamitatum* is missing, replaced by a gentler, if equally insistent, one; in this, in his franker confessions of guilt, in his greater concern for Heloise, and in his rewriting of his presentations of himself, her, and their relationship, the letters move toward a more convincing posture of Christian humility, one that successfully emulates the posture of his opponent.

Abelard begins by enumerating the charges he must answer, a tactic again recommended in Cicero's *De inventione* and a rhetorical imitation of the method Heloise had used to open her first letter.[85] The charges are four in number: her complaint against his subordination of himself to her both in the salutation of *Ep.* 2 and in the natural order; her complaint against his failed consolation in *Ep.* 2; her "old perpetual complaint against God concerning the manner of [their] entry into the religious life and the cruelty of the act of treachery performed on" Abelard [veterem illam et assiduam querelam tuam in Deum . . . de modo videlicet nostrae conversionis ad Deum et crudelitate proditionis illius . . . commissae];[86] and last her complaint against his praise of her. All are related to the issues of humility and arrogance. In promising to answer each of these, he implicitly acknowledges some of her criticisms: he will answer not to justify himself (as he had often done in the *Historia calamitatum*) but to enlighten and encourage her, as he is bound to do.

In essence, Abelard concedes much of the argument to her in his response to her first charge, namely that, contrary to custom and natural order, he put her name above his in his last salutation, thus according her the superior status. He defends his practice by recourse to Jerome, who had thus addressed Eustochium because, like Heloise, Eustochium was Jerome's superior as the bride of Christ. While such a defense would seem to ground Heloise's superiority in something other than her own worth, to return her to a monastic circumscription, the ensuing comparison between this bride of Christ and the bride in the Song of Songs also recognizes many of the superior virtues of Heloise's confession. Moreover, since this charge is, in part, a protest against Abelard's rhetorical inadequacies, it is striking that in this section, he imitates Heloise's rhetorical use of *exempla*. In the past, his *exempla* had often seemed ill chosen, fraught with implications that contradicted his arguments. In contrast, while Heloise's *exempla* also implied more than was at first apparent, the subtext supported her contentions or backfired to her benefit. In the same way, the comparison between the black bride of the Song of Songs and the nuns (in general) or Heloise (in particular) cleverly asserts a more positive view of Abelard himself, to whom the *exemplum* also applies.

All these qualities are developed analogically through the contrast between the bride's exterior blackness and her inner beauty. On the surface, of course, this is a graceful refutation of Heloise's hypocrisy. It also acknowledges the superiority of her overall change in values, to wit the change from Abelard's unwise valorization of exterior reputation at the expense of inner worth. Even more interesting, however, is the imitation of Heloise's rhetorical sleight-of-hand, for when speaking of the nuns as "black but lovely" [Nigra . . . sed formosa], bruised by tribulations that strengthen their spiritual worth, Abelard extends the comparison to himself, whose bruised physical form after the castration is evidence of the tribulations that were meant to purify and beautify his soul.[87] Thus the *exemplum,* contrary to those of his first letter, works toward a unity with Heloise, a relationship of parity rather than dominance and subordination. In support of his estimate of *her* worth through the *exemplum* of the black bride, Abelard, in a lovely gesture of humility, now quotes 2 Timothy 3.12, the passage that he had used in the *Historia calamitatum* to argue for *his* virtue.[88] He explicitly pays tribute to her humility, the striking aspect of her second letter, by noting that the nun's black garb shows that "while she is still an exile on life's pilgrimage, she keeps herself humble and abject in this life so that she may be exalted in the next" [in hac peregrinatione adhuc exsulat, vilem et abiectam se tenet in hac vita ut in illa sublimetur].[89] He thus implies that this road is Heloise's despite her disclaimers, for he suggests that hers is the true monastic life of contemplation and retirement. He likens her relationship with Christ to that of a man and wife in the bedchamber, thus according her the greater virtue. Moreover, he attributes the love of Christ to the blackness that represents her bodily tribulations and so relates the pains she suffers from carnal desire to his pain from castration, equating their suffering for the first time as a mutual and just expiation for their sins. This note of mutuality carries over into the conclusion, when he explains that he asks for her prayers because of their purity. He notes that they must be uttered devoutly since "we are bound together in such great mutual love" [quanto maiore nos invicem caritate colligati sumus].[90] Conspicuously absent is the self-centered stance of his initial letter to her, to which Heloise's letters so directly object.

As he responds to her complaint that his mention of imminent death brought her desolation, not comfort, he quite rightly objects that he was merely responding to her own request. But he also recognizes the undercurrents of her protest, for he shows a new awareness of her feelings and a new humility. This too responds to Heloise's example. Instead of touching upon *his* fears and misfortunes, he appeals to *her* love and obligation to share both good and bad times; he further promises her that death will not be a tragedy for him but a liberation. He concludes by telling her if she is his friend, she must not "prefer me to live on in great misery rather than be happier in death" [Nec nisi tuis in me commodis aliquid provideas, cur me miserrime vivere malis quam felicius mori non video].[91] Again the tone has changed from the fearful one characteristic of *Ep.* 3 and the *Historia calamitatum*. Moreover, by appealing to the tragedy of his life, he does what one should do in a consolation and what Heloise had done in *Ep.* 4: console one's readers by convincing them others have greater trials. By embedding these remarks within a calmer approach to his death and a better confession of his past sins, he also responds to the more convincingly Christian posture of Heloise's confession and thus concedes the accuracy of her critiques of genre and pose.

In response to the third complaint, her rejection of his praise, Abelard demonstrates how thoroughly he has understood and applied her stance of humility to his case. He tells her that if she really believes in the words she has written, "yours is the true humility and will not vanish with anything I say" [vera est humilitas tua nec pro nostris evanuerit verbis];[92] and he quotes passages of scripture to approve her example and acknowledge her method: Proverbs 18.17: "He who is first in accusing himself is just" [Iustus in primordio accusator est sui], and Luke 18.14: "Whoever humbles himself will be exalted" [Qui se humiliat, se exaltat].[93] He goes even further by implementing her advice immediately and playfully acknowledging her methodology. He does not rest with praise but is "fearful for [her] always" [Time . . . semper] as she requested.[94] He advises her not to "seek praise when you appear to shun it" [hoc ipso laudem quaeras quo laudem fugere videris] and gives the example of Galatea, who "by feigning rejection led on her lover" [simulatione repulsae, amplius in se amantem incitabat].[95] That, of course, is just what Heloise has been doing in *Ep.* 4, even if for rhetorical rather than carnal reasons. That Abelard realizes this crucial difference is shown when he assures her, "I mention this because it is a common occurrence, not because I suspect such things of you; I have no doubts about your humility" [Et haec quidem quia saepe accidunt dicimus non quia de te talia suspicemur qui de tua non haesitamus humilitate].[96] His additional warning, "I want you to refrain from speaking like this, so that you do not appear to those who do not know you so well to be seeking fame by shunning it" [Sed ab his etiam verbis te temperare volumus ne his, qui te minus noverint, videaris . . . fugiendo gloriam quaerere], shows a concern for her reputation and safety that had been conspicuously absent from other letters, a concern that is not at all out of place considering the frequency with which readers have concentrated on the sensational details of Heloise's confession and ignored their utility as rhetorical ploys.[97]

Most important, when he comes to the most intimate of the charges, the one relating to the manner of their entry into religious life, he offers his own response to her confession by essentially retelling the story in the *Historia calamitatum* and rewriting his self-representation there. This revision is marked by two important differences: Abelard's increased concern for Heloise's salvation and the more intense and stark revelation of his own guilt in relation to the events of that time. In both these changes he is clearly following Heloise's lead and adopting a new modesty.

As she had claimed to be distressed by his physical danger, so now he claims to be distressed by her spiritual one, and he echoes her words: "The more dangerous such bitterness is to you in wearing out body and soul alike, the more pitiful it is and distressing to me" [Quae, quanto tibi periculosior est, corpus tuum pariter et animam conterens, tanto miserabilior est et mihi molestior].[98] He is now eager to show that what happened was not only "salutary" [*saluberrima*] for him but also for her (another example of his new emphasis on mutuality).[99] Far from being his ruin, she was, he says, "the cause of so great a good, for which you must not doubt you were specially created by God" [Nec te tanti boni causam esse doleas].[100] This presentation of her role in the marriage completely reverses the one that appears in the *Historia calamitatum*. Even more significant, he adopts her stance and shows himself to be as willing to go to extremes for her as she had been for him. Just as she did not spare her reputation to bring him to his senses, so he is willing to investigate and confess to his total guilt to console her. He notes that if the punishment had fallen on him justly, it would not have distressed her less, and in fact he is willing to prove that it fell justly.

In this letter Abelard presents a different picture of their love from that he offered in the *Historia calamitatum;* here Heloise's role and his own are fully acknowledged. He blames not her lasciviousness but his own for their many "wanton impurities," [impudentissimas . . . pollutiones] including (in a memorably daring confession that parallels Heloise's remarks about lascivious memories at mass) an encounter that occurred in a corner of the refectory at the nunnery of Argenteuil.[101] He notes that he even forced her to consent to "fornication" [fornicationes] when she was "unwilling" [te nolentem], so intense was his bondage to lust.[102] The word "fornication" is significant. In the *Historia calamitatum,* Abelard uses the more euphemistic term "lovemaking" [*passio*];[103] in *Ep.* 4, Heloise had not only written "fornication" [*fornicationi*] but had underlined its use by adding "if I may use an ugly but expressive word" [ut turpiore, sed expressiore vocabulo utar].[104] She had been as blunt when she noted that she would rather be his "concubine or whore" [concubinae vel scorti] than another's "wife" [uxoris].[105] He had used the term "mistress" [*amicam*]. There are no more euphemisms; Abelard presents himself as able to speak in as honest a voice as hers. And like the

Heloise of *Ep.* 4, he sees a similar continuity between his past sins and current difficulties, for now he finds his present "daily unending torment" [quotidie indesinenter sustineo] the true punishment for his earlier excesses.[107]

However, it is while comparing the true and false spouse that he most forcefully concedes the truth of Heloise's points. In the *Historia calamitatum,* Abelard often draws implicit parallels between himself and Christ. In this letter, that comparison is completely rescinded. He appears to regret his earlier boasts when he quotes Galatians 6.14: "God forbid that I should boast of anything but the Cross of our Lord Jesus Christ, through whom the world is crucified to me, and I to the world" [Absit mihi . . . gloriari nisi in cruce Domini nostri Iesu Christi per quem mihi mundus crucifixus est et ego mundo].[108] When he contrasts himself with Christ, Abelard shows a new humility. He claims Christ is her true spouse, the one who loved her for herself, suffered for her willingly, and bought her not with money but with himself. In fact, Abelard humbly confesses to his inadequacies as her lover, quite a change from his earlier assertions and a direct concession to charges Heloise made in *Ep.* 2: "It was he who truly loved you, not I. My love, which brought us both to sin, should be called lust, not love" [Amabat te ille veraciter, non ego. Amor meus, qui utrumque nostrum peccatis involebat, concupiscentia, non amor dicendus est].[109] He warns her to direct her remorse toward Christ, not toward himself; and in a final revision, he repudiates her quotation of Cornelia's words from Lucan's *Pharsalia.* Where the Heloise in the *Historia calamitatum* had compared herself to the woman whose failings had brought low her husband, now Abelard warns the Heloise of the correspondence to be careful *lest* he apply to her Pompey's reproach to Cornelia: "The battle ended, Pompey the Great / Lives, but his fortune died. It is this you now mourn / And loved [Vivit post proelia Magnus! / Sed fortuna perit. Quod defles, illud amasti].[110] The injunction cleverly asserts he would not now apply such words to her (she who has been at such pains to reject concerns for worldly reputation), nor does he persist in overly valuing his reputation.

While concluding, he neatly summarizes by conceding her main points and affirming her superiority in humility. In examining the castration, he notes that since hers was the weaker nature yet hers was the stronger resistance, she was less deserving of punishment. And he insists that the very arguments she brings for her unworthiness prove her worth: "The many greater sufferings of the heart through the continual prompting of the flesh of your own youth He has reserved for a martyr's crown. Though you may weary of hearing this and forbid it to be said, the truth of it is clear" [refrigeravit ne corruam, multas adolescentiae tuae maiores animi passiones ex assidua carnis suggestione reservavit ad martyrii coronam. Quod licet te audire taedeat et dici prohibeas, veritas tamen id loquitur manifesta].[111] In place of his arrogant assumption of his own victory, Abelard now echoes Heloise's words and again follows her advice: he wishes merely "to escape further punishment" [nonnullam tamen evitam poenam].[112] He affirms their continuing connection and the resurrection of the love on the terms she had demanded originally: "we are one in Christ, one flesh according to the law of matrimony. . . . Now you have as a servant me whom in the past you recognized as your master, more your own now when bound to you by spiritual love than one subjected by fear" [Unum quippe sumus in Christo, una per legem matrimonii caro . . . Et nunc, ut supra memini, me habes servum quem olim agnoscebas dominum magis tibi tamen amore nunc spirituali coniunctum quam timore subiectum].[113] The word "master" [*dominum*] is significant since Heloise had applied it to Abelard in the salutation of *Ep.* 2 to indicate his former role as teacher. Now the reversal of roles suggests it is Heloise who is "dominus," a title she has won through a disputation on the meaning of their lives.

At the close of *Ep.* 5, Abelard provides a prayer for Heloise. Unlike the prayer of *Ep.* 3, this one is offered for both rather than for Abelard alone and seeks their spiritual rather than physical salvation. In this mutuality, in its defense of marriage through biblical sources, in its humility and tone, one can read Abelard's concession and rhetorical conversion. Indeed, he has proven a worthy recipient of her instruction. Responding to her arguments, he has adopted both her pose and many of her rhetorical strategies. As in any successful doctorate exam, the laws of equity have been reversed: the pupil has mastered the debate, the teacher has followed the pupil's lead, and, it is argued by the letters, both have thus paradoxically succeeded.

Notes

1. Beginning with Orelli's 1841 edition of the *HC,* several theories have been advanced in an attempt to establish that the letters were, in part or in whole, forged. These were refuted perhaps most compellingly by Étienne Gilson in *Héloïse et Abélard;* see especially pp. 150–71. The controversy, however, has continued to provoke frequent and at times acerbic debate. For the principal arguments against authenticity, see Ludovic Lalanne, "Quelques doutes sur l'authenticité de la correspondance amoureuse d'Héloïse et Abélard"; Bernhard Schmeidler, "Der Briefwechsel zwischen Abälard und Heloise: eine Fälschung," "Der Briefwechsel zwischen Abaelard und Heloise dennoch eine literarische Fiction Abaelards"; and Charlotte Charrier, *Héloïse dans l'histoire et dans la légende* (1933). The most recent contribution to the forgery theory included, most notably, John Benton, "Fraud, Fiction, and Borrowing in the Correspondence of Abélard and Héloïse," pp. 469–512 and the ensuing discussion on pp. 507–11. Soon after, Benton retracted this theory and advanced another, much more elaborate one, that asserted Abelard actually wrote the Heloise letters. See "A Reconsideration of the Authenticity of the Correspondence of Abelard and Heloise," in Trier 1980, pp. 41–52. Among later supports for the forgery theory are Hubert Silvestre, "Die Liebesgeschicte zwischen Abaelard und Heloise: der Anteil des Romans," pp. 121–65, and Deborah Fraioli, "The Importance of Satire in Jerome's *Adversus Jovinianum* as an Argument Against the Authenticity of the *Historia calamitatum,*" pp. 167–200. For the most important arguments brought against the letters' forgery, see not only Gilson but also Peter Dronke, *Abelard and Heloise in Medieval Testimonie* and "Excursus: Did Abelard Write Heloise's Third Letter?" in *Women Writers,* pp. 140–43, and most recently in "Heloise, Abelard, and Some Recent Discussions," in *Intellectuals and Poets in Medieval Europe.* See also Barbara Newman's textual arguments for authenticity in "Authority, Authenticity, and the Repression of Heloise." Although not concerned directly with the correspondence, another rebuttal to Benton is to be found in C. Stephen Jaeger, "The Prologue to the *Historia calamitatum* and the 'Authenticity Question.'"
2. See, for example, D. W. Robertson, *Abelard and Heloise,* especially pp. 120–23; Robertson argues that the text, far from celebrating erotic passion, is an exemplary story of a conversion, narrated by Abelard.
3. Among the most prominent sources in this respect are Dronke, *Women Writers;* Peggy Kamuf, *Fictions of Feminine Desire: Disclosures of Heloise;* Linda Kauffman, *Discourses of Desire: Gender, Genre, and Epistolary Fictions;* Glenda McLeod, "'Wholly Guilty, Wholly Innocent': Self-Definition in Héloïse's Letters to Abélard," pp. 64–86; and Peter von Moos, "Le Silence d'Héloïse et les idéologies modernes," pp. 425–68. Several scholars also have contributed to this line of argument while dismissing the question of Heloise's

authenticity and limiting themselves to a study of the body of the text. This approach has been aptly described by Claire Nouvet in "La castration d'Abélard: impasse et substitution." She notes, "tels que je les comprendraie ici, les noms d''Abélard' et 'Héloïse' ne se réfèrent plus aux deus corps historiques qui les portèrent mais au 'corpus' de lettres auquel ils sont désormais chacun attachés" (p. 260). See also Paul Zumthor, "Préface" in *Abélard et Héloïse, Correspondance,* trans. Zumthor; Jean-Charles Huchet, "La Voix d'Héloïse"; and Claire Nouvet, "The Discourse of the 'Whore': An Economy of Sacrifice."

4. For our stance on the authenticity of the letters, see the argument that follows. In reference to the historical Abelard and Heloise, there exists ample evidence of the high regard in which Heloise was held: Abelard himself remarks upon this in the *HC.* See especially Radice 97. Even more famous is Peter the Venerable's tribute to Heloise in a letter where he tells her that "You are indeed the disciple of truth, but in your duty towards those entrusted to you, you are the teacher of humility" (Radice 279). As Newman points out in "Authority, Authenticity, and the Repression of Heloise," even Abelard's enemy Roscelin called her *puella prudentissima,* and late in Heloise's life Hugh Métal, a canon who wished to enhance his own reputation by association with her, wrote her two letters of praise (p. 129, n.2). Newman also notes that despite the early scandal and the Abbé Suger's eviction of the nuns at Argenteuil for alleged misconduct, the Paraclete thrived under Heloise's thirty-five-year-long administration, adding five new priories and an abbey (p. 136). This would have been impossible without Heloise's command of the respect of local dignitaries. Finally, Penelope Johnson in *Equal in Monastic Profession: Religious Women in Medieval France,* records other evidence for this respect: the frequency with which the name "Heloise" was taken by nuns and noblewomen in the generation after Heloise's death (p. 234). All of this stands in stark contrast to Abelard's own, stormy relations with both his teachers and superiors and those entrusted to his care. For example, in the *HC,* he details a number of problems with the church, his teachers and superiors, and often the monks entrusted to his care.
5. For another view, see Catherine Brown's essay "*Muliebriter:* Doing Gender in the Letters of Heloise," pp. 25–51.
6. This change in focus from textual authenticity to textual analysis was first recommended by Peter von Moos in *"Post Festum:* Was kommt nach der Authentizitätsdebatte über die Briefe Abaelards und Heloisen?" Trier 1980, pp. 19–39. Dronke's argument can be found in *Intellectuals and Poets in Medieval Europe.*
7. *Ep.* 2, ed. Muckle 68 (Radice 109). In the original Latin, this reads "Domino suo immo patri, coniugi suo immo fratri."
8. The terms of this debate may well have been set by Abelard's *Historia calamitatum,* which, as Nouvet points out in "La castration d'Abélard," is essentially the autobiography of a *magister* (p. 260).
9. For a review of this early scrutiny, see Peter Dronke, *Abelard and Heloise in Medieval Testimonies* and Newman in "Authority, Authenticity, and the Repression of Heloise," especially pp. 145–57. The first and arguably the seminal reaction is found in Jean de Meun's *Roman de la Rose,* lines 8765–66, 8773–75, and 8825–30, which later served as a source for Chaucer's mention of the story in Jankyn's *Book of Wikked Wyves* in the Wife of Bath's *Prologue.*
10. To appreciate Heloise's confession of her failings as a rhetorical critique of Abelard's *HC,* one should bear in mind Abelard's melding of the confession and the letter of consolation in the *HC.* Chris Ferguson in "Autobiography as Therapy: Guibert de Nogent, Peter Abelard, and the Making of Medieval Autobiography" notes that in promising a consolation, Abelard essentially chose a pagan genre, the *epistola consolatoria* associated with Seneca and Boethius (202). In our view, the Heloise letters present the argument that if the basis of the consolation is to work—that is, if the addressee is to believe that

in suffering unjust wrongs he and Abelard are expiating their sins—then Abelard must demonstrate a full understanding of his sins and their magnitude. He must offer a full and humble confession. It is this failure that she faults; because his confession fails, he fails to console. In his discussion of the confession, Ferguson identifies three types: the *confessio fidei,* the *confessio peccatorum,* and the *confessio laudis* (p. 196). Specifically, Heloise charges that Abelard has made an incomplete and flawed *confessio peccatorum* (confession of sins designed to convey to the reader the author's sense of sinfulness and humility) and thus has rendered incomplete and flawed his closing *confessio laudis* (an elaborate praise of divine attributes, particularly mercy and grace, and particularly as they were of benefit to the confessor.)

11. See Catherine Brown's "*Muliebriter:* Doing Gender in the Letters of Heloise," for a commentary on Heloise's use of multiple voices.
12. For this account see the *Vita Adae et Evae* 3: 2–3 translated by R. H. Charles in *The Apocrypha and Pseudepigrapha of the Old Testament in English,* Vol. 2. In various literary treatments, this embellishment of the Genesis story can also be found, in part or in whole. See, for example, the *Mystère d'Adam,* especially lines 329–450, 560–90; the *Ludus Coventriae,* 2. 300–500; and *Genesis B,* 823–25. This refashioning also influences the picture of Eve in later texts, most famously, the account of the Fall in Book 10 of Milton's *Paradise Lost.* For a comprehensive treatment of this tradition, see John M. Evans, *Paradise Lost and the Genesis Tradition,* especially pp. 55–56, 162, 204–206, 214–15.
13. *Ep.* 2, ed. Muckle 71 (Radice 113). The Latin reads "ut quo me videlicit pro te amplius humilirem ampliorem apud te consquerer gratiam."
14. See Dronke's chapter on Heloise in *Women Writers* and his "Heloise's *Problemata* and *Letters,*" in Trier 1980, pp. 53–73. See also Peter von Moos in "Le Silence d'Héloïse et les idéologies modernes" in Colloque, pp. 425–68; and Linda Georgianna, "'In Any Corner of Heaven': Heloise's Critique of Monastic Life," in this volume.
15. See Ferguson, "Autobiography as Therapy," especially p. 202, and D. K. Frank, "Abelard as Imitator of Christ."
16. *HC,* ed. Monfrin 70 (Radice 65).
17. *HC,* ed. Monfrin 71 (Radice 65).
18. Abelard himself points out at the beginning of the *HC* that he was punished for conceit by the burning of his book at Soissons; but in his discussion of this episode, nothing of that recognition emerges. Without once pointing out or referring to his earlier observation, Abelard focuses instead on his bitterness and despair at the wrongs heaped on an innocent man. Mary Martin McLaughlin remarks on this lifelong tendency to arrogance and a curious lack of self-knowledge in "Abelard as Autobiographer: The Motives and Meaning of His 'Story of Calamities.'" She notes that in his life he saw "the inevitable outcome of the arrogance of spirit, fostered by his intellectual prowess and the fame it had won him, in which he had embarked on the seduction of Heloise and by which, still earlier, he had aroused the antagonism that triumphed in his condemnation at Soissons" (p. 470). As she astutely adds, he was "sharp enough in discerning the faults of others, yet lacking the deeper insight that is so impressive in the letters of Heloise . . . he was also tempted to lighten the burden of his own responsibilities by projecting it on those around him. . . . His consciousness that his sufferings were at least partly self-inflicted did not move him to that probing of their deeper sources for which he would have found so superb an example in the *Confessions* of St. Augustine" (p. 470–71).
19. McLaughlin also comments on the images of the warrior (p. 473) and the brilliant scholar (p. 473). For his self-defined piety, see the account of his problems with the monks of Saint-Micard [*HC,* ed. Monfrin 90–91 (Radice 85–86)] and at Saint-Gildas [*HC,* ed. Monfrin 98–99 (Radice 95–96)].
20. The comparison with Job is implicit in the form of the complaint; Heloise later explicitly refers to Job twice [*HC,* ed. Muckle 80 (Radice 95–96)]. Interestingly, the *planc-*

tus tradition was connected most frequently not with Job but with the Virgin Mary. See Sandro Sticca, *The Planctus Mariae in the Dramatic Tradition of the Middle Ages.* Comparisons with Christ are drawn when Abelard compares Anselm to the fig tree and himself to Christ, who cursed the fig [*HC,* ed. Monfrin 68 (Radice 62)]. Later, after the castration, when Abelard is teaching at the Priory at Maisoncelle-en-Brie, he records that his students' complaints about other teachers, who do not use dialectic to speak of matters of faith, include Christ's own condemnation of and imply His difficulty with similar "blind guides" [duces cecorum, *HC,* ed. Monfrin 83 (Radice 78)]. He also echoes Christ's words at Gethsemane when closing the book [*HC,* ed. Monfrin 108 (Radice 105)] and compares his companionship with women at the Paraclete to Christ's companionship with women [*HC,* ed. Monfrin 103–105 (Radice 100–102)]. For other comparisons see Radice, especially pp. 79 and 90, and *HC,* ed. Monfrin 84; for a discussion of the identification, see D. K. Frank, "Abelard as Imitator of Christ." Identifications with St. Jerome can be found in *HC,* ed. Monfrin 101 and 108 (Radice 98 and 105).

21. These revelations had surfaced at the time of his injury and were related to the injunction in Leviticus 22.24 that a eunuch is an unclean abomination and prohibited from entering church. See *HC,* ed. Monfrin 80 (Radice 76).
22. *Ep.* 4, ed. Muckle 79 (Radice 131).
23. See Cicero, *De inventione,* I.xvi.22.
24. See Cicero, *De inventione,* I.viii.10 and I.xiii.18.
25. *Ep.* 2, ed. Muckle 71 (Radice 76).
26. See Cicero, *De inventione,* II.xxxiii.101.
27. *HC,* ed. Monfrin 75 (Radice 70).
28. *Ep.* 2, ed. Muckle 71 (Radice 113).
29. *Ep.* 2, ed. Muckle 70 (Radice 113).
30. *Ep.* 2, ed. Muckle 71 (Radice 114).
31. *HC,* ed. Monfrin 77 (Radice 72).
32. *HC,* ed. Monfrin 77 (Radice 72).
33. *Ep.* 2, ed. Muckle 69 (Radice 110). Seneca's position as the "archetype for the *epistolae consolatoriae* throughout the Middle Ages" (Ferguson, "Autobiography as Therapy," p. 201) makes this a particularly telling rebuke given Heloise's complaint that Abelard's *Historia* failed to console.
34. *HC,* ed. Monfrin 78 (Radice 73).
35. *HC,* ed. Monfrin 78 (Radice 74).
36. Radice identifies this source (114 n.2) as does Muckle (71 n. 91). For the quotation in Cicero, see *De inventione* I.31.52.
37. *Ep.* 2, ed. Muckle 71 (Radice 114).
38. *Ep.* 2, ed. Muckle 71 (Radice 114).
39. *Ep.* 2, ed. Muckle 71 (Radice 114).
40. *Ep.* 2, ed. Muckle 72 (Radice 116).
41. *HC,* ed. Monfrin 84 (Radice 79).
42. *Ep.* 2, ed. Muckle 72 (Radice 116).
43. *HC,* ed. Monfrin 89 (Radice 85).
44. *Ep.* 2, ed. Muckle 72 (Radice 114).
45. *HC,* ed. Monfrin 88 (Radice 83).
46. *Ep.* 2, ed. Muckle 72 (Radice 117).
47. *HC,* ed. Monfrin 89 (Radice 84).
48. *Ep.* 2, ed. Muckle 73 (Radice 117).
49. *Ep.* 3, ed. Muckle 74 (Radice 120); *Ep.* 3, ed. Muckle 74 (Radice 158); *Ep.* 3, ed. Muckle 74 (Radice 121).
50. *Ep.* 3, ed. Muckle 70 (Radice 113).

51. *Ep.* 3, ed. Muckle 77 (Radice 114). Among the comparisons that Abelard draws are the fact that women cared for the tomb of Christ, came ahead of and followed after the body, brought ointments, watched at the tomb, and were the first to hear of the resurrection.
52. *Ep.* 3, ed. Muckle 77 (Radice 114).
53. See Ferguson, "Autobiography as Therapy," p. 201.
54. *HC,* ed. Monfrin 63 (Radice 57).
55. This identification of sources is noted both in Radice's translation (72 n. 1) and Monfrin's edition of the *Historia calamitatum* (77 n. 487).
56. *Ep.* 4, ed. Muckle 77 (Radice 128).
57. *Ep.* 4, ed. Muckle 78 (Radice 128).
58. *Ep.* 4, ed. Muckle 78 (Radice 128).
59. *HC,* ed. Monfrin 68 (Radice 62).
60. *Ep.* 4, ed. Muckle 81 (Radice 62).
61. *Ep.* 4, ed. Muckle 79 (Radice 130).
62. *HC,* ed. Monfrin 89.
63. *HC,* ed. Monfrin 70–71 (Radice 65).
64. Radice 84; *HC,* ed. Monfrin 85 (Radice 84).
65. *Ep.* 4, ed. Muckle 79 (Radice 131).
66. *Ep.* 4, ed. Muckle 80 (Radice 131).
67. *Ep.* 4, ed. Muckle 80 (Radice 131).
68. *Ep.* 4, ed. Muckle 80 (Radice 132).
69. *Ep.* 4, ed. Muckle 80 (Radice 132).
70. *Ep.* 4, ed. Muckle 80 (Radice 132).
71. *Ep.* 4, ed. Muckle 81 (Radice 133).
72. The quotation reads: "I have more easily found men who have presented their innocence than men who have known repentance" [*Ep.* 4, ed. Muckle 80 (Radice 132)]. It is from *De paenitentia II.10.*
73. See especially passages in *HC,* ed. Monfrin 108–109 and (Radice 104–105).
74. For Abelard's use of Romans 8.28 see *HC,* ed. Monfrin 108 (Radice 105). Heloise's quotation of Romans 7.24 is found in *Ep.* 4, ed. Muckle 81 (Radice 133).
75. *Ep.* 4, ed. Muckle 81 (Radice 133).
76. *Ep.* 4, ed. Muckle 82 (Radice 135).
77. *Ep.* 4, ed. Muckle 82 (Radice 135).
78. *Ep.* 4, ed. Muckle 82 (Radice 135).
79. *Ep.* 4, ed. Muckle 82 (Radice 135).
80. *Ep.* 4, ed. Muckle 82 (Radice 135).
81. *Ep.* 4, ed. Muckle 82 (Radice 136).
82. *Ep.* 4, ed. Muckle 82 (Radice 136).
83. *Ep.* 4, ed. Muckle 82 (Radice 136).
84. *Ep.* 4, ed. Muckle 82 (Radice 136).
85. *HC,* ed. Monfrin 73 (Radice 67); See Cicero, *De inventione,* I.xxii.31.
86. *Ep.* 5, ed. Muckle 83 (Radice 137).
87. *Ep.* 5, ed. Muckle 83 (Radice 138).
88. See Radice, 105; *HC,* ed. Monfrin 108 (Radice 139); *Ep.* 5, ed. Muckle 84.
89. *Ep.* 5, Muckle 87 (Radice 139).
90. *Ep.* 5, ed. Muckle 87 (Radice 144).
91. *Ep.* 5, ed. Muckle 87 (Radice 139).
92. *Ep.* 5, ed. Muckle 87 (Radice 144).
93. *Ep.* 5, ed. Muckle 87 (Radice 143); 94. *Ep.* 5, ed. Muckle 87 (Radice 143–44).
94. *Ep.* 5, ed. Muckle 82 (Radice 135).
95. *Ep.* 5, ed. Muckle 87 (Radice 144).

96. *Ep.* 5, ed. Muckle 87 (Radice 144).
97. *Ep.* 5, ed. Muckle 87 (Radice 144).
98. Ep. 5, ed. Muckle 87 (Radice 144).
99. *Ep.* 5, ed. Muckle 87 (Radice 145).
100. *Ep.* 5, ed. Muckle 88 (Radice 145).
101. *Ep.* 5, ed. Muckle 88 (Radice 146).
102. *Ep.* 5, ed. Muckle 88 (Radice 146); *Ep.* 5, ed. Muckle 89 (Radice 147).
103. *HC,* ed. Monfrin 108 (Radice 69).
104. *Ep.* 4, ed. Muckle 79 (Radice 130).
105. *Ep.* 4, ed. Muckle 71 (Radice 113).
106. *HC,* ed. Monfrin 78 (Radice 74).
107. *Ep.* 5, ed. Muckle 88 (Radice 146).
108. *Ep.* 5, ed. Muckle 92 (Radice 152).
109. *Ep.* 5, ed. Muckle 92 (Radice 153).
110. *Ep.* 5, ed. Muckle 92 (Radice 135).
111. *Ep.* 5, ed. Muckle 93 (Radice 154).
112. *Ep.* 5, ed. Muckle 93 (Radice 154).
113. *Ep.* 5, ed. Muckle 93 (Radice 154).

CHAPTER 6

HELOISE, DIALECTIC, AND THE *HEROIDES*

Phyllis R. Brown and John C. Peiffer II

In her letters to Abelard, Heloise employs her special sensitivity to pagan classical works, especially Ovid's Heroides, *to explore potential new identities, not imagined by classical authors, that she and Abelard might assume.*

M. T. Clanchy's recent *Abelard: A Medieval Life* pushes analysis of Heloise's letters into new territory. First, he suggests "it may have been Heloise who gave Abelard's writing its distinctive character"[1]: "She is a 'writer' in the modern sense of creative author and also in the sense of a stylist and rhetorician, who has been instructed in—and delights in performing variations on—the most advanced manoeuvers in Latin composition. She is steeped in Latin literature, both in the modes of expression of its classical authors and in their subject matter, particularly their discussions of exemplary heroes and heroines. . . . For her, these noble Romans are living presences and an inspiration even though they were pagans."[2] Next Clanchy attributes to Heloise's influence on Abelard's writings not only stylistic and rhetorical features but also fundamental philosophical and theological concepts. Thus he writes: "In her first extant letter to him (in response to his 'history of calamities' in c. 1132) she told him she was both 'very guilty and very innocent' [*nocens/innocens*], since 'it is not the doing of a thing but the intention of the doer which makes the crime.' This is a fundamental premise of Abelard's *Ethics* and nothing he says there expresses the problem more succinctly than Heloise's paradox *nocens/innocens*."[3] In addition, Clanchy writes, "More significant in its consequences for European culture than the castration and persecution of Abelard (the 'calamities' which followed his marriage) was the silencing of Heloise, as that was a prelude to the silencing of academic women as a class for the next eight centuries."[4] Clanchy concludes his study with the idea that the one and only person in Europe Abelard tolerated as an intellectual equal or superior was Heloise.

Our study of Heloise's uses of Ovid's *Heroides* in her letters to Abelard agrees with the arguments of Clanchy and others, especially those represented in this volume: Heloise uses her Latin literary models in major ways that are unusual for her time and that have not only literary significance but also have philosophical and theological significance. In other words, while Heloise faces "the world with a 'self' constructed out of bits and pieces of great authors of the past," as Mary Carruthers argues, she also employs her special sensitivity to pagan, classical authors in her exploration of possibilities for new identities she and Abelard may assume, identities not imagined by her pagan models.[5] In this she creates parallels not only between herself and Ovid's heroines but also between herself and Ovid. More specifically, our examination of echoes of and parallels to Ovid's *Heroides* in Heloise's letters reveals that in the course of writing her three letters to Abelard, Heloise moves beyond the binary oppositions of legitimate and illegitimate, victor and victim, suggested by Ovid's heroic women and intensified by some medieval commentaries, to explore the latent content that dialectical processes disclose.

In addition, Abelard's insistence in his letters on points of views that directly oppose hers and his pressure for her to adopt the persona of a victor in place of the stance of victim that she borrows from Ovid's *Heroides* seem to contribute to her success in exploring the middle ground between victim and victor.[6] Thus while our study corroborates Clanchy's suggestion that Heloise "saved Abelard's monastic reputation by inviting him—in response to his 'history of calamities' and the letters that followed—to write a rule and numerous other works, most notably his hymns, for her nuns at the Paraclete" and that "Heloise seems to have set the agenda which Abelard addressed in his theological writings," it also illuminates some of the ways that Abelard's intelligence and perceptivity contributed to Heloise's accomplishment.[7]

Although Heloise never cites Ovid's *Heroides* the way she does Ovid's *Art of Love* in *Ep.* 6, Seneca's letter to Lucilius, and Cicero's "Contra Catilinam," many critics have noted similarities between her letters to Abelard and the *Heroides,* a series of fictional letters from women who played minor or supporting roles in ancient epic, drama, and other forms of literature, to the men whom they loved. For instance, D.W. Robertson suggests the Heloise of the letters "makes of herself another Dido, abandoned by a man whose *pietas* demanded more honorable pursuits" and also points out similarities between Heloise's account of her amorous dreams and Sappho's letter to Phaon.[8] Barbara Newman remarks, "Heloise, like an Ovidian heroine, gestures toward the whole world as witness to her woes," and "she knew of the passionate women in love, seduced and abandoned yet eternally ardent—Dido, Sappho, Medea, Oenone. These utterly committed lovers of the *Heroides,* rather than the playful and manipulative coquettes of the *Ars amatoria,* powerfully appealed to her."[9] Linda S. Kauffman precedes her chapter on Heloise's letters with a chapter on Ovid's *Heroides* and points out similarities between Heloise's situations and Hypsipyle's, Ariadne's, and Phaedra's.[10] Peter Dronke remarks at the beginning of his chapter on Heloise that she in a sense "writes her own *Heroides*"; later Dronke explores similarities between Ovid's letter from Briseis to Achilles and Heloise's first two letters to Abelard.[11] In chapter 5, in this volume, Katharina Wilson and Glenda McLeod note parallels between Heloise's insistence on a variety of roles for herself and relationships to Abelard and Ovid's *Heroides,* especially Medea's letter to Jason. Michael Calabrese explores some of the differences between Andreas Capellanus' and Abelard and Heloise's uses of Ovid in what Calabrese sees as a "movement from Ovid's *Ars amatoria* to his *Remedia amoris,*" with Andreas, Abelard, and Heloise substituting "medieval, Christian remedy" for Ovidian remedy.[12]

W. S. Anderson's overview of similarities among Ovid's women further clarifies significant parallels. First, he points out that "The plaintive heroine regards herself as alone, deserted, abandoned [*sola, deserta, relicta*]." Even more significant is Anderson's generalization that

> all the heroines believe that they have a claim on the man: an explicit or implicit *foedus* or bond links the two, which imposes *fides,* loyalty, on them both. The heroines have remained faithful [*fida*] and regularly represent themselves as still loving [*amans*], but the long absence of the man, perhaps also information about his disloyal behaviour, leads to complaints, unhappy charges that he is anywhere from slow to respond [*lentus*] and iron-hearted [*ferreus*] all the way to cruel [*crudelis*], criminal [*sceleratus*] and faithless [*perfidus*]. The heroine hopes, usually in vain as we know, by these complaints to stir the conscience of her beloved and so bring him home, to re-create the *foedus* and the once-glorious context of reciprocal passion.[13]

In writing "her own *Heroides,*" Heloise picks up on many of these motifs but to radically different ends. While many of Ovid's mythological heroines respond to their abandonment destructively, with suicide or revenge, Heloise uses references to them as part of her process of shaping for herself and for Abelard possibilities for productive and successful lives as leaders exerting powerful influences on the church and society as a whole.

Heloise and Abelard both would have known Ovid's writings from their years studying the *trivium*. In the twelfth century, students normally encountered Ovid's *Remedia Amoris* shortly after learning the alphabet, the Lord's Prayer, and the psalter. Evidence for this is its appearance in many redactions of the *Libri Catoniani,* the first anthology of classical texts students used for learning Latin grammar.[14] Other *Libri Manuales,* anthologies of readings for preuniversity students, also often include Ovid's works as grammatical or rhetorical models. In his study "Ovid at School: From the Ninth to the Fifteenth Century," James H. McGregor examines "five major sources of information on medieval grammar curricula," each of which "gives Ovid significant place in the curriculum."[15] Both McGregor's and Eva Matthews Sanford's earlier study, "The Use of Classical Latin Authors in the Libri Manuales," demonstrate that Ovid's *Heroides* consistently plays an important role in the school texts. Ralph Hexter suggests one reason for the popularity of the *Heroides* as a school text may have been that they offered a more "manageable number of tales" (twenty in most medieval manuscripts) than did the *Metamorphoses.*[16] Commentary in several medieval manuscripts (Codex latinus Monacensis [clm]19475, sometimes called the Munich manuscript, clm 19474, clm 29208 (19, Palatinus lat. 242, and Hafn. 2013) reveals that Ovid's *Heroides* were read as texts with multiple uses: to study grammar, rhetoric, the art of letter writing, and mythology and to learn moral and ethical judgment.[17] Perhaps of particular significance to an understanding of Heloise's uses of Ovid is the fact that some medieval commentators read Ovid's *Heroides* as offering double messages that students could study for their rhetorical and moral/ethical significance. For instance, Ralph Hexter cites marginal comments in Hafn. 2013, f. 67r, specifying that each letter should be understood both in terms of the intention of the female speaker (or in the double letters the male speaker as well) and the intention of the author, Ovid.[18] Some of the moralizing was heavy-handed, but at least one manuscript, the Munich manuscript, offers a range of interpretation.

The Munich manuscript is particularly revealing about uses of the *Heroides* as a school text because it includes not just one introduction to the collection of letters but three, the second and third increasingly longer and more complex than the first, each specifying the moral/ethical lessons the texts were to teach. In Huygens's edition the first *accessus* occupies twelve lines of text, the second, twenty-seven lines, and the third, ninety-two lines. *Accessus* II moralizes the *Heroides* as follows:

> Intencio sua est legitimum commendare conubium uel amorem, et secundum hoc triplici modo tractat de ipso amore, scilicet de legitimo, de illicito et stulto. de legitimo per Penolopen, de illicito per Canacen, de stulto per Phillidem. sed has duas partes, scilicet stulti et illiciti, non causa ipsarum, uerum gratia illius tercie commendandi interserit et sic commendando legitimum, stultum et illicitum reprehendit[19]
>
> [Its intention is to commend legitimate marriage or love, conducting its discussion of love precisely according to three categories, legitimate, illicit and foolish—about legitimate love through Penelope, about illicit love through Canace, and about foolish love through Phyllis. But he inserts these two parts, namely of the foolish and illicit [love], not for the sake of these but in favor of the third (love) to be commended, and so by commending the legitimate (love) he rejects the foolish and illicit.]

Accessus III gives a slightly more complex moral system, subdividing illegitimate love into three categories: *stultus, incestus,* and *furiosus.* Even more important, this *accessus* goes on to list five different explanations of the author's aim in writing these letters, introducing the alternatives offered after the first explanation with the word *aliter.* To conclude, the compiler offers a summary comment, as Hexter points out "not to exclude any explanation mentioned so far but to add an over-arching aim: 'Sciendum quoque est quod cum in toto libro hanc et supradictas habeat intentiones, preterea duas habet in hoc libro, unam generalem et aliam specialem'" [It is also to be noticed that when in the entire book (The *Heroides*) he has this and the aforesaid intentions, he furthermore has two intentions in this book (Penelope's letter), one general and the other specific.][20]

Remarkably, this one manuscript offers a range of interpretation. Readers find here the simple binary oppositions of legitimate/illegitimate love and Ovid's aim/letter writer's aim, which in Hexter's words "rides roughshod over the subtle differences among the heroines and the situations in which each finds herself."[21] However, readers also find an example of multiple, conflicting yet unresolved interpretations of text that may confirm Clanchy's suggestion that Abelard's "innovation" in composing his *Sic et Non* is that he took "an existing structure, that of the *Liber Pancrisis* or something like it, and improved it almost out of recognition."[22] The idea of introducing students to contradictory interpretations that result from a dialectical exploration of complexities, instead of editing to create a unified view condoned by the church, may have been developing at that time.

In this chapter we analyze some of the ways Ovid's *Heroides* and medieval commentaries contributed to Heloise's self-construction in her letters to Abelard. In addition to pointing out some surprising verbal echoes, we illuminate the way dialectical processes contribute to complexity of her borrowings from Ovid. We argue that, finally, Heloise is much more like Ovid himself than like his fictional heroines.

Penelope

Parallels between Heloise and Penelope are less obvious to a modern reader than the parallels between Heloise and Ovid's more unconventional heroines. However, medieval commentaries suggest that it was usual for medieval readers to read the *Heroides* "intertextually," with Penelope not only figuring as the first of the letter writers but also as the ideal against whom all the other women were evaluated. Twentieth-century commentators also read the *Heroides* intertextually, not only understanding the individual letters in the larger context of the collection but also reading Ovid's treatment of myth and legend against treatments by other classical authors. Thus, for example, according to Howard Jacobson, Ovid uses the Homeric characterization of Penelope, the "paragon of wifely devotion and loyalty," to set off his own characterization of her "as a dissatisfied lover who feels wronged by her man."[23] Penelope opens her letter, written shortly after the end of the Trojan War, with a strong reproach, which Jacobson argues derives from a very different literary tradition that turned "the obviously loyal Homeric heroine into a slut": Penelope calls Ulysses *lento,* suggesting he is delaying deliberately, and insists that he not even take time to write, just return immediately. Jacobson continues, "here is a different world, a different Penelope: complaints, utterances of self-pity, ungracious allegations all issue from her mouth with consistent regularity. . . . In harsh terms she condemns the Greek expedition to Troy, essentially because it conflicts with her self-interest."[24]

By setting up this tension between an idealized Penelope, who willingly accepts her role as subordinate to the "larger good" that Ulysses must serve in order to be worthy to be her husband, and a more human woman who has the audacity to question the importance of the wars occupying the Homeric and Vergilian gods and men and to insist on the importance of loyalty to wife and homeland, Ovid offers Heloise rich material to draw from as she writes her letters of reproach and complaint to Abelard. Abelard, like Ulysses, has left his wife to pursue a higher calling, in Abelard's case turning to a monastic life after his castration. And Heloise, like Ovid's Penelope, resists subordination to that higher calling, although she is willing to subordinate herself to Abelard himself. Penelope's letter introduces a theme of the *Heroides* as a whole, in which Ovid explores and undermines, through the women's voices, the moral stance that values the sacrifice of self for higher ends. Heloise's letters to Abelard translate that exploration into an explicitly Christian context without simplifying any of the issues involved. Significantly, moreover, dialectical processes provide Heloise with ways, in the course of her correspondence with Abelard, to move beyond the options available even to Penelope, who may be Ovid's most fortunate woman.[25]

Although medieval commentators emphasize the binary opposition of Penelope and most of the other women writing letters in the *Heroides,* other parallels between Heloise's self-characterization in her letters and Ovid's characterization of Penelope tend to illuminate ways that both women are like the other less fortunate Ovidian heroines. Thus while headnotes in the medieval commentaries stress the differences between what commentators consider legitimate love and what they consider foolish love, a close examination of the parallels Heloise creates suggests she, like twentieth-century readers, sees the underlying problems with medieval commentators' simple systems of moral categories. Heloise's insistence on bridging what medieval commentators constructed as a gap between Penelope and most of the other women in Ovid's *Heroides* is made explicit in her insistence on the double nature of Abelard's obligation to her: "Cui quidem tanto te maiore debito noveris obligatum, quanto te amplius nuptialis foedere sacramenti constat esse astrictum et eo te magis mihi obnoxium, quo te semper ut omnibus patet immoderato amore complexa sum" [Yet you must know that you are bound to me by an obligation which is all the greater for the further close tie of the marriage sacrament uniting us, and are the deeper in my debt because of the love I have always borne you, as everyone knows, a love which is beyond all bounds].[26] Marriage and duty, Ulysses' obligations to Penelope, bind Abelard to Heloise, and at the same time Abelard is in her debt because of her "love which is beyond all bounds," like the love experienced by Phyllis, Canace, Dido, and Medea, for instance.

Other examples confirm that Heloise is drawing examples from women the medieval commentators see as diametrically opposed. For instance, Ulysses and Abelard on the surface may seem more justified in having left Penelope and Heloise than are Demophoon, Paris, and Hercules for abandoning Phyllis, Oenone, and Deianira, who apparently were motivated more by whim or personal desire than by a higher duty. Nevertheless, the parallels between Heloise's letters and Penelope's letter point as much or more to similarities to the other ladies than to difference. So when Heloise chastises Abelard for neglecting his responsibilities to her and to the Paraclete, she is simultaneously establishing a parallel to the virtuous Penelope and to the foolish heroines whose letters follow Penelope's. Indeed, the parallels to Phyllis and Ariadne, for example, who provide much more dramatic examples of the vulnerability of abandoned victims than Penelope does, are more immediately evident than the parallels to Penelope.

Another similarity between Heloise and Penelope that highlights similarities to a number of other Ovidian heroines in the *Heroides* is their shared fear of real and imagined dangers that their husbands are facing. Penelope writes: "Quando ego non timui graviora pericula veris? / res est solliciti plena timoris amor [When have I not feared dangers graver than the real? / Love is a thing ever filled with anxious fear].[27] Heloise, like Penelope, expresses terror at the idea that Abelard's life may be in danger. Although shipwreck does not pose a literal threat for Abelard, Heloise's shipwreck metaphor, "fluctuas naufragiis,"[28] intensifies the parallel between her fears and Penelope's while at the same time suggesting parallels to other Ovidian heroines whose absent lovers literally are traveling by sea. Heloise's fears that Abelard may never have felt anything more than lust for her provides another link not only to Ovid's Penelope but even more dramatically to Phyllis, Oenone, Hypsipyle, Deianira, Ariadne, and Medea, all of whom are faced with the reality that lust has been a primary influence on their beloved men.

Heloise shares the fears of these women but ultimately finds ways to construct herself that are radically different from any of Ovid's women (even though Ovid may have given other readers the sense that he explored the full range of possibilities for heroic women). The rather simplistic resolution of Penelope's situation—Ulysses does finally return home—is not available to Heloise any more than it is to Phyllis, Oenone, or Ariadne. The other alternatives suggested by Ovid's women are rather discouraging. Phyllis, Dido, Deianira, Canace, and Leander all commit suicide; Hypsipyle and Medea both resort to terrible cursing and/or vengeance. While Ariadne's, Hermione's, and Cydippe's marriages to Dionysius, Orestes, and Acontius are more positive, they are not options for Heloise. In her first letter especially, Heloise insists, in ways that make Abelard very uncomfortable, on the ways she is like the women medieval commentators label as illegitimate and, at the same time, like Penelope, the model of legitimate behavior. Significantly, in that letter Heloise is using Ovid's *Heroides* in a way similar to the use of Ovid's *Ars Amatoria* that Donna Bussell sees in Heloise's third letter to Abelard, suggesting not only that weak and strong are yoked by the Benedictine Rule but also that "the nature of Philosophy and the wanton woman (or man) can abide in the same body"[29]

Phaedra and Canace

At first glance there might seem to be no connection between Heloise and Phaedra, who is attempting to lure her stepson Hippolytus into an incestuous relationship, or Canace, who, imprisoned by her father as a punishment for the incestuous relationship with her brother Macareus, will commit suicide after completing the letter. However, both Ovid's Phaedra and his Canace demand of readers that we—in contrast to medieval commentators—rethink simple moral categories. The medieval commentators label Phaedra as either foolish or unchaste, Canace as foolish or mad, both as reprehensible contrasts to Penelope. Heloise, however, chooses to construct herself using a dialectical process that draws on the traditionally exemplary and the conventionally reprehensible. Phaedra says to Hippolytus, in an exclamation remarkably like Heloise's famous avowal that she would rather be Abelard's whore than Augustus's wife, "Si mihi concedat Iuno fratremque virumque, / Hippolytum videor praepositura Iovi!" (IV.35–36) [Should Juno yield me him who is at once her brother and her lord, methinks I should prefer Hippolytus to Jove!] Note, though, that Phaedra's verb *concedat* sidesteps the moral issue of a love relationship outside of wedlock versus virtuous marriage, contextualized as it is by the mores of Jove, a pagan god. Heloise takes the suggestion offered by Ovid's poem, Phaedra's preferring Hippolytus to Jove, presumably with neither relationship resulting in marriage, and exaggerates it by preferring the role of Abelard's whore to the role as wife to Emperor Augustus.[30]

Also relevant is the fact that Ovid allows Phaedra to explore her love for her stepson in ways that explode conventional morality. Thus she insists, "Non ego nequitia socialia foedera rumpam; / fama—velim quaeras—crimine nostra vacat" (IV.8–9). [It will not be through wanton baseness that I shall break my marriage bond; my name—and you may ask—is free from all reproach]. At the very moment when she proposes a relationship that will earn her general reproach, she insists she is beyond reproach. Heloise goes a step further, admitting to guilt and insisting on her innocence in the same sentence: "Quae plurimum nocens, plurimum ut nosti sum innocens" [Wholly guilty though I am, I am also, as you know, wholly innocent].[31] In an argument that explicitly challenges conventional morality, both medieval and modern, Heloise defends her relationship with Abelard as better for both of them than marriage, using the "ethic of pure intention" that Abelard later elaborates in his *Ethics.*

Canace's refusal to see her experience simply as moral deviation also may have contributed to Heloise's self-construction in her letters to Abelard. Contrasts between Canace and Phaedra are significant as well, for Ovid's Canace succeeds in convincing many readers that she is beyond reproach, while Phaedra's insistence that she is beyond reproach is far from convincing. Howard Jacobson asks, "Who could be heartless enough not to commiserate with, even shed a tear for, the wretched girl [Canace]?" after pointing out her role as an innocent victim of cruel fate.[32] Heloise's letters, especially the first two, have evoked similar sympathy from readers.

Furthermore, in contrast to most of the other women in the *Heroides,* Canace does not use her letter as a medium within which to berate Macareus. Rather, too late, she tries to understand how her tragic situation has come to be. Katerina Philippides points out that Canace refers only once in the letter to the incestuous nature of her relationship with Macareus, and that comes in a passage not concerned with an exploration of moral issues but rather in the context of an amoral philosophic questioning.[33] Canace asks, "O utinam, Macareu, quae nos commisit in unum, venisset leto serior hora meo! / cur umquam plus me, frater, quam frater amasti, / et tibi, non debet quod soror esse, fui? (XI.21–24) [Ah, Macareus, would that the hour that made us two as one had come after my death! Oh why, my brother, did you ever love me more than brother, and why have I been to you what a sister should not be?] Canace wants to know *why* she and her brother chose this path of doom, *why* they fell in love, *why* they acted upon it, but she does not express guilt or shame for her act; she regrets only that she was so unfortunate as not to have died before the incest occurred. Neither Heloise nor Canace sees her situation as a simple punishment for moral deviation. Thus just as Canace asks her brother *why* they acted as they did, Heloise's first letter is riddled with questions to Abelard and an overall request that he help her understand his treachery and her situation.

Indeed, Heloise refuses to interpret her misfortune or Abelard's simply as justified punishment for their sinfulness. Although she identifies changing her clothing and her mind to enter the convent as madness, and thus identifies herself with Canace who is the epitome of mad love in at least one medieval commentary, her uses of language convey the strong sense of a philosopher struggling to make sense out of complex evidence and demanding that Abelard assist her in her effort. Here she is simultaneously like Canace and different from her. Many readers have assumed that Heloise was as innocent as Canace when Abelard first seduced her. Heloise is explicit in emphasizing, as Canace does, that the extramarital love relationship, however it began, was a reciprocal one, that she too felt the flame of passion. Jacobson writes: Canace had "no reason to find fault with Macareus, this was reciprocated love. She too felt the flame of love and passion. Any responsibility, any guilt, she shares—and understands that she shares."[34] However, whereas Canace understands she shares the responsibility, underlying her characterization as "loving, gentle, delicate, pitiful, yet with a carriage of dignity, quiet resolve, and resignation," according to Jacobson, are qualities very different from Heloise's passionate resistance to conventional morality.[35] Ovid's Canace relates that near death in childbirth, she was revived by Macareus' promise that they would marry. She seems at the time to have accepted marriage as a simple solution to the problem of her pregnancy. Not so Heloise, who, according to both Abelard's account in the *Historia Calamitatum* and her own fuller account in her first letter, clearly saw that marriage would not solve their problems.

Furthermore, Heloise, who as Glenda McLeod has pointed out, "presents her case logically, linguistically, committing the public side to an Abelard who will judge 'all' and 'in everything,'" demands, in return for all she has given him, that he explain one thing, why he has neglected her.[36] Like Canace, Heloise asks why, but not from a stance of resignation: "Dum unum si vales cur, post conversionem nostram quam tu solus facere decrevisti, in tamtam tibi negligentiam atque oblivionem venerim ut nec colloquio praesentis recreer nec absentis epistola consoler" [Tell me one thing, if you can. Why, after our entry into religion, which was your decision alone, have I been so neglected and forgotten by you that I have neither a word from you when you are here to give me strength nor the consolation of a letter in absence?].[37] Like Canace, Heloise is concerned to make sense of what might simply be interpreted by a less thoughtful woman as senseless fortune; both women—in sharp contrast to the medieval commentators—resist seeing their misfortune as related to moral deviation. But

Heloise, unlike Canace, ultimately finds an alternative to self-destruction as a way to deal with her tragic situation. Not only does she "make a space for her erotic experience which does not reduce an unruly otherness—both hers and Abelard's—to a symbolic and ordered identity," as Peggy Kamuf suggests[38]; through her letters to Abelard and his responses, Heloise also constructs for herself an identity that occupies a middle ground between the stance of victim suggested by the *Heroides* and the role of victor suggested by Abelard when he writes, "Refero Domino et in hoc grates, qui te tunc et a poena liberavit et ad coronam reservavit" [For this I give thanks to the Lord, who both spared you punishment then and reserved you for a crown to come].[39] Significantly, Heloise has already informed Abelard in *Ep.* 3 that she does not "seek a crown of victory," that she wants only "whatever corner of Heaven" God deems appropriate for her. Heloise uses the humility topos in a dialectical exploration of new philosophic and theological ground.

Dido

Recently Michael Calabrese has explored parallels between the self-constructions in the correspondence between Heloise and Abelard and Ovid's construction of the relationship between Dido and Aeneas in the *Heroides.* For example, Calabrese writes: "Abelard plays the role of the male lover engaged in other pursuits who refuses to recognize, validate, or satisfy female desire. His higher calling, like Aeneas's, absents him from his lover's life. Like a *Heroides* heroine, Heloise speaks her desire, complains of his absence, and demands redress."[40] Calabrese then goes on to argue that Abelard offers Heloise a Christian remedy for her love: "Abelard's neo-Ovidian *remedia amoris* seeks to liberate Heloise from the *amor furiosus* that has driven her to complain as Ovid's poor scorned women do."[41] He concludes: "Together, Abelard and Heloise finally do what Dido longs to do with Aeneas—they build a Carthage, not a city but a spiritual community, a spiritual temple which has needs that Abelard, responding to Heloise's requests, is manifestly ready to meet. Its high towers rise out of the ashes of Ovidian craft and Heroidian desire."[42] However, there are at least two problems with this conclusion. First, Heloise chose, after receiving Abelard's writings on the monastic life and his suggestions for a rule for women, to model her own rule at the Paraclete more closely on Cistercian adaptations of the Benedictine Rule than on Abelard's prescriptions.[43] Thus the actual developments in Heloise's administration of the Paraclete after the correspondence occasioned by the *Historia calamitatum* owe at least as much to thinkers such as Bernard of Clairvaux, Abelard's archenemy, as to Abelard.

Second, the main activities of building a new spiritual community at the Paraclete had already occurred before Abelard wrote his *Historia.* Heloise did spend some three years working with Abelard at the Paraclete between 1129, when he returned to Champagne from Saint-Gildas to turn his hermitage over to Heloise and her nuns, and about 1132, when his *Historia* and the subsequent letters seem to have been written. It is conceivable that Heloise could have understood these events, their working together to create a spiritual community when her beloved returned to her after an absence of about ten years, as Calabrese suggests. However, Heloise says of their time together since entering into their monastic vocations: "Unde non mediocri admiratione nostrae tenera conversationis initia tua iam dudum oblivio movit quod, nec reverentia Dei nec amore nostri nec sanctorum patrum exemplis admonitus, fluctuantem me et iam diutino moerore confectam vel sermone praesentem vel epistola absentem consolari tentaveris" [I was not a little surprised and troubled by your forgetfulness, when neither reverence for God nor our mutual love nor the example of the holy fathers made you think of trying to comfort me, wavering and exhausted as I was by prolonged grief, either by word when I was with you or by letter when we had parted].[44]

Moreover, evidence from Abelard's own *Historia calamitatum* and his life after the correspondence makes it quite clear that he never really departed from his life pattern of seeking for himself positions that would reflect his self-assessment as the greatest philosopher in the world but consistently throwing away his hard-earned success almost as soon as he had established himself in what could be a secure position. In sharp contrast to Abelard's self-centeredness combined with a self-destructive streak is Heloise's self-abnegation and her gifted administration of the Paraclete. This is not a Christian reworking of the Dido-Aeneas story in which they finally are reunited and construct a spiritual community where they can live happily ever after. Although Abelard himself emphasizes the parallel between himself and Vergil's Aeneas, as Jane Chance argues in chapter 7 in this volume, Ovid's Dido story invites us to see ways in which Abelard's mixture of brilliant reasoning and self-destruction is Dido-like, while Heloise's ultimate acceptance that her spiritual responsibilities must take precedence over her personal feelings is parallel not to Ovid's Aeneas so much as to Vergil's.

Yet there are some significant parallels between the Heloise–Abelard correspondence and Ovid's letter from Dido to Aeneas. Ovid's Dido fears—wrongly—that she may be a cause of danger for Aeneas if he feels obliged to leave her: "Perdita ne perdam, timeo, noceamve nocenti, / neu bibat aequoreas naufragus hostis aquas (VII.61–62) [Undone myself, I fear lest I be the undoing of him who is my undoing, lest I bring harm to him who brings harm to me, lest my enemy be wrecked at sea and drink the waters of the deep]. Heloise regrets that the marriage which she foretold would be harmful to both of them has been more harmful to Abelard than to her and exclaims in her second letter: "O me miseram in tanti sceleris causa progenitam!" [What misery for me—born as I was to be the cause of such a crime!].[45] She also dwells in her second letter on the irony that Abelard's punishment came not when they were fornicating but after they were married, thus emphasizing the role of marriage to her as a source of danger.

Furthermore, Heloise, like Dido (and several other Ovidian heroines), willingly accepted an extramarital relationship. Toward the end of her letter Dido writes, "si pudet uxoris, non nupta, sed hospita dicar; / dum tua sit, Dido quidlibet esse feret (VII.167–68) [If you shame to have me your wife, let me not be called bride, but hostess; so she be yours, Dido will endure to be what you will]. Heloise takes this further. She corrects Abelard's paraphrase of her argument against marriage, specifying that she argued it was *more honorable to her,* not to him, for her to be his whore than to be his wife.

In addition, Dido's anguished request that Aeneas at least delay his departure in order to give her a little time to learn strength and thus to endure bravely is also like Heloise's final argument in her first letter to Abelard, when she writes: "Per ipsum itaque cui te obtulisti Deum te obsecro ut quo modo potes tuam mihi praesentiam reddas, consolationem videlicet mihi aliquam rescribendo, hoc saltem pacto ut sic recreata divino alacrior vacem obsequio" [And so, in the name of God to whom you have dedicated yourself, I beg you to restore your presence to me in the way you can—by writing me some word of comfort, so that in this at least I may find increased strength and readiness to serve God].[46] Perhaps more important than these parallels, however, is Heloise's reasonableness, even when she is describing herself as mad. Ovid's Dido similarly calls herself foolish (suggesting the category in which some medieval commentators classified her) to want an ingrate like Aeneas to stay with her, but at the same time is "a model of common sense," to borrow Jacobson's words. In sharp contrast to Vergil's Dido, Jacobson points out, Ovid's Dido "is no ranting epic heroine but a lover with a repertoire of traditional elegiac poses and arguments, capable of seeing the immediate realities and coping with them."[47]

Jacobson also points out that the argument Ovid's Dido articulates "far surpasses the speeches of Dido in the *Aeneid*. Not only are the arguments persuasive but—above all—they are reasonable, both in their content and in the manner of presentation."[48]

Jacobson goes on to give examples of Dido's talent at disputation, "her ability to argue a point, concede some hypothetical objection, and then counter it by introducing a new argument." Moreover, Jacobson argues that as important to Dido's character as her reasonableness is her "tendency to give her arguments erotic shades, a quality totally absent in Vergil's Dido who mentions *noster amor* (r.307; cf. 370, 429, and 479) and feels no need to harp on the obvious. Ovid's utilizes every erotic conceit she can marshal."[49] Jacobson concludes that Ovid's Dido is "a model of common sense in the erotic-elegiac vein" who uses her common sense to question the very Vergilian and Augustinian ideal of a divine mission taking precedence over personal considerations, which by definition is beyond common sense.[50] Heloise, too, combines logical reasonableness with erotic overtones in surprising ways, exploding the seeming polar oppositions of reason and emotion, logic and love.

Deianira

Ovid creates a particularly dramatic situation in *Heroides* IX out of the essentially static literary form of the epistle. As Deianira gets to line 143 of her letter to Hercules, a messenger arrives bearing the news that Hercules is dying from the poison that was in the cloak she sent him. The refrain she repeats four times in the final twenty-five lines of the poem, "inpia quid dubitas Deianira mori?" [O wicked Deianira, why hesitate to die?"] has a parallel in Heloise's second letter to Abelard: her horror at his supposition that she and her fellow nuns will outlive him. The parallel is heightened by her subsequent ejaculation, "O me miseram in tanti sceleris causa progenitam!" [What misery for me—born as I was to be the cause of such a crime!].[51] The crime itself is her uncle's causing Abelard to be castrated, not her being the immediate cause of his death, as is Deianira's case. Nevertheless, Heloise insists on seeing herself as responsible for the crime. The parallel highlights the accuracy of Heloise's prediction about their marriage in contrast to Deianira's inability to see that her gift would destroy Hercules.

Deianira and Heloise also share the common dilemma that Heloise expresses with her statement, "Sed quo te amplius nunc securum reddidi, negligentiorem sustineo" [But as it is, the more I have made you feel secure in me, the more I have to bear with your neglect].[52] When Hercules saw a threat to his relationship with Deianira, as when Nessus abducted her, he came to her rescue, but when she is enacting her wifely duties at home, he pursues other women and dishonor. Abelard insisted that Heloise take her monastic vows before he took his but neglects her when she is dutifully carrying out the responsibilities incumbent on her as an abbess.

Perhaps even more important, however, is Harold Jacobson's observation that Ovid's Deianira "lives through and in her husband's greatness," that she "finds honor and meaning in her husband's preeminence."[53] Jacobson's observation suggests a parallel to Heloise's insistence in her first letter that she has abnegated her own identity through her love for Abelard so that she no longer exists except in relation to him. Thus the treachery (which McLeod points out could be Abelard's insistence that she enter the monastery as well as the more obvious crime of his castration) "robbed me of my very self in robbing me of you."[54] Heloise describes their former relationship in ways that emphasize her having exchanged her identity as the most learned woman in Europe for the new identity as Abelard's whore. For both Heloise and Deianira, identity is dependent on more than the legal tie of marriage. Fundamental to Deianira's lament about Hercules' self-degradation through his affairs with Iole and Omphale is her belief that by behaving so Hercules denies her "the vicarious self-importance she had cherished," especially when he dresses and acts like a woman instead of like a hero.[55]

Heloise re-creates the spirit of Deianira's situation when she writes, "Et quod maius est dictuque mirabile, in tantam versus est amor insaniam ut quod solum appetebat, hoc ipse sibi sine spe recuperationis auferret, cum ad tuam statim iussionem tam habitum ipsa quam animum immutarem ut te tam corporis mei quam animi imicum possessorem ostenderem" [My love rose to such heights of madness that it robbed itself of what it most desired beyond hope of recovery, when immediately at your bidding I changed my clothing along with my mind, in order to prove you the sole possessor of my body and my will alike].[56] The fact that she has addressed Abelard at the beginning and ending of letter one as *unice* and by the phrase *unicae tuae* midway through the letter[57] and her repetition of *solus* in this particular section further contribute to the parallel to Deianira, suggesting that Heloise depends on Abelard's making a success of his life, putting his mind to philosophical and theological reasoning instead of complaining about all his problems, as fundamental to her own successful self-construction.

Helen, Hero, and Cydippe

The last six letters of the *Heroides,* written later than the first fifteen, have their own structural unity. Both Helen and Cydippe contrast sharply with Hero, whose response to Leander comes between their responses to Paris and Acontius. Hero is especially notable for her lack of insight into the power of rhetoric.[58] Whereas most of the women in the *Heroides* fail in their attempts to alter the behavior of the men they love, Leander's tragedy results from her successful persuasion combined with a complete inability to foresee the negative consequences of her influence over Leander.

Though Helen's story ultimately ends even more tragically than Hero's, in her case the tragedy ensues despite her ability to see and articulate very clearly what will be the negative consequences of the elopement Paris has proposed to her in his letter. She has the foresight Hero lacks, but her ability, unlike either Hero or Paris, to see beyond selfish desires to the potential negative effects they will have both personally and more generally fails to deter the proposed action. Thus Ovid's Helen offers a particularly interesting example of the complexities of love for an intelligent and self-confident woman.

As Heloise composed her first letter to Abelard, several parallels to Helen may have suggested themselves. Most important, both women eventually do marry, despite their objections. Neither Helen's letter nor any of Heloise's letters specifies whether the woman finally was forced or whether she gave in to the persuasion of the man. Although Helen's letter flatly rejects Paris's marriage proposal, it suggests that she is willing to entertain the idea of an affair because she clearly is attracted to him and flattered by his proposal. Heloise, too, has argued at length against a marriage, although she has willingly reciprocated Abelard's advances in an extramarital affair. Heloise's letter goes a step further than Helen's, though, when she insists it was an honor for her to be his whore.

Heloise also may have seen similarities between Ovid's Paris and Abelard. Abelard himself sets up his similarity to Paris, when he describes in his *Historia calamitatum* how public was his seduction of Heloise. He concludes by saying "Few could have failed to notice something so obvious, in fact no one, I fancy except the man whose honour was most involved—Heloise's uncle."[59] Later Abelard recalls, "we became even more abandoned as we lost all sense of shame and, indeed, shame diminished as we found more opportunities for love-making."[60] This is like Helen's account of the way Paris's behavior has put them both at risk of exposure. Both Abelard and Paris seem to have enjoyed the risk of seducing a woman within her own home. Paris is self-centered and unwilling or unable to see beyond his own selfish desires to the potential effect they will have on the world around him, despite Apollo's prophecy. Heloise may well have seen in Paris's self-depiction something of Abelard's tendency to rush into trouble without taking account of the consequences.

Heloise differs sharply from Helen as well. Although both marriages had disastrous after-effects, Heloise's letters to Abelard had a real potential to affect their future not possible for Helen, since Ovid's Helen lived a course of events that had worked themselves out to tragic conclusions long before. This contrast gives Heloise's expression of helplessness to combat Fortune an ironic resonance. Helen writes to Paris with a confidence that she is in control of her life; Heloise expresses helplessness in the face of Fortune. In her first letter she writes: "Nosti carissime, noverunt omnes quanta in te amiserim et quam miserabili casu summa et ubique nota proditio me ipsam quoque mihi tecum abstulit ut incomparabiliter maior sit dolor ex amissionis modo quam ex damno" [You know, beloved, as the whole world knows, how much I have lost in you, how at one wretched stroke of fortune that supreme act of flagrant treachery robbed me of my very self in robbing me of you].[61] Her second letter develops a striking metaphor that attributes to Fortune imagery usually associated with Love: "O infortunatam fortunam, quae iam in me universi conaminis sui tela in tantum consumpsit ut, quibus in alios saeviat, iam non habeat; plenam in me pharetram exhausit ut frustra iam alii bella eius formident" [O Fortune who is only ill-fortune, who has already spent on me so many of the shafts she uses in her battle against mankind that she has none left with which to vent her anger on others].[62] Later in the same letter she invites the reader to think about other great and noble women who have been similarly miserable: "Quam mihi nobilium ac potentium feminarum fortuna umquam praeponere potuit aut aequare? Quam denique adeo deiecit et dolore conficere potuit? Quam in te mihi ruinam intulit? Quam mihi vehemens in utramque partem exstitit ut nec in bonis nec in malis modum habuerit?" [Has Fortune ever set any great or noble woman above me or made her my equal, only to be similarly cast down and crushed with grief? What glory she gave me in you, what ruin she brought upon me through you! Violent in either extreme, she showed no moderation in good or evil].[63] However, in the course of her letters Heloise does find ways to construct a new identity out of the ruins of her past, unlike Helen, who is inexorably destroyed by her tragic fate.

Cydippe's letter to Acontius closes Ovid's *Heroides* in most medieval editions.[64] Like Helen, Cydippe is reasonable. Even more than Helen, Cydippe can argue her case like the best of attorneys. Particularly important to our understanding of Heloise's letters to Abelard is Cydippe's self-characterization as a victim who clearly understands both the illogic and the illegality of the claim Acontius makes on her but nevertheless falls in love and finally agrees to the marriage against which she has so cogently argued. Like Cydippe, Heloise eloquently argued against marriage as the means of resolving conflict. However, having made their cases, both women capitulate and consent to marriage, it seems for love.

Several details in Cydippe's letter suggests it influenced Heloise's self-construction in her letters. For example, Cydippe asks Acontius: "haec nobis formae te laudatore superbae / contingit merces? et placuisse nocet? (XXI. 33–34) [Is this the reward that falls to my beauty, proud in your praise? Must I suffer for having pleased]? Heloise in a sense inverts this when she writes, "Sed quo te amplius nunc securum reddidi, negligentiorem sustineo" [Consider then your injustice, if when I deserve more you give me less, or rather, nothing at all].[65] Both women suffer for having been pleasing to the men—Cydippe experiences attentions that are making her ill, and Heloise experiences neglect that is making her miserable.

Even more striking is the similarity between Cydippe's insistence that even if her illness seems to be an indication that she is guilty of neglecting the vow she has read out in Diana's temple, nevertheless she is innocent: "nil ego peccavi, nisi quod periuria legi / inque parum fausto carmine docta fui (XXI. 181–82) [I have sinned in naught except that I have read a false oath, and been clever with unpropitious verse]. Cydippe also writes: "iam pudet, et timeo, quamvis mihi conscia non sim, / offensos videar ne meruisse deos (XXI. 47–48) [I already am shamed, and in fear, though I feel no guilt within, lest I appear to have merited the displeasure of the gods]. Heloise's "Wholly guilty though I am, I am also, as you know, wholly innocent" is remarkably similar. Even more striking, Cydippe explains that her innocence is dependent on intention: "sed si nil dedimus praeter sine pectore vocem, / verba suis frustra viribus orba tenes. / non ego iuravi—legi iurantia verba / vir mihi non isto more legendus eras (XXI. 141–44) [but if I have given you naught but my voice, without my heart, you possess in vain but words without a force of their own. I took no oath—I read words that formed an oath; that was no way for you to be chosen to husband by me]. Heloise explains to Abelard: "Non enim rei effectus sed efficientis affectus in crimine est. Nec quae fiunt sed quo animo fiunt aequitas pensat" [It is not the deed but the intention of the doer which makes the crime, and justice should weigh not what was done but the spirit in which it is done].[66] Furthermore, the legalistic language throughout both their writings accentuates the parallels. Is it possible that Ovid *and* Heloise should be credited when Abelard writes in his *Ethica,* "our actions must be judged good or bad solely through the spirit in which they are performed and not by their effects. The deed itself is neither good nor bad?"[67]

In *Les intellectuels au Moyen Âge,* Jacques Le Goff declares that Abelard learned everything he knew about love from Ovid. When his career was about to be badly disrupted by his relationship with Heloise, Abelard "n'a connu de l'amour que les livres d'Ovide et les chansons qu'il a composées—par esprit goliardique et non par expérience"[68] [knew love only through the books of Ovid and the songs he had composed—in true goliard spirit, but not through experience]. This study of the ways Ovid's *Heroides* contributed to Heloise's self-construction in her letters to Abelard suggests that both of them learned much more than the art of love from Ovid. Especially when combined with the evidence from Dronke's analysis of parallels between Heloise and Briseis and Wilson and McLeod's discussion of the ways Ovid's Medea contributes to Heloise's self-construction, the examples provided in this chapter demonstrate that Heloise was powerfully affected by her reading of Ovid's fictional letters and that she used her source materials in remarkable ways. Presenting unresolved conflict in tension—what Thomas Reed has called an "aesthetics of irresolution"[69]—for instance, is an Ovidian rhetorical technique as well as a characteristic of Abélard's *Sic et Non.* Perhaps even more important, though, is Heloise's gift for using dialectical processes to discover through the tension between conflicting ideas new ways of thinking about herself, her relationship to Abelard, and her role as abbess of the Paraclete.

Despite obvious differences between them—Ovid, a first-century man impersonating the voices of a group of legendary women in elegiacs; Heloise, a twelfth-century nun writing prose letters to her husband and mentor—Heloise has incorporated an extraordinary amount of Ovid in her letters: his rhetorical skill, his wit, his nuance in characterization, and most of all his willingness to tolerate, even exaggerate, contradictions and complexities in theme and character. A consummate synthesizer, she draws on all the subjects of the *trivium*—the literary texts that provided the means to learn Latin grammar, the processes of dialectic, and rhetoric not only as an approach to Christian truth but also as a source of persuasive force—and in doing so moves beyond each of the sources she draws on. Thus ultimately it is the differences between Ovid's accomplishment and Heloise's that is most striking. Ovid (with the Emperor Augustus), like Abelard (with Bernard of Clairvaux and the church), got himself into serious political difficulties. Although Abelard managed to extricate himself from difficulties again and again, his final trial for heresy, his withdrawal to Cluny to die, and his earlier self-exile at the Abbey of Saint-Gildas are remarkably like Ovid's exile. One may admire their writings yet see them as heroic victims, paradoxically literary victors because of their victimization. Heloise, in contrast, refused the choice between victim (offered by Ovid's tragic women) and victor (offered by Abelard's understanding of the Christian alternatives). Not only does she create verbal and topical resonances that have made many readers think of Ovid's women; she employs the processes of what we now call Hegelian dialectic to show the way beyond the choices available to Ovid's victims and beyond the traditional choices the church and Abelard recommend, to new possibilities for herself and for Abelard. In doing so, she is part of the twelfth-century affirmation of human invention realized through powerful relationships among grammar, dialectic, and rhetoric.

Notes

1. M.T. Clanchy, *Abelard: A Medieval Life,* p. 169.
2. Clanchy, *A Medieval Life,* p. 170.
3. Clanchy, *A Medieval Life,* p. 279. See also chapter 5 by Wilson and McLeod in this volume.
4. Clanchy, *A Medieval Life,* p. 46.
5. Mary J. Carruthers gives Heloise's citation of Lucan's Cornelia "quoted" in Abelard's *HC* as an example of the way reading shaped identity for educated people in the Middle

Ages, in *The Book of Memory: A Study of Memory in Medieval Culture,* p. 180. Donna Bussell in chapter 10 in this volume explores ways that Heloise goes beyond constructing an identity from her readings to the idea that the "male textual space" of the Benedictine Rule provides not only the foundation for a new formulation of the Rule but also for new identities for herself and for Abelard.

6. Thomas L. Reed, Jr.'s study of the "purposeful irresolution the debate poem is capable of" in *Middle English Debate Poetry and the Aesthetics of Irresolution,* p. 3, is relevant here.
7. Clanchy, *A Medieval Life,* pp. 222; 278.
8. D. W. Robertson, *Abelard and Heloise,* pp. 125; 130–31. Similarities between Heloise's self-construction and Ovid's Sappho pose special problems, however, since most medieval redactions of the *Heroides* did not include Sappho's letter. See Ralph J. Hexter, *Ovid and Medieval Schooling: Studies in Medieval School Commentaries on Ovid's* Ars Amatoria, Epistulae ex Ponto, *and* Epistulae Heroidum, p. 141.
9. Barbara Newman, "Authority, Authenticity, and the Repression of Heloise," *Journal of Medieval and Renaissance Studies* 22, pp. 135, 150.
10. Linda S. Kauffman, *Discourses of Desire: Gender, Genre, and Epistolary Fictions.*
11. "Heloise" in *Women Writers,* pp. 107, 126–27.
12. Michael Calabrese, "Ovid and the Female Voice in the *De Amore* and the *Letters* of Abelard and Heloise," pp. 1–2.
13. W. S. Anderson, "*The Heroides,*" pp. 69, 70.
14. James H. McGregor, "Ovid at School: From the Ninth to the Fifteenth Century," p. 29, and Eva Matthews Sanford, "The Use of Classical Latin Authors in the Libri Manuales," pp. 198–200.
15. McGregor, "Ovid at School," p. 39.
16. Hexter, *Ovid and Medieval Schooling,* p. 143.
17. See Hexter, *Ovid and Medieval Schooling,* and R. B. C. Huygens, ed., *Accessus ad auctores.*
18. "In qualibet epistula habetur duplex intentio actoris et mittentis." The same commentary says of Letter 1, from Penelope to Ulysses, "In prima epistula intendit actor commendare amorem legitimum. Intentio Penelopes est reuocare Vlixem"[In the first letter the agent/author intends to commend legitimate love. The intention of Penelope is to call back Ulysses.] Continued in Hexter, *Ovid and Medieval Schooling,* p. 163. According to Hexter, the introductions to each of the letters end with a similar identification of double purpose.
19. Huygens, ed., *Accessus ad auctores,* p. 25. (Our translation).
20. Hexter, *Ovid and Medieval Schooling,* p. 161.
21. Hexter, *Ovid and Medieval Schooling,* p. 157.
22. Clanchy, *A Medieval Life,* p. 81.
23. Howard Jacobson, *Ovid's* Heroides, pp. 243, 250.
24. Jacobson, *Ovid's* Heroides, pp. 250–51.
25. The understanding of what dialectic is for Heloise and how it relates to rhetoric is a complex question because the term has shifted at various times in history. Heloise was probably influenced by the tension between Boethius' belief that rhetoric is a subordinate part of dialectic and Augustine's belief that dialectic serves and is a part of rhetoric, the only category of the *trivium* adequate to treatment of the word of God. Educators following the Augustinian model might advocate teaching dialectic after rhetoric because study of rhetoric could form a good foundation for study of the more intellectually challenging dialectic, but even then dialect was subordinated to rhetoric's goals in the Christian context. Although Heloise may not have known that Aristotle saw dialectic and rhetoric as parallel contributors to different parts of the same process, she probably was familiar with the Ciceronian basis of Augustine's belief that dialectic is subordinate to rhetoric. It is possible to see in Heloise's letters to Abelard evidence of a belief (like Gilbert of Reims') that, for a Christian, rhetoric is fundamental to a virtuous life, in contrast to the distrust of more conservative monastic thinkers who feared

the power of rhetoric to serve evil ends as well as virtuous ends. In that sense, Heloise might join Augustine in seeing dialect as subordinate to rhetoric. She may also, however, be moving back to an Aristotelian sense of dialectic and rhetoric as coequals. Many readers will confirm a sense that the logical elements of her discourse outweigh the rhetorical. For the purposes of this chapter, we will take advantage of hindsight and apply a Hegelian understanding of dialectic as "a process whereby a *thesis,* when countered by an *antithesis,* leads to the *synthesis* of a new idea" (*The Bedford Glossary of Critical and Literary Terms*). For overviews of changes in understanding of dialectic and rhetoric in the Middle Ages, see chapter 4 of Thomas M. Conley, *Rhetoric in the European Tradition,* and James Jerome Murphy, *Rhetoric in the Middle Ages: A History of Rhetorical Theory from Saint Augustine to the Renaissance.*

26. *Ep.* 2, ed. Muckle 70 (Radice 112–13).
27. Citations from and translations of Ovid's *Heroides* are from the Loeb edition, *Ovid: Heroides and Amores,* trans. Grant Showerman. Subsequent citations will be parenthetical.
28. *Ep.* 2, ed. Muckle 68.
29. Donna Bussell, in chapter 10 in this volume, p. 249.
30. The parallel to Phaedra invites the question, why Augustus? The emperor's role in Ovid's exile may be significant, especially since there are so many parallels between Abelard's and Ovid's lives.
31. *Ep.* 2, ed. Muckle 72 (Radice 115).
32. Jacobson, *Ovid's* Heroides, p. 159.
33. Katerina Philippides, "Canace Misunderstood: Ovid's *Heroides* XI," p. 427.
34. Jacobson, *Ovid's* Heroides, p. 163.
35. Jacobson, *Ovid's* Heroides, p. 163.
36. Glenda McLeod, "'Wholly Guilty, Wholly Innocent': Self-Definition in Héloïse's Letters to Abelard," p. 70.
37. *Ep.* 2, ed. Muckle 72 (Radice 116).
38. Peggy Kamuf, *Fictions of Feminine Desire,* p. 8.
39. *Ep.* 4, ed. Muckle 93 (Radice 154).
40. Calabrese, "Ovid and the Female Voice," p. 16.
41. Calabrese, "Ovid and the Female Voice," p. 21.
42. Calabrese, "Ovid and the Female Voice," p. 26.
43. See David Luscombe, "Monasticism in the Lives and Writings of Heloise and Abelard," vol. 2, pp. 1–11.
44. *Ep.* 2, ed. Muckle 70 (Radice 112).
45. *Ep.* 4, ed. Muckle 79 (Radice 130).
46. *Ep.* 2, ed. Muckle 73 (Radice 117).
47. Jacobson, *Ovid's* Heroides, p. 90.
48. Jacobson, *Ovid's* Heroides, p. 89. See also Marilynn Desmond, *Reading Dido: Gender, Textuality, and the Medieval* Aeneid, pp. 37–45.
49. Jacobson, *Ovid's* Heroides, p. 89.
50. Jacobson, *Ovid's* Heroides, p. 90.
51. *Ep.* 4, ed. Muckle 79 (Radice 130).
52. *Ep.* 2, ed. Muckle 73 (Radice 117).
53. Jacobson, *Ovid's* Heroides, p. 240.
54. McLeod, "'Wholly Guilty, Wholly Innocent,'" pp. 67–68; Radice 113.
55. Jacobson, *Ovid's* Heroides, p. 242.
56. *Ep.* 2, ed. Muckle 70 (Radice 113).
57. Muckle 70.
58. Having received a letter from Leander expressing his unwillingness to risk swimming to her on account of the weather, Hero writes a letter back that causes him to ignore the very reasonable fears he has of the probable consequences and thus to die tragically.

59. Radice 68.
60. Radice 69.
61. *Ep.* 2, ed. Muckle 70 (Radice 113).
62. *Ep.* 4, ed. Muckle 78 (Radice 129).
63. *Ep.* 4, ed. Muckle 78–79 (Radice 129).
64. The story behind the letters is that Acontius has seen Cydippe, who is visiting Delos, and fallen in love with her. Therefore, he writes a vow on a piece of fruit ["malum"] and throws it so that it falls at Cydippe's feet. According to Cydippe, her nurse picked it up and handed it to her, asking what it said. The result is that Cydippe reads out loud the words: "I swear by the sanctuary of Diana that I will wed Acontius." Cydippe is thus caught in a bind, for her parents have betrothed her to an unnamed suitor and Acontius has elicited from her a vow that she will marry him. According to Harold Isbell, Ovid derived the little-known story behind the final pair of letters from the *Priapea* (XVI.5), "a collection of erotic stories circulating in Rome at the time of Ovid" (Ovid, *Heroides,* trans. Harold Isbell, p. 229). Pierre Grimal points out similarities between the stories of Acontius and Cydippe and of Hermochares and Ctesylla in *The Penguin Dictionary of Classical Mythology.*
65. *Ep.* 2, ed. Muckle 73 (Radice 117).
66. *Ep.* 2, ed. Muckle 72 (Radice 115).
67. Continued in Radice 115.
68. Jacques Le Goff, *Les intellectuels au Moyen Âge,* p. 43.
69. Thomas L. Reed, Jr., *Middle English Debate Poetry and the Aesthetics of Irresolution,* p. 27.

CHAPTER 7

CLASSICAL MYTH AND GENDER IN THE LETTERS OF "ABELARD" AND "HELOISE": GLOSS, GLOSSED, GLOSSATOR

Jane Chance

Within the narrative of the letters, Heloise, acting as master to "Abelard" as grammar school pupil, inverts the clerical methodologies of reading the classical auctores *to "instruct" her pupil in self-understanding. For the self-glossation on himself as mythological hero whose life is epic in its battles, culminating in the castration and his ruin, Heloise substitutes a Boethian authorizing of the hero as Christian.*

The figure of Heloise, whether historical or fabricated, from the earliest juncture to the present moment has dominated in varying and extreme ways subsequent poetic or fictional re-creations and learned discussions of her relationship with Abelard.[1] Although Heloise herself penned but three letters to him, apparently composed in the mid-1130s and found in eight manuscripts, her voice also is sounded by Abelard in his own memoir/autobiography, currently known as the *Historia calamitatum,* or the "Story of calamities," composed about 1132;[2] we might well identify this voice as "Heloise," although over the years, even Heloise in her own letters has been viewed by scholars as constructed by Abelard. Heloise also wrote a letter to Peter the Venerable, abbot of Cluny, and a set of *Problemata,* or theological problems, with a prefatory letter, intended for Abelard.[3]

In relation to the dialogue between Abelard and Heloise in their letters, the construction of "Heloise" has evolved in the literary criticism, especially during the course of the past twenty or thirty years. As Abelard's concubine, she is construed to exist in the written testimony only as a gendered cipher, a fictional construction, with all the *Epistolae* (her three and his five, including the *Historia calamitatum* as the first) understood to have been written by Abelard himself (according to Bernhard Schmeidler [1913, 1935, 1940] and, later, in a more ironic literary construction of Abelard's self, D.W. Robertson, Jr. [1972]),[4] or forged, in whole or in part, by some other scholar either contemporary with Abelard or later (according to John F. Benton [1975, 1980]),[5] to the most recent polar extreme (Barbara Newman [1995]), in which a historical Heloise not only wrote her letters to Abelard (an argument originally put forth by Étienne Gilson in 1948)[6] but did so out of desire for authenticity lacking in that monastic *conversatio* she had accepted out of obedience to her master, Abelard. Newman argues against Benton's (and Robertson's) repressive reading of "Heloise" as a "submissive, sensual creature" because of the Paraclete documents associated with Heloise as abbess that depict her as a person historical, holy, and intellectual.[7] Even so, Michael Calabrese (1997) echoes anew the old, misogynist interpretation of "Heloise" by positioning her in the Ovidian role of the *Heroides* heroine who "speaks desire, complains of [Abelard's] absence, and demands redress"; worse, cast into a role similar to that of the "imaginary Ovidian pupil" in the *De amore* of Andreas Capellanus, "Heloise" is aided by "Abelard," "acting as an Ovidian *doctor amoris,*" in overcoming "the obsession that binds her to her love for him."[8]

More promising for understanding the complex articulation of gender, voice, and persona in these letters is the recent rereading and reassessment of Abelard in the *Historia calamitatum* in relation to the issue of subjectivity, which has been followed by a similar rereading and reassessment of the letters of Heloise. Medieval feminist scholars, such as Glenda McLeod (1993), have argued for viewing the *Historia calamitatum* as one of the most important medieval "experiments in self-definition, . . . broadening the enterprise to include Hèloïse herself . . . Shaped by the *confessio peccatorum* and epistolary genres such as the *epistolae consolatoriae,* Hèloïse's letters not only investigate and reinterpret Abélard's story but also help reveal the components of, and pressures surrounding, a twelfth-century woman's self-definition," that is, "self" defined as both abbess and wife, both public and private.[9] Certainly the *Historia calamitatum* has been understood to signal the twelfth-century advent of individual subjectivity, along with other forms of the personal, such as the *planctus,* letter writing, autobiography, and memoir.[10] Thus Heloise also voices female authority by taking up the role of the normally masculine "investigator," "reinterpreter," and "self-definer" in this gendered epistolary interchange, just as those twelfth-century French scholars such as Marbod of Rennes and Baudri of Bourgueil inscribe similar Latin dialogic letters with female personae or respondents (whether fictional or historical).[11] To read "Heloise"—the persona of Heloise that she herself constructs in the *Epistolae*—in this way reinforces R. W. Southern's point (1970), that, "far from being one-sided, both sides of the correspondence are represented, and they are so arranged that they tell a single story ending in a climax or (as some might think) an anti-climax. They must be read straight through if they are to be understood."[12] Further, as Linda Georgianna (1986) has noted, in her important essay on Heloise's third letter, "we can understand better both Heloise and those aspects of twelfth-century spirituality which she epitomizes if we treat her works as a coherent and imaginative whole. . . . Heloise . . . challenges Abelard and later spiritual writers to provide a new kind of rule for the inner life."[13]

In this gendered and inverted sense, Heloise's "Heloise"[14] appropriates the very role of ecclesiastical authority that belongs by definition to Abelard. Thus, medieval feminist scholars such as Catherine Brown (1996) have cautioned against misreading "Heloise" in Abelard's "story" as submissive in her roles of whore, misogynist, and *castrata,* for "[a]ll of these discursive positions are part of the epistolary disputation with Abelard, and they share a common rhetorical agenda: to assert Heloise's mastery (over words, over herself, over the *auctoritates,* over Abelard) by seeming to humiliate her."[15] Put another way, "mastery," according to Claire Nouvet (1990), depends ironically on

Heloise's self-humiliation before Abelard as a means of winning gratitude, in that "the master is master only to the extent that the 'whore,' through self-humiliation, recognizes him as such. . . . [T]he whore is true master of a master who precisely could not be master without her."[16] Other feminist critics have argued similarly for the irony of Heloise's apparent submissiveness. For example, Bonnie Wheeler (1997) views Heloise's seeming submissiveness as a gender performance in an "epistolary seduction" intended to enable Abelard's sense of his own masculinity in the face of criticisms of his authority by his peers.[17] In chapter 10 of this volume, Donna Alfano Bussell focuses in particular on the third letter as a paraenetic letter in an epistolographic relationship, to compel Abelard's figurative participation in a Benedictine Initiation ritual that would reinforce his return to the corporeal body. In all these feminist approaches, Heloise occupies the role of a powerful ecclesiast who may adopt a gendered demeanor of apparent submission within their epistolary relationship in line with her own political and spiritual strategies.[18]

In light of these new interpretations and to extend the conclusions of Nouvet and Brown, I would argue that *puella prudentissima* "Heloise,"[19] acting as master to "Abelard" in the role of grammar school *puer,* also inverts the clerical methodologies of reading to "instruct" her pupil in self-understanding. "Mastery," a means of domination, also can be defined as overlaid with the clerical and latinate practice of the *magister,* "teacher"; in these terms, "mastery" must be understood as gendered male, the role of *magister* being barred to women except through fictional appropriation by means of rhetorical inversion and irony. Heloise performs this scholastic act by reversing the usual commentary procedure. That is, if glossation of classical mythology clarifies for the *puer* the *involucrum,* or "cover," of the fable, then the *fabula*—the fiction of the Greek and Roman poets that conceals truth—clarifies by means of the exposure of the levels of allegorical meaning in a text, a *littera,* with a literal, or historical, meaning. So also the "glossation" of "Heloise" of the story of "Abelard" story in the *Historia calamitatum,* that is, of his "lies" or his "fictions," must analogously expose the concealed truth therein, both in the *Historia calamitatum* and in her letters—to invert allegory, as it were.

The irony in this reversal derives from the emergence of literal, or historical, truth from the allegories used by "Abelard" in what appears to be an *historia,* a chronicle, or a truthful accounting of his life, a secularized "self-hagiography." To return to the literal, or historical, truth in scholastic commentary is to return to the place of the Other, *aliena,* a gendered place in the text, marginalized as if female by its subordinate place.[20] Not only does literal, or historical, truth emerge, but it is a privileged and valorized type of meaning dominant over more figurative *sententia* conventionally vaunted by patristic commentators—the *magistri.* Within the hierarchy of allegorical meaning, the lowly *historia* provides a necessary foundation for the *moralia, allegoria,* and *anagogia,* but the dominant three occupy the commentator's attention in the commentaries of the twelfth century, whether those by Bernard Silvestris on Vergil and Martianus Capella, by Bernard of Utrecht on the anonymous *Ecloga Theoduli,* or by Arnulf of Orleans on Ovid's *Metamorphoses.*

Heloise, or "Heloise," then, occupies the role of a Boethian Philosophy, or a Nature as portrayed by Alanus ab Insulis or Jean de Meun; she is an instructive and moralizing teacher for a suffering, foolish persona adopted by the poet in order to learn more about himself—in this case, Abelard, or "Abelard." But it also may be that the *Historia calamitatum,* this *epistola consolataria,* "letter of consolation," can be read only as the sign of one Boethian voice in a dialogue or disputation, that of "Abelard." This Boethian voice therefore must be complemented by the voice of a Philosophy-like figure, in this case, "Heloise," persona of the author of three letters that "gloss" his own *historia,* as if in imitation of the commentary of the *magister* who glosses the myths of the epic story of Vergil. The role of "Heloise" as *magister* is gendered by means of her own return to the literal truth as an anodyne against the pomposity, pride, and self-delusion of "Abelard," whose very wit and reason become weapons to use against himself, against self-understanding, in the visionary tale of his troubles. Against overwrought masculine fancy and conceit are set practical and therapeutic truths offered by an "Heloise" who has been well instructed by her instructor in scripture. Against self-allegory and mythological rhetorical figuration as concealment and self-deceit she wields the surgical tools of the literal and scriptural truth.

To characterize this role reversal in another way: this dialogue between lovers in letters is so clearly modeled on the epistolary exchanges between Dido and Aeneas, Medea and Jason, and other couples in which the female is betrayed by a lover, found in Ovid's *Heroides* and Andreas's *De amore.* Thus, if we look at "Abelard" instead of "Heloise," while it is ironic that "Abelard" appears initially and historically to be victimized by his love for a woman like those whom he misogynously characterizes as responsible for the downfall of man at various points in human history, as Calabrese notes, on another level "Abelard" functions more figuratively as the Other, the "female" who must be led, educated, or converted.[21] That is to say, if "Heloise" appropriates the masculinized role of the authority, the *magister,* and therefore of the victimizing lover, then what Calabrese has omitted in his interpretation is what I am calling "Heloise."

To push this argument further: Whatever the biological, cultural, or historical reality behind such dialogic constructions of subject, in the texts of Abelard and Heloise there is an ironic and gendered presence—a trace of feminine difference—that belies the possibility of any essentially "masculine" construction of "Abelard," as the scholastic mythological ramifications of his letters will demonstrate; That is, the entire epistolary construction of his role (in the examples from the *Historia calamitatum* I will present) is feminized. Four times in the *Historia calamitatum* Abelard uses mythological exempla to which "Heloise" in the *Historia calamitatum* and Heloise herself in her own letters will respond. The latter letters are remarkably lacking in mythology and learned or scholastic reference. Abelard casts himself in his rise to power in the first part of his story as the Trojan hero Aeneas and the Greek hero Ajax who fights with Ulysses, describes his downfall because of Heloise and her uncle in terms of the myth of the god Mars caught by Vulcan with his wife Venus, and refers to his fame, toward the end of his career, as Echo-like. When "Heloise" responds in the *Historia calamitatum* (and when Heloise does use a mythological reference, in one later letter), she subverts the scholastic appropriation of "Abelard" by means of a feminizing and subversive or ironic instruction: in response to his early life and his identification of self as hero, she subtly casts herself as a type of Minerva; in response to his midlife fall and castration, she identifies "Abelard" with Venus and herself with Vulcan as Revealer. Once she has accomplished this role reversal, she can "instruct" him in his feminized position and regenerate his manhood, understood figuratively. The inversion of the glossator's role to that of the glossed (and concomitantly of the role of the glossed to that of glossator) is accompanied by a gender reversal that allows "Heloise" to subvert the masculine and egotistical and empower the feminine, the marginal and humble—herself and other women. The mythological image, then, offered up as an illustration of Abelard's subjectivity, or what we might term a gloss on himself as his main text, is ignored, deflated, or made literal; in her reglossation she functions in this gender reversal within the scholastic role of a glossator whose "text" is her lover, whom she must correct and/or interpret.

After examining Heloise's role as *magister* and glossator in relation to "Abelard" as her epic text, or *auctor,* I then turn to the classical myths each uses to advance these roles: Abelard's use of each mythological reference, the traditions and sources on which he is drawing, and the way their deployment advances his rhetorical strategies, particularly as a means of fictionalizing his self or of formalizing what might be termed his projection of subjectivity within the narrative of his rise and fall; and the magisterial response of "Heloise" to each reference, to her specifically descholasticized and demythologized focus on the literal as a means of gender balance, in particular, the references that she appropriates, reglosses, and resubmits to him as a correction of himself as text. Finally I demonstrate how she appropriates the sacerdotal and ecclesiastical tools to educate and reman him—to make him "whole" again.[22]

I. "Heloise" as Glossator, "Abelard" as Glossed: The Unmanning of the Epic Hero

The relationship between "Abelard" and "Heloise" is vexed, unnatural, and inverted, if she serves now as *magister* to his pupil, for "Heloise" is no allegorical personification of wisdom, Philosophy; no mythological deity, or Minerva; no *magister,* like Abelard; instead she is the *puella,* the feminized *homunculus,* the "little man," the Other. Their mutual identity crisis is signaled by the polysemous address, in the salutation of her first letter, to Abelard in multiple roles, "Domino suo immo patri, coniugi suo immo fratri, ancilla sua immo filia, ipsius uxor immo soror, Abaelardo Heloisa" [To her master, or rather her father, husband, or rather brother; his handmaid, or rather his daughter, wife, or rather sister; to Abelard, Heloise].[23] How confused she seems: What exactly is the role in which the authority of "Abelard" inheres? Master? Father? Husband? Brother? And, therefore, what is her role? Handmaid? Daughter? Wife? Sister? If "Abelard" is nobody, no man, Unman, then can he be master? Father? Husband? As adulterer, can he be brother? Is she handmaid, then, to the master? And as an unmanned (unnatural equals irrational) man, can he be said to be "master," either of himself or anyone else? Later, when she reveals her understanding of the appropriate rhetorical form of salutation in the *ars dictaminis,* that is, when she reveals that the name of the person of greater authority should appear first in the address, in *Ep.* 4, she inadvertently glosses her own opening in that first letter, where she has reversed the order.[24]

As the "master" of "Abelard," "Heloise" instructs him by means of a position dialectically opposite to his, a *non* set against his *sic.* Heloise's "voice" in the three letters, unlike that of "Abelard," is personal; her advice, practical and therapeutic, down-to-earth; and her tone, sweetly corrective and scolding. The comparative lack of scholastic, mythological, and learned reference is notable, although she supplies scriptural reference as a moral corrective.

Most important is the commentary of "Heloise" on his "text," supplied as if "Abelard" were her *auctor* and the *Historia calamitatum* bore the kind of classical *auctoritas* of his three mythological references from antique texts. Early in her first letter (*Ep.* 2), "Heloise" comments on the point and purpose "Abelard" had in writing his "letter of consolation," typing it by genre, author, effect, purpose, and contents. According to Alastair Minnis, such a process was considered necessary in an introduction to a university lecture course on an *auctor,* when "the text would be considered as a whole, and an outline provided of those literary and doctrinal principles and criteria considered to be appropriate to it."[25] This introduction became the *accessus* to the commentary at the time of its publication in manuscript form.

The headings under which a literary text were considered in the twelfth century included the title of the work, author's name, author's purpose, subject, literary mode, order of topics, usefulness, and educational rubric.[26] Note that "Heloise" follows these headings in the sequence of topics in her first letter, what might be termed her *accessus* to the *Historia calamitatum.* (Note also that it comes at the end of the *Historia calamitatum,* not at the beginning, the conventional position for an *accessus* as introduction or abstract of the text.) Her first literary gloss on the genre of Abelard's text is, in fact, the first sentence of the first letter, when Heloise acknowledges that it is a "letter of consolation." Although his own *historia,* his autobiography, is styled in the earliest manuscripts as a "letter of consolation" to a (possibly imaginary) friend in response to the friend's own misfortunes—his title reads "Abaelardi ad amicam suum consolatoria <epistula>"[27]—Heloise acknowledges this text as an epistolary *consolatio,* indeed, a "letter of consolation" to his friend brought to her by chance.[28] She identifies the author and her own reaction: "Quam ex ipsa statim tituli fronte vestram esse considerans, tanto ardentius eam coepi legere" [I saw at once from the superscription that it was yours, and was all the more eager to read it].[29] She pictures the *intentio* of the author to be in fact the consolation—*imagine recreer* [renewal of strength]—that she hopes for, but instead, she remarks with disappointment, "[e]rant memini huius epistolae fere omnia felle et absinthio plena" [nearly every line of this letter was filled, as I remember, with gall and wormwood].[30] She summarizes the subject and design of the letter: "Complesti revera in epistola illa quod in exordio eius amico promisisti ut videlicet in comparatione tuarum suas molestias nullas vel parvas reputaret" [In that letter you did indeed carry out the promise you made your friend at the beginning, that he would think his own troubles insignificant or nothing, in comparison with your own],[31] and she designates the order of topics as the persecutions by his teachers, the castration, the attacks by his fellow students, the treatment of his work of theology, his prisonlike sentence, the plotting against him by the abbot and monastic brothers, the slanders against him by the pseudoapostles and his rivals, and the persecutions by the tyrant and monks in the abbey where he served as abbot. She ends her *accessus* by correcting his reading of his own work: she notes that his "letter" is more the story of misfortunes of "Abelard" than consolation for that of his friend, as he has described them as being, and that its effect on his audience of her and her nuns is not what he had intended: "Quas videlicet tuas diligenter commemorans cum eius intenderes consolationi nostrae plurimum addisti desolationi et, dum eius mederi vulneribus cuperes, nova quaedam nobis vulnera doloris inflixisti et priora auxisti. Sana, obsecro, ipsa quae fecisti qui quae alii fecerunt curare satagis" [The detailed account you gave of these may have been intended for his comfort, but it also greatly increased our own feeling of desolation; in your desire to heal his wounds you have dealt us fresh wounds of grief as well as re-opening the old. I beg you, then, as you set about tending the wounds which others have dealt, heal the wounds you yourself have inflicted].[32] Most important, "Heloise" distinguishes between the wounds others have inflicted (his castration) and his own "wounds," the ones he has inflicted on himself.

Much of his story, and her explication of it, will serve to differentiate the two kinds and their signification, one physical and one spiritual.

"Heloise" seems to insist that the memorial record of "Abelard," like Boethius' Philosophy, may be a history of his life, but, like all works of poetry, it has adversely affected the emotions of its auditors—it has a literary function and nature that does not teach and inform so much as alarm and distort. If "Abelard" is her text, her classical *auctor,* then in what way is the *Historia calamitatum* an epic narrative of the hero? Let us return to the *Historia calamitatum* and Abelard's constructions of his self, which "Heloise" will gloss first in her memorialized voice in his own recording in the *Historia* and then in her letters.

Historia calamitatum, Stage 1, the Rise to Power: "Abelard" as Aeneas and Ajax

In his autobiography, Abelard presents himself as a type of Vergil's masculine hero, Aeneas. Abelard may be invoking, by means of a mythological shorthand well known to grammar scholars of his day, the troping of his own spiritual and psychological life as heroic in exactly the same way that Aeneas' journey was interpreted within the schools. By overlaying the story of his own life with the epic analogy of the hero Aeneas, Abelard can suggest the dual levels of *historia:* one, a surface "history," or chronicle, of actual events that occurred during his life; and the other, an *allegoria,* its more figurative, if concealed, meaning, which moralizes the sequences of steps in that life in line with the psychology of the scholastic journey toward wisdom and *moralitas.*

In Abelard's first gloss, early in the *Historia calamitatum,* when describing his early life as the firstborn son of a Breton noble (himself a scholar-warrior), he explains the reason for his choice of learning and the contemplative life over that of war and the active life by setting Mars as god of war against Minerva as goddess of wisdom: he withdrew from the public *curia,* the "court of Mars," in order to be educated in the private *gremium,* literally the "bosom of Minerva": "Ego vero quanto amplius et facilius in studio litterarum profeci, tanto ardentius eis inhaesi, et in tanto earum amore illectus sum ut, militaris gloriae pompam cum hereditate et praerogativa primogenitorum meorum fratribus derelinquens, Martis curiae penitus abdicarum ut Minervae gremio educarer" [For my part, the more rapid and easy my progress in my studies, the more eagerly I applied myself, until I was so carried away by my love of learning that I renounced the glory of a soldier's life, made over my inheritance and rights of the eldest son to my brothers, and withdrew from the court of Mars in order to kneel at the feet of Minerva].[33]

Abelard's Latin articulates a gender binary of a masculinized "Mars" and a feminized "Minerva" by means of a spatial metaphor, that is, "Abelard" moves from a public domain acculturated as masculine to a private, internalized, embodied domain acculturated as feminine. By "Minerva" Abelard means not just wisdom but the scholastic practice of philosophy, in which the sequence of education from the *trivium* to the *quadrivium* culminates. What appears to be missing is the epic figure of the protagonist hero Aeneas—the hero yet to be named or born or designated—although the mythological allegory, once parsed, clearly centers on the missing hero.

But in moving to this more feminized space, "Abelard" moves as in a text, a fabulous narrative: he has become an allegorical hero instead of a man, for he retains his masculinized martial activities within rational disputation: "[*D*]*ialecticarum rationum armaturam* omnibus philosophiae documentis praetuli, *his armis* alia commutavi et trophaeis bellorum *conflictus* praetuli *disputationum*" [I preferred the *weapons of dialectic* to all the other teachings of philosophy, and *armed with these* I chose the *conflicts of disputation* instead of the trophies of war].[34] Arms and the man [*arma virumque*] is of course the subject of which Vergil sings in the *Aeneid,* although as a subject of Abelard's *epistula consolatoria* (as Southern defines this rhetorical type of letter)[35] it seems a strangely fictional and heroized diversion in an ostensible mission to console a friend for his misfortunes, unless that "friend" is in fact himself.[36] Even in Boethius' consolation by Philosophy, the lessons Boethius learns from his own *magister* can be perceived as part of a dialogue, or debate, between two sides of himself, but not literally as epic or as fable, *fabula* (even though, it is true, author Boethius intersperses songs with classical epic and heroic imagery among his more didactic and learned prose sections, in a work whose genre has been termed a *prosimetrum,* or *satura,* a mixture of poetry and prose).

Why would Abelard need to cast himself as a Novus Aeneas, a hero setting out on his journey? And why is the choice of "Abelard" between the *literal* weapons of Mars and the *figurative* weapons of Minerva? We will consider these questions in order. Part of his problem, as prototype of Aeneas, is that "Abelard" keeps resorting to the natural and the corporal (Mars or Venus) when he should be embracing the intellectual (Minerva). If the mythological glosses in Abelard's story function as the song of "arms and the man," then "Abelard" does not progress easily and readily from the corporal to the intellectual phases. As hero Aeneas, "Abelard" should end his story happily, a tripartite exercise like that involved in the Fulgentian allegorization of the Vergilian journey, well known as a text and a paradigm in the twelfth century.[37] In Fulgentius' sixth-century commentary on the *Aeneid,* a fictionalized "Vergil," or *magister,* debates with a *homunculus,* "little man," or pupil, that is, the insignificant "Fulgentius" the grammarian, about the subject of Vergil, *arma virumque . . . primus,* or human life.[38] This Vergilian phrase "of arms and the man . . . first" is divided by "Vergil" into three parts to signify the three stages of each man's life, *historia,* his "story." Or, rather, each stage in human life relates to one of the three terms represented by the Vergilian phrase *arma* [arms], *virum* [the man], and *primus* [first]: man's birth and early life, dictated by his *natura,* that is, his parentage, family, background, called by Fulgentius *virtus animi,* "strength of soul"; followed in order by *doctrina,* his "learning" or his education; and his *felicitas,* his "attaining to prosperity," the lessons provided by experience during the course of life. The word *arma* refers to the first stage, *virtus,* "manliness," or early nature, identified as the "corporeal substance"; the word *virum* refers to the second stage, *sapientia,* "wisdom," the essence of manliness, and therefore the "intellectual substance," in both of which human perfection inheres; and the word *primus* refers to the third stage, the *princeps,* "the ruler," or the power of judgment.[39] These three stages reappear in what seem to be distinct parts of Abelard's life: first, the early youth and the coming to education and the church; second, the tutelage of Heloise, their subsequent affair, and Abelard's castration; and third, the aftermath. In relation to Abelard's self-glossation, at this point in his story "Abelard" has progressed from the first phase, in his early life, *arma,* "arms," manliness, or nature, to the second, *virum,* "wisdom," "the man," that is, to education and learning—in other words, from "Mars" to "Minerva," mythological equivocations for these abstractions traced in any number of early mythological commentaries and handbooks, including Fulgentius' own *Mitologiae.*

To turn then to the second question: Why does "Abelard" choose between the *literal* weapons of Mars and the *figurative* weapons of Minerva? To explain, we must first ascertain the significance of Minerva in the Vergilian mythographies on Aeneas. Minerva is one is the signal figures in book 2 of Fulgentius' other famed work, the *Mitologiae;* she is one of the three goddesses from whom Aeneas's half brother Paris must select the most beautiful.[40] Minerva becomes, in commentaries on the *Aeneid,* including that of Fulgentius, the tutelary deity associated with Italy as the goal to which Aeneas must journey, rejecting the early counsel of his mother, Venus, in Troy, and the blandishments of Dido, in Carthage (Juno's nation).[41] But Minerva reappears in Abelard's use of another myth in this same first part, on the education and rise in fame of "Abelard," that is, his involvement in the second stage of the Fulgentian heroic journey. As wisdom Minerva is rejected by Ajax, the Greek (Telamonian) hero of arms with whom Abelard identifies because he wishes to paint a scholastic competition as a "battle" in which he struggles heroically. Abelard likens the conflict between himself and his previous teacher William of Champeaux (in 1113), along with their supporters and students, to a battle over "arms"—in the Fulgentian sense, education and learning—that "Abelard" appears to win. "Abelard" mouths Ajax's argument to Ulysses for the arms of the slain Greek hero Achilles after the latter had killed the Trojan prince and brother of Paris, Hector, that depends on a *litotes* preserved in Ovid's *Metamorphoses* (13.89–90): "Illud vero Aiacis, ut temperantius loquar, audacter proferam: ' . . . si quaeritis huius / Fortunam pugnae, non sum superatus ab illo'" [I shall not go too far if I boldly say with Ajax that "If you demand the issue of this fight, / I was not vanquished by the enemy"].[42] "Abelard" omits the fact that Ajax loses the contest and thereupon kills himself and that Minerva does not want proud, brutal Ajax to have his arms because she is outraged by his killing of Hector. Like Ajax, Abelard lost and retreated to Le Pallet; like Ulysses, Abelard's adversary William apparently also "won" the arms, in that he became Bishop of Châlon.[43] By use of this Ovidian exemplum, "Abelard" may wish to demonstrate his learning and his awareness of the new contemporary interest in Ovid as a school author. His text, however, and its literary associations convey instead his very nature as a foolish man who chooses ill even in his mythological exempla.

Magister *"Heloise" as Minerva in the* Historia calamitatum. To expose the pride and fatuity of "Abelard" in his heroic (if ironic) portrait of self, the response of "Heloise" to "Abelard" in the *Historia calamitatum* by means of her first mythological image—Minerva—provides an inverse mirror image of the glosses "Abelard" has used thus far. She does this by means of having "Abelard" voice her own words. First she uses an *occupatio:* in explaining that the pagan philosophers were known as wise because of their lives and not their learning, she acknowledges, "Quam sobrie autem atque continenter ipsi vixerint non est nostrum modo ex exemplis colligere ne *Minervam ipsam* videar docere" [There is no need for me to give examples of their chaste and sober lives—I should seem to be teaching *Minerva herself*].[44] She means there is no need for her to remind the philosopher "Abelard" of what he knows about those philosophers, presumably because he has taught her those truths, but by using the name "Minerva" to type what he knows, as if he were the goddess of wisdom herself, she refers the reader back to the first gloss of "Abelard," where he prophetically describes himself preferring the lap/womb of Minerva to the court of Mars. Of course he is not wise—his life represents a travesty of wisdom—nor is he female, except in his emasculated state, which, of course, can be read figuratively as unmanned rationality and, therefore, according to conventional misogynistic definitions, as indeed feminine. If he has pursued "Minerva," it is the body of Minerva as exemplified in "Heloise." Further, she is teaching "Minerva"—if "he" would only listen. More likely "Heloise" is, in this current lecture, "Minerva," that is, a female authority expressing a wisdom that must be understood through antiphrasis, or irony, a technique celebrated by Christine de Pizan in the *Livre de la Cité des Dames.* That "Abelard" is himself revoicing her lecture, no doubt accurately, adds to the humor of his density. Like many men, he just does not get it. Better still, she inverts the conventional and misogynistic portrait of woman as a schemer intent on marriage by inserting this gloss into an expostulation against marriage for "Abelard," for reasons laid down by the Apostle Paul and St. Jerome and based on common sense and the example of the very lives of the contemporary monks and ancient philosophers, Nazirites, sons of the prophets, the Pharisees, Sadducees, and Essenes (all tutees, so to speak, of wisdom, or Minerva).

Historia calamitatum, Stage 2, The Discovery and Castration: "Abelard" as Mars, "Heloise" as Venus

That "Abelard" in the *Historia calamitatum* is still lying to himself—covering up his sins, as if in shame or denial—is clear from the use of the names "Mars and Venus" in the dominant mythological *exemplum* in his second section, as if "Abelard" were heroized as Mars, god of war, and "Heloise" as Venus, goddess of love. As shorthand, the myth would immediately communicate to a clerical and learned audience the nature of the crime of "Abelard"—but because the emphasis falls on the discovery, even in the original story, "Abelard" seems to berate himself less for the sin of lechery and fornication than for the loss of shame that contributes to the openness of the act. "Abelard" returns explicitly to the god Mars, with whom he identifies himself as lover of "Heloise" in the role of the hapless Venus, only he refers now to the adultery of Mars and Venus discovered by Venus' husband, Vulcan; "Abelard" is interested less in describing how they are discovered than in conveying the fact of the revelation of the illicit act. Indeed, while it is the uncovering of the truth that is most clear from the narrative in the well-known story, of greatest interest here is that very truth that "Abelard" is covering up by means of the mythological cloak.[45] He might have articulated the occurrence of the sexual act explicitly and literally. Instead, "Abelard" relays the story of their increasing passion for one another, which culminates in the loss of "all sense of shame": "[Et] verecundiae transacta iam passio inverecundiores reddebat" [{A}nd, indeed, shame diminished as we found more opportunities for love-making].[46] The trope "Abelard" uses for the uncovering of their passion is mythological: "Actum itaque in nobis est quod in Marte et Venere deprehensis poetica narrat fabula" [And so we were caught in the act as the poet says happened to Mars and Venus], after which "the girl" [*puella*] becomes pregnant. Heloise's son, Astralabe, is born at Abelard's sister's house after Abelard takes Heloise secretly from her uncle's house.[47]

To use this very myth points the finger of blame not so much at Mars but at the married goddess Venus, whose spouse Vulcan discovers them; in reality, it is "Abelard," as cleric, *magister,* and mentor of "Heloise," who is at fault, and who continues to resist understanding his own vaunted pride. In this instance the implicit role of the husband, Vulcan, is assumed, at first glance, by Heloise's uncle, who went, on his return, "quasi in insaniam conversus" [almost out of his mind],[48] and at second glance, by

Abelard, who takes it on himself to inform the uncle of his own deceit—his cover-up—in the action. This confession to the uncle, again ironically, is itself subverted by Abelard's refusal to see his own motives clearly: beginning with a self-rationalizing blame placed on all women that thinly disguises the *puella* "Heloise," the confession ends with a promise to marry her if it is kept secret in order to protect Abelard's reputation.

> Tandem ego eius immoderatae anxietati admodum compatiens, et de dolo quem fecerat amor, tamquam de summa proditione, me ipsum vehementer accusans conveni hominem supplicando et promittendo quamcumque super hoc emendationem ipse constitueret, nec ulli mirabile id videri asserens, quicumque vim amoris expertus fuisset, et qui quanta ruina summos quoque viros ab ipso statim humani generis exordio mulieres deiecerint memoria retineret. Atque ut amplius eum mitigarem supra quam sperare poterat, obtuli me ei satisfacere eam scilicet quam corruperam mihi matrimonio copulando, dummodo id secreto fieret ne famae detrimentum incurrerem

> [In the end I took pity on his boundless misery and went to him, accusing myself of the deceit love had made me commit as if it were the basest treachery. I begged his forgiveness and promised to make any amends he might think fit. I protested that I had done nothing unusual in the eyes of anyone who had known the power of love, and recalled how since the beginning of the human race women had brought the noblest men to ruin. Moreover, to conciliate him further, I offered him satisfaction in a form he could never have hoped for: I would marry the girl I had wronged. All I stipulated was that the marriage should be kept secret so as not to damage my reputation].[49]

The deceit of "Abelard" in love is as nothing when compared to his self-deceit. But the uncle, according to "Abelard," agrees only in order to betray him. Further, "Heloise" herself is opposed: this marriage would bring disgrace to her and to him, in that she would be blamed for his downfall.[50] That "Abelard" has covered up his own guilt by means of the "lies of the poets" is clear enough to the reader; that he has thought only of himself in his justification is clear enough to "Heloise," who sees herself as the scapegoat in the projected marriage-as-cover-up. Further, the use of the myth of Mars and Venus is itself a distortion, in that "Heloise" is not married to another, while in fact "Abelard" is, in a sense—although he was not required to be—to the church. Indeed, the ironic self-gloss of "Abelard" on this incident by means of the mythological imagery stresses the insistence of the truth to be made manifest despite concealment. The truth, the more profound truth about himself—his pride and lechery—emerges although he apparently refers only to the fact of their sexual union, the literal couplingand the scholastic truth about the Mars, Venus, and Vulcan allegory. Abelard acknowledges, "Sed quod novissime scitur utique sciri quandoque contingit, et quod omnes deprehendunt non est facile unum latere" [But what is last to be learned is somehow learned eventually, and common knowledge cannot easily be hidden from one individual].[51] For some reason, self-understanding eludes him.

"Abelard" as Venus, "Heloise" as Minerva, in the* Historia calamitatum *(The Myth of Charybdis). The second myth of "Heloise" in the *Historia calamitatum,* within the next sentence following the Minerva reference, still in this same bracketed intervention within the narrative of "Abelard," presents the whirlpool Charybdis as a sign of the mutability of sexual desire and all earthly things, that is, the things of Venus. The mythological image is used here to gloss the inadvisability of marriage for a man committed not to *Venus* but to *Minerva:* "Si autem sic laici gentilesque vixerunt, nulla scilicet professione religionis astricti, quid te clericum atque canonicum facere oportet ne divinis officiis turpes praeferas voluptates, ne te praecipitem haec Charybdis absorbeat, ne obscoenitatibus istis te impudenter atque irrevocabiliter immergas?" [But if pagans and laymen could live in this way, though bound by no profession of faith, is there not a greater obligation on you, as clerk and canon, not to put base pleasures before your sacred duties, and to guard against being sucked down headlong into this Charybdis, there to lose all sense of shame and be plunged forever into a whirlpool of impurity?][52] The "whirlpool" in which "Abelard" may be immersed forever is secret marriage—not fornication without legitimation—in this strange inversion of expectation. If lechery and the excessive fulfillment of sexual desire are normally associated with other changeable and mutable activities, just as Venus is often linked with the goddess Fortune, one would naturally expect fornication to be linked with "Charybdis," who represents the Wheel of Fortune, according to Hugutio of Pisa's late-twelfth-century dictionary, the *Magnae derivationes.*[53] Yet "Heloise" rightly suggests that marriage, or at least covert marriage, for "Abelard," led as he is by desire, will up-end his reputation and change his fortune. She is later perceived as a prophet by "Abelard" because he ignores her sage advice, marries her, and, as she predicted, continues on his downward spiral.

"Heloise" as Vulcan, the Revealer (Ep. 2). Heloise responds to "Abelard" and in particular this myth of downfall in his journey narrative in *Ep.* 2, her first letter, by means of a reference to Vulcan, the third party in the allegory of the revelation of their sexual union, as if "Abelard" and "Heloise" had continued as Mars and Venus. Initially it was her uncle who appeared to play the role of Vulcan in the myth of "Abelard," and then "Abelard" himself. What she uncovers here by means of the only mythological reference in her own letters is that *she* has played a double role: first as Venus and then as the uncoverer, the cuckold Vulcan. She has revealed not the shame of their congress, but the shame of her own betrayal by "Abelard"—that is, at the point when she inserts this rhetorical figure into her text, she has similarly been cuckolded by her "wife," "Abelard," who has abandoned her for the church and, worse still, had insisted she become a nun before he became a monk, a mistrust that galls her: "In quo fateor uno minus te de me confidere vehementer dolui atque erubui. Aeque autem Deus scit ad *Vulcania loca* te properantem praecedere vel sequi pro iussu tuo minime dubitarem" [Your lack of trust in me over this one thing, I confess, overwhelmed me with grief and shame. I would have had no hesitation, God knows, in following you or going ahead at your bidding to the *flames of hell*].[54] Although the circumlocution reads *Vulcania loca,* "regions of Vulcan," and figuratively suggests "the lengths of the earth," or "to any lengths," including the place of the damned,[55] I would argue instead that "Heloise" means she would, if necessary, follow "Abelard" into the Vulcanian regions, the "smithy of Vulcan." By using the strange trope, she invokes once again his second mythological analogy, that of the discovery of Mars and Venus by Vulcan. Ironically, it was Aeneas, guided by the Sibyl, and not "Heloise" guided by "Abelard," who actually descended into hell, in book 6 of the *Aeneid,* where he encountered the shades of his abandoned lover Dido and his father, Anchises. I say "ironically" because Aeneas is the heroic figure "Abelard" has chosen, in his self-delusion, to represent himself; here it is "Heloise" he mistrusts rather than himself. Commentators such as Bernardus Silvestris understood the descent into hell by Aeneas to represent self-understanding, knowledge, the achievement of virtue. That Aeneas in hell confronts his abandoned lover, the suicide Dido, suggests the nature of his treachery toward her.

Historia calamitatum, Stage 3, Ruin and Fall from Power: "Abelard" as Echo

The third and last mythological gloss of "Abelard," which appears in relation to the third major phase of his life, his persecution by rivals after the castration, refers to Echo, who loved Narcissus unto death, and thereby suggests most ironically his own essentialized feminine nature in the third stage of his life, his ruin and decline. "Abelard" uses this myth of Echo to describe the curious paradox of his fame spreading more and more widely, as if in echo of his importance, while in fact he remains poor and isolated—reduced to bone, indeed—at his school in the oratory dedicated to the Holy Trinity that he has named the "Paraclete": "Hic autem loco me corpore latitante sed fama nunc maxime universum mundum perambulante, et illius poetici figmenti quod Echo dicitur instar penitus recinente, quod videlicet plurimum vocis habet, sed nihil substantiae" [Meanwhile, though my person lay hidden in this place, my fame travelled all over the world, resounding everywhere like that poetic creation Echo, so called because she has so large a voice but no substance].[56] "Abelard" here refers to the nymph who was condemned by Juno, in Ovid's *Metamorphoses* (3.359ff.), for delaying by means of conversation Juno's search for her own adulterous husband, Jupiter, and thereby allowing the guilty nymphs to flee; for this, Echo always must repeat what someone has just said and is never able to initiate conversation. Although "Abelard" uses the image to refer to his fame, "Echo" glosses him in two ways, based on other details in her myth. When Echo later falls in love with Narcissus and is ignored and spurned, her unquenched desire leads to sleeplessness and loss of appetite, so that she wastes away to bone and eventually to sound alone: "[V]ox tantum atque ossa supersunt: / vox manet, ossa ferunt lapidis traxisse figuram" [Only her voice and her bones remain; then, only voice; for they say that her bones were turned to stone].[57] So also, as Echo, "Abelard" will divest himself of both "arms" and "the man"—he will have neither the corporal nor the intellectual nature of a man, of Aeneas. Like Echo in love with Narcissus, "Abelard" as a result of his desire for "Heloise" has diminished physically—he has been unmanned; he has indeed been feminized and transformed into a poetic creation as unnatural as Echo.[58] That this unmanning deliberately inverts the second Fulgentian stage, *virum,* "manliness," coincides with his downfall, into *luxuria* and the flesh, or his ironic return to the first stage, that of the body and nature.

And yet Echo is deprived of her body and her autonomy by Juno (not Venus or Mars, who have cost "Abelard" everything, nor the "Minerva" who was, but is at this point no longer, an option for our hero). The goddess of fame and the active life, Juno is the third goddess involved in the Judgment of Paris and at this juncture, therefore, also responsible for depriving the feminized "Abelard" of his "voice," his *vox.* Ironically, this deprivation also occurs because of an adultery, but his own, not Jupiter's. Attacked by his enemies for celebrating but one Person of the Trinity, "Abelard" suffers from the slanders and persecutions of his fellow clerics.

> . . . [P]riores aemuli cum per se iam minus valerent, quosdam adversum me novos apostolos quibus mundus plurimum credebat excitaverunt, quorum alter Regularium Canonicorum vitam, alter

> monachorum se resuscitasse gloriabatur. Hi praedicando per mundum discurrentes et me impudenter, quantum poterant, corrodentes non modice tam ecclesiasticis quibusdam quam saecularibus potestatibus contemptibilem ad tempus effecerunt, et de mea tam fide quam vita adeo sinistra disseminaverunt ut ipsos quoque amicorum nostrorum praecipuos a me averterent; et si qui adhuc pristini amoris erga me aliquid retinerent, hoc ipsi modis omnibus metu illorum dissimularent
>
> [My former rivals could do nothing by themselves, and therefore stirred up against me some new apostles in whom the world had great faith. One of these boasted that he had reformed the life of the Canons Regular, the other the life of the monks. They went up and down the country, slandering me shamelessly in their preaching as much as they could, and for a while brought me into considerable disrepute in the eyes of the ecclesiastical as well as secular authorities; and they spread such evil reports of my faith and of my way of life that they also turned some of my chief friends against me, while any who up till now had retained some of their old affection for me took fright and tried to conceal this as best they could].[59]

As a result, "Abelard" falls into despair, accepts a position as an abbot at a monastery in Brittany, where he is subjected to incessant demands for taxes and income by external secular and internal ecclesiastical authorities, learns that Heloise's abbey had been seized by an abbot and the nuns dispossessed, returns to the hermitage at the Paraclete and gives it to Heloise and her nuns, and suffers further calumny for what appears to be his uxoriousness. He describes his situation as a *diminutio,* or "mutilation," both of body and of name, which resembles that of Echo in a second sense: "[P]lus ex detrimento famae quam ex corporis crucior diminutione" [My agony is less for the mutilation of my body than for the damage to my reputation].[60] He is thereafter in danger physically, from the threat of poison, and ends his history on a note of false courage and heartiness: his suffering friend could not have suffered as much as he did; they must think of God's will, knowing these wrongs were undeserved.[61] He has indeed fallen into the whirlpool of Charybdis, as foretold by "Heloise."

The image of Echo that dominates this whole last section bears yet another signification, of course, that we have left unexamined: Is not the Echo of the fame of "Abelard" similarly linked with the Narcissus of his own self-love? If "Abelard" is Narcissus, full of himself and deceived by his desire for the image he sees, in actual despair of God's help, as he appears to be at the end of the *Historia calamitatum,* then this third image signals that his narrative, nearing its end, lacks the allegorical and theological closure provided in more visionary poems such as Boethius' *Consolation of Philosophy* and certainly the Fulgentian allegory of human life found in the exposition on the *Aeneid.* Echo loved Narcissus, after all, whose doom was to love only himself or, rather, the image of himself reflected in the pool into which he gazed, and who represents self-love, selfishness, in all the Ovidian commentaries, beginning with those of twelfth-century Arnulf of Orleans and thirteenth-century John of Garland, just as Echo represents the loss of self, self-destruction. Narcissus, described by John of Garland in his epitome of Ovid as "greedy" [*cupidus*] and deceived by the apparent glory of the material world, is also responsible for the naming of the Mirror Perilous in the

Roman de la Rose of Guillaume de Lorris, that fountain into which he peered and saw himself and in which Amaunt can see only half of the courtly garden of love reflected.[62]

II. "Heloise" as Dame Philosophy to "Abelard"—Boethius: The Remanning of the Epic Hero (Ep. 2–8)

Heloise has attempted to educate "Abelard" by making him confront his own self-glossation, or cover-up; his anger has made him want to blame her, her uncle and brothers, or his rivals for his "wounds" and mistakes in judgment. Because his wounds are physical (the castration), public and secular (the blow to his fame), and also spiritual (his sinful soul), he has been "unmanned" on many different levels. So Heloise has chastised him, as we have already noted, at the end of her first letter, her "letter of request," or *epistola deprecatoria,*[63] for sending his long autobiographical letter addressed to his "friend" to her and the other nuns: "Quas videlicet tuas diligenter commemorans cum eius intenderes consolationi nostrae plurimum addisti desolationi et, dum eius mederi vulneribus cuperes, nova quaedam nobis vulnera doloris inflixisti et priora auxisti. Sana, obsecro, ipsa quae fecisti qui quae alii fecerunt curare satagis" [The detailed account you gave of these may have been intended for his comfort, but it also greatly increased our own feeling of desolation; in your desire to heal his wounds you have dealt us fresh wounds of grief as well as re-opening the old. I beg you, then, as you set about tending the wounds which others have dealt, heal the wounds you yourself have inflicted].[64]

With this admonishing advice, "Heloise" here takes up the explicit literary role of *magister* Philosophy to pupil Boethius in his sixth-century *Consolation.* In her description of the mutilation and suffering of "Abelard," "Heloise" describes the very despair of a Boethius who can no longer remember he is more than a man and who replies, when Philosophy asks, "Nihilne aliud te esse novisti?" [And you do not know you are anything more (than a man)?], "Nihil" [I am nothing more].[65] "Heloise" glosses the state of "Abelard" as Philosophy does the state of Boethius, as one in which he no longer remembers his identity as *homo,* at once a rational animal, but also as one that is more than a rational animal: "[Q]uid ipse sis, nosse desisti . . . [T]ui oblivione confunderis, et exsulem te et exspoliatum propriis bonis esse doluisti. Quoniam vero quis sit rerum finis ignoras, nequam homines atque nefarios potentes felicesque arbitraris" ({Y}ou have forgotten what you are . . .{Y}ou are wandering, forgetful of your real self, you grieve that you are an exile and stripped of your goods; since indeed you do not know the goal and end of all things, you think that evil and wicked men are fortunate and powerful].[66] But "Heloise" identifies forgetfulness of self of "Abelard" in his unmanned state as spiritually different from that of Boethius, although equally distorted. Bearing the *cruces assiduas* [cross of unending suffering], "Abelard" in his "Passion," according to "Heloise," occupies the role of the crucified Christ.[67]

"Heloise" reveals the *superbia* of "Abelard" in an incisive and authoritative gloss or comment on the man as if he were a text she was reading, construed here as feminized, that is, helpless, unmanned, deficient in the masculine and requiring rational guidance, like Boethius, and literally feminine, that is, castrated. Indeed, the boundaries between the *auctor* and his creation—whether "Abelard" and his *historia* or the oratory held by the nuns, the Paraclete, or "Heloise" and the community of nuns themselves—slip and merge: "Heloise" says to "Abelard," "Huius quippe loci tu post Deum solus es fundator, solus huius oratorii constructor, solus huius congregationis aedificator. . . . Totum quod hic est tua creatio est" [For you after God are the sole founder of this place, the sole builder of this oratory, the sole creator of this community. . . . Everything here is your own creation].[68] For this reason, he is bound by obligation to his *amicissimas* [dearest friends], what she terms in this same passage *filias* [daughters], to cultivate his creation, his oratory, his community, his text, himself.

> Satis ex ipsa feminei sexus natura debilis est haec plantatio et infirma etiam si non esset nova. Unde diligentiorem culturam exigit et frequentiorem iuxta illud apostoli: *Ego plantavi, Apollo rigavit, Deus autem incrementum dedit.* Plantaverat apostolus atque fundaverat in fide per praedicationis suae doctrinam Corinthios quibus scribebat. Rigaverat postmodum eos ipsius apostoli discipulus Apollo sacris exhortationibus et sic eis incrementum virtutum divina largita est gratia. Vitis alienae vineam quam non plantasti in amaritudinem tibi conversam admonitionibus saepe cassis et sacris frustra sermonibus excolis. Quid tuae debeas attende qui sic curam impendis alienae
>
> [Through its feminine nature this plantation would be weak and frail even if it were not new; and so it needs a more careful and regular cultivation, according to the words of the Apostle: "I planted the seed and Apollos watered it; but God made it {Radice = 1 Corinthians 3.6}grow" . The Apostle through the doctrine that he preached had planted and established in the faith the Corinthians, to whom he was writing. Afterwards the Apostle's own disciple, Apollos, had watered them with his holy exhortations and so God's grace bestowed on them growth in the virtues. You cultivate a vineyard of another's vines which you did not plant yourself and which has now turned to bitterness against you{Radice = Jeremiah 2.21} so that often your advice brings no result and your holy words are uttered in vain. You devote your care to another's vineyard; think what you owe to your own].[69]

Here "Heloise" inserts into her instruction an appropriate biblical and monastic allegory, that of the vineyard, and cites the New Testament directly and by paraphrase, in order to suggest that Abelard must now convert himself.

In other words, "Heloise" is preaching to "Abelard," commenting on the Word of God, like any patristic commentator, to correct the man and his mythological and exegetical errors. That she is masculinizing her own role here in contradistinction to the Pauline prohibitions against women preaching and glossing the Bible completes the gender reversal of the situation, which involves a feminized "Abelard"/text/pupil instructed and converted by a masculinized "Heloise"/glossator/*magister.* I say "converted" because Abelard has converted Heloise, at an earlier moment, and now "Heloise," by using the cultivation and vineyard or planting imagery to describe herself and the other nuns, as part of the self or creation of "Abelard," is also invoking another Creation, that of God, as described in Genesis, as a reminder of man's fall (and that of "Abelard"). If "Abelard" has not tended his garden, then, like any fallen Adam, he must accept the consequences. If Adam disobeyed God's injunction not to eat of the fruit of the Tree of Knowledge of Good and Evil and fell because of his uxoriousness toward Eve, then he must depart Eden, just as "Abelard," who similarly disobeyed his obligation to tend his nuns, his tender plants, must return to his duty and think of them instead of himself, revise his "text" of misfortune and affliction.

"Heloise" provides the anodyne of Gospel truth for the wounds of "Abelard"—his unmanning—in order to remasculinize and heal him. To use scripture as a *specu-*

lum animae [mirror of the soul] is indeed advice provided by "Abelard" himself, in the letter of direction for the community of the Paraclete (*Ep.* 8): "Speculum animae scripturam sacram constat esse, in quam quilibet legendo vivens, intelligendo proficiens, morum suorum pulchritudinem cognoscit vel deformitatem deprehendit, ut illam videlicet augere, hanc studeat removere" [It is agreed that Holy Scripture is a mirror of the soul, in which anyone who lives by reading and advances by understanding perceives the beauty of his own ways or discovers their ugliness, so that he may work to increase the one and remove the other].[70] Like the twelfth-century commentators Bernard of Utrecht and Arnulf of Orleans, who combine in their exegeses of classical myth a layering of moral (psychological) allegoresis set against Christian (scriptural) allegorization, "Heloise," by use of biblical citation and allegory in this letter, complements the inscription of "Abelard" of classical myth within a personal story in the *Historia calamitatum*.[71]

To borrow a rhetorical term from postmodern critic Gregory L. Ulmer, "Abelard" "invaginates" pagan and heroic analogy within the pseudohagiography of his text, a text both identified by "Heloise" as his self and identified by "Abelard" *with* himself.[72] Like Philosophy disclosing to Boethius, "Heloise" reveals the source of his unmanning, or self-mutilation, *as* "Abelard" himself. To correct his pride, his selfishness, she reminds him of his sin and asks for his conversion. So she informs him that it was desire and lust and not affection that impelled his advances; so she asks for "words" now, "some sweet semblance of yourself": "Dum tui praesentia fraudor verborum saltem votis quorum tibi copia est tuae mihi imaginis praesenta dulcedinem" [While I am denied your presence, give me at least through your words—of which you have enough and to spare—some sweet semblance of yourself].[73] To tend his community he must write them; by so doing, of course, he tends (and renews) himself.

The whole remaining dialogue illustrates what might be termed the conversion, or shift, from self to Other, from male to female, from classical to Christian, from unmanning to *novus homo,* that is involved in this *magister*'s instruction of her pupil. The process of the education of "Abelard" can be measured by the shift in subject, from the male self to the female "body," that is, the community of nuns. This process also can be witnessed in the shape and progression of their overall correspondence, namely, in relation to the proportion of classical to biblical and patristic reference and allusion and the change of tone, from despair to peaceful joy—that is, in regard to the shape and progression of their correspondence, if "Abelard" begins with himself in his "letter of calamities," the *Historia calamitatum,* he ends in *Epistolae* 3, 5, 7 with "Heloise" and the nuns, biblical women, the origin of nuns, woman herself, and ultimately, in *Ep.* 8, with the construction of their gender-specific religious rule, for all history.

The salutations in each remaining letter affix the respective state of spiritual progress from the subject of self to Other, from male to female. The subterfuge evident in the *Historia,* when "Abelard" addresses an imaginary male friend, and the confusion in the first letter, when "Heloise" addresses "Abelard" as master, father, husband, and brother and herself as handmaid, daughter, wife, and sister, are gradually repaired. In *Ep.* 4, "Heloise" addresses Abelard as "Unico suo post Christum" [her only one after Christ] and identifies herself as "unica sua in Christo" [she who is his alone in Christ][74] as a reminder of the only appropriate relationship they share. In *Ep.* 4, "Abelard," having renounced all personal ties with her, sees her as "Sponsae Christi servus eisidem" [the bride of Christ, Christ's servant];[75] consequently, "Heloise" acknowledges the return of Abelard's manhood (that is, his humanity) to God in *Ep.* 6, where he is addressed as "Suo [Domino] specialiter" [God's own in species], and also as an individual male, "sua singulariter" [his own as individual].[76] In *Epistolae* 7 and 8 "Abelard" omits any personal address or salutation to her at all, as if to signal his return to a rational and spiritually correct state. Further, by *Ep.* 6, "Heloise," as Jean-Charles Huchet has noted, begins to speak essentially like "Abelard": the "echo of the masculine word has returned to its source and is not lost."[77] But I would disagree that at this point she is "enfin obéissante au Maître": he has in fact obeyed her in her role as master, which has enabled him to return to his own masculinized identity and simultaneously to empower her and all nuns and abbesses like her by means of the articulation of a female *regula*—female rule, indeed, set side by side with masculine rule in an appropriate cultural binary—which he will soon provide.

"Abelard" is progressing in self-understanding and therefore in the acquisition of humility, but slowly, slowly. Within the context of this *Ep.* 7 as a response to her *epistola deprecatoria,* her "letter of request" for information on the origin of nuns and for a female *regula* for the community of the Paraclete, he has (one might say) just begun—by honoring *her* rather than himself. For example, in another ironic mythological reference, "Abelard" mentions the Erechthean and Cumaean sibyls in *Ep.* 7 (On the origin of nuns) in a paragraph celebrating the honoring of women by the church, chief of whom is Mary, mother of God, and Elizabeth, mother of John the Baptist. He mentions the sibyls because of their gift of prophecy: the Erechthean who prophesized the birth of Christ and the Cumaean who prophesized a miraculous birth that would take away the world's sins.[78] The laudatory mythological reference is ironic given Abelard's lack of self-understanding and his failure to honor "Heloise" as a learned woman, as mother of his son, as nun, and as *magister,* that powerful "sibyl" who in the course of their dialogue is attempting to transform and "convert" him back into a man.

The use of classical reference and allusion to any classical text and not just to classical mythology in the epistolary sequence, both in the *Historia calamitatum* and in the *Epistolae,* also gradually diminishes, with a corresponding increase in biblical and patristic references and allusions, especially in relation to the New Testament.[79] In succeeding letters, the only differences to be remarked from this clearly articulated progression from classical to biblical and patristic—from the mythologized words and classical learning of "Abelard" to the Word of God—are in *Ep.* 5, his sudden sensitivity and response to the letters of "Heloise," just as she has always referred, from the beginning of her own letters, to his *Historia calamitatum.*[80] This change from self-obsession suggests a helpful and gender-balanced interest in her writing and in the *auctoritas* of the Other. He also cites two classical references in *Ep.* 5, one from that very Vergil he has plundered earlier to design himself previously as a hero within an epic narrative and whom he now cites as author of *Eclogues* 3.65 and uses judiciously to validate the apparent rejection of praise of "Heloise." "Abelard" cautions "Heloise" not to appear humble while concealing proud desire, like the manipulative and lascivious shepherdess Galatea of Vergil: "Talem et lascivae calliditatem Galateae Virgilius describit, quae quod volebat fugiendo appetebat et, simulatione repulsae, amplius in se amantem incitabat: 'Et fugit ad salices, inquit, et se cupit ante videri.' Antequam lateat cupit se fugientem videri, ut ipsa fuga qua reprobare consortium iuvenis videtur amplius acquirat" [Such artfulness Vergil describes in wanton Galatea, who sought what she wanted by flight, and by feigning rejection led on her lover more surely towards her: "She flees to the willows and wishes first to be seen." Before she hides she wants to be seen fleeing, so that the very flight whereby she appears to reject the youth's company ensures that she obtains it].[81] The emphasis on doubleness—concealment and revelation, self-duplicity, public dishonesty—might well serve to gloss his own previous behavior in its apparent probity while concealing gross pride and lust. The female figure here once again appropriately types "Abelard," "feminine" in his wiles and his sexual negation, rather than "Heloise"; she becomes only the pretext for his proof of invulnerability against the seduction of the classical text. Second, "Abelard" cites Lucan's *Pharsalia* in *Ep.* 5 as an admonishment to "Heloise" not to indulge in memories of the past.[82] Such use of the classical to instruct and guide her evidences his increasing charity and appropriate use of historical epic text as exemplum. These lines from Lucan's *Pharsalia* (8.84–85) represent what Radice terms a near rebuke to "Heloise" for mourning the wrong things, in that Pompey here reproaches Cornelia for mourning his ruined fortune after the war ended.[83]

Note, however, early on in the *Historia calamitatum,* that "Heloise," in a self-dramatizing appropriation of words (but not of figuration), has invested herself with Cornelia's situation by invoking lines also taken from Lucan's *Pharsalia,* when Cornelia offers to die for her husband. This famous appropriation, occurring as it does at the moment when "Heloise" obeys the plea of "Abelard" to take up the veil before he becomes a monk and thereby earn penance for her sin, sounds her own guilt over causing the downfall of "Abelard":

> O maxime coniunx!
> thalamis indigne meis! Hoc iuris habebat
> In tantum fortuna caput? Cur impia nupsi,
> Si miserum factura fui? Nunc accipe poenas,
> Sed quas sponte luam
>
> [O noble husband,
> Too great for me to wed, was it my fate
> To bend that lofty head? What prompted me
> To marry you and bring about your fall?
> Now claim your due, and see me gladly pay.][84]

"Heloise" also has cited lines from Lucan (2.14–15) in *Ep.* 4, about the necessity for human hope to continue in the face of fear and adversity, as a reminder to "Abelard" to be strong by refusing to convey to her and the other nuns his bitterness and despair, which makes them grieve for him—that is, she reminds him to consider his audience. By appropriating wife Cornelia's voice at the beginning, "Heloise" dramatizes her own situation as abandoned wife; by appropriating Pompey's voice at the end, "Abelard" as head—and not just as husband—instructs "Heloise" and her nuns in the necessary *remedium* for ill fortune suffered because material things have become too valued. In a sense, this is also Philosophy's position in the *Consolatio,* so that "Abelard" here doubly communicates his own restoration of clear understanding. In *Ep.* 6, "Heloise" cites from the Rule of St. Benedict, which she is using to show to "Abelard" the gender specificity of that rule, or rather the lack of gender applicability to her own community, and thereby she encourages him to construct a "rule" for them. *Ep.* 7, from "Abelard" (On the origin of nuns), consists entirely of a list of examples from biblical and patristic texts in which women appear. And finally, *Ep.* 8, the feminized *Regula* "Heloise" has asked him for, is appropriately bolstered throughout by references to biblical and patristic texts and to classical texts like Lucan's *Pharsalia,* which appear to document Roman history.

The conversion of "Abelard" is complete when his tone and attitude toward "Heloise" and himself change from worldly despair to the peace that comes from an acceptance of self, a love for the entire human community, both male and female, and a faithful love of God as Truth. At the very end, in *Epistolae* 7 and 8, "Abelard" has divorced the personal almost wholly from his text, left behind "Heloise" as a person and as a woman, so that *Ep.* 7 can end with an address to "soror in Christo carissima" [{d}earest sister in Christ].[85] By means of such closure "Abelard" acknowledges that he has answered appropriately her request to legitimate the order of nuns so that they may "tanto studiosius vestrae professionis propositum amplectamini, quanto eius excellentiam amplius noveritis" [warmly embrace the calling of your profession through better understanding of its excellence].[86] In *Ep.* 8, which appears to end abruptly, "Abelard" has so fully reclaimed his manhood as a doctor that he can, presumably without irony, refer "Heloise" and her nuns in the search for Truth to the love of Mary, sister of Martha, a blessed woman who sat at Christ's feet to learn, to God Himself, and to the love of the Word, scripture, as represented by Jerome's disciples, Paula and Eustochium.

Of course "Heloise" initially found herself sitting at the feet of "Abelard" in her desire to read scripture and love the truth; and as ecclesiasts "Heloise" and "Abelard" in their dialogue resemble Paula and Jerome, a couple upon whom "Abelard" originally modeled their relationship.[87] The point of his analogy is to reinscribe that vexed and mutilated relationship of "Heloise" and "Abelard" within his text—to right it, by writing now the appropriate scriptural and patristic figures he might have invoked to her so long ago, had he been both man and manly enough to have done so.

Notes

I am indebted to Theresa Munisteri for her help in editing this chapter.

1. For the history of the interpretation of Heloise and her reception from the Middle Ages on, see the brief discussion by J. T. Muckle, "The Personal Letters between Abelard and Heloise," (1953) pp. 49–50; and, for the Middle Ages to the nineteenth century, Charlotte Charrier, *Héloïse dans l'histoire et dans la légende* (1933). See also the more focused treatments of reception, ranging in date from the seventeenth to the eighteenth centuries, in Peggy Kamuf, *Fictions of Feminine Desire: Disclosures of Heloise* (1982); for the fourteenth and fifteenth centuries, in Colette Jeudy, "Un Nouveau Manuscrit de la Correspondance d'Abélard et Héloïse" (1991); for the twelfth century, in Helen C. R. Laurie, "Cligès and the Legend of Abelard and Heloise" (1991); from the eighteenth to the twentieth century, in Andrew Louth, "The Image of Heloise in English Literature" (1993); for a fifteenth- to sixteenth-century manuscript, in Véronique Wakerley, "Heloys: André or Andreas? A Problem of Authorship in MS Royal 16F II in the British Museum Library" (1996); and for seventeenth- and eighteenth-century French imitations of love correspondence in which male writers impersonate female writers like Heloise, in Nancy May Arenberg, "Epistolary Transvestism: (Re)Visions of Heloise (Seventeenth-Eighteenth Centuries) (1996)."
2. *HC,* ed. Muckle 163–213.
3. On the *Problemata,* see Peter Dronke, "Heloise's *Problemata* and *Letters:* Some Questions of Form and Content"; and Maria Cipollone, "In margine ai *Problemata* Heloissae," 227–44.

4. Bernhard Schmeidler published three articles at different times, "Der Briefwechsel zwischen Abälard und Heloise eine Fälschung?" (1913) "Der Briefwechsel zwischen Abälard und Heloise dennoch eine literarische Fiktion Abälards"(1935) and "Der Briefwechsel zwischen Abälard und Heloise als eine literarische Fiktion Abälards" (1940); D.W. Robertson, Jr. *Abelard and Heloise;* and Barbara Newman, "Authority, Authenticity, and the Repression of Heloise."
5. See John F. Benton, "Fraud, Fiction and Borrowing in the Correspondence of Abelard and Heloise" (1975); and also his "A Reconsideration of the Authenticity of the Correspondence of Abelard and Heloise" (1980). Because the manuscripts are dated later in time than that of the historical Abelard and contain references that appear to come from the thirteenth century, the authenticity of the text has remained a vexed issue, although previous scholarly responses have tended to validate the legitimacy of at least some of the correspondence (especially the *HC*) as being by Abelard himself: see Peter Dronke, *Abelard and Heloise in Medieval Testimonies* (1976); Peter von Moos, "Le Silence d'Héloïse et les idéologies modernes,"(1975); and also "*Post festum:* Was kommt nach der Authentizitätsdebatte über die Briefe Abaelards und Heloises?" (1980); and C. Stephen Jaeger, "The Prologue to the *Historia calamitatum* and the 'Authenticity Question'" (1980).
6. Étienne Gilson, "L'Authenticité de la correspondance d'Héloïse et d'Abélard," in Gilson, *Héloïse and Abélard,* 2nd ed., 1948, pp. 150–71.
7. Barbara Newman, "Authority, Authenticity, and the Repression of Heloise," p. 49.
8. Michael Calabrese, "Ovid and the Female Voice in the *De Amore* and in the Letters of Abelard and Heloise," 17, 19.
9. Glenda McLeod, "'Wholly Guilty, Wholly Innocent': Self-Definition in Héloïse's Letters to Abélard," p. 64.
10. This has been noted by critics such as Mary Martin McLaughlin, "Abelard as Autobiographer: The Motives and Meaning of His 'Story of Calamities'"; Peter Dronke, *Poetic Individuality in the Middle Ages: New Departures in Poetry, 1000–1150;* Jean Leclercq, "Modern Psychology and the Interpretation of Medieval Texts"; John F. Benton, "Consciousness of Self and Perceptions of Individuality"; Chris D. Ferguson, "Autobiography as Therapy: Guibert de Nogent, Peter Abelard, and the Making of Medieval Autobiography"; and Gerald A. Bond, *The Loving Subject: Desire, Eloquence, and Power in Romanesque France,* among others.
11. See Bond and some of his earlier articles, especially "Composing Yourself: Ovid's *Heroides,* Baudri of Bourgueil and the Problem of Persona"; and "*Iocus amoris:* The Poetry of Baudri of Bourgueil and the Formation of the Ovidian Subculture."
12. R.W. Southern, "The Letters of Abelard and Heloise," p. 88.
13. Linda Georgianna, "'Any Corner of Heaven': Heloise's Critique of Monasticism," 224, 226, revised as chapter 8 in this volume.
14. I am using quotation marks now to distinguish the persona of Heloise, "Heloise," from the historical person and abbess, in the same way we distinguish Chaucer from his persona, "Geffrey," and Langland from his "Will." That women writers might construct voice and mask for strategic reasons is an approach recently taken up by Lynn Staley, *Margery Kempe's Dissenting Fictions.*
15. Catherine Brown, "*Muliebriter:* Doing Gender in the Letters of Heloise," p. 35.
16. Claire Nouvet, "The 'Discourse of the Whore': An Economy of Sacrifice," 761. For the extension of Nouvet's arguments on role-playing, see Juanita Feros Ruys, "Role-Playing in the Letters of Heloise and Abelard," 53–78.
17. See Bonnie Wheeler, "Origenary Fantasies: Abelard's Castration and Confession".
18. Rather curiously, John Marenbon in chapter 2 of this volume, "Authenticity Revisited," appears to equate what he terms the "feminist" interpretation of Heloise with the role of the disempowered victim, an interpretation he attempts to correct by attention to

what he views as a more scholarly reworking of the authenticity question in several recent articles by male scholars. Ironically, Marenbon's conclusion, of Heloise's authentic and powerful voice in the correspondence, actually confirms the most recent feminist interpretations of Heloise's role (many of them included in this collection), even though he may have intended to undermine earlier feminist interpretations as "political" and unscholarly because motivated by a desire to grant a more powerful role to women in the Middle Ages. I see no incongruity between his conclusions and those of Catherine Brown, Bonnie Wheeler, Alcuin Blamires, Donna Alfano Bussell, Katharina Wilson and Glenda McLeod (in this volume), and my own. Also ironically, Marenbon supposedly traces a kind of inductive and objective investigation of the subjectivity of the *scholars* who have examined the authenticity question, one that concludes in favor of viewing Heloise as herself authentic but hardly as a victim of Abelard, and without conscious attention to his own subject position.

19. The term was used by Abelard's old master Roscelin to describe Heloise.
20. "Allegory," *allegoria,* according to Dante in his *Letter to Can Grande,* derives from Greek *alleon,* Latin *alienus,* "strange," "different," or "other." See the discussion, "Margin as Text, Text as Image," in Jane Chance, *Medieval Mythography: From Roman North Africa to the School of Chartres, A.D. 433 - 1170,* especially pp. 5f.
21. "The voice of Abelard functions, oddly enough, like the voices of the women in Andreas's *De amore,* becoming the force of authority, purifying love, reforming the error and folly of his interlocuter in the dialogue." Calabrese, "Ovid and the Female Voice," 20.
22. Because I have broken up the "narrative sequence," of *HC* followed by the separate *Epistolae* to clarify the argument I am making here about Heloise as glossator, titles for sections of this chapter in which discussion involves the responsive voice of "Heloise" as constructed by Abelard in *HC* will be signaled by the use of roman font, as opposed to the use of italic font for titles of sections in which Heloise's own glosses in her *Epistolae* appear.
23. *Ep.* 2, ed. Muckle 68 (Radice 109).
24. *Ep.* 4, ed. Muckle 77 (Radice 127 and note).
25. Alastair J. Minnis, *Medieval Theory of Authorship: Scholastic Literary Attitudes in the Later Middle Ages,* p. 2.
26. Minnis, *Medieval Theory of Authorship,* p. 4.
27. *HC,* ed. Muckle 79 (Radice 57, n. 1).
28. *Ep.* 2, ed. Muckle 68 (Radice 109).
29. *Ep.* 2, ed. Muckle 68 (Radice 109).
30. *Ep.* 2, ed. Muckle 68 (Radice 109).
31. Ep.2, ed. Muckle 68 (Radice 109).
32. *Ep.* 2, ed. Muckle 69 (Radice 109, 110–11).
33. *HC,* ed. Muckle 175 (Radice 58; my emphasis).
34. *HC,* ed. Muckle 175–76 (Radice 58; my emphases).
35. Southern, "The Letters of Abelard and Heloise," p. 89. Other scholars have focused on the consolatory aspects of this text within the rhetorical or epistolary tradition instead of the grammatical and philosophical tradition. If the *HC* can be considered a *narratio fabulosa* in a more Macrobian sense, or at least a *prosimetrum* like that of Boethius, the opportunities for recovery of self become more pronounced.
36. Mary Martin McLaughlin argues that, "[b]rought face to face with the defeats and failures of his later life, Abelard himself was the friend whom he wanted to console and in writing a letter that was evidently designed to arouse the sympathy of others, he could also find some relief for his own emotions." McLaughlin, "Abelard as Autobiographer," p. 469. However, she does not explore the literary or philosophical implications of this insight and adheres to the historical and biographical facts that can be corroborated. As

"affirmation of self," the *HC* does, she concludes, celebrate Abelard "at once its author and its subject, . . . the autonomous individual who carries his world within, who faces constantly the private decisions and dilemmas, as well as the struggles with his environment, that force him repeatedly to define himself anew, the individual who by choice and action shapes himself" (p. 488). Unfortunately, she also ignores the role of the remainder of the letters in that shaping, and with it the concomitant role of Heloise as shaper/shaped, author/subject.

37. In the early twelfth century, although Chartrian philosopher Bernardus Silvestris had not yet written his commentary on the first six books of the *Aeneid,* it is true that Fulgentius, the influential sixth-century Roman African grammarian who penned his exposition on the content of the *Aeneid,* would have been well known. See Chance, *Medieval Mythography,* vol. 1, especially chap. 2.
38. The "first" refers to the arrival of Aeneas in Italy in *Aeneid* 1.1–2. Fulgentius portrays "Vergil" as stating: "[In] omnibus nostris opusculis fisici ordinis argumenta induximus, quo per duodena librorum volumina pleniorem humanae vitae mostrassem statum" [In {of the *Aeneid*} all my writings I have introduced themes of natural order, whereby in the twelve books I have shown the full range of human life]. Fulgentius, *Expositio Virgilianae Continentiae,* in *Opera,* ed. Rudolf Helm, pp. 86–87; trans. Leslie George Whitbread, *Fulgentius the Mythographer,* no. 6.
39. The full passage reads: "Ergo tres gradus istos in uno versu nostro considera positos, id est: 'arma', 'virum' et 'primus': 'arma', id est virtus, pertinet ad substantiam corporalem, 'virum', id est sapientia, pertinet ad substantiam sensualem, 'primus' vero, id est princeps, pertinet ad substantiam censualem, quo sit ordo huiusmodi: habere, regere, ornare. Ergo sub figuralitatem historiae plenum hominis monstravimus statum, ut sit prima natura, secunda doctrina, tertia felicitas." Fulgentius, *Expositio Virgilianae,* ed. Helm, pp. 89–90. (Think of these three stages as arranged in my one-verse line, as "arms," "man," and "the first." "Arms," that is, manliness, belongs to the corporeal substance; "man," that is, "wisdom," belongs to the intellectual substance; and "the first," that is, a ruler [*princeps*], belongs to the power of judgment; whence this order, to possess, to control, to ornament. Thus in the guise of a story [*historia*] I have shown the complete state of man: first, his nature; second, what he learns; third, his attaining to prosperity.) Fulgentius, *Exposition on the Content of Virgil,* no. 10, trans. Whitbread, *Fulgentius the Mythographer.*
40. See Fulgentius, *Mitologiae,* in *Opera,* ed. Helm.
41. See Jane Chance, "The Medieval Sources of Cristoforo Landino's Allegorization of the Judgment of Paris"; and Margaret J. Ehrhart, *The Judgment of the Trojan Prince Paris in Medieval Literature.*
42. *HC,* ed. Muckle 179 (Radice 62).
43. D. W. Robertson, Jr., *Abelard and Heloise,* pp. 112–13.
44. *HC,* ed. Muckle 188 (Radice 73; my emphasis).
45. Radice glosses the myth of Mars and Venus as derived from Homer's *Odyssey* 8 and known to Abelard through Ovid's *Ars amatoria* 2.561ff. and *Metamorphoses* 4.169ff. (p. 69, n. 1).
46. *HC,* ed. Muckle 184 (Radice 69).
47. *HC,* ed. Muckle 184–85 (Radice 69).
48. *HC,* ed. Muckle 185 (Radice 69).
49. *HC,* ed. Muckle 185 (Radice 69–70).
50. *HC,* ed. Muckle 185 (Radice 70).
51. *HC,* ed. Muckle 184 (Radice 68).
52. *HC,* ed. Muckle 188 (Radice 73).
53. See, for example, Hugutio of Pisa, *Magnae derivationes.* This dictionary has not yet been edited. Excerpts have appeared in Claus Riessner, *Die 'Magnae derivationes' des Uguccione da Pisa und ihre Bedeutung für die romanische Philologie.*
54. *Ep.* 2, ed. Muckle 72–73, my emphasis (Radice 117; my emphasis).

55. Radice believes Heloise refers here to the fires of hell, which may be correct, because Vulcan was a smith born from a volcano; "regions of Vulcan" is therefore meant to be identified with Tartarus.
56. *HC,* ed. Muckle 202 (Radice 93).
57. Ovid, *Metamorphoses* 3.395–99.
58. A similar treatment of the myth, including an analogous gender reversal, appears in Chaucer's "Franklin's Tale." See Chance, *The Mythographic Chaucer: The Fabulization of Sexual Politics,* pp. 251–62.
59. *HC,* ed. Muckle 202 (Radice 93).
60. *HC,* ed. Muckle 207 (Radice 99).
61. *HC,* ed. Muckle 211 (Radice 105).
62. Guillaume de Lorris and Jean de Meun, *The Romance of the Rose,* trans. by Charles Dahlberg, ll. 1560ff.
63. Southern, "The Letters of Abelard and Heloise," p. 97.
64. *Ep.* 2, ed. Muckle 69 (Radice 109, 110, 111).
65. Boethius, *Consolatio* 1.38; from *Tractates; De consolatione Philosophiae,* pp. 168–69.
66. *Consolatio* 1.40–46; from *Tractates; De consolatione Philosophiae,* pp. 168–71.
67. *Ep.* 2, ed. Muckle 68 (Radice 109).
68. *Ep.* 2, ed. Muckle 69 (Radice 111).
69. *Ep.* 2, ed. Muckle 70 (Radice 111–12).
70. *Ep.* 8, ed. Muckle 285 (Radice 257).
71. See the definitions, especially in the preface and introduction, and the bibliography provided for this ample field in Chance, *Medieval Mythography,* vol. 1.
72. Gregory L. Ulmer, *The Anti-Aesthetic,* pp. 83–110.
73. *Ep.* 2, ed. Muckle 72 (Radice 116).
74. *Ep.* 4, ed. Muckle 77 (Radice 127).
75. *Ep.* 4, ed. Muckle 82 (Radice 137).
76. *Ep.* 6, ed. Muckle 241, 241, n. 2 (Radice 159, 159, n. 1). Alternatively, the line might be translated as "To him who is especially her lord, she who is uniquely his," as Radice observes.
77. "L'écho de la parole masculine est retourné à sa source et s'y est perdu," in Jean-Charles Huchet, "La voix d'Héloïse," 287.
78. *Ep.* 7, ed. Muckle 272 (Radice 181).
79. In his *HC* (according to the notes in Muckle and Radice), the very learned Abelard refers to or cites or paraphrases the writings of Seneca, Cicero, Porphyry, Diogenes Laertius, Juvenal, Lucan, Ovid, Horace, Priscian, and Quintillian, among others; the writings of the Church Fathers Augustine and Jerome and then Eusebius and Bede; the Old Testament books of Genesis, Leviticus, Numbers, Deuteronomy, Judges, Kings, Esther, Psalms, Proverbs, and Jeremiah; Susannah; and finally, a handful of New Testament books, especially the Gospels of Matthew, Luke, and John and then the Pauline books of Romans, 1 and 2 Corinthians, Galatians, Timothy, and Peter. Heloise's first letter (*Ep.* 2) cites or refers to or invokes, in a much less scholarly and abstruse manner, the *HC,* of course, as major text, along with Seneca and Cicero, among the classical authorities, and then Genesis and Jeremiah from the Old Testament, followed by Matthew, John, Romans and Corinthians. Only then, in the second letter (*Ep.* 3), do we see Abelard responding to her instruction by citing only biblical or prophetical texts, in acknowledgment of the authority of God's Word—in order of first mention, Thessalonians, Exodus, Jeremiah, the Psalms, the prophet Habbakuk, Judges, Ephesians, James, Samuel, Matthew, Hebrews, Kings, Luke, John, Mark, Proverbs, Corinthians, and Ecclesiasticus. Heloise's third letter (*Ep.* 6) is similarly intermeshed with biblical and patristic citations and allusions, from Matthew, Lucan, Proverbs, Ecclesiastes, Samson, Kings, Job, Church

Fathers Gregory and Ambrose, Romans, the Psalms, Isaiah, Ezekiel, Jeremiah, Proverbs, Ecclesiasticus, Corinthians, Timothy, and Church Father Jerome; she also cites Seneca.

80. *Ep.* 5, ed. Muckle 87–88 (Radice 145).
81. *Ep.* 5, ed. Muckle 87 (Radice 144).
82. *Ep.* 5, ed. Muckle 92 (Radice 153).
83. Radice 153.
84. *HC,* ed. Muckle 191 (Radice 76).
85. *Ep.* 7, ed. Muckle 281 (Radice 182).
86. *Ep.* 7, ed. Muckle 281 (Radice 182).
87. See also, in this volume, chapter 12, by Alcuin Blamires, which retraces the relationship of Heloise and Abelard in the light of the epistolary and scholarly relationships of various women with Jerome, including Furia, Eustochium, and Marcella.

CHAPTER 8

"IN ANY CORNER OF HEAVEN": HELOISE'S CRITIQUE OF MONASTIC LIFE

Linda Georgianna

This chapter argues that Heloise's third letter should be read not as proof of a prior conversion but rather as a reasoned critique of monastic life in light of her own history as well as her evolving, experiential theology.

Traditionally, readers have sought to cast Heloise as a modern romantic heroine, defiant, candid, courageous, tragic, and above all unyielding in her passionate attachment to Abelard. Her modernity has been variously construed; if one admirer associates her achievements with the Italian Renaissance, another views them as a precursor of the Enlightenment.[1] But the thrust invariably is to praise Heloise for her precocity in rebelling against the mores of her age. Henry Adams, in *Mont-Saint-Michel and Chartres* (1904), turned to Abelard's works for clues to "the Gothic thought and philosophy" embodied in the famous cathedral; but he excuses Heloise from his study, saying: "Neither art nor thought has a modern equivalent; only Héloïse, like Isolde, unites the ages."[2] Much more recently Barbara Newman wrote: "While [Heloise] wages impassioned war with Abelard under the guise of submission, she never ceases to fascinate; but when she actually submits, she dwindles into virtue as a heroine of romance might dwindle into marriage."[3]

The effort to construct Heloise as a romance heroine has produced some insightful readings of her letters, especially in Étienne Gilson's *Héloïse and Abélard,* first published in 1938 and still essential reading. Nevertheless, the romanticizing of Heloise, typified by the popular Caedmon recording featuring Claire Bloom as Heloise opposite Claude Rains's Abelard (with selections from the Song of Songs on the flip side!) has had its price. As Peter Dronke remarked some years ago, and Neil Cartlidge has recently reiterated, the most damaging arguments against the authenticity of Heloise's letters—damaging not because they were persuasive but because they sidetracked serious study of her work for many years—were themselves reactions against the sentimental portrait constructed by Heloise's admirers.[4] John Benton's extended attack on the letters as forgeries and D. W. Robertson's characterization of the correspondence as a pious fiction are misguided in all kinds of ways and have, for good reason, fallen by the wayside. Nevertheless, both readers, steeped in the history and literature of the period, had reason to be suspicious of what was, and I would argue still is, the prevailing image of Heloise as the tragic heroine of a love affair gone bad, heroically persisting, even glorying, in her unrequited love to the bitter end.[5]

The most important change to be noted in Heloise studies in recent years is the effort to *historicize* Heloise, to see her less as a passionate rebel against contemporary conditions than as a superbly educated writer who was produced by, and an important contributor to, the complex intellectual environment of early twelfth-century Paris. Transhistorical or essentialist notions of love or passion or the feminine are now giving way to attempts to study Heloise's discourse in terms of her education, contemporary debates over marriage laws, actual marriage practices among clerics, and scholastic developments in theology and philosophy, particularly in the growing field of moral theology to which her work is now being viewed as a major contribution, both in its own right and in its impact on Abelard's mature writings.[6]

This chapter, first published in 1987 and now updated, began with my frustration at being asked to drop from a book a section on Heloise as a twelfth-century religious innovator because readers of the manuscript felt that the letters might be thirteenth-century forgeries. The chapter originally began with remarks about the authenticity debate, which I have dispensed with here, since they have been rendered unnecessary by the recent work of Barbara Newman, M. T. Clanchy, and especially the balanced assessment of John Marenbon (in chapter 10 of this volume) that, I hope, will close this debate for now or at least relegate it to the fringes unless someone discovers far more persuasive evidence of forgery or fiction than has yet been produced. My chapter works to "authenticate" Heloise's letters by another route, one less concerned with silencing a seemingly profane Heloise than with hearing more of what she had to say. Preference for the sentimental Heloise has led critics to canonize her first two letters to Abelard and ignore her third one, a detailed analysis of monasticism, the institution within which she struggled to authenticate herself for most of her life. My aim is to historicize Heloise's letters in several ways, first by closely analyzing the argument of her critique of monasticism in light of contemporary debates over the theory and practice of monastic life and then by showing how her institutional analysis proceeds from and extends the experiential analysis of her far more famous "personal" letters. The result, I hope, is a fuller and more historical account, both of the intellectual development of Heloise's thought and of the complex cultural milieu that her work reflects and shapes.

While the coherence and development of Abelard's thought, including his letters to Heloise, have often been explored, it is the incoherence of Heloise's letters that dominates criticism.[7] Even though most scholars now see no reason to doubt the historical authenticity of her letters, they have frequently raised questions concerning authenticity of a different sort, asking, in effect, which is the more "authentic" Heloise, the "très sage Heloys" so admired by her medieval contemporaries as the holy abbess of the Paraclete and apparent author of the last two extant letters to Abelard dealing with monastic and biblical questions, or the "woman of sensuous mind" apparently revealed in the early letters, the tragic, inconsolable lover of Abelard trapped in her memories of the past and whose persistent, unrequited passion is so familiar to readers throughout the Western world.[8] A sharp break between what we might call a serious and a sensuous Heloise is reinforced by editors who divide the correspondence into two distinct halves and invent separate titles for them, such as "The Personal Letters" and "The Letters of Direction."[9]

Most criticism has focused on the so-called personal letters, whose dramatic, detailed self-analysis makes them anomalous in the literature of the period. Heloise's third letter, her longest and most learned by far, in which she examines the monastic life of women and requests a new religious rule for the nuns of the Paraclete, is treated far less often and with much less enthusiasm.[10] R. W. Southern's estimate of Abelard's two responses to Heloise's request might well be extended by most readers to apply equally to Heloise's third letter: "They are by no means readable and they are seldom read. They have no personal interest."[11] Although sharply divided on ideological grounds, feminist, romantic, and more clerically minded readers alike view Heloise's third letter as an act of submission or repression of her personal experience, a willed silence on the subject of her love for Abelard and her grief over losing him. Whether hailed as proof of Heloise's conversion or dismissed as proof of her capitulation to Abelard's mastery and subsequent "dwindl[ing] into virtue," this densely argued text is routinely read as a form of "silence," that is, for what it does *not* say.[12] Étienne Gilson is one of the few earlier critics to analyze this letter in any detail, but he does so apart from his extensive and subtle reading of the first two letters and in a very different historical context, reserving his remarks on Heloise's ideas about religious life for his conclusion, where he depicts her as a proto-Renaissance thinker.[13] Among more recent critics, Peter Dronke stands out as one of the few readers to treat Heloise's third letter as worthy of serious attention, especially as it sheds light on the consistency of her thought throughout the letters.[14]

This chapter explores the significance of Heloise's third and most neglected letter, especially when viewed in the context of contemporary controversies concerning the monastic life as well as other, newer forms of spirituality. My aim is to show that Heloise's concerns in this letter follow from and develop ideas expressed in her earlier letters and that we can understand better both Heloise and those aspects of twelfth-century spirituality that she epitomizes if we treat her works as an intellectual and imaginative whole rather than as a disjointed series of documents, explicable only in terms of forgery, fiction, or repression. In the end, I believe that close investigation of the contents, context, and style of Heloise's letters will cast more light on the authenticity debate than more narrowly conceived studies of authorship.[15]

In arguing for the consistency of Heloise's letters, we need not assert the simple and neatly sequential development that some readers have found there, namely, the exemplary story of how Abelard was first converted himself, then converted Heloise from worldly love to the religious life. The literary model invoked by these readers is the popular conversion narrative, and the supposed rupture between Heloise's second and third letters is to be explained by her private and unrecorded moment of conversion, in which she abruptly renounces her past and embraces a new life of devotion.[16] No evidence anywhere in her works suggests that Heloise renounces her past or that she translates her previously complex analysis of her history into the sharply delineated "before" and "after" narrative pattern so prominent in conversion stories of the period, including Abelard's own. On the contrary, the difficulty of converting or dismissing one's memories lies at the heart of Heloise's argument throughout her work; it is the *absence* of a traditional conversion experience that drives her debate with Abelard and her notion of the spiritual life as well. Heloise is as eager to "authenticate" her experience as scholars are to authenticate her letters. But she rejects all externally imposed models, literary as well as spiritual, that presume a conventional conversion, seeking instead a new spiritual model that can adequately describe and account for her complex spiritual state.[17]

In her first two letters, Heloise examines her personal history as Abelard's mistress and wife. She dwells particularly on the devastating emotional and spiritual consequences of her inability to repent of loving Abelard, in spite of having lived for many years, outwardly at least, the penitential life as defined in the Rule of St. Benedict. In her third letter, rather than repressing or converting her past, Heloise begins to generalize from her own experience, transforming what once had seemed a unique spiritual predicament into a theoretical exploration of some of the most basic assumptions of the monastic life as conceived by St. Benedict. Her assessment of the institution of monasticism grows directly out of her own experience, detailed in her earlier letters, of the wide gap between her turbulent spiritual life and the seemingly static, external religious rule that she professes and teaches as abbess of the Paraclete. In her third letter, Heloise moves away from viewing hers as solely a personal predicament caused by a particular and unjust set of circumstances and toward a highly sympathetic view of all Christians alike, men and women, monks and laymen, called to spiritual love yet weak and troubled, bending frequently under the heavy burden of the Law and more in need of spiritual comfort and direction than of prescriptive rules governing external behavior. Taken together, Heloise's three letters trace the progress of a kind of evangelical awakening, to use M. D. Chenu's term for the twelfth-century apostolic movement that eventually brought widespread spiritual and institutional reform, especially in the area of lay spirituality.[18] In her analysis of the relationship between external religious rules and an unruly inner life, between the most revered, traditional spiritual goals on the one hand and the most profane memories and desires on the other, Heloise moves away from a theology of perfection as defined by Abelard and St. Benedict as well; instead, she challenges Abelard and later spiritual writers to provide a new kind of religious rule for the inner life.[19]

What many would see as the rupture between the sensuous and the serious Heloise, or the unconverted and the converted Heloise, occurs immediately after the opening paragraphs of her third letter. Because this passage is often referred to but rarely quoted, it deserves to be given here in full:

> So that you cannot reprove me as disobedient in any way, I have imposed the curb of your injunction even on the words of my immoderate grief, so that in writing at least I may temper what is not so much difficult as in fact impossible to control in speaking. For nothing is less under our control than the heart; rather than being able to command it, we are forced to obey it. And so when its desires stimulate us, no one can repel their sudden impulses from easily breaking forth into action and more easily flowing into words, which are the ever-ready signs of the heart's passions. Thus it is written: "Out of the overflowing of the heart, the mouth speaks." I will restrain my hand, therefore, from writing words that I cannot hold back my tongue from speaking. Would that the heart that grieves were as ready to obey as the hand that writes!
>
> Yet you have the power to bring some remedy for my grief, even if you cannot entirely remove it. For, as one nail is inserted to drive out another, so a new thought expels the old, when the heart intent on other things is forced to dismiss or interrupt its remembrance of the past. But, in fact, so much the more does any thought occupy the heart or lead it away from other things as *what* is thought is judged the more worthy and *where* we direct our heart seems the more compelling (*necessarium,* emphasis mine).[20]

Although readers all agree that this passage marks a turning point in the correspondence, there is no consensus on what this turning signifies. Those who would see the correspondence as a spiritual conversion narrative locate the signs of it here. Yet these readers rarely provide any textual analysis to support their claim, resting instead on the argument of "silence." Robertson takes this paragraph as proof of Heloise's conversion, but the only evidence he cites is the fact that she never again writes of her passion: "Abelard's [second] letter proved efficacious, for in her reply Heloise says nothing further about her personal difficulties, but asks instead for instruction on the origin of nuns, and for a rule that she and her nuns may follow at the Paraclete. . . . There is no further talk about abandoning the Paraclete, but instead an expressed desire for Abelard, the founder, to establish its rule. . . . Heloise, that is, has now resolutely turned away from worldly joy and worldly sorrow to devote herself wholeheartedly to her profession."[21] Dronke, however, committed, unlike Robertson, to reading literary texts closely, points out that in this passage Heloise's silence on the subject of her grief is imposed from without, by Abelard, and accepted by her reluctantly at best, hardly characteristics to be desired in a conversion exemplum. Furthermore, Heloise explicitly and repeatedly distinguishes here between interior and exterior reality, between the words that issue from the heart and those written by the hand. Since genuine conversion, as Heloise well knows, is an affair of the heart, it would seem that she is pointedly forewarning her reader not to confuse what Robertson calls a "sincere interest in her profession" with proof of interior conversion.[22] Heloise's willed silence concerning her heart's grief does not justify reading into that silence proof of conversion. In fact, as Dronke has pointed out, silence about the details of one's conversion would be unusual, to say the least, in a conversion exemplum, the climax of which is typically some unmistakable sign of God's grace. (The miraculous voice of a child singing "Take up and read" in St. Augustine's conversion story is a good example.) If Heloise's correspondence is to be classed as an exemplary conversion narrative, it is of a kind so different from those preceding it as to require a redefinition of the genre.[23]

If Robertson reads Heloise's silence as evidence of her conversion, many others have read the same silence as evidence that she persisted heroically in her passion for Abelard.[24] Even Gilson, more attentive than most to the subtleties of Heloise's thought, finally interprets her silence to mean that she persisted faithfully in her passion and even "gloried" in it. Following his compelling analysis of the spiritual torment described in Heloise's first two letters, Gilson writes:

> Nothing, not a single line, justifies our thinking that she ever changed [in her grief over her loss of Abelard]. Urged by Abélard to adopt an attitude towards God more in conformity with her state, she prefers to change the topic; for as long as Abélard was there, it would be quite impossible for her not to start in all over again. Thus Héloïse is reduced to silence, but for the same motives that ruled all her other acts—obedience. . . . We never know whether this was a disciplinary silence, once more carrying out the will of Abélard, or whether it was a kind of reconciliation to the will of God. We shall never know, and there are few reasons, humanly speaking, to suspect the latter. The iron will she everywhere displayed would hardly allow her to betray the passion in which she gloried. She could refuse to speak about it. But nothing from her pen has ever denied it.[25]

In this passage Gilson struggles not to draw conclusions impossible to prove from Heloise's silence. Yet the question of Heloise's conversion is most intriguing, and it is difficult, once drawn into it, not to choose sides. Such choices, however, based as they are on "reading" silences, go beyond the limits of literary analysis and become what Gilson labels his "human" choices. Perhaps less critical concern with Heloise's silence would lead us to examine more closely the subjects about which she chose *not* to be silent. Her third letter does not offer evidence of a conversion in any conventional sense. But read closely, it does suggest that the kind of conversion she seeks is not the traditional event, sudden and miraculous, but rather an intellectual, emotional, and spiritual process, slow and painful at times, whose success is always reversible and always in doubt.

Only if we are intent on reading what is not there can we fail to follow the logic of this letter's *exordium,* in which Heloise lends urgency and force to her request by closely linking her personal with her institutional concerns. Her argument seems rather straightforward: I can and will control my written words to you, but thus far, Heloise says, I have found it "difficult," even "impossible," to control my spoken words, which issue directly from my heart's immoderate grief. My situation is not unusual, for the heart is notoriously uncontrollable. But a remedy is still possible and is entirely in your power. A new subject for reflection, one as compelling as my preoccupation with our past, might "dismiss or interrupt" my old thoughts. The subject that Heloise proposes concerns religious history and monastic rules for women, and she asks Abelard to provide her with specific materials for thought: a history of the order of nuns and a new rule for the women of the Paraclete.

Although clear and forceful, Heloise's request is not without ironies that become evident only if we attend closely to the logic of the letter that follows. Heloise's request to Abelard, couched in the tender terms of courtly love, claims that Abelard alone has the power "to bring some remedy" for her grief by redirecting her thoughts. Yet, in the long, closely argued and immensely learned letter that follows, Heloise demonstrates that she is prepared to do the job herself.[26] As she becomes increasingly engaged in her analysis of the monastic duties imposed upon women, she writes with the same passion and intensity of thought that she earlier brought to her analysis of her personal life.[27] Such intensity is not surprising once we see how closely related the two subjects are in fact. Heloise here as elsewhere draws on Abelard's thought for key ideas in her argument.[28] Not only is Abelard's dialectical style evident in the spirit of open inquiry that Heloise brings to her examination of the Benedictine Rule, but also several of his most fundamental moral principles underlie her analysis of the religious life. Yet the fact remains that it is Heloise, not Abelard, who first applies these principles to the subject of monastic life. Abelard's reputation as a monastic reformer rests largely on his two treatises written in response to Heloise's letter, treatises in which Abelard frequently makes use of slightly altered versions of her arguments.[29] Thus, knowing that she is challenging him as much as she is beseeching him, the grieving wife's modest request to her illustrious husband for guidance is not quite as humble and submissive as it might first appear. There is a further and perhaps greater irony in this request, which will become apparent after we have studied in more detail the substance of Heloise's critique of the Rule of St. Benedict as a guide to the spiritual life.[30]

We will return again to the opening of Heloise's third letter, but here only one further observation should be made, and that concerns the serious claims Heloise makes for the subject of this often-neglected letter. Having established her heart's grief as an extremely powerful and, up to now at least, inevitable preoccupation, Heloise works here to persuade Abelard that her new concern is equally compelling. In a sentence awkward to translate because it is so repetitive in its emphasis, Heloise forcefully asserts an equality between her old subject and her proposed new direction: "So much the more fully does any thought occupy the heart and lead it away from other things as what is thought is judged the more worthy, and where we direct our heart seems the more compelling [*necessarium*]." Her new project, she reiterates a few lines later, is "absolutely necessary" [*admodum necessaria*], perhaps as commanding as the subject of her grief had been.[31]

Thus, unlike many readers who would dismiss or slight Heloise's new concerns, she herself does not grant to her preoccupation with the past a higher degree of authenticity or importance than the subject of monastic life. She does say that the process of shifting from personal to institutional analysis is not easy: the image of one nail driving out another, when applied to the human heart, suggests a painful ordeal.[32] But the process can succeed, Heloise argues. Rather than being "cynical" in her request, as she has been described,[33] Heloise in fact moves from near despair to hope in the great turn of this passage, in which she resolutely proposes a possible remedy for her grief, even as she describes the process of diverting her heart as difficult. Although she portrays herself here as the victim of an uncontrollable heart, she neither glorifies her position nor assumes it is irremediable. If, as some critics argue, Heloise is awaiting either Abelard's return or God's call to conversion, she does not propose to wait in hopeless silence. The process Heloise proposes in the elaborate opening of this letter involves a willed act of imagination and intellect, her own more than Abelard's. Her study of the monastic life of women is not a dry, disinterestedly chosen piece of research nor a sign of repression or submission, but a subject chosen because Heloise judges it to be as "necessary" to her life as her passion for Abelard, and, for that reason, perhaps able to affect and even cure her grief.

Heloise was by no means alone in judging the subject of religious rules and the monastic life as a "worthy" subject at this time. For her own reasons and from her own perspective, Heloise in this third letter to Abelard joins the growing contemporary debate among religious groups over the meaning and purpose of the religious life. Beginning early in the twelfth century, with the rise of conservative Cistercian influence on the one hand and the demands of the newly reformed Augustinian canons on the other, questions concerning the authority and the appropriateness of religious rules, especially the influential Rule of St. Benedict, began to reshape monastic intellectual life and ultimately redefined lay spirituality as well.[34] The quarrel between traditional Black Benedictines and the newer White Cistercians centered on their varying interpretations of the Benedictine Rule; each group justified its particular practices as more true to the spirit or the letter of St. Benedict's venerated Rule. The nonmonastic canons, under pressure from both monastic groups to reform by allying themselves with an established religious order, added fuel to the controversy and expanded its scope by rejecting the Benedictine Rule model and inventing an altogether new rule, the so-called Rule of St. Augustine. Ultimately, the controversy over the legitimacy of this or that rule, and over this or that interpretation of the Benedictine Rule, had effects beyond the religious houses themselves, as first preachers and schoolmen and then the new friars at the beginning of the thirteenth century denounced the legalism and presumption of all man-made rules and turned instead to the Gospel as the only truly "legitimate rule" for Christians to follow.[35]

But in spite of such broad, long-range effects, the debate over the authenticity and meaning of the Rule of St. Benedict was often, especially in its early phase, highly polemical and sometimes petty. Benedictine and Cistercian commentaries of the early and mid-twelfth century strongly suggest that this was, in its beginning at least, an insider's quarrel, one in which criticism concerning the length of another order's sleeves could carry real bite.[36] Heloise's contribution to the debate is especially noteworthy because she takes up the position of an informed and interested outsider and thus avoids the provincialism of so many monastic commentaries of the period. And, indeed, she is an outsider in many ways. The peculiar circumstances of her entry to the monastery made her in the beginning, at least, a detached participant in monastic life. In addition, in her education, dialectical style and habit of mind, indeed, in her self-image as a whole, she has far more in common with academics or schoolmen than with monks.[37] It is a connection she seems almost to flaunt at times, as when she frequently pairs biblical quotations and passages from pagan poets in support of an argument.[38] Yet although she shares many interests with schoolmen, she writes on this issue of religious rules long before the schools take up the controversy.[39] Her critique of St. Benedict's Rule is learned, eclectic, somewhat contentious perhaps, but above all reasoned and theoretical. Although she clearly means her analysis of religious rules to have practical effects, so fully informed is her letter by what can only be called scholarly concerns of accuracy, thoroughness, and careful judgment that she easily avoids the more parochial extremes of both Benedictine and Cistercian apologists. Indeed, both Bernard of Clairvaux and Peter, the abbot of Cluny, monks who disagreed sharply in their attitudes toward the Rule of St. Benedict, honored the Paraclete with personal visitations and lavished praise upon the monastery's young abbess.[40] Heloise's strategy in persuading Abelard to provide a new rule is to demonstrate the inadequacy of the Rule of St. Benedict as a suitable guide for religious women, and she brings to her task all of the objectivity and detachment that her dialectical training had evidently taught her. Consistently, she treats the Rule as a historical document, distanced in time and circumstances from her own age. Such a clear sense of history is unusual regarding any text in the Middle Ages, but particularly so regarding the venerated, almost sacred Rule of St. Benedict. Although Heloise demonstrates great respect for Benedict as a wise legislator in his time, her chief concern is with the Rule as a current, practical guide for religious women. By paying close attention to the document itself, its background, form, and above all its particulars, Heloise builds a case against the widespread practice of interpreting Benedict's text as a universal rule, equally suitable to all religious men and women and to all times.

She does so first by showing that the work was the product of its own time. She points out, for example, that Benedict composed his rule against the backdrop of earlier rules and institutes that influenced him to alter certain details, and she even engages in speculation about his possible sources and influences.[41] Furthermore, she deduces from her study of particular phrases that Benedict himself was strongly influenced by contemporary circumstances to make certain concessions "according to the quality [or condition] of men or the times" [*pro qualitate hominum aut temporum*], such as allowing wine and some meat to his monks, when they refused to be persuaded that such luxuries are inappropriate to the monastic life.[42] In describing the Rule as the product of its own particular history, Heloise strips it of the timeless aura that monastic writers so often ascribed to it. In addition, she isolates numerous details in the text that suggest that it was written with a particular audience in mind. St. Benedict's Rule,

Heloise asserts categorically, was clearly written "for men alone" [*viris solummodo*], and she amasses details scrupulously collected from the text itself that amply demonstrate her conclusion.

For Heloise then, one cannot profess this or any other rule without first having studied the document itself, as she has, in a fairly rigorous way:

> If indeed many of those who these days profess monastic vows rashly would attend more carefully and consider beforehand what it is that they promise in their vows, and examine diligently the actual tenor of the Rule, they would offend less through ignorance and sin less through negligence. But now nearly all alike rush without discretion to the monastic life, are received in disorder, and live in more disorder. Disdaining the Rule they are ignorant of with the same ease with which they profess it, they set up whatever customs they prefer as though they were law.[43]

Her complaint is primarily that of a scholar, not a partisan, and should not be confused with either the typical Cistercian or Benedictine position, although it has points in common with both. In its emphasis on strict discipline, and in associating such discipline with strict observance of the details of the Rule of St. Benedict, Heloise seems to echo the Cistercian argument that monastic reform requires a return to the "purity" of the Rule, observed in every detail "to the last dot."[44] Heloise's sensitivity to the particularity of Benedict's Rule, however, rather than leading her to embrace it as a tool for monastic reform, instead leads her to question its appropriateness to her own circumstances as a nun, which for her take precedence. Often she associates particulars of the Rule with specific conditions not relevant to current circumstances, a historical argument usually ignored by Cistercian apologists. In fact, the very specificity of the Rule, which the Cistercians stressed as the key to its authenticity, becomes her strongest argument for rejecting Benedict's text as unsuitable to be a common rule for all religious. Furthermore, the particulars Heloise most often emphasizes concern Benedict's numerous references to the need for flexibility and adaptation of monastic practice according to individuals and to circumstances. This emphasis on flexibility associates Heloise more closely with Cluniac arguments used to defend their sometimes extremely loose interpretation of the Rule. Peter the Venerable and other traditional Benedictines argued that Benedict intended his rule as a spiritual ideal rather than as a literal, universal guide.[45]

But Heloise seems as unwilling to accept wholeheartedly the Cluniac position as she was to align herself exclusively with the Benedictine view. When she castigates those who disregard what she calls "the actual tenor of the Rule," she seems to be speaking specifically of those who fail to attend to the original text of the Rule, which Cluniacs especially were often accused of ignoring in favor of "whatever customs they prefer," as Heloise puts it. Such disdain for the particulars of the Rule, Heloise asserts in the strongly worded passage just quoted, proceeds from ignorance and a lack of diligence in studying the Rule as written, and such carelessness, she argues, leads to a growing "disorder" in place of the *ordo* of the monastic life.

Once again Heloise is not taking sides in a bitter, political dispute; rather, it is her critical sense of what it means to "know" the Rule that is offended by loose readings of Benedict's highly particular text. For Heloise, to know the Rule is to study it closely, from both a historical and a practical perspective, before taking any religious vows. Women in particular, she argues, cannot be instructed adequately by a mere three readings of the text, as Benedict prescribes.[46] Her own thorough study of the Benedictine Rule, although completed over thirteen years after her unexpected entrance into religious life, leads her to conclude that, whether strictly or loosely interpreted, it is at best inappropriate to the nuns of the Paraclete. Never intended as a common rule, Heloise argues, it should not be used indiscriminately by every variety of religious group.

Viewed in light of the controversy over the meaning and authority of the Rule of St. Benedict, Heloise's intentions in this letter seem clear. The religious rule that she was forced by circumstances to adopt is inappropriate as a suitable, contemporary guide for women, she argues. Other religious groups have created new and more appropriate rules, she notes, referring specifically to the Augustinian canons, and so Abelard should, as founder of the Paraclete, provide a new rule for his charges. Some specific changes are necessary, and Heloise outlines them in some detail.

The most particular changes grow out of the need Heloise sees to adapt the monastic life to the special circumstances of women, whom she frequently calls "the weaker sex."[47] In arguing this need, Heloise is, in fact, transforming into a more general version a personal complaint that she has made previously to Abelard. Her complaint against the Rule of St. Benedict, as currently practiced, is similar to her complaint against Abelard in her previous letters: both overlook differences between individuals. Throughout her first two letters, Heloise laments the differences between Abelard's circumstances and her own: he is converted, she is not; he is strong, she is weak; he is thoroughly holy, she is a hypocrite; he is castrated, and therefore without desire, while she is tormented by desire. Abelard rarely acknowledges these differences, instead repeatedly emphasizing "*our* conversion from the world to God" (my emphasis), with the hope of persuading Heloise to adopt his rhetoric.[48] In her third letter, after agreeing to set aside the subject of her personal complaint to Abelard, Heloise turns to a generalized and institutional version of the differences between his circumstances and hers. Her analysis of the Rule of St. Benedict is built on the most fundamental and general example possible of the differences between men and women that make some particulars of the Benedictine Rule clearly inappropriate as a common rule. In a strategy designed to shock Abelard into recognizing their differences, Heloise begins her new, institutional complaint with a boldly contentious example. How can we women be expected, she asks, to follow a religious rule that requires long underwear [*femoralia*] and close-fitting wool clothes when the "monthly purging of [our] superfluous humors" [*humoris superflui menstruae purgationes*] makes such an injunction impossible to keep? Adding example after example, ranging from the physical weakness of women that makes the required harvest work inappropriate, to the reputed humidity of the woman's body, which makes her less susceptible to the intoxicating effects of wine, Heloise argues with a flood of observed details that Benedict did not have women in mind when he composed his Rule.[49]

This extraordinary sensitivity to the particularity of life is a hallmark of Heloise's thought and provides another strong link between her personal and institutional concerns. In his previous letter Abelard had asked his wife, whom he addresses as "the bride of Christ," to replace her worldly attachment to him with an analogical, spiritual love of Christ, providing her with meditations on the black bride of the Song of Songs, the passion of Christ, and a moving prayer on the marriage bond. Yet when Heloise responds, agreeing not to write again of her personal grief, the subject she chooses as a "worthy" replacement is not the elaborate spiritual analogy outlined by

Abelard (love Christ as you would a husband) but the basic, everyday details of monastic life, with which this letter, especially its first half, is saturated: tunics and underwear, work and sleep, meat and wine, guests and pilgrims, apple juice and date palms. And not one of these subjects is treated in the least bit metaphorically by Heloise. Her substitution of actual for Abelard's metaphorical details is telling. Religious rules, as a genre, are almost obsessive in their concern for minute details, and perhaps it is this obsession with the particular that Heloise finds so "necessary" in her new theme.

Seen in this way, her concern for the particular in religious rules seems closely related to her attitude toward her memories as described in her previous letters. Indeed, what Heloise stresses about her memories and their effects on her is their particularity: "Not only what we did, but also the times and places in which we did it, are so fixed along with your image in my heart that in those recalled details I reenact all with you."[50] Similarly, early in her first letter, after summarizing in some detail Abelard's autobiographical letter, she complains that the sorrows renewed by his account were the greater the more carefully "each single event" [*singula*] was described.[51] In Abelard's case, the singular events of his life are convertible, or at least they have been converted by him, into spiritual analogies or signs of God's providential power. That his life can be read as a providential narrative is the argument of his autobiographical letter that precipitates the correspondence between Abelard and Heloise some years after the events themselves have occurred. But, for Heloise, the same detailed memories remain wholly intact, "singular," unmanipulable, and thus they retain all of their original associations with pleasure, guilt, and desire. At the risk of oversimplifying, I would suggest that while Abelard's is fundamentally a philosophical or logical temperament, Heloise's habit of mind is primarily influenced by imagination and memory.

Perhaps it is this distinction in their attitudes toward the past that Heloise alludes to in the famous but enigmatic superscription to her third letter: "Domino [or suo] specialiter, sua singulariter," usually translated as To Abelard, her lord (or hers) in a special sense, from Heloise, who is singularly his.[52] There is considerable play in this as in all of Heloise's superscriptions, which she seems to treat as a rhetorical skills contest with her former teacher and husband.[53] Of particular interest here is Heloise's allusion to her differences with Abelard in terms of his own philosophical language.

First of all, as Dronke has observed, in using the term *specialiter* Heloise is echoing a phrase from the close of Abelard's previous letter, in which he asks Heloise to remember him "who is specially yours" [*qui specialiter est tuus*]. While Abelard had used the word in its most general sense, Heloise responds by playing on the subtle philosophical distinctions between what is special and what is singular. Abelard, both in his dealings with Heloise after their marriage and in his work as a logician, is especially interested in *species* or classes of things. In his letters to Heloise, he also works to confine references to his wife to terms of species or classes. For example, he conspicuously avoids forms of personal address, addressing Heloise instead as a spiritual sister or as a bride of Christ. In distinguishing between Abelard's "special" relation to his spiritual bride and her "singular" relation to him, Heloise wittily reminds Abelard of an important difference in their relationships toward the particulars of their past.[54]

Heloise's complaint to Abelard, especially as described in her second letter, is that the details of her past remain *singular* and thus less easy for her than for him to coerce into some logical pattern.[55] Indeed, it is the particulars of her past that coerce Heloise, rather than the abstract pattern that Abelard would impose on those images, times and places that remain "fixed" in her heart. The image of Heloise driven by the singular events of her past, so often alluded to in her first two letters, is recalled not only in her salutation but also in her request for a new thought to serve as a nail: "As one nail is inserted to drive out another," she says, emphasizing how much force will be required to ensure that a new but equally "necessary" thought will drive out the old. The necessaries in Heloise's life, it seems, are the particulars, and she insists that they be accounted for and dealt with, whether they be the current details of her monastic life, the prescribed details of the monastic rule, or the highly charged details of her personal past.

If Heloise had ended her third letter to Abelard with her argument for the necessity of specific changes that he should include in his new monastic rule, she would have performed the important service for the nuns of the Paraclete of realigning their rule and their religious life and also reserved for herself a place in the religious reform movement of the twelfth century. In addition, even had she stopped here, a strong link between her previous letters and this one would be clear: Heloise is as committed to her new subject as to her old because both concern what we might call the power of the particular. Yet despite her knowledge of and interest in the details of monastic life, Heloise is not so naive as to assume that particular rules concerning food and clothing have the same emotional force as the particulars of one's memories and desires. When she begins to examine the end or goal of regulating the details of daily life in monasteries, namely, the spiritual ideal that religious rules are meant to serve, she then begins to question the very particularity that normally defines the genre of religious rules. Just as Heloise's request to Abelard in the beginning of her letter was not as straightforward as it seemed at first (since her object in this letter is less to request guidance than to offer it), so too the guidance that she offers Abelard proves contradictory. Less than halfway through her letter, Heloise slowly begins to turn her argument dialectically against itself: what begins innocently enough as a request for specific and relatively minor changes in an existing monastic rule becomes, as Gilson observed long ago, a broad, speculative argument questioning the whole enterprise of attempting to regulate the interior, spiritual life by means of external, bodily rules.[56]

The first signal of a change in emphasis comes quite early in the letter. While pursuing the argument that "weak women" should not be subjected to a common rule with monks, Heloise begins to equate religious rules with the Old Law of retribution, not only the Rule of St. Benedict but all rules that go beyond the precepts of the Gospel in regulating spiritual life. Glossing a passage from a sermon by John Chrysostom that asserts that laymen must conduct themselves like monks in all matters except for continence, Heloise writes:

> From these words we can easily gather that whoever adds the virtue of continence to the precepts of the Gospel will achieve monastic perfection.
>
> And would that our religious life could reach as high as to fulfill the Gospel, rather than go beyond it, and would that we not seek to be more than Christians. Indeed, if I am not mistaken, this is why the holy Fathers decided not to fix for us as for men any general rule, as though it were a new law, nor to burden our infirmity with a great many vows. . . .[57]

Heloise's remarks are curious in a number of ways. What John Chrysostom gives as a complaint against laymen who assume too much freedom from strict religious observance, Heloise sees in a very different light, as extending the definition of monastic perfection beyond the walls of the monastery to include all those who combine celibacy with a virtuous life lived according to the precepts of the Gospel, which are available and equally applicable to all Christians. Heloise's complaint is directed not at laymen but at monks who, by adding numerous and burdensome man-made rules to the precepts of the Gospel, become presumptuous and perhaps hypocritical in attempting to be "more than Christians." The conclusion Heloise draws here, that perhaps the early Church Fathers did not provide a rule for women because they saw the danger of presuming to improve on the Gospel, seems incongruous with the rest of the passage. Although it does serve to bring Heloise back to her ostensible argument concerning the "infirmity" of women, the conclusion seems illogical in being restricted to rules for women. Obviously the dangers in trying to outdo the Gospel inhere equally in rules for men and for women, and writers of the later twelfth and early thirteenth centuries will not hesitate to say so.[58] But Heloise here is making an argument against elaborate rules and observances well before the evangelical movement really has taken hold, and her hesitancy to draw the most radical conclusion is therefore understandable.

Nevertheless, this tendency to equate man-made rules with a "new law," with all of the associations of legalism and presumption that that term carried with it, grows stronger as Heloise's letter continues, and by the end the distinction between the particular needs of men and women drops out altogether. Pitting what she calls "the freedom of the Gospel," a popular tag of the coming evangelical movement, against the burdening constraints of the Law, Heloise mounts an argument that love, not the law, is the object of the spiritual life; thus rules regulating outward behavior are inadequate and perhaps irrelevant to the ideal of personal, spiritual perfection. They may even be counterproductive, Heloise suggests, in that they tend to confuse "spirit" with "matter," inner virtue with the mere "show of virtue."[59]

Examples abound of Heloise's tendency to shift her argument from the special needs of women to the spiritual needs of all religious men and women. She refers several times to the new Augustinian canons whose simple rule and unencumbered way of life, although far from following strict, monastic observances, have won them favor and respectability. There is more than a hint of rebellion in her tone when she reminds Abelard that the canons are men "who consider themselves not at all inferior to monks, although we see them wearing linen and eating meat."[60] Again, she does not distinguish between men and women when she castigates those religious who hastily profess the detailed Rule of St. Benedict, then ignore its precepts. However, immediately following her reproval Heloise writes:

> We must take precautions not to presume for women a burden under which we see nearly all men fall or else they abandon it. We observe that the world has grown old, and man himself along with everything else of the earth has lost his natural vigor. And so too, in the words of Truth, the love not just of many but of nearly all men has grown cold, so that clearly it is necessary to temper or change according to man's condition in the present those rules which were written for men.[61]

Here Heloise seems to return to the premise of feminine weakness only to abandon it within a few lines, moving quickly from the weakness of women to the weakness of all men and all living things of the world. Clearly, it is "man's condition" that has become Heloise's subject; the need for spiritual redirection is universal in an aging world where nearly all Christians fall beneath their burdens.

In the final third of Heloise's letter, she grows more bold and drops all pretense of arguing from the sole premise of women's weakness. Instead, she appropriates terms developed in Abelard's theology for her argument regarding monastic life.[62] Using rules regarding the eating of meat as an example of the misdirected effort to control unimportant details, Heloise pleads in Abelardian terms for less emphasis in religious rules on "those areas lying between good and evil, which are called indifferent."[63] Echoing Abelard's views so closely that her editor concludes either that Heloise is quoting Abelard directly or that Abelard's later works draw from her letter, she repeatedly distinguishes between intentions, which determine sinfulness, and outward actions, which are always morally neutral.[64] In language reminiscent of a basic premise of Abelard's *Scito te ipsum,* Heloise points out that what distinguishes Jew from Christian, and Old Law from New Dispensation, is that "true Christians are totally occupied with the inner man" rather than with outward works.[65] Relying frequently on passages from Paul to the Romans, also a key text in Abelard's moral theology, Heloise argues that "love alone distinguishes between the children of God and those of the devil."[66] And the love that God requires is not necessarily achieved by adhering to man-made and therefore arbitrary religious rules but by accepting the grace and "freedom of the Gospel" [*evangelicae libert(as)*].[67]

Heloise boldly assigns to the category of morally indifferent acts a host of subjects ordinarily regulated by traditional religious rules. She not only rejects the rules governing the eating of meat but implies that all fasting regulations that go beyond what the church generally requires of Christians may be inappropriate, since Christians should seek "to abstain more from vice than from food."[68] On the subject of physical labor, Heloise is even more strident, perhaps in response to increasing complaints during this period, especially from male Cistercian houses, about "idle" nuns who expected nearby monks to attend to their material needs. Heloise attacks this argument directly and on several fronts. Noting that she in no way intends to shirk labor "when necessity demands it," she nevertheless flatly denies that work in itself has any spiritual value, a denial that seems to fly in the face of the Cistercian emphasis on the value of physical labor. Using battle imagery, not inappropriate given the hostility that often obtained between male and female Cistercian houses, Heloise derides those who "bitterly complain less about what tyrants take from them by force" [*rapiunt*] than about their obligation, sanctioned by apostolic concession and even by Christ himself, to provide for the material needs of holy women who are wholly occupied with spiritual things.[69]

Heloise's argument concerning the primacy of the interior life over rules governing external behavior captures remarkably well the essence of the coming evangelical movement, which will rebel against overly elaborate and elitist religious rules in favor of an ideal of personal perfection as defined by the simple precepts of the Gospel. Nevertheless, her argument also seriously undermines the modest request, with which her letter began, for certain specific changes in the existing rule model. It certainly puts Abelard in a difficult position. On the one hand, Heloise has requested of him a new religious rule, and she has framed her request in terms of the most urgent obligation: if Abelard wants her to set aside her immoderate grief and preoccupation with their past, he has it in his power, she says, to offer a worthy replacement for her loss, in the form of a suitable and workable religious rule. On the other hand, she seems to reject, as either irrelevant or at least inadequate, much of the stuff of which religious rules are made, specific precepts regulating the external lives of monks and nuns, their food, drink, clothes, and work. Furthermore, her rejection takes a peculiarly Abelardian form, showing how Abelard's own moral theology casts considerable doubt on what she sees as a basic premise of the Rule of St. Benedict: that the inner life can to some extent be controlled and perhaps even judged by outward behavior. Thus Heloise's letter seems to fall into rather disjointed halves: one questions whether certain particulars of the Benedictine Rule are appropriate for women, while the other questions whether most rules regarding external particulars can affect the inner lives of Christians.

The object of Heloise's request, then, seems not to be a traditional religious rule at all but some new form of rule that will help more directly to guide the inner life. But how? For Heloise, the goals of the spiritual life are absolute and strictly interior. The passages discussed earlier, as well as numerous others concerning the worthlessness of works without faith or love make that much clear. Yet religious rules, as Heloise knows them, have more to do with works than with love. Although she never doubts that certain works are essential to religious life—namely, celibacy and poverty—she in fact has very little to say about them. The only facet of traditional religious rules in which Heloise shows much interest is prayer. Close to the very end of her third letter, she begins to emphasize what she has only mentioned in passing until now: that her rejection of bodily regulations is meant to foster increased attention to the *Opus Dei,* or divine office. In the area of prayer, Heloise actually requests more detailed prescriptions, asking Abelard to concern himself especially with directions regarding the order and distribution of psalms and who should read the night offices.[70] Heloise's continuing interest in prayer is attested indirectly by the many prayers, hymns, and sermons that Abelard composed and delivered to the Paraclete at what he says was her "urgent request."[71] Thus the religious life that Heloise imagines can be defined, outwardly at least, quite simply. "It should be enough for our infirmity," she reasons, if religious women live "continently and without possessions, wholly occupied with the divine office."[72]

It may seem surprising that in spite of Heloise's request for rules regarding prayer and her ample arguments against rules regarding exterior things, we hear very little in this letter about what she implies is the only goal of the religious life, that is, a loving spiritual relationship with God. The absence of this topic is especially noticeable in light of Abelard's previous letter, in which he invites Heloise to join in a rich, spiritual relationship with Christ, urging her, for example, to participate imaginatively as one of the women who witnessed the passion and death of Christ. His meditation on the Passion, in its vivid detail and in its emotionalism, is reminiscent of the justly famous meditations of Aelred of Rievaulx (d. 1167), included as part of his religious rule for recluses, *De institutione inclusarum*. A close contemporary of Heloise, Aelred seems to have shared some of her concerns regarding religious rules, for he divides his rule for women into an "outer" followed by an "inner" one. For Aelred, however, the relationship between the two rules is not problematic: the richly sensuous meditations on the life of Christ, which compose his inner rule, serve as a kind of reward for the recluse who has achieved success in living the ascetic life defined in the outer rule. Aelred's emphasis on detailed, external rules follows directly from his faith in the Cistercian ideal of exact observance of the Rule of St. Benedict.[73]

But in Heloise's case, as we have seen, the ascetic life as defined in the Benedictine Rule has not led to the withdrawal from the world that both Aelred and Abelard have assumed. Unconvinced of any automatic relationship between the interior life and the observance of a religious rule, Heloise consistently avoids the meditative mode in her works. Even in her last extant communication with Abelard, the so-called *Problemata,* Heloise is still taken up with particular, probing, and scholarly questions about scripture. In the letter that we have been examining, instead of ending with a description of, or even a yearning for, the rich spiritual love that Abelard had depicted, Heloise provides as if in its place the image of a severe, probing God who demands our love but who seems to judge its quality by searching out our "hidden thoughts" or "secret places," where "evil thoughts" of "adultery or murder" may be lurking in our hearts. He is a God who demands pure, disinterested love but who also "tests the hearts and loins."[74] In an earlier letter, where Heloise refers to the same phrase from Psalm 8, it is no wonder that she speaks not of God's love but of his judgment.[75] The rule that Heloise imagines, then, is far from Aelred's inner rule or the inner rule of love later composed by the author of the *Ancrene Wisse,* who borrows the term "inner rule" from Aelred.[76] Heloise focuses on the interior life more as a theoretical than as an applied principle. In comparison with Abelard's or Aelred's meditations, or the emphasis on love in the *Ancrene Wisse,* Heloise's argument for a new rule seems rather technical.

Other readers, most effectively Gilson, have noted the "absence" of God in Heloise's first two letters, where the subject matter of her continuing desire and torment makes obvious the gap she experiences between herself and God. But in her third letter also, in spite of its religious subject, God is at least far distant, if not altogether absent, not because Heloise has defiantly excluded him but because she has yet to find him. Her third letter provides proof that she is still searching, intellectually as well as emotionally, and is best understood as a more institutionally centered version of what she has asked of Abelard all along: consolation and guidance for an unruly heart, her own as well as the hearts of others who might fear God's judgment even as they seek his love. While some might believe that professing and following an established religious rule ensures salvation, throughout her letters Heloise proves herself as not the sort to take consolation so easily, nor is her faith in the institution of monasticism so secure. Abelard has reasoned that Heloise ought to take what consolation the religious life has to offer, redirecting her heart and her desire to Christ. Nowhere in her letters does Heloise refuse; instead, she asks, in effect, *how?* She prefaces her request for a religious rule with a thought reminiscent of a passage in Gregory's *Regula pastoralis:* "Nothing is less under our control than the heart," to which Heloise adds emphatically, "rather than being able to command it, we are forced to obey it."[77]

This aphorism provides a key to understanding not only Heloise's third letter but all of her letters to Abelard. The immediate context bears repeating: Abelard has asked Heloise to stop dwelling on her loss and turn her attention instead to her current spiritual life. Heloise, in fact, *has* focused in her first two letters on her current spiritual life, complex and imperfect, and unidealized though it might be, but Abelard has rejected her version of herself because it is unconverted, still "turning" toward the past. In her third letter, Heloise agrees willingly to change the direction of her letters to Abelard, but she also emphasizes that she cannot so easily change her heart's turning, because her heart is not yet subject to her will. The clear implication in her request for a new religious rule is that neither Abelard nor St. Benedict's Rule has as yet taught her and her charges a way to control their hearts.

This statement is not meant to make Heloise sound perverse, and certainly not "cynical," any more than Augustine is perverse or cynical in wondering in Book 8 of his *Confessions* why he can will his hand but not his heart to obey his commands.

Heloise's supposed blasphemy and defiance in her two most famous letters are misreadings stemming from unfamiliarity with her contentious, dialectical style and, perhaps, with her third letter. At heart, Heloise is certainly not a libertine, nor is she primarily the Roman heroine that Gilson (and even Heloise herself) portrays her at times to be.[78] Instead, she remains throughout her letters a thoroughly Christian thinker, steeped in the most sophisticated and nuanced theology of her day, a moral rigorist like her husband and former teacher, Peter Abelard, one of the twelfth-century's least compromising moral theologians.[79] At times she seems to outdo the master in her spiritual demands. Indeed, it is primarily *because* she is so uncompromising in her spiritual goals that she seems so sinful and sensuous in her two early letters and that she boldly demands a new religious rule in her third letter to Abelard. While Abelard depicts her as winning the heavenly "crown" by continually overcoming her desire, Heloise sees herself in her first two letters as having lost the battle because, in spite of her efforts, her desire continues, or at least her memory of the pleasures of satisfying carnal desire. Unlike Abelard, who distinguishes between desire and consent, the constitutive element of sin, Heloise seems to equate the two and thus to damn herself as unworthy of God's forgiveness.[80] While Abelard repeatedly pictures Heloise as the model bride of Christ because she appears to be a successful abbess, Heloise presents herself as ungrateful and offensive to God, using ideas that feature prominently in Abelard's redemptive theory, where he argues that Christ's death was purely an act of love, calling for an equally pure and disinterested love on man's part.[81] Heloise, having searched her heart, judges that while she has loved Abelard disinterestedly, she has yet to respond to God with the wholly disinterested act of love that she believes He requires.[82]

Thus the argument that Heloise uses in her third letter as the basis of her plea for a new religious rule, namely, that outer works can add nothing to faith, is not finally a comforting or liberating thought for her. A simpler religious rule, rather than being merely a concession to female weakness, as Heloise sometimes characterizes it, may in fact make more acute the problem of her own salvation, because it demands that its followers focus squarely on the interior life that has caused her so much torment. Although she seeks a less burdensome exterior rule, she remains uncompromising in her belief that her salvation depends on fulfillment of the most basic and irreducible requirements of the spiritual life. In her second letter, she defines what she sees as the only legitimate spiritual goal in its most absolute form: "to do good and to turn from evil," as the psalm says, and to do both, Heloise adds, for the love of God alone.[83] While Abelard writes consistently of their mutual conversion "from the world," Heloise will not consider herself converted until she can "turn from evil" absolutely by means of "true contrition" [*vera poenitentia*] for her sins, the same condition that Abelard argues in his *Ethics* is essential to forgiveness.[84] But pure contrition, as it will come to be called later in the century, the sorrow that springs solely from love of God rather than fear of punishment, is very rare, Heloise realizes, agreeing with Ambrose that it is easier to find an innocent man than a truly repentant one.[85] Indeed, Heloise reminds Abelard in her second letter, absolute contrition and conversion came to Abelard through the "grace" of his castration, which literally and spiritually cut him off from his past and what he calls the sole source of his desire.[86] In fact, for Abelard, castration is an accurate emblem for true conversion, and in a remarkable passage he associates both castration and conversion with cleansing, freedom from desire, and a return to innocence.[87]

This sudden, complete conversion, although rarely achieved so violently, was a popular motif in eleventh- and twelfth-century literature. And it is precisely what Heloise has not yet experienced. Neither her earlier life in the world nor her penitential life in the monastery has taught her a way of cutting herself off, so to speak, from her past and her desires. Yet that is what both she and Abelard believe God requires of those who love him and what St. Benedict's Rule hopes to encourage by means of strictly regulating the exterior life. Lacking pure contrition and pure love, Heloise can find no place for herself in the spiritual landscape created for her. Abelard in his letters and Benedict in his Rule describe that landscape in terms of heroic armies, combat, victories and losses, strength and power, weapons and crowns.[88] In fact, Heloise finally rejects this traditional heroic description of her spiritual life. At the very end of her second letter, Heloise writes: "I do not wish you to exhort me to virtue and call me forth to the battle, saying 'Virtue is made perfect in weakness' and 'He will not be crowned who has not struggled rightfully.' I do not seek the crown of victory. It is enough for me to avoid danger. Avoiding danger is safer than engaging in battle. In whatever corner of heaven God places me, it will be enough for me. None will be envious of another there, where whatever each has will be sufficient."[89] Heloise caps this essentially nonheroic view of spirituality with a quotation from Jerome, an ironic choice considering that Jerome is Abelard's favorite model of spiritual heroism: "I confess my weakness; I do not wish to fight in the hope of victory lest I lose the victory at some time. What need is there to let go of what is certain and strive after what is uncertain?"[90] Here Heloise, who herself has often described her struggle in hyperbolic terms, finally rejects Abelard's larger-than-life portrayal of her spiritual state, probably for the same reason that she had rejected Abelard's abstract, providential view of their conversion, because it does not adequately account for the complex, unidealized particulars of her life, which for Heloise still have extraordinary power. Measured by Abelard's absolute standards of pure love, true contrition, final conversion, and victories over desires, Heloise judges herself to have lost her spiritual battle for perfection. But this does not mean that she capitulates to Abelard's arguments; still less does she glorify her failure. On the contrary, here and especially in her third letter, Heloise begins, at first tentatively and then more surely, to break free from the very notion of absolute victory as a suitable spiritual ideal and to begin to seek "any corner whatever of heaven" reserved for herself and those like her who have quit the battle for perfection but who struggle on in weakness without any definitive victories or signs of spiritual progress.

Heloise's third letter to Abelard marks a turning point not because it demonstrates her conversion or even predicts it but because in this discursive exploration of the meaning of the religious life she begins to move away from those definitions of spirituality that depend on an absolute break with the world and the past. The theory of Heloise's conversion, so often evoked to "explain" her third letter, seems extraneous once we examine more closely the supposed gap between her personal confessions of weakness and her request for a new religious rule. It is not that God is absent in the early letters but present in the later ones. As we have seen, Heloise's critique does not depend on her experience of a rich interior spiritual life. On the contrary, she avoids the popular meditative mode of Abelard and Aelred as surely in her third letter as in her previous ones.

Nor can Heloise be described as sensuous in one half of the correspondence and serious in the other. She is highly serious, even scholarly, throughout, whether analyzing her own spiritual inadequacies or those of the Benedictine Rule. In her personal letters she concerns herself primarily with her failure to achieve Abelard's model of spiritual perfection, embodied in his heroic terminology, his logical but highly abstract treatment of their past, especially their conversions, and his theology of pure contrition and disinterested love. In her third letter, she directs her attention toward a different but related model of perfection embodied in the Benedictine Rule, which in her reading becomes another example of a kind of misplaced heroism, depending as it does on highly regulated asceticism to achieve spiritual perfection. Arguing first of all that such an athletic approach to spirituality is inappropriate for religious women (and it may help to recall that *ascesis* comes from the Greek verb meaning 'to exercise'), she moves toward a reformulation of the same critique she had used in her so-called personal letters, except that now the issue is not how Abelard has treated her spiritual dilemma but how the Benedictine Rule treats the spiritual life in general. Heloise argues that the Benedictine Rule as practiced, like Abelard in his dealings with her, ignores crucial differences between weak and strong, overvalues morally neutral external works, and, most important, fails adequately to guide the often unruly inner life, even though for Christians the interior life is all that matters. In Heloise's view, the result of both Abelard's and St. Benedict's spiritual models is the same, a kind of inauthenticity that she experiences as a wide gap between her interior experience and her external circumstances.

In her third letter Heloise's search for her own authenticity takes the form of a forcefully presented request that Abelard define the rules for attaining that "corner of heaven" that she has described as her goal. The rule that she requests, although simpler than most religious rules, is not necessarily easier, for Heloise knows full well that the new rule cannot serve as a substitute for the rich spiritual life that Abelard has falsely presumed she already enjoys. In fact, that the one cannot possibly be confused with the other is, for Heloise, a strong point in the new rule's favor, because it lessens the danger she sees in all religious rules, namely, that they tend to substitute works for faith. What the new rule emphasizing the simple apostolic life of celibacy and prayer can do, Heloise suggests, in addition to providing some practical guidance on the subject of prayer, is to help the nuns of the Paraclete, including herself, to focus more directly on the Gospel's irreducible demands that true Christians seek to do good and avoid evil for the love of God, requirements that entail an ongoing interior struggle with one's motives, memories, and desires. Most of what is needed in the new rule can be summarized, Heloise asserts, in a line from Persius: "Do not look outside of yourself."[91] Most other rules are superfluous. Heloise asks for guidance concerning prayer, because she sees prayer as providing her only hope not of perfection but of salvation. Fearful of God's judgment and sure that he judges only the "hidden places" of the heart, whose secrets she has already revealed, Heloise hopes yet for grace, realizing that God accepts not only prayers of praise but also those asking for help. Only rarely does she refer directly to this modest hope, but in the climax of her third letter she begs Abelard to substitute interior for exterior rules, reminding him that God Himself says that he prefers cries for help to outward sacrifices, saying "Call on me in time of trouble and I will rescue you, and you shall honor me."[92]

Heloise's call to Abelard for help is a sign neither of defeat nor conversion. It is instead a reasoned, learned critique of contemporary monastic life in light of her own history as well as her theology. Few writers in the twelfth century were prepared, either by experience or by education, to offer such a balanced theoretical and practical appraisal of the monastic life.

Notes

1. Étienne Gilson, *Héloïse and Abélard,* 1938, 2nd rev. ed., 1948; trans. L. K. Shook 1960, pp. 124–44, takes issue with Jacob Burkhardt's famous claims for the Italian Renaissance, arguing that Heloise's "story of flesh and blood, carried along by a passion at once brutal and ardent" is a far better example of individuality "developed to its highest point" than Burkhardt's examples. Peggy Kamuf, *Fictions of Feminine Desire* studies the eighteenth-century French novel in terms of the "residue of a woman's excessive desire" that she discovers first in the letters of Heloise.
2. Henry Adams, *Mont-Saint-Michel and Chartres,* pp. 283–84.
3. Barbara Newman, "Authority, Authenticity, and the Repression of Heloise," in *From Virile Woman to WomanChrist: Studies in Medieval Religion and Literature,* p. 74.
4. *Women Writers,* p. 108; Neil Cartlidge, *Medieval Marriage: Literary Approaches, 1100–1300,* pp. 158–59.
5. John Benton, "Fraud, Fiction and Borrowing in the Correspondence of Abelard and Heloise," in Colloque, pp. 469–506; see also the extensive debate following this controversial address, Colloque, pp. 507–11, and "A Reconsideration of the Authenticity of the Correspondence of Abelard and Heloise" in Trier 1980; D. W. Robertson, *Abelard and Heloise.* The most recent, and most persuasive, account of the authenticity debate is by John Marenbon, *The Philosophy of Peter Abelard,* pp. 82–93. See also chapter 2 herein.
6. Admittedly, all descriptions of Heloise's education are, at this point, speculative, but see M. T. Clanchy's plausible accounts in *Peter Abelard: A Medieval Life,* pp. 12–14, 169–72, 277–82. Clanchy and others (see *A Medieval Life,* pp. 173–74, 369 n. 4) recently have questioned the widespread assumption that Heloise was an impressionable teenager of sixteen or seventeen when she met Abelard; no contemporary evidence supports this idea, and, in addition, Heloise's prior education and reputation for learning would suggest that she was much closer to Abelard in age and in education when they met, although their training, hers in literature, his in logic, differed. On Heloise's classical and biblical reading and the uses to which she put it, see Newman, "Authenticity, Authority, and the Repression of Heloise," pp. 69–75. Heloise's analysis of the marital bond is read in light of contemporary debates over marriage law and custom by Christopher Brooke, in *The Medieval Idea of Marriage,* pp. 103–18, and by Cartlidge in *Medieval Marriage,* pp. 58–75. For Heloise's contribution to contemporary developments in ethics, particularly in Abelard's ethical writings, see Marenbon, *The Philosophy of Peter Abelard,* pp. 72–79, 298–303, 310–14; Clanchy, *A Medieval Life,* pp. 169–72, 251–60, and 277–82, and Constant J. Mews, chapter 3 in this volume. Recent investigations of Heloise's impact on the development of Abelard's thought cast doubt on the widespread but unexamined assumption, of which I am sometimes guilty in the chapter that follows, that Heloise was necessarily the borrower, and Abelard the inventor, of theological and philosophical ideas. Of particular interest, in light of my argument below, is Marenbon's claim (*The Philosophy of Peter Abelard,* pp. 310–14), that Abelard moderates his earlier "perfectionist views of human society" in response to Heloise's nonheroic view of the moral life.
7. Linda Georgianna, "In Any Corner of Heaven: Heloise's Critique of Monasticism" first appeared in *Mediaeval Studies* 49 (1987): 221–53 and is reprinted here in revised form with permission of the editors.

   On the consistency of Abelard's concerns in his responses to Heloise, see Mary Martin McLaughlin, "Peter Abelard and the Dignity of Women: Twelfth Century 'Feminism' in Theory and Practice," pp. 287–333. Recent major studies by John Marenbon (*The Philosophy of Peter Abelard*) and M. T. Clanchy (*A Medieval Life*) have broken new ground in our understanding of the development of Abelard's ideas.
8. Robertson, *Abelard and Heloise,* pp. 54, 120–24, argues that medieval readers would have responded only to the holy and wise Heloise (whom he identifies as the "historical

Heloise") and that the notion of a passionate Heloise is an anachronism, a theory that Dronke forcefully counters in *Abelard and Heloise in Medieval Testimonies.* Muckle, Heloise's editor, is suspicious of the authenticity of parts of Heloise's first two letters primarily because of the split they suggest between "a religious superior bound by religious vows, and . . . a woman of sensual mind, serving Abelard and not God" (*Ep.* 2–5, p. 59). On the "myth of Heloise" tragically bound to her love for Abelard, see Peter von Moos, "Le silence d'Héloïse et les idéologies modernes," in Colloque, pp. 425–30 and passim, who calls this romantic myth "a vulgarization" of the more complex story that the letters tell.

For *Ep.* 2–7, I have used Muckle's edition, which I cite by page number. For Abelard's *Historia calamitatum,* I have used Monfrin's third edition, which I cite by line number. The *Problemata* appear in PL 178:677–730. Numbering of the letters follows D. E. Luscombe's *Checklist* rather than Muckle and Radice (i.e., *HC* is numbered *Ep.* 1 and Heloise's letters are *Ep.* 2, 4, and 6).

9. Radice uses these titles. Muckle's edition distinguishes similarly between "The Personal Letters" and those "on Religious Life." Muckle is so concerned to keep the "personal" material intact that he prints the opening of Heloise's third letter twice, at the end of the so-called personal letters and again at the beginning of the so-called religious letters, because he judges it to be "of a personal character" (*Ep.* 6–7, ed. Muckle 240).
10. For earlier discussions or descriptions of this letter, see: Gilson, *Héloïse and Abélard,* pp. 134–40; Charlotte Charrier, *Héloïse dans l'histoire et dans la légende,* 1933, pp. 220–29; Peter M. Dronke, "Heloise and Marianne: Some Reconsiderations," pp. 236–40 and *Women Writers,* pp. 127–34. See also the chapters in this volume by Bussell, McCracken, McGuire, and McLeod and Wilson.
11. R. W. Southern, "The Letters of Abelard and Heloise," p. 101.
12. Newman, "Authority, Authenticity, and the Repression of Heloise," p. 74, argues that Heloise submits to a "double repression," both of her desire and of her love: "when she actually submits, she dwindles into virtue as a heroine of romance might dwindle into marriage. The second repression of Heloise does entail a silencing, not only of her desire and her rebellion, but of all that is most 'literary' about her." Newman's conclusion, echoed in most readings, summarizes well the position I question in the pages that follow. See also the similar judgement of Kamuf in *Fictions of Feminine Desire* that in her third letter Heloise "capitulates to Abelard's consistent substitution of the Christian symbolic context for the personal, erotic one." Kamuf calls Heloise's tone in the opening of her third letter "almost cynical" (pp. 8–9), while I argue below that Heloise may be artful and strategic, but she is always serious and not cynical.
13. Gilson, *Héloïse and Abélard,* pp. 134–43.
14. Dronke, "Heloise and Marianne: Some Reconsiderations," pp. 236–40, and especially *Women Writers,* pp. 127–34.
15. Leclercq's study of the relationship between psychology and rhetoric in the letters is a good example of how more broadly based studies can help to resolve the authenticity question. See "Modern Psychology and the Interpretation of Medieval Texts." See also C. Stephen Jaeger, "The Prologue to the *Historia calamitatum* and the 'Authenticity Question,'" and D. E. Luscombe, "The Letters of Heloise and Abelard Since 'Cluny 1972,'" pp. 23–31. Recent studies by Marenbon, *The Philosophy of Peter Abelard,* and Clanchy, *A Medieval Life,* often analyze Heloise's views on particular issues in order to compare them with Abelard's, thus providing a more coherent account of Heloise's thought.
16. On the correspondence as an exemplary narrative, see: Robertson, *Abelard and Heloise,* pp. 119–35; Benton, "Fraud, Fiction and Borrowing," p. 473; von Moos, "Le silence d'Héloïse," pp. 431, n. 12, and 456–68; and most recently Chrysogonus Waddell, *The Paraclete Statutes: Institutiones Nostrae: Introduction, Edition, Commentary,* pp. 48–50. Luscombe's review of the issue, in "Letters of Heloise and Abelard," pp. 25–31, is useful.

17. *Women Writers,* p. 130 makes a similar point. On the absence of a traditional conversion experience, see also Gilson, *Héloïse and Abélard,* pp. 95–97.
18. M. D. Chenu, *Nature, Man, and Society in the Twelfth Century. Essays on New Theological Perspectives in the Latin West,* especially "Monks, Canons, and Laymen in Search of the Apostolic Life," pp. 202–38, and "The Evangelical Awakening," pp. 239–69.
19. For somewhat differing but often compatible views of the structure of Heloise's work, see: Jacques Monfrin, "Le problème de l'authenticité de la correspondance d'Abélard et d'Héloïse" in Colloque, pp. 419–21; von Moos, "Le silence d'Héloïse," pp. 425–68; and *Women Writers,* pp. 127–39.
20. *Ep.* 6, ed. Muckle 241–42: "Ne me forte in aliquo de inobedientia causari queas, verbis etiam immoderati doloris tuae frenum impositum est iussionis ut ab his mihi saltem in scribendo temperem a quibus in sermone non tam difficile quam impossibile est providere. Nihil enim minus in nostra est potestate quam animus, eique magis obedire cogimur quam imperare possimus. Unde et cum nos eius affectiones stimulant, nemo earum subitos impulsus ita repulerit ut non in effecta facile prorumpant, et se per verba facilius effluant quae promptiores animi passionum sunt notae, secundum quod scriptum est: *Ex abundantia enim cordis os loquitur.* Revocabo itaque manum a scripto in quibus linguam a verbis temperare non valeo. Utinam sic animus dolentis parere promptus sit quemadmodum dextra scribentis.

    "Aliquod tamen dolori remedium vales conferre si non hunc omnino possis auferre. Ut enim insertum clavum alius expellit, sic cogitatio nova priorem excludit cum alias intentus animus priorum memoriam dimittere cogitur aut intermittere. Tanto vero amplius cogitatio quaelibet animum occupat, et ab aliis deducit, quanto quod cogitatur honestius aestimatur, et quo intendimus animum magis videtur necessarium."

    Translations from the Latin are my own, although they are often indebted to Radice's excellent translation; I have also consulted *The Letters of Abelard and Heloise,* trans. C. K. Scott-Moncrieff.
21. Robertson, *Abelard and Heloise,* pp. 134–35. It is difficult to see what in Heloise's previous letters could be interpreted as "talk about abandoning the Paraclete." On the contrary, her loyalty to the Paraclete and to her responsibilities as fosterer of the abbey's interests are evident throughout the correspondence. On Heloise as an effective patroness of the Paraclete, see Luscombe, "The Letters of Heloise and Abelard," pp. 22–23 as well as chapter 13 by McGuire in this volume.
22. Robertson's description of Heloise's turn as "whole-hearted" is particularly misinformed given what Heloise says here about her heart.
23. See *Women Writers,* p. 129. For a useful account of the popular conversion narrative in the eleventh and twelfth centuries, see Jean-Charles Payen, *Le motif du repentir dans la littérature français médiévale des origines à 1230,* pp. 33–44.

    Lester K. Little, "Intellectual Training and Attitudes toward Reform, 1075–1150," p. 245, notes "an obvious and great need for a study of medieval conversion experience," a need met only partially by Karl Morrison's rather narrowly conceived *Understanding Conversion* and the essays collected by James Muldoon, *Varieties of Religious Conversion in the Middle Ages.*

    In the twelfth century, the term *conversio* [literally 'turning'] could refer to several quite different events or states: the dramatic and often sudden change of heart so often described in conversion stories; the less dramatic change marked by one's entry to life in a monastery; or, simply, the monastic life itself. Abelard and Heloise frequently use the term (they use *conversio* and *conversatio* interchangeably) to refer to their entrance into religious life, and both make clear that this original *conversio* bore no relationship to true spiritual conversion or change of heart, because, as Abelard says, their change of life was instigated by shame alone rather than by grace (*HC,* ed. Monfrin, ll. 623–25). While in his later letters Abelard prefers to gloss over the differences between the two kinds of conversion, implying that spiritual conversion inevitably follows upon entrance to monastic life, Heloise almost always follows her use of the term *conversio* with some ironic reminder of the gap she continues to perceive between true conversion and her hasty entrance into religious life at Abelard's command. These terms and their meanings became embroiled in early debates over the authenticity of the correspondence; see Gilson, *Héloïse and Abélard,* pp. viii, 151–55.

24. For abundant evidence of the tendency by critics to "read" Heloise's silence as the sign of her heroic passion, see von Moos, "Le silence d'Héloïse," pp. 425–30, who himself goes on to read Heloise's silence as a sign of her conversion.
25. Gilson, *Héloïse and Abélard,* pp. 101–102.
26. Kamuf, *Fictions of Feminine Desire,* p. 17, argues also that Heloise offers only "the pretext of submission," but she believes that Heloise's strategy is designed to "keep alive the possibility of an erotic subtext." I argue here that Heloise's motives are intellectual, spiritual, and emotional, rather than simply erotic. See *Women Writers,* p. 134, and more recently, Cartlidge, *Medieval Marriage,* pp. 58–73, for a study of the topicality and urgency of Heloise's debate with Abelard over implications of the marital bond.
27. Dronke, in a stylistic analysis of Heloise's letters, notes frequent examples of the same "highly-wrought diction" in her third letter as that which predominates in her previous letters; see "Heloise's *Problemata* and *Letters:* Some Questions of Form and Content," p. 55.
28. As I note above in n. 5, recent readers have suggested that Abelard may often be the borrower and Heloise the originator of some key ideas discussed here.
29. McLaughlin argues in "Peter Abelard and the Dignity of Women" that Abelard is deeply indebted to Heloise's arguments for key ideas in his treatment of the religious life of women. Brooke goes even further (perhaps too far) in depicting Abelard as almost slavish in following Heloise's instructions when he composes a new rule for the Paraclete: "He dutifully did what he was told, . . . picked up every hint in her letter and solemnly carried her own arguments to their logical conclusion—occasionally misinterpreting wishes not fully expressed." Brooke describes Abelard's contributions to the rule "comparatively rare" (*Medieval Idea of Marriage,* p. 117).
30. See also Gilson, *Héloïse and Abélard,* pp. 134–40, on the ironies of Heloise's apparently "harmless" request. In seeming to disguise her intent, Heloise is by no means being coy. Instead, she may see herself caught between two conflicting ideologies described by Penny Schine Gold as follows: "The Christian monastic experience for women was characterized by a basic contradiction entirely absent from the male experience. On the one hand, monastic life offered one of the few non-domestic outlets for women's capabilities and talents and provided for both education and a certain degree of autonomy. . . . On the other hand, female religious in the Christian tradition rarely, if ever, were able to achieve full autonomy or independence from male scrutiny, and women's ability to enter and enjoy the religious life was circumscribed by an ideology of feminine weakness that implied that female religious were unable to manage their own affairs." (*The Lady & the Virgin: Image, Attitude, and Experience in Twelfth-Century France,* p. 76).
31. *Ep.* 6, ed. Muckle 245; see above, n. 20. See also Bussell (chapter 10 in this volume) for an alternate translation and discussion of this passage.
32. She may borrow the aphorism from either Cicero or Jerome. Muckle cites Cicero, *Tusc. disp.* 4.35.75 (*Ep.* 6, ed. Muckle 242 n. 12), but both Gilson, *Héloïse and Abélard,* p. 188 n. 21, and *Women Writers,* p. 305 n. 39 suggest that Heloise's wording more closely resembles Jerome, *Epistle* 125.14, which she also cites in the *Problemata.*
33. See above, n. 12.
34. On the Cluniac-Cistercian debate, see: Louis J. Lekai, *The Cistercians: Ideals and Reality,* pp. 21–32; David Knowles, "Cistercians and Cluniacs: The Controversy between St.

Bernard and Peter the Venerable," pp. 50–75; Adriaan H. Bredero, "Cluny et Citeaux au xii(eme) siècle: les origines de la controverse." See also the lucid account of R. W. Southern, *Western Society and the Church in the Middle Ages,* pp. 230–72, and the somewhat opposing view of Cistercian ideals in Jean Leclercq, "Profession according to the Rule of St Benedict," pp. 117–49. For the early history of the Augustinians and their quarrel with the Rule of St. Benedict, see J. C. Dickinson, *The Origins of the Austin Canons and Their Introduction into England,* pp. 49–72. See also Giles Constable's excellent overview of the larger context of the religious reform movement of the twelfth century, especially its rhetorical component, "Renewal and Reform in Religious Life: Concepts and Realities," pp. 37–67.

35. On the evangelical movement, see Chenu as cited above, n. 18.

36. Gilson, *Héloïse and Abélard,* p. 111, refers to the Cluniac-Cistercian debate as a "little monastic quarrel." If we consider some of its more extreme polemics, his is not an entirely unfair characterization. Nearly a century after the debate had begun, this parochial element in the debate was still prominent enough to arouse the indignation of the anonymous author of Ancrene Wisse: "ȝef ei unweote easkeð ow of hwet ordre ȝe beon, as summe doð, þe telleð me, þe siheð þe gneat & swolheð þ flehe, ondswerieð of Sein Iames, þe wes godes apostel . . . ȝef him puncheð wunder & sullich of swuch ondswere, easkið him hwet beo ordre, & hwer he funde in hali writ religiun openlukest descriueþ & isutelet þen is i Sein Iames canonial epistel. He descriueþ religiun nowðer hwit ne blac, ne nempneð he in his ordre. Ah moni siheð þe gneat ant swolheð þe flehe, þet is, m.akeð muche strengðe þer as is þe leaste. Pawel þe earste ancre, Antonie & Arsenie, Makarie & te oþre neren ha religiuse & of Sein Iames ordre? wið hare greate matten & hare hearde heren neren ha of god ordre, & hweðer hwite oðer blake as unwise ow easkið þe weneð þet ordre sitte i þe curtel" (J. R. R. Tolkien, ed., *Ancrene Wisse: Edited from ms. Corpus Christi College Cambridge 402,* pp. 9–10).

37. Little, "Intellectual Training and Attitudes toward Reform," pp. 235–49, speaks generally of what could be called a dialectical or urban style that arises in the twelfth-century urban schools and that is often described in terms of the opposing monastic habit of perception. On the monastic style, see the classic study of Jean Leclercq, *The Love of Learning and the Desire for God: A Study of Monastic Culture,* trans. Catherine Misrahi, pp. 233–86, and Chenu, *Nature, Man, and Society,* pp. 300–309.

38. See *Ep.* 6, ed. Muckle 242, for example, where Heloise sets side by side quotations from Jerome's letters to holy women and Ovid's *Ars amatoria,* and later (p. 251) Heloise juxtaposes a phrase from a psalm with a line from Persius' satires on the necessity of self-knowledge. Gilson, *Héloïse and Abélard,* p. 135, finds particularly ironic Heloise's use of Ovid, whom she calls "the doctor of sensuality and shame," to support the highly ascetic St. Jerome. Clanchy, who emphasizes that Heloise's training in literature set her apart from Abelard's more narrow logical habits of mind, has recently described Heloise's style specifically in terms of the "dazzling wit" with which she raises "disconcerting questions" (Clanchy, *A Medieval Life,* pp. 149–54); see also Newman, "Authority, Authenticity, and Repression," pp. 68–71, who speculates that Heloise's reading of Ovid, Seneca, Jerome, Cicero, and Lucan provided her with a variety of "personae" that she could adopt and manipulate for effect. On the importance of Ovid in particular in Heloise's letters, see Michael Calabrese, "Ovid and the Female Voice in the *De Amore* and the *Letters* of Abelard and Heloise."

39. Although the subject was widely discussed in the monastic context beginning in the eleventh-century monastic reform movement, Chenu's earliest examples of academic interest in the *vita apostolica* occur in the last decade of the twelfth century. See *Nature, Man, and Society,* p. 250, and Constable, "Renewal and Reform in Religious Life," pp. 53–56. Heloise's letter on monastic life was written sometime after 1132, the approximate date of Abelard's *Historia calamitatum,* and before Abelard's death in 1142. The cor-

respondence as a whole is usually dated 1132 to 1135. (See Muckle's introduction, *Ep.* 2–5, ed. Muckle 47–48.)

40. St. Bernard's best-known attack upon traditional Black monks, the *Apology,* has been translated in *The Works of Bernard of Clairvaux,* vol. 1. Abelard, in a letter to Bernard, describes the latter's visit to the Paraclete as related to Abelard by Heloise (*Letters IX–XIV,* ed. E. R. Smits, Letter no. 10, p. 239), and see Radice, pp. 37–38. For Peter's famous encomium to Heloise, see *The Letters of Peter the Venerable,* ed. Giles Constable, Letter 115, vol. 1:303–308 and the translation by Radice, pp. 277–84.
41. See *Ep.* 6, ed. Muckle 246–47, the paragraph beginning "Cuius quidem discretionis." Later (p. 248) Heloise analyzes a brief passage from chapter 40 of the Rule as evidence of Benedict's concessions to the times and speculates that Benedict was probably referring in the passage to a section of the *Lives of the Fathers,* which she quotes for comparison.
42. Heloise refers repeatedly to Benedict's "discretion," to his sensitivity both to the needs of individual monks and to the particular times in which he lives. See especially *Ep.* 6, ed. Muckle 244, 246–47, 248.
43. "Quod quidem hoc tempore multi monasticae religionis temerarii professores, si diligentius; attenderent, et in quam professionem iurarent antea providerent, atque ipsum Regulae tenorem studiose perscrutarentur, minus per ignorantiam offenderent, et per negligentiam peccarent. Nunc vero indiscrete omnes fere pariter ad monasticam conversionem currentes, inordinate suscepti, inordinatius vivunt, et eadem facilitate qua ignotam Regulam profitentur eam contemnentes, consuetudines quas volunt pro lege statuunt" (p. 246).
44. On the Cistercian impulse to follow or even outdo St. Benedict in regulating every detail of daily life, see the opposing views of Southern, *Western Society and the Church,* pp. 251–59, and Leclercq, "Profession according to the Rule," pp. 138–39, and the balanced compromise of Constable, "Renewal and Reform in Religious Life," pp. 57–59. Many of the relevant early Cistercian documents have been translated by Bede K. Lackner as an appendix in Lekai, *The Cistercians: Ideal and Reality,* pp. 442–66. Most recently Martha G. Newman, *The Boundaries of Charity: Cistercian Culture and Ecclesiastical Reform, 1098–1180,* offers a stimulating reconsideration of the politics of early Cistercian history.
45. See especially Peter the Venerable's famous letter to St. Bernard in Constable, *The Letters of Peter the Venerable,* 1.52–101.
46. Although there were numerous exceptions including, of course, Heloise herself, women who entered the convent were generally less well trained in the *trivium* than their male counterparts. They thus came to Benedict's Rule less well prepared than Heloise to study it with the rigor she seems to demand. On female education in the Middle Ages, see Joan M. Ferrante, "The Education of Women in the Middle Ages in Theory, Fact, and Fantasy," pp. 9–42.
47. On the "ideology of feminine weakness" in monastic literature, see Gold, *The Lady and the Virgin,* pp. 76–115. Barbara Newman recently speculated that Heloise's antifeminist strain may explain the reluctance of "modern feminist scholars . . . to insist on the authenticity of her letters" ("Authority, Authenticity, and Repression," p. 70). See also Cartlidge, who notes with dismay that Heloise's letters "sugges[t] that she really saw herself in terms of antifeminist stereotypes . . ." (*Medieval Marriage,* p. 67). Discovering Heloise's antifeminism is one of the results of historicizing Heloise. In studying Heloise's thought in light of her contemporaries, insofar as we can, instead of seeking evidence only of her precocity in anticipating the modern, we are bound to discover our own differences with her beliefs and values.
48. Kamuf, *Fictions of Feminine Desire,* pp. 10–43, is especially sensitive to the sexual dialectics of the letters, the rhetorical strategies used by both Heloise and Abelard to gain the

upper hand in the ongoing debate that runs through the correspondence. In Kamuf's view, Heloise consistently tries to reestablish "the destabilizing experience of the erotic" (p. 19) while Abelard "adopts the aim of bringing Heloise to embrace castration—her own as well as his" (p. 36).

49. *Ep.* 6, ed. Muckle 242–46. *Women Writers,* p. 130, makes a similar point. See also chapter 9 by McCracken in this volume.
50. *Ep.* 4, ed. Muckle 81. "Nec solum quae egimus, sed loca pariter et tempora in quibus haec egimus, ita tecum nostro infixa sunt animo, ut in ipsis omnia tecum agam, . . ."
51. *Ep.* 2, ed. Muckle 68.
52. *Domino* appears in Troyes, Bibliothèque Municipale 802, the most reliable manuscript among the seven extant copies of this letter, but in the other manuscripts the more symmetrical *suo* is found. For varying interpretations of these superscriptions, see: Gilson, *Héloïse and Abélard,* pp. 102–103; Dronke, "Heloise and Marianne," pp. 236–37 and *Women Writers,* pp. 127–28; Radice, p. 159 and n. 1.; and Mews in chapter 3 in this volume. *Domino* is a particularly interesting reading in light of Heloise's arguments concerning her relation to Abelard, because it is an ambiguous term whose confusion is compounded by its context. In his previous letter, Abelard had repeatedly used the terms *Dominus* referring to God and *domina* referring to Heloise, especially in the beginning of his letter, where he argues that Heloise was mistaken in thinking of Abelard as her *domino* (*Ep.* 4, 77) because she became his *domina* when she became the bride of Christ, her true *Dominus* (*Ep.* 5, 83). Again, at the end of this letter, Abelard repeats the term *Dominus* no fewer than five times (pp. 93–94), always referring unmistakably to Christ, whom he has asked Heloise to take instead of Abelard as her only lord. Thus, when Heloise responds with a letter addressed to her *Domino,* we cannot help but wonder whether she refers to God or to Abelard. One suspects that the ambiguity is intentional but that her primary referent is still Abelard. Gilson, *Héloïse and Abélard,* pp. 102–103, interprets *Domino* in the superscription to refer to God and suggests that the salutation signifies Heloise's acknowledgement that "in so far as concerns the logical species—the nun—she is the Lord's." Radice's translation follows Gilson's closely: "God's own in species, his own as individual" (p. 159). However, this interpretation not only overlooks the previous play upon the term in the letters, as just outlined, but also would argue for a radical departure from Heloise's usual style of address. In all of her letters the first term of Heloise's salutation consists of some form of address to Abelard. In her first salutation, in fact, she addresses her letter "Domino suo," but there she modifies that ambiguous phrase by further defining her addressee as her "master," "father," "husband," and "brother," a conundrum whose only solution could be Abelard, Heloise's earthly husband and master at the same time that he is her spiritual father and brother. Given Heloise's consistency in always addressing her letters to Abelard, however elliptically, it seems unlikely that suddenly in her third letter she would adopt a new form of salutation. It should also be added that at the very end of her third letter Heloise refers unambiguously to Abelard as her *domino* (*Ep.* 6, ed. Muckle 253). It would seem, then, that in her superscription *domino* refers his absolute mastery. In all likelihood, however, Heloise would welcome any confusion on the reader's part between Abelard and God as the appropriate referent for the first term of her superscription, in that it might serve to remind Abelard of the profound differences in their respective frames of reference. On the form of Heloise's salutations, see also Muckle's introduction (*Ep.* 2–4, ed. Muckle 50–51).
53. This is especially true in the superscription of Heloise's first letter (*Ep.* 2, ed. Muckle 68): "Domino suo immo patri, coniugi suo immo fratri, ancilla sua immo filia, ipsius uxor immo soror, Abaelardo, Heloisa." While Abelard had ended his letter of consolation to a friend with an orderly series of pious reflections on the nature of divine providence and the clear path of righteousness, Heloise, in her superscription, reminds

Abelard of the less orderly human perspective, particularly how very confusing her circumstances are, now that Abelard is both her secular master and her spiritual father, her husband and her brother. Heloise continually scrambles what Abelard depicts as clear, logical relationships. On Heloise's tendency to undo Abelard's logical statements, both in her salutations and elsewhere, see Kamuf, *Fictions of Feminine Desire,* pp. 9–19.

54. Dronke, "Heloise and Marianne," p. 237, states without further explanation that "the philosophical sense of 'specialiter' would seem forced" and prefers to translate the term simply as "especially." But Dronke has revised his view in *Women Writers,* pp. 127–28. It seems to me that Heloise, in juxtaposing "specialiter" and "singulariter," is precisely forcing a distinction upon the reader that can best be explained with reference to the philosophical distinction between species and individuals. This issue was, of course, of more than passing interest to Abelard, who not only treats the issue thoroughly in his philosophical writings but also builds the whole structure of his autobiographical letter upon the debate with his teacher, William of Champeaux, over the relation between individual things and universals. Abelard portrays himself as the winner of the debate and champion of the integrity of individual things as quite distinct from universals. Here Heloise, addressing her teacher, is perhaps subtly replaying that debate with herself in the starring role of defender of singulars, while Abelard is identified with William's old position. Mary Bartholemy, a former graduate student at the University of California, Irvine, pointed out to me the various ways in which Heloise, as much as or even more than Abelard, could appropriately be called a "nominalist."

For a recent thorough discussion of Abelard's nominalism and his position on the closely related problem of universals and *species,* see Marenbon, *The Philosophy of Abelard,* pp. 101–23, 174–201.

55. I would interpret what Abelard calls "Heloise's old perpetual complaint" (Radice 145) more broadly than most readers. Abelard refers twice in Letter 5 to Heloise's "veteram illam et assiduam querelam" (*Ep.* 5, ed. Muckle 83, 87). In both cases he interprets the complaint as being directed against God's justice and as having to do with Heloise's questioning of the divine order of things. Heloise does specifically complain that God treated Abelard unjustly, but her attention is directed more toward the human rather than the divine order, for the human order to her way of seeing is full of incongruous details. For instance, she asks why God chose to punish Abelard with castration *after* he had married Heloise and not before, and why God punished one partner to the crime and not the other. It is the incoherence of the *details* of their life viewed as a providential narrative that vexes Heloise. Abelard's letters to Heloise suggest that it is much easier for him than for her to ascend to the eighth sphere, as it were, ignoring details in order to concentrate on God's grand scheme. At least, this is true in his later letters. In the preceding story of his own calamities, Abelard too is torn between the providential view of his history and a more limited, less idealistic view embodied in the figure of Fortune.

56. Gilson, *Héloïse and Abélard,* pp. 134–40, discusses Heloise's critique of monastic rules in light of the Renaissance emphasis on reason in religion.

57. *Ep.* 6, ed. Muckle 245: "Ex quibus quidem verbis aperte colligitur quod quisquis evangelicis praeceptis continentiae virtutem addiderit, monasticam perfectionem implebit.

"Atque utinam ad hoc nostra religio conscendere posset ut Evangelium impleret, non transcenderet, nec plusquam christianae appeteremus esse. Hinc profecto, ni fallor, sancti decreverunt Patres non ita nobis sicut viris generalem aliquam regulam quasi novam legem praefigere, nec magnitudine votorum nostram infirmitatem onerare . . ."

58. Gilson, *Héloïse and Abélard,* pp. 137–38, makes a similar point but views Heloise's remarks in light of Erasmus and other Renaissance thinkers. We need not look so far ahead to find strongly worded objections to overly exclusive man-made rules for religious life. See Chenu, *Nature, Man, and Society,* pp. 221–22, and especially his analysis of the views of

Peter the Chanter, pp. 256–57; Jean Leclercq, François Vandenbrouke, and Louis Bouyer, *A History of Christian Spirituality,* vol. 2: *The Spirituality of the Middle Ages,* pp. 257–58; and Linda Georgianna, *The Solitary Self: Individuality in the Ancrene Wisse,* pp. 15–18.

Clanchy, *A Medieval Life,* p. 256, notes that although Abelard eventually espoused many of Heloise's ideas about monastic life, he had little use for her more radical argument against the privileging of religious orders: "Abelard did not follow Heloise down this fundamentalist road, probably because he was too attached to his own standing as a monk and *religiosus;* he had preached a sermon on the theme that 'monk' is the name of religion itself."

59. *Ep.* 6, ed. Muckle 249–50, 252.
60. *Ep.* 6, ed. Muckle 245. See Bussell's chapter 10 in this volume for further discussion of the shift in Heloise's third letter from specifically female to universal "infirmitas."
61. *Ep.* 6, ed. Muckle 245: "Providendum itaque nobis est ne id oneris feminae praesumamus in quo viros fere iam universos succumbere videmus, immo et deficere. Senuisse iam mundum conspicimus hominesque ipsos cum ceteris quae mundi sunt pristinum naturae vigorem amisisse, et iuxta illud Veritatis ipsam caritatem non tam multorum quam fere omnium refriguisse ut iam videlicet pro qualitate hominum ipsas propter homines scriptas vel mutari vel temperari necesse sit Regulas."
62. See above, n. 6, for references to recent arguments that suggest that Heloise might be the originator and Abelard the appropriator of some of these ideas.
63. See *Ep.* 6, ed. Muckle 248. Heloise's tone grows quite indignant as she asks: "Ubi umquam, quaeso, carnes a Deo damnatae sunt vel monachis interdictae?"
64. See especially *Ep.* 6, ed. Muckle 251: "Non itaque magnopere quae fiunt sed quo animo fiant pensandum est, si illi placere studemus, qui cordis et renum probator est, et in abscondito videt . . ." and Muckle's introduction, *Ep.* 2–5, ed., Muckle 55–56. While Muckle cites Abelard's Rule for the Paraclete as the closest approximation of Heloise's wording, his *Ethics* may provide an even closer parallel, in that it repeats even the same biblical quotations in support of the notion of intentionality: "Deus uero solus qui non tam quae fiunt, quam quo animo fiant adtendit, ueraciter in intentione nostra reatum pensat et uero iudicio culpam examinat. Vnde et probator cordis et renum dicitur, et in abscondito uidere" (*Peter Abelard's Ethics,* ed. D. E. Luscombe, p. 40.9–12; see also p. 29.9–11 for very similar phrasing of the same idea). On Abelard's theory of intentionality, see Robert Blomme, *La doctrine du péché dans les écoles théologiques de la première moitié du xii(e) siècle,* pp. 115–44, and the more recent analysis in Marenbon, *The Philosophy of Peter Abelard,* pp. 251–64.
65. *Ep.* 6, ed. Muckle 250: "Unde quicumque sunt vere Christiani sic toti circa interiorem hominem sunt occupati . . ."
66. *Ep.* 6, ed. Muckle 248.
67. *Ep.* 6, ed. Muckle 251.
68. *Ep.* 6, ed. Muckle 252. Marenbon, *The Philosophy of Peter Abelard,* pp. 312–14. Abelard in time rethinks his views on the monastic life along precisely the lines Heloise here sets down, replacing his earlier emphasis on austerity and perfection with Heloise's view of moderation in religious practices.
69. On the hostile relations between male and female Cistercian houses, see: Lekai, *The Cistercians: Ideals and Reality,* pp. 347–63; Gold, *The Lady and the Virgin,* pp. 76–115; Southern, *Western Society and the Church in the Middle Ages,* pp. 314–18; and Sally Thompson, "The Problem of Cistercian Nuns in the Twelfth and Early Thirteenth Centuries," pp. 227–52.
70. *Ep.* 6, ed. Muckle 252–53.
71. Abelard prefaces his hymns with a typical note of urgency: "Ad tuarum precum instantiam, soror mihi Heloisa . . ." See *Peter Abelard's* Hymnarius paraclitensis, ed. Joseph Szövérffy, 2.9, and Radice, pp. 32–34.

72. *Ep.* 6, ed. Muckle 246: "Satis nostrae esse infirmitati et maximum imputari debet, si continenter ac sine proprietate viventes et, officiis occupatae divinis, ipsos Ecclesiae duces vel religiosos laicos in victu adaequemus, vel eos denique qui regulares canonici dicuntur et se praecipue vitam apostolicam sequi profitentur." Note how quickly Heloise moves from women's "infirmity" to their ability to equal the new canons and the very leaders of the church in their religious practice.
73. For the text of Aelred's rule, see Charles Dumont, ed., *La vie de recluse. La prière pastorale.* On Aelred's meditations, see Dumont's introduction, pp. 29–39. On the form of Aelred's rule, see Georgianna, *The Solitary Self,* pp. 42–49.
74. *Ep.* 6, ed. Muckle 251.
75. *Ep.* 4, ed. Muckle 81.
76. On the *Ancrene Wisse* as a religious rule, see Georgianna, *The Solitary Self,* pp. 18–31.
77. PL 77:72B. In a section on guarding one's thoughts and keeping silence, Gregory writes: "Nil quippe in nobis est corde fugacius, quod a nobis toties recedit, quoties per pravas cogitationes defluit."
78. Gilson, highly sensitive to Heloise's use of classical models and texts, speaks frequently of Heloise as a Roman heroine, characterizing the sentiments motivating her to take the veil at Abelard's command as "not Christian [but] completely Roman" (*Héloïse and Abélard,* p. 91).

    Earlier Gilson opposes "Abelard's Christian submission to Providence" to "Héloïse's acceptance of Stoic principles which she found in Seneca and Lucan" (p. 86). However, Gilson also writes what remains the most illuminating study of Heloise's *Christian* crisis in his chapter called "The Mystery of Heloise." He perhaps comes closest to the truth when he describes Heloise as "haunted by the double ideal of Roman and Christian greatness" (p. 141).
79. On the rigor and idealism of Abelard's moral theology, especially in terms of human responsibility and accountability, see Richard E. Weingart, *The Logic of Divine Love: A Critical Analysis of the Soteriology of Peter Abailard,* pp. 169–84, and Paul L. Williams, *The Moral Philosophy of Peter Abelard.* Williams argues for a close connection between Abelard's study of logic and his moral theology, and that in both areas Abelard remained throughout his life the moral "perfectionist—uncompromising in his demands and single-minded in his purpose" (p. 37).
80. Compare *Ep.* 4, ed. Muckle 80–81, with Abelard's *Ethics,* especially pp. 4–21, where Abelard repeatedly distinguishes between desire (or will) and consent. In order to "win a crown," as Abelard puts it, one must "restrain" or "resist" desire, not "extinguish" it (p. 6). Marenbon examines the differences in their views of intentionality in *The Philosophy of Peter Abelard,* pp. 91–92, 53–64.

    Although Heloise's confusion of desire and consent is not Abelard's legacy, her constant self-searching seems closely related to the internal state fostered by Abelard's *Ethics,* alternately known as *Scito te ipsum.* Williams notes that, above all, "Abelard stressed the importance of knowing one's self in regard to the quality and rightness of one's intentions. This constant self-scrutiny, this hounding search for self-knowledge, was the legacy of Abelard's ethics . . ." (*The Moral Philosophy of Peter Abelard,* p. 145).
81. Much of Abelard's teaching on the Incarnation and Redemption is found in his *Commentaria in epistolam Pauli ad Romanos.* See the analysis of Weingart, *The Logic of Divine Love,* pp. 66–96. In his recent biography, Clanchy argues that Abelard's redemptive theory was developed very late in his career, making it possible that Abelard's emphasis on love as Christ's motive in the act of redemption might have been influenced by Heloise's letters (*A Medieval Life,* pp. 283–87). On Heloise's development and use of the notion of disinterested love, see also Gilson, *Héloïse and Abélard,* pp. 47–65, and A. H. C. Downes, trans., *The Mystical Theology of Saint Bernard,* pp. 158–66; Weingart, *The Logic of*

Divine Love, pp. 169–76; Williams, *The Moral Philosophy of Peter Abelard,* pp. 159–63, and most recently Marenbon, *The Philosophy of Peter Abelard,* pp. 298–303.

82. See *Ep.* 4, ed. Muckle 81; see Gilson, *Héloïse and Abélard,* pp. 95–96, especially n. 7.
83. See *Ep.* 4, ed. Muckle 81.
84. Peter Abelard's *Ethics,* pp. 76 ff. See also the analysis of Weingart, *The Logic of Divine Love,* pp. 196–200, and Williams, *The Moral Theology of Peter Abelard,* pp. 145–60.
85. *Ep.* 4, ed. Muckle 80. On the concepts of perfect and imperfect contrition, see Payen, *Le motif du repentir,* pp. 81–83, and Amédée Teetaert, *La confession aux laïques dans l'église latine depuis le viii(e) jusqu'au xiv(e) siècle,* pp. 258–60.
86. *Ep.* 4, ed. Muckle 81.
87. *Ep.* 5, ed. Muckle 93.
88. On Abelard's use of military imagery in the *Historia calamitatum,* see Clanchy, *A Medieval Life,* pp. 141–45. Throughout his career, Abelard is drawn to classical and biblical quotations that employ battle images. Heroic language is such an indispensable habit of mind for Abelard that, even after Heloise's rejection of it, he continues to describe her spiritual state in epic terms. See especially *Ep.* 5, ed. Muckle 92–93, beginning with Abelard's allusion to Pompey's reproach to Cornelia after his defeat at Pharsalia. Since according to Abelard, Heloise had recalled Cornelia's lament to Pompey when she (Heloise) entered the convent of Argenteuil (*HC,* ed. Monfrin, 11. 632–38), he probably felt it appropriate to quote a nearby passage from the same work (Lucan's *Bellum civile*). But as I argue here, Heloise ultimately rejects such heroic portrayals of her situation. St. Benedict's Rule also often relies on battle imagery to describe the spiritual life, especially in the prologue, which is addressed to "you, whoever you may be, who are renouncing your own will to do battle under the Lord Christ, the true King, and are taking up the strong, bright weapons of obedience." The translation is that of Leonard Doyle, *St. Benedict's Rule for Monasteries,* p. 1.
89. *Ep.* 4, ed. Muckle 82: "Nolo, me ad virtutem exhortans, et ad pugnam provocans, dicas: *Nam virtus in infirmitate perficitur;* et: *Non coronabitur nisi qui legitime certaverit.* Non quaero coronam victoriae. Satis est mihi periculum vitare. Tutius evitatur periculum, quam committitur bellum. Quocumque me angulo coeli Deus collocet, satis mihi faciet. Nullus ibi cuiquam invidebit, cum singulis quod habebunt suffecerit."
90. *Ep.* 4, ed. Muckle 82: "Tateor imbecillitatem meam; nolo spe victoriae pugnare ne perdam aliquando victoriam. . . . Quid necesse est certa dimittere, et incerta sectari?" (*Adversus Vigilantium* [PL 23:367B]).
91. *Ep.* 6, ed. Muckle 251: "Ne te quaesiveris extra" (*Satires,* 1.7).
92. *Ep.* 6, ed. Muckle 252: " invoca me in die tribulationis; et eruam te, et honorificabis me" (Ps 49: 15).

CHAPTER 9

THE CURSE OF EVE: FEMALE BODIES AND CHRISTIAN BODIES IN HELOISE'S THIRD LETTER

Peggy McCracken

This chapter examines the way in which Heloise uses the material female body to describe authentic religious experience.

Heloise's third letter to Abelard has long been considered a sort of end point for the correspondence, even though it is not the last letter in the exchange.[1] Here Heloise abandons the passionate speech of desire that characterizes her first two letters and makes two requests of Abelard: that he explain the origin and authority of monastic foundations for women and that he write a monastic rule appropriate for nuns.

It is certainly true that the third letter is radically different from the first two. It does not continue the explicit recollections of the love affair found in the letters of both Abelard and Heloise up to this point in the correspondence, and for some readers, Heloise's third letter is less a continuation of the previous exchange than the beginning a new correspondence, one unrelated to the love story and its aftermath.[2] While it clearly marks an interruption in the tone of the correspondence, Heloise's third letter also continues a conversation begun in the earlier letters, and I will follow recent critics in focusing on the relationship of this letter to those that precede it.[3] In particular, I will examine the way that both Abelard and Heloise describe the body in monastic experience. In the letters of both correspondents, the exemplary Christian body is a female body. Both use the female body to illustrate the relationship between body and spirit for the Christian subject; both use the female body in a definition of authentic religious identity; and both insist on the materiality of the body, although in crucially different terms.[4]

Strongly marked by the memory, loss, or deliberate forgetting of shared passion, the letters of Abelard and Heloise maintain a constant tension between personal experience and the monastic rule, and the female body is the privileged illustration of this tension in the letters. Abelard describes an abstract body-as-metaphor; Heloise counters with a concrete image of the menstruating body.[5] Both use the female body to describe the Christian subject. Yet while Abelard subsumes gender into the figural meaning of the body, Heloise insists on gender as part of the body's experience; while Abelard effaces gender in the description of the Christian subject, Heloise describes the female body as a literal and inescapable site of identity.[6]

The Body as Metaphor

Heloise begins her third letter to Abelard with an ostensible acceptance of his repeated exhortation to put aside her "bitterness of heart" and to "seek piety."[7] She describes her submission to Abelard's instruction with a metaphoric division of her body, opposing the voice of the heart to the writing of the hand:

> Ne me forte in aliquo de inobedientia causari queas, verbis etiam immoderati doloris tuae frenum impositum est iussionis ut ab his mihi saltem in scribendo temperem a quibus in sermone non tam difficile quam impossibile est providere. Nihil enim minus in nostra est potestate quam animus, eique magis obedire cogimur quam imperare possimus. Unde et cum nos eius affectiones stimulant, nemo earum subitos impulsus ita repulerit ut non in effecta facile prorumpant, et se per verba facilius effluant quae promptiores animi passionum sunt notae. . . . Revocabo itaque manum a scripto in quibus linguam a verbis temperare non valeo. Utinam sic animus dolentis parere promptus sit quemadmodum dextra scribentis
>
> [I would not want to give you cause for finding me disobedient in anything, so I have set the bridle of your injunction on the words which issue from my unbounded grief; thus in writing at least I may moderate what it is difficult or rather impossible to forestall in speech. For nothing is less under our control than the heart—having no power to command it we are forced to obey. And so when its impulses move us, none of us can stop their sudden promptings from easily breaking out, and even more easily overflowing into words which are the ever-ready indications of the heart's emotions. . . . I will therefore hold my hand from writing words which I cannot restrain my tongue from speaking; would that a grieving heart would be as ready to obey as a writer's hand!][8]

In this passage Heloise inverts the metaphoric opposition between body and heart used by Abelard in his first letter where he encouraged her to "listen . . . with the ear of [her] heart to what [she has] so often heard with [her] bodily ear."[9] Whereas Abelard locates spiritual love in the heart and sexual desire in the body, Heloise here makes the heart the locus of a desire that cannot be renounced and the body the instrument of containment: "I will . . . hold my hand from writing words which I cannot restrain my tongue from speaking; would that a grieving heart would be as ready to obey as a writer's hand!" In her appropriation of Abelard's metaphor, Heloise introduces the problematic relationship of body and spirit that will implicitly structure the whole of her third letter. Does the heart rule the body, or is the heart to be ruled by the contrite, chaste body, a body whose excesses are contained by a religious rule?

The relationship between the body and desire dominates the correspondence of Abelard and Heloise. Abelard repeatedly encourages Heloise to renounce carnal desire, which he locates in the body, and to embrace the desire for God, which he locates in the heart. The separation between the body and the spirit receives an extended development in Abelard's second letter to Heloise, where he addresses what he calls "[her] old perpetual complaint against God concerning the manner of [their] entry into religious life and the cruelty of the act of treachery performed on [him]."[10] In Abelard's letter spiritual perfection is described as the renunciation of the body. There is nothing surprising in this, of course: the repression of the needs and desires of the material body characterizes the Christian quest for spiritual perfection in its earliest forms.[11] What is worth remarking in the *Correspondence* is Abelard's representation of an idealized renunciation of the body in the figure of the Ethiopian bride of the Song of Songs.

Taking the bride's body as a metaphor, Abelard stresses the opposition between exterior appearance and interior worth, between the black skin that symbolizes adversity and the white bones that represent the strength and virtue of the soul.[12] In Abelard's discussion the blackness of bodily tribulation is a blessing because it provokes a humility that is not the vain abjection of hypocrites, but a true turning away from the love of earthly things and an attachment to the desire for eternal life. The black bride disdains her body, she "keeps herself humble and abject" [*vilem et abiectam se tenet*].[13]

In Abelard's discussion of the Ethiopian bride, sanctity is figured as a gendered position that includes the abjection of a racially defined body. In other words, the Christian subject comes into being through the abjection of a body defined as black and female. Abelard's concept of abjection seems clear enough: by denying or rejecting the black body that represents worldly tribulation, and by rejoicing in the white interior that signifies purity, the Ethiopian bride realizes the glory of humility and the pleasures of spiritual love that are the rewards of the Christian subject. Yet at the same time, Abelard describes the abject body as an ever-present sign of "the adversity of bodily tribulations," and he extends that sign to Heloise: the black monastic habit that she wears, like the bride's black body, identifies the soul that renounces the world and seeks a contemplative life.[14] The black habit is an ever-present sign of "the life of humility and withdrawal" that characterizes the monastic profession.[15]

The always present, ever-to-be-rejected body posits an abjection that is always haunted by its object, and in this tension it conforms to theorist Julia Kristeva's description of the abject as that which disturbs identity, system, and order, as that which "does not respect borders, positions, rules."[16] The abject is that which must be cast off in order to attain subjecthood yet that haunts the borders of the subject as its other and as its potential annihilation. I do not wish to assimilate Abelard's idea of the abject body to Kristeva's psychoanalytically informed definition of abjection; however, I do wish to stress the way that her description of what abjection does may elucidate what is implicit in Abelard's use of abjection. Both Abelard and Kristeva see abjection as part of the process of becoming a subject. In Abelard's letter, abjection defines the specifically Christian subject, a subject that is also represented as female.

As Catherine Brown has noted, Abelard's discussion of the Ethiopian bride subsumes Heloise's personal experience of pleasure and desire into allegory.[17] In Abelard's description of the bride's secret sexual pleasure, he repeats and recontextualizes Heloise's discourse of desire from her previous letters: "because she is black, as we said, and lovely, she is chosen and taken into the king's bedchamber, that is, to that secret place of peace and contemplation, and into the bed" [quia nigra est, ut diximus, et formosa, dilectam et introductam se dicit in cubiculum regis, id est, in secretum vel quietem contemplationis, et lectulum illum].[18] Abelard's representation of carnal desire as an allegory of spiritual desire is yet another instance of his repeated exhortation that Heloise turn her desire for him into a desire for God. What is newly apparent in Abelard's extended discourse on the black bride, and what Heloise seems to respond to in her third letter, is the way that Abelard acknowledges the material body only to call for its abjection; he acknowledges desire and sexual pleasure, but only in a spiritual state attained through the abjection of the material body—a body that, in its association with secret pleasures and with the marriage bed, may be recognizable as Heloise's own body. Again, it is not surprising that Abelard would suggest that Heloise renounce her body and its desires—he has done that explicitly and repeatedly in his previous letter. What is surprising is that—as Brown points out—Abelard *does* acknowledge and respond to Heloise's discourse of desire. Through the metaphor of the bride's body, he implicitly transforms the material body—Heloise's body—as a body to be abjected in order to find pleasure in the soul.

A similar move, and one that goes deeper into their common experience, characterizes Abelard's allegorical representation of maternity as spiritual reproduction. In the same letter he laments his own barren state and exults in the many spiritual daughters Heloise has born to the Lord:

> Quam lamentabile incommodum, si carnalium voluptatum sordibus vacans paucos cum dolore pareres mundo, quae nunc multiplicem prolem cum exsultatione parturis coelo! Nec esses plus quam femina nunc etiam viros transcendis et quae maledictionem Evae in benedictionem vertisti Mariae. O quam indecenter manus illae sacrae, quae nunc etiam divina revolvunt volumina, curae muliebris obscenitatibus deservirent! Ipse nos a contagiis huiuis caeni, a voluptabris huius luti dignatus est erigere . . . et hoc ipso fortassis exemplo nostro alios quoque litterarum peritos ab hac deterrere praesumptione
>
> [What a hateful loss and grievous misfortune if you had abandoned yourself to the defilement of carnal pleasures only to bear in suffering a few children for the world, when now you are delivered in exultation of numerous progeny for heaven! Nor would you have been more than a woman, whereas now you rise even above men, and have turned the curse of Eve into the blessing of Mary. How unseemly for those holy hands which now turn the pages of sacred books to have to perform degrading services in women's concerns! God himself had thought fit to raise us up from the contamination of this filth and the pleasures of this mire and draw us to him by force . . . and by our example perhaps to deter from our audacity others who are also trained in letters].[19]

Abelard explicitly praises Heloise's metaphorical maternity as an avoidance of the pollution associated with "women's concerns" [*curae muliebris obscenitatibus*]. By transcending "the curse of Eve," Heloise becomes "more than a woman" [*plus quam femina*].

In order to render Heloise exemplary of her sex and, at the same time, to praise her exemplary transcendence of her sex, Abelard has to repress an important part of their shared past. Heloise is not only the spiritual mother of God's daughters, she is also the mother of Abelard's son, and it was her pregnancy that led to the secret marriage and, arguably, to Abelard's castration and the couple's entry into religion. Nowhere is Heloise's nonspiritual maternity acknowledged in Abelard's exultation of the spiritual childbirth that permits her to rise above her physical body. The price of Heloise's exemplarity—of becoming "more than a woman"—is the abjection of the material body that is also a maternal body, an abjection that Abelard constructs as a renunciation of past shared sexual pleasures but also of a part of their past that Heloise has not mentioned: their son.

Abelard exhorts Heloise to accept abjection—to imitate the black bride in holding her body "vile and abject," and to rejoice in her avoidance of "degrading women's concerns." Like the black bride, the spiritual mother is a metaphorical representation of the female body that reveals a neat division between inside and outside, between physical adversity and spiritual worth, and between the desiring, copulating maternal body marked by childbirth, lactation, the tears and excrement of children, and the chaste, contained, transcendent body that reproduces spiritually.

Heloise's third letter to Abelard is characterized in part by a resistance to the metaphorical representation of the female body—and of *her* body. That is, where Abelard subsumes Heloise's desiring maternal body into the allegory of a body that rejects its materiality and rejoices in spirituality, Heloise insists on the body's experience of its materiality. As Linda Georgianna notes in chapter 8 of this volume, in her third letter Heloise responds to Abelard's figurative discussion with "the basic everyday details of monastic life" and "not one of these subjects is treated in the least bit metaphorically by Heloise." One of the "everyday details" on which Heloise insists is the life of the body, emphasized in the form of the material female body, a body characterized by precisely those "degrading women's concerns" that Abelard had counseled her to avoid by becoming more than a woman. Heloise responds to Abelard's call for exemplary abjection, his praise of her as "more than a woman," with a return to "the curse of Eve," the messiness of reproduction that Abelard claims she has transcended. Heloise invokes a female body characterized by its materiality, a wasting, purging body defined by what Abelard calls "degrading women's concerns."

The Menstruating Body

In her third letter Heloise asks Abelard to prescribe a rule for his spiritual daughters since the Rule of St. Benedict is unsuitable for women. She cites a number of exceptions to the Rule allowed by Benedict in recognition of the different qualities and abilities of men, and she asks why there should be no consideration of sexual difference in the Rule:

> Benedictus . . . pro qualitate hominum aut temporum cuncta sic moderatur in regula ut omnia sicut ipsemet uno concludit loco mensurate fiant. . . . Quid, obsecro, ubi iste qui sic ad hominum et temporum qualitatem omnia moderatur ut ab omnibus sine murmuratione perferri queant quae instituuntur? Quid, inquam, de feminis provideret, si eis quoque pariter ut viris regulam institueret? Si enim in quibusdam regulae rigorem pueris, senibus et debilibus pro ipsa naturae debilitate vel infirmitate temperare cogitur, quid de fragili sexu provideret cuius maxime debilis et infirma natura cognoscitur?
>
> [St. Benedict . . . moderates everything in the Rule according to the quality of men or the times, so that, as he himself says at one point, all may be done in moderation. . . . What, I wonder, when he adapts everything to the quality of men and seasons, so that all his regulations can be carried out by everyone without complaint—what provision would he make for women if he laid down a Rule for them like that for men? For if in certain respects he is obliged to modify the strictness of the Rule for the young, the old and weak, according to their natural frailty or infirmity, what would he provide for the weaker sex whose frailty and infirmity is generally known?][20]

Georgianna has shown that Heloise's focus on individual status and ability is part of a twelfth-century debate about the meaning and purpose of monastic life, and she suggests that Heloise's critique of the Benedictine Rule is "similar to her complaint against Abelard in her previous letters: both overlook differences between individuals." In the first part of Heloise's letter, difference is represented as sexual difference, and I want to emphasize the way that her description of women's material bodies corresponds to and counters Abelard's descriptions of women's metaphorical bodies.

To highlight the particular unsuitability of the Benedictine Rule for women's communities, Heloise refers twice to the menstruating female body.[21] First she cites "the monthly purging of women's bodies" that makes the vestimentary requirements of the Benedictine Rule impossible for women to follow: "how can women be concerned with what is written there about . . . tunics or woolen garments worn next to the skin, when the monthly purging of their superfluous humours must avoid such things?" [Quid denique ad ipsas de tunicis aut de laneis ad carnem indumentis, cum earum humoris superflui menstruae purgationes haec omnino refugiant?][22] Heloise uses the purging female body to show the inadequacy of the universal prescriptions of the Benedictine Rule.

Later in her letter when she turns to the question of whether women should be governed by the same dietary restrictions as men, Heloise again uses menstruation to demonstrate the difference between women's bodies and men's bodies. Citing Macrobius as her authority on Aristotle, Heloise claims that women should be allowed food and drink because they are not intoxicated as easily as men are:

> Aristoteles mulieres inquit raro ebriantur crebro senes. . . . Mulier humectissimo est corpore; docet hoc et levitas cutis et splendor, docent praecipue assiduae purgationes superfluo exonerantes corpus humore. Cum ergo epotum vinum in tam largum ceciderit humorem, vim suam perdit . . . nec facile cerebri sedem ferit fortitudine eius exstincta. Item: Muliebre corpus crebris purgationibus deputatum pluribus consertum [est] foraminibus ut pateat in meatus et vias praebeat humori in egestionis exitum conduenti; per haec foramina vapor vini celeriter evanescit. Contra senibus siccum est corpus, quod probat asperitas et squalor cutis
>
> [Aristotle says that women are rarely intoxicated, but old men often. Woman has an extremely humid body, as can be known from her smooth and glossy skin, and especially from her regular purgations which rid the body of superfluous moisture. So when wine is drunk and merged with so general a humidity, it loses its power and does not easily strike the seat of the brain when its strength is extinguished. . . . A woman's body which is destined for frequent purgations is pierced with several holes, so that it opens into channels and provides outlets for the moisture draining away to be dispersed. Through these holes the fumes of wine are quickly released].[23]

Heloise uses menstruation as the privileged example of the unsuitability of the Benedictine Rule for nuns in a logical appeal for a rule written specifically for women, and she situates her appeal in the context of the many modifications of the Rule allowed by Benedict himself. Heloise's third letter offers a lucid and powerful critique of monastic practice, a critique based on sexual difference, on the different strengths and abilities of men and women. As Georgianna notes, this focus on "the power of the particular" is a strong link between Heloise's first two letters and her third. I want to emphasize this link: the third letter continues an implicit debate about the representation of the female body introduced in the letters that precede it. Heloise's representation of the menstruating female body is surely provoked, at least in part, by Abelard's use of the female body as metaphor. She responds to Abelard's second letter by countering the bodies of Abelard's black bride and spiritual mother, neatly divided between a spiritual inside and an abjected material outside, with an unruly female body, a body that does not escape "women's concerns" and whose unruly materiality cannot be contained by its dress or by its outward appearance.

If Heloise insists on material sexual difference and on the experience of the gendered body, it is not in order to exclude women from monastic rule; nor does she link women's bodies to some sort of intellectual inferiority. The correspondence reveals Heloise's views on women—and on gender—as complex and multivalent.[24] Her third letter contains a wide-ranging discourse on bodies and, implicitly, on gender, and I suggest that it is not only a strong voice within a growing critique of monastic practice, as Georgianna has shown, but that it also challenges Abelard's definition of the value of the body and of embodied experience within monasticism. Heloise's menstruating body represents the body that lives with its humors, its products, its wastes, even—potentially—its blackness, and cannot cast them off or abject them because they are part of the experience of subjectivity. This appeal to embodied experience rejects the metaphoricization of the body and the elimination of difference that Abelard's metaphors imply, and it defines the authentic subject of religious devotion as a subject with a body.

The Abject Body

The menstruating female body that Heloise introduces into the correspondence is more than a female counterpart to the male body that is the object of the Benedictine Rule. It is defined by cultural notions of pollution and defilement, the "degrading women's concerns" that Abelard identifies with "the curse of Eve."[25] Notably, however, Heloise does not acknowledge cultural notions of pollution associated with the female body. She does not mention restrictions on menstruating women in the religious community, nor does she repeat Abelard's characterization of women's role in reproduction as a curse. She ignores characterizations of menstruation as polluting or as dangerous, and describes women's monthly purgings as a positive process.

What is interesting in Heloise's representation of the purging female body is that menstruation is *not* part of what makes women's bodies weak or inferior to men's bodies. In a limited sense, menstruation is identified as a strength of women's bodies: because of monthly purging, women are not intoxicated as easily as are men. Yet Heloise does not aim to prove the superiority of one body over another; rather she focuses on the demonstration of difference. I suggest that it is not a coincidence that in this letter about differences between individual abilities, illustrated in the first part by a focus on the physical differences between men and women, Heloise cites menstruation as a privileged example of sexual difference: Heloise transforms a "degrading women's concern" into a strength of women's bodies.

Heloise cites the body that purges as one that cannot be contained by the clothing prescribed by the Benedictine Rule. Her example is a literal one (during menstruation the close-fitting clothing prescribed by the Rule is inappropriate), but it also has a more general importance. The body that escapes its clothing also demonstrates the failure of the Rule to constrain the inside by regulating the outside, and here the menstruating body figuratively illustrates Heloise's repeated assertion that belief cannot be shaped by practice, that outward adherence to monastic rule does not reflect or form interior piety.

Heloise's insistence on the bleeding body reinscribes in the correspondence the abject body that Abelard had attempted to efface through metaphor, and she seems to protest the abjection of the material body that he requires in his definition of the authentic subject of religion as a disembodied subject. Heloise's third letter insists on the instability of an identity that depends on the abjection of the body as a merely metaphoric exterior, and she uses the purging female body as an emblem of the body that cannot be contained or repressed by a change of clothing—or by a change of heart.

Indeed, in her first letter Heloise describes her desiring body in precisely the same terms that she uses to introduce the unruly body in her third letter: the body's relationship to its clothing. In this passage Heloise describes the events that led to Abelard's castration: the marriage, her subsequent removal to a convent, and her adoption of religious dress:

> Solus quippe es qui me contristare, qui me laetificare seu consolari valeas. Et solus es qui plurimum id mihi debeas et nunc maxime cum universa quae iusseris in tantum impleverim ut cum te in aliquo offendere non possem me ipsam pro iussu tuo perdere sustinerem. Et quod maius est dictuque mirabile, in tantam versus est amor insaniam ut quod solum appetebat, hoc ipse sibi sine spe recuperationis auferret, cum ad tuam statim iussionem tam habitum ipsa quam animum immutarem ut te tam corporis mei quam animi unicum possessorem ostenderem. . . . Non matrimonii foedera, non dotes aliquas expectavi, non denique meas voluptates aut voluntates sed tuas, sicut ipse nosti, adimplere studui. Et si uxoris nomen sanctius ac validius videtur, dulcius mihi semper exstitit amicae vocabulum aut, si non indigneris, concubinae vel scorti, ut, quo me videlicet pro te amplius humiliarem, ampliorem apud te consequerer gratiam et sic etiam excellentiae tuae gloriam minus laederem
>
> [You alone have the power to make me sad, to bring me happiness or comfort; you alone have so great a debt to repay me, particularly now when I have carried out all your orders so implicitly that when I was powerless to oppose you in anything, I found strength at your command to destroy myself. I did more, strange to say—my love rose to such heights of madness that it robbed itself of what it most desired beyond hope of recovery, when immediately at your bidding I changed by clothing along with my mind, in order to prove you the sole possessor of my body and my will alike . . . it was not my own pleasures and wishes I sought to gratify, as you well know, but yours. The name of wife may seem more sacred or more binding, but sweeter for me will always be the word mistress, or, if you will permit me, that of concubine or whore. I believed that the more I humbled myself on your account, the more gratitude I should win from you, and also the less damage I should do to the brightness of your reputation].[26]

Heloise's equation of sexual desire and the desire to submit to Abelard, explicitly evoked in other passages of the letters, is signaled here by her willingness to change clothes, to put on religious dress. In his first two letters to Heloise, Abelard repeatedly admonishes her to make a similar submission to God. Heloise claims that she cannot—while she might put on religious dress and live chastely, her desire cannot be restrained: "How can it be called repentance for sins, however great the mortification of the flesh, if the mind still retains the will to sin and is on fire with its old desires?" [Quo modo etiam poenitentia peccatorum dicitur, quantacumque sit corporis afflictio, si mens adhuc ipsam peccandi retinet voluntatem, et pristinis aestuat desideriis?][27] In her third letter, Heloise changes registers: she no longer speaks of a persisting desire, but she continues to insist on the relationship between the body and the soul, between the flesh and the mind.

Women's association with the flesh is a commonplace of medieval theological thinking and of medieval misogyny. Karma Lochrie has discussed this association at length, underscoring the way that medieval writers define the flesh as neither fully body nor soul, a permeable boundary that threatens the integrity of the body and soul.[28] Lochrie suggests that the characterization of woman as flesh also provides a potential position of subversion for the female mystic: "By occupying and exploiting her position as flesh, the woman writer has recourse to a power derived from the taboo which defines her and which she breaks with her speech."[29] Caroline Walker Bynum has richly documented and analyzed the bodily practices of medieval women mystics, demonstrating that in the discourse and religious practice of these women, bodilyness provided access to the sacred. She links the importance of the experience of the body in late medieval religious experience to a new view of the person as a psychosomatic unity, as body *and* soul.[30] While the association of women with flesh, along with the potentially subversive speech that this association makes possible, and the view of the body as a site of access to the sacred are descriptions of women's religious practice similar to the ones I have used to describe Heloise's presentation of the body in her third letter, I maintain that Heloise is insisting on something different. She does not valorize the body or the experiences of the body as an access to the sacred. Although she stresses the different strengths and abilities of individual men and women, she situates them in a common experience of the body. Indeed, Heloise adamantly does not seek heroic or extraordinary spiritual experiences. Rather, she seeks to integrate the body as a site of individual experience into the definition of the religious subject; she seeks to show that the experiences of outside and inside cannot be neatly separated into an abjected exterior and a cherished interior. She reclaims the material body that Abelard had effaced through metaphor.

As Georgianna argues in chapter 8, the female body introduces and grounds the extended questioning of the possibility of shaping an interior spiritual life through exterior regulation that dominates the second half of Heloise's third letter. Even as she requests a new rule, one better suited to women's bodies, she rejects the idea that the regulation of the exterior is a sign of interior worth: "we should care little for what is performed outwardly and called indifferent" [quae fiunt exterius, et indifferentia vocantur, non magnopere curanda esse docemur]; "it is not so much what things are done as the spirit in which they are done that we must consider if we wish to please him who tests the heart and the loins, and sees in hidden places . . ." [Non itaque magnopere quae fiunt sed quo animo fiant pensandum est, si ille placere studemus, qui cordis et renum probator est, et in abscondito videt . . .].[31] Like Abelard, Heloise locates authentic subjectivity in intention, in the spirit; unlike Abelard, she rejects the idea that subjectivity can be formed or transformed by actions.

Heloise's use of the menstruating body in her third letter is an essentializing move whose rhetorical force is directed toward Abelard's effacement of gender. She valorizes the experience of the material body, of the body whose materiality is defined according to biological functions. The experience of the material body is not limited to menstruation in Heloise's letter, however, but extends to the portrayal of women's lack of physical strength and their inability to work as hard as men. Heloise replies to

Abelard's metaphoricization of the female body and call for a life of the mind, with a call for a rule that acknowledged the life of the body, a body that menstruates, a body characterized by "the curse of Eve."

The Gendered Body

If Heloise's bleeding body is a prominent image in her third letter, it displaces the body that dominates the earlier letters and for which the love story is perhaps best known. Abelard's castrated body is the subject of Heloise's "old perpetual complaint against God" and the reason for the couple's entry into religion. It is a body whose identity is founded on an anatomical lack, and it stands alongside the female body described by Heloise as a body defined by its (lack of) reproductive organs.[32] Yet although the castrated body is defined according to essential gender identity, the healing experience of castration is available to Heloise.[33]

> Perpende altissimum in nobis divinae consilium pietatis, et quam misericorditer iudicium suum Dominus in correptionem verterit et quam prudenter malis quoque ipsis usus sit et impietatem pie deposuerit ut unius partis corporis mei iustissima plaga duabus mederetur animabus. Confer periculum et liberationis modum. Confer languorem et medicinam. Meritorum causas inspice et miserationis affectus admirare
>
> [Consider the magnanimous design of God's mercy for us, the compassion with which the Lord directed his judgment towards our chastisement, the wisdom whereby he made use of evil itself and mercifully set aside our impiety, so that by a wholly justified wound in a single part of my body he might heal two souls. Compare our danger and manner of deliverance, compare the sickness and the medicine].[34]

Abelard's castration has the paradoxical status of a medicinal wound, an injury that has healing powers. It is a sacrifice that is figuratively available to Heloise—Abelard has suffered so that both may be saved, as he repeatedly emphasizes in his exhortation to renounce the body for the heart.[35] Castration thus enacts a literal casting off of the body, an experience that Abelard invites Heloise to share and to imitate.

Abelard's figural representations of the black bride and the spiritual mother are also models of the renunciation of the body. Whereas the racial position in Abelard's rhetoric might appear uniquely available to the female subject—it is gendered by the passive sexual position of the bride and by the analogy with the couple's secret marriage[36]—the maternal position (once the body has been abjected) can be assumed by the male subject: the gendering of Abelard's model of reproduction does not restrict it to women. Abelard does not become a spiritual mother, but it is a position to which he had aspired. He exults in Heloise's "numerous progeny for heaven" while lamenting his own failure to reproduce: "How great an interest the talent of your own wisdom pays daily to the Lord in the many spiritual daughters you have borne for him, while I remain totally barren and labor in vain among the sons of perdition" [Tuae vero prudentiae talentum quantas quotidie Domino refert usuras, quae multas Domino iam spirituales filias peperisti, me penitus sterili permanente, et in filiis perditionis inaniter laborante].[37] Abelard's claim to sterility places him in the (failed) position of the spiritual mother that he holds out to Heloise as the desired alternative to messy maternity.

Abelard's repeated exhortations to renounce the body's desire and to live in the desire for God would seem to have provoked an assenting response in Heloise's third letter. Despite the lack of an extended explanation for why she finally consents to abandon the passionate discourse of desire that characterized her earlier letters—Peter von Moos calls this omission the "silence of Heloise"—the abbess's change of subject and of tone are often regarded as, in Barbara Newman's words, "the ultimate victory of the masculine voice over the female voice: not only a personal triumph of Abelard over Heloise, but a victory for the poetics of castration over the discourse of desire."[38] However, if "authenticity becomes a question of proper monastic observance under an appropriate Rule" in Heloise's third letter, as Newman suggests, Heloise seems to argue that the definition of an "appropriate Rule" depends on an appropriate recognition of the body.[39] Her descriptions of the bleeding female body are simultaneously a response to and a refusal of Abelard's denial of embodied experience in his metaphoricization of the female body and in his invitation to share his castration symbolically.

Christian Bodies

Heloise repeatedly cites the menstruating body as a concrete exception to a monastic rule that does not recognize gender difference, and as an emblem of difference the menstruating body figures the many individual weaknesses and particular needs that she cites in support of her request for a rule written especially for women. Georgianna's nuanced reading, in chapter 8, of how Heloise's arguments fit into a nascent evangelical movement emphasizes the importance of her insistence on the particular strengths and weaknesses of individual men and women. The insistence on sexual difference and on menstruation plays a dual role in Heloise's argument. The menstruating body is an emblem of difference—women menstruate, men do not—but at the same time it seems to figure a more general materiality, the embodied experiences of both women and men that are the basis for Heloise's call for exceptions to the Benedictine Rule.

As she reiterates her call for a monastic rule that accounts for differences among individuals, and especially between men and women, Heloise turns to the goal of all such regulation in the Christian life: "Perpende itaque quam longe absistat ab omni rationis discretione eiusdem regulae professione tam feminas quam viros obligari, eademque sarcina tam debiles quam fortes onerari. Satis esse nostrae arbitror infirmitati, si nos ipsis Ecclesiae rectoribus et, qui in sacris ordinibus constituti sunt clericis tam continentiae quam abstinentiae virtus aequaverit" [Consider then how far removed it is from all reason and good sense if both women and men are bound by profession of a common Rule, and the same burden is laid on the weak as on the strong. I think it should be sufficient for our infirmity if the virtue of continence and also of abstinence makes us the equals of the rulers of the Church themselves and of the clergy who are confirmed in holy orders].[40] Heloise goes on to cite a sermon of John Chrysostom in which he locates the difference between laymen and monks only in the layman's freedom to sleep with his wife, and she concludes:

> Ex quibus quidem verbis aperte colligitur quod quisquis evangelicis praeceptis continentiae virtutem addiderit, monasticam perfectionem implebit. Atque utinam ad hoc nostra religio conscendere posset ut Evangelium impleret, non transcenderet, nec plusquam christianae appeteremus esse. Hinc profecto, ni fallor, sancti decreverunt Patres non ita nobis sicut viris generalem aliquam regulam quasi novam legem praefigere, nec magnitudine votorum nostram infirmitatem onerare

[From these words it can easily be inferred that anyone who adds the virtue of continence to the precepts of the Gospel will achieve monastic perfection. Would that our religion could rise to this height—to carry out the Gospel, not to go beyond it, lest we attempt to become more than Christians! Surely this is the reason (if I am not mistaken) why the holy Fathers decided not to lay down a general rule for us as for men, like a new law, or to burden our weakness with a great number of vows].[41]

In chapter 8 Georgianna notes that Heloise's conclusion does not seem logically to follow from the passage she has cited from Chrysostom: Heloise's suggestion that the Church Fathers may have chosen not to write a rule for women because they feared going "beyond" the Gospel would seem to apply equally well to rules for men. Georgianna explains Heloise's restriction of her conclusion as a hesitation on Heloise's part to draw radical conclusions—rather than characterizing all monastic rules as an excess, Heloise suggests merely that the choice not to write a women's rule may be due to a hesitation to go beyond the guidance offered by the Gospel. However, it also might be possible to see Heloise's rhetorical return to the particular status of women religious as a recollection of Abelard's negation of gendered bodies in his metaphor of spiritual maternity: Heloise's call for moderation in the monastic rule, the rejection of the goal of becoming "more than Christians" [*plusquam Christianae*] surely echoes Abelard's valorization of spiritual motherhood as a way of becoming "more than a woman" [*plus quam feminina*] by avoiding the "degrading women's concerns" associated with the material maternal body.[42] This association is further suggested by the discussion that follows this passage: after citing Chrysostom, Heloise goes on to discuss women's weaknesses in terms of their reluctant continence and their rashness in taking vows, examples that recall Heloise's willing seduction by Abelard, her precipitous and reluctant entry into religion, and her claims to hypocritical chastity in her earlier letters.

Heloise continues her argument in favor of a new monastic rule for women by moving from the weaknesses of women to a strength: "It is well known that women can be sustained on less nourishment and at less cost than men, and medicine teaches us that they are not so easily intoxicated" [Constat quippe multo parciore sumptu et alimonia minore feminas quam viros sustentari posse, nec eas tam leviter inebriari physica protestatur].[43] And here Heloise introduces the menstruating body as a positive value.

In her third letter to Abelard, Heloise does not dispute the place of continence in monasticism. What she does seem to protest is the image of a body that transcends itself, as in Abelard's description of the abjection of the body as a material "outside" that is less real than a spiritual "inside." Yet Heloise's repeated references to a body that bleeds are more than a rewriting of Abelard's metaphors that continues the questioning, correction, and disputing of images exchanged in the first four letters. If Heloise rejects the Christian heroics located in the renunciation of the body, as Georgianna discusses, it is no longer because she insists on her physical desire for Abelard. In her third letter desire has been relocated to the heart and constrained by the body—the writing hand that bends to her will when her heart will not—and the body has become the emblem of a common experience of individual weaknesses and abilities. Heloise argues for the body as a universal condition with particular experiences, and she makes embodied experience a condition of authentic identity. Neither more than a Christian nor more than a woman, Heloise claims the identity of a Christian woman.

Notes

I am very grateful to colleagues who offered perceptive readings of this chapter in an earlier version. Thanks to Catherine Brown, Deborah Covino, Karma Lochrie, Patricia A. Renda, and James A. Schultz. Errors and inconsistencies that remain are all my own.

1. For a complete list of the extant correspondence, see Martin Irvine, "Heloise and the Gendering of the Literate Subject," p. 89. Irvine stresses that the correspondence "developed both intertextually, presupposing the genre of the Latin literary epistle, specific letter collections, and other classical and Christian literature, and intratextually, constructed with self-reflexive gestures and references to earlier statements in their own exchange." (p. 89). In chapter 10 of this volume Donna Alfano Bussell situates the letters in the medieval *ars dictaminis* and emphasizes the third letter's place in that tradition.
2. Modern editors and translators have impressed on readers the seeming rupture that Heloise's third letter causes in the correspondence. Muckle classifies the first four letters as "Personal Letters" and Heloise's third letter as a "Letter on Religious Life." Radice's translation divides the correspondence into "Personal Letters" and, beginning with Heloise's third letter, "Letters of Direction." A popular paperback translation into modern French ends after the fourth letter and does not include what the translator calls the "impersonal" letters relating to the administration of the Paraclete. *Abélard et Héloïse: Correspondance,* Paul Zumthor, trans., n., p. 9. Linda Georgianna discusses this assumption and implications of this practice in chapter 8.
3. See Catherine Brown, "*Muliebriter:* Doing Gender in the Letters of Heloise," pp. 25–51; Irvine, "Heloise and the Gendering of the Literate Subject"; Barbara Newman, *From Virile Woman to WomanChrist: Studies in Medieval Religion and Literature,* pp. 46–75; and Peter Dronke, "Heloise and Marianne: Some Reconsiderations"; and *Women Writers,* pp. 127–34. See also Donna Bussell (chapter 8) and Linda Georgianna (Chapter 10) in this volume.
4. The use of female imagery to represent religious sentiment is not newly invented by Abelard and Heloise, of course. Indeed, Caroline Walker Bynum's *Jesus as Mother: Studies in the Spirituality of the High Middle Ages* demonstrates the prominence of maternal imagery in Cistercian writing, pp. 110–69.
5. I am considering the correspondence as an authentic exchange of letters between Abelard and Heloise. Barbara Newman's nuanced and definitive study of the letters' authenticity is the most recent intervention into the debate over who wrote the letters, and she offers a thorough history of the question. (*From Virile Woman to WomanChrist,* pp. 46–75). Irvine affirms the authenticity of the collection based on an examination of the manuscripts. ("Heloise and the Gendering of the Literate Subject," pp. 87–89). See also Georgianna's discussion in chapter 8 of the critic's desire to prove which Heloise is most authentic, the passionate lover of the first two letters or the abbess who composed the letters dealing with questions of religious life and devotion. In chapter 10 of this volume, Bussell also discusses the desire to find an "authentic" Heloise. For an exploration of ideological and methodological questions in the authenticity debate, see chapter 2 by John Marenbon in this volume.
6. Several recent studies have explored the rhetorical gendering of the writing subject in the letters of Abelard and Heloise, suggesting various ways in which the correspondents construct identities based on culturally defined gender positions: Brown, "*Muliebriter*"; Irvine, "Heloise and the Gendering of the Literate Subject" and "Abelard and (Re)Writing the Male Body: Castration, Identity, and Remasculization"; Bonnie Wheeler, "Origenary Fantasies: Abelard's Castration and Confession," pp. 107–28; and Claire Nouvet, "The Discourse of the 'Whore': An Economy of Sacrifice," pp. 750–73, especially 173–43 on Heloise's manipulation of definitions.
7. Radice 145.

8. *Ep.* 6, ed. Muckle 241 (Radice 159).
9. "Exaudi, obsecro, aure cordis, quod saepius audisti aure corporis." *Ep.* 3, ed. Muckle 75 (Radice 123).
10. "Tertio vero veterem illam et assiduam querelam tuam in Deum adiecisti, de modo videlicet nostrae conversionis ad Deum et crudelitate proditionis illius in me commissae," *Ep.* 5, ed. Muckle 83 (Radice 137). See also *Ep.* 5, ed. Muckle 87 (Radice 145): "Superest tandem ut ad antiquam illam, ut diximus, et assiduam querimoniam tuam veniamus qua videlicet de nostrae conversionis modo Deum potius accusare praesumis quam glorificare, ut iustum est, velis" [I come at last to what I have called your old perpetual complaint, in which you presume to blame God for the manner of our entry into religion instead of wishing to glorify him as you justly should].
11. Peter Brown, *The Body and Society: Men, Women, and Sexual Renunciation in Early Christianity;* Aline Rousselle, *Porneia: On Desire and the Body in Antiquity.*
12. Abelard's discussion of the Ethiopian bride takes place in the context of numerous medieval commentaries of the Song of Songs. For an examination of this tradition see Ann W. Astell, *The Song of Songs in the Middle Ages,* and E. Ann Matter, *The Voice of My Beloved: The Song of Songs in Western Medieval Christianity.* Abelard's discussion of the black bride has yet to be examined in light of the implicit relation among blackness, abjection, and the racially defined female subject that it constructs. For a discussion of the bride and racial difference in English Renaissance lyrics, see Kim F. Hall, *Things of Darkness: Economies of Race and Gender in Early Modern England,* p. 115.
13. *Ep.* 5, ed. Muckle 84 (Radice 139).
14. Radice 138.
15. Radice 141. On the notion of mastery inherent in Heloise's humility and submission, see Nouvet, "The Discourse of the 'Whore,'" pp. 761–63.
16. Julia Kristeva, *Powers of Horror: An Essay on Abjection,* p. 4.
17. Brown, "*Muliebriter,*" pp. 38–39.
18. *Ep.* 5, ed. Muckle 84 (Radice 140).
19. *Ep.* 5, ed. Muckle 90–91 (Radice 150).
20. *Ep.* 6, ed. Muckle 244 (Radice 162–63).
21. In chapter 8 Georgianna suggests that Heloise's rhetorical strategy may have been intended "to shock Abelard into recognizing their differences." Peter Dronke sees it as "a touch of humour" (*Women Writers,* p. 130).
22. *Ep.* 6, ed. Muckle 242 (Radice 169).
23. *Ep.* 6, ed. Muckle 246; ellipses in original (Radice 166).
24. Brown, "*Muliebriter,*" pp. 39–43; Newman, *From Virile Woman to WomanChrist,* pp. 68–75.
25. Cultural constructions of pollution and defilement are not static or self-evident, but I cannot explore the historical and cultural associations of pollution with the female body in the space of this chapter. The best overview of medieval ideas about menstruation is still Charles T. Wood, "The Doctors' Dilemma: Sin, Salvation, and the Menstrual Cycle in Medieval Thought." Jocelyn Wogan-Browne discusses the leaky body in the context of treatises on virginity in "Chaste Bodies: Frames and Experiences," pp. 24–42. The classic study of notions of pollution associated with the body (and the one against which dissenting views are articulated) is Mary Douglas's *Purity and Danger: An Analysis of the Concepts of Pollution and Taboo.* In an extension of Douglas's work, Julia Kristeva emphasizes that what is abjected in rituals of containment that accompany pollution taboos are bodily wastes—excrement, blood, the decaying body: precisely those bodily secretions which transgress the boundaries of inside and outside (*Powers of Horror,* pp. 56–89). The castrated body may also be constructed as polluting, as Claire Nouvet shows in her discussion of Abelard's castration in the context of Old Testament rituals of sacrifice ("La castration d'Abélard: impasse et substitution").
26. *Ep.* 2, ed. Muckle 70–71 (Radice 113).

27. *Ep.* 4, ed. Muckle 80 (Radice 132).
28. Karma Lochrie, *Margery Kempe and Translations of the Flesh,* pp. 11–55, especially p. 38.
29. Lochrie, *Margery Kempe,* p. 4.
30. Caroline Walker Bynum, "The Female Body and Religious Practice in the Late Middle Ages," in *Fragmentation and Redemption,* pp. 222–23.
31. *Ep.* 6, ed. Muckle 251 (Radice 176); *Ep.* 6, ed. Muckle 251 (Radice 175).
32. In "Abelard and (Re)Writing the Male Body: Castration, Identity, and Remasculization," Martin Irvine has discussed how the gender of Abelard's body is questioned by his contemporaries. Whether Abelard is male or less than male, the castrated body is still defined in relation to its masculinity. See also Wheeler, "Origenary Fantasies."
33. Brown notes that Heloise "repeatedly reaches for a properly gendered analogue to [Abelard's] mutilation," and argues, along with Nouvet, that Heloise's apparent self-abasement is part of a rhetorical contest with Abelard in which the correspondents share the rhetorical agenda of "[asserting] Heloise's mastery (over words, over herself, over Abelard) by seeming to humiliate her" ("*Muliebriter,*" p. 34). See Nouvet, "The Discourse of the 'Whore,'" p. 761.
34. *Ep.* 5, ed. Muckle 89 (Radice 147).
35. Nouvet offers a nuanced reading of the castration in terms of sacrifice in "La castration d'Abélard."
36. Brown, "*Muliebriter,*" p. 39; Peggy Kamuf, *Fictions of Feminine Desire,* pp. 29–31. Astell discusses the feminine position of self-surrender in *The Song of Songs in the Middle Ages,* especially pp. 10–15.
37. *Ep.* 5, ed. Muckle 90 (Radice 150).
38. Peter von Moos, "Le silence d'Héloïse et les idéologies modernes," In Colloque, pp. 425–68; Newman, *From Virile Woman to WomanChrist,* p. 74.
39. Newman, *From Virile Woman to WomanChrist,* p. 74.
40. *Ep.* 6, ed. Muckle 244 (Radice 163–64).
41. *Ep.* 6, ed. Muckle 245 (Radice 164–65).
42. *Ep.* 6, ed. Muckle 245; *Ep.* 5, ed. Muckle 90.
43. *Ep.* 6, ed. Muckle 245 (Radice 166).

CHAPTER 10

HELOISE REDRESSED: RHETORICAL ENGAGEMENT AND THE BENEDICTINE RITE OF INITIATION IN HELOISE'S THIRD LETTER

Donna Alfano Bussell

Heloise's third letter is her treatise on the relation between infirmitas *and* virtus. *Using a request formulated in an* imitatio *of the Benedictine Initiation Rite, she draws on both pagan and monastic literary traditions to propose that men and women religious in general, and she and Abelard in particular, must share the material and relational* habitus *of the monastic life if they are to experience the spiritual* communitas *and enduring* amicitia *that is its goal.*

> [Heloise] herself was not ashamed to write in her letters to her beloved, whom she loved so well that she called him father and lord, strange words that many people would think absurd.
>
> —Jean de Meun, "The Advice of a Friend," *The Romance of the Rose*

In the history of criticism on Heloise (when her letters have been regarded as authentic), the twelfth-century abbess's display of passion in her first two letters of correspondence with Abelard, captivates us as a natural, unfeigned expression.[1] However, her later response to Abelard in her third letter, the seemingly arid exegesis of scripture, and other texts, to support her request for a woman's rule makes her a much less enchanting literary subject. Nonetheless, the analytical tone Heloise adopts in *Ep.* 6 represents an intriguing departure from the impassioned *voces* she employs in her first two letters. This change, however, has proven difficult for many scholars to accept at face value without thinking of it as representing either a form of emotional (and female) manipulation or evidence of some repression of Heloise's passion.[2] The psychobehavioral meaning assumed to be operating behind Heloise's shift in rhetorical strategy is discernible in the critical effort to determine whether it is Abelard or Heloise who exerts the stronger influence on the other partner in their debate (presumably Abelard in much of the critical discussion until now).[3]

These debates have transpired in response to a surplus of relatively recent theories that try to explain Heloise's third letter as a work signifying a rather puzzling "conversion." Linda Georgianna, in her perceptive reading of *Ep.* 6 as Heloise's critique of monastic life, observes that the difference between Heloise's first two letters and her third presents critics with a gap that they often try to fill by imposing a linear psychological unity on Heloise's letters. (See chapter 8.) When her letters are used to trace the social-cultural phenomena of misogyny, the Heloise of *Ep.* 6 is transformed (or transforms herself) from the spirited lover of her two earlier letters to a stoic abbess who bends herself to Abelard's will. To interpret *Ep.* 6, a priori, as a work that charts Heloise's progressive attempt to salvage or manipulate her previous relationship (even for some greater purpose such as a collusion with Abelard) has left the content of her argument to languish relatively unexamined, as if this were a matter of secondary rather than primary importance.

An experienced abbess like Heloise needs little guidance from Abelard on the pragmatic issues she raises in *Ep.* 6, such as the comportment required of nuns when they receive guests or the specifications for female undergarments to accommodate menstruating women. Why Heloise would bring up such issues in this letter is as mystifying as the apparent minimization of her ardor. There are two usual answers to this question. The alleged discrepancy between Heloise's "passion" and her "competence" has suggested to some scholars, as I have noted, that her technical discussion of the religious life in *Ep.* 6 signifies her capitulation to Abelard's attempt to silence her desire, expressions that reveal a weakness not only troubling to Abelard but also to recent scholars. Although Georgianna argues in chapter 8 that *Ep.* 6 does not represent any kind of "defeat or conversion" in Heloise, for example, she nonetheless regards Heloise's argument in *Ep.* 6 as unsettling because of the neediness implied by the request for a woman's rule: "Heloise's argument for a new rule seems rather technical. . . . Her third letter provides proof that she is still searching, intellectually as well as emotionally, and is best understood as a more institutionally centered version of what she has asked of Abelard all along: consolation and guidance for an unruly heart. . . ." Other scholars explain this apparently dispassionate request for a woman's rule by theorizing that Heloise has some programmatic agenda, perhaps in collaboration with Abelard, and composes these works to teach the nuns at the Paraclete about some aspect of proper behavior or God's grace or, perhaps, to support Abelard's status as a teacher in the face of the feminizing ridicule aimed at him by his enemies.[4] While I agree with Alcuin Blamires' argument in chapter 12 of this volume that Heloise "plays on . . . Abelard's misplaced sense of security about her religious role" and his negligence toward the Paraclete, I do not think, as Blamires does, that Heloise is seeking a rule that is "seriously operable by women such as herself." Critics who invoke Heloise as a woman seeking guidance (even only as a show of support or as a partner in education) find in *Ep.* 6 a woman who cannot help but finally subject her woman's heart to patristic constructs of control, institutional or otherwise.

The ensuing critical discussion often has been limited, implicitly or explicitly, by imagining Heloise in these terms; we pose questions that address how Heloise either reinforces or challenges rigid patristic definitions of sexual identity. These kinds of questions invoke three problematic, and as I will argue from *Ep.* 6, erroneous premises: first, and most important, that Heloise's rhetorical strategy primarily informs us of her interior state; second, that as a woman subjected to cultural and theological expressions of misogyny, Heloise has internalized (or otherwise accepts) certain misogynist tenets of sexual identity without question or with minimal modulation; and, third, that the formulaic and rigid constructs of gender identity articulated in some Christian and classical texts are in fact enacted in the ways Abelard and Heloise interact and communicate with one another.[5] Although the problem of sexual identity is central to Heloise's third letter, I would like to propose that she takes up this concern as one part of a larger and nuanced ethical debate with Abelard on the relationship between the body and sin, a topic that she examines through her exegesis of two important texts: the Song of Songs and the Rule of St. Benedict.[6]

I propose that *Ep.* 6 should be read as a work of medieval epistolography in the tradition of a paraenetic letter, and would like to add to the argument that Heloise be regarded as an exegete in her own right.[7] She responds specifically to the definitions of *infirmitas* and *virtus* Abelard advances in his exegesis of the Song of Songs in *Ep.* 5 and, as I will argue, uses the structural and textual topoi of the Rule to rebut Abelard's construct of the monastic habit as a signifier of penance. Her interpretation counters Abelard's argument that the penitent's subsequent acceptance of separation from the material-social world is the proper response to wearing the habit. Heloise proposes that the habit is a signifier of a new wedding between the body and a distinct, local *communitas.* The social relations with other corporeal beings in a monastic community are essential to the practice of their spirituality.

Heloise posits that their personal past is contiguous with their corporate religious present because the spiritual expression open to them in the religious life requires that they accept all the physical and social realities of monastic life. These material and corporeal realties of their current existence are not burdens, but potentially good and necessary for the practice of spirituality. Moreover, Heloise argues that the creation of such a community locally in the Paraclete is a duty that she and Abelard are uniquely equipped to share because the Paraclete itself is a consolation born out of their personal history. (See chapter 7 herein for Jane Chance's analysis of creation and garden imagery). The primary secular paradigms of Christian community are to be brought into play. The relational dyads of secular marriage and the secular household ("husband-wife," "parent-child," "lord-servant," and "brother-sister") should be considered thoughtfully as the models for their regular life. In Abelard's reading of the Song of Songs in *Ep.* 5, he treats the paradox of *infirmitas* as that which is necessarily associated with the body, and particularly represented in the feminized figures such as the Bride whose sensuality requires that she be cloistered. *Virtus* is associated with the noncorporeal spiritual state toward which he strives postcastration. In this state, Abelard can adopt a distinct, advantageous persona: the masculinized eunuch figure who is another manifestation of the Christian warrior facing danger. Heloise responds in *Ep.* 6 by arguing that Abelard's distinctions and subsequent interpretation of the habit's significance for both of them contradicts the principles of *modus* outlined in the Rule.

Heloise uses the Benedictine initiation ceremony to complicate Abelard's privileging one member of the dyad over the other, male over female or vice versa, so that she may challenge his notion of the body as an object of penitence. The Benedictine Rule, particularly Chapter 58, *De Disciplina Suscipiendorum Fratrum* [The discipline of receiving brothers], gives her a theological and monastic model from which she illustrates the necessary connection between body and soul in the creation of the social body that forms the local monastic community. Chapter 58 of the Rule outlines the three elements of the Rite of Initiation, a ceremony whose elements enact this union of the individual body into the corporate body. The ceremony is conducted before the entire Benedictine community. A novice begins by stating that he understands and agrees to follow the Rule; this is his *promissio.* He then conveys his body and property to the local Benedictine community in a written document laid on the altar, his *petitio.* Third, he requests that the abbot accept his pledge in a prayer, his *oratio,* addressed to the abbot. The Rite of Initiation thus invokes a double movement of social-physical incorporation before the altar. In the first movement, the novice is active, a suitor seeking admission to the house, with the abbot the attentive and receptive patron. Once the novice has offered his *promissio* and *petitio,* the abbot must signal his acceptance of the novice by removing the *petitio* from the altar. In the second movement, the novice is surrounded by his new brothers; he is now the attentive and responsive new member. The novice allows himself to be stripped of his earthly clothes and redressed in the habit. In this act that serves as a guiding image in Heloise's argument in *Ep.* 6, the novice is physically invested with the community's identity in an intrusive manner that suggests the totality of the commitment required: "Then and there in the oratory, he is to be stripped of everything of his own that he is wearing and clothed in what belongs to the monastery. The clothing taken from him is to be put away and kept safely in the wardrobe, so that, should he ever agree to the devil's suggestion and leave the monastery—which God forbid—he can be stripped of the clothing of the monastery before he is cast out."[8] The Latin original below conveys the material essence of this spiritual act in the verbs of stripping [*exatur*] that suggest that the outsider's, the novice's, physical being is necessarily intertwined with that of his new spiritual family. By discarding more neutral terms for dressing, such as *vestire,* or undressing, such as *nudare, deponere,* in favor of terms such as *induatur,* the Rule's language suggests that the novice's new corporate, spiritual identity is merged with his particular physical body: "Mox ergo in oratorio exuatur rebus propriis quibus vestitus est et induatur rebus monasterii. Illa autem vestimenta quibus exutus est reponantur in vestiario conservanda, ut si aliquando suadenti diabolo consenserit ut egrediatur de monasterio—quot absit—tunc exutus rebus monasterii proiciatur."

Investiture under the Rule, then, is neither a private act nor an act of contrition for past sins of the body invested with the habit, but rather a willing dispossession of one kind of material body for the sake of embracing a body of a higher order that is not entirely noncorporeal. If the new monk were to reject the habit, he would repudiate the local, material body to which he had wed himself.

Heloise is sensitive to the physical as well as the spiritual resonances in this dance of initiation and submission between the novice and the abbot and the potential in this imagery for understanding the fluid nature of "masculine" (dominant, spiritual) and "feminine" (weak, corporeal) roles adopted in the course of monastic life. Abelard, not unlike his patristic model Jerome, characterizes the Bride in *Ep.* 5 as one whose feminized and desiring body requires a strict cloistering through which she rightfully exists only for the Bridegroom in their bedchamber. Consequently, the Bride must flee the table outside where the corporeal familial and social bodies are manifested. This position impoverishes the habit by turning this sign of communal inclusion into one of exclusion: "Ipsa quippe nigredinis deformitas occultum potius quam manifestum, et secretum magis quam publicum amat. Et quae talis est uxor, secreta potius viri gaudia quam manifesta desiderat et in lecto magis vult sentiri quam in mensa videri . . . et earum viri ut illis oblectentur, magis eas in cubiculum introducunt quam ad publicum educunt" [Indeed the disfigurement of her blackness makes her choose what is secret and not known to all, and any such wife desires private, not public delights with her husband, and *would rather be known in bed than seen at the table* . . . their husbands take them into a bedroom to enjoy them rather than parade them before the world].[9] Heloise challenges Abelard's argument that the habit signifies the decision to separate from a larger community in favor of an exclusive, private relation with the Bridegroom. By receiving the coarse clothing of the community, she argues, the religious do not agree to isolate themselves. Rather, they agree to bind themselves to a complex of interconnected relationships: spousal, fraternal, paternal, student-master. The novice's contract with the local community is what constitutes his special relationship within the hierarchies of the larger church. To borrow a term from Peggy McCracken's discussion in chapter 9, Heloise adopts an "essentializing" strategy. Heloise uses the rigid construct of woman's special weak nature (always the lesser member in these dyads due to her menstruating body) as the starting point from which to formulate a more subtle definition of *infirmitas* from texts written by and for men.

The *Ars Dictaminis* and the "Male Textual Culture" of the Rule

For Abelard and Heloise, theories of masculine and feminine personae provide a range of commonplaces that permit them to make their letters performative in the ways learned people "played" themselves in twelfth-century rhetoric. The Rule, scripture, and a variety of classical and patristic texts are freely used to distinguish the various forms of weakness and strength found in any human community. What Heloise ostensibly begins as a petition for a woman's rule is a rebuke to Abelard for his nonmaterial and nonrelational analysis of the habit as a mark of disfigurement and his uncritical adherence to the interpretation that prescribes vilification and isolation of the body in order to promote spiritual maturation of that interiority beneath the habit. The gap that Heloise addresses is the logical inconsistency she finds in the difference Abelard suggests exists between the corporeal feminine domain and the spiritual masculine domain. Heloise's counterproposal in *Ep.* 6 is a thoughtful treatise on *infirmitas* and *virtus,* and the *ex infirmitate* topos is a tool she employs effectively to structure her exhortations to Abelard

As the writer of a paraenetic letter, Heloise uses a recognized topos, *ex infirmitate feminarum* [arguing from the weakness of women], to continue a conversation with Abelard for reasons beyond her own loss and discontent. She directs the exhortation at Abelard first and foremost as his friend. This should not be surprising, except that we have so infrequently considered Heloise as a scholar in her own right with full access to the means of address and redress available in the dictaminal tradition. Abelard uses his first letter to Heloise (*Ep.* 3) to respond to her request for consolation using familiar formulas of exhortation and admonition. There is nothing unexpected or unusually harsh in this response. In fact, his letters of exhortation are written because a substantial relationship exists between the two of them that allows Abelard to write as a teacher advising his student, or as an elder addressing a younger friend or family member. The extended literary and philosophical topics treated in epistolary form are supposed to comfort and encourage grief-stricken recipients by advising them to subdue grief through the writer's rebuke and appeal to reason. The writer's social authority over the recipient permits him to frame the recipient's previous state of mind as logically and morally untenable. It is notable that the hortatory mode Heloise chooses in *Ep.* 6, in and of itself, demonstrates that she too assumes this privilege of social authority that has long been thought to exist only in friendships between men.

Heloise's use of her own social authority is evident in all her letters. It is not a matter of whether the emotions expressed there are "true" or "false," whether Heloise or Abelard present themselves as "weak" or "strong" in relation to each other, or whether their letters are "personal" or "public." These interpretive parameters do not account for the ways practitioners of medieval epistolography structured their letters to elicit particular responses and actions on the part of the recipient(s). Martin Irvine has observed that Heloise's participation in "male textual culture" is evident in her use of "genre encoding" in her first two letters. She writes, Irvine argues, as Abelard's fellow *litteratus* and *amicus* by choosing a Senecan style of expression synonymous with that of a friend speaking to an equal.[10] Abelard, on the other hand, continues to assert the paternal authority of a man speaking to a woman that is evident in his "Jeromian" responses to Heloise.[11] Joan Ferrante, however, challenges any notion of strict gender distinctions in epistolary practice.[12] Ferrante's argument is supported by Heloise's and Abelard's attention to the Senecan model in the *Epistolae ad Lucilium*.

This invocation of Seneca is threaded throughout their correspondence. Abelard and Heloise each cite Seneca's letters to Lucilius (many of which, not coincidentally, are paraenetic letters) to emphasize the right each of them has to exhort the other.[13] In her first letter, for example, Heloise uses an extensive passage from *ad Lucilium* on the importance of letters as an expression of friendship in order to defend her request for a letter of consolation from Abelard and justify the writing of her own apology.[14] Heloise adopts an even stronger Senecan admonitory tone in her response to Abelard's anxiety about the dangers he faces, reminding him of this passage: "'Why is it necessary,' says Seneca, 'to summon evil' and to destroy life before death comes?"[15] To our ears, Heloise's reaction is curiously unsympathetic. She spends little time reinforcing Abelard's anxieties and instead reminds him that Seneca refused to coddle Lucilius with any "sweet hope" because Lucilius must stop destroying his present life by worrying about the future.[16] Heloise thus counters Abelard's argument that he must absent himself from her and the Paraclete in order to face his own spiritual battles.[17] By citing Seneca, Heloise emulates the wise elder in her second and third letters and adopts a paternal position toward Abelard. In *Ep.* 6, she presents another fully developed paraenetic to argue that the obligations of their friendship in the material here-and-now are expanded by her role as abbess rather than diminished by it.

In a *transmotio* and *refractio* of Abelard's prescription for her in *Ep.* 5, "would that your written words be reflected in your heart," Heloise continues in the dual mode of friend and elder when she informs Abelard that she has made her overflowing passion subject to reason, "so that in my writing at least, I might restrain from that which is not so much difficult as impossible to guard against in speech."[18] When compared to Abelard's advice to her in *Ep.* 5: "Atque utinam sic sit in animo tuo sicut et in scripto" [May your written words be reflected in your heart], it is apparent that Heloise is mirroring and inverting his prescription for her: "Utinam sic animus dolentis parere promptus sit quaemadmodum dextra scribentis" [Would that the heart of the one grieving would be as ready to yield to the hand with which one writes].[19] With this inversion, Heloise highlights how her reasoned written arguments have been modulated and expanded through her *infirmitas.* The grieving speech over which she has little control finally compels her to embrace moderation. So, too, Heloise will argue, the body may be a locus of *infirmitas* (evident in her desire for Abelard and in his disfiguring castration), but *infirmitas* also can be understood as a vital antecedent to and companion of the life that is still possible for them under the Rule, a life possible without despising the bodies they have or once had. The explicit display of her *infirmitas,* the uncooperative grieving heart, in Heloise's *exordium* underlies the also explicit display of her *virtus,* the writing hand. The exchange, she suggests, is predicated on a symbiotic consolidation of "desirable" displays of strength with the "undesirable" displays of weakness that Abelard thinks ought to be relegated to their past. As Heloise points out to Abelard, it is the heart that puts the hand into motion so that "uncontrollable" speech and the written word are transformed. In this textualization of speech into written rhetoric, reason and passion struggle with one another but nonetheless, are merged and continue to transform the mind:

> Revocabo itaque manum a scripto in quibus linguam a verbis temperare non valeo. Utinam sic animus dolentis parere promptus sit quemadmodum dextra scribentis. Aliquod tamen dolori remedium vales conferre si non hunc omnino possis aufere. Ut enim insertum clavum alius expellit, sic cogitatio nova priorem excludit cum alias intentus animus priorum memoriam dimittere cogitur aut intermittere. Tanto vero amplius cogitatio quaelibet animum occupat, et ab aliis deducit, quanto quod cogitatur honestius aestimatur, et quo intendimus animum magis videtur necessarium"
>
> [I will retract the hand from what has been previously written, the tongue from words which I do not have the power to refrain. Would that the heart of the one grieving would be as ready to yield to the hand with which one writes! This grief can be assuaged if it cannot be removed completely. Certainly just as a new nail expels the previous one, a new way of thinking displaces the one before it. The attentive mind is compelled to dismiss or interrupt a prior memory with other things. Truly, the more fully a new way of thinking is allowed to fill the mind and turn it away from the previous preoccupations, the more highly esteemed (the new object of our attention is), and the more necessary it seems (to us) that we pursue this new direction of thought].[20]

Heloise's prescription for Abelard is one of negotiation with past weaknesses rather than their abnegation. I would like to expand on Blamires's observations in chapter 12 of this volume that Heloise purposefully mixes the modes of *doctrina, exhortatio,* and *consolatio* by examining how she makes her own grief and womanly weakness an example of how to use *infirmitas.*

As has already been noted, Heloise's image of the new nail being used to drive out the old nail exemplifies the extreme painfulness of displacing carnal desire with divine love, but, in advancing the Christian adaptation of the classical trope, she also insinuates the satirical trope of displacement in which one disorder is traded for another, "emovit veterem mire novus."[21] Radice's translation suggests that Heloise is addressing Abelard specifically and asking for his assistance when she declares, "You can assuage this grief, if you would not remove it completely."[22] However, I think the context of this statement (especially the Ovidian images that follow in Heloise's argument) and her repetitive usage of *intentus* indicates that she is not merely reproaching Abelard for ignoring her grief but instead suggesting that he should regard her argument as presenting a new guide for their behavior toward one another. She posits that new ways of thinking from the perspective of weakness, *ex infirmitate,* are created and valued because it is the previous life that continues to shape the new one. Heloise thus suggests that out of their love and grief, new identities under the Rule can be formed. The ground for this formulation can be found in the male textual space of the *veteres.*

Heloise suggests that Abelard misunderstands the quality of his *infirmitas* and her *virtus* when he supposes that he, chastened by his castration, and she, seeking a higher life in her office of abbess, should be separated from each other as the Bride is from the table outside the garden in Abelard's strictly allegorical reading of the Song of Songs. Wearing the habit in the Benedictine tradition should, as we have seen from the Rule, symbolize inclusion in the community that provides a nexus of the material and spiritual worlds.[23] In the litany of unanswered questions echoing the Benedictine *promissio,* Heloise emphasizes that the relationship between human weaknesses and commitment to the religious life are inextricably bound: "Quid rursum stultius quam viam ignotam nec adhuc demonstratam aggredi? Quid praesumptuosius quam eligere ac profiteri vitam quam nescias, aut votum facere quod implere non queas? . . . Quis autem ab omni ratione ac discretione seiunctum not videat, si ad imponenda onera eorum, quibus imponuntur, valitudines prius non discutiantur ut naturae constitutionem humana sequatur industria" [What could be so foolish as to take an unknown path, not yet defined, or so presumptuous as to choose and profess a way of life of which you know nothing, or to make a vow you cannot fulfill? . . . Who would not see the complete absence of reason and discretion in imposing burdens on these (men and women) without first investigating the strength of those who are to bear these burdens, so that human work may correspond to one's natural constitution]?[24] A full understanding of the community's monastic commonplaces (the inscription of the *promissio, petitio,* and *oratio* in communal life) can be achieved only through a careful study of the relationship of the Rule to those who profess it. As Catherine Brown observes, "Abelard's allegory [of the Bride of Christ], ideally, effects [an artificial] harmonization by embodying divine love and disembodying (and, perhaps, degendering) the human."[25] Heloise emphasizes that Abelard's neglect of her and the Paraclete is a result of his confusion of the appearance of *virtus,* wearing the habit, with a genuine *virtus,* the *habitus* derived from the understanding of human weakness.

One of Heloise's shrewdest decisions in *Ep.* 6 is her choice of the Benedictine Rule as the central text for suggesting that *infirmitas* and *virtus* are qualities that are not necessarily associated with a particular kind of body. Although she recognizes that certain constitutional differences exist between men and women that allow women to be designated as the "weaker sex," the substance of her argument is concerned with explicating the subtleties of weakness and strength as these are manifested in both men and women. This is evident, for example, in Heloise's comparison of women's natural propensity toward sobriety with men's propensity toward drunkenness. She uses the comparison of constitutional differences to call attention to the carnal nature of humanity and to clarify the necessity for new interpretations of the Rule. A look at her rhetorical strategy is useful for appreciating how Heloise employs a clever semiotic shift of subject to change the emphasis from women to men and from men to humanity: "Providendum itaque nobis est ne id oneris *feminae* praesumamus in quo *viros* fere iam universo succumbere videmus, immo et deficere. Senuisse iam mundum conspicimus *homines*que ipsos cum ceteris quae mundi sunt pristinium naturae vigorem amisisse, et iuxta illud. Veritatis ipsam caritatem non tam multorum quam fere omnium refriguisse ut iam videlicet pro qualitate *hominum* ipsas propter *homines* scriptas vel mutari vel temperari necesse sit Regulas" [We must be cautious, therefore, not to presume women can carry the burden that we now universally see men sinking under, indeed defeated by it. We see what the world has already perceived, and that is that humanity itself, along with other things in the world, has lost its former natural vigor. In truth, charity itself, not just in many but in nearly everyone, has grown cold. Thus, it is now clear that rules, just as they were written on account of humanity, should be changed or modified in accordance with the temperament (of humanity as it is now)].[26] Bringing men *and* women into the circle of human weakness, Heloise defines the problem of human carnality as that which cannot be ameliorated simply by adding requirements to the Rule and depending on the hope of spiritual perfection to carry you toward that higher state. Heloise regards the Rule as a guide sympathetic toward human fragility. Its purpose is to compel the corrupted body toward the corporate body divine. Abelard's notion of Heloise as Bride treats the Rule as if it were silent on the topic of human weakness and potentially silencing of any future weaknesses (i.e., female nature) of those who would profess it.

To do its work of freeing the religious to practice the *opus dei* in their communities, the Rule must be adapted in a spirit of *conversatio* by those who seek to follow its precepts. Abelard, interestingly, is not completely cut off in *Ep.* 5 from this paradoxical notion of *conversatio* as a permanent spiritual bond accomplished in the material body (marriage). On one hand, he regards his carnality as that which inadvertently has fitted him for a new role as a spiritual warrior, a persona not much different from his image of himself as a warrior of dialectic: "Unum quippe sumus in Christo, una per legem matrimonii caro. Quidquid est tuum, mihi non arbitror alienum. Tuus autem est Christus quia facta est sponsa eius. . . . Unde et de tuo nobis apud ipsum patrocinio amplius confidimus ut id obtineam ex tua quod non possum ex oratione propria. Et nunc maxime cum quotidiana periculorum aut perturbationum instantia nec vivere me nec orationi sinat vacare" [for we are one in Christ, one flesh according to the law of matrimony. Whatever is yours cannot, I think, fail to be mine, and Christ is yours because you have become his bride . . . through your prayer, I may be granted what I cannot obtain through my own; especially now, when the daily pressure of dangers and disturbances threaten my life and give me no time for prayer].[27]

On the other hand, even though a solitary warrior, Abelard still regards Heloise as sufficiently bound to him by the marriage sacrament that they may both gain from prayers he has no time to pray. Nor does he have the luxury of meditative reading like that enjoyed by the "blessed eunuch": "nec illum beatissimum imitari eunuchum potentem in domo Candacis reginae Aethiopum qui erat super omnes gazas eius et de tam longinquo venerat adorare in Ierusalem. Ad quem revertentem missus est ab angelo Philippus apostolus ut eum converteret ad fidem, quod iam ille meruerat per orationem vel sacrae lectionis assiduitatem. A qua quidem ut nec in via tunc vacaret licet ditissimus et gentilis, magno divinae dispensationis actum est beneficio ut locus ei Scripturae occurreret qui opportunissimam conversionis eius occasionem apostolo praeberet" [Nor can I imitate that blessed eunuch, the high official of Candace, Queen of Ethiopia . . . the apostle Philip was sent by the angel to convert him to the faith, as he had already deserved by his prayers and his assiduous reading of the Scriptures. Because he did not want to take time from this . . . it came about through the great goodness of Providence that the passage of Scripture was before him which gave the apostle the perfect opportunity for conversion].[28]

Lacking the eunuch's usual opportunities and possessing one advantage most eunuchs do not, the marriage sacrament, Abelard is certainly unique. He tacitly assumes that Heloise should obey his request for her prayer and engage in the meditation he cannot. Her first statement in *Ep.* 6 indicates that she has constructed a response to fill this expectation: ""Ne me forte in aliquo de inobedientia causari quas, verbis etiam immoderati doloris tuae frenum impositum est iussionis" [I would not want to give you cause for finding me disobedient in anything, so I have set the bridle of your injunction on the words which issue from my unbounded grief]."[29] Ironically, it is Heloise who must point out the obvious inconsistency between bidding her farewell and expecting, indeed, depending on her obedience.

Establishing the nature of their relationship to one another is necessary to Heloise's argument, not only for the sake of dictaminal practice per se but also to represent her interpretation of the Rule.[30] In Heloise's enigmatic *salutatio,* "Suo specialiter, sua singulariter," she reinforces the inviolable connection between them. Abelard's position, and a centerpiece of their debate, is that they both possess a new unidimensional and noncorporeal source of strength in their spiritual persona because they are now related only in Christ: "To Heloise, his dearly beloved sister in Christ, Abelard her brother in Christ"; and "To the bride of Christ, [from] Christ's servant.[31] However, Heloise's description of their bond in her first two letters is pointedly mobile, crossing spiritual and secular lines of devotion: "To her only one after Christ, she who is his alone in Christ."[32] The bond they share, according to Heloise, consists of the secular and spiritual identities that culminate in their names. It is as if their proper names were titles denoting each and every one of these bonds: "To her master, or rather her father, husband, or rather brother; from his handmaid, or rather his daughter, wife, or rather sister, to Abelard, Heloise."[33] In *Ep.* 6 Heloise cuts short their rhetorical tug-of-war over title by telescoping the identities of her *dominus* to cover the secular and spiritual realms. With two linguistic strokes, she captures the breadth of their bond to each other and Christ so neatly that there is no clear boundary between their secular and the spiritual lives. There is purposefully no way out of the circular and ambiguous inflections: "Suo specialiter, sua singulariter" [To him in particular, from her own as individual].[34] Constant Mews notes, in chapter 3 of this volume, that *specialis* is a philosophical term denoting both the particular and essential nature of Heloise's beloved. Heloise uses a play on Abelard's concept of universals, making the most of her love of wordplay and attention to lexemes (as Mews also observes), so that she may blur the nature of secular and spiritual spheres that Abelard has so carefully drawn. Heloise reinforces the ongoing bond between them by declaring her desire for obedience and, just as quickly, indicating that she and the Paraclete cannot be obedient without her, and their, particular *dominus.*

Since Abelard lacks the time for meditative study, Heloise obliges him with the results of her own study on their place in the religious life. She invokes two other segments of the Benedictine Rule in her *exordium* in addition to Chapter 58 to clarify this relationship further: Chapters 2 and 68. Heloise highlights the problem of being obedient when the one to whom she, and the Paraclete, owe obedience absents himself by claiming a lack of resources: "we handmaids of Christ, who are your daughters in Christ, come as suppliants to demand of your paternal interest."[35] In counting herself and the Paraclete as Abelard's daughters, she recalls for Abelard chapter 2 of the Rule, *Qualis Debeat Esse Abbas* [Qualities the abbot must possess]:

> Christi enim agere vices in monasterio creditur, quando ipsius vocatur pronomine, dicente apostolo: *Accepistis spiritum adoptionis filiorum, in quo clamamus: abba, pater.* . . . Meminere debet semper abbas quod est, meminere quod dicitur, et scire quia cui plus committitur, plus ab eo exigitur . . . et secundum uniuscuiusque qualitatem vel intellegentiam, ita se omnibus conformet et aptet. . . . Ante omnia, ne dissimulans aut parvipen-

dens salutem animarum sibi commissarum, ne plus gerat sollicitudinem de rebus transitoriis et terrenis atque caducis, sed semper cogitet quia animas suscepit regendas de quibus et rationem redditurus est. Et ne causetur de minori forte substantia meminerit scriptum. . . . *Nihil deest timentibus eum*"

[The abbot is believed to hold the place of Christ in the monastery, since he is called by His name, as the Apostle says: *You have received the spirit of adoption of sons by which we cry out: Abba father.* . . . The abbot must always remember who he is and what he is called and know that to whom much has been committed, much will be demanded . . . and [he must] conform and fit himself to each one's qualities and intelligence. . . . Before everything, he must not ignore or hold inferior the health of the souls entrusted to him, nor care for transitory or perishable earthly affairs, but always be aware of the care of the souls he has undertaken, whom he will be returning and accounting for . . . and so that he may not plead a lack of resources as an excuse, he shall remember the scripture. . . . *Those who fear him lack nothing*].[36]

Abelard stands in, as it were, for the holy Bridegroom with whom he wants Heloise to cloister herself. He must hold himself answerable, therefore, to those whose strengths and weaknesses are different from his own by analyzing the nature of *virtus* and *infirmitas* in all those who follow the Rule: "Cuius quidem rei defectu et indigentia nunc agitur ut ad eiusdem regulae professionem tam mares quam feminae in monasteriis suscipiantur, et idem institutionis monasticae iugum imponitur infirmo sexui aeque ut forti. Unam quippe nunc Regulam beati Benedicti apud Latinos feminae profitentur aeque ut viri. Quam sicut viris solummodo constat scriptam esse ita et ab ipsis tantum impleri posse tam subiectis pariter quam praelatis" [Through lack and need of this (Rule for women) it is the practice today for men and women alike to be received into monasteries to profess the same Rule and the same yoke of monastic ordinance is laid on the weaker sex as on the stronger. At present the one Rule of St. Benedict is professed in the Latin Church by women equally with men, although, as it is clearly written for men alone, it can only be fully obeyed by men, whether subordinates or superiors].[37] Heloise employs the epistolary rhetoric of social familiarity ("friend writing to friend" or "teacher to student") in the context of family relationships created in the religious life. The relationships created through profession of the Rule and nourished in dictaminal practice allow her to position herself at advantageous, flexible points in regard to Abelard.

The simple appeal to Abelard to fulfill his paternal duties allows Heloise to speak as both daughter and brother, or son, as far as the Rule is concerned. She interprets the Rule as a text that should be adapted to accommodate *infirmitas* and *virtus* not only in both sexes but also in superiors as well as inferiors. Chapter 68 of the Rule indicates St. Benedict's recognition that those who live the *Opus Dei* may encounter the abbot's weaknesses as well as their own. This injunction requires the abbot to modify instructions if his commands prove too strenuous for a weaker monk to follow. Conversely, this chapter also grants the monk a degree of autonomy in relation to the abbot. It stipulates that a monk may approach the abbot and request a modification if the brother has done his best to obey the abbot's orders but is still unable to do so. The basis for the monk's request is his personal *infirmitas:* "Si cui fratri aliqua forte gravia aut impossibilia iniunguntur, suscipiat quidem iubentis imperium cum omni mansuetudine et oboedientia. Quod si omnino virium suarum mensuraum viderit pondus oneris excedere impossibilitatis suae causas ei qui sibi praeest patienter et opportune suggerat, non superbiendo aut resistendo vel contradicendo" [A brother may be assigned a burdensome task or something he cannot do. If so, he should, with complete gentleness and obedience, accept the order given him. Should he see, however, that the weight of the burden is altogether too much for his strength, then he should choose the appropriate moment and explain patiently to this superior the reasons why he cannot perform the task. This he ought to do without pride, obstinacy, or refusal].[38]

This requires, of course, that the abbot be introspective. He must consider his own actions and spiritual failings, and decide whether he was harsh toward those in his care, inattentive to their weaknesses, or, perhaps, proud in his strength and authority. Through the Rule's text Heloise may selectively simulate parity ("abbess to abbot," "friend to friend," or "male brother to male abbot") and disparity ("female to male," "supplicant to lord," or "Bride to Bridegroom") in ways that resonate with the spousal and teacher-student valences of their own past and allow them to be renegotiated in the present. Her old complaint is reason enough to merit Abelard's reconsideration of his previous command. Thus, by virtue of her already declared weaknesses, Heloise makes her old *infirmitas* the door through which she enters the male authoritative space of the Rule. When she enters this male textual space wearing the habit of womanly weakness, Heloise does so to take the metonymy of the habit in a different direction than Abelard does in his discussion of the Ethiopian bride in *Ep.* 5. The habit that they all wear, Heloise argues, represents the means by which each of them participates in multiple discursive positions through the consideration of *infirmitas,* that is, an outward movement as vital to the practice of *communitas* as the inward, solitary practice of the penitent.

Heloise has a fine ear for the absurd. Nowhere is this more evident than in her use of clothing. In pointing to the inadequacies of woman's monastic garments designed for men, Heloise has a delightfully concrete, and ironically literal, images from which she may draw attention to the larger problem apparent in Abelard's exegesis of the Song of Songs: his explication of the table and the garden, and notions of sensuality. Abelard employs the figures of the table and garden to suggest that these two disparate discursive spaces necessarily exist because of the Bride's sensuality. He renders the habit as the mark of disfigurement that both emphasizes her sensuality, the epitome of their carnal *infirmitas,* and necessitates the movement into the garden. The Bride's sensuality is not diminished, just displaced to a new venue so that she has no contact with the public table and secular world outside the cloister walls. She is implicitly and simply dislodged from the table right outside her chamber, i.e., *emovit veterem mire novus.* This fine distinction that Abelard makes between the garden and the table is subtle but important. Heloise bluntly counters this argument by pointing out that this needless exclusion arises from a myopic focus on sensuality rather than attention to the larger practices of communal spirituality: "How are [women who experience monthly purgings of their superfluous humours] affected by the Ruling for the abbot, that he shall read the Gospel himself and afterwards start the hymn?"[39] The abbot is blind to *infirmitas* of the community right in front of him. This passage is not about the practicality of clothing but the truth of investiture.[40] Heloise is asking Abelard to pay attention to the kind of commitment that makes the investiture articulated in the *promissio* and *petitio* meaningful as that which is practiced communally. She structures an exhortation from the metaphor of female enclosure that employs the very gender constructions on which such "privileged" enclosure of weakness is based.[41]

Rhetorical Redress and the *Modus* of Initiation

Heloise adopts mobile positions of power and humility in *Ep.* 6 to suggest that the relationship between the Rule and classically inspired notions of moderation, *modus,* should be the model for the relationship between *virtus* and *infirmitas.* Abelard imbues Heloise's habit (and his own) with an almost magical ability to transform each of them into abstracted spiritual personae in ways that Heloise, I believe, finds very disturbing. Her insistence on the religious life as a nexus of secular and spiritual identities formed from their past and present lives is her way of redressing the terrible memory of their investiture. For both of them, taking orders enshrined the habit as the symbol of their pain and mutilation and an endless inscription of anger and remorse. In spite of his claims to the contrary, the habit as a symbol of enduring what is intolerable is no less part of Abelard's memory than it is for Heloise. Recalling their lovemaking in the refectory at Argenteuil, Abelard sanctions the habit as a form of flagellation, memorializing their past carnality in the fabric of the present spirituality: "sacro te habitu indutam monialem te finxisse, et tali simulatione tuae, quam nunc habes, religioni irreverenter [*sic*] illusissse. Unde etiam pensa quam convenienter ad hanc te religionem divina iustitia, immo gratia traxerit nolentem, cui verita non es illudere, volens ut in ipso luas habitu quod in ipsum deliquisti, et simulationis mendacio ipsa rei veritas remedium praestet et falsitatem emendet" [you disguised yourself in the sacred habit of a nun, a pretense which was an irreverent mockery of the religion you now profess. Consider, then, how fittingly divine justice, or rather, divine grace brought you against your will to the religion which you did not hesitate to mock, so that you should willingly expiate your profanation in the same habit, and the truth of reality should remedy the lie of your pretense and correct your falsity].[42]

The ghost of the illicitly worn habit clings to the true habit Heloise wears. It is her (and his) own peculiar act of repentance. Abelard returns several times to his memories of Heloise's true and false investitures to consider the nature of the sin they committed. In the *Historia calamitatum,* Abelard recalls his role in disguising Heloise at Argenteuil as an active one and Heloise as passive: "I prepared the religious clothing for her in the manner of monastic women who were taking vows, except for the veil, and dressed her in them."[43] A look at the Latin underscores the importance of the moment of investiture to Abelard: "Vestesque ei religionis quae conversationi monasticae convenirent, excepto velo, aptari feci et his eam indui." Étienne Gilson has observed the emphasis Abelard places on presenting himself as a figure of spiritual authority during this deceptive act: "I hesitate to translate the Latin text literally—*et his eam indui,* . . . [*sic*]—because it suggests that Abélard gave Héloise the religious habit—without the veil—in a sort of formal ceremony."[44] The dynamics of the subject-object relationship that Gilson is hesitant to articulate (Abelard as directing subject, Heloise as acted-upon object) are unchanged in Abelard's account of the actual ceremony: "Heloise had already agreed to take the veil in obedience to my wishes . . . she broke out as best she could through her tears and sobs into Cornelia's famous lament. . . . So saying she hurried to the altar, quickly took up the veil blessed by the bishop, and publicly bound herself to the religious life.[45] Although the bishop grants Heloise the veil, Abelard suggests that Heloise's state of dress, her habit, is still his doing. Once again Heloise undergoes a ritual disappearance under the habit, but this time both her and Abelard's bodies are forever buried in that coarse garment. Heloise argues in *Ep.* 6 that they must temper the grief this moment holds for them by reconsidering the meaning of *modus.*

In a pun on *modus* ("rule" as well as "measure" or "moderation"), Heloise cleverly cites Jerome's protreptic comments on the sin of excess virtue. In a fitting antidote to Abelard's Jeromian prescription of the severe enclosure for Heloise, she prescribes a feminized *modus:* "Sed et cum omnium virtutum discretio sit *mater,* et omnium bonorum *moderatrix* sit ratio, quis aut virtutem aut bonum censeat quod ab istis dissentire videat? Ipsas quippe virtutes excedentes *modum atque mensuram* sicut Hieronymus asserit inter vitia reputari convenit" [But since discretion is the *mother* of all virtues, and reason the *moderator* of all good, who may express an opinion on either a virtue or a good that seems to be inconsistent with these? Certainly these virtues that exceed moderation and measure, as Jerome asserts, are fit only to be counted as vices].[46] Through an intriguing redundancy of synonyms for moderation, Heloise inverts and conflates the definitions of virtue and vice. Excessive virtue violates the Rule's precepts: the textual inscription of moderation vis-à-vis human *infirmitas.* Heloise advises Abelard that the attempt to punish the flesh beneath the habit through a tyrannical regulation of the body is itself a sin. Likewise, Abelard's desire to seek a solitary path, fighting against his enemies and regrets, may seem virtuous, but, in reality, this response foolishly separates him from a community that he needs and that needs him. As Brown comments, there is a discrepancy "between virtue and its exhibition," and Heloise is aware of the hypocrisy in Abelard's advice that she practice virtue of her office when the bodily *infirmitas* metonymically represented by "woman" is unacceptable.[47] Heloise is sensitive to the conflict between Abelard's desire for virtue and his inability to integrate *infirmitas* and *virtus* in his own body, much less a single community.

To Heloise, moderation and the Rule may exist either in opposition or in synonymity. Abelard's exclusionary excesses arise from his far too literal definition of her (and their) weakness as carnal and his far too allegorical definition of their strength as spiritual. She illuminates this rigidity by superimposing images of purity and sin on the figure of the table. The refectory table, already an erotically loaded image from their personal past, is given a synecdochical relation to *infirmitas* that defies any neat corporeal and spiritual boundary (not unlike the strategy of Heloise's enigmatic *salutatio*). As she does with her image of humanity stumbling under burdensome regulations as if drunk, Heloise begins with the usual suspect: woman and her propensity to seduce and be seduced. She exaggerates a gender dynamic of *infirmitas,* familiar in Jerome's letters, to emphasize female carnality so that cupidity, gluttony, and drunkenness are not limited to that which occurs between men and women, or that which happens outside the cloister:

> Numquid nostrae convenit religioni ut vel numquam hospitium viris praebeat aut cum his quos susceperit viris abbatissa comedat? O quam facilis ad ruinam animarum virorum ac mulierum in unum cohabitatio! Maxime vero in mensa ubi crapula dominatur et ebrietas et vinum in dulcedine bibitur in quo est luxuria. . . . Numquid et si feminas solas hospitio susceptas ad mensam admiserint, nullum ibi latet periculum? Certe in seducenda muliere nullum est aeque facile ut lenocinium muliebre

> [Which is more fitting for our religious life, for an abbess never to offer hospitality to men, or for her to eat with men she has allowed in? It is all too easy for the souls of men and women to be destroyed if they live together in one place, and especially at the table, where gluttony and drunkenness are rife, and wine which leads to lechery is drunk with

> enjoyment. . . . And even if [nuns] admit to their table only women to whom they have given hospitality, is there no lurking danger there? Surely nothing is so conductive to a woman's seduction as women's flattery, nor does a woman pass on the foulness of a corrupted mind so readily to any but another woman].[48]

Heloise expands Abelard's notion that the Bride is protected from the temptation of the table to point of paradox. By erasing the boundary separating the safety of the garden and the danger of the table, Heloise reveals that the real ugliness at work at the table is neither carnal nor secular. In much of her extended argument in the *narratio* that follows, Heloise minimizes the kind of danger posed by the physical body proffered in the *promissio* and *petitio,* and compares the supposed danger of carnality with the greater one posed by the undiscriminating mind or heart. Heloise does not stop with beautifully articulating Jerome's statement of the danger posed by women. Her table is expanded to make room for another woman.

The seductress of the Ovidian table is juxtaposed with another paradoxical image of the Bride noted earlier, that of the *mater* and *moderatrix:* "Sed et cum omnium virtutum discretio sit *mater,* et omnium bonorum *moderatrix* sit ratio, quis aut virtutem aut bonum censeat quod ab istis dissentire videatur" [But since discretion is the mother of all virtues, and reason the moderator of all good, who may express an opinion on either a virtue or a good that seems to be inconsistent with these]?[49] Heloise invests the bride figure with a persona far removed from both the exotic Ethiopian maid and the lascivious Ovidian seductress in the term *moderatrix. Moderatrix,* I think, is another example of the unusual semantic choices that Mews argues are characteristic of Heloise's writing. The intriguing image of the female judge amplifies a competing association of woman in that of the mother and source of reason that Heloise emphasizes in the *modus* and *mensuram* passage. Playing off Abelard's advice that she embrace her current position as abbess in a passage that Heloise uses to intimate his excesses, she intertwines the old proverb on discretion with the female figure as the chief arbiter of virtue. She reminds Abelard that the Bride also can work as a figural corollary of matronly wisdom by recasting the figure of the Bride in the form of Abelard's true lady love: Philosophy, referring to book seven of Macrobius' *Saturnalia.*[50] By citing this authority on women's natural sobriety, Heloise alludes to the context in which this conversation occurs: Symmachus' concern that Philosophy ought to keep a "cloistered modesty" like a good wife because the conversation at the table, a public place, should be shared only with that openly carnal woman, the concubine. But it is poor Symmachus, the curmudgeonly dinner guest sounding much like Abelard in his second letter, who unwittingly excludes from the table the guest who ensures the best conversation: the matron Philosophy. As Heloise and Abelard know, Symmachus is only the foil for Eustathius' declamation on the necessity of Philosophy's presence: "Heaven forbid that Philosophy . . . should herself shun the banquet and so suggest that she is incapable of practicing what she preaches or that she does not know how to observe moderation whose bounds she has herself prescribed."[51] Heloise's playful reference once again to *modus* in this *mater* figure suggests an intersection between these alternate female figures and the physical and allegorical bodies subject to the *promissio* and *petitio.*

In Heloise's imagery, nuns travel from the sacred table (where the abbot reads the Gospel) to the lusty table (where they receive guests) simply in the course of the convent's daily business. Consequently, these nuns must be thought of as capable of conducting that business at various tables and in the constant presence of their natural *infirmitas.* Rather than minimizing the erotic signification of women's carnal weaknesses, Heloise chooses to emphasize that the nuns are always in danger of manifesting their natural *infirmitas* whether they are attending the Sunday vigil or receiving secular guests. The bleeding that inevitably disrupts the sacred reading prefigures the sensuality of the physical table where the nuns also must show hospitality toward their benefactors. Abelard hopes that Heloise's response to her persistent carnality will be to accept a greater distance between them, and he encourages her to think of this distance as the justifiable prohibition of the Bride from the secular table. Heloise replies, a bit tongue-in-cheek, by dragging Ovid's table into the cloister:

> Vinaque cum bibulas sparsere Cupidinis alas
> permanet et <capto> stat gravis ille loco . . .
> Tunc veniunt risus tunc pauper cornua sumit:
> Tunc dolor et curae rugaque frontis abiit . . .
> Illic saepe animos iuvenum rapuere puellae
> Et Venus in vinis ignis in igne fuit
>
> [When wine has sprinkled Cupid's thirsty wing
> He stays and stands weighed down in his chosen place . . .
> Then laughter comes, then even the poor find plenty,
> The sorrow and care and wrinkles leave the brow . . .
> That is the time when girls bewitch men's hearts,
> And Venus in the wine adds fire to fire].[52]

The result is a luxurious and almost salacious revision of Abelard's figure of the habit-as-penitence. This verse is not a paean to lust, or even a warning against it. It is Ovid's ironic commentary on the perils of self-delusion awaiting Love's "warrior" at his own pseudo-victory celebration. Heloise's selection from the *Ars Amatoria* suggests to Abelard that he is subject to the same warrior's blindness, mistaking homeliness for beauty because he thinks he can see the women clearly. The next several lines of Ovid's verse describe the warrior's faulty vision:

> hic tu fallaci nimium ne crede lucernae:
> iudicio formae noxque merumque nocent.
> luce deas caeloque Paris spectauit aperto,
> cum dixit Veneri 'uincis utramque, Venus.'
> nocte latent mendae utioque ignoscitur omni,
> horaque formosam quamlibet illa facit
> consule de gemmis, de tincta murice lana,
> consule de facie corporibus diem
>
> [Night and drink can impair your eye for beauty:
> Don't trust the lamplight too much
> It's deceptive. When Paris examined those goddesses, when he said 'you
> Beat them both, Venus' he did it in Broad
> Daylight. But darkness hides faults, each blemish is forgiven:
> Any woman you name will pass
> As a beauty at night. Judge jewels or fine fabrics,
> A face or a figure, *by day*].[53]

Her desire and *infirmitas,* however uncontrollable her grieving tongue may seem, have not caused Heloise to disregard either her life as an abbess mother or her devotion to Abelard. Rather, it is she who is clear-sighted because she knows that neither she nor the women of the Paraclete have the option of retreating from the table set for them (as Abelard, and Symmachus, might recommend): "Denique si viris ab hospitalitate nostra exclusis solas admittamus feminas, quis non videat quanta exasperatione viros offendamus quorum beneficiis monasteria sexus infirmi egent, maxime si eis a quibus plus accipiunt minus aut omnino nihil largiri videantur" [if we exclude men from our hospitality and admit women only, it is obvious that we shall offend and annoy the men whose services are needed by a convent of the weaker sex, especially if little or no return seems to be made to those from whom most is received].[54] For all the Ovidian opportunities lurking at (or under) the cloister's table, the possibility of cupidity in the Brides of Christ should not be considered their determinate characteristic. The bond all members share under the Rule's *petitio* means that the weak and strong always will be yoked together. Thus, Heloise suggests that both the nature of Philosophy and the wanton woman (or man) can abide in the same body.

Heloise uses these Ovidian poetics to suggest that the excesses brought to the secular *and* the spiritual table must be counterbalanced by the knowledge that the body is not an object to be read as if it were an *exemplum* of either *virtus* or *infirmitas.* The intersections of *infirmitas* and *virtus* are vital places of *conversatio* in which the character of virtue can be revealed. In the series of illustrations that follow Heloise's figure of the Ovidian table, she presents the range of virtues and weaknesses in the rulers of the church.[55] Using Macrobius' medical theories on food and wine, she examines three primary physical appetites (eating, drinking, and sex) in men and, in doing so, reverses the association of these appetites with the deceptive women in Ovid, to argue that neither the presence of these appetites nor their fulfillment has any relation of spiritual maturity. Heloise juxtaposes Macrobius' theories on the advantages of the female body's excessive moisture with those of the *Saturnalia*'s matronly Philosophy in the Natura figure. Nature knows all about *modus,* and she gave a share to women, who, as it turns out, have a natural advantage over men in combating two out of the three carnal appetites:

> Ex his itaque perpende quanto tutius ac justius naturae et infirmitati nostrae cibus quilibet et potus indulgeri possit, quarum videlicet corda crapula et ebrietate gravari facile non possunt, cum ab illa nos cibi parcitas, ab ista feminei corporis qualitas, ut dictum est, protegat
>
> [And Nature herself has made provision for our being safely granted a mild indulgence in any kind of food, for our sex is protected by greater sobriety. It is well known that women can be sustained on less nourishment and at less cost than men, and medicine teaches that [women] are not so easily intoxicated . . . in fact we cannot easily fall victims to gluttony and drunkenness, seeing that our moderation in food protects us from the one and the nature of the female body . . . from the other].[56]

Menstrual blood and natural sobriety are two sides of the same coin: a curse and an advantage bestowed by Nature. Natural *infirmitas* makes certain natural strengths possible. Heloise's *dominus* has had difficulty connecting what he reads in the Gospel, the Rule, Philosophy, and Nature with the woman he knows. He, therefore, remains ignorant of the physical advantages signaled by menstruation and insensible to the value of the community to which he should be attending, since there is no impediment to his living in communion with these women regardless of his, or their, disfigurement. The *petitio* that Heloise proposes in her request for a women's rule is one in which no material or corporeal hindrance can be thought to prevent her, Abelard, and the Paraclete from joining one another in the regular community.

This union that Heloise proposes is cemented through an ongoing dialogue. The Rule defines the *promissio* thus: "promittat de stabilitate sua et conversatione morum suorum et obedientia."[57] The ordering of these ideas indicates that a dynamic relationship exists among stability, behavior, and obedience. The phrase "conversatione morum suorum" [through the frequent reconsideration of one's way of life] presents the means through which the "promittat de stabilitate" [the promise of stability] and "obedientia" [obedience] are achieved. The link between the *promissio* (knowing the Rule) and the *petitio* (binding one's self to the community) is a function of *conversatio:* the frequent sojourn to Rule and a return to engagement with fellow religious. The Rule's syntax emphasizes a circular, continuous, and mutually dependent relation among body, mind, and text. In chapter 8 Georgianna observes that Heloise is concerned with the importance of *conversatio* in the Rule but finds that Heloise's division of interiority and outward behavior clouds the argument: "Heloise's letter seems to fall into rather disjointed halves: one [half] questions whether certain particulars of the Benedictine Rule are appropriate for women, while the other questions whether most rules regarding external particulars can affect the inner lives of Christians." However, there is no confusion here but rather, a rhetorical mirroring of the initiation rite. Heloise structures her argument in these "halves" to suggest that this process of *conversatione* works as a dialectic between obedience and stability. The division found in the initiation rite's *promissio* reflects the *conversatione* between exterior life (marked by obedience to the community and the Rule) and one's interior life (stability achieved through an intimate understanding of the Rule). The *petitio,* the ability of cede oneself completely and permanently to the religious life in a local community, is a process constantly renewed through the daily practice of the *promissio.* It is a dialectic familiar to those who understand the Rule because, in the Rule the Benedictine religious profess, their *modus* and *habitus* perpetually weave together outward behavior and the inner life.

The highest expression of this dialectic is the marriage trope central to the Song of Songs imagery and the Benedictine initiation.[58] Heloise speaks *suo specialiter* and *sua singulariter* throughout her third letter to suggest that Abelard's model of allegorical marriage must invoke a *petito* that realigns gendered and material claims of strength and weakness. Even her initial request for the woman's rule is structured with this in mind. She places the figure of the husband parallel to weakness and that of the wife parallel to strength: "tam mares [husbands] quam feminae [wives] . . . idem institutionis monasticae iugum imponitur infirmo sexui [weak sex] aeque ut forti [strong sex]." Radice translates this passage as a more general admonition: "men and women alike to be received into the monasteries to profess the same Rule, and the same yoke of monastic ordinance is laid on the weaker sex as on the stronger." Radice translates *mares* as men, but I think *mares* in the context of Heloise's argument also connotes the allegorical and (in Heloise's case) secular spousal relationship.[59] The connotations of *maritus* that Heloise invokes are those related to the verb *maritare* in which the act of marriage abounds in rich horticultural imagery: the fertilization of plants and the binding, or "wedding," of vines to increase the structural stability of two branches by uniting them. By weaving the request for a woman's rule into the initiation rite and her position as spouse and mother, Heloise indicates the Song of Songs allegory can be used as their personal allegory of reintegration.

Heloise's use of Song of Songs imagery is confined, and defined, by her names for Abelard. He is the Bridegroom. His *virtus* is to be found in realigning himself with Heloise and the Paraclete. In the closing words of her third letter, Heloise offers the flourish of the initiation's *oratio.* It is her prayer to the abbot to conclude the initiation rite by accepting her *petitio* and *promissio* and bring them all together in the fullness of his care. She calls out to him over and over. Abelard is not only her *dominus* [lord] and *fundator* [founder] but also her, and their, *plantor* [sower of seeds, gardener] and *institutor,* another synonym for creator and gardener. In the cadences of the *oratio*'s thrice repeated plea, Heloise concludes: "Tu quippe post Deum huius loci fundator, tu per Deum nostrae congregationis es plantor, tu cum Deo nostrae sis religionis institutor" [Certainly, you, after God, are the founder of this place; you, through God, are the gardener of our community; you, with God, should be the director of our religious life].[60]

Plantor, fundator, and *institutor* are the linguistic and metaphoric mirrors of *maritus.* There is no difference between the allegorical Bridegroom and the material one. Never mind where the table is located. To Heloise, the important *locus* is the garden, and the garden is found in relationships of the material present. By addressing Abelard in her letters, she has been in the bedchamber with the Bridegroom. She treats their particular marriage and painful separation as analogous to the disjunctions between men and women religious whose contractual commitment is paradoxically severed through rigid exclusionary practices. The new nail with which Heloise replaces the old one is forged in a present built on their past. It is made through the initiation of the body, weak and feminized as it is, into the Rule. In her sublimely technical rhetoric, Heloise transforms the words of Cornelia's remorse into those of the Bride's *conversatio* with her Bridegroom.[61]

Notes

1. The authenticity question, outside the scope of this chapter, has been taken up at length elsewhere. I find the arguments for authenticity made by scholars such as Peter Dronke and Barbara Newman persuasive. See chapter 2 by John Marenbon in this volume for a detailed discussion on the history of this question.
2. There have been some vigorous scholarly debates on whether the image of Heloise as a stoic, repressed woman is compatible with that of the sensuous and defiant Heloise of her first two letters. In comparison to these earlier letters, *Ep.* 6 has, thus, been characterized as evidence of: (1) Heloise's skillful articulation and submissive acceptance of the dilemmas she faces vis-à-vis gender inequality and the "principle of male superiority" in Eileen Kearney, "Heloise: Inquiry into the sacra pagina," pp. 70–71; (2) the "conversion of Heloise's passion" in Peggy Kamuf, *Fictions of Feminine Desire: Disclosures of Heloise,* p. 38; (3) Heloise's scolding of Abelard to attend to the needs of the Paraclete in M. E. Waithe, "Heloise," p. 82; (4) the "gradual transition to reconciliation with her destiny as a nun," in Shulamith Shahar, *The Fourth Estate: A History of Women in the Middle Ages,* p. 166; (5) the letter "encouraging Abelard to think of himself as an educator of women," in Wanda Cizewski, "*In Saeculo Quondam Cara Nunc in Christo Carissima:* Heloise and the Spiritual Formation of the Convent of the Paraclete," p. 69; (6) Heloise's skill in finding "just the right note of entreaty to snare her former lover and husband into continuing their correspondence and their collaboration" although her

"real" character is evident in her competent administration of the Paraclete, as pointed out by Penelope Johnson, *Equal in Monastic Profession: Religious Women in Medieval France,* pp. 243–44; and (7) the letter in which many readers find that "[Heloise's] spirit dies, or at least goes underground forever . . . when she actually submits, she dwindles into virtue as a heroine of romance might dwindle into marriage . . . a silencing, not only of her desire and her rebellion, but of all that is most 'literary' about her" in Barbara Newman, "Authority, Authenticity, and the Repression of Heloise," p. 74. For a further consideration of this 'conversion' question, see Katharina Wilson and Glenda McLeod's analysis in chapter 5 of this volume.

3. Some recent considerations of Heloise's impact on Abelard's thought and writings include: Alcuin Blamires, *The Case for Women in Medieval Culture;* M. T. Clanchy, *Abelard: A Medieval Life;* Joan Ferrante, *To the Glory of Her Sex: Women's Roles in the Composition of Medieval Texts;* Martin Irvine, "Heloise and the Gendering of the Literate Subject," pp. 87–114; and John Marenbon, *The Philosophy of Peter Abelard.*
4. Barbara Newman calls Heloise's third letter "a victory for the poetics of castration over the discourse of desire" ("Authority, Authenticity, and the Repression of Heloise," p. 74). Bonnie Wheeler disagrees with Newman's conclusion and expands on the possible uses Abelard and Heloise make of the "poetics of castration." Wheeler argues that Heloise's is an example of "gender as act and performance" through which Heloise completes an epistolary seduction through a "stunning submissiveness" (pp. 123–24). In so doing, Heloise colludes with Abelard in an attempt to reinforce his masculinity in the face of male peers who denigrate that authority by ridiculing Abelard as a creature that is neither male nor female. See Wheeler, "Origenary Fantasies: Abelard's Castration and Confession," pp. 107–28.
5. As Alcuin Blamires notes in chapter 12 of this volume (in his consideration of Joan Ferrante's examination of epistolary practice in *To the Glory of Her Sex*), the model of Jerome and Marcella so important to understanding Abelard and Heloise's rhetorical practice defies this conclusion.
6. The edition of the Rule used here is: *The Rule of Saint Benedict: In Latin and English with Notes* (henceforth cited as: RB), ed. Timothy Fry. Fry's edition is based on the Sangellenis 914/Codex A. This manuscript, according to C. H. Lawrence, is the text "derived at only once [*sic*] remove from the author's original" and made at Charlemagne's request. See Lawrence's *Medieval Monasticism: Forms of Religious Life in Western Europe in the Middle Ages,* p. 22. This version was widely disseminated by the twelfth century and was likely known to Abelard and Heloise. English translations are from Fry, unless otherwise noted.
7. See Stanley Stowers, *Letter Writing in Greco-Roman Antiquity,* especially pp. 51–152. A paraenetic letter served two complementary purposes: an exhortation to the recipient to lead a better life and the writer's attempt to dissuade the recipient from a wrong course of action. Abelard and Heloise employ both hortatory and dissuasive modes in their letters, and often cite Jeromian and Pauline letters in ways that suggests they are familiar with the paraenetic letter. Giles Constable has observed in "Letters and Letter-Collections," pp. 21–25, that medieval letters are so varied in form as to defy classification using classical terms. However, Carol Lanham has recently argued that the persistence of certain forms and conventions "implies a powerful, stable tradition and its transmission by teaching" through the early Middle Ages (p. 118). See "Freshman Composition in the Early Middle Ages: Epistolography and Rhetoric Before the *Ars Dictaminis.*"
8. RB 58: 26–28.
9. *Ep.* 5, Muckle 85 (Radice 140, emphasis added).
10. Irvine, "Heloise and the Gendering of the Literate Subject," p. 87.
11. Irvine, "Heloise and the Gendering of the Literate Subject," p. 91.

12. Ferrante, *To the Glory of Her Sex,* pp. 56–61. Ferrante also points out that women were often adept at asserting their power within the patristic belief system, pp. 28–29: "it is also likely that as a woman who has achieved success in the world (and an abbess was a worldly as well as religious figure), [Heloise] had enough experience of female effectiveness and male hostility to have serious doubts about the clichés of womanly weakness. . . . Abelard's occasional misogynist outbursts may be more deeply ambivalent. Medieval correspondence gives many examples of men who can attack women in one context and praise them in another, who can speak of women as an inferior sex but treat them as political or intellectual equals and even superiors, who seem to have one view of the sex in general or in theory and another of the individuals they knew. In this, despite his great intellect, Abelard is like men of his and other times."
13. Irvine posits Heloise does not refer to Seneca in *Ep.* 6 because she is modifying the "form in her third letter [*Ep.* 6] to match Abelard's [Jeromian style]" ("Heloise and the Gendering of the Literate Subject," p. 92). However, Heloise and Abelard use St. Jerome to defend their admonitions to one other or support theological positions. For example, Heloise quotes Jerome in her third letter to argue that women can be as corrupted by the flattery of other women as they can by the flattery of men, *Ep.* 6, ed. Muckle 242–43 (Radice 161). Abelard cites Jerome in a similar manner in *Ep.* 5 to warn Heloise that excessive expressions of humility can be seen as ostentatious pleas for praise *Ep.* 5, ed. Muckle 87 (Radice 144).
14. Seneca, *ad Lucilium* 40.1. *Ep.* 2, ed. Muckle 68–69 (Radice 110).
15. Seneca, *ad Lucilium* 24.1, Radice 128, n. 2.
16. Seneca refused to address Lucilius' concerns about a pending lawsuit. Also, note the dissuasive element in this admonition.
17. *Ep.* 3, ed. Muckle 76 (Radice 124–25).
18. *Ep.* 5, ed. Muckle 87 (Radice 144; my translation); *Ep.* 6, ed. Muckle 241 (Radice 159; my translation).
19. *Ep.* 5, ed. Muckle 87 (Radice 144); *Ep.* 6, ed. Muckle 241 (Radice 159; my translation).
20. *Ep.* 6, ed. Muckle 241–42 (Radice 159; my translation).
21. Blamires attributes this figure to Jerome's letter to Rusticus. Cf. Horace, *Satires* 2.3.28.
22. *Ep.* 6, ed. Muckle 241–42 (Radice 159).
23. Cf. RB 58: 7–16. The study required for the *promissio* is extensive. The emphasis on knowledge of the Rule is apparent when it is compared with the *Regula Magistri* in this regard. The novitiate under the *Regula Magistri* is completed in two months while one year is required by the Rule of St. Benedict.
24. *Ep.* 6, ed. Muckle 243 (Radice 162; my translation).
25. Catherine Brown, "*Muliebriter:* Doing Gender in the Letters of Heloise," p. 39.
26. *Ep.* 5, ed. Muckle 246 (Radice 167; my translation, emphasis added).
27. *Ep.* 5, ed. Muckle 93 (Radice 154).
28. *Ep.* 5, ed. Muckle 93 (Radice 154–55).
29. *Ep.* 6, ed. Muckle 241 (Radice 159).
30. See Carol Lanham, *Salutatio Formulas in Latin Letters to 1200: Syntax, Style, and Theory,* pp. 89–109; and James Murphy, *Rhetoric in the Middle Ages: A History of Rhetorical Theory from Saint Augustine to the Renaissance,* pp. 194–201 and 205–16.
31. *Ep.* 3, ed. Muckle 73 (Radice 119). *Ep.* 5, ed. Muckle 82 (Radice 137).
32. *Ep.* 4, ed. Muckle 77 (Radice 127).
33. *Ep.* 2, ed. Muckle 68 (Radice 109).
34. *Ep.* 6, ed. Muckle 241 (Radice 159; my translation).
35. *Ep.* 6, ed. Muckle 241 (Radice 159).
36. RB 2.2–3, 2.30–35 (my translation).
37. *Ep.* 6, ed. Muckle 242 (Radice 160).
38. RB 68.1–3.

39. *Ep.* 6, ed. Muckle 242 (Radice 160).
40. The Rule is more than sufficiently broad regarding clothing to accommodate any modifications women might need. Chapter 55.1–14 is a general provision directing that economical clothing should be obtained locally, suited for the climate, provide sufficient warmth, and fit reasonably well. The only comment on undergarments is that any undergarment borrowed for the purposes of proper dress on a journey should be returned clean.
41. See Brown, "*Muliebriter,*" pp. 28–29, 40–41. In her intriguing reading of Heloise's letters, Brown observes that Heloise integrates bodily desire with textual exhibition to invoke a course of strategic (and theatrical) transgression of the female body. Through this transgression, Brown argues, Heloise defines the "authentic feminine."
42. *Ep.* 5, ed. Muckle 88 (Radice 146).
43. *HC,* ed. Muckle 189 (Radice 74; my translation).
44. Étienne Gilson, *Heloise and Abelard,* trans. L. K. Shook; repr. 1992, p. 40–41.
45. *HC,* ed. Muckle 191 (Radice 76–77; my translation).
46. *Ep.* 6, ed. Muckle 243 (Radice 162; my translation; emphasis added).
47. Brown, "*Muliebriter,*" p. 41.
48. *Ep.* 6, ed. Muckle 242–43 (Radice 160–61).
49. *Ep.* 6, ed. Muckle 243 (Radice 162; my translation; emphasis added).
50. *Ep.* 6, ed. Muckle 246 (Radice 166).
51. Macrobius, *Saturnalia* 7.1.2, 5, pp. 440–41.
52. *Ep.* 6, ed. Muckle 242 (Radice 160).
53. Ovid, *The Art of Love,* Book 1.244–52, p. 173.
54. *Ep.* 6, ed. Muckle 243 (Radice 161).
55. *Ep.* 6, ed. Muckle 244–45 (Radice 164–65).
56. *Ep.* 6, ed. Muckle 246 (Radice 165–66).
57. RB 58.17.
58. See Fry, *The Rule of Saint Benedict,* p. 453. He notes that the Benedictine *petitio* is particularly metonymic of the marriage contract and is based on Pauline descriptions of marriage in 1 Cor. 7.4.
59. *Ep.* 6, ed. Muckle 242 (Radice 160). This is another instance of Heloise's careful word choice. The term *maritus* represents a deviation from her general use of the term *vir* to denote 'man' or 'men' in most of this letter. In French and other continental administrative and legal documents in the tenth through twelfth century, *femina* is sometimes used as a term denoting dependent relationships vis-à-vis a lord in a manner distinct from the usage of the general term *mulier* for woman. J. F. Niermeyer's *Mediae Latintatis Lexicon Minus,* for example, defines *femina* as wife and gives the usage with *maritus.* Similarly, the Bride of Christ image for women religious is connoted with the phrase *femina regia aut ecclesiastica,* and female villains or vassals are called *femina* (Niermeyer, *Mediae Latintatis,* pp. 412–13). R. E. Latham's lexicon of British and Irish sources, *Revised Medieval Latin Word-List from British and Irish Sources,* indicates the same trend in Britain; *maritus* and *femina* denote marriage or other relationships of social and feudal dependence as early as the mid-eleventh century.
60. *Ep.* 6, ed. Muckle 253 (Radice 178; my translation).
61. Mary J. Carruthers proposes that medieval rhetoric and ethics emerges from practices of active reading, imitation, and the internalization of literary tropes and figures. Through this process, medieval readers and their audiences carry on a "hermeneutical dialogue" (p. 186) that allows them to experience and articulate dynamic and transformative expressions of character. See especially Carruther's discussion of Heloise and the use of Cornelia's lament, pp. 179–86.

CHAPTER 11

LISTENING TO HELOISE AT THE PARACLETE: OF SCHOLARLY DIVERSION AND A WOMAN'S "CONVERSION"

Morgan Powell

By reading the Letters of Abelard and Heloise as a text compiled and used at the Paraclete, this chapter argues that the correspondence serves to justify and generate a model of the monastic life for women.

What happened to Heloise? With what image of her continuing life are we to fill the "silence" that is supposed to begin after the close of her second letter? Did she "convert" into an authentically religious abbess? Did she persist as the incorrigible and uncompromising romantic heroine? Another question—Did she write at all?—posed by those who would resolve this dilemma by rendering her voice entirely inauthentic, has recently and, I believe, appropriately been put to rest, by consensus if not by proof.[1] But the apparent contradictions between Heloise "before and after" that have repeatedly abetted theories of forgery have not been explained away, and more recent attempts to historicize Heloise, to read her as a writer on her own terms in her own time, often become thinly disguised, if more prudently circumspect, versions of the old debate. By insisting on an authentic Heloise, an integral historical self that can be encountered and reconstructed through the texts that bear her name, these readings still run the risk of being called to explain the psyche they conjure and thus of confronting the old contradictions they have in reality only sidestepped.[2]

The fate of Heloise twisting in the winds that scholars have martialed to address her supposed contradictions has been summarized many times as a prelude to new contributions—some of them within this volume. I will not linger over another account of the same. My argument is not so much directed at others' attempts to answer the questions I cited at the outset as it is at the assumptions that led them to be posed at all. The preoccupation with the question of "what happened to Heloise" and its various offspring arises from an experience of identification with the voices of the text—generally with the voice of Heloise—that constitutes a modern displacement of an experience the text itself delineates, and one that its very existence also calls us to investigate: the experience of its monastic readers. Rather than attempting to historicize Heloise, we should attempt to historicize the text to which our images of her are indebted. I have no doubts in the likelihood, still less in the authenticity, of the authorship of letters such as these by the twelfth-century woman and abbess, Heloise, but this text is not, or is no longer only, those letters. As we have them, Heloise's letters are part of a composed whole, compiled for, and doubtless adapted to, a new communicative function.[3] By historicizing the text I mean reading it in relationship to this function or reconstructing its relationship to its intended audience.

The extent of the text at issue here can be defined both internally and through the circumstances of its manuscript transmission as beginning with Abelard's first letter of consolation to a friend (known as the *Historia calamitatum*) and ending with his rule, which completes his fulfillment of the requests made by Heloise in her last letter. This is the collection as it is transmitted to us by the best and (possibly) oldest manuscript, Troyes, *Bibliothèque Municipale* MS 802 (hereafter Troyes 802).[4] As Jacques Monfrin's study of the manuscript tradition showed, the sparse evidence we have on the origins of the compilation as it is found in Troyes 802 points to the same origin that its contents would lead us to suppose: the community of the Paraclete.[5] It is indeed difficult to imagine another origin and justification for such a collection: the life of the founder, the life of its celebrated and highly successful first abbess,[6] a letter on "how the order of nuns began and what authority there is for our profession," and "a rule which shall be suitable for women."[7] Troyes 802 most likely represents one surviving example of a compilation that existed in multiple copies distributed among the Paraclete and its daughter houses;[8] no fewer than six such dependencies were established in Heloise's lifetime.[9] While the Troyes manuscript dates from the end of the thirteenth century or the beginning of the fourteenth, the compilation of the correspondence now can be placed with some confidence to the mid-twelfth century.[10] The dating of the compilation to the lifetime of Heloise has important implications for its relationship to her life and legacy as abbess, but while I consider it both probable and appealing, it is not crucial to my own reading.

Two of the most widely acknowledged authorities on the correspondence, Jacques Monfrin and Peter von Moos, long ago called for the letters to be read as a compiled whole related to the foundation and direction of the Paraclete, a functionalization of the text that would imply reading from the position of its monastic audience.[11] But Monfrin never offered such a reading himself, and von Moos's assiduous efforts at preparing the ground for his own were abandoned in the face of the renewed authenticity debate that followed the unveiling of John Benton's provocative forgery theory at the Cluny conference of 1972.[12] The approach has found no significant echo since. In fact, all readers who have not removed the letters to the realm of forgery have tended to assume they had no audience.[13] Modern critics have imagined themselves in the privileged position of voyeurs to an intimate exchange that anticipates neither this presence nor any other.[14] The assumption that the letters represent an intimate exchange produces the modern experience of identification with its voices that is so very foreign to the experience the text offers its monastic audience.

The degree of difference between these two experiences can be grasped through a simple observation: for Heloise's monastic readers, the nuns of her community and perhaps its daughter houses, our open-ended conclusion was a forgone conclusion. Heloise was, alive or dead, revered as founder and spiritual mother of her community; our questions can hardly have preoccupied her communal daughters. But another question will have been their daily and continuous preoccupation, that is, how to apply the directional legacy of the correspondence, the monastic life it defines, justifies, and prescribes explicitly for them, to their own continuation in that life. They were not so much concerned with what happens to Heloise after the curtain falls as they were enjoined to complete their own lives according to the legacy of this text, its programmatic presentation of the female monastic life, and its rule to govern the same.

For the readers of modern posterity, the Heloise who emerges from the parchment of Troyes 802 is sandwiched between one of history's first autobiographies and one of its first rules for the female monastic life. In between lies what might be called history's first epistolary novel, for whether fact or fiction, the arrangement of these letters in chronological order with each following that to which it responds is something of a medieval *unicum*.[15] The experience of medieval monastic readers, however, was not shaped by our retrospective awareness of genre; most likely these readers apprehended these novelties as the consequences of an elaborate embedding of personal lives in a communal whole. From such a perspective, the letter compilation was indeed an interesting book. It begins with a narrative recapitulation of the past and ends with prescriptive instruction for the future. In between is a fascinating window onto the present moment, a suspended parenthesis between "how we got here" and "where we are going," "who we are" and "who we shall become." Autobiography, indeed: it tells not one but three lives, those of Abelard, Heloise, and the Paraclete—or rather four, for the life of its reader is fused with the future it prescribes. "Let her who has not yet begun think it over, and her who has made a start, continue," writes the *discipula veritatis* and *magistra humilitatis,* reflecting on "women's inherent weakness" and the nature of monastic vows in her final letter.[16] Her choice of textual authority is, as so often, strategic and telling: the statement is from Augustine's *On the Continence of Widows* [*De bono viduitatis*]. As will emerge in the argument that follows here, the appeal to a treatise on widows to figure Heloise's commitment to her monastic life, and to instruct others on that commitment, reflects tellingly on her past and allows it to define her present and future, and implies this past, present, and future are all in some way transferable to the nuns living under the rule she requests. The key to this transfer and to the assimilation of past into future that it requires are in fact articulated in the Letters through the strategic implementation of the idea of women's weakness and its relationship to an understanding of the widow as the figure of a woman's bereaved desire.

In what follows I first examine the relationship the text sets up between its individual voices and the community. This examination exhibits the way a communal audience is written into the text and its responses are prescribed there; the posture assumed by Heloise, her voice or voices, is predicated on the notion of reaching out to her community and including it in a redefinition of her monastic life. The question of identification between Heloise and her community is one with a question of identity: Heloise seeks a monastic identity that adequately assimilates the needs of her spiritual daughters to her own and defines their common relationship to Abelard such that his spiritual direction can be equally appropriate to her needs and theirs. Next I demonstrate how this new identity is negotiated, that is, on what terms Heloise's understanding of her position converges with Abelard's to form their agreement on the "remedy" [*remedium*] for her grief. The basis for this agreement is found in the prerogative of women's weakness, "infirmioris sexus praerogativa," as Abelard calls it.[17]

The structures of identification in the text assure that this is a communal remedy—the basis for a monastic commitment specific to the community's needs, just as the agreement itself allows abbess and spiritual director to commence their project of defining the community's future. Finally, I reassess Abelard's much-maligned and misunderstood black, or widowed, bride as the focal point of agreement on the women's inner monastic lives and show how, when read in relationship to the contemporary metaphors of the female religious life in which it is couched, the black bride figures as a reversal of Heloise's self-professed hypocrisy, a reconciliation of her desire past and present with a religious life grounded in the principle of inner commitment.

This argument will seem surprising enough to readers familiar with the scholarship on these letters and the habits of mind that it has formed. But the conclusions reached here are only the logical consequences of a fundamental difference introduced by historicizing the text. For readers who assume the voices of the Letters have no audience, the exposition of each voice, whether Abelard's or Heloise's, aims at persuading or coercing its respective interlocutor. This has led, in turn, to motives being habitually ascribed to both Abelard and Heloise that are nowhere explicitly supported in the text—they are rather supplied as necessitated by the original assumption: Heloise, supposedly, seeks some resumption of the lovers' erotic adventures (what she can have in mind in view of Abelard's self-professed physical and psychological eunuchry is not clear),[18] and Abelard supposedly seeks to perform some metaphorical equivalent of his castration upon Heloise.[19] In fact, these purported motives are all but contradicted by the text. They are not so much readings as extrapolations of a predisposition to the text that constitutes a decision as to how it makes meaning or its internal hermeneutic.

For the monastic audience, however, these texts do not represent a lovers' dispute unknowingly overheard but a performance that stages the foundation of their monastic lives. The motive so eagerly attributed to Heloise by latter-day readers never even enters their horizon of expectations. Her advocacy of her community's needs, on the other hand, offers an immediate opportunity for identification. The motive attributed to Abelard does, for its part, have a place on this horizon, not least because Heloise defines her dilemma as the inability to emulate Abelard's conversion, or castration narrative. But then the text no longer confronts us (its voyeuristic latter-day readers) with a struggle between two lovers over the renunciation or resumption of their erotic past; rather it confronts its monastic audience with an unresolved problem in which that audience is implicated and which is defined by the man's narrative of renunciation and the woman's incapacity to accomplish the same. It is indeed the problem of "conversion," although only if a modern semantic imposition is allowed to displace what the text calls conversion: the entry into the monastic life.[20] For the text, *this* conversion is decisive and irreversible. The problem the text delineates, or performs, is better put as—and always has been implicitly understood as—that of human sexual desire in relationship to a life devoted to God. But the text and its audience assume that the latter fact—a life devoted to God—is immutable, while our conversion hermeneutic always has toyed with an assumption, implicit or explicit, that as Heloise's desire is immutable, her monastic commitment must be negotiable. What is or must become negotiable in terms of the text's dialogic structure is instead the principle of conversion as renunciation, which Abelard's narrative embodies as castration.

Heloise twice tells us that Abelard's letters, both his letter of consolation to a friend and his first reply (*Ep.* 3), are "heard" by the entire convent. She thus inscribes a communal response and mode of reception in the text, one that presumably refers to reading aloud in chapter or refectory. Commentators on these letters have ignored the implications of this mode of reception, whether considered internal to the text or as a reflection of its possible function within the community. Similarly, Heloise's insistent inclusion of her sisters in her own distress over Abelard's letters, even at its highest pitch, has been mentioned in the literature only to be dismissed as a "pretense," an "ambivalence," or a rhetorical device. These omissions are typical of a tendency to suppress the voice of the abbess in favor of that of the passionate lover. The two voices are curiously inconsistent, and here I refer not to the inconsistency Heloise points out herself, that between her religious office and authority and the state of her soul, but to the simultaneity of the abbess's "we" and the lover's "I," of the abbess's confidence and clarity and the lover's despair and confusion, of a voice that suggests a future beyond the present conflict and one that adamantly refuses to relinquish the past.[21] That readers habitually have ignored or dismissed this simultaneity, necessarily repressing one voice or the other, is again a reflection of a model of reading imposed on the text, one that goes hand in hand with the judgment that Heloise's confessions of hidden sexual desire, her rhetorical espousing of whoredom, her panegyric despair over the thought of her lover's death, or her *planctus* against God could not have been fitting reading for devout nuns. Assuming the compilation had a communal function, daily monastic practice with texts in medieval monasteries—Abelard's ambitious plans for his daughters' literacy notwithstanding—would have seen the compiled Letters read aloud to the community in the same way Heloise suggests they were upon being received (if they ever were "received"). This does not mean they were not also read or studied by individuals alone, but it does alert us to a functional role of the text in its community and to the necessity of maintaining a flexible view of its internal hermeneutics. Communal monastic reading experience served to develop and affirm community identity. Segments or chapters as well as whole Letters excerpted from this text may have served as the stuff of such communal sessions, during which texts were read aloud and then commented upon, possibly discussed. The experience and the interpretation of the text is the locus and result of something like a classroom experience in the presence of an authority. The Letters may have been heard over and again in this way. It is the function of such texts to construct gaps in which continual reactivation of their meaning could take shape, to juxtapose antithetical arguments and manipulate their positioning such that resolution, the completion of meaning, occurs outside the text in a communally determined reading experience.[22]

The idea of the text as a performance allows us to consider its various voices in varying relationship to each other and to their audience. The monastic audience may hear the voice of a present or past Heloise, a present or past Abelard, with varying implications for the resolution of the problem. In general, while Heloise's conflicting voices have been recognized by modern scholars and explained away, the possibility of any such duplicity of voice is disallowed for Abelard. Abelard's Letters are assumed to issue from a monolithic and unchanging personality, one constructed more often than read, providing a convenient foil against which to read Heloise. But read with their monastic audience the opposite assessment of these voices applies: the abbess's upfront requests for spiritual counsel are not mere facades, but just what they seem to be: an appeal for the attention of the spiritual director whose assistance the abbess sees as equally—and even equivalently—indispensable to herself and her entire community. Nowhere in the text do we find support for the assumption that these two needs are incommensurable; on the contrary, the text insists, and sensationally so, that they are one and the same. On the other hand, the monolithic voice of the Abelardian boogieman is split into at least two identities by the very speech act that is seen to produce the entire text: a voice addressed to an *amicus* is "overheard" by another audience, one seeking the voice of its spiritual director and one that defines its needs in terms of the inadequacy of the voice it hears and the absence of the voice it requires: "Sana, obsecro, ipsa [vulnera] quae fecisti qui quae alii fecerunt curare satagis. Morem quidem amico et socio gessisti et tam amicitiae quam societatis debitum persolvisti. Sed maiori te debito nobis astrinxisti quas non tam amicas quam amicissimas non tam socias quam filias convenit nominari vel si quod dulcius et sanctius vocabulem potest excogitari" [I beg you, then, as you set about tending the wounds which others have dealt, heal the wounds you have yourself inflicted. You have done your duty to a friend and comrade, discharged your debt to friendship and comradeship, but it is a greater debt which binds you in obligation to us who can properly be called not friends so much as dearest friends, not comrades but daughters, or any other conceivable name more tender and holy].[23] In Abelard's consolation narrative for a male friend, the shamed and humiliated philosopher consciously performs his comedy of errors, or history of calamities, in order that its recipient should be reassured as to the lesser nature of his own suffering.[24] The text reveals that the same narrative has precisely the opposite effect on the (ostensibly) unintended audience of his wife, sister, and spiritual daughters—it deals them grievous wounds. From the outset, the incommensurability of a male discourse of conversion and the spiritual needs of a female community is exhibited—without, however, calling into question Abelard's ability to serve properly—through a different voice—as the women's spiritual director.

Heloise's request for "healing" of the "wounds" the women are caused displays her own difficulties in defining the relationship that justifies it: she can construct this relationship only in analogy to the very discourse to which she so strongly objects. She seeks to establish the claim of the women of the Paraclete on the same but higher ground and, in so doing, reveals an inability to name adequately the relationship that binds Abelard to them. The sisters are his *amicas,* or better, his *amicissimas,* or perhaps *socias* or *filias,* "or any other conceivable name more tender and holy." At the conclusion of the epistolary dialogue, the beginning of Heloise's third letter, she repeats the same request, couched in similar but shifted terms: "Aliquod tamen dolori remedium vales conferre si non hunc omnino possis auferre. Ut enim insertum clavum alius expellit, sic cogitatio nova priorem excludit cum alias intentus animus priorum memoriam dimittere cogitur aut intermittere. . . . Omnes itaque nos Christi ancillae et in Christo filiae tuae duo nunc a tua paternitate supplices postulamus, quae nobis admodum necessaria providemus" [And yet you have it in your power to remedy my grief, even if you cannot entirely remove it. As one nail drives out another hammered in, a new thought expels an old, when the mind is intent on other things and forced to dismiss or interrupt its recollection of the past . . . And so all we handmaids of Christ, who are your daughters in Christ, come as suppliants to demand of your paternal interest two things which we see to be very necessary for ourselves].[25] Both requests are for healing [*Sana obsecro, dolori remedium*] and both are made on behalf of the communal whole. They form a parenthesis around a present moment, a moment Heloise calls a wound. Preceding the first request is a narrative that brings us to this wound; after the second request we presumably find the prescription for its healing. The binding of the codex, which sews Abelard's account of the past together with the joint construction of a future, constitutes a suture that makes Heloise's wound into the very substance that bridges them. The present is a space in which the wound is revisited in its relationship to the voice or voices of Abelard before and after. Not only the compiler but also the epistolary Heloise makes this construction quite explicit: she introduces her first request only after recapitulating Abelard's narrative ("how we got here"), and she follows her second request with a precapitulation of what he should now provide ("where we are going").

Heloise's second request evinces none of the same struggle adequately to name her and her community's relationship to Abelard that is found in the first; she confidently stakes their claim to his attentions with the words "Omnes itaque nos Christi ancillae et in Christo filiae tuae" [All we handmaids of Christ and your daughter in Christ]. Simultaneously she suggests a difference from her earlier view of what he can provide. If her grief still remains to be healed, she implies that the voice she has heard in the interim, that of the spiritual director, is one to which she can safely entrust the continuation of her monastic life and that of her community.

As has been observed often enough, the terms *amicus* and *amicitia* that Heloise evokes to launch her first request place the relationship between Abelard and the recipient of his letter of consolation under the Ciceronian ideal of disinterested love between friends united *cum benevolentia et caritate consensio* [in harmony of love and good will].[26] By constructing her own claim on this ground, she is claiming a place for women—and for love between the sexes—within an exclusively male club[27]: there is no term, as her search for an adequate name reveals, to gender this ideal in the feminine. *Amica,* also defined by relationship to the man, is generally understood as "mistress."[28] Her well-known use of the term in her passionate plea against marriage relies on a coalescence of the male and female gendered meanings to offer a very similar progression of names for the female friend, a progression in the opposite direction, insisting on sexual love: "Non matrimonii foedera, non dotes aliquas expectavi, non denique meas voluptates aut voluntates sed tuas, sicut ipse nosti, adimplere studui. Et si uxoris nomen sanctius ac validus videtur, dulcius mihi semper exstitit amicae vocabulum aut, si non indigneris, concubinae vel scorti . . ." [I looked for no marriage-bond, no marriage portion, and it was not my own pleasures and wishes I sought to gratify, as you well know, but yours. The name of wife may seem more sacred or more binding, but sweeter for me will always be the word mistress, or, if you will permit me, that of concubine or whore].[29]

Here, too, she seeks a name "sweet enough" for an unnamable love, but where earlier this name united sanctity and sweetness—"quod dulcius vel sanctius vocabulum"—here she demonstratively allows the two criteria to stand in opposition, an opposition between roles prescripted for women's love of men. The terms she invokes, whether meant to characterize feelings between the community (herself included) and Abelard or her sacrifice for him, whether exhibited by the spiritualized *amicissima* or the whore, are meant to serve one and the same ideal, and yet she cannot resolve the tension between them within the terms offered her by a male monastic discourse. In fact, Heloise's dilemma is constructed in the correspondence to arise from an imperative emulation of a male ideal that she cannot fulfill.

These two naming progressions are bound up in one in the salutation that opens Heloise's letter. Initiating the dialogue that will bridge past and future, she is at a loss to assimilate the various bonds that join her and Abelard in this venture: "Domino suo immo patri, coniugi suo immo fratri, ancilla sua immo filia, ipsius uxor immo soror,

Abaelardo Heloisa" [To her master, or rather her father, husband, or rather brother; his handmaid, or rather his daughter, wife, or rather sister; to Abelard, Heloise].[30] The woman who is handmaid, daughter, sister, and wife all to one "man" was only too well known to twelfth-century monastic spirituality: she is Mary, the *sponsa* or bride of the Song of Songs. This echo may have been heard by the female monastic audience, and it has in its turn a certain echo in Abelard's salutation to the "bride of Christ" at the opening of *Ep.* 5, the decisive letter in which he uses the black bride of the Songs of Songs to define the identity of his spiritual daughters.[31] The "bride of Christ" is not mentioned in the correspondence before that point, a fact that hints at its role in resolving the identity question. But the echo of the position of the biblical bride in Heloise's salutation is most instructive here because the *sponsa*'s naming is predicated on a convergence of what is consistently divergent in Heloise's naming confusion: a spiritualized and an erotic love, a human and a divine beloved, and marriage and religious devotion. By seeking a place within *amicitia* for the monastic lives of women and their male *magister,* a place for love freely given within the institutional confines of marriage, and a place for sexual desire within spiritual love, Heloise's exposition to her abbot, husband, and beloved causes the vows taken in such rapid succession in her past to become constitutive for her monastic present, as she relates to Abelard, as she relates to the nuns in her charge, and as they relate to him. The varying and divergent identities of Heloise and the women of the Paraclete converge in one ideal of love; this love in turn is recognizable as the justification of convergence in the varying female identities of the *sponsa,* also the expression of a convergence between human (erotic) and divine (spiritualized) love. Between the plaintive despair of desire in search of a name and the available referent of both this desire and the names it invokes an unspoken identity is circumscribed and thus made to take shape through the collusion of identities inside and outside the text. When this unspoken identity finally speaks within the text as the *sponsa nigra* [black bride], it is not Abelard's creation but the result of a continuously unfolding negotiation of identity and desire conducted between the voices of the text.

As mentioned earlier, the coalescence of the "I" and the "we" addressing Abelard in each of Heloise's letters has received very little attention. For Dronke, the "we" is but the façade of decorum on the way to becoming an "I"; more recent and feminist readings brand it a "pretext to the erotic transgression,"[32] or find in it the public voice that is defined in opposition to the private self.[33] Among earlier commentators, even von Moos regards this rhetorical merger as an "ambivalence" that is sooner to be explained and excused than believed.[34] These cursory and dismissive readings are nonetheless the exception to a rule of silence: most do not address the issue at all. But the text speaks a clear message: each of Heloise's three letters opens with this same identification. The discourse then becomes (except in the last letter) progressively more interiorized. But the progression from plural to singular, exteriority to interiority, does not exempt the sisters from partaking in the depths of Heloise's suffering or from sharing the desperation of her love for Abelard or even from implicit inclusion in her personal narrative. The climactic second letter begins just as did her first, by evoking the nuns' "desolate" and tearful state "upon hearing the words you wrote towards the end of your letter."[35] To outlive him would be harder than death for his "humble handmaids"; he should sooner expedite them on the journey beforehand. The community would join her in raging against God himself, "the soul will lose its power of reason and the tongue its use of speech."[36] Finally, she intimates that the convent would commit mass suicide: "Quae, cum in te nostram amiserimus vitam, vivere te recedente nequaquam poterimus. Atque utinam nec tunc usque possimus. Mortis tuae mentio mors quaedam nobis est. Ipsa autem mortis huius veritas quid si nos invenerit, futura est" [If we lose our life in you, we shall not be able to go on living when you leave us. I would not even have us live to see that day, for if the mere mention of your death is death for us, what will the reality be if it finds us still alive]?[37] Such blasphemies can hardly be dismissed as a legitimizing disguise. The identification between the community and its suffering representative is made as undeniable as the consequences are made sensational.

Heloise begins this letter with an expression of individual surprise: "I am surprised, my only love. . . ."[38] She then cites a parallel reaction among the communal whole: "We were also greatly surprised. . . ."[39] From here she launches into the communal lamentation just summarized. At the culmination of this first cycle of communal desolation and desperation, the "I" reemerges from the "we," but as its singular representative: "And so, I beg you, spare us—spare her, at least. . . ."[40] This leads to a renewed lamentation, now focused on her own condition, spoken by the "I." No less panegyric than the first, this interior focus is more inwardly wrenching. But the spiraling self-recrimination that ensues does not isolate Heloise as an individual so much as it makes her into a superlative example of the general case, the "wickedness" of her sex: "O summam in viros summos consuetam feminarum perniciem" [Oh how great is the ruin that women invariably bring on great men]![41] Heloise moves back and forth between details of her own story and misogynist generalization, including all women in her fate ("You . . . had raised me and all my kind to your own level"), or setting her story next to that of Eve and various of her biblical daughters: "It was the first woman in the beginning who lured man from Paradise. . . ."[42]

Heloise and *her* daughters share one wound, they seek one remedy and they define their identity in a mutual relationship to a narrative of which hers is the *exemplum.* The requests for consolation from their spiritual director are made simultaneously on behalf of the communal whole and its representative speaker, and the petitioning abbess leaves no room for even the most careful surgical analysis to extricate the "I" from the "we." This is not to say that she has managed to bring them together without internal contradiction: her struggle with the suitable *vocabuli* amply attest to unresolved issues. But the fact of the sisters' full participation is simply assumed, not only by Heloise but by Abelard as well. This "we" is beyond question, even as the other two relationships, or the one other relationship, between the "we" and Abelard, is under negotiation. To negotiate this last relationship, however, is to unite marriage, the monastic life, spiritual friendship, and erotic love under one term, one love. It is, quite simply, the negotiation of Heloise's past against her present, with the stakes the *communal* future. The negotiation over the terms on which she married and continues in marriage, on which she took her monastic vows and continues to live them, is the site of a newly conceived monastic "we," a rule—and a spiritual life—appropriate to women. No lesser *remedium* will heal the mistress or rather the *amicas,* indemnify the wife or rather the handmaids, nor satisfy the abbess or rather the daughters.

For a monastic audience, the communal reception of Abelard's letters, as represented by Heloise, mirrors their own act of reading (or listening), that is, the communal "we" that fuses with Heloise's "I" in the act of receiving Abelard's letters inscribes the "present" audience in the text and in the articulation of Heloise's "private" anguish. Each and every nun who hears these letters becomes a new witness to their articulation of desire as her own. This fact is initially somewhat astonishing, but our astonishment is due primarily to an overexposure to critical misapprehensions and several centuries of romanticizing reception of the texts and the historical personages. Abelard, too, subscribes to the idea that the expression of Heloise's desire speaks for the community as a whole. Commentators have not hesitated to point with distaste to the assumption in his first reply that the entire convent should share equally in Heloise's mourning of his death and ardent prayers for his soul and the way in which this results in an identification between their devotion to him and their devotion to Christ. What Heloise's Letters say on this point has quite simply been ignored, hopelessly obscured by a preoccupation with their "heroine," a desire to identify with her in ways that simultaneously deny the overt offer of identification made by the abbess to her community.[43]

Taken on its own terms, the insistent assimilation of Heloise's "I" to the communal "we" (and vice versa) indicates that when the relationship between Abelard and his spiritual daughters emerges as stabilized at the opening of *Ep.* 6, the same is equally true of his relationship to Heloise. In the same way, the personal concerns of the first two letters must be assimilated to the project of communal direction. Linda Georgianna's detailed analysis in this volume of Heloise's third letter demonstrates abundantly that the personal concerns voiced in the earlier letters are transposed onto the regulation of community life in her third letter.[44] The newly engaged activity of the monastic foundation is, as Heloise says, only a different way of engaging the same concerns, a different nail driven through the same hole, such that earlier thoughts may be supplanted by new ones. That is, where here the abbess speaks for the community of nuns in order to establish the regulation of their outer lives as a function of the specific [*specialiter*] needs of women, there the grieving wife, mistress, and *amica* spoke *singulariter* for her sisters in suffering in order to require direction of their spiritual lives that would respond to the inner needs of a woman. The difference between the two is not one between private and public, or between personal and directional, or still less between published and unpublished, edifying and intimate, communal and individual.[45] It is only that between the inner and the outer life, the spiritual and regulatory dimensions of direction. Just as Aelred of Rievaulx divided his direction of his sister's life as a recluse into an outer and an inner rule,[46] the foundation of the communal life of the Paraclete focuses first on the inner struggle of each one and then on the outer governance of the whole. The task confronting this reading, then, is to examine whether and how Heloise's crisis is negotiated such that it becomes constitutive for the spiritual needs of the community. It is the question of how the *remedium* comes to be defined and how it relates to her past and the community's future.

The epistolary dialogue witnessed in this text as the performance—what it presents to its audience as the present moment—takes place as a wound inflicted on a female community when it overhears a male conversion narrative. The community's representative speaker then exemplifies this wound by recalling its imbedding in her own past and her monastic life. Heloise formulates her moment of commitment to the monastic life as at once an emulation of the male ideal of *amicitia* and an emulation of her husband's castration. As articulated by twelfth-century monastic writers, the Ciceronian ideal requires that the beloved be loved "for himself alone" or, as Heloise puts it, "Nihil umquam, Deus scit, in te nisi te requisivi, te pure non tua concupiscens" [God knows I never sought anything in you except yourself; I wanted simply you, nothing of yours].[47] This ultimately means love for love's sake, for possession of the beloved must be secondary to the ideal expressed by disinterested love.

Thus Heloise makes her greatest commitment to love by depriving herself of her beloved: "in tantam versus est amor insaniam ut quod solum appetebat, hoc ipse sibi sine spe recuperationis auferret" [my love rose to such heights of madness that it robbed itself of what it most desired beyond hope of recovery].[48] The heroic act of self-deprivation named here is Heloise's original "wound," and both the verb she uses and the terms in which she describes the act show that she sees it as analogous to, and simultaneous with, Abelard's castration, which wounded and healed him at once. Abelard designates his castration in the *Historia calamitatum* with the words "facultate ablata," a physical fact that, he says, removes all suspicion of either his continuing desire or his ability to fulfill it.[49] Heloise uses the same verb, *auferre,* whether speaking of the self-inflicted separation from the object of her own desire or of the more complex mutual loss imposed by the treacherous act of others. In the continuation of the just cited passage, she makes clear that her heroic sacrifice was also to affirm both a bodily and a spiritual commitment, but in the opposite direction from that forced on Abelard: "ad tuam statim iussionem tam habitum ipsa quam animum immutarem ut te tam corporis mei quam animi unicum possessorem ostenderem" [at your bidding I changed my clothing along with my mind, in order to prove you the sole possessor of my body and my will alike].[50] A few lines earlier she names the separation imposed from without such that her loss and his are indistinguishable: "Nosti, carissime, noverunt omnes quanta in te amiserim et quam miserabili casu summa et ubique nota proditio me ipsam quoque mihi tecum abstulerit ut incomparabiliter maior sit dolor ex amissionis modo quam ex damno" [You know, beloved, as the whole world knows, how much I have lost in you, how at one wretched stroke of fortune that supreme act of flagrant treachery robbed me of my very self in robbing me of you; and how my sorrow for my loss is nothing compared with what I feel for the manner in which I lost you].[51]

The ambiguity of this passage—is it the castration alone, or at all, that is meant, or other events Heloise equates with it?[52]—perfectly suits the conflation of her loss with his and unites them in the verb *auferre.* The possibility of fulfilling her desire is torn from her—or rather she tears it from herself as Abelard's potency was torn from him—but the text insists on the assumption that castration also eradicated Abelard's desire while leaving hers intact. The woman's emulation of this male conversion remains, and must remain, incomplete; that is, the text locates the difference between her conversion and his in a fact of anatomy and thus makes it insurmountable. The emulative act is itself a consequence of, or required by, the ideal of love to which Heloise subscribes but that enforces the same gender-determined exclusion.

The appraisal of Abelard's castration conversion in the secondary literature has never recognized it as a possible foil for the construction of an alternative—because the position of the audience has been left out of account.[53] Instead, most readings supply the assumption mentioned above, which sees the "castration solution" as one imposed by Abelard on Heloise, one he persistently attempts to bring her to accept for herself as well as for him.[54] In fact, the text reveals the opposite is true: it is Heloise who consistently identifies with Abelard's loss and tries to make it her own, and who assumes that grace is denied her because of her simultaneous exclusion from the spiritual transformation offered by the bodily mutilation. Despite the urgent plea Heloise makes in the passages just cited for Abelard to address their differing experience of one loss, his first reply remains completely silent on this point. It is then Heloise, not Abelard, who, in her second letter, proceeds from her earlier recognition to the belief that the healing she seeks is a completion of his transformation as yet incompletely effected upon herself: "O vere me miseram, et illa conquestione ingemiscentis animae dignissimam. 'Infelix ego homo, quis me liberabit de corpore mortis huius?' Utinam et quod sequitur veraciter addere queam: 'Gratia Dei per Jesum Christum Dominum nostrum' [Rom. 7.24]. Haec te gratia, carissime, praevenit, et ab his tibi stimulis una corpora plaga . . . sanavit, . . . more quidem fidelissimi medici qui non parcit dolori ut consulat saluti. Hoc autem in me. . . ." [In my utter wretchedness, that cry from a suffering soul could well be mine: 'Miserable creature that I am, who is there to rescue me out of the body doomed to this death?' Would that in truth I could go on: 'The grace of God through Jesus Christ our Lord.' This grace, my dearest, came upon you unsought—a single wound of the body by freeing you from these torments has healed many wounds in your soul . . . like an honest doctor who does not shrink from giving pain if it will bring about a cure. But for me . . .].[55] The placement of this last passage is crucial to the argument on Heloise's *remedium*. It is the culmination of her confession that memories, specific memories tied to times, places, and actions of their illicit lovemaking obsess her even in the act of prayer and devotion, even in the Mass. As a result she seeks liberation from the body, a removal of herself from her desire. She sees her desire as Abelard presents his—as something that must be excised from the self. But this recognition occurs within a desperate confession of her own weakness; the entire letter, from its portrayal of the pitiful state of the Paraclete community unable even to contemplate the death of its male protector through the misogynist invective to the final confession, is a demonstration of incapacity.[56] As the woman rails against her sex for the failings of which she (she says) is also guilty, so the community's desperation exhibits its weakness such that the final confession is spoken for all, and the entire exposition articulates an impasse that confronts woman and all women when measured as Heloise measures herself—against the accomplished removal of desire, exhibited in Abelard's castration. But the impasse is then inscribed not only as one between Heloise's desire and Abelard's purification but also, and inescapably, as one between the female and the male body. Both the bodily reality of castration and its metaphorical significance apply, but the one cannot be separated from the other. This recognition is at the root of Heloise's misogynist invective: the woman is in a double bind, deprived of the "cure" that can be effected on the male body, while her desire, as Heloise goes on to insist, is the more intense by reason of her "weaker nature": "Hoc autem in me stimulos carnis haec incentiva libidinis ipse iuvenilis fervor aetatis, et iucundissimarum experientia voluptatum plurimum accendunt, et tanto amplius sua me impugnatione opprimunt, quanto infirmior est natura quam impugnant. Castam me praedicant qui non deprehendunt hypocritam. Munditiam carnis conferunt in virtutem, cum non sit corporis, sed animi virtus" [But for me, youth and passion and experience of pleasures which were so delightful intensify the torments of the flesh and longings of desire, and the assault is the more overwhelming as the nature they attack is the weaker. Men call me chaste; they do not know what a hypocrite I am. They consider purity of the flesh a virtue, though virtue belongs not to the body but to the soul].[57]

Heloise's confession of weakness stands in opposition to the formulation of her earlier sacrifice as a heroic emulation of her husband's loss, as an emulation of the man's castration and of her own ideal of love. This singular dilemma, one that confronts her ethic of sacrifice for love with an incapacity fully to accomplish what it requires, converges with a representation of the community and of the "weaker sex." Castration and the ideal of *amicitia* both define an understanding of desire, love, and conversion that is intrinsically male; weakness comes increasingly to mark the incommensurability between this understanding and the female case. As demonstrated earlier, the movement of Heloise's second letter between the "I" and the "we" brings about a convergence of what she once saw as her singular needs arising from singular circumstances with the special needs of her sex as a whole (*singulariter/specialiter*). Through the convergence of communal, sexual, and personal (that imbedded in narrative events) identity in the idea of the weakness of the woman's body, or of the woman as body, Heloise's particular hypocrisy becomes gendered, located in the inability to renounce what arises from the nature of her sex, and applies potentially to all women. This is the point that her letter must reach in order for Abelard to respond such that the new remedy applies equally to herself and to her entire sex.

In her analysis of Heloise's third letter in chapter 8, Georgianna provides excellent insights into the continuity between Heloise's insistence on the "particularity" of her memories and experiences, their grounding in time, place, and body, and the nature of her commitment to her new subject, the conception of an appropriately female monastic life. The attempt to define the difference of an appropriate rule emerges as one that is continuous with the difference defined between the "bodily" continuity of her desire and Abelard's renunciation.[58] Georgianna speculates that this perhaps demonstrates that "while Abelard's is fundamentally a philosophical or logical temperament, Heloise's habit of mind is primarily influenced by imagination and memory."[59] The characterization may stand, but only insofar as it reveals the voices of the dialogue as types that correspond to the medieval understanding of the ontological dimension of gender. The woman's affinity with the particular, the material and the body, is contrasted here with the man's affinity with the abstract and the spiritual. At the moment when Heloise consigns her desire to an incontrovertible and unconvertible weakness of her sex, the positions in the dialogue become realigned in accordance with the equation "woman is to man as flesh is to spirit." In her groundbreaking work, historian Caroline Walker Bynum has demonstrated in detail how this equation is exploited with increasing force and consistency in the definition of women's spirituality—beginning with contemporaries of Heloise—such that the woman's position becomes, in all its gendered specificity, simultaneously identified with a weakness common to all humanity.[60] The man's position is posited as the *vir* in Paul's *factus sum vir:* a condition of spiritual perfection not easily attainable within, or even removed from, this world.[61] Male writers exploit the woman's position in a symbolic reversal that demonstrates their humility before God: by identifying with the abject body of woman, they partake of the privilege of the weak who will inherit the earth.[62] For women, however, this position is not one of reversal or renunciation but of continuity with their bodily selves and secular roles, their social and biological identities, "a deepening of ordinary human experience that came when God impinged upon it."[63] The hallmark feature of this continuity, indeed, its driving force is "to realize the *opportunity* of physicality," such that "bodily impulses and emotions—the person's full sensuality—were released into new experience."[64] Man is to woman as spirit is to flesh, as renunciation is to integration or fusion between human desire and the love of God. The impasse at which Heloise arrives at the end of her second letter, and beyond which no amount of critical speculation has been able to move her, is the same one that a contemporary monastic discourse on gendered desire was beginning to articulate—and to overcome, but not through a notion of contrived and contrite conversion or a Magdalene fantasy of tearful repentance; no *medicus ex machina* intervenes to perform a surgical correction on the body-that-is-woman. The solution was found in continuity between past and present, as between profane and sacred desire, between a desire fulfilled in the body and a bodily cognizance of desire for God.

The Letters as text construct a dialogue that pits the voice of "male" renunciation against "female" desire, that is, in terms of the medieval understanding of gender, the voice of spiritual perfection against bodily imperfection. Woman is to man as weakness is to strength as desire/hypocrisy is to renunciation (or conversion in our modern sense): thus Heloise sees her own position. But the identification of renunciation with castration forces an inversion within the terms in which the problem is initially posed: Woman is to man as weakness is to strength as desire is to castration and . . . humanity is to divinity. The miraculous conversion narrative is inemulable, this case by reason of woman's bodily imperfection or weakness in the flesh. The position of the man becomes one unattainably aligned with spiritual perfection, and that of the woman is, as a result, redefined as the weakness of humanity measured against the divine.

The solution just evoked, one of integration as opposed to renunciation, is articulated in the text through the black bride. But the value of this figure to the exposition as a whole cannot be fully appreciated without first considering the way the voices of both Abelard and Heloise undergo a correction that allows them to converge in the idea of woman's weakness as her special dispensation, or the prerogative of human sexual desire before God.

Heloise's final request to Abelard, at the outset of her third letter, makes a distinction between what she now believes he can and cannot provide. Tellingly, this distinction is denoted by the opposition between the phrases *remedium conferre* and *dolorem auferre.* Shortly before she makes her parallel request for healing in *Ep.* 2, Heloise speaks of the consolation she envisions as both the removal [there: *deferre*] and the alleviation [*conferre remedium*] of suffering.[65] The later request intensifies the contrast between the removal of and the remedy for grief and recognizes that the former cannot be accomplished. The substitution of *auferre* to signal this recognition—the only clear statement she makes of a change in her position—echoes the identification made elsewhere by both her and Abelard between *auferre* and castration, most particularly the discussion of castration finally offered by Abelard in the letter immediately preceding her request. What Heloise is saying, in the context of these statements, is that there can be no extinguishing of her desire equivalent to Abelard's, but she nonetheless perceives a remedy for her grief.

The text does not support the habitually touted claim that Abelard seeks metaphorically to castrate Heloise. In fact, Abelard has said nothing and has apparently had nothing to say on his castration *to Heloise* until she reaches the impasse of her second letter. Moreover, as has been noted more than once within the discussion of the religious credibility of the letters, Abelard never chides or reproves Heloise for the expression of her desire[66]; not once does he admonish her to suppress confession of the carnal memories that, she says, torment her.[67] He does chide and reprove her for her "old perpetual complaint" on "the manner of our entry into the religious life," for railing against the "mercy" of his castration, and for her betrayal of "true love" in requiring that he remain silent on the perceived danger to his life.[68]

Where in her second letter (*Ep.* 4) Heloise envisions a removal [*auferre*] of the *stimuli carnis* as the only relief adequate to her case, the *castratus* responds in such a way as to make the unavailability of his solution explicit and also to deny it any usefulness.

In his discussion of castration, a topic that he feels "may relieve the bitterness of your grief," Abelard never encourages Heloise in her belief that his solution is or ought to be emulable.[69] Not a few wise men, he says, sought to execute the same act upon themselves, so fervently did they aspire to the purity granted him by divine grace.[70] But then the presentation takes a different tack. The examples Abelard cites do not serve to illustrate the opening statement, but rather show that those who sought such a solution of their own will were in error. God denied the Apostle who, "stimulo carnis auferendo" [in order to be to be rid of the promptings of the flesh], sought the favor granted Abelard. Origen was seriously to blame for seeking a *remedium* for sin in punishment of his own body, "per poenam corporis remedium culpae quaerit."[71] This misguided fervor—"Suggestione diabolica vel errore maxima" [at the suggestion of the devil or in grave error]—is referred to a misunderstanding of Scripture that does not see beyond the literal sense.[72] The word *remedium* as applied to Origen's error is a negative corrective, for despite the repeated evocation of God as doctor and Abelard's castration as a sort of cure, *remedium* elsewhere always applies only to the relief envisioned for Heloise, a relief that cannot be found in castration. Abelard goes on to explain that he escapes Origen's guilt, because his castration was not sought of his own will but was rather the effect of divine grace.[73]

The similarity between Heloise's diction and Abelard's (*auferre stimulos carnis, remedium*) conceals a tautological comparison, because neither the Apostle's nor Origen's case applies to Heloise any better than Abelard's does. It can hardly be any comfort to Heloise that she need not cut off a member she does not have. Abelard's exposition is spoken by the voice of the fallible and punished philosopher; the spiritual director will come to the fore shortly. But the voice of the man testifying to his own case does reflect in opposition on her own: it aims not at a commensurate comparison with Heloise's case but rather at a removal of Abelard's from the realm of human will. The recurrence of Heloise's terms serves to underline this point: what she seeks, the Apostle and Origen sought, and even they, as men for whom this action is physically realizable, cannot partake of the grace given Abelard. Abelard's "male" solution is not, in fact, a human solution. For Heloise and her sisters, who represent the weakest of humanity, another must be envisioned.

Where Abelard's letter aims at directly addressing Heloise's irrepressible desire, he represents his own state rather differently. While castration still accomplishes the "removal" of desire, this in itself is no model of perfection or guarantee of reward: "Mihi vero nulla superest corona quia nulla subest certaminis causa. Deest materia pugnae, cui *ablatus est* stimulus concupiscientiae" [But no crown is waiting for me, because the proddings of the flesh *have been removed*].[74] Her task is thus not to excise her desire nor to continuously overcome it, but to live with the "torment" caused her by her memories.[75] Invoking first, as she did, the "weakness of her nature" and "the greater weakness of her sex" as apologies available to her for their past indulgences, he then echoes her mention of the greater susceptibility of her youth. Acknowledging all these as reason for the greater intensity of her carnal desires, he makes these desires into her guarantee of the crown that will elude him: " . . . multas adolescentiae tuae maiores animi passiones ex assidua carnis suggestione reservavit ad martyrii coronam" [. . . the many greater sufferings of the heart through the continual prompting of the flesh of your own youth he has reserved for a martyr's crown].[76]

Abelard's argument thus insists on a point the secondary literature has continually suppressed: he understands his castration and its consequences for his desire in a way that he fully acknowledges cannot apply to Heloise, and his remarks on her martyr's crown are thus not a call to follow him in some metaphorical sense but an insistence on difference that itself depends on a continuity between her memories of human passion and her salvation. The assumption that Abelard requires of Heloise a kind of continually repeated victory over desire modeled by his castration denies the premises on which the argument is built: hers is a struggle he never encountered; its value derives from the weakness or susceptibility of the woman in which he does not share. The myth of his castration as a complete cleansing of soul and body is constructed to attest to the necessity of an alternative for the woman's voice, the voice defined from beginning to end by the continuity of desire as opposed to its extrahuman renunciation. Abelard's miraculous conversion thus becomes the contrafact to the real dilemma: how to define conversion in real "human" terms, as a complex reorientation from a past life onto a future one. This inversion depends on the overt gendering of Heloise's specific impasse, in which both voices concur and participate; indeed, agreement on the convergence between her crisis and its gender-specific understanding *allows* them to communicate: where the first exchange (*Ep.* 2 and 3) exhibits a crisis of opposition and divergence, the second enables convergence and resolution; where Abelard initially overlooks entirely the urgent petitions of Heloise's first letter, in his second reply he declares himself ready to address comprehensively the content of the entire exchange.

The secondary literature, especially in recent years, has expanded the claim that Abelard imposes his castration on Heloise to the idea that he also denies her the position of difference between the male and the female sex from which she proposes to channel his spiritual direction in her third letter (*Ep.* 6).[77] There is, in fact, one passage that could support this idea. In Abelard's initial presentation of the power of women's prayer, which makes up nearly the entire content of his first reply, he writes: "Vitae vero nostrae conservationem multiplex vestrae devotionis oratio facile obtinebit. Quarum tam abstinentia quam continentia Deo sacrata, quanto ipsi gratior habetur, tanto ipsum propitiorem inveniet" [. . . the multiplied prayers of your shared devotion should easily win the preservation of my own life. The more God is pleased by the abstinence and continence which women have dedicated to him, the more willing he will be to grant their prayers].[78] Abelard's rhetoric here summons Heloise to a more sublime form of his own renunciation. Following this statement, she can only despair of any expediency of her prayers for him, lacking as she does the stated precondition. But while the power of women's prayer and women's special favor with God are ideas Abelard will repeat over and again, after Heloise's response they never recur in this form, but rather are paired with a new precondition, the one Heloise insists on: women's carnal weakness.[79] The gap in Abelard's initial understanding of her position, his simultaneous assumption of the efficacy of his wife's prayer and of her "abstinence and continence"—his idea of the abbess's interior and exterior perfection—places him, and the audience with him, before a stunning *refutatio* of this conception of his "widow's" devotion to him and to God, which is the manifest demonstration of woman's weakness.

Once this demonstration is made, it determines the content and direction of the remaining correspondence. In chapter 8 of this volume Georgianna has analyzed the central importance of women's weakness to Heloise's third letter. Abelard's reply, *Ep.* 7—the Letter it seems no one reads—becomes a veritable treatise on woman's weakness as the *fons et origo* of a special grace and dignity with God.[80] Woman's weakness stands behind the idea of the purity of the Magdalene's desire as expressed in the excesses of her devotion at the letter's outset.[81] Weakness justifies the ensuing emphasis on women's bodily closeness to Christ and serves to make their steadfastness at His grave all the more laudable, for, as is well known, "Sunt et viri naturaliter tam mente quam corpore feminis fortiores" [Men are naturally stronger than women in both mind and body].[82] The complementary obverse of this statement, twice repeated, insists on women's continuous bodily and spiritual proximity to the bridegroom they mourn: "a quo nec in morte vel mente vel corpore feminae sunt disiunctae" [from whom even in death the women were separated neither in mind nor in body].[83] Farther on, the letter builds to a resounding repetition of the theme of grace derived from weakness,[84] and makes women's flesh, indeed the vulva itself, the cause of man's salvation, even as it was the cause of the Fall: "Ut autem cetera omnia praetermittamus, quid tamen necessarium nostrae redemptioni et totius munde salute fuerit quam sexus femineus, qui nobis ipsum peperit Salvatorem? . . . Posset utique, si vellet, redemptor noster de viro corpus assumere. . . . Sed hanc suae humilitatis singularem gratiam ad infirmioris sexus transtulit honorem. Posset et alia parte muliebris corporis digniore nasci quam ceteri homines, eadem qua concipiuntur vilissima portione nascentes. Sed ad incomparabilem infirmioris corporis honorem longe amplius ortu suo consecravit eius genitale, quam viri fecerat ex circumcisione" [But leaving all of this out of account, what was more necessary for our redemption and for the salvation of the entire world than the female sex, which bore us the Savior himself? . . . Our Redeemer, had he desired, could have assumed his body from a man. . . . But instead he accorded this singular grace of his humiliation to the weaker sex. And he could have made himself be born by another, more worthy part of woman's body than that vile organ through which other men are both conceived and born. But to the incomparable honor of the weaker sex, he made the woman's genital organ far more sacred than he had the man's through circumcision].[85]

How does this elevation of woman's sexual physicality and the specific focus on the organ that previously defined her insufficiency, her exclusion from the man's castration solution, "read" in the context of the reorientation of the *remedium?* Bodilyness is abject but redeemed, apparently *vilissima* but reserved for the highest honor, approached by reason of its very exterior baseness to the divinity of Christ—that is, woman's inability to excise her desire, to remove her bodilyness, demonstrates a need for a corporeal proximity to Christ as for a corporeal understanding of her desire for Him. Implicit in this exposition is a reversal of Heloise's understanding of her hypocrisy, of the adversarial relationship between appearance and truth, exterior and interior, body and soul, that has likewise gone unnoticed. If the weakness for which she condemns herself is not damning but rather redeeming, then what she calls her hypocrisy is in fact a misapprehension of the dilemma that confronts her sex.

The "personal correspondence," or the present moment witnessed by the audience, performs woman's weakness; it is a demonstration *in re* of the inadequacy of a monastic inner life founded on the idea of renunciation to subjects posited as weak in the flesh. The confrontation with this fact brings about a reorientation to the "conversion" question on both sides of the dialogue to allow an agreement on an inner spiritual life that acknowledges this weakness. Abelard is in fact the first to evoke women's weakness, in the *Historia calamitatum*. There it is little more than the familiar monastic rhetoric applied a priori to a female community.[86] But this topos does not reemerge in the dialogue until it has been redefined by the articulation of woman's desire and the impasse at which it arrives. It is part of the genius of the text that it is constructed such that the shamed philosopher is made to witness a performance in his turn, the same performance offered the Paraclete audience, and that this performance shapes both the emergent voice of the spiritual director and the audience's identification with the textual recipients of his instruction.

The conventional monastic rhetoric of women's weakness uses it either to abjure men to shun female company or to exhort women to a more glorious victory over their own innately more grievous vice. "Vince mulierem, vince carnem, vince libidinem" [Conquer the woman, conquer the flesh, conquer desire]—thus Osbert of Clare exhorts Ida of Barkening in his letter of direction for nuns written in the mid-twelfth century.[87] Heloise's recrimination of herself and her sex voices this rhetoric from the opposite position, and thus reverses its relevance to her case: it now expresses what cannot be accomplished, just as Abelard's castration serves as the image of an unattainable renunciation. When Abelard then reaffirms woman's sexual identity as a vilified whose very infirmity is dear to God, he replaces the idea of the more glorious victory with that of an "infirmioris sexus praerogativa" [privilege of the weaker sex], grace accorded the meek ipso facto, predicated on the humility of continuous and self-acknowledged inadequacy.[88]

Self-acknowledged inadequacy and a refusal to seek a glorious victory—a willingness to be content with "whatever corner of heaven"—describe precisely the position from which Heloise makes her final plea at the end of her second letter.[89] At the same time she insists on the imperative of inner truth and submits her conscience—with no dissembling of its abject state—to the sole true Judge, "he who searches our hearts and loins and sees in our darkness."[90] This position, which she despairingly also castigates as that of an inveterate hypocrite, is in fact the perfect complement to Abelard's black bride; it is also an eloquently, if paradoxically, self-indicting portrayal of herself as the figure of female monastic virtue after which the black bride is modeled: the Wise Virgin. By the end of Heloise's second letter, the voice of the woman confronting her own weakness has been brought fully into line with the image she will be offered of her continuing monastic life. The nature of this image itself dictates that its virtue can be stated only by another, or through the self-effacing inversion of its own sincerity that is Heloise's self-indictment for hypocrisy.

Apparently previous commentators have regarded Abelard's identification of the *sponsa nigra* with a "widowed" bride as conventional, which it is not, or they simply have chosen to ignore it.[91] But Abelard introduces it such that there can be no mistake: with the tripartite and narrowing distinction *generaliter, specialiter, expressius tamen* he offers the figure of the widowed bride as an identity especially and uniquely appropriate to the community whose desire is now identical with that of its representative member.[92] This widowed bride is placed at the meeting point between memory of lost human love ("like the mourning worn by good widows who weep for the dead husbands they loved")[93] and hope for spiritual fulfillment, her monastic future, figured in the same terms ("The women sitting at the tomb wept and lamented for the Lord").[94] Her defining attribute is the habit that is the mark of her monastic and communal identity. That is, the exterior mark of vocation, "Ipse . . . cultus exterior nigrorum" [This same outward donning of blackness], is made into a symbol of the continuity between desire for an earthly and a divine beloved;[95] the experiential continuity between the past loss of one bridegroom and unachieved union with the other assures the very integrity of her position, a potential dissolution of Heloise's hypocrisy.

The blackness of the bride is indeed seen as a condition that is imposed from without, a disfigurement that is executed by the bridegroom upon his bride that is also her special grace. But there is no indication that this abject exterior is to be taken as the metaphor for a repression of desire that it is so often seen to represent.[96] The text aligns it with several ideas: self-effacing humility, the desire to shun public acclaim, women's bodily imperfection or weakness, and the enhanced sensuality of hidden lovemaking. All of these, with the exception of the last, are anticipated by Heloise's plea at the end of her preceding letter. The black bride in effect speaks Heloise's position from one of exegetical authority, assigning it the very scriptural locus that was circumscribed by the salutation of her opening letter. The "I" and the "we" recur here as the *sponsa* and her followers, the daughters of Jerusalem, united in the blackness that exhibits her singular as well as her communal identity, a distinguishing mark as well as a flaw that is common to her *species:* "Sic vero eam sol verus decolorat quia coelestis amor sponsi eam sic humiliat. . . . Bene autem filias Jerusalem, id est, imperfectiores alloquens fideles qui filiarum potius quam filiorum nomine digni sunt, dicit: Nolite mirari [quod fusca sim].[97] Ac si apertius dicat: Quod sic me humilio vel tam viriliter adversitates sustineo, non est meae virtutis, sed eius gratiae cui deservio" [So indeed the true sun changes her color because the heavenly love of the bridegroom humbles her in this way. . . . And she rightly told the daughters of Jerusalem, that is, the weaker amongst the faithful who deserve to be called daughters rather than sons, 'Take no notice of my darkness, because the son has discolored me.' She might say more openly: 'The fact that I humble myself in this way or bear adversity so bravely is due to no virtue of mine, but to the grace of him whom I serve'].[98] The black bride speaks to the Daughters of Jerusalem from the Song of Songs such that their youth and their gender are identified with their "less complete" or weaker nature. The text formulates this analogy, however, so that the weaker among the faithful are appropriately gendered as female, or "daughters," rather than the other way around, with women appropriately called the weaker. What has been observed of Heloise's writing, that it proceeds from a statement of women's weakness to one that embraces all humanity, is here also true of Abelard's use of the same idea.[99] In either case, what we witness is the broader understanding of the metaphor, woman as "man's humanity," emerging within the formulation of its gender-specific application. The specific exchange of the correspondence is embedded in a larger, contemporary discourse.

The image of the widowed bride "explaining" her blackness to her "daughters" performs Heloise "speaking" to her audience, the community of the Paraclete, through a figure of continuity between her secular and monastic identity, or personal and communal selves. The bride speaks to her own kind, the weak in nature, as Heloise speaks to her sisters in desire: the widowed bride answers the identity question that was posed in such confusion in Heloise's first letter. The bride's "instruction" refers back to Heloise's statement equating the torments of physical desire with her "youth" and "weaker nature," and then explains how the blackness of the bride's exterior makes this same fact into the sign of her special grace [*eius gratiae cui deservio*]. The same blackness, a few lines earlier, is identified as "the repeated adversity of corporeal tribulation" [in hac vita crebris adversitatum tribulationibus corporaliter afflicta].[100] It is her weakness, alternately understood as the pain of a continuous dependence on the flesh—a pain to which Heloise eloquently testified—that is identified with the abject exterior and in turn is offered to the "daughters" as their means of identification with her. Then again, the same weakness, or blackness, is associated with the enhanced sensual pleasure the bridegroom finds in her. Abelard pauses over the idea of the bride's abject appearance to elaborate its inverse erotic appeal: "Et frequenter accidit ut nigrarum caro feminarum quanto est in aspectu deformior, tanto sit in tactu suavior; atque ideo earum voluptas secretis gaudiis quam publicis gratior sit et convenientior. . . ." [Moreover it often happens that the flesh of black women is all the softer to touch though it is less attractive to look at, and for this reason the pleasure they give is greater and more suitable for private than for public enjoyment. . . .].[101] Whether on the inside or the outside, the woman's infirmity it always simultaneously her greatest "beauty." The black flesh is at once the mirror of an inner weakness and the contrafact of an inner beauty; it is her unworthy carnality and the enhanced attraction of a desire expressed through this weakness. In the same way, as will be seen shortly, Heloise's self-indictment is a "blackening" of her outer self that by its very sincerity redeems her desire. Bereaved desire, the widow's blackness, is made the point of continuity that assimilates Heloise's love, marriage, and loss into a vocation for the love of Christ and thus the point of continuity that also assimilates her past to the community's future. The *ancilla, filia, uxor,* and *soror* are adequately assimilated to the biblical *sponsa* and to a monastic identity by the blackness that grounds both in a devotion of the widow.

Abelard defines the opposition between the abject and the exalted exterior not as one between desire and renunciation but as one between a "private" and a "public" desire, what is secret, hidden, experienced in the interior, as opposed to what is open, public, directed to the exterior. A distinction that has so often been anachronistically imposed on the text emerges here on its own terms. It is within this shifted opposition that the unmitigatedly erotic expression of desire is allowed a place in Abelard's exposition. Blackness makes this woman "choose what is hidden rather than open, what is secret and not known to all, and any such wife desires private, not public delights with her husband, and would rather be known in bed than seen at table."[102] The desire expressed by Heloise to shun public acclaim and seek some hidden space in heaven suited to her own unworthiness is taken up here as the special privilege of a disfigured woman who is granted and provides all the more sensuous rewards. The weakness that Heloise acknowledges and condemns becomes in Abelard's formulation the quality that guarantees not only grace but also a place in her religious life for the very desire she believes she must excise.

The introduction at this point of the "private" versus the "public" is no attempt to "detour Heloise back into the cloister" (from which she never even hints at departing); still less does it represent an attempt to bring her "to embrace castration."[103] It defines the widowed bride's relationship to her bridegroom in the same terms that Heloise herself requested. But Abelard takes up the space Heloise identifies with shamed withdrawal and privileges it with an erotic intimacy that is itself the result of, again, her "black flesh."

It is, above all, this equation between an imperative of interiority and the woman's carnal weakness that reveals the way the black bride recasts Heloise's dilemma, as she defines it, in terms of the metaphors of specifically female monastic experience. The text explicitly identifies the biblical *exemplum* against which it is to be read as the monastic exegesis of the parable of the Wise and Foolish Virgins.[104] The false or Foolish Virgins are in fact the true hypocrites. This topos serves to redefine hypocrisy in the gendered terms of women's relationship to the body and exterior manifestation of virtue, and as such it frames the bride's self-presentation to her intra- and extratextual daughters, which occurs between the following two statements:

> Decolorat eam sic, id est, dissimilem eam a ceteris facit quae terrenis inhiant, et saeculi quaerant gloriam ut sic ipsa vere . . . [non] efficiatur . . . sicut illae videlicet *fatuae virgines* quae de munditia carnis, vel abstinentia exteriore, apud se intumescentes, aestu tentationum aruerunt. Bene autem filias . . .
>
> . . . eius gratiae cui deservio. Aliter solent haeretici vel hypocritae, quantum ad faciem hominum spectat, spe terrenae gloriae sese vehementer humiliare, . . . Qualis quidem fatuarum virginum continentia est, quae a ianua sunt exclusae
>
> [He changes her color, that is, he makes her different from other women who thirst for earthly things and seek worldly glory, so that she may [not] become . . . like those foolish virgins who pride themselves on purity of the flesh or an outward show of self-denial, and then wither in the fire of temptation. And she rightly told the Daughters . . .
>
> . . . him whom I serve. This is not the way of heretics and hypocrites who (at any rate when others are present) humiliate themselves to excess in hopes of earthly glory, . . . Such self-denial is that of the foolish virgins who found the door shut against them].[105]

The first treatise of the High Middle Ages to be devoted to women's instruction in the monastic life, the *Speculum virginum* (c. 1130–1140), devotes the sixth of its twelve books entirely to the Wise and Foolish Virgins.[106] Most striking from the outset is the insistence on the idea that the Wise and the Foolish are indistinguishable in their outer piety: fasting, vigils, abstinence—"outward actions" writes Heloise, "common to the damned and the elect" alike, and "performed more eagerly by hypocrites than saints."[107] The error of the Foolish lies not in a failure to behave virtuously but in their belief that their virtue derives from their own merit [quicquid boni fecerunt, propriis meritis ascripserunt], an idea explicitly contradicted by the black bride when she says "non est meae virtutis, sed eius gratiae cui deservio" and mirrored in reverse by Heloise's denial of her own *virtus* ['strength' and 'virtue'].[108] The Foolish thus make an outward show of a humility they inwardly lack. Heloise's inward humility causes her to burn with shame over her perceived outward piety. As the *Speculum* repeats over and again, the decisive determiner of integrity is not virtuous behavior, but the virgin's inner intention, whether her actions proceed from a desire for the praise of men ("in appetitu vanae gloriae vel laudis" or "laudes ab hominibus") or are directed solely to Christ as the source of her grace.[109] The desire to please Abelard and him alone is precisely the failing of which Heloise accuses herself, and it is this turn that, in seeming paradox, aligns her most convincingly with the Wise. Wise Virgins are not defined by their works, the successful outward manifestation of inner virtue, but by their avoidance of ostentation. Inward humility is evinced by an exterior that abnegates its exteriority, its representational value, seeking hidden places and shunning the public eye.[110] The true voice of humility therefore can manifest virtue only in self-condemnation and can condemn others only by way of confessing its own unworthiness. Heloise's self-acknowledged hypocrisy at the end of her second letter is thus peculiarly complicit with the indictment of hypocrisy of a different kind. She, like Abelard, names the true hypocrites, but where he does so in opposition to an identity shaped to her requirements, she must do so as if identifying herself. Her rhetorical gesture is motivated entirely, however, by an abhorrence of the false praise that is sole motivator of the

Foolish. The Wise Virgin emerges in the gap constructed between Heloise's self-assessment and the more eloquent testimony this makes to her true motivations or inner intention.

Just as the correspondence brings its voices to converge around a mutual acknowledgment of women's weakness, thus enabling or, in fact, forcing the consideration of difference, so, too, the *Speculum virginum* emphatically genders its argument on the seductive power of worldly acclaim when it is considered in relationship to women's weakness. Women's proclivity for exterior ornament and flattering self-representation is a continuous assumption in the *Speculum virginum,* which makes extensive use of an analogy with the seductive practices of worldly women to articulate the spiritual life of God's virgins.[111] That self-effacing humility is the only tenable behavior for women is made clear in Book 6 by the example of great men who fell to the allure of fame: "Si vir formae prestantis et staturae divitiarum gloria, linea nobilitatis ceteris eminentior et clarus vanitatis huius umbram captaverit, mirum non est, etiamsi humilitatis callem professus est, quod vero mulier, quo sexu nihil fragilius est, in alta levatur, monstro simile est" [If even the great man who surpasses all others in noble extraction as in renown for outstanding nature and extent of his wealth seeks after the shadow of this vanity, it is no wonder that, even when she has sworn herself to the path of humility, a woman—than whom by her sex none is weaker—elevated in praise is truly a monstrosity].[112]The susceptibility of women to this temptation is so great that the author concludes, just as Heloise confesses to Abelard at the end of her second letter in much more personal terms: "Vere ipsi vos seduxerunt, qui vos benedixerunt" [In truth they seduce you who speak well of you].[113]

The discourse on women and praise affirms woman's proclivity for the exterior, the seduction of the body and its ornament and, in its monastic articulation, sees this proclivity as continuous with women's monastic lives, not altered by their conversion.[114] The same tendencies to which women in the world are subject are evident in the Foolish Virgins' behavior, although they appropriate a different idea of outer beauty. Ostentatious self-denial becomes a seductive exterior belying an inherently weak nature. To acknowledge inadequacy is, therefore, to renounce all aspiration to exterior excellence, to virtue manifest as perfect continuity between exterior and interior such as *the text* understands Abelard's castration. Like the castration theme, then, "worldly praise" is a textual flag to women's carnal weakness that relocates sincere commitment in an acknowledgment of the incapacity to perform "manly" virtue, *tam viriliter adversitates sustinere,* as the black bride puts it—a point that Heloise makes the undeniable leitmotif of her instructions to Abelard on the proper direction of the female monastic life. In the *Speculum virginum* it corresponds to an ethical imperative of interiority that resounds throughout the work: "Totum intra est, quod quaeris extra te" [All is found within, that you seek outside yourself]—the same statement Heloise makes by quoting Persius' "Ne te quaesiveris extra" [Do not look outside yourself].[115]

Heloise is in fact a Wise Virgin; her confession is presented as the contrafact of women's hypocrisy as defined by the Foolish. The sincere *desire* she expresses for repentance defines a properly oriented intention that, consigned to the bodily vessel of her sex, cannot rise above this struggle. Her humility, her desire to avoid ostentation, her acknowledgment of her weakness—all these are echoed in the black bride's self-presentation in explicit opposition to a redefined hypocrisy, that of the Foolish Virgins. The voice of the woman whose identity as mistress, wife, handmaid, and sister was "emptied out" in her first letter (*Ep.* 2),[116] finding no adequate name for a self suspended between desire and an unrealizable renunciation, is here affirmed by its act of self-negation in a new identity, that of the *sponsa vidua et desolata,* an identity that assimilates her past to the biblical bride whose "name" was circumscribed by the search for identity that initiates the epistolary dialogue. "Domino specialiter, sua singulariter" [The/her Lord's own in species, his/His own as individual][117]: Heloise's "final" salutation is all the verification she offers, or needs to offer, of her acknowledgment and assent. This "narrative" continually plants figures of its own progression, in dramatically condensed form, as it goes along and then unpacks these in the rhetorical positioning of its protagonists.[118] It is art, not life, executed by a master (no gender intended) of composition.

Abelard significantly enhances the monastic understanding of the biblical *exemplum* as a reversal of the hypocrisy of carnal weakness by placing the Foolish Virgins not opposite the Wise but opposite the black and widowed bride, the abject and self-effacing exterior that is the "singular" mark of a selfhood predetermined by human, conjugal love, by an attachment to the memories of a "human" past defined as ineffaceable through her very blackness. The Wise Virgins are neither mentioned nor defined in Abelard's exposition; that is, they are redefined implicitly both by the black bride who displaces them and by Heloise's testimony that anticipates, or even enables, the convergence with the monastic topos. Heloise's monastic followers are thus instructed to read the black bride as the inversion of her "hypocrisy" and as the adequate assimilation of her "weakness" to a monastic identity "suitable for women." The epistolary exchange commonly known as the "Personal Letters" brings about a reorientation of the inner life of the woman that is fully analogous and indispensable to the function Heloise states for proposed regulation of the outer life. The negotiation of the past, the successful assimilation of Heloise's "I" to a monastic "we," is the precondition for, and generator of, the "we" that engages the project of a reformed monastic future. The famed "silence of Heloise" is indeed no aposiopesis, no unarticulated rupture or stoic self-repression.[119] It is simply agreement on the established basis of continuation, exactly what the unique structure of this text would indicate it to be.

This "weakness of woman" that the text makes the lynchpin of its exposition is no more an accurate, limiting, or defining description of female individuals than the heroic transformation of Abelard's castration is an accurate representation of male conversion. Both are exploited in the text as the means through which "outer" and "inner" conversion become manifest as male and female attributes respectively, opposite and irreconcilable visions of the human condition. The woman serves, then, as the justification for a reformed view of commitment to the religious life, one that is in step with the evangelical movements of its own time in an attempt to embrace the laity, the spiritually imperfect or infirm, and ultimately to define their position as the only truly human stance before God.[120] The spiritual athleticism of the man, or *vir,* as spiritual elite is removed to the realm of the legendary, the miraculous and inemulable, and is finally the idol that the text seeks implicitly to displace.

To historicize the text of Troyes 802 or read it with its monastic audience is to discover a unified conception that brings the voices of the so-called "Personal Letters" fully into line with the objectives and strategies recently articulated for the "Letters of Direction" by authors such as Linda Georgianna and Peggy McCracken in this volume. The differences between these readings—attempts to historicize Heloise—and my own are at times so significant as to make the two seem diametrically opposed, but it would be a missed opportunity to obscure their essential complementarity. When the assumptions stemming from misplaced identification with the voices of the text are erased and when the strategies of audience identification modeled in the text are considered in their place, the abbess who so confidently wields the rhetorical shield of gender difference to take control of her future religious life is not only fully compatible with the passionate lover and her irrepressible desire, she is the lover's compelling fusion with the voice of a nascent spirituality that seeks the assimilation of human sexual desire to the love of God.

This is the offer of identification that the abbess of the Letters makes to her female charges, present and future. Those who have claimed that this text cannot have been edifying "reading" for monastic women have, in effect, only proclaimed the unsuitability of their own hermeneutic bias to the text itself. This bias confronts a priori several glaring contradictions that have been systematically "silenced" in same way as it invented a silence of Heloise to fill its own hermeneutic gap: the Paraclete "reader" is inscribed in this text such that both her response of the moment and her monastic future are identical to that of her spiritual mother. The correspondence the text contains is undertaken for the express purpose of communal *consolatio*—the very delivery of which Abelard repeatedly makes synonymous with his monastic foundation[121]; and the whole culminates in perhaps the most programmatic advancement of a specifically female monastic life known to the Middle Ages. Finally, the text makes an eloquent if implicit statement of its public or communal function: "*Cogita et recogita* in quantis ipsi nos periculis constitueramus et a quantis nos eruerit Dominus et *narra semper* cum summa gratiarum actione quanta fecit Dominus animae nostrae; et quoslibet iniquos de bonitate Domini desperantes *nostro consolare exemplo. . . .*" [*Think and think again* of the great perils in which we were and from which the Lord rescued us; *tell always* with the deepest gratitude how much the Lord has done for our souls. *Comfort by example* any unrighteous who despair of God's goodness. . . .].[122]

At the outset, I cited the difference between our preoccupation with an "open-ended" conclusion and the foregone conclusion that confronted Heloise's monastic audience. But the monastic "reader," too, was aware of an open-ended conclusion, differently conceived, because it assumes her participative reading act. At the junctures in the text that place Heloise's dilemma in irreducible opposition to the resolution posed as her dialogic obverse, when the voices of woman's desire and that of male monastic renunciation sound hopelessly dissonant chords, this reader recognizes a hermeneutic task; that is, these very moments define and implement her presence. Her life completes the open-ended meaning, speaks the resolution, even as the compilation speaks resolution only as the definition and prescription of this life. "Let her who has not yet begun think it over, and her who has made a start, continue." The debate over Heloise as the romantic heroine, a voice extinguished in a tragic abyss between irrepressible desire and inexpressible fulfillment and Heloise as the able and respected abbess is not, finally, a question of textual interpretation but one of textual hermeneutics, a decision as to the way the text makes meaning that is preliminary to any interpretative act, as it was no doubt preliminary to the compositional act that caused the text to be delivered to us as it is.

Notes

1. The authenticity debate reached something of a moratorium with Newman's *refutatio*, Barbara Newman, "Authority, Authenticity, and the Repression of Heloise." For an ap-

praisal of the most recent renewal of the debate, see D. E. Luscombe, "The Letters of Heloise and Abelard Since 'Cluny 1972,'" and Peter von Moos, "*Post Festum:* Was kommt nach der Authentizitätsdebatte über die Briefe Abaelards und Heloises?" pp. 19–39 and 75–100. A detailed critique of earlier literature is found in Peter von Moos, *Mittelalterforschung und Ideologiekritik: Der Gelehrtenstreit um Heloise.*

2. See Catherine Brown's critique of the following readings in "*Muliebriter:* Doing Gender in the Letters of Heloise," pp. 27–29; Newman, "Authority, Authenticity, and the Repression," pp. 121–44; Peggy Kamuf, "Marriage Contracts: The Letters of Heloise and Abelard," pp. 1–43; Glenda McLeod, "'Wholly Guilty, Wholly Innocent': Self-Definition in Héloïse's Letters to Abélard," pp. 64–86; Nancy Partner, "No Sex, No Gender," pp. 419–44.
3. The idea is indeed compelling, although impossible to prove, that Heloise herself was this compiler and adapter. First suggested in Étienne Gilson, *Héloïse and Abélard,* pp. 165–66, this hypothesis has been reiterated by others since. But this is no authorization to read the Letters as intimate autobiography or as a key to their author's psyche. It would, however, make them all the more compelling as testimony to twelfth-century women's monasticism.
4. Troyes 802 is not identical to this definition of the text. For one thing, the manuscript that concerns us was bound together with two others unrelated to it in the eighteenth century. Second, this first manuscript of the three (fols. 1–103), adds the *Institutiones nostrae* (fols. 89–94), a Paraclete customary now thought to have been written largely by Heloise herself; another female monastic rule extraneous to the Paraclete (fols. 94–102); and, as later additions, Abelard's epitaph and absolution. None of this evidence speaks against the consideration of the correspondence (*Ep.* 1–8) as an integral whole, nor do any of these other texts have internal relevance to the correspondence. For the sake of expediency, I speak of this first manuscript, fols. 1–103, both as Troyes 802 and "the codex," meaning, in fact, the compilation as it was originally bound. See the full description in *HC,* ed. Monfrin 9–13. Paris, *Bibliothéque nationale* lat. 2923 may in fact be older than Troyes 802 by a generation. See Luscombe, "The Letters Since 'Cluny 1972,'" p. 29; and *HC,* ed. Monfrin 19.
5. *HC,* ed. Monfrin 13–18. Monfrin's conclusions were reiterated in 1988 by Luscombe, "From Paris to the Paraclete: The Correspondence of Abelard and Heloise," pp. 270–71; and recently reaffirmed by Martin Irvine, who writes, "The . . . correspondence was almost certainly compiled and edited at Heloise's convent of the Paraclete" ("Heloise and the Gendering of the Literate Subject," p. 88).
6. This description of the *HC* and the Letters as "lives of the founders" is not intended as a genre classification but only as a characterization of content that will evolve later in this chapter.
7. Radice 160–61. *Ep.* 6, ed. Muckle 242: "unde sanctimonialium ordo coeperit, et quae nostrae sit professionis auctoritas. Alterum vero est . . . regulam . . . quae feminarum sit propria."
8. *HC,* ed. Monfrin 17.
9. Charlotte Charrier, *Héloïse dans l'histoire et dans la légende* (edn: 1933), pp. 244–77.
10. Luscombe, "From Paris to the Paraclete," pp. 272–73; and his "The Letters Since 'Cluny 1972,'" pp. 20–23.
11. Jacques Monfrin, "Le problème de l'authenticité de la correspondance d'Abélard et d'Héloïse," pp. 409–24, especially 421–24; von Moos, "*Post Festum,*" pp. 84–86 and passim.
12. John Benton, "Fraud, Fiction and Borrowing in the Correspondence of Abelard and Heloise." See the bibliography for a complete listing of von Moos's contributions. I cite the article listed there as "Le Silence d'Héloïse et les idéologies modernes" in its later, revised German version, "Die Bekehrung Heloises."

13. See von Moos, *Mittelalterforschung und Ideologiekritik,* pp. 21–28; and his "Die Bekehrung Heloises," 100, on this point particularly; see also Luscombe, "The Letters Since 'Cluny 1972,'" p. 24, where D. W. Robertson, *Abelard and Heloise,* is discussed as another exception. More recent readings are accounted for below.
14. In *Women Writers,* p. 138, Dronke considers briefly the question of Heloise's audience, "half-consciously" recognized in her "allusions to the outer world." Oddly, this leads him to the conclusion that "The later writing, in a sense, is more private than the so-called 'personal' letters—it concerns only Abelard and the Paraclete, whereas in the first two letters we see Heloise determined publicly to set a particular human record straight." Here, as elsewhere, the monastic audience is fully effaced. For Newman, on the other hand, the early letters are "relentlessly private" and could never have been "published"—an act that would have resulted in "the wanton destruction of her own reputation [and] endangered the Paraclete and all its priories"—nor even read by the nuns of the Paraclete, although she speculates that the last three were ("Authority, Authenticity, and the Repression," pp. 134–35). Distinctions such as public and private, published and unpublished are of little use applied to this text without careful definition of what they mean in the twelfth-century context. In these arguments the terms are crutches for assumptions that are preliminary to the critics' reading of the text.
15. Von Moos, "*Post Festum,*" p. 85; Monfrin, "Le problème de l'authenticité," p. 419. On medieval letter collections, see Giles Constable, "Letters and Letter Collections."
16. Radice 165. *Ep.* 6, ed. Muckle 245: "Quae non coepit, deliberet; quae aggressa est, perseveret" (Augustine, *De bono viduitatis* 9.12). Peter the Venerable conferred these titles on Heloise in a letter to her: Petrus Venerabilis, *Epistola* 21, PL 189.349.
17. "Quae est ista, quaeso, Domini benignitas, aut quae mulierum dignitas. . . . Quae est ista, obsecro, infirmioris sexus praerogativa . . . ?" [What special grace of the Lord, I ask, is this, or what special dignity of woman. . . . What, I implore, is this special privilege of the weaker sex . . . ?] *Ep.* 7, ed. Muckle 254; my translation.
18. See, e.g., Kamuf, "Marriage Contracts," p. 19 and passim. This idea goes hand in hand with another that sees Heloise contemplating abandoning the Paraclete, also utterly lacking in textual support. Cf. Kamuf, "Marriage Contracts," p. 32, Brown, "*Muliebriter,*" p. 34, and Robertson, *Abelard and Heloise,* pp. 134–35.
19. "Castration becomes the index of a mastery which is unassailable and intact" (Kamuf, "Marriage Contracts," p. 32). See also Brown "*Muliebriter,*" p. 34; Newman, "Authority, Authenticity, and the Repression," p. 156; and, in this volume, Linda Georgianna, chapter 8; and Peggy McCracken, "Curse of Eve," chapter 9.
20. Gilson, *Héloïse and Abélard,* pp. 151–53.
21. Von Moos, "*Post Festum,*" pp. 88–89, emphasized the paradox immanent in the work's construction poised between a historical point of departure and an ideal even utopian aspiration that points beyond its own frame as a major uncharted field in the analysis of the letters.
22. Von Moos made a similar point with regard to the structure of the Letters in "Die Bekehrung Heloises," 116.
23. *Ep.* 2, ed. Muckle 69 (Radice 111).
24. Cf. *HC,* ed. Muckle 175 and 210–11.
25. *Ep.* 6, ed. Muckle 242 (Radice 159).
26. Gilson, *Héloïse and Abélard,* pp. 47–63, especially pp. 56–58. The point has been reiterated many times since then and finds a new and insightful analysis in Irvine, "Gendering of the Literate Subject."
27. Irvine, "Gendering of the Literate Subject," pp. 90–101, offers a detailed analysis of this point. On the exclusively male discourse of *amicitia,* see Brian Patrick McGuire, *Friendship and Community: The Monastic Experience 350–1250,* pp. 40–42, 89–90; and Barbara

Newman, "Flaws in the Golden Bowl: Gender and Spiritual Formation in the Twelfth Century," pp. 136–41.

28. Irvine, "Gendering of the Literate Subject," p. 96.
29. *Ep.* 2, ed. Muckle 71 (Radice 113).
30. *Ep.* 2, ed. Muckle 68 (Radice 109).
31. The consistently Marian interpretation of the Song in its entirety was inaugurated by Rupert of Deutz's influential commentary c. 1125. The currency of the Marian interpretation and its implementation in monastic instruction for women are amply attested to in the *Speculum virginum* (see below, n. 105).
32. *Women Writers,* pp. 114, 115, 122, 136. Kamuf, "Marriage Contracts," p. 20. For Kamuf, the first-person plural address, the communal response to the letters, and the obligations of Heloise's religious office are part of a "public domain as the domain of pretense and pretext to the erotic 'truth'" (p. 18; see also pp. 11, 17, and passim).
33. Glenda McLeod writes, "In all the letters Héloïse switches between her roles as abbess and lover by switching the number of the speaking pronoun. First person singular indicates her private role as Abélard's wife; first person plural speaks as the more public abbess" ("'Wholly Guilty, Wholly Innocent,'" p. 65); see also p. 78 in McLeod, where this distinction becomes one opposing "personal" and "spiritual matters." These distinctions are applicable in themselves, especially as McLeod makes an attempt to historicize the ideas of public and private, but because the object of "this dialectic between inner and outer, singular and plural, . . . public and private" is assumed to be "self-realization," the public voice is likewise assumed once again to be only the foil of the private one (McLeod, "'Wholly Guilty, Wholly Innocent'," pp. 80, 77). Most recently, Bonnie Wheeler writes that Heloise "uses the feminine community of the Paraclete as a metaphor for her own state" in "Origenary Fantasies: Abelard's Castration and Confession," p. 120.
34. Von Moos, "Palatini quaestio quasi peregrini: Ein gestiger Streitpunkt aus der Abelard–Heloise–Kontroverse nochmals überprüft," pp. 138–39.
35. Radice 127. *Ep.* 4, ed. Muckle 77: "Quae enim nostrum siccis oculis audire possit, quod circa finem epistolae posuisti . . ."
36. Radice 128. *Ep.* 4, ed. Muckle 78: "cum nec anima rationis sensum, nec lingua sermonis retinebit usum."
37. *Ep.* 4, ed. Muckle 78 (Radice 128).
38. Radice 127*Ep.* 4, ed. Muckle 77: "Miror, unice meus. . . ."
39. Radice 127. *Ep.* 4, ed. Muckle 77: "Illud non parva admiratione suscepimus. . . ."
40. Radice 128. *Ep.* 4, ed. Muckle 78: "Parce itaque, obsecro, nobis; parce unicae saltem tuae . . ."
41. *Ep.* 4, ed. Muckle 79 (my translation).
42. Radice 130. *Ep.* 4, ed. Muckle 79: " . . . et me pariter et totum genus meum sublimaveras." Radice 131. *Ep.* 4, ed. Muckle 79: "Prima statim mulier de paradiso virum captivavit . . ."
43. As Catherine Brown shows ("*Muliebriter,*" pp. 27–29), this omission is as characteristic of the most recent attempts to recuperate the "true and truly female speaker"—as she correctly characterizes the contributions of McLeod, Newman, and Partner—as it was of the readings that become the object of their polemic (see especially Newman, "Authority, Authenticity, and the Repression," pp. 123–31). In my view, however, Brown does not entirely succeed in dodging her own bullet. Whether the critic reconstructs a self that is continuous with Heloise's gendered rhetoric or one that consciously manipulates this rhetoric "in a high-stakes struggle for erotic and intellectual power" (Brown, "*Muliebriter,*" pp. 28, 46, n. 29), he or she is still reading with the assumption of being the audience to a "closed" communication, reconstructing an authorial self, and

potentially effacing the text's rhetorical construction. Not surprisingly, Brown makes no mention of Heloise's use of the first-person plural.

44. Despite making this valuable contribution, Georgianna's reading cannot reconcile the prescription Heloise makes with her own case; the rule she seeks becomes a kind of fire cure, its refusal to recognize the value of any outward virtue condemning first and foremost Heloise herself. This shortfall is a necessary result of Georgianna's laudable attempt to analyze the third letter in its own right, avoiding the old conversion question. But when she attempts to reconstruct the emotional state of the writer who was able to request a rule that was "not finally a comforting or liberating thought for Heloise," (Georgianna, chapter 8, p. 203), the same "biographizing" reflex emerges that mars other readings (Georgianna, chapter 8, pp. 204–205).
45. See nn. 14 and 33 above.
46. Aelred of Rievaulx, *De institutione inclusarum*. There are other parallels between the two texts; most striking is Abelard's vividly visualizing description of Christ's Passion in *Ep.* 6, very like the series of meditations that Aelred offers his sister as part of his inner rule.
47. *Ep.* 2, ed. Muckle 70 (Radice 113). On the monastic reception of Cicero's *amicitia,* see McGuire, *Friendship and Community,* pp. 40–42, 89–90.
48. *Ep.* 2, ed. Muckle 70 (Radice 113).
49. *HC,* ed. Muckle 206.
50. *Ep.* 2, ed. Muckle 70 (Radice 113).
51. *Ep.* 2, ed. Muckle 70 (Radice 113).
52. Also pointed out by McLeod, "'Wholly Guilty, Wholly Innocent,'" pp. 67–69.
53. See n. 19, above. Wheeler, considering the meaning of Abelard's castration for a construction of masculinity in the text, comes to a conclusion I understand as close to my own when she rewrites Newman's statement to say "the poetics of castration *is* the discourse of their desire" (Wheeler, "Origenary Fantasies," p. 123). My thinking on the castration question is indebted to an unpublished essay by John Frymire, "*Petrus Imperfectus:* Abelard and the *Sermo de Eunuchis* Late in the Early High Middle Ages."
54. In addition to the instances cited in note 19, above, see Kamuf, "Marriage Contracts," p. 36; McLeod, "'Wholly Guilty, Wholly Innocent,'" pp. 74–5; and McCracken in this volume, pp. 224 ff. Brown is more nuanced on this point, recognizing Heloise's own "gestures of discursive self-mutilation" ("*Muliebriter,*" p. 35).
55. *Ep.* 4, ed. Muckle 81 (Radice 133).
56. *Ep.* 4, ed. Muckle 80 (Radice 132): "Si enim vere miserrimi mei animi profitear infirmitatem . . ." [For if I truthfully admit to the weakness of my unhappy soul . . .]
57. *Ep.* 4, ed. Muckle 81 (Radice 133).
58. Georgianna, chapter 8; see also McCracken, chapter 9.
59. Georgianna, chapter 8, p. 197..
60. In what follows I summarize from Caroline Walker Bynum, *Holy Feast and Holy Fast: The Significance of Food to Medieval Women.* The most important points are also argued at length in " . . . And Woman His Humanity': Female Imagery in the Religious Writing of the Later Middle Ages," and "The Female Body and Religious Practice in the Later Middle Ages," both in her *Fragmentation and Redemption: Essays on Gender and the Human Body in Medieval Religion,* pp. 151–89 and 181–238.
61. 1 Cor. 13.11. Paul compares the imperfect knowledge of the *parvulus* [boy] gained in the mirror of this world, and perfect knowledge of the man, gained "face to face" with the godhead.
62. As Bynum emphasizes, these "feminine metaphors and symbols" are not new in conception but only in their implementation; they do not redefine the terms in which the woman's position is articulated, but are rather "the inverse, the mirror image, of earlier medieval language" (Caroline Walker Bynum, *Jesus as Mother: Studies in the Spirituality of the High Middle Ages,* p. 138).

63. Bynum, *Holy Feast and Holy Fast,* p. 295.
64. Bynum, *Holy Feast and Holy Fast,* pp. 246, 250. It is true that Bynum's argument aims primarily at a corrective reappraisal of what to us are sensationally somatic practices of late medieval female spirituality. But she consistently traces the beginnings of the argument from the time of Abelard and Heloise and the context of twelfth-century reformed women's monasticism. Moreover, the misapprehension she seeks to obviate, which assumes that the somatic religious practices of women aim at mortification and vilification of the flesh, is precisely the same one that plagues assessment of these letters. The assumption that Heloise is to imitate Abelard's castration repeatedly results in statements that reveal a simplistic opposition between voluptuous indulgence of the flesh and its flagellation.
65. *Ep.* 2, ed. Muckle 68.
66. For Muckle, this silence was so complete as to form the only notable inconsistency in a "logical sequence with no inherent contradictions" ("The Personal Letters Between Abelard and Heloise," p. 66).
67. Heloise does not "revel in erotic nostalgia" (Newman, "Authority, Authenticity, and the Repression," p. 138). This all-too-frequent misunderstanding fails to distinguish between the way Heloise consistently describes the irresistible appeal of her memories, and their relationship to her current state, which she apostrophizes with the words "O vere me miseram. . . ." (cited above, n. 51).
68. *Ep.* 5, ed. Muckle 87 (Radice 145): "antiquam . . . et assiduam querimoniam tuam . . . qua videlicet de nostrae conversionis modo." *Ep.* 5, ed. Muckle 87, 86 (Radice 145, 143).
69. Radice 145. *Ep.* 5, ed. Muckle 88: "Ut tamen et hoc modo huius amaritudinem doloris leniamus."
70. *Ep.* 5, ed. Muckle 89 (Radice 149).
71. *Ep.* 5, ed. Muckle 148 (my translation); *Ep.* 5, ed. Muckle 90.
72. *Ep.* 5, ed. Muckle 90 (Radice 149).
73. *Ep.* 5, ed. Muckle 90.
74. *Ep.* 5, ed. Muckle 93 (Radice 154 [translation altered]; emphasis added).
75. "Abelard depicts her as winning the heavenly 'crown' by continually overcoming her desire." (Georgianna, chapter 8, p. 203).
76. *Ep.* 5, ed. Muckle 93 (Radice 154).
77. Georgianna, chapter 8. Newman claims that Abelard contradicts Heloise's plea from weakness by arguing for women's dignity, failing to recognize that these are two sides of the same coin (Newman, "Flaws in the Golden Bowl," pp. 112, 121). Dronke, on the other hand, cannot reconcile Heloise's argument from the position of weakness with her earlier heroism, and thus excuses it as a rhetorical expediency that "is probably a concession to Abelard"! (*Women Writers,* p. 132).
78. *Ep.* 3, ed. Muckle 75 (Radice 122–23).
79. In *Ep.* 5, the letter in which the spiritual director fully emerges, Abelard invokes the idea of women's weakness four times: once as in the passage already cited on the "martyr's crown," where he uses it as an apology for the continuous torments of the flesh; again in excusing her acquiescence to his passion in the past (*Ep.* 5, ed. Muckle 89); and once more in association with the black bride, to which I will turn shortly. Finally, he "returns" the idea to Heloise in the prayer that assimilates their conjugal love to her devotional practice. In a clear echo of her final plea for his acknowledgment of her weakness—"Now particularly you should fear, now when I no longer have in you *a remedy* for my incontinence" (Radice 135, my alteration in italics)—the prayer she is to speak as a widow petitioning God "to reunite in heaven those he has parted on earth" (Radice 156) begins with a moving presentation of marriage both as a sacrament and as "hoc remedium fragilitatis incontinentiae" [this remedy for the incontinence of my frailty] (*Ep.* 5, ed. Muckle 93 [Radice 155]).

80. Both Jean Leclercq and Mary Martin McLaughlin studied this letter and Abelard's rule, and both pointed to Abelard's argument on the dignity of women as a mark of the novelty and singularity of his writing for the Paraclete. Only McLaughlin, however, made any mention of the emphasis on women's weakness and its importance to the argument, and this in a somewhat apologetic tone: Mary Martin McLaughlin, "Peter Abelard and the Dignity of Women: Twelfth-Century 'Feminism' in Theory and Practice," pp. 301–302 and 310; and Jean Leclercq, "'Ad ipsam sophiam Christum': Le témoignage monastique d'Abélard, pp. 161–81. More recent readings, despite their avowed interest in gender and the monastic life, have largely ignored these contributions, possibly a reflection of both authors' overemphasis of a "feminist" Abelard.
81. *Ep.* 7, ed. Muckle 254.
82. *Ep.* 7, ed. Muckle 257 (my translation).
83. *Ep.* 7, ed. Muckle 257 (my translation).
84. *Ep.* 7, ed. Muckle 270–73.
85. *Ep.* 7, ed. Muckle 271 (my translation).
86. *Ep.* 1, ed. Muckle 205. Von Moos took this instance as a point of departure for a detailed analysis of the manipulation of the position of feminine weakness opposite masculine strength and pastoral care but limited his view to the construction of mutual need as justification and authority for the letter exchange itself: "Der Paraklet braucht allem *invidiae murmur* zum Trotz dringend die Präsenz seines Seelsorgers . . . Die weibliche Schwäche wird derart heilsam-heilend für den leidenden, sie stärkenden Mann. Hilfe und Hilfsbedürfdigkeit werden gewissermaßen austauschbar" (von Moos, "Palatini quaestio," p. 135).
87. Cited in Newman, "Flaws in the Golden Bowl," p. 116; see also pp. 115–22 on the monastic rhetoric generally. Newman's characterization of Abelard's treatment of the same question does not recognize the reversal I have attempted to demonstrate here. See also Penny Schine Gold, *The Lady and the Virgin: Image, Attitude, and Experience in Twelfth-Century France,* pp. 76–115.
88. Ep. 7, ed. Muckle 254. See n. 17, above, for the text.
89. *Ep.* 4, ed. Muckle 82 (Radice 135–36).
90. Radice 133. *Ep.* 4, ed. Muckle 81: "qui cordis et renum probator est, et in abscondito videt."
91. Von Moos, "Die Bekehrung Heloises," 119, pointed to the possibility that the correspondence might represent an attempt to address the spiritual needs of women whose experience of sexual love would make them "widows," and Luscombe, "The Letters Since 'Cluny 1972,'" pp. 20–21, tends in the same direction, but these are the only exceptions I know and even they do not deal specifically with the black bride.
92. *Ep.* 5, ed. Muckle 83 (Radice 138): "In quibus quidem verbis cum generaliter anima describatur contemplativa quae specialiter sponsa Christi dicitur, expressius tamen ad vos hoc pertinere ipse etiam vester exterior habitus loquitur." [In general it is the contemplative soul which is described in these words and especially called the bride of Christ, but your outer habit indicates that they have particular application to you all].
93. Radice 138. *Ep.* 5, ed. Muckle 83: " . . . instar lugubris habitus bonarum viduarum mortuos quos dilexerunt viros plangentium."
94. Radice 138. *Ep.* 5, ed. Muckle 84; "Mulieres sedentes ad monumentum lamentabantur flentes Dominum." Abelard uses this passage, cited from the Roman Breviary, three times in his first two letters to equate women's monastic vocation with the mourning of widows for Christ. The idea is then enlarged upon in *Ep.* 7, ed. Muckle 256–57.
95. *Ep.* 5, ed. Muckle 83 (my translation).
96. Kamuf, "Marriage Contracts," pp. 27–32; and McLeod, "'Wholly Guilty, Wholly Innocent,'" pp. 74–75; and McCracken, chapter 9 of this volume. Brown, "*Muliebriter,*" pp.

38–40, 48, n. 51, corrects this dismissal of the figure as another instance of Abelard's purported "castration" of Heloise's desire, but I cannot see why she insists that the figure "disembodies" and "degenders" the same desire. Bereavement implies neither.

97. The text reads "Nolite mirari, etc.," and is alluding to its own previous citation of a pre-Vulgate version of Cant. 1.5. See *Ep.* 5, ed. Muckle 83 nn. 30 and 31.
98. *Ep.* 5, ed. Muckle 84 (Radice 139).
99. *Women Writers,* pp. 130–33, and Georgianna in this volume.
100. *Ep.* 5, ed. Muckle 84 (Radice 139).
101. *Ep.* 5, ed. Muckle 85 (Radice 140).
102. Radice 140. *Ep.* 5, ed. Muckle 85: "Ipsa quippe negredinis deformitas occultum potius quam manifestum, et secretum magis quam publicum amat. Et quae talis est uxor, secreta potius viri gaudia quam manifesta desiderat et in lecto magis vult sentiri quam in mensa videri."
103. Kamuf, "Marriage Contracts," pp. 32 and 36, in words equally representative of others after her. In particular, McLeod and Brown concur with Kamuf's view that the emphasis on secrecy constitutes a continuation of the suppression and silencing of the legitimate rights of a wife that they find manifest in Abelard's earlier insistence on a clandestine marriage. The denial of any development in the voice of Abelard is, here again, an idea arbitrarily imposed on the text. Why should not equal emphasis be placed on the idea of continuity expressed in the widow's bereaved desire?
104. Matt. 25.1–13.
105. *Ep.* 5, ed. Muckle 84 (Radice 139).
106. Seyfarth, ed., *Speculum virginum,* CCCM 5. All translations from the *Speculum virginum* are my own. This work apparently represents the distillation of years of practice on the part of its author of the very instruction that is modeled in its pages. There is no known manuscript transmission of the text west of the Rhine before the end of the twelfth century, when it was avidly copied by the Cistercians at no less a center than Clairvaux. Two copies survive that are know to have been made there. But both the nature of the work as a universal model for women's male instructors and the testimony it gives to a model of orally delivered instruction make it probable that the ideas it contains were far more broadly disseminated than we can assess today through the surviving manuscripts. On these points see Morgan Powell, *The Mirror and the Woman: Instruction for Religious Women and the Emergence of Vernacular Poetics 1120–1250,* pp. 99–173; and, for a detailed appraisal of the work's contents, Matthäus Bernards, *Speculum Virginum: Geistigkeit und Seelenleben der Frau im Hochmittelalter.*
107. Radice 135. *Ep.* 4, ed. Muckle 82: "Nulla quidem meriti apud Deum obtinerit, quae reprobis aeque ut electis communia sunt. Haec autem ea sunt quae exterius aguntur, quae nulli sanctorum tam studiose peragunt, quantum hypocritae."
108. *Speculum virginum* 6, ll. 9–10.
109. *Speculum virginum* 6, ll. 104, 370. Examples could easily be multiplied. The text is tireless in its repetition of the idea.
110. *Speculum virginum* 6, ll. 355–71. The text articulates this idea through a collation of phrases from several biblical passages.
111. The analogy is most evident in the presentation of the ornaments of the Daughters of Sion in Book 3, but it also occurs repeatedly by way of explicating the titulary metaphor of the *speculum.* See Powell, *The Mirror and the Woman,* pp. 249–57.
112. *Speculum virginum* 6, l. 394.
113. *Speculum virginum* 6, ll. 399–400. As Heloise puts it in *Ep.* 4, ed. Muckle 82 (Radice 135): "Tanto autem mihi tua laus in me periculosior est, quanto gratior, et tanto amplius ea capior et delector, quanto amplius tibi per omnia placere studeo" [To me your praise is the more dangerous because I welcome it. The more anxious I am to please you in everything, the more I am won over and delighted by it].

114. This observation reflects the formulation, as Bynum sees it, of women's religious experience generally: Bynum, " . . . And Woman His Humanity," p. 175.
115. *Speculum virginum* 9, l. 1008. *Ep.* 6, ed. Muckle 251 (Radice 176).
116. Brown, "*Muliebriter,*" p. 31.
117. I cite the salutation as it occurs in the text at issue here, that of Troyes 802. See *Ep.* 6, ed. Muckle 241 n. 2 (my translation). On the salutation and its discussion in the secondary literature, see the contributions of Georgianna (chapter 9) and Mews (chapter 3) in this volume.
118. This was another of the many overlooked insights put forward by von Moos, "Palatini quaestio," p. 125 and passim.
119. The idea of a "silent conversion," one made implicit by a rupture in the text, was advanced by von Moos, "Die Bekehrung Heloises," 117–88; and disputed in *Women Writers,* p. 129.
120. See Georgianna, chapter 8.
121. Cf. *HC,* ed. Muckle 201 and 205; *Ep.* 3, ed. Muckle 77.
122. *Ep.* 5, ed. Muckle 88–89 (Radice 147; emphasis added).

CHAPTER 12

NO OUTLET FOR INCONTINENCE: HELOISE AND THE QUESTION OF CONSOLATION

Alcuin Blamires

Heloise renegotiates Abelard's role and her own by invoking consolatory patristic letters to educated women, which clarify the "remedy" that would properly match their own situation.

It is rather well known that in the course of her indignant response to the *Historia calamitatum,* Heloise protests her surprise that after the earlier trauma of their separation and her abrupt entry into religious life, Abelard had not thought of comforting her through the medium of letters. Here he was, sending a *Consolatory Letter to a Friend* ("Abaelardi ad amicum consolatoria," as two manuscripts identify what we now call the *Historia*)[1] that presumed to include dispassionate comment on herself, yet there was no sign of any consolatory epistles to her—a once-intimate friend upon whom he might be expected to lavish rather more concern. She hardly need remind him, she pointedly remarks—"Your superior wisdom knows better than our humble learning" [tua melius excellentia quam nostra parvitas novit]—of the "many serious treatises" that the holy Fathers carefully compiled "for the instruction or exhortation or even the consolation of holy women" [in doctrina vel exhortatione seu etiam consolatione sanctarum feminarum].[2] Perhaps because it seems to generalize or because it takes knowledge for granted, this allusion has been greeted by most readers with only a vague nod of recognition. Yet as is now becoming increasingly apparent, Heloise and her husband conduct sinuous and probing disputations through the medium of their shared reading, through their mutual sense of specialized vocabularies and discourses, through their deployment of cultural masks.[3] So, should we not ask the logical questions: *What* treatises of instruction, exhortation, consolation? by whom? and what models are available there for adaptation by the present correspondents? Above all, how might such "treatises" have helped configure the process or dynamic that the correspondence enacts?

I emphasize "process," because speculation about the couple's modeling of their relationship on the precedent of interactions between early Christian women and patristic theologians has been confined largely to two focal points. One is Abelard's justification in *Ep.* 5 of the deference to Heloise implied by the salutation he had used to introduce his previous letter. He specifically invokes Jerome's mode of address to Eustochium, and this ushers in further adaptations of Jerome's advice to her.[4] The second is near the culmination of the extant correspondence—that is, in Heloise's letter introducing the *Problemata* where she invokes the precedent of Marcella, Roman matron and then ascetic widow who conducted a scholarly relationship with Jerome. Joan Ferrante recently has emphasized how Heloise conspicuously cites Jerome's commendation of Marcella's extensive studies, her questioning intelligence, and her probing critical mind. The passage "reveals a lot about Heloise's intellectual independence—there is no humility topos here," comments Ferrante. "Apparently identifying with Marcella, as Abelard clearly did with Jerome, [Heloise] notes that Jerome proposed that Marcella teach others, but she reminds Abelard that the responsibility for her nuns is his" in the sense that he brought them to the Paraclete, whence they look to him for clarification of scriptural puzzles.[5]

Before Ferrante, Peter Dronke, too, had briefly noted Heloise's interest here in Marcella and had suggested that her allusion signals a new stage in her awareness of her intellectual relationship with Abelard. Dronke spots the clue to what might be a suggestive echo of the earlier appeal to the Fathers' writings for women with which we began. When she refers Abelard to Marcella, she does so with studied deference. Dronke points out that

> the expression Heloise uses—"your wisdom knows this better than does my simplicity" [*vestra melius prudencia quam mea simplicitas novit*]—takes us back to a similar moment in her first letter: there too she had mentioned the exemplar of the Fathers writing to holy women, adding "Your excellence knows this better than my littleness" [*tua melius excellentia quam nostra parvitas novit*]. Then it had been a matter of persuading Abelard to write at all; now the relationship between Jerome and Marcella portends something more complex.[6]

Commentary has begun to develop, therefore, some perception of the eventual significance of Jerome's Marcella for Heloise and an incipient perception of a trajectory that might be traced from Heloise's first mention of such precedents to her last. There is more to be discovered, as this chapter will propose. I believe it can be shown that Heloise and Abelard found in self-assimilation to figures and strategies in patristic letters, or sometimes in deliberate self-distancing from them, one important means of defining, refining, and redefining their own self-models as their correspondence evolved.

In *Ep.* 2 Heloise explains how her hopes of being refreshed by rediscovering the image of her husband in his words in the *Historia* were dashed by the general misery of the piece. Worse than that, if in the *Historia* Abelard ostensibly has offered his friend *consolatio,* its impact on herself is the opposite: *desolatio.*[7] Famously, she now pleads for consolation from him at least in the form of letters. Letters could restore something of his presence; they could do something to clear the double debt that he owes her—the huge debt incurred by her personal sacrifice in taking the veil at his command and, encompassing that, his corporate debt to the whole community of nuns settled at the Paraclete, a place of which he is, she declares emphatically, "the sole founder."[8] Heloise here of course invokes, without needing even to state it, the distinctive name given by Abelard to this his sole foundation after arriving near Troyes in the depths of despair. He had emphasized in the *Historia* that he chose the name "Paraclitus" meaning *consolator* [comforter] because he had found divine *consolatio* there.[9]

Heloise elaborates her insistence that Abelard must be considered the founder of the Paraclete through an extended horticultural metaphor:

> Tua itaque vere tua haec est proprie in sancto proposito novella plantatio cuius adhuc teneris maxime plantis frequens ut proficiant necessaria est irrigatio. Satis ex ipsa feminei sexus natura debilis est haec plantatio et infirma etiam si non esset nova. Unde diligentiorem culturam exigit et frequentiorem iuxta illud apostoli: *Ego plantavi, Apollo rigavit, Deus autem incrementum dedit.* Plantaverat apostolus atque fundaverat in fide per praedicationis suae doctrinam Corinthios quibus scribebat. Rigaverat postmodum eos ipsius apostoli discipulus Apollo sacris exhortationibus et sic eis incrementum virtutum divina largita est gratia
>
> [And so it is yours, truly your own, this new plantation, for God's purpose, but it is sown with plants which are still very tender and need watering if they are to thrive. Through its feminine nature this plantation would be weak and frail even if it were not new; and so it needs a more careful and regular cultivation, according to the words of the Apostle: 'I planted the seed and Apollos watered it; but God made it grow.' The Apostle through the doctrine that he preached had planted and established in the faith the Corinthians, to whom he was writing. Afterwards the Apostle's own disciple, Apollos, had watered them with his holy exhortations and so God's grace bestowed on them growth in the virtues].[10]

She goes on to allege Abelard's "neglect" of his own "vineyard": his failure to meet his obligation to comfort her—and through her the whole community of the Paraclete—by writing those treatises of "instruction," "exhortation," or "consolation," which (as already quoted) the Fathers formerly penned for holy women.

The association between "plantation" and "exhortation by the Fathers" is more immediate than criticism has discovered. It is advisable not to be diverted by what sometimes has been supposed the surprising "sexual overtone" of the irrigation figure.[11] Quite apart from the fact that sexual irrigation would be a sick joke in the context of a castrated "founder," it is precisely this metaphor that is to be used by Jerome when he talks about strengthening the resolve of women converts. As early as Letter 7 Jerome mentions to three other colleagues the conversion of his own sister by a deacon called Julian at Aquileia: "He planted, you must water, the lord will give the increase." Despite the optimism of the biblical saying, Jerome discloses through a counterquotation from Vergil that he is still apprehensive about his sister's spiritual welfare: "omnia etiam tuta timeo" [All things, though safe in semblance, I do fear]. However safe things appear, everyone knows "how treacherous is the path of youth," and it is above all now, as she enters upon that path, that she needs to be supported and encouraged by all—"in other words, strengthened by such frequent letters as your saintliness will suggest."[12]

In this instance Jerome is looking to others to do the watering: in the case of Demetrias, one of Rome's wealthy women who had recently dedicated herself to virginity when he wrote to her in A.D. 414, he represented himself as the irrigator. Demetrias was actually a stranger to him, and her profession of virginity had been confidently made, with the enthusiastic support of her mother and grandmother. Yet in the letter Jerome argues that, writing at the family's request, he can still quicken her pace, rouse her determination, fire up her valor: "The grandmother and the mother have planted, but it is I that water and the Lord that giveth the increase."[13] Later in the letter he warns Demetrias of the dire consequences of backsliding—but only, he adds tactically, because he is "an apprehensive and prudent monitor who in your case fears even what is safe."[14]

Although Heloise perhaps needed no intermediary to see how the Pauline plantation metaphor lent itself to a context such as hers,[15] the possibility that she knowingly alludes to Jerome's applications of the verse is deeply interesting. Representing herself and her community in her letter as "tender plants," she partly invokes gender stereotype, of course.[16] But she is also playing on what she conceives as Abelard's misplaced sense of security about her religious role. Whereas Jerome was acutely anxious for the "safety" of new female spiritual recruits (hence concerned for their "watering"), Heloise finds in Abelard a baffling lack of anxiety on her account, which leads him not into exhortatory activity but *negligentia.* She pointedly reminds him that it was *not* "any sense of vocation" [religionis devotio] that brought her to accept monastic asperity, but only his own bidding.[17] She wants to shake his misplaced trust. If only he would trust her less, so that he would be more anxious about her. She underlines the irony: the more outwardly competent is her handling of her religious role, the more he is able to "feel secure in [her]" and the more she herself sustains his negligence [quo te amplius nunc securum reddidi, negligentiorem sustineo].[18]

That last expression is translated by Betty Radice "the more I have to bear with your neglect." I think that *sustineo* is more nuanced than that. By unwittingly contributing to Abelard's feeling of security about her vocation, she not only "endures" his neglect; she "supports" or even "nourishes" that neglect (for these are competing senses of the verb). So far is she from being the recipient of the sort of encouragement liberally offered by Jerome to female correspondents, therefore, that she somehow has ended up encouraging the silence of her own husband, founder, and mentor. Her response to this predicament in the letter is to recall strategies from Jeromian letters of exhortation within her own appeal for such letters. She represents her likeness to Jerome's female protégés, for she is a tender plant requiring sustenance, but also calculatedly emphasizes her unlikeness. She is no Demetrias for she has no vocation, is handicapped in the religious life, has even been *mis*planted there and by one who does not acknowledge how "unsafe" she is. In short, she is an extreme case for epistolary consolation, which—as she once more urges at the end of the letter—is urgently required in order to strengthen her toward a greater alacrity in serving God.

Ep. 2 is an extraordinary phenomenon, not least in that Heloise borrows from memories of Jerome's letters to women to write the sort of letter that is not extant from any woman to him. (This does not mean that such letters were not written. When Jerome writes to Furia that "In your letter you beg and beseech me to write—or rather to write by return—and tell you how you ought to live, keeping your crown of widowhood," the details of his reply strongly imply that Furia's letter has expressed an emotional appeal for his backing amid a crisis of parental pressure upon her to remarry).[19] But, given that Heloise gestures toward the Fathers' own letters, what reply from Abelard might be envisaged if he were indeed to turn to patristic models?

If he looked to Augustine, he could find some letters of instruction (i.e., to Proba, concerning prayer, at her request) and some of consolation to women who had lost loved ones (i.e., to Sapida). Often the letters of consolation are a pretext for instruction (as is Letter 92, to Italica, on seeing God).[20] If he thought of Ambrose, he would recall that the *De virginibus* was written for Ambrose's sister Marcellina and that a consolatory treatise on the death of Valentinianus (mainly instructional again) was written for the latter's sisters. Incidentally, a perusal of letters such as these soon removes all thoughts of trying to sustain distinctions between "instruction, exhortation and consolation." *Consolatio* certainly was understood sometimes as a genre with defined rules. Jerome noisily identifies some of the rules even as he transgresses them. Yet in practice, perhaps especially in a context governed by the gender asymmetry of male writing to female, consolation blended readily into *doctrina* and *exhortatio.* In this chapter I have not found it useful to insist on distinctions among the three terms that Heloise uses because I believe that she means by them to accommodate the mixture, not the separation, of modes in the discourses she is naming.

Despite the presence of relevant letters among other patristic writers, it was above all Jerome's letters to women that would come first to mind, both because they were so numerous and because Jerome drew attention to their numerousness[21] and also because he wrote self-consciously about the whiff of scandal that they drew upon him. (Abelard in his own acute sense of being victimized described himself as "Jerome's heir . . . as regards slanders and false accusations," including the accusations stemming from the saint's relationship with Paula, which Abelard likened to those he incurred by trying to help Heloise after she was installed at the Paraclete.[22]) And yet how aptly could Jerome's intentions in his letters be appropriated by Abelard for the current situation? Heloise is not literally "bereaved" (a prospect that fills her with horror in *Ep.* 4). Since her husband is not dead, the relevant consolatory strategy—that he has gone ahead, to be rejoined in eternity—cannot operate fully, although one can see the possibility of adapting Jerome's consolation of Theodora, that her departed husband still has her in mind and "supports" her in her "struggle."[23] Heloise's desire for moral strengthening eminently qualifies her for that kind of Jeromian response in a sense. However, she eludes his chief categories for exhortation: consecrated virgins whose resolve and purity needs vigilant defense or widows whose dedication to religious life needs shoring up against enticements of worldliness and remarriage.

If it were a question of looking for personal emotional empathy, one would look largely in vain in Jerome. It is a rare moment when he writes of Blesilla, the dead daughter of his associate Paula, that "as I think of her my eyes fill with tears, sobs impede my voice."[24] It is even unusual that he offers a gentle closing reassurance to Theodora: "May the watcher and the holy one who came down to Daniel come also to you."[25] More characteristic of Jerome are bracing exhortations, prickly or even lurid admonitions, pungently satirical reflections. The principle that Abelard owed Heloise epistolary *consolatio* on the patristic model was one thing in theory; in practice, there would be some difficulty in locating a tone and a strategy to emulate.

In *Ep.* 3 Abelard sidesteps the problem, although not perhaps as comprehensively as sometimes thought. First, apparently ignoring her invitation to him to mistrust her strength, he reasserts his confidence in her own wise sense. Second, he agrees to write at her future request on any specific matter of religious instruction.[26] Third, he interposes his own extreme need of her support, as if she had no need of his. Expatiating on his need, he exasperatingly incorporates complimentary remarks on her own sanctity and on the efficacy of women's (and especially wives') prayers *for men.*[27] Actually I think it may be that Abelard nevertheless intends this discourse on prayer and on prayer's power to curb divine rigor to do double duty—to be partly a reminder of the efficacy of prayer to help her in her own distress. It is notable that he refers her, for instance, to a same-sex example in St. Gregory, concerning "how much support the prayers of his fellow brethren quickly brought a brother, although he was unwilling and resisted" in his "utter despair"—an example that *mutatis mutandis* obviously offers a prospect of Heloise's nuns sustaining her through their prayers.[28]

If Abelard was, perversely, smuggling in that kind of encouragement under the banner of urging her to pray for himself, Heloise was unimpressed by such indirection. In *Ep.* 4 she repeats again that Abelard, by anticipating his death, brings her not *consolatio* but *desolatio.* But it continues to be a subtle facet of her own writing that she seeks to sharpen his understanding of her predicament by herself appropriating the topoi of Jerome's letters of encouragement to women. In *Ep.* 4 she configures herself according to four such topoi in particular: "Climb and Fall," "Inner Depravity," "Unsafe Conversion," and the "Crown of Victory."

The first has already drawn astute comment from Barbara Newman. When Heloise begins to articulate the cruelty of her fate in this letter, she imagines herself toppled from the very zenith to the very bottom of Fortune's wheel. "The higher I was exalted when you preferred me to all other women, the greater my suffering over my own fall and yours, when I was flung down; for the higher the ascent, the heavier the fall."[29] Newman compares Heloise's brilliant application of this motif with its rather different normative use "to warn virgins of their precarious stature," as by Ivo of Chartres in an epistle on virginity. Since Heloise is projecting herself as exalted while a mistress and flung down by marriage, she has turned the topos "on its head."[30] One classic patristic precedent is Jerome's dark warning to Demetrias that although she is ennobled by her holiness, "the higher she climbs the more terrible will be her fall": that is, if she falls into sensuality and severance from Christ.[31]

The reason for harking back to Jerome's epistle even for such a commonplace would be that it is closely followed there by a typically theatrical warning to Demetrias not to allow evil into her thoughts. (There is a somewhat similar passage in Jerome's letter of exhortation to the aristocratic consecrated virgin Eustochium. Jerome caps his stern advice to her to stifle sexual reveries with a memory of his own vulnerability to fantasies while living as a hermit. His mind hot with desire, he found himself imagining girls performing erotic dances.[32]) Like Eustochium, Demetrias is to guard against the presence of the serpent in her *cogitationes* and concentrate on keeping out secret faults, "slay the allurements to vice while they are still only thoughts."[33] Guarding thoughts becomes a key to keeping the body inviolate, a huge task given the power of sensual will as lamented by St. Paul in his famous outcry, "who shall deliver me from the body of this death?"[34]

Catherine Brown has argued that in *Ep.* 4 Heloise wields the *persona* of the hypocrite.[35] I would add that within that *persona,* she here projects her inner state as that of the endangered female ascetic besieged by those thoughts against which Jerome warns his protégés. She discloses that she is prey to sexual fantasies, fired with sexual desires, fed by "lewd visions" that take over her thoughts and keep them intent on "wantonness instead of on prayers"; thoughts so ungovernable that she, too, would echo St. Paul's despairing cry.[36]

Again, while Jerome exhorts Demetrias because he fears even what is safe, and while he sets out to warn Eustochium against complacency (her dedication of herself to God is a basis not for pride but for fear[37]), Heloise has to articulate *for* Abelard her *unsafe* state, her insecure conversion, to which he seems oblivious in his praises of her. In this letter she unexpectedly brings this protest to the brink of threat. She insists that her inner depravity belies her outward piety. Thus his high estimate of her, while it dangerously tickles her vanity, is misguided. One more time, but now more urgently than before, she appeals to him to view her moral state with an appropriate *anxiety* (i.e., to fear for her ascetic durability in the manner of a Jerome). She begs him for sustained apprehension, not confidence: "Time, obsecro, semper de me potius quam confidas." It is only his anxiety that can help her, and now especially there should be anxiety "when I no longer have in you an outlet for my incontinence." Radice's expression "outlet for incontinence" is an astute translation of Heloise's "incontinentiae remedium."[38] Heloise is invoking one of the traditional theological justifications of marriage, as a "remedy" for the suspect human drive to fornicate. But does Abelard's wife just mean that he must fear the vulnerability of her mind to dreams of a sexual satisfaction she can no longer obtain from him? Or is there a dark hint that, unless he fears for her enough to reinforce her religious commitment, she may physically seek an outlet for sexual incontinence?

Conjoined with this challenge is another, the fourth of the topoi in *Ep.* 4 that have long patristic roots. In *Ep.* 2 she already has asserted that she merits no reward from God for taking up the religious life wholly at Abelard's behest.[39] Now again she dissociates herself from the prospect of glamorous celestial reward, repudiating talk of winning a celestial crown. She imagines herself at best creeping into some obscure corner of heaven.[40] "She will not march into a high seat in heaven like the champions of the ascetic life," as Peter Dronke puts it.[41] Her clinching authority for this is a sentiment quoted from a polemical treatise by Jerome himself, that one should not attempt spiritual warfare beyond one's strength.[42]

Yet in this allusion there is a certain irony, of which Heloise cannot have been unaware, since Jerome often encouraged his female correspondents precisely by holding out the prize of the "crown of victory."[43] In his letter to Demetrias he reflects on a succession of misfortunes that befell her grandmother Proba and concludes "It is for this end that we labour, it is for this end that we risk our lives in the warfare of this world, that we may be crowned in the world to come."[44] What I think Heloise has recalled, however, is on one hand the kind of qualification that Jerome registers when counseling Demetrias about how far she should give away all her wealth: "it is for you to choose whether you will enter the arena and win the crown."[45] On the other hand, more conclusively, in the very epistle that closes with the invitation to Eustochium to imagine for herself a magnificent reception in heaven, Heloise would find a salutary warning about the fallen virgin: God "has no power to crown one who has been corrupted."[46] Heloise's little corner of heaven is her solution to this, a concessionary reward sought by someone who is less like Eustochium than like Jerome's protégé Fabiola, a woman who transgressed the ideal categories because she had repudiated one husband and married a second. After her death Jerome supposed that he could not automatically predict for her the sublime rewards for those "stained by no defilement"; she would be reliant on God's grace and on the comfort of the words "In our father's house are many mansions."[47]

In *Ep.* 5 Abelard carefully counters these challenges by Heloise. Consciously transgressing her prohibition on the subject, he proposes her as a far greater candidate for a "martyr's crown" than he on the grounds that whereas he is now excluded from struggle against the temptation of the flesh, her struggle has necessarily continued. At the same time he argues that his own erstwhile desires were much more uncontrollable than hers. "Incontinence," he implies, is a word that befitted his mentality more than hers. (She was "fortior continentia," his incontinence was "immoderata."[48]) It is partly this that inspires his persistent confidence in her.

There is room for cynicism about this consolation, not only because it competitively seeks to downsize the capacity of her passionate sexual psyche but also because it designates for Heloise a future of toiling chastity that will well suit him as her defunct husband. It portends "her own castration as well as his," in Peggy Kamuf's decisive phrase.[49] But I have no doubt that Abelard means in this letter to meet, in part, her need for strengthening. Moreover, he begins exactly where one might expect him to begin—with Jerome's most famous exhortation to a woman, the letter to Eustochium. There is clear incidental proof of this in Abelard's sophisticated commentary on Heloise's resistance to praise. He expressly draws from Jerome some observations on the risk of cultivating praise precisely by seeming to shun it.[50]

However, more centrally, Abelard begins where Jerome begins, with a meditation on his addressee as the bride of the Song of Songs and hence on her commitment to a celestial marriage. Although the underlying concept is absolutely routine in the case of a convertee or nun, the immediate focus on the description of the bride as "black and beautiful" is less so, and in both Abelard and Jerome it is linked with a further meditation on the seclusion of the bride.[51] Abelard's innovation is to compare Heloise's black religious habit with the outward blackness of the bride and to interpret her loveliness as interior and hidden. It is (as Glenda McLeod has noted) a brilliant inversion of Heloise's preferred self-construction whereby she envisaged herself as a facade of sanctity covering inner depravity.[52] In terms of patristic *exhortatio,* she receives what she has asked for in this epistle. She receives assurances about a super-husband to replace the one she can no longer be with, including the clever assurance that this bridegroom fulfills her criterion for an ideal marital partner, namely one who desires her absolutely in herself rather than anything else that is hers.[53] She is also exhorted to sublimate her grief and her resentment into a mourning for injustices against Christ. In terms of *consolatio* there are some adaptations of universal commonplaces (such as the suggestion that, although giving up sexual fertility, she can rise instead to spiritual and intellectual fertility). More personally, she gains some acknowledgment of their continuing, even if separate, companionship and of an intertwined destiny. Above all, she at last successfully prompts Abelard to try to erase her deep sense of the injustice of what befell them—but only at the cost of an injunction never to raise the matter again.

In consenting to this prohibition at the beginning of *Ep.* 6, Heloise articulates the harshness that may be required to force down grief by invoking the image of one nail used to drive out another fixed in wood. (Anyone who has actually tried this knows just what a last-ditch, drastic method of removing a nail it is.) This is Abelard's new responsibility: forcibly to expel her old emotions with new preoccupations, writing to herself and her nuns on topics in an instructional way as he previously promised.[54] I agree with Gilson and Dronke that she most likely recalls the nail image not from Cicero (as editors suggest) but from Jerome's letter to Rusticus, a man who had recently taken monastic vows and whose vocation therefore required encouragement. Jerome applies the nail analogy to the difficulty a monk may encounter in driving out the vice of carnal desire unless he can replace it with a more sublime love.[55] As Dronke has noticed, Heloise quotes another similar maxim from the same epistle in her letter introducing the *Problemata:* "love the knowledge of the Scriptures and you will not love the sins of the flesh."[56]

The usage in *Ep.* 6 not only supplies good evidence of her familiarity with Jerome's exhortatory epistles, it also expertly appropriates from one of them in the very moment of inviting Abelard to contribute further to the genre of instructional writing for women. Typically she sets new tasks in this old genre. One will be to explain the origins and authority of the nun's profession; the other (never accomplished by the Fathers, she points out) will be to design a rule for women religious.

On closer analysis the introduction to *Ep.* 6 holds one crucial but seemingly hitherto unnoticed detail. In suggesting to Abelard "dolori remedium vales conferre" [you have it in your power to remedy my grief], she appears to me to be recalling and varying the concept of the *remedium incontinentiae,* the remedy for the sex drive or "outlet for incontinence" over which we paused before. At first sight this marks a purposeful shift. If it is no longer possible for him to "remedy" her libido either sexually or even by writing, he can at least "remedy" her grief by writing. But behind the shift from *incontinentia* to *dolor* there is continuity too. The one is really the other. That is why it seems apt to argue that *all* the consolatory options that Heloise urges her husband to exercise are "outlets for incontinence," strategies for diverting thwarted energies, not only hers but perhaps his also by implicit extension. Her echo of the *remedium* in this context tends, at least, to substantiate Linda Georgianna's thesis that *Ep.* 6 really constitutes "a more institutionally centered version of what she has asked of Abelard all along: consolation and guidance for an unruly heart."[57]

I shall not dwell on the rest of *Ep.* 6 except to say two things. First, Heloise further seeks "consolation" in the sense that, resigned to the religious life but intensely aware of the inadequacies of the current Benedictine Rule, she asks for a rule that is seriously operable by women such as herself—one that is not impossible or obsessed with outward formalities and that will make sense of the strain that she alleges "continence" actually imposes on women. (Here it will be noted that she carries on her debate with Abelard over the question of gender and continence.) The second point is that there is a veritable rush of allusions to Jerome's letters here, and it is instructive to see which ones she has been reading. Not surprisingly she refers twice to Letter 22, to Eustochium, once on avoidance of worldly company and again on nuns who fail the test of continence.[58] Not surprisingly again, she draws on Letter 130, to Demetrias, for an ethical *sententia.*[59] Rather unexpectedly she quotes also from Jerome's letter "To a Mother and Daughter Living in Gaul," with regard to the difficulty of preserving modesty at the dining table. This reference substantiates the idea that she herself has assiduously gone back to epistles written for the exhortation of women, but it carries an extra hint. The letter is written to encourage a religious mother and daughter to live together rather than apart as they are currently living each with a male advisor, or "holy man." Jerome seizes the opportunity to write a devastating critique of the idea that a twenty-five-year-old woman of pious intentions can cohabit with a "holy man" without either forming a sexual liaison or provoking mass suspicion that she has done so.[60] Perhaps no Jerome letter would have seemed so poignantly apposite to Heloise and Abelard alike.

The Rule that Abelard provides in *Ep.* 8 is chiefly of interest in the present context for its conclusion. Prior to that, Jerome's epistles are invoked a dozen times, but only with reference to details of the monastic life. The letter's abrupt end is most intriguing, however. Abelard has expatiated on the nuns' duty to meditate silently on Christ's words—like the Virgin Mary or Mary, sister of Martha. If they are unable to match those women's fervent devotion, he suddenly concludes, let them at least in their study of scriptures emulate Jerome's disciples Paula and Eustochium, at whose request Jerome wrote so many books "to bring enlightenment to the Church."[61] Should we read here within the plurality of the nuns some special comfort for Heloise? Does Abelard imply that whatever any ultimate shortcoming she claims in her devotional zeal, her intellectual pursuits can provide a substitute religious identity? Or is any such thought crowded out by a characteristically egotistical hint that her best service will be to continue to prompt him to writings that (contrary to the aspersions of his theological enemies) will illuminate all Christendom?

Before ending where we began, late in the uncollected correspondence, the importance of *Ep.* 7 as a consolation should be noted. This letter is the essay commissioned by Heloise *On the Authority and Dignity of the Nun's Profession*.[62] In general, it is a celebration of the centrality of women in the early history of religious life, so probing and so positive that Abelard may be said to have made here a tremendous effort to endow Heloise with a sense of the *auctoritas* of her calling commensurate with her talents, in order to foster her commitment to that calling.[63] For its time it is therefore a profoundly consolatory discourse, although of a novel type.

In a way Abelard underlines how distinctive this form of consolation is and simultaneously offers mild criticism of conventional *consolatio,* when he offers concluding comment on the lengths to which admiration took some of the Fathers when they extolled particular women. Jerome is found to have gone "some way beyond the bounds of truth" in saying that he could never utter enough of the virtues of Paula even if every limb of his body turned into a separate tongue. Jerome is likewise suspected of committing excessive "adulation" in commenting on the virtues of Demetrias. The "compassion" of Ambrose is observed to have led him to the margins of orthodoxy in "promising" their brother's salvation to the sisters of Emperor Valentinianus.[64] If Abelard has dragged his feet before in response to the demand that he emulate the Fathers in consolation, these reflections explain some of his reluctance. His previous "praise" of Heloise's good sense is eminently sensible, compared with Jerome's more unwary encomiastic moments.[65] Anyway, one cannot imagine that Heloise would ever have welcomed the kind of tributes that Abelard here insinuates that he would never dish out. *Ep.* 7 surely constitutes a significant critical pause along the trajectory of the couple's attempts to appropriate patristic modes of writing for women.

As in the end of the Rule (*Ep.* 8), so in *Ep.* 7 Abelard's mind runs on the significance of women as mobilizers of the output of Jerome. "Who does not know what a harvest of divine books" he left to the Church at the instigation of Paula and Eustochium?[66] There can be no doubting the enormous affinity Abelard felt with Jerome, whom he called "the greatest doctor of the Church and glory of the monastic profession."[67] Clearly he now felt that under Heloise's prompting he was embarking on a new harvest of divine books. In the remaining correspondence the assimilation of Abelard to Jerome and of Heloise to his women associates becomes yet more palpable, although the preferred model now for Heloise is Marcella, the most informed and critical of these women. This choice seems particularly apt at a point when (as *Ep.* 6 shows) Heloise has assumed a greater intellectual initiative, not just asking for a new rule but elaborately anticipating its emphases.

Marcella counts as the last in a succession of cultural models that Heloise's learning and her relationship with Abelard enabled her—as Barbara Newman puts it—to "actualize."[68] Heloise specifically adopts the Marcella identity when she moves on to send Abelard her series of questions on scriptural (often implicitly ethical) problems, her *Problemata.* She begins by reminding Abelard how "vehemently" Jerome approved of Marcella's desire to pose scriptural questions and to examine his replies in a way that showed herself as much critic as pupil. Heloise describes Marcella as a "woman professor" (*magistra,* a word that at this period was sometimes used of prioresses). She is using her to epitomize her own sense of intellectual confidence, even if accompanying gestures of deference to Abelard as *doctor* remain rhetorically and doctrinally necessary.[69]

Marcella was one of the most influential and erudite of the Christian circle of women colleagues with whom Jerome became acquainted during his sojourn at Rome. Behind Heloise's allusion lie Jerome's numerous epistles to Marcella; for example, on the ten names for the deity in the Hebrew Scriptures (Letter 26) and on the meaning of other particular Hebrew words (Letters 28–29), also on the task of critically editing the scriptures (Letters 27 and 32).[70] One letter that gives an insight into the range of Marcella's scriptural inquiry on one hand and the extent of her correspondent's self-consciousness of his role as theological mentor and pedagogical censor on the other is Letter 37.[71] Marcella has asked Jerome to lend her a copy of a commentary by Rhetitius on the Song of Songs, but Jerome refuses. Rhetitius is not, as it were, recommended for her reading list, the grounds being that the commentary contains too many errors, of which he mentions examples.

It is in *Ep.* 9 that Abelard formally takes up the prompt about Marcella, with characteristic ostentation. This letter is clearly addressed to the nuns of the Paraclete although it lacks a salutation.[72] Often referred to as the *De studio litterarum,* it was once thought to have preceded the *Problemata,* but it can certainly be more logically placed after Heloise's letter introducing them.[73] It is an exhortation on reading and a discussion of what books and languages the nuns should study in particular. Jerome is trawled for suggestions, particularly a letter to Laeta (daughter-in-law of another of his disciples, Paula), which offered a junior syllabus for the education of Laeta's daughter. Then, hypersensitive as ever to the suspicions that Jerome's communings with women aroused, Abelard recalls that Jerome thought it right to advise even a single Roman virgin in order that she might become herself a *magistra* to others, and that his justification for keeping on writing to women was that women, not men, bothered to ask him about scripture.[74]

In the center of the Epistle Abelard quotes extensively from the letter to Principia that is a memoir of Marcella as widow, ascetic, and scholar. Although it is characteristic of Abelard to try to supply a ton of quotation for every ounce offered by Heloise, I think that he is actually pursuing the opportunity she has created, through her own self-identification with Marcella, for them to discuss themselves. Jerome describes how he found himself won over from initial modest diffidence (*pudor,* even) by Marcella's intellectual commitment, her striking persistence, and her critical questioning.[75] We should be alert here for reverberations of Abelard's description in the *Historia* of how he held aloof from women in Paris until he met Heloise with her gift for letters.[76] Meanwhile in *Ep.* 9 Abelard continues to rehearse Jerome, quoting his observation that what he himself had learned, Marcella so absorbed and possessed that "after [his] departure from Rome" people sought her verdict on problems of scriptural meaning. Abelard chops out part of a paragraph of the letter to Principia that he is following here but is careful to preserve the rest: "Absenciam nostri mutuis solabamur alloquiis at quod carne non poteramus, spiritu tenebamus. Semper obuiare se epistule, superare officiis, salutacionibus preuenire. Non multum perdebat absencia que iugibus sibi litteris iungebatur" [Meanwhile we consoled ourselves for our separation by an interchange of conversation, discharging in the spirit the debt that we could not pay in the flesh. Our letters always crossed, outvied in courtesies, anticipated in greetings. Separation brought no great loss, since it was bridged by a continual correspondence].[77] Is not this passage an extraordinary concise summary of much that has been at issue, and only gradually resolved, between Heloise and Abelard? The "debt" [*debitum*] that she felt he owed her is matched by the "debt" (although not a sexual one) of obligations between Marcella and Jerome; for mutual obligations are implicit (as the translator realizes) in the *quod non poteramus . . . tenebamus* construction. Then the power of letters to conjoin what absence separates is stunningly expressed by Jerome in a vocabulary (*iugibus . . . iungebatur*) that also sustains a subliminal suggestion of marital connection.

Up to this point in *Ep.* 9 it seems that Abelard is recognizing what Heloise has implicitly asserted, that she has graduated from the status of a Demetrias, recipient of her religious mentor's wisdom, to the status of a Marcella stimulating exchanges of discourse by her independent knowledge and scrupulous interrogation. But now in this passage we have a more far-reaching recognition. Through Jerome, Abelard acknowledges that, all along, Heloise has been *right* about consolation. Her demand for communication to continue through letters, for them to "hold in spirit" what they could not in the body, has patristic authority at the highest level.

The passage is thus the culmination of a process (one not unfamiliar in medieval literature) whereby autobiographical narrative is constructed around a metanarrative. At Heloise's instigation they have used the great inherited saga of Jerome and his women friends to describe themselves to themselves and to propel each other forward. Most often the impulse (here, Jerome's approbation of Marcella) comes first from Heloise. Abelard obliges by discovering in his reading, perhaps, exactly what she hopes he will discover. We may even find ourselves pondering an enticing final question. Was Heloise already remembering this passage when she first responded to the *Historia* and chastised Abelard for failing to compensate for his absence by consoling her, as the Fathers did, with letters?

Notes

1. See *HC,* ed. Muckle, 163, 175 n. 2.
2. *Ep.* 2, ed. Muckle 70 (Radice 112). In this chapter, I adhere to the view (propounded variously by Peter Dronke, David Luscombe, and Barbara Newman) that the correspondence is authentic.
3. As M. T. Clanchy in *Abelard: A Medieval Life,* p. 16, has recently reminded us, medieval letter writing in general presupposed a rhetorical cultivation of "artificial voices." Catherine Brown vigorously argues Heloise's deliberate adoption of varying identities or "cultural masks" in her "disputation" with Abelard in "*Muliebriter:* Doing Gender in the Letters of Heloise," pp. 25–51 (especially pp. 28, 33, 42).
4. *Ep.* 5, ed. Muckle 83 (Radice 137–38). Jerome, *Epistle* 22.2, PL 22:412, trans. F. A. Wright, *Select Letters of St Jerome,* pp. 56–57. Wright's translation is cited. For letters not covered in his volume I use the translation by W. H. Fremantle, *The Principal Works of St Jerome.* The relevance of Jerome's writings to the Heloise–Abelard correspondence has often been mentioned but not much analyzed. A controversial exception (somewhat oblique to the present discussion) is Deborah Fraioli, "The Importance of Satire in Jerome's *Adversus Jovinianum* as an Argument against the Authenticity of the *Historia calamitatum,*" pp. 167–99.

5. Joan Ferrante, *To the Glory of Her Sex: Women's Roles in the Composition of Medieval Texts,* pp. 59–60 (see also p. 28). For the letter introducing the *Problemata,* see PL 178:677–78. Heloise's quotation of the admiration Jerome expresses (in a commentary on Galatians) for Marcella's intellect is in column 677.
6. *Women Writers,* p. 135.
7. *HC,* ed. Muckle 69 (Radice 110–11).
8. *Ep.* 2, ed. Muckle 69–70 (Radice 110–13).
9. *HC,* ed. Muckle 201 (Radice 90–91). Abelard makes further comments on the appropriateness of the name in *HC,* ed. Muckle 205 (Radice 97), and in *Ep.* 3, ed. Muckle 77 (Radice 125).
10. *Ep.* 2, ed. Muckle 70 (Radice 111–12). Cf. 1 Cor. 3.6, 7–10.
11. Glenda McLeod, "'Wholly Guilty, Wholly Innocent': Self-Definition in Héloïse's Letters to Abélard," p. 66, following a lead by Dronke, *Women Writers,* p. 116.
12. Jerome, *Epistle* 7.4 ("Ad Chromatium, Iovinum, Eusebium,") PL 22:340 (trans. Wright, pp. 24–25). The Vergilian reference is to *Aeneid* IV.298.
13. Jerome, *Epistle* 130.2, PL 22:1108 (trans. Fremantle, p. 261).
14. "Haec dicta sint, non infausto contra te vaticinio, sed pavidi cautique monitoris officio, ea quoque in te, quae tuta sunt formidantis," Jerome, *Epistle* 130.8, PL 22:1114 (trans. Fremantle, p. 265).
15. Conceivably, Abelard himself is the intermediary since he himself applies the plantation metaphor to the nuns in *Sermon* 30, PL 178:569; but whether this postdates *Ep.* 2 or precedes it as Clanchy thinks (*A Medieval Life,* p. 250), I am not sure.
16. The stereotyping includes deference to a masculinity that lays claim to superior creative *intellectual* power, as cogently discussed by Bonnie Wheeler, "Origenary Fantasies: Abelard's Castration and Confession," pp. 107–28 (especially pp. 118–20). Further suggestions about the "plantation" passage will be found in chapters 7 and 10 in this volume.
17. *Ep.* 2, ed. Muckle 72 (Radice 116).
18. *Ep.* 2, ed. Muckle 73 (Radice 117).
19. Jerome, *Epistle* 54.1, PL 22:550 (trans. Wright, p. 229).
20. Respectively PL 33:493–507, 1092–94, 318–21. For translations see Augustine of Hippo, *The* Confessions *and* Letters *of St. Augustine,* ed. Philip Schaff.
21. In "To Demetrias" Jerome remarks that he has "written short exhortations to several virgins and widows," *Epistle* 130.19, PL 22:1123 (trans. Fremantle, p. 271).
22. *HC,* ed. Muckle 211, 206 (Radice 105, 98) respectively.
23. Jerome, *Epistle* 75.2, PL 22:686 (trans. Fremantle, p. 155).
24. Jerome, *Epistle* 39.1, PL 22:466 (trans. Fremantle, p. 47). The exception proves the rule: Jerome goes on to criticize displays of grief as non-Christian phenomena.
25. Jerome, *Epistle* 75.5, PL 22:688–89 (trans. Fremantle, p. 156).
26. Compare, however, Jerome, *Epistle* 75.5: "if there is any spiritual work of which you think me to be capable, boldly command me to undertake it," PL 22:688 (trans. Fremantle, p. 156).
27. On some of the profeminine topoi involved, see Alcuin Blamires, *The Case for Women in Medieval Culture,* pp. 84–89, 145–48.
28. *Ep.* 3, ed. Muckle 75 (Radice 122). The impression of coded comfort here arises partly through the suggestion that the details of this example are already "known" to Heloise and "cannot have escaped" her.
29. *Ep.* 4, ed. Muckle 78 (Radice 129).
30. Barbara Newman, "Authority, Authenticity, and the Repression of Heloise," p. 143.
31. Jerome, *Epistle* 130.7, PL 22:1113 (trans. Fremantle, p. 265).
32. Jerome, *Epistle* 22.6–7, PL 22:398 (trans. Wright, pp. 63–67).
33. Jerome, *Epistle* 130.8–9, PL 22:1114–15 (trans. Fremantle, p. 266).

34. Rom. 7.24.
35. Brown, "*Muliebriter,*" pp. 35–37. Heloise's preoccupation with evil thoughts in the "hidden places" of the heart continues on into *Ep.* 6, ed. Muckle 250–51 (Radice 174–75) as Linda Georgianna observes in chapter 8 in this volume.
36. *Ep.* 4, ed. Muckle 80–81 (Radice 132–33).
37. "Nolo tibi venire superbiam de proposito, sed timorem," Jerome, *Epistle* 22.3, PL 22:395 (trans. Wright, p. 57). Subsequently in the same epistle further emphasis is given to the perpetual insecurity of religious continence: "do you think you ought to lay aside all fear?" [tu te putas securam esse debere?] (*Epistle* 22.5), PL 22:397 (trans. Wright, p. 63).
38. *Ep.* 4, ed. Muckle 82 (Radice 135). In addressing the doctrinal echo in *remedium,* I do not exclude the possibility that Heloise also has in mind the Ovidian *Remedia amoris,* as argued by Michael Calabrese, "Ovid and the Female Voice in the *De Amore* and the *Letters* of Abelard and Heloise," pp. 16–20.
39. *Ep.* 2, ed. Muckle 72 (Radice 116–17).
40. *Ep.* 4, ed. Muckle 82 (Radice 136).
41. *Women Writers,* p. 126.
42. Jerome, *Adversus Vigilantium* 16, PL 23:367.
43. The biblical origin is 2 Tim. 4.7–8: "I have fought a good fight, I have finished my course, I have kept the faith. Henceforth there is laid up for me a crown of righteousness, which the Lord, the righteous judge, shall give me at that day."
44. Jerome, *Epistle* 130.7, PL 22:1112 (trans. Fremantle, p. 264).
45. Jerome, *Epistle* 130.14, PL 22:1118 (trans. Fremantle, p. 268).
46. Jerome, *Epistle* 22.41 and 22.5 respectively, PL 22:424–25 and 22:397 (trans. Wright pp. 155–59 and p. 63).
47. Jerome, *Epistle* 77.12, "To Oceanus," PL 22:698 (trans. Fremantle, p. 162).
48. *Ep.* 5, ed. Muckle 92–93 (Radice 154).
49. Peggy Kamuf, "Fictions of Feminine Desire," p. 36.
50. *Ep.* 5, ed. Muckle 87 (Radice 143–44); Jerome, *Epistle* 22.27, PL 22:412–13 (trans. Wright, pp. 113–17).
51. *Ep.* 5, ed. Muckle 82–86 (Radice 137–42): compare Jerome, *Epistle* 22.1–2, 25–26. The basis is Song of Songs 1.4–5: "I am black but lovely, daughters of Jerusalem; therefore the king has loved me and brought me into his chamber" [Nigra sum, sed formosa filiae Hierusalem. Ideo dilexit me rex et introduxit me in cubiculum suum].
52. McLeod, "'Wholly Guilty, Wholly Innocent,'" p. 74.
53. *Ep.* 5, ed. Muckle 92 (Radice 152): cf. *Ep.* 2, ed. Muckle 71 (Radice 114).
54. *Ep.* 6 and 7 of the correspondence are cited from the edition by J. T. Muckle, "The Letter of Heloise on Religious Life and Abelard's First Reply." See here *Ep.* 6, ed. Muckle 241–42 (Radice 159).
55. "Worldly philosophers are wont to drive out an old passion by a new one, as you drive out an old nail by hammering in another," Jerome, *Epistle* 125.14, PL 22:1080 (trans. Wright, p. 421). See Alcuin Blamires, "*Caput a femina, membra a viris:* Gender Polemic in Abelard's Letter 'On the Authority and Dignity of the Nun's Profession,'" p. 57. Étienne Gilson, *Héloïse and Abélard,* 2nd ed., trans. L. K. Shook, p. 188, n. 21, and *Women Writers,* p. 305, n. 39, both make the case for Jerome as the source of the analogy.
56. "Ama scientiam scripturarum et carnis vitia non amabis." See *Women Writers,* p. 136 and n. 55, and Jerome, *Epistle* 125.11, PL 22:1078 (trans. Wright, p. 417).
57. See chapter 8 herein. An alternative view of this letter as a subtle ungendering of the concept of *infirmitas* is developed by Donna Alfano Bussell in chapter 10.
58. *Ep.* 6, ed. Muckle 243, 245 (Radice 161, 165).
59. *Ep.* 6, ed. Muckle 243 (Radice 162).
60. *Ep.* 6, ed. Muckle 242 (Radice 160); and Jerome, *Epistle* 117.5–6, 9, PL 22:956–57, 958–59; (trans. Wright, pp. 381–85, 391–93).

61. *Ep.* 8, ed. McLaughlin 241–92, 292 (Radice 269).
62. For an explanation of this title, see Blamires, *The Case for Women,* p. 201 and n. 9. The text is translated by C. K. Scott-Moncrieff, *The Letters of Abelard and Heloise,* 1942: repr. 1974, pp. 131–75.
63. This is the objective he lays out in the last few lines of the letter, although ostensibly directed to the nuns in the plural: *Ep.* 7, ed. Muckle 281 (Scott-Moncrieff 175). For a discussion of the pro-feminine qualities of the letter, see Mary Martin McLaughlin, "Peter Abelard and the Dignity of Women: Twelfth-Century 'Feminism' in Theory and Practice," pp. 287–334; and Blamires, *The Case for Women,* pp. 199–208.
64. *Ep.* 7, ed. Muckle 279–80 (Scott-Moncrieff 172–74), and citing Jerome, *Epistle* 108.1, PL 22:878 and *Epistle* 130.1, PL 22:1107; and Ambrose, *De obitu Valentiniani consolatio,* PL 16:1435.
65. For further comment on *Ep.* 7 as a discourse of consolation which critiques other consolations, see Blamires, "*Caput a femina,*" p. 71.
66. *Ep.* 7, ed. Muckle 279 (Scott-Moncrieff 172).
67. *Ep.* 8, ed. McLaughlin 289 (Radice 264).
68. Newman, "Authority, Authenticity," p. 151.
69. PL 178:677–78. Deference remained doctrinally necessary on the same grounds that it had been (as Jerome writes) for Marcella, who would attribute her own insights to himself or others rather than seem to infringe the Pauline injunction "not allowing a woman to teach." *Epistle* 127.7, PL 22.1091–92 (trans. Wright, p. 455).
70. PL 22:430–431, 433–41, 431–33, and 446 respectively.
71. PL 22:461–63, summarized in Fremantle, p. 47.
72. *Ep.* 9 is edited in Edmé Renno Smits, *Peter Abelard, Letters IX-XIV. An Edition with an Introduction,* pp. 219–37; see also PL 178:325–36.
73. Damien van den Eynde, "Chronologie des écrits d'Abélard a Héloïse," pp. 340–43. However, Constant Mews, "On Dating the Works of Peter Abelard," pp. 131–32, still tentatively dates the *Problemata* "c. 1137–38," and *Epistles* 2–10 "1132–37(?)."
74. *Ep.* 9, ed. Smits; and PL 178:328.
75. "cum . . . uerecunde nobilium feminarum occulos declinarem, ita egit, secundum Apostolum, 'importune oportune', ut pudorem meum sua superaret industria," *Ep.* 9, ed. Smits 226.
76. *HC,* ed. Muckle 183 (Radice 66).
77. *Ep.* 9, ed. Smits 227; from Jerome, *Epistle* 127.8, PL 22.1092 (trans. Wright, p. 457).

CHAPTER 13

HELOISE AND THE CONSOLATION OF FRIENDSHIP

Brian Patrick McGuire

The word consolatio *is a key concept in explaining what Heloise sought from Abelard: the Christian friendship between clerical men and holy women, a tradition going back to late antiquity and one that the papal reform movement of the eleventh century challenged but did not succeed in removing.*

In the mid-1980s when I was working on a book concerning friendship in monastic life in the Middle Ages, I deliberately left out the relationship between Abelard and Heloise.[1] I did not even try to consider whether their bond was one of friendship. At the time it seemed too problematic to delve into the question of their love affair, the witness of the letters and their authenticity, as well as the monastic element in their relationship. In what follows here I want to answer this unasked question of friendship and look at it in terms of the concept of consolation.[2] I can do so only in fear and trembling, for the letters of Abelard and Heloise, the foundation of any speculation about the relationship of the two, have in the last decades been one of the most controversial areas of medieval studies.[3]

As a young undergraduate at Berkeley in the 1960s I read with fascination the account of the letters in Étienne Gilson's version.[4] From that time I was aware of the debate about whether Heloise had written the letters ascribed to her. For me Gilson's most convincing argument was the one he took from a Benedictine he once met in the manuscript room of the Bibliothèque Nationale. According to this monastic scholar, the letters had to be genuine because of their beauty: "It is impossible for that to be unauthentic. It is too beautiful."[5]

Beauty was not the criterion for R. W. Southern, who came to Berkeley in the spring of 1968 as visiting professor of medieval studies and taught a memorable graduate seminar. Here he read a paper on the letters of Abelard and Heloise, later included in his *Medieval Humanism and Other Studies.*[6] Southern accepted the letters as genuine, but what I remember about his oral presentation was his concern with the amount of sexual passion in the relationship. At one point he turned aside from his carefully prepared manuscript and pointed to Abelard's description in *Ep.* 5 of visiting Heloise at Argenteuil and making love to her in a corner of the refectory. Abelard claimed to regret what he did. Southern could not help being fascinated with Abelard's audacity. In the age of "sexual liberation" that the 1960s were supposed to be, subjects were being discussed openly that long had been outside public discourse.

A decade later, when I returned to the United States for the first time after a seven-year self-imposed exile, I made the acquaintance and later became the friend of John F. Benton, who then taught at the California Institute of Technology in Pasadena. My interest in psychological understanding of medieval people had led me to Benton, whose introduction to his revised translation of Guibert of Nogent, however controversial, was also a pioneering effort to make psychohistory respectable.[7] In the last years of the 1970s Benton was still engaged in an attempt to show that the letters of Abelard and Heloise are a falsification, probably invented in thirteenth-century Paris, although Benton retracted most of his earlier hypotheses in a paper given at the Abelard conference at Trier in 1980: there were too many loose ends, and it was easy to make his suppositions look ridiculous.[8]

The great, and also controversial, monastic historian Jean Leclercq once described to me how he had come across John Benton during the Trier conference and found him distraught. I can understand and sympathize. After Trier, Benton still insisted that Heloise had not written the letters attributed to her but claimed Abelard had written all the letters. This point of view is severely criticized in recent research, where Benton is portrayed almost as a male chauvinist for not being willing to attribute to Heloise the degree of literary brilliance that he reserved for Abelard.[9]

John Benton was a tireless seeker of historical truth, and I think he would have welcomed the results of the past years, during which many scholars have argued that the letters are genuine.[10] This point of view makes it possible to return to the question of the bond between Heloise and Abelard in order to understand the content of a human relationship in the period. At the same time, however, I must admit a certain unease about the authenticity debate. Amid the plethora of arguments for and against, I have to entrust myself to those who know the letters better than I do. In what follows, I consider the letters to be a unique document of a love affair without parallel in medieval literature. Here for once we hear a woman's voice as well as a man's.

In acknowledging the uniqueness of the letters, I would like to relate them to a tradition so rich and common that it almost might be called banal: the literature of friendship.[11] If we assume that Heloise did write the letters attributed to her, then we can use the collection in order to trace the development of a relationship where the expression of friendship was a central factor. Frustrated lovers eventually became good friends.

Such an interpretation might seem like an idealization of what must have been a painful and traumatic process. I want in no way to deny the difficulties that Heloise and Abelard faced, but I want in what follows to show how Heloise to a great extent "called the shots," directing Abelard's direction of her and telling him what she needed from him. Abelard to a great extent responded to her instructions. Abelard did so, I think, because he came to realize how much he loved Heloise: she was one person in whom he could invest his talents and abilities, his thoughts and emotions. The involvement of Abelard with the Paraclete and with Heloise its abbess can be seen in terms of the growth of a spiritual friendship in the ruins of a sexual love affair.

By describing the development of such a relationship, I intend in no way to deny that for Heloise herself, friendship at a distance may have been far less than what she really wanted from Abelard. If we take the assertions of the magnificent *Ep.* 4, in which

Heloise revealed her inner state of being, then she had not reconciled herself with being a bride of Christ instead of Abelard's lover. But the fact remains that Heloise remained at the Paraclete and followed the very monastic principle of obedience, as she herself pointed out in the opening of *Ep.* 6. Her acceptance of her situation as the fulfillment of Abelard's will can indicate that Heloise conformed only because of her passionate love for Abelard. Heloise nevertheless made use of Abelard and her bond with him to find a new meaning in her monastic commitment.[12]

I make no attempt in what follows to solve the old dilemma of Heloise's intentions. What I want to show is that Heloise in her letters compelled Abelard to face the content and meaning of his bond with her. She did so by showing Abelard that his form of *consolatio* was insufficient and had to be reworked.[13] From consoling a friend by telling him about his own troubles, Abelard was forced first to do the same to Heloise and then to give a new type of consolation in listening to her troubles and responding to them. Heloise insisted that *consolatio* means more than rhetorical advice in formal letterwriting. It became a means of compelling the correspondent to acknowledge the situation of the person addressed and to respond to what he was being told.

In what follows I present the elements in the letter collection that deal less with consolation and more with the topic of monastic concern for women. I show how Abelard came to describe the importance of close male-female bonds in the spiritual and religious life. This use of consolation in a male-female spiritual bond marks a new departure in the history of medieval religion, even though it harkens back to late antiquity and especially to the letters of Jerome to holy women.[14]

The consolation that Abelard offered to his friend in *Ep.* 1, the so-called *Historia calamitatum,* was of a type that might be expressed thus in colloquial American: "You think you got troubles; hey, man, take a look at me." Toward the end of the letter, however, Abelard used the term *consolationem* in another context. Speaking of the suspicion under which Jerome labored because of his bond with the young Paula, Abelard said that it has been a matter of consolation for him to see that the Church Father Jerome was looked upon with the same skepticism that now was being shown towards his relationship to Heloise at the Paraclete: "When, as I say, I recalled the injustice of such a calumny against so great a man, I took no small comfort from it."[15] Abelard used this reference to emphasize his own condition of physical impotence. As a eunuch, he thought he would be beyond suspicion, but somehow his enemies still believed that his bond with Heloise was sexual. As usual, Abelard put himself at the center of the discourse and emphasized his own pain and trials. But he also pointed out that it is natural for men and women to find closeness of a non-sexual type to each other. Once he considered castration and impotence, he returned to this idea in emphasizing how the apostles and "other holy fathers" engaged in close contact with women [*tam familiari conversatione feminis praecipue videret sociatos*].[16]

Abelard revealed a knowledge of patristic literature on the subject by quoting Augustine's *On the Work of Monks* to show how "women were the inseparable companions of our Lord Jesus Christ and the apostles."[17] He used the term *inseparabiles comites* where the adjective qualifies and intensifies the meaning of the noun. He did not use the term *amici,* friends, a term normally reserved for bonds between men. Even here, however, changes were on the way.

This section of Abelard's first letter in the collection was intended as a defense of his own involvement with the Paraclete, but it developed also into a plea for male supervision of female monastic life. In attacking double monasteries where "the natural order is overthrown to the extent that we see abbesses and nuns ruling the clergy,"[18] Abelard was very much in harmony with the reform movements of his time.[19] But in explaining his decision to look after the needs of the sisters of the Paraclete, Abelard was also linking himself with the church fathers of late antiquity who cared for holy women and their religious communities. Here he found consolation, just as he gave consolation to his anonymous friend in telling about the calamities of his life.

In the opening of her first letter to Abelard, Heloise made it clear that she expected consolation from the man whose many roles in her life she described in her elaborate salutation. She had been disturbed and upset by Abelard's narrative of the dangers he experienced and asked to be able to share his sorrow as well as his happiness. At this point she defined the kind of consolation she expected and needed:

> It is always some consolation in sorrow to feel that it is shared, and any burden laid on several is carried more lightly or removed. And if this storm has quietened down for a while, you must be all the more prompt to send us a letter that will be the more gladly received. But whatever you write will bring us no small relief in the mere proof that you have us in mind. Letters from absent friends are welcome indeed, as Seneca himself shows us by his own example when he writes these words in a passage of a letter to his friend Lucilius . . . [20]

Heloise made use of commonplaces about friendship that at first glance can seem almost innocuous, and yet she was laying the foundation for the new relationship she sought with Abelard in the aftermath of their love affair. The consolation she asked for consisted in Abelard's making himself available to her through correspondence. In using a quotation from Seneca's fortieth letter to Lucilius, she could assert that when a letter from a friend comes, then there arises a feeling of the friend's presence. By referring to Seneca's words on friendship through correspondence, Heloise could assert that Abelard was an absent friend. Friendship by letter could provide the consolation that Heloise needed.

This assertion of classical friendship, however, was not sufficient for Heloise. She added that the very act by which Abelard concentrated on consoling a friend had been at her expense. Abelard's gesture of consolation for his friend was painful for Heloise, as her wordplay on *consolatio* and *desolatio* shows: "The detailed account you gave of these <misfortunes> may have been intended for his comfort, but it also greatly increased our own feeling of desolation."[21] If Abelard looked after his one friend, then he should be even more concerned about those sisters at the Paraclete who were his closest friends [*quas non tam amicas quam amicissimas*].[22] Heloise used the term *amicas* to describe her relationship not only with Abelard but also with the nuns of the Paraclete. One might claim that this generalization watered down the meaning of the bond of personal friendship, but later in the letter Heloise changed her approach and went from plural to singular, highlighting her individual feelings and situation more than that of the monastery. Here she made it clear she was appealing to Abelard as the friend who owed consolation and not desolation to his Heloise.

All through the remainder of the letter, Heloise's argument is consistent: Abelard must remember what he owes those to whom he is closest: " . . . consider the close tie by which you have bound yourself to me and repay the debt you owe a whole community of women dedicated to God by discharging it the more dutifully to her who is yours alone" [. . . quanto erga me te obligaveris debito pensa ut quod devotis communiter debes feminis unicae tuae devotius solvas].[23] Here Heloise moved from the care of community to the requirement of Abelard's individual care for her. She criticized Abelard for "forgetfulness, when neither reverence for God nor our mutual love nor the example of the holy Fathers made you think of trying to comfort me." He might, she thought, have encouraged her either in person or by letter.[24]

What began as a seemingly conventional request for a letter of consolation has turned into an accusation against Abelard for increasing Heloise's grief. Since Abelard was the sole cause of her grief, then he is the only one who could provide consolation [*Solus sis in gratia consolandi*].[25] In a few lines, Heloise repeated three times various forms of the word "consolation": consolationis adhibenda remedia . . . solus sis in gratia consolandi . . . seu consolari valeas, ending with the assertion: "You alone have the power to make me sad, to bring me happiness or comfort" [Solus quippe es qui me contristare, qui me laetificare seu consolari valeas].

Heloise here changed her strategy. Instead of talking of the consolation she needed from Abelard, she concentrated on what he owed her. She pointed out how she had given him everything and had had no reservations. Now he had to reciprocate. Since it is the intention that matters, not the deed, she was wholly guilty and wholly innocent in her actions, for she performed them not out of lust but out of love for her Abelard.[26] This section has been noticed, and rightfully so, as an assertion of Heloise's identity in terms of the ethics of intention she shared with Abelard and with which she may have inspired his ethical thinking.[27] But this theme is only one element in a larger argument asking and insisting that Abelard make himself present again to Heloise: "I beg you to restore your presence to me in the way you can, by writing me some word of comfort" [te obsecro ut pro modo potes tuam mihi praesentiam reddas, consolationem videlicet mihi aliquam rescribendo].[28] This is the petition of the letter, the request which Abelard could not ignore. Having consoled a friend with his own story, he was now being asked to console a much greater friend through his presence by letter.

Abelard, like the rest of us, chose to read the text before him in the way that best suited him. He conceded the point that Heloise deserved the consolation he could give her. He addressed her as "dearly beloved sister in Christ"[29] and set about to define that bond. First he explained that he had not tried to console Heloise because he did not think she was in need of such comfort. So far as he had known, it was Heloise who provided others with consolation in the way she dealt with her sisters at the Paraclete. So why should she need to get "any teaching or exhortation" from Abelard when she was the teacher and exhorter: [. . . ut iam omnino superfluam doctrinam vel exhortationem nostram arbitremur]?[30] For the first of many times Abelard here linked consolation with the functions of teaching and exhortation. Abelard claimed that he had admired the way Heloise taught and exhorted the nuns at the Paraclete and insisted that his lack of attention was due to his trust in her.

If she still felt in need of his advice, however, Heloise was welcome to "write what you want" [super his quae velis scribe mihi].[31] She, after all, was his "sister once dear in the world and now dearest in Christ" [soror in saeculo quondam cara, nunc in Christo carissima]. Abelard here declared his love for Heloise but qualified it in a manner so that there would be no mistaking the nature of the bond that had developed between the two of them. As in his first letter, he was looking over his shoulder at a world that automatically suspected him of sexual motives for keeping in touch with Heloise and the Paraclete.

With these opening lines Abelard had seemingly fulfilled Heloise's request: he had shown her that he cared about her and her concerns and had conveyed his presence to her through the letter. He could go further and add some instruction, in the tradition from the church fathers he had already mentioned at the end of *Ep.* 1. What could be better than to point out the value of prayer, especially prayer for those in need, and so Abelard provided examples of the power of prayers, "especially those of women on behalf of their dear ones and of wives for their husbands."[32] Abelard thus provided Heloise with an acknowledgment of his status with her: as her beloved and as her husband. He suggested that the prayers of Heloise and her sisters could function as prayers had done in examples from the Old and New Testaments showing what the prayers of women could do, even in raising the dead.[33] These miracles took place at the request of only a few people. The presence of the many sisters will make even a greater difference, he insisted.

Having remarked on the power of community prayer, Abelard then pointed out his special need for Heloise's prayers: "Remember me specially in your prayer, I who am specially yours" [Memento itaque semper in orationibus tuis eius qui specialiter est tuus].[34] In the remainder of the letter Abelard drives home his point that the prayers of women and especially of Heloise can make a difference. Since he finds himself in danger of death, he can only turn to Heloise and ask her to pray for him.

The consolation Abelard provided in this letter is thus the same type of consolation he offered his anonymous friend: if Heloise thought she had so many problems, in missing Abelard so terribly, then she should remember her Abelard and know that he was far worse off then she. The request for prayer thus reasserted the traditional function of consolation between friends: the one consoled the other by telling how badly off he was and how much he deserved the other's sympathy. The friend, in this case, Heloise, would thus forget her own troubles. The only addition to the classical commonplace is the additional request for prayers.

As lovers time again have done through history, Heloise could only reply that what she was being given was not good enough. She started by complaining about bad form: Abelard had put her name first in his salutation, contrary to common practice. Bad grammatical practice was a point of departure for Abelard's failure to offer the consolation that Heloise needed: " . . . instead of bringing us the remedy of consolation, you increased our desolation" [. . . quibus consolationis remedium afferre debuisti, desolationem auxisti].[35] Here we find once again the opposition between consolation and desolation. The tears that Abelard had been asked to stop he had instead increased. The immediate cause of Heloise's sense of devastation was Abelard's speculation over the possibility of his death. By doing so, Abelard "had made women who already were miserable even more miserable" [miseras miserrimas facias]."[36]

Speaking here in the plural, as representative of the entire community, Heloise soon turned to specifying her own individual situation. Without Abelard, she would have nothing: "Of all wretched women I am the most wretched, and amongst the unhappy I am unhappiest."[37] So begin the complaints of Heloise. She could not understand the fact that she and Abelard had not been punished while they sinned, while after their marriage and pursuit of chaste lives, the wrath of God had been visited upon Abelard: "It was then that you alone paid the penalty in your body for a sin we had both committed."[38]

Here Heloise went beyond the commonplaces of spiritual friendship and revealed an inner life still dominated by the desire of what we would call passionate love. She described her misery and blamed herself for ruining a great man. But how could she repent what she had done and felt, for she still felt the same: "I should be groaning over the sins I have committed, but I can only sigh for what I have lost" . . . "Men call me chaste; they do not know the hypocrite I am."[39]

These passages deserve our admiration, as a rare, perhaps unique, instance of a medieval woman admitting that she could not conform to the expectations of religious life. But Heloise was doing so not because she expected Abelard to come and "rescue her" from the monastery. She pointed out herself what it was she wanted: "I beg you, be fearful for me always, instead of feeling confidence in me, so that I may always find help in your solicitude" [Time, obsecro, semper de me potius quam confidas ut tua semper sollicitudine adiuver].[40] In other words: do not assume that I am someone you can keep at a distance; I am a human being of flesh and blood who needs your care and concern.

If this reading of Heloise's complaints against Abelard is correct, then the key to her bond with him is once again the question of consolation. Heloise felt entitled to loving attention and intellectual guidance from Abelard. She turned Abelard's consolation upside down to reveal to him that she was far more wretched than he, no matter what he thought or felt about himself and her. She moreover accused Abelard of making her situation all the more wretched: instead of giving consolation, he had left her in desolation. It was not acceptable for Abelard to continue to dwell on his own misery and to ignore the misery of Heloise. "Do not take me for granted, so that you stop helping me by praying for me," she cried out: [Noli, obsecro, de me tanta praesumere, ne mihi cesses orando subvenire].[41]

In our understanding of such an appeal, it might be tempting to conclude that Heloise remained nun and abbess against her will solely because of Abelard. She could be interpreted as a sexually frustrated woman fixated on a man who (in our eyes) hardly was worth it. But Heloise was a daughter of the twelfth century, not the twentieth. She believed in the power of prayer and of salvation, and she was asking for her own "corner of heaven," whatever God might give her.[42] She was a believer in fighting battles with the flesh and in transforming carnal bonds into spiritual ones. But at the same time she was a harbinger of a new culture that insisted on the inner person with his or her intentions leading to actions. She demanded that Abelard consider that inner person and not turn her into some sort of projection of what he needed. If he was going to provide consolation, then he had to know to whom he was writing. Heloise wanted the truth and so she had to tell the truth. In doing so, she was telling the truth and asking for genuine consolation from the spiritual friend who no longer could be her passionate lover.

Abelard in *Ep.* 5 gave Heloise what she had requested. First of all, he provided her with an explanation for his salutation that had placed her name first. Secondly, he had to deal with the assertion that instead of providing consolation, he had inflicted desolation on Heloise. In the third place came her "old perpetual complaint against God concerning the manner of our entry into religious life."[43] Finally he felt called upon to answer Heloise's request that he stop praising her for what she was not. "I have decided to answer you on each point in turn, not so much in self-justification as for your own enlightenment and encouragement. . . ."[44] The Latin terms are *doctrina* and *exhortatione,* referring back to the statement at the beginning of the third letter that Abelard then had considered it superficial to provide *doctrinam vel exhortationem nostram* for the community. He had assumed Heloise was taking care of these functions for the sisters. Now he accepted that Heloise needed both, in order to get the consolation that he conceded she required and deserved from him.

We thus see a logical development: in the first letter Abelard consoled the anonymous friend. In the second Heloise accused him of failing to console her. Abelard tried to provide that consolation in the third letter. Heloise informed him in the fourth letter that his kind of consolation was worse than useless. Finally, in the fifth letter, Abelard formally took on responsibility as teacher of the nuns and consoler of Heloise.

Concerning the complaint about his previous salutation to Heloise, where he had placed her name before his, Abelard returned to the male-female world of the late antique Church and pointed to St. Jerome and his bonds with holy women. In his letter (22) to Eustochium, Jerome had called her his "mistress" [*domina mea*].[45] This reference in itself would have been enough of an answer but Abelard expanded the question by explaining what he meant by the salutation of his present letter to Heloise as "bride of Christ." He placed this term in the context of the Song of Songs and provided an explication of the image in terms of the contemplative soul and its closeness to God. What might appear to be a long digression to show Abelard's exegetical abilities is actually an attempt to relate the Song of Songs to the contemplative life.[46] Abelard already here assumed the role of teacher of doctrine for Heloise and her sisters: in defining Heloise's new identity, Abelard provided a mini-treatise on the contemplative element of monastic life.

At the end of this part of his letter, Abelard reasserted his confidence in the lives Heloise and her sisters were leading and once more turned to them for their prayers. This time, however, he asked for their prayers not because of the danger he experienced but because of the love he shared with them: " . . . I believe these prayers are offered more devoutly on my behalf because we are bound together in such great mutual love" [Quas etiam tanto devotius pro me faciendas esse credimus, quanto maiore nos invicem caritate colligati sumus].[47] Abelard had allowed himself to return to his earlier request, but rephrased it in harmony with Heloise's own insistence that he not mention his imminent death. As a good Christian, he provided a motivation for prayer based not on fear but on love.

But Abelard to some extent remained unrepentant about his prior reference to his own dangerous situation. He pointed to Heloise's own encouragement of him in *Ep.* 2 to write about his situation and cited her words that "It is always some consolation in sorrow to feel that it is shared."[48] Whatever he told Heloise in his response, then, was at her own request: "Why then do you accuse me of making you share my anxiety when I was forced to do so at your own behest?" If our friendship is true, he adds, then we must share both happiness and sadness: "There is no wider distinction between true friends and false than the fact that the former share adversity, the latter only prosperity" [Nulla maior verorum et falsorum differentia est amicorum quam quod illi adversitati, isti prosperitati, se sociant].[49]

Abelard here was drawing on Cicero's *De amicitia,* as well as the commonsense idea that a friend in need is a friend indeed.[50] But he was not just using a commonplace in the great European tradition of friendship: he was redefining his bond with Heloise in terms of the language of friendship. Until now it had been Heloise who had made use of the terms of friendship. Now Abelard turned to that same language. One could almost accuse him of emotional pressure on Heloise to accept friendship according to his own terms: " . . . anyone who takes special pleasure in the presence of a friend would rather have him happy in absence than present and unhappy, for he finds suffering intolerable if he cannot relieve it."[51] In other words, Heloise had to resign herself to the possibility of Abelard's impending death, for it might be an improvement in his situation. If she really was his friend, then she would want only what was best for him and not for her.

In these passages Abelard addressed Heloise with the same directness that she had shown him in the previous letter. Just as she had warned him about her interior state of mind, he told her that she had to take his situation into consideration: "If you see your advantage in prolonging my miseries, you are proved an enemy, not a friend" [Quod si nostras protendi miserias in commoda tua desideras, hostis potius quam amica convinceris].[52] So Abelard could conclude this section not by commiserating with Heloise but with a request bordering on an order: "I beg you, as I said before, to cease your complaints."

Thus Abelard disposed of Heloise's request that he not speak of his impending death. Now he could turn to another of Heloise's complaints, the question of his praising her. He claimed to accept her point of view but, as in the former matter, ended by defending himself. If Heloise ran away from praise, then she might be accused of seeking it. Here Abelard failed to come to grips with what Heloise had actually been saying: that she was a hypocrite and not at all the person he claimed her to be.

In answering the final question, however, Abelard to a certain extent did acknowledge the significance of what Heloise had been saying. This was her "old perpetual complaint" about how they had entered the religious life. Here Abelard had but a single answer to give: it was useless for Heloise to proceed with these regrets. If Heloise wanted to do what he wanted, as she claimed she did, then she had to stop complaining. Abelard refused to let Heloise claim that God's treatment of him had been unjust. He saw himself as rightly punished after his misuse of Heloise when he demanded lovemaking at Argenteuil.[53] In everything that had happened, Abelard saw the imprint of God's will and purposes, as well as his compassion. Abelard and Heloise could rise above their mutual consolation and provide consolation to others. Our example, he claimed, should console other people who despair of God's goodness" [et quoslibet iniquos de bonitate Domini desperantes nostro consolare exemplo].[54]

It may seem odd to make a castration into a divine blessing. Abelard's concentration on his own bodily loss is a theme that he develops to such an extent and to which he returns so frequently that I at times have trouble believing he genuinely understood what Heloise was suffering. Much of the time he seems to have been far more absorbed in his own thoughts and feelings than in hers. There is no doubt that he felt obliged to assert the traditional medieval Christian view of all sexual activity outside of marriage: "those wretched, obscene pleasures, which we blush even to name" [. . . miseras illas et obscenissimas voluptates, quas etiam nominare confundimur].[55] But in rejecting his past in a way that Heloise refused to do, Abelard asserted a lasting bond with Heloise, who had become his "inseparable companion,"[56] the term he once before had used, in referring to the women who were with Jesus.[57] As his *inseparabilis comes,* Heloise should rejoice with Abelard for the grace God gave them. She could now both bring spiritual daughters to God and turn to the example of Christ's suffering and love for us: "Think of him always, sister, as your true spouse and the spouse of all the Church" [Hunc semper, soror, verum tuum et totius Ecclesiae sponsum prae oculis habe, mente gere].[58]

Abelard's evocation of the scenes of the crucifixion and of the women at the tomb calls to mind what Aelred of Rievaulx described in his "Rule of Life for a Recluse."[59]

But Abelard was writing in the 1130s, perhaps two decades before Aelred. He personalized the bond to Jesus as that with someone who is a friend: "He is the true friend who desires yourself and nothing that is yours, the true friend who said when he was about to die for you, 'There is no greater love than this, that a man should lay down his life for his friends.'"[60]

Abelard tried to place Jesus at the center of Heloise's spiritual life because "it was he who truly loved you, not I." This observation, however true, might have provided Abelard with the perfect excuse for making his exit. But instead Abelard made clear his commitment. He would not leave her behind and for the first time really faced what she had been telling him about herself. Since Christ should have all Heloise's "devotion . . . compassion . . . remorse," then she was obliged to blush at what she once had done, "unless you would commend the wanton vileness of our former ways."[61] Here Abelard expressed a sense of responsibility for Heloise's state of mind and told her what she must do. In offering Christ to her, he was not abandoning her. Indeed, he was embracing her in the one way he could allow himself, as her spiritual lover: "Now . . . you have as a servant me whom in the past you recognized as your master, more your own now when bound to you by spiritual love than one subjected by fear" [Et nunc . . . me habes servum quem olim agnoscebas dominum, magis tibi tamen amore nunc spirituali coniunctum quam timore subiectum].[62]

Abelard was not casting Heloise aside or buying her off with pious nothings. He was expressing a bond that we can rightly call a spiritual friendship. "Listen to the prophet and take comfort," Abelard had written Heloise earlier in the same letter [Audi prophetam et confortare].[63] The comfort could be expressed at the end of the letter in a new prayer, now concentrating less on Abelard's situation and considering Heloise's development. Abelard called on God's mercy for her and asked him to come "as a redeemer, not an avenger."[64] If we have faith, Abelard assured her, we will not be tempted beyond our powers, as St. Paul had promised: "You have joined us together, Lord, and you have separated us when it pleased you and in the way it pleased you" [Coniunxisti nos, Domine, et divisisti quando placuit tibi et quo modo placuit].[65]

Everything that had happened to Abelard and Heloise could be acknowledged in terms of divine will and mercy. God in the end is "our hope, our portion, our expectation and our consolation."[66] It can be no accident that Abelard's prayer for Heloise ends with the word *consolatio.* He was once again making the theological point that our only true consolation comes from God. But he was also offering Heloise the consolation of friendship, by imparting to her true doctrine and helpful exhortation. Abelard had taken on the role of spiritual friend, leading his friend and former wife to Christ and eternal life.

Did Abelard give Heloise what she wanted and needed? Within the boundaries of the monastic life that she for whatever reason had chosen, Abelard offered genuine consolation. He was not going to do what men have done to their lovers before and since: disappear into the sunset and remain a legend and a memory. At the same time, he would not allow Heloise to dwell any longer on the pain of her loss and separation from him He would take Heloise at her word and give her sisters the advice and instruction she said they needed.

I read the enigmatic opening of the sixth letter as Heloise's indication of acceptance. She promised not to return to the cause of her grief but would control her difficult heart and in turn ask Abelard to give her other matters for reflection. This was not a question of being distracted but of finding something worthwhile and important to think about: "the more worthy should be the subject of such a thought and the more important it is where we direct our minds" [quanto quod cogitur honestius aestimatur, et quo intendimus animum magis videtur necessarium].[67]

Thus began a series of questions about the origins of the monastic life for women and its content. Heloise's queries are not my concern here. In the context of this chapter it is enough to point out that Heloise now also was asking for consolation, the consolation earlier mentioned by Abelard as coming from teaching (*doctrina*) and encouragement (*exhortatione*). In this connection I can only agree with recent researchers who have emphasized the unity of the letter collection, instead of the traditional division, as that used by J. T. Muckle and Betty Radice, between the "Personal Letters" and the "Letters of Direction."[68] All that Abelard wrote to Heloise was personal, and everything was meant as part of her instruction and monastic discipline. Heloise's close reading of the Rule of Saint Benedict enabled her to make a careful evaluation of the places in it that showed little or no awareness of communities of women and their special needs. She could add her own thoughts about inner intention and emphasize that "devotion of the heart is valued the more highly by God the less it is concerned with outward things" [Quae quidem animi devotio, tanto maior in Deo habetur, quanto in exterioribus minus est animus occupatus].[69]

Heloise partly answered some of her own questions at the end of her letter. She defended the contemplative life and exemption from manual labor so long as the life of prayer was the central concern of a community of women. She remembered Benedict's warning about avoiding idleness but added the greater authority of the New Testament, where Jesus said that Lazarus's sister Mary had the "better part" than her sister Martha (Luke 10.41). Mary sat at Christ's feet and listened to his words while Martha made the food. The contemplative life is higher, and so nuns have a worthy vocation and do not have to apologize for not engaging in manual labor.

It was up to Abelard to deal with such matters in his reply: Heloise reminded him, as she had already done in her first letter, what his role was in the Paraclete: " . . . after God you are the founder of this place, through God you are the creator of our community, with God you should be the director of our religious life."[70] As *fundator . . . plantator . . . institutor* of the religious life at the Paraclete, Abelard could now go ahead with the teaching function that Heloise asked him to carry out.[71] Personal consolation for Heloise was a point of departure for general instruction to an entire community concerning the basis for its life.

Betty Radice chose not to translate Abelard's first reply to Heloise and only provided a summary of what he wrote about the origin of nuns, arguing that Abelard's treatment of the subject "seems prolix and not very logical."[72] For anyone patient enough to work through the text, however, the contents are fascinating. They provide much more than a response to Heloise's query concerning the historical origins of women in the religious life. Abelard expanded this question into a collection of examples intended to show the religious life and spirituality of women in general, as manifested in their devotion to Jesus, the apostles, and the church fathers. One might well entitle this letter "In praise of women in the spiritual and religious life."

The origin of women in the religious life is with Jesus Christ, Abelard began. The women who surrounded him stayed with him to the bitter end. They stuck it out, while almost all the men fled: " . . . sanctarum devotio feminarum perstitit immobilis."[73] In this function they became like apostles to the apostles: " . . . has sanctas mulieres quasi apostolas super apostolos esse constitutas."[74] Later in the desert communities women were present and were not segregated from the men: "Unde nec a clericorum ordine mulierum religio disjuncta videtur."[75] The very name "deaconesses" shows the close bond such women had to the men who were named "deacons."

Here Abelard started a long discourse on the role of deaconesses in the church, but he eventually returned to his larger theme, "in praise of women," emphasizing their strength, as seen both in Old and New Testament examples. Strong women, such as in the Second Book of Machabees, provide a lesson for the monks of Abelard's own day, as in the question of eating meat: "O brothers and fellow monks, who so impudently daily against the institution of the Rule and our profession open your mouths wide for consuming meat, what will you say to the constancy of such a woman" [O fratres et commonachi, qui tam impudenter quotidie contra Regulae institutionem ac vestram professionem ad carnes inhiatis, quid ad huius mulieris constantiam dicturi estis]?[76]

Even though the contents of this letter is not organized in a manner that makes it easy to follow, Abelard did keep returning to one central point. Whatever men can do, women have done, and often better. They have shown their abilities, for example, as prophets. Prophetic gifts have not been limited to women in the church. Abelard pointed to pagan women, such as the Sibyls, and their powers, as in prophesying the birth of Christ.[77] But returning to the Christian tradition, the Samaritan woman provides an important example of the virtue and desire for salvation of women.[78] Such a poor woman was more receptive to the words of Christ than the rich and well-connected Nicodemus. As for Martha and Mary, they had the same privilege as John alone among the apostles was given, that of being called the Lord's beloved: " . . . hoc ipso privilegio quod nulli aliorum ascripsit apostolorum, feminas insignivit."[79]

Having emphasized Christ's bonds with women, and after reviewing examples of the chastity women had shown through history, Abelard turned to their bonds with doctors of the Church: "If we wish to see how much care, what great diligence and love the holy doctors by the examples of the Lord himself and the apostles have always shown to devout women, we will find that their devotion has embraced and cherished these women with the greatest zeal of love. They have instructed them and increased their religious life with frequent teaching and attentive exhortation" [Quod si perscrutari velimus quantam curam, quantam diligentiam et caritatem sancti doctores, ipsius Domini et apostolorum exemplis incitati devotis semper exhibuerint feminis, reperiemus eos summo dilectionis zelo devotionem earum amplexos fuisse et fovisse et multiplici doctrinae vel exhortationis studio earum religionem iugiter instruxisse atque auxisse].[80] I have quoted this passage in full because it summarizes Abelard's teaching on the bonds of women and men in the church. Here he repeated what he already had written at the end of his first letter. But there he was engaged in a polemic with those who were suspicious of his involvement with the sisters of the Paraclete and especially with Heloise. Now he made the same assertion about the importance of providing teaching and exhortation for women, but with much greater confidence and without special application to his own situation. What once had been part of Abelard's apparatus of self-consolation now was placed in the context of the religious and spiritual bonds manifested through the history of Christian life. Abelard here acted almost as a church historian, singling out an important theme that he insisted remained relevant for his own time.

Not surprisingly, however, Abelard could not leave himself out entirely. Reference to Origen's self-castration in order to avoid "suspicion in teaching or encouraging women" [ne ulla eum suspicio a doctrina vel exhortatione mulierum abduceret] reflected also on Abelard's situation.[81] But from here he moved on quickly to the seemingly less problematic example of Paula and Eustochium in their bond with Jerome. Abelard quoted from Jerome's letters to show how the Church Father could deny nothing to them. In fact, Jerome spent more time and effort in answering their requests than those of St. Augustine: "We know that he worked hard with composing and handing over so many works at the petition of these women that he showed far greater reverence for them than for the bishop" [Quam quidem ad petitionem praedictarum feminarum in tot et tantis voluminibus vel transferendis vel dictandis sudasse cognovimus, longe eis maiorem quam episcopo reverentiam in hoc exhibens].[82] Sometimes, in fact, Jerome's zeal in his love seems almost have gone too far, Abelard admitted, providing appropriate citations from Jerome's writings. There is no doubt that he had studied Jerome's letters carefully and saw them as a model for his own relationship with women.

Some of the fathers concerned themselves "not only with doctrine and exhortation of holy women but also in their consolation" to such a degree that "their wondrous compassion" would bring them to the very limits of church doctrine [Nec solum in doctrina vel exhortatione feminarum mira sanctorum Patrum caritas innotuit, verum etiam in earum consolatione ita vehemens nonnumquam extitit ut ad earum dolorem leniendum nonnulla fidei adversa promittere mira eorum compassio videatur].[83] As an example, Abelard pointed to the *consolatio* shown by St. Ambrose when he "dared" to write on the death of the Emperor Valentinian to his sisters that even though their brother had been only a catechumen, he would have attained salvation. "This seems to be a long way from catholic faith and gospel truth," Abelard insisted [quod longe a catholica fide atque evangelica veritate videtur dissidere]."

There were thus limits for care and concern for women, but Abelard summed up the history of instructing and exhorting women in the church through the concept of consolation. Abelard did not use the word *amicitia:* he could make use of the more common expression for spiritual bonds *familiaritatem,* as in describing the relationship between Christ and "the holy prostitute": "Legimus et Dominum ipsum tantam beatae meretrici familiaritatem exhuibuisse. . . ."[84] Abelard ended this letter with the same defense of spiritual bonds between men and women found at the end of his first letter, but the earlier sections of *Ep.* 7 provide a much richer context. These relationships were now seen as an integral part of the *history* of Christianity.

Abelard thus gave Heloise much more than she had asked for. He answered the question about the history of consecrated women by pointing out that the women who followed Jesus could be seen as the first nuns. But going far beyond Heloise's request, Abelard offered a history of religious women in the church. An integral part of the lives of these women had been their close relationships with clerical and monastic men who had rightly spent time and effort in teaching, exhorting, and thus consoling such women.

After this treatment of the importance of religious women and their spiritual bonds with men, Abelard could in *Ep.* 8 fulfill Heloise's second request by providing a rule for nuns that took into account the special needs of women. There is no need here to review what Abelard proposed. I wish solely to point out that in providing such a rule, he was patterning his work on that of earlier doctors of the church, who had provided women with teaching and exhortation. This function fulfilled his intention to provide the consolation for which Heloise had asked, not by holding her in his arms but by offering a pattern for the Paraclete's way of life.

To many of us it might seem as if Abelard was getting off cheaply. Instead of living with the wife who wanted him, he kept her at a distance. But Abelard was, in effect, doing what Heloise had asked him to do, providing a scriptural, legal, and historical basis for her foundation. He was obeying her as she earlier had obeyed him, and so their bond could take on the spiritual characteristics of every human bond where sexual passion for one reason or another cannot be expressed but where there remains a foundation of genuine love. Such a relationship, Heloise had insisted, must not deny what the former lovers could still feel, but this love could manifest itself through mutual support.

Heloise had excoriated Abelard for neglecting her and had insisted on his giving her consolation in friendship. He had done his best to concentrate on his own needs, but eventually he acknowledged what Heloise had written and responded to it. In his letters, Abelard did not even mention his physical son, but for his spiritual daughters at the Paraclete he took on paternal tasks in terms of their instruction and care. He gave them not only an elaborate and detailed rule but also the monument of his hymns, which are hardly known today and deserve more attention. These were written also at the request of Heloise, as we can see from his introduction.[85] Here Heloise seems once again to have been Abelard's muse, inspiring him to set out in new directions and to rethink and reformulate traditional elements in the monastic life. For the brilliant logician who had impressed a world of competitive men, this was by no means an unworthy task.

So far as we can tell from the religious intensity and stylistic beauty of the hymns, Abelard believed in what he was doing and here left a monument of himself indicating the depths of his own religious experience. In writing about Mary Magdalene, for example, Abelard was telling about himself: "The solemnity of this blessed sinner / greatly encourages sinners / After her, no one need despair of forgiveness / No matter what sins they come with / So long as the cries of penance reach the place of the Victim."[86]

Elsewhere in two remarkable hymns, Abelard also praised the strength of holy women.[87] Here again he was providing *doctrinam* that could be a source for *consolationem*. He was doing so at the request, or order, of Heloise. She gave Abelard in the 1130s a function and a meaning in a life that otherwise he described as a kind of martyrdom. Because of their renewed bond, now based on religious instruction and spiritual contacts, Heloise could still have her Abelard.

And so what? as my skeptical teenage son might say in his challenge to any happy ending or moment of sentiment. Yes, so what! Abelard's consolation of Heloise through teaching and exhortation does make a difference in the history of medieval religion and thus in the formation of European culture. From about 1080 and until about 1120, the reform of the church had tried to separate men from women. Clerics could no longer be married or have concubines. Double monasteries were suspected and strong abbesses were put down. This institutional development is well known and documented, but it also had an emotional side. Spiritual bonds between men and women in the church, so important in late antiquity and in the early Middle Ages, were no longer favored. The tender sentiments of a Goscelin of Saint-Bertin for his beloved Eve from about 1080 are the last manifestation of a practice going back to the church fathers and continuing in Anglo-Saxon monastic life.[88]

The exception to this development might seem to be Robert of Arbrissel, known for his contacts with women. But recent work has indicated that Robert's involvements were marginal: even though women are found in his company, there is very little evidence that he encouraged or cultivated such bonds.[89] His apparent desire to keep women at a distance is matched by the first monks of Cîteaux, who wanted to find an isolated place where they would not be called upon to care for the religious needs of women or peasants. In reality, we know that the first Cistercians soon became involved with women, but officially they kept them at a distance for as long as possible.[90] Only by the end of the twelfth century did they begin acknowledging an interdependence, which also could include spiritual bonds. I have elsewhere documented this "transformation of monastic friendships," a harbinger of the type of male-female bonds found among the mendicants.[91]

In the last decades of the eleventh century and the first decades of the twelfth, reformers, whether clerical or monastic, emphasized the separation of men from women. For Pope Gregory VII, the sin of simony, the purchase of church office, went together with that of nicolaitism, clerical marriage. Writing to William the Conqueror about the scandalous life of a bishop, Gregory complained that the man "in the very bishopric which he had so destructively obtained . . . was not ashamed to enter openly into marriage and to take a harlot rather than a wife, prostituted his soul to the debaucher of souls by his simoniacal trafficking." In marrying, this bishop had handed over "his body in shame to the devil by his lewd and foul lust."[92] One of the most avid reformers, Peter Damian, was equally worried about the bonds of the flesh, and in his few letters to women he is full of disgust and warnings against the functions of the body: "Call to mind that the flesh that now is nourished by dainty food will in a little while be swarming with worms; that it will then become the meat of rodents . . . that it will emit an overwhelmingly fetid and putrefying odor proportionate to the gentle sweetness on which it was reared."[93]

Anselm of Canterbury had perhaps more contacts with women, but there is a kind of cold formality in his letters, in stark contrast to the glowing words he sent to his monastic friends. At times there is the same revulsion toward male-female sexuality that we find in Peter Damian, as when Anselm wrote to an Anglo-Saxon princess, Gunhilda, warning her to return to her monastery and describing graphically what her former lover's body now had become: "Go now, sister, lie down with him on the bed in which he now lies; gather his worms to your bosom; embrace his corpse; press your lips to his naked teeth, for his lips have already been consumed by putrefaction."[94]

In the world of church reform, male clerics emphasized separation from women, not union with them. However, by no means do I want to claim that close spiritual bonds between men and women in the church disappeared completely because of the reform movement and its desire to put women at a distance from clerical or monastic men. But there is a dearth of literature of male-female friendship between about 1080 and 1120. Only at the end of this period do we find the phenomenon of Christina of Markyate, who insisted on finding a way of life outside of marriage and had to turn to clerical men for their protection and friendship.[95] The care she received was often reluctant, and only in the end did she win the affections of a churchman who could make a difference for her, the abbot of Saint-Albans.

Christina's story might be seen as an isolated incident that has little bearing on the general development of male-female relationships in the new reformed church. Or it might be considered the tip of an iceberg, a manifestation of a male-female bonds always present in the church. But if we look at Christina's life in the 1120s in terms of what Heloise was asking Abelard for in the 1130s, we can conclude that it was not a matter of course for clerical men to go out of their way to help women who sought a religious or spiritual way of life. Women were automatically under suspicion, and clerical men were taught to be wary of their own sexual drives and of attaching themselves to women.

With good reason, one might add, in thinking of what Abelard did to Heloise. But this is precisely my point: Heloise showed the way to a reconciliation of sexuality with Christian love. She insisted that a physical relationship could grow into a spiritual one. Thus she refused to let Abelard go. She demanded his concern and consolation. In so doing, she could have cared less about the reservations and purposes of churchmen. And she succeeded, winning the attention and support of Abelard and the admiration of so central a church figure as the abbot of Cluny, Peter the Venerable.[96]

Heloise gave male-female friendship a voice, a legitimacy, a vocabulary. She inspired Abelard to revive the classical and patristic description and celebration of such friendships. Southern once pointed out how Abelard's pragmatic description of his exploitation of Heloise shows how the first decades of the twelfth century were "untouched by the ideals of romantic love which emerged in the next generation."[97] The same can be said about a Christian language applying to marriage as a desirable and worthy state. That, too, would come later. But there was already at the time a rich language of male-female spiritual friendship. It was available, especially in the letters of Jerome to his female friends. But it had to be rediscovered and reformulated.

Abelard went ahead and did so, apparently because Heloise insisted. This was the consolation she asked for, the expression of the bonds between them in terms of a spiritual love. Thanks to Abelard's response and her obedience to his advice, Heloise was able to continue as abbess and consoler of her nuns. By provoking Abelard to give what he had within him, Heloise thus did more than renew her own vocation. She provided a new beginning for spiritual friendships between men and women in the religious life. These friendships were based not on sentimental feeling alone but could involve the affectivity that grows through intellectual contact and advice.

Heloise got what she asked for. In Abelard's consolation, she secured a lasting bond of friendship.

Notes

1. Brian Patrick McGuire, *Friendship and Community: The Monastic Experience 350–1250.* See also *Friendship in Medieval Europe,* ed. Julian Haseldine.
2. For a full treatment of the concept of *consolatio* as a literary phenomenon, see Peter von Moos, *Consolatio: Studien zur mittelalterlichen Trostliteratur.* For *consolatio* in terms of Abelard and Heloise's use of Jerome's letters, see Alcuin Blamires, chapter 12 in this volume.
3. Glenda McLeod provides a helpful treatment of the debate until the early 1990s in her excellent article, "'Wholly Guilty, Wholly Innocent': Self-Definition in Héloïse's Letters to Abélard," pp. 64–86, especially n. 2, pp. 82–83.
4. Étienne Gilson's *Héloïse et Abélard* was originally published in Paris in 1938. I used the 1963 second printing Ann Arbor Paperback, *Heloise and Abelard.*
5. Gilson, *Héloïse and Abelard,* p. xiii. It should be added, however, that Gilson added a careful appendix on the authenticity of the Letters, where he reviewed the arguments.

6. R.W. Southern, "The Letters of Abelard and Heloise," pp. 86–104 (edn: Oxford: 1970).
7. John F. Benton, ed. *Self and Society in Medieval France: The Memoirs of Abbot Guibert of Nogent.* Benton's approach and translation are challenged in a new introduction and translation by Paul J. Archambault, *A Monk's Confession: The Memoirs of Guibert of Nogent.*
8. Benton's incomplete paper is entitled "A Reconsideration of the Authenticity of the Correspondence of Abelard and Heloise," in Trier 1980, pp. 41–52. This article as well as Benton's other studies on the correspondence is included in the convenient collection of Benton's most significant work, edited by Thomas N. Bisson, *Culture, Power and Personality in Medieval France.*
9. As in Barbara Newman's otherwise superb *From Virile Woman to WomanChrist: Studies in Medieval Religion and Literature,* "Authority, Authenticity and the Repression of Heloise," pp. 46–75, as p. 49 where she refers to Benton indirectly: "One may perhaps be pardoned for asking if this preoccupation with putting women in their place, establishing male control, and giving a man the final say is exclusively Abelard's."
10. *Women Writers,* pp. 107–43, especially pp. 140–43, "Excursus: Did Abelard Write Heloise's Letters?"; M. T. Clanchy, *Abelard: A Medieval Life,* especially pp. 327–29. See also John Marenbon's chapter 2 herein.
11. For background, see McGuire, *Friendship and Community;* C. Stephen Jaeger, *The Origins of Courtliness: Civilizing Trends and the Formation of Courtly Ideals, 939–1210,* and *The Envy of Angels: Cathedral Schools and Social Ideals in Medieval Europe, 950–1200,* has a different evaluation of the origins of friendship, placing it in court culture. In *Ennobling Love: In Search of a Lost Sensibility,* Jaeger expands on this thesis, which I do not think necessarily excludes my view that the celebration of friendship in monastic life is a central theme of medieval culture.
12. In what follows, when the page number from Radice is not given, this indicates the translation is my own.
13. For the *epistola consolatoria,* see R.W. Southern, *Medieval Humanism,* pp. 89–90. For the Roman origins of the *consolatio* genre, see *The Oxford Classical Dictionary,* p. 226.
14. See chapter 12 in this volume.
15. *HC,* ed. Muckle 206 (Radice 98).
16. *HC,* ed. Muckle 207.
17. *HC,* ed. Muckle 207 (Radice 99).
18. Radice 101.
19. R.W. Southern, *Western Society and the Church in the Middle Ages,* pp. 310–12.
20. *Ep.* 2, ed. Muckle 68–69 (Radice 110).
21. *Ep.* 2, ed. Muckle 69 (Radice 110–11).
22. *Ep.* 2, ed. Muckle 69.
23. *Ep.* 2, ed. Muckle 70 (Radice 112).
24. [Vel sermone praesentem, vel epistola absentem consolari tentaveris]: *Ep.* 2, ed. Muckle 70 (Radice 112).
25. *Ep.* 2, ed. Muckle 70.
26. *Ep.* 2, ed. Muckle 72 (Radice 115).
27. See Glenda McLeod, "Wholly Guilty, Wholly Innocent."
28. *Ep.* 2, ed. Muckle 73 (Radice 117).
29. *Ep.* 3, ed. Muckle 73 (Radice 119).
30. *Ep.* 3 ed. Muckle 73.
31. *Ep.* 3, ed. Muckle 73 (Radice 119).
32. *Ep.* 3, ed. Muckle 74 (Radice 120).
33. *Ep.* 3, ed. Muckle 75 (Radice 122–23).
34. *Ep.* 3, ed. Muckle 75.
35. *Ep.* 4, ed. Muckle 77.
36. *Ep.* 4, ed. Muckle 77.

37. *Ep.* 4, ed. Muckle 78 (Radice 129).
38. *Ep.* 4, ed. Muckle 79 (Radice 130).
39. *Ep.* 4, ed. Muckle 81 (Radice 133).
40. *Ep.* 4, ed. Muckle 82 (Radice 135).
41. *Ep.* 4, ed. Muckle 81.
42. *Ep.* 4, ed. Muckle 82 (Radice 135).
43. *Ep.* 5, ed. Muckle 83 (Radice 137).
44. Radice 137.
45. *Ep.* 5, ed. Muckle 83.
46. Ann W. Astell, *The Song of Songs in the Middle Ages* and E. Ann Matter, *The Voice of My Beloved: The Song of Songs in Western Medieval Christianity.*
47. *Ep.* 5, ed. Muckle 86 (Radice 142).
48. *Ep.* 2, ed. Muckle 68. *Ep.* 5, ed. Muckle 86 (Radice 110, 142).
49. *Ep.* 5, ed. Muckle 86 (Radice 142–43).
50. As in *De amicitia* 17.64, where Cicero quoted Ennius: "Amicus certus in re incerta cernitur."
51. *Ep.* 5, ed. Muckle 86 (Radice 143).
52. *Ep.* 5, ed. Muckle 86–87 (Radice 143).
53. *Ep.* 5, ed. Muckle 88 (Radice 146).
54. *Ep.* 5, ed. Muckle 89 (Radice 147).
55. *Ep.* 5, ed. Muckle 89 (Radice 147).
56. *Ep.* 5, ed. Muckle 90 (Radice 149).
57. *HC,* ed. Muckle 207.
58. *Ep.* 5, ed. Muckle 91 (Radice 151).
59. Aelred of Rievaulx, *Treatises and The Pastoral Prayer,* trans. Mary Paul Macpherson, especially "A Threefold Meditation," pp. 90–92.
60. Jn 15.13. *Ep.* 5, ed. Muckle 92 (Radice 152).
61. *Ep.* 5, ed. Muckle 92 (Radice 153).
62. *Ep.* 5, ed. Muckle 93 (Radice 154).
63. *Ep.* 5, ed. Muckle 91.
64. Radice 155.
65. *Ep.* 5, ed. Muckle 94.
66. *Ep.* 5, ed. Muckle 94 (Radice 156).
67. *Ep.* 6, ed. Muckle 242 (Radice 159).
68. See especially Dronke on Heloise in *Women Writers,* particularly his conclusion, pp. 138–39.
69. *Ep.* 6, ed. Muckle 251 (Radice 175).
70. Radice 178; cf. 111.
71. *Ep.* 6, ed. Muckle 253.
72. Radice 180.
73. *Ep.* 7, ed. Muckle 257.
74. *Ep.* 7, ed. Muckle 258.
75. *Ep.* 7, ed. Muckle 262.
76. *Ep.* 7, ed. Muckle 269.
77. *Ep.* 7, ed. Muckle 272.
78. Jn 4.31–32; *Ep.* 7, ed. Muckle 273.
79. *Ep.* 7, ed. Muckle 274.
80. *Ep.* 7, ed. Muckle 278–79.
81. *Ep.* 7, ed. Muckle 279.
82. *Ep.* 7, ed. Muckle 279.
83. *Ep.* 7, ed. Muckle 280.
84. Lk 7.39; *Ep.* 7, ed. Muckle 280.

85. "Praefatio," in *Hymn Collections from the Paraclete II. Edition of Texts,* ed. Chrysogonus Waddell, Cistercian Liturgy Series 9 (Gethsemani Abbey; Trappist, Kentucky, 1987), p. 5.
86. *Hymn Collections II,* p. 134: "Peccatricis beate sollemnitas / peccatores maxime letificat / post hanc nemo desperet de uenia, / quantumcumque precedant flagitia, / si lamenta penitentie / subsquentur loco victime."
87. *Hymn Collections II,* pp. 128–29. In the first of these, for example, Abelard makes the same point that he did in *Ep.* 7, concerning the strength and constancy of women in religion as compared to men: "Si cum viris feminas contendere / de virtute liceat constantie, / quis uirorum mentis fortitudine / adequari possit . . ."
88. For Goscelin and Eve, see McGuire, *Friendship and Community,* pp. 201–204.
89. Jacqueline Smith, "Robert of Arbrissel: *Procurator Mulierum,*" pp. 175–84.
90. Brigitte Degler-Spengler, "The Incorporation of Cistercian Nuns into the Order in the Twelfth and Thirteenth Century," pp. 85–134.
91. McGuire, "The Cistercians and Friendship: An Opening to Women," in *Hidden Springs,* pp. 171–200, an abbreviated and revised version of "The Cistercians and the Transformation of Monastic Friendships," *Analecta Cisterciensia* 37 (1981): 1–63.
92. The *Epistolae Vagantes* of Pope Gregory VII, ed. and trans. H. E. J. Cowdrey, Oxford Medieval Texts (Oxford: Clarendon Press, 1972), Letter 16, p. 45.
93. This is from Letter 66 from 1059–60, to the former Countess Blanche, warning her not to leave her monastery in Milan, trans. Owen J. Blum, *Peter Damian. Letters 61–90,* The Fathers of the Church. Mediaeval Continuation (Washington DC: The Catholic University of America Press, 1992), p. 59.
94. *The Letters of Saint Anselm of Canterbury* 2, trans. Walter Fröhlich (Kalamazoo; Cistercian Publications, 1993), Letter 169, p. 70.
95. *The Life of Christina of Markyate,* ed. C. H. Talbot, Oxford Medieval Texts (Oxford: Clarendon Press, 1959 and 1987).
96. Radice 277–78.
97. R. W. Southern, *Medieval Humanism,* p. 91.

CHAPTER 14

QUAE MATERNAE IMMEMOR NATURAE: THE RHETORICAL STRUGGLE OVER THE MEANING OF MOTHERHOOD IN THE WRITINGS OF HELOISE AND ABELARD

Juanita Feros Ruys

Heloise and Abelard contend over the meaning and practice of motherhood using biblical quotations and allusions. Heloise's persistently personalizing rhetorical practices, which focus on the experience of mothering, compel Abelard to a reconsideration of his position and an examination of his own fatherhood.

It has long been thought that the issue of Heloise's motherhood in general and her mothering of her son, Astrolabe, in particular were not issues of great importance to Heloise and Abelard. Scholars point to Abelard's mention of Astrolabe in his *Historia calamitatum,* his later verses of advice to his son, and Heloise's entreaty to Peter the Venerable regarding Astrolabe's future as representing the sum total of their interest in the subject.[1] Nothing could be further from the truth. As I intend to show, the issue of Heloise's status and practice as mother was a topic of great contention between Heloise and Abelard throughout their monastic careers.

This chapter examines the competing rhetorical positions vis-à-vis motherhood adopted by both Heloise and Abelard. It notes that Heloise insistently personalizes the figure of the mother and grounds it in her own experience of mothering, most consistently representing herself as the biological mother of a living child. Conversely, Abelard attempts to abstract and Christianize the figure of the mother, representing Heloise only as spiritual mother to her monastic family.

This proposition acknowledges these postures as primarily rhetorical positions. Indeed, the chapter as a whole recognizes the distinction between the biological fact of maternity and the more problematic cultural construction of motherhood, which varies according to time and place.[2] Heloise was undeniably a mother. Here I explore her ideological construction of that motherhood and her insistence on her own reading of it in the face of the competing models so forcefully presented by Abelard. In addition, this study is based on a reading of the correspondence between Heloise and Abelard as rhetorically contestatory. This view has been increasingly recognized over the past decade by several scholars such as Linda Kauffman, Claire Nouvet, Barbara Newman, myself, Glenda McLeod, Catherine Brown, and Bonnie Wheeler.[3] These studies have revealed a correspondence founded on complex strategies of persuasion and negotiation, with the "selves" deployed by Heloise and Abelard best understood as shifting, game-playing, and multiple. Because of the disputatious nature of the correspondence, the texts that comprise it must be read in chronological order. This allows the development of an idea or image, along with its negotiations, to be traced. As Martin Irvine has observed, the writings of Heloise and Abelard must be read "dialogically," because "the letters represent stages in a sequence of responses, not isolated statements."[4]

My analysis of the struggle that ensues between Heloise and Abelard over the meaning and practice of motherhood is indebted to Barbara Newman's examination of the figure of the "maternal martyr" as a woman who sacrifices her children to the will of God and/or her husband.[5] Newman identifies two paradigms of the maternal martyr as functioning within Western medieval culture. The first, and earlier, paradigm is the mother whose children are given up without her consent, usually by her husband, and who is consequently "inscribed in the narrative as a figure of grief or protest." The second, and later, paradigm is the mother "whose holiness is enhanced by her willingness to abandon her children or, in extreme cases, consent to their deaths as the Virgin did to Christ's."[6] Heloise and Abelard contend across precisely this divide. Heloise represents herself as the grieving, unwilling, maternal martyr, while Abelard strives to write her as the willing, spiritual, maternal martyr. That Heloise and Abelard are writing at the chronological point that Newman identifies as the transitional period between the two paradigms adds to the significance of Heloise's rhetorical struggle and victory.[7] It is also striking to recognize just how many of the standard medieval antimaternal and antifamilial motifs identified by Newman—such as the figures of the daughter of Jephthah and the mother of the Maccabees, Christ's injunction to would-be followers to hate their families, and the letters of Jerome to his female disciples—appear in Abelard's writings to Heloise.[8] Indeed, all four of these appear in Abelard's *Ep.* 7 to Heloise alone.

While Astrolabe does not appear by name in their writings, with the three exceptions mentioned at the outset, I would argue that he remains at the heart of the discussions of motherhood that ensue between Heloise and Abelard. Their writings on motherhood are replete with images, largely biblical allusions, of children and particularly of only sons as well as of the sacrificing mothers and rashly vowing fathers through whom such children are either destroyed or dedicated to God. The rhetorical struggle over the meaning of motherhood erupts most forcefully in Abelard's *Ep.* 5 and it is negotiated consecutively through *Ep.* 6, 7, and 8 and Problems 31 to 35 and 42 of the *Problemata Heloissae.* Heloise's rhetoric of a personalized, biological motherhood wins over Abelard and eventually leads him to adopt a similar pose with regard to his own fatherhood. This results in his composition of the strikingly beautiful *Planctus* 2 and 3. *Planctus* 2 (The Lament of Jacob over his Sons) can be read as a moving statement of paternal love by Abelard and an admission of Heloise's status as *mater dolorosa. Planctus* 3 (The Lament of the Maids of Israel over the Daughter of Jephthah the Gileadite) represents, I believe, Abelard's recognition of his action in depriving Heloise of the ability to mother her son and his apology for this. In arguing this point, I hope to suggest that these positions of personalized parenthood may begin to represent to us the feelings of Heloise and Abelard with regard to their own son, Astrolabe.

Certainly historians and literary critics to date have overlooked, diminished, or dealt harshly with Heloise's ability to mother her son.[9] For example, Clarissa W. Atkinson, in her study of medieval Christian motherhood, dismisses Heloise's maternal feelings with the observation that "Neither of them [Heloise and Abelard] was interested in motherhood as a concept or a reality," and adds: "As parents, Heloise and Abelard did not ask very much of themselves. They found a home for their infant son, and when he was old enough, his mother helped him find a job."[10] Even those most devoted to Heloise's cause have been hard-pressed to justify her apparent lack of maternal devotion. Her first English-language biographer, Enid McLeod, could offer in Heloise's defense only that her introduction to motherhood may have been "somewhat overwhelming for a young and studious girl whose life from babyhood had been spent in surroundings of cloistered calm."[11] This position in which motherly love and scholarly ability are incompatible is also present in the writings of Hubert Silvestre, who recognized Heloise's mothering of her son, but then denied her the authorship of her letters.[12] What is even more telling is that this ideological divide first appeared in the writings of Abelard himself.[13]

When McLeod opined that "if women can be divided into two types, the maternal and the conjugal, Héloïse was unquestionably always much more a lover and a wife than a mother,"[14] she was revoicing the suspicions of Heloise's earlier French biographer, Charlotte Charrier.[15] Indeed, Charrier found the lack of maternal sentiment in Heloise's writings so disturbing that to her it provided compelling evidence against the authenticity of the letters attributed to her.[16]

The Discourse of Motherhood: *Epistle 5*

Abelard's *Ep.* 5 is a pastiche of antimaternal motifs and constitutes a deliberate and comprehensive attempt on his part to write Heloise as willing maternal martyr and spiritual mother. From *Ep.* 5 throughout the remainder of their correspondence, Abelard consistently designates Heloise as his monastic sister [*soror*] but as the mother [*mater*] of her nuns. This strategy of nominalization marks the commencement of his rhetorical struggle with Heloise over the meaning of her status as mother, and it is a strategy fiercely contested by Heloise as, with equal persistence in the ensuing letters, she refers to herself as Abelard's daughter and as the sister of her nuns.[17] However, the most striking and unambiguous statement of intent made by Abelard in *Ep.* 5 is his panegyric to Heloise's spiritual motherhood: "Tuae vero prudentiae talentum quantas quotidie Domino refert usuras, quae multas Domino iam spirituales filias peperisti, me penitus sterili permanente. . . . O quam detestabile damnum! Quam lamentabile incommodum, si carnalium voluptatum sordibus vacans paucos cum dolore pareres mundo, quae nunc multiplicem prolem cum exsultatione parturis coelo! Nec esses plus quam femina nunc etiam viros transcendis et quae maledictionem Evae in benedictionem vertisti Mariae" [How great an interest the talent of your own wisdom pays daily to the Lord in the many spiritual daughters you have borne for him, while I remain totally barren. . . . What a hateful loss and grievous misfortune if you had abandoned yourself to the defilement of carnal pleasures only to bear in suffering a few children for the world, when now you are delivered in exultation of numerous progeny for heaven! Nor would you have been more than a woman, whereas now you rise even above men, and have turned the curse of Eve into the blessing of Mary].[18] This passage has perplexed scholars by Abelard's apparent insensitivity toward Heloise in praising her spiritual motherhood while failing to mention her biological motherhood. Atkinson states: "Astralabe's father seems to have forgotten that Heloise ever did bear a child; their living son was subsumed in the abstract representation of the curse of Eve."[19] Far from overlooking Astrolabe, however, Abelard's polemical exhortation refers directly to him. This passage constitutes a quite deliberate attempt on Abelard's part to efface Heloise's natural biological motherhood and refigure it as spiritual motherhood.

The paragraphs that follow this exposition are replete with filial imagery, the purpose of which is twofold. First, it confirms Heloise in her separation from her son by arguing that it is the just will of God. Indeed, as Abelard points out, in theological terms, the apparently harsh treatment of a child by a parent can be beneficial: "Ne te id igitur, soror, obsecro, moveat, nec patri paterne nos corrigenti sis molesta, sed attende quod scriptum est: *Quos diligit Deus, hos corrigit, castigat autem omnem filium quem recipit.* Et alibi: *Qui parcit virgae, odit filium.* Poena haec momentanea est non aeterna, purgationis, non damnationis" [I beg you then, sister, do not be aggrieved, do not vex the Father who corrects us in fatherly wise; pay heed to what is written: 'Whom the Lord loves he reproves' and 'He lays the rod on every son whom he acknowledges.' And elsewhere: 'A father who spares the rod hates his son.' This punishment is momentary, not eternal, and for our purification, not damnation].[20] Second, just as Abelard in *Ep.* 5 recasts Christ as Heloise's true spouse in place of himself, so in like manner he recasts Christ as Heloise's one true son and only proper object of maternal pity in place of Astrolabe.[21] This is a typical technique of antimaternal texts, and Newman describes its function thus: "Like erotic longings, which could more safely be lavished on Christ than on an earthly spouse, maternal feelings won praise if they were displaced from one's own children onto the Child of Mary."[22] Because, like Christ, Astrolabe can be described as a firstborn son and only-begotten child, Abelard's imagery is powerful and persistent: "Hic pro te occisus est unigenitus Dei, *oblatus est quia voluit.* Super hoc uno compatiendo dole. . . . Et quod per Zachariam prophetam de animibus devotis praedictum est comple: *Plangent,* inquit, *planctum quasi super unigenitum, et dolebunt super eum ut doleri solet in morte primogeniti.* Vide, soror, quantus sit planctus his qui regem diligunt super morte primogeniti eius et unigeniti" [for you, the only begotten Son of God was killed; he was made an offering because he wished it. Grieve with compassion over him alone. . . . Fulfil what was foretold of devout souls through the prophet Zachariah: 'They shall wail for him as over an only child and shall grieve for him as for the death of a first born son.' See, sister, what great mourning there is amongst those who love their king over the death of his only and first begotten son].[23] Toward the end of this letter, Abelard multiplies and emphasizes the maternal martyr imagery. He recalls Christ's words, addressed to the women of Jerusalem: "Happy are the barren, the wombs that never bore a child, the breasts that never fed one."[24] Newman points out that this passage was used in medieval times to argue against excessive parental love for a child.[25] Abelard follows this with a depiction of the laments of the women over Christ's cross and tomb, thus invoking the figure of the Virgin Mary as maternal martyr, willing to sacrifice her son to God's will.[26]

Newman also identifies a shift "which began to win favor in the twelfth century" toward the importance of the maternal martyr's obedience to her husband rather than to God. Newman sees this obedience as founded on "the indissoluble loyalty of the wedded pair," which now "takes precedence over their fertility."[27] Abelard appeals to just such loyalty in his plea to Heloise: "Accede et tu, inseparabilis comes, in una gratiarum actione, quae et culpae particeps facta es et gratiae . . . ipse, inquam, clementer disposuit in uno duobus consulere. . . . Paululem enim antequam hoc accideret, nos indissolubili lege sacramenti nuptialis invicem astrinxerat. . . ." [Come too, my inseparable companion, and join me in thanksgiving, you who were made my partner both in guilt and in grace. . . . In his mercy, I say, he intended to provide for two people in one . . . since a short while before this happening he had bound us together by the indissoluble bond of the marriage sacrament].[28]

While Abelard's rhetoric is expansive on the "two" who are to be saved, it appears to elide the third member of this family—or does it? Abelard goes on to assert to Heloise that without the bond of marriage, "facile in discessu meo a saeculo vel suggestione parentum vel carnalium oblectatione voluptatum saeculo inhaesisses" [you might easily have clung to the world when I withdrew from it, either at the suggestion of your relatives, or in enjoyment of carnal delights].[29] Significant here is the use of the term "carnal delights" [*carnalium voluptatum*], which notably is the same phrase Abelard used to characterize the biological childbirth Heloise had escaped by means of her spiritual motherhood (discussed earlier). It is my contention that this term indicates a fear (perhaps even a jealousy) on Abelard's part that Heloise may have been tempted to stay in the world in order to raise her son. This term has often been taken to have a solely sexual signification and to indicate that Abelard was motivated in his claustration of Heloise by sexual jealousy.[30] Yet no evidence for this conclusion, nor any comparable usage in Abelard's other writings, has been adduced. Indeed, it appears to have been based largely on assumptions made about the sexuality of a castrated man. On the contrary I believe that for Abelard, the term "carnal delights" was not confined to sexual relations but encompassed all delights of the flesh in which human contact and fleshly gratification took precedence over divine service. These delights included sexuality but extended beyond to include, for example, excessive maternal love and enjoyment of a child.

Such an understanding of the term was in fact widespread in medieval antifamilial texts, as Newman's study of the maternal martyr shows. In addition, as I reveal later, Abelard's own terminology supports this reading. In *Ep.* 7 and 8 and the *Ethics,* his sentiments and language indicate that he adhered to standard medieval antifamilial ideas in which excessive maternal love was viewed as a distracting and selfish worldly vice. Thus the "carnal delights" that Abelard feared would hold Heloise in the world may not have been (or been limited to) sex and marriage but may have included the love of her child.

Throughout *Ep.* 5 Abelard adduces the figure of the maternal martyr in a range of guises in order to spiritualize Heloise's motherhood and focus it onto the figure of Christ. The persistence of Abelard's rhetoric indicates that he was aware of and seeking to resolve problems that Heloise was experiencing in reconciling her own construction of motherhood with both her own status and practice as mother and that of the monastic ideal to which she was bound.

Epistle 6

How does Heloise respond to this insistent and specific construction of her motherhood? She establishes an alternative, although still Christian, construction, using scriptural authorities to show that women are intended to live in the world and particularly within the bounds of human relationships as wives and mothers. She does this by making extensive use of Paul's First Epistle to Timothy, claiming, for example: "Idem quoque maximus continentiae praedicator de infirmitate nostra plurimum confidens, et quasi ad secundas nuptias urgens iuniores viduas: *Volo,* inquit, *iuniores nubere, filios procreare, matresfamilias esse, nullam occasionem dare adversario*" [The same great preacher of continence also shows great consideration for our weakness and appears to urge the younger widows to a second marriage, when he says 'It is my wish, therefore, that young widows shall marry again, have children and preside over a home. Then they will give no opponent occasion for slander'].[31] Here Heloise contrasts the idyll of the family home with the "occasion for slander," should it become known, of her present monastic hypocrisy, revealed to Abelard in her last letter (*Ep.* 4). Whereas, she argues, she and Abelard could have lived together in a chaste union (necessarily, given his castration) and raised their son as St. Paul and other biblical authorities decree, now she is forced to live in an unvocational claustration, denied both husband and son, daily bearing the burden of failing to measure up in her heart with her external reputation. Is this really the more holy option? she asks. There are scriptural precedents for women continuing to live in the world even when widowed. Heloise quotes: "Unde ad Timotheum Paulus: *Si quis fidelis habet viduas, subministret illis, et non gravetur Ecclesia ut his, quae vere viduae sunt, sufficiat.* Veras quippe viduas dicit quascumque Christo devotas, a quibus non solum maritus mortuus est, verum etiam mundus crucifixus est et ipsae mundo" [Thus Paul writes to Timothy: 'If any among the faithful has widows in the family, he must support them himself: the Church must be relieved of the burden, so that it may be free to support those who are widows in the full sense.' By widows in the full sense he means all women devoted to Christ, for whom not only are their husbands dead but the world is crucified and they too to the world].[32] The implication here is that Heloise does not class herself as a "widow in the full sense" whose only available refuge is the church. Such a woman would be one "devoted to Christ," which Heloise has forcefully shown throughout her previous letter that she is not, one whose husband is dead, which is not the case for Heloise, and one for whom "the world is crucified." Clearly the world cannot be crucified for Heloise when it contains her only child still living. In this passage Heloise argues against the need for her monastic enclosure and argues for the right to have remained in the world with her son at least, regardless of her husband's desire to withdraw from it. A recent analysis of the contemporary canon law by the French psycho-historian Yves Ferroul confirms the veracity of Heloise's claim, with Ferroul concluding that: "Abelard could have permitted his wife to remain a laywoman, without asking her to enter a convent."[33] Moreover, Heloise's citation of this passage is an intentional correction of Abelard's approximation of its meaning in *Ep.* 5, where he spoke of "good widows" who are "truly widowed and desolate and such as the Church should be charged to support."[34] Heloise's more accurate quotation reveals that Paul enjoined widows to be supported by the church *only* when they are lacking male family members to keep them.

Heloise ends this passage with the cutting observation that "the Lord provided his own mother with an apostle to care for her instead of her own husband."[35] By this she refutes the suggestion that Christ is the prime cause for her monastic enclosure, because (as Abelard has argued) of the reparation she owes him for her sins and in reverence of his suffering. Instead, she contends, Christ himself would have had her remain in the world within the realm of human relationships. Abelard should at least acknowledge that it was his will alone that she be sequestered in the monastic life.

Threading through these Pauline defenses of Heloise's position is a discourse, strikingly elucidated by Peggy McCracken in chapter 9 in this volume, of the menstruating monastic female body. McCracken explains this discourse as Heloise's polemical reply to Abelard's evocation in *Ep.* 5 of the figures of the spiritual mother and the "black but beautiful" bride of Christ. She argues that "Heloise's descriptions of the bleeding female body are simultaneously a response to and a refusal of Abelard's denial of embodied experience in his metaphorization of the female body. To this analysis I would simply add that Heloise's evocation of the menstruating body reminds Abelard that the adult female body, whether cloistered or not, is also, by God and nature intended, a potentially maternal body.

These passages show that Heloise determinedly refutes Abelard's spiritualized construction of her motherhood. Heloise produces a model of mothering that is situated outside the close bounds of monasticism while maintaining the approval of both God and church, and, as McCracken has noted at several points in her chapter, Heloise bases her arguments in the personal and experiential. These strategies force Abelard to confront the fact that she is, biologically as well as spiritually, a mother.

Epistle 7

Abelard's *Ep.* 7 (On the origin of nuns) is less the mild treatise on the history of nuns it purports to be and more a fiercely argued polemic on the figure of the maternal martyr and the place of widows in the church, all aimed directly against Heloise and the arguments expressed in her previous letter.

Abelard's use of biblical maternal martyrs is quite striking. He adduces Hannah who willingly gave her son Samuel into the service of God and cites cases of actual child sacrifice, such as the Old Testament story of Jephthah's daughter, in order to emphasize that even rash vows to God must be fulfilled and that doing so brings glory to both the victim and God.[36] However, he expends the greatest rhetorical energy eulogizing the mother of the Maccabees who stood by as seven of her sons were put to death rather than break the Law: "Quae maternae immemor naturae et humanae affectionis ignara nec nisi Dominum prae oculis habens quot sacris exhortationibus suis ad coronam filios praemisit tot ipsa martyriis triumphavit, proprio ad extremum martyrio consummata" [And she, forgetful of her natural maternal love and untouched by human affections, having nothing before her eyes but the Lord, sent her children with so many exhortations to their crown, and herself triumphed in so many martyrdoms, and finally ended in her own martyrdom].[37] Abelard's most persistent strategy in *Ep.* 7 is his exposition of Paul's First Epistle to Timothy regarding the place of widows in the church. Abelard is stung by Heloise's correction in *Ep.* 6 of his reference to "widows indeed" [*vere viduae*] and now expends pages analyzing the meaning of Paul's words, defining and redefining the term, and binding Heloise within his web of terminology.[38] One of the most telling moments comes toward the end of the discussion where Abelard deals with the issue of widows who have young children: "*Si quis,* inquit, *suorum et maxime domesticorum curam non habet, fidem negavit, et est infideli deterior.* In quibus quidem verbis simul et debitae providet humanitati et propositae religioni ne videlicet sub obtentu religionis parvuli deserantur inopes et carnalis compassio erga indigentes sanctum viduae perturbet propositum et retro respicere cogat, et nonnumquam etiam usque ad sacrilegia trahat et aliquid suis porrigat quod de communi defraudet" ['But if any provide not for his own, and especially for those of his own house, he hath denied the faith, and is worse than an infidel.' Now in these words he provides at the same time for the obligations of humanity and the purposes of religion, lest under cover of religion the young should be left unprovided for, and human compassion towards the needy should disturb the holy intentions of the widow and compel her to look back and not infrequently lead her to sacrilege *and to giving something to her family by which she defrauds the community*].[39] Here we see clear evidence of Abelard's adherence to an ideology in which care and concern for one's family, and especially one's children, was viewed as a detriment to holy service. This passage acts as a reminder to Heloise that as her own son is safely provided for, she is now free, and indeed obliged, to look to the spiritual care of others. Such thinking on Abelard's part is not limited to writings to Heloise. For example, in his *Ethics,* Abelard argues that a mother who has accidentally smothered her child through an excess of parental care and love is guilty of a crime and should be punished. His language reveals the strength of his feeling: "infirmitate eius ui naturae superata, opprimere cogitur quem amore summo amplectitur" [in her weakness overcome by the force of nature, she unavoidably smothers (literally: 'is compelled to crush') the one she clasps with the utmost love].[40] The use of the term *amore summo* is telling, for it indicates that in Abelard's opinion, this woman's love for her child is her "highest" or "greatest" love. It is therefore necessarily greater than her love for God and so a sin. Moreover, Abelard concludes this *exemplum* by observing that God is the judge of "all the intentions which come from an affection of the soul or from a *weakness or a pleasure of the flesh.*"[41] That love of a child and "weakness" or "pleasure of the flesh" are so readily allied in Abelard's thought substantiates the contention that his reference in *Ep.* 5 to the "carnal delights" that might have held Heloise in the world could have comprised her maternal feelings.

In this powerfully antimaternal letter, Abelard has paraded before Heloise an army of maternal martyrs for emulation, argued the definition of widows, and proclaimed that the proper place for such widows, even those who are mothers of young children, is in the church.

Epistle 8

In *Ep.* 8 (his Rule for the Paraclete), Abelard maintains his antifamilial rhetoric and continues to promote a construction of motherhood that is solely spiritual and monastic. In contrast to Heloise's critique of the limitations of female monasticism in *Ep.* 6, which she based on the discrepancies between the Benedictine Rule and the physicality of women, Abelard argues that the primary requirement for successful monastic observance is not the reasonableness of the Rule but complete obedience to it beyond any personal considerations. Several times in his opening remarks he stresses the need for monastic members to forsake human ties and submit to the will of their superiors and God, and much of this discussion is phrased in terms of the renunciation of family. For example, Abelard argues that those in the monastic profession follow naked a naked Christ: "cum propter eum non solum terrenas possessiones aut carnalis propinquitatis affectiones, verum etiam proprias postponimus voluntates" [when for his sake we put behind us not only our earthly possessions and affection for our kindred in the flesh, but also our own wishes].[42] A few sentences later he quotes and comments on that most famous of antifamilial statements, the injunction of Christ to his would-be followers that: "*Si quis venit ad me et non odit patrem suum aut matrem et uxorem et filios et fratres et sorores, adhuc autem et animam suam, non potest meus esse discipulus.* Hoc autem est odire patrem vel matrem, etc., affectiones carnalium propinquitatum nolle sequi" ['If anyone comes to me and does not hate his father and mother, wife and children, brothers and sisters, even his own life, he cannot be a disciple of mine.' Now, to hate father or mother, etc. is to refuse to yield to affection for kindred in the flesh].[43] Later in his Rule Abelard returns to a quotation Heloise had adduced in *Ep.* 6 in criticism of him, when she argued that Jesus appointed a second son to minister to his mother. Abelard quotes the identical passage but interprets it spiritually, reading it as an injunction to abbesses to stay secluded and allow their work in the world to be done by lay monks.[44] In this way he subverts Heloise's personalization of the passage, emphasizes her claustration, and reminds her that her only family now is the monastic one she rules. In these and other similar quotations, Abelard insists to Heloise that her monastic profession requires her to cease proposing a construction of Christian motherhood in which devotion to her own biological son is the paramount concern and instead dedicate herself to the service of God and her spiritual children. His tone in *Ep.* 5, 7, and 8 has remained didactic, remote, and philosophical, eschewing the more personal and experiential mode of Heloise's expression.

Problemata Heloissae, Problems 31 to 35 and 42

Abelard has insisted on a construction of motherhood in which child and mother are separated according to the will of God and for the benefit of the church. In Problems 31 to 35, Heloise accepts these limitations on the conceptualization of motherhood but continues to impress upon Abelard that maternal love and the act of mothering do not necessarily cease therefore. Heloise does this by considering the Old Testament story of Hannah, who gave up her son Samuel to the service of God and the Temple. Whereas Abelard had used this story in *Ep.* 7 to explain the practice of child oblation, Heloise now refocuses it, raising in her questions to Abelard such female-centered issues as a woman's joy in pregnancy and the practice of mothering.

For example, Heloise's Problem 31 adduces Hannah's despair at her barrenness and devout wish for a son; Problems 32 and 33 speak of Hannah's great joy in her pregnancy; Problem 34 observes that Hannah remained in the world after the dedication of Samuel and bore several other children; and Problem 35 is a deeply touching vignette of Hannah bringing little presents to her son in the Temple, by which Heloise considers the practice of mothering a son who has been separated from her by the will of God.[45]

Abelard's replies remain aloof from the obvious personal intent of such questions and maintain his ideological position on the spiritualization of motherhood. For example, on the barrenness of Hannah, he observes that "virgins of Christ . . . strive for a spiritual and far better fruit"[46]; he speaks of the song of praise uttered by Hannah on learning of her pregnancy (which must have evoked memories of Heloise's similar song of praise, as reported in his *Historia*) as simply a foretelling of Jesus' birth and as "instructive of the Virgin's faith"[47]; even the gifts brought by Hannah to her son are turned into a disquisition on monastic garb.

Abelard's discussion of the spiritual function of children in his reply to Problem 42, dealing with the theology of conception and childbirth, appears intended to reprove Heloise. Here Abelard characterizes both the construction of motherhood centered on a biological child and the mothering of that child as a selfishness that is unacceptable to God: "Tanquam ergo melius fit, concubitum quoque conjugalem Deo magis quam nobis impendi, ut ei scilicet filios generare magis quam utilitati nostrae intendamus providere" [So it is as if it might become better that conjugal copulation be expended for God rather than for ourselves, so that we should intend to beget children for God rather than to provide for our own utility.][48] In her *Problemata,* as in *Ep.* 6, Heloise attempts to personalize the issue of motherhood, grounding her discussion of the scriptures in her own experiences and raising the implications of the mothering of a biological son, even though that son may be separated from her due to divine will. This persistently personal rhetorical position does not elicit a matching response from Abelard in the *Problemata,* where he maintains an impersonal didactic stance on the spiritualization of motherhood, but it does eventually bear fruit.

Planctus 2: The Lament of Jacob Over His Sons

In his *Planctus,* the deeply personal nature of which has long been recognized,[49] Abelard at last relinquishes his remote philosophical tone and matches Heloise in speaking of parenthood with an honesty and beauty that appears to spring from personal experience. In memorable poetry he admits to Heloise both his own deep feelings of love for their son and indeed for her (*Planctus* 2) and his guilt in depriving her of the ability to mother her son (*Planctus* 3).

In *Planctus* 2 Abelard speaks through the voice of Jacob in order to express paternal love. The argument of Guiseppe Vecchi, drawn from F. Laurenzi, that Jacob actually represents Abelard's father, Berengar, mourning his own son's misfortunes, is not convincing.[50] Abelard characterizes Jacob in the *Planctus* as wretched (ll. 2 and 29) and sinful (l. 14),[51] hardly the depiction we would expect him to provide of his noble and beloved father, a man who ended his life in monastic piety. In addition, the *Planctus* extols Jacob's son Benjamin as the delight of Jacob's old age. Surely even Abelard's legendary arrogance would have balked at describing himself thus. On the contrary, I believe that the correspondences of Jacob/Abelard, Rachel/Heloise, and Benjamin/Astrolabe are compelling.[52] For example, the fact that Jacob's marriage to Rachel was the subject of a trick, or a betrayal, by Rachel's father must have held resonance for Abelard.[53]

However, in scripture and in biblical allusion, the figure of Jacob as grieving parent is substantially overshadowed by that of his wife, Rachel, who was used to typify the grieving mother as early as the scriptures themselves. A verse in Jeremiah (31.15) that refers to Rachel bewailing her lost children is repeated in Matthew 2.18, where it is used to contextualize the Slaughter of the Innocents by Herod. Abelard himself adapts the same passage in his Hymn 104 commemorating the Slaughter of the Innocents.[54] Generally, scholars have noted that Rachel is "the biblical figure who best incarnates the intercessional power of the female suppliant's tears" and "the Old Testament type of sorrowing motherhood" who "seized the imaginations of early Christian and mediaeval writers."[55] Therefore, for Abelard to write a lament, a *Planctus,* over a child in the voice of Rachel's husband, Jacob, is a powerful representation of, and insistence on, a paternal, as distinct from a maternal, grief. As such, it may stand as Abelard's polemical reminder to Heloise that her grief is not unique and that he also has been deprived of the joys of children and family life by forces beyond his control. Nevertheless, for Abelard then to write Heloise into the role of Rachel is a concession to her arguments and an admission that her rhetorical struggle has won her the right to be read as an unwilling maternal martyr, a *mater dolorosa*.

Everywhere in the *Planctus* are powerful images of fatherly love. None is more moving than the strophe in which Abelard declares: "Pueriles nenie / super cantus omnes / orbati miserie / senis erant dulces" (ll. 33–36) [Childhood lullabies / were sweet / beyond all songs / to the wretchedness of a bereaved old man].[56] This strophe contains a striking reconsideration of the arguments against marriage expounded by Heloise and reported by Abelard in his *Historia*. There the question was asked: "Quis denique sacris vel philosophicis meditationibus intentus pueriles vagitus, nutricum quae hos mitigant nenias . . . sustinere poterit" [Who can concentrate on thoughts of Scripture or philosophy and be able to endure babies crying, nurses soothing them with lullabies]?[57] Perhaps with the hindsight of the bereavement of the last fifteen years, Abelard now recognizes that the *pueriles neniae,* which he and Heloise in their younger childless state saw as potential impediments to philosophic study, in reality comprise a great delight and a privilege to be treasured.

Abelard does not insist on the exclusivity or primacy of his love but acknowledges Rachel's/Heloise's motherhood, and even confesses that a great part of his love for his child springs from his love for her. Abelard appears to compare Astrolabe most particularly with Benjamin, the youngest son of Jacob, who was, significantly, the son to whom Rachel died giving birth.[58] Abelard declares that: "post matrem et Beniamin / nunc amisi gaudia (ll. 15–16) [After Benjamin and his mother, / now I have lost all joys]. Later he says of Benjamin/Astrolabe: "blanditiis tuis miserum / relevabas patris senium (ll. 29–30) [By your charms you were in the habit of lightening the wretched old age of your father]. He adds that a great part of his joy in this son resides in the fact that he restores to him "the face of your beautiful mother" [mihi reddens . . . decore matris faciem (l. 32)]. A strikingly powerful evocation of the healing that Astrolabe's existence brings his unfortunate parents is expressed in two later strophes:

> Duorum solacia
> perditorum maxima
> gerebas in te, fili.
> Pari pulcritudine
> representans utrosque
> reddebas sic me mihi. (ll. 41–46)
>
> [The greatest consolations
> of two lost souls,
> you bear in yourself, my son.
> Representing each of them
> with equal beauty,
> in this way you are accustomed to restore me to myself].

In this *Planctus* Abelard has finally accepted both Heloise's construction of a parenthood that encompasses deep personal love for a biological (as opposed to spiritual) child and her challenge to express his feelings for that child. However, he still has not dealt with the fact that he was the agent of depriving Heloise of the ability to mother her son. That step he will undertake next in what is widely considered to be his poetic masterpiece, the *Planctus* over Jephthah's daughter.

Planctus 3: The Lament of the Maids of Israel over the Daughter of Jephthah the Gileadite

The Old Testament story of the daughter of Jephthah[59] comes from Judges 11.30–40, where the military leader Jephthah rashly vows to sacrifice whatever he may first see on his return if he is successful in battle. Unfortunately, this proves to be his daughter, described in the Bible as "his only child."[60] She does not permit him to break his vow to God and demands the right to die for him, asking only a period of two months in which she may roam the hills and lament her unmarried state, which will never now be fulfilled with husband and children. The similarity between Abelard's depiction of the noble and fearless daughter of Jephthah and Heloise has long been recognized, in terms of the willingness of both women to die to the world for the sake of a man's vow.[61] What has not been recognized, however, is the correspondence between Heloise's loss of the ability to mother Astrolabe (and indeed to bear any other children) and the lost opportunity to become a mother over which Jephthah's daughter mourns.

The figure of Jephthah's daughter is one used frequently by Abelard.[62] She appears in his *Ep.* 3, *Ep.* 7, Hymns 125 and 126, the solution to Problem 42 of the *Problemata Heloissae,* and this third *Planctus,* which are all texts written to Heloise and/or the nuns of the Paraclete.[63] Abelard's earlier preoccupation with Jephthah's daughter is with her unswerving courage and integrity in pursuing the vow of her father, and it is only in the later references that he begins to consider the significance of her potential loss of motherhood. In *Ep.* 7 he inaccurately describes the two-month period spent by Jephthah's daughter as a time granted by her father for freedom rather than as a time requested by the girl herself to mourn her childless state.[64] It is not until his solution to Problem 42 of the *Problemata Heloissae* that Abelard recognizes the childlessness of Jephthah's daughter as at all significant: "Hoc maledictum legis Jephte filia considerans, virginitatem suam deflebat, quod virgo moritura semen in Israel non esset relictura" [The daughter of Jephthah, contemplating this malediction of the Law, mourned her virginity, because she was to die a virgin leaving no seed in Israel].[65] It may be that this realization then combined with Abelard's dawning understanding of Heloise's construction of motherhood to produce the intermeshed figure of Jephthah's Daughter/Heloise whose powerful presence impels *Planctus* 3. This *Planctus* contains the following poignant portrayal of Jephthah's daughter bewailing her childlessness: "peragrans et plorans vacem planctibus, / quod sic me semine privet dominus" (ll. 77–78) [wandering and weeping I may devote myself to laments, / that thus my lord should deprive me of children]. It is interesting that Abelard should use the term *dominus.* Throughout the *Letters* Heloise and Abelard have argued over the correct attribution of this term, with Heloise persistently referring to Abelard alone as her "lord," and Abelard attempting to transfer this term solely onto God.[66] Here perhaps Abelard indulges a little in that ambiguity. While he does not back away from his assertion that it is the Lord God who has demanded Heloise's claustration and the consequent loss of her ability to mother her child, nevertheless, he does leave room for a hint that his own will and role as Heloise's "lord" may have played some part in that decision.

Jephthah's daughter is specifically referred to as an only child. Astrolabe is an only child, and the image of Christ as a firstborn and only-begotten child was employed in *Ep.* 5. Therefore, it is my contention that in *Planctus* 3, Jephthah's daughter bears a double signification, standing both for Heloise, as a woman who loses her ability to be a mother by a rash vow, and for Astrolabe, as the only-begotten child who is lost due to that vow. For example, in the strophe that compares Abraham's intended sacrifice of his son with Jephthah's offering of his daughter (ll. 38–43), the roles become fluid. The God who demands this sacrifice can be God demanding that Abraham/Abelard sacrifice Isaac/Heloise, or the positions can be filled by a God/Abelard demanding that Abraham/Heloise sacrifice Isaac/Astrolabe.

Abelard does suggest some mitigation for his own guilt. For example, as Abraham was granted the covenant of circumcision and thereafter asked to sacrifice his son, so Abelard appears to suggest that he received the divine mark of castration and was thereafter obliged to sacrifice his wife and son. Martin Irvine has detailed Abelard's interest in circumcision and its relation to his own castration and notes that in Abelard's *Dialogue,* it is the opinion of the Jew that: "Circumcision is also God's punishment in the male genitals equivalent to female pain in childbirth."[67] On the whole, however, Abelard does confess his guilt in the claustration of Heloise and abandonment of Astrolabe. This is most strikingly and unambiguously stated in the final strophe of the poem:

> O mentem amentem iudicis!
> O zelum insanum principis!
> O patrem sed hostem generis,
> unice quod nece diluis! (ll. 149–52)[68]
>
> [O senseless mind of the judge!
> O insane zeal of the general!
> O father, but enemy of your kind,
> which you destroy by the death of your only one!]

Abelard's apology becomes the more remarkable if *zelus* bears the suggestion not only of 'zeal' but also of 'jealousy.' This then would correspond with the implication first expressed in *Ep.* 5 that it was a certain amount of jealousy over their son which prompted Abelard to insist on Heloise's claustration rather than allowing her to remain in the world when he became a monk. The endearment *unica* is also significant. In chapter 3 in this volume, Mews notes that the term is much more a feature of the man's (that is, Abelard's) than the woman's letters in the *Epistolae duorum amantium,* those letters that Mews recently has reclaimed as the early "love letter" correspondence of Heloise and Abelard.[69] Abelard's reversion to a term reminiscent of his more personal and less didactic correspondence with Heloise endows it with a personal history that increases its overtones of reconciliation and confirms that in the struggle for the correct rhetorical tone in which to discuss their plight, Heloise's insistence on the personal and experiential has triumphed. As a result, this strophe stands as the closest Abelard ever comes to an apology to Heloise for the arrogation of her right to be a mother to her son.

Heloise insists on the right to base her ideological construction of motherhood on her own biological maternity of Astrolabe and the right to be read as an unwilling maternal martyr, deprived of the ability to mother Astrolabe by the actions of Abelard. She speaks of motherhood from the standpoint of personal experience and demonstrates that the status and practice of mothering continue regardless of the physical contiguity of mother and child and despite the fact that their separation may have been willed, whether by God, church, or man (that is, Abelard). It is remarkable that Heloise manages to maintain this position in the face of sustained and even quite brutal rhetoric by Abelard on the subject of the willing maternal martyr and his attempted effacement of natural biological maternity in its spiritual and monastic counterpart. What is even more remarkable, however, is that Heloise's insistence on her position triumphs, and she induces Abelard to move from his impersonal and philosophical rhetoric to a powerful expression of paternal love and an apology for her lost ability to mother Astrolabe as she would have wished. A recognition of this hitherto unexplored rhetorical struggle waged by Heloise for the right to speak of herself as the biological mother of a child not only grants a fuller representation to this medieval woman; it begins to concede a greater emotional complexity to medieval women in general.

Notes

I would like to thank John O. Ward and Constant J. Mews for reading and commenting on earlier drafts of this chapter and Bonnie Wheeler for her assistance and advice regarding the theorizing of motherhood. An earlier version of this chapter was read at the Fourth Annual Arizona Center for Medieval and Renaissance Studies Conference in February 1998. I would like to thank the organizers of that conference for granting me a travel bursary that allowed me to present my paper in person.

1. For the relevant sections see Abelard's *HC,* ed. Monfrin 74 ll. 391–99, 79 ll. 559–60 Hicks 13 ll. 348–54, 17 ll. 496–97, Muckle 163–213 (Radice 184–85). For the *Carmen* see Josepha Marie Annaïs Rubingh-Bosscher, *Peter Abelard. Carmen ad Astralabium. A Critical Edition.* For Heloise's letter to Peter the Venerable see Constable, vol. 1, Letter 167, pp. 400–401; translated by Radice, p. 285. In Latin the child's name is *Astralabius,* sometimes transliterated into English as Astralabe. However, more commonly in modern English texts the spelling is given as Astrolabe, and that is the spelling I follow here.
2. For the theorizing of motherhood with specific reference to medieval mothering, see John Carmi Parsons and Bonnie Wheeler, "Introduction: Medieval Mothering, Medieval Motherers," pp. ix-xvii, especially pp. ix-xi. On the need to approach medieval women's representations of maternity "by examining the evasions, omissions, and oblique allusions" in their texts, as I do in this chapter, see Wendy Harding, "Medieval Women's Unwritten Discourse on Motherhood: A Reading of Two Fifteenth-Century Texts," pp. 197–99.
3. Linda Kauffman, *Discourses of Desire: Gender, Genre, and Epistolary Fictions,* pp. 63–89. Claire Nouvet, "The 'Discourse of the Whore': An Economy of Sacrifice," pp. 750–73; Barbara Newman, "Authority, Authenticity, and the Repression of Heloise," in *From Virile Woman to WomanChrist: Studies in Medieval Religion and Literature,* pp. 46–75. Juanita Feros Ruys, "Role-Playing in the *Letters* of Heloise and Abelard," pp. 53–78. Glenda McLeod, "'Wholly Guilty, Wholly Innocent': Self-Definition in Héloïse's Letters to Abélard," pp. 64–86; Catherine Brown, "*Muliebriter:* Doing Gender in the Letters of Heloise," pp. 25–51. Bonnie Wheeler, "Origenary Fantasies: Abelard's Castration and Confession," pp. 107–28.
4. Martin Irvine, "Heloise and the Gendering of the Literate Subject," p. 89.
5. Barbara Newman, "'Crueel Corage': Child Sacrifice and the Maternal Martyr in Hagiography and Romance," pp. 76–107.
6. Newman, "'Crueel Corage,'" p. 77.
7. In "'Crueel Corage'" Newman speaks of the earlier paradigm as prevalent up to the thirteenth century, the later paradigm as well established in thirteenth-century texts.
8. Abelard's use of these motifs will be discussed as they occur. For Newman's analysis of them, see "'Crueel Corage,'" pp. 79–81.

9. Indeed, with the lack of interest on the subject by scholars, it has largely been left to fiction to explore the issue of Heloise's motherhood. Novels such as George Moore's *Héloïse and Abélard* (1921), Marion Meade's *Stealing Heaven: The Love Story of Heloise and Abelard* (1979), Christa Laird's *The Forgotten Son* (1990), and Sharan Newman's *The Devil's Door* (1994) offer perceptive portrayals of the relationship between Heloise and her son, from his infancy to his adulthood. For a discussion of these and other texts, see my *Genre, Gender and Authenticity: Reading Heloise in the Twentieth Century.*
10. Clarissa W. Atkinson, *The Oldest Vocation: Christian Motherhood in the Middle Ages,* p. 128. For similar views see Mary Martin McLaughlin, "Survivors and Surrogates: Children and Parents from the Ninth to the Thirteenth Centuries," pp. 101–81, and p. 144, n. 30; Shulamith Shahar, *The Fourth Estate: A History of Women in the Middle Ages* (edn: Methuen, 1983), p. 142; as well as Shahar's *Childhood in the Middle Ages,* p. 154; and John Boswell, *The Kindness of Strangers: The Abandonment of Children in Western Europe from Late Antiquity to the Renaissance,* p. 283, n. 37.
11. Enid McLeod, *Héloïse: A Biography,* p. 64.
12. Hubert Silvestre, "Héloïse et le témoignage du 'Carmen ad Astralabium,'" pp. 644 and 656.
13. *Ep.* 5, ed. Muckle 90, Hicks 82 ll. 417–19 (Radice 150): "O quam indecenter manus illae sacrae, quae nunc etiam divina revolvunt volumina, curae muliebris obscenitatibus deservirent!" [How unseemly for those holy hands which now turn the pages of sacred books to have to perform degrading services in women's concerns!].
14. McLeod, *Héloïse: A Biography,* p. 69.
15. "Nous la soupçonnons pourtant d'avoir toujours été beaucoup plus amante encore que mère." Charlotte Charrier, *Héloïse dans l'histoire et dans la légende,* pp. 134–35.
16. Charrier, *Héloïse dans l'histoire,* pp. 18, 27, 117–18.
17. For a more detailed description of this contest, see my "Role-Playing in the *Letters,*" p. 68ff.
18. *Ep.* 5, ed. Muckle 90, Hicks 82 ll. 409–17 (Radice 150).
19. Atkinson, *The Oldest Vocation,* p. 128.
20. *Ep.* 5, ed. Muckle 91, Hicks 82 ll. 423–28 (Radice 150).
21. See, for example, my "Role-Playing in the *Letters,*" pp. 65–70.
22. Newman, "'Crueel Corage,'" p. 93.
23. *Ep.* 5, ed. Muckle 91–92, Hicks 84 ll. 471–77 (Radice 152).
24. *Ep.* 5, ed. Muckle 91, Hicks 83 ll. 450–51 (Radice 151): "Beatae steriles, et ventres qui non genuerunt et ubera quae non lactaverunt"; the verse is Luke 23.28–29.
25. Newman, "'Crueel Corage,'" p. 84.
26. *Ep.*5, ed. Muckle 91, Hicks 83 ll. 456–58 (Radice 151). See Newman, "'Crueel Corage,'" pp. 77 and 82–83.
27. Newman, "'Crueel Corage,'" p. 97.
28. *Ep.* 5, ed. Muckle 90, Hicks 81–82 ll. 389–97 (Radice 149).
29. *Ep.* 5, ed. Muckle 90, Hicks 82 ll. 400–402 (Radice 149).
30. On Abelard's sexual jealousy see Radice, pp. 22–23, McLeod, "'Wholly Guilty, Wholly Innocent,'" p. 84, n. 17, and M. T. Clanchy, *Abelard: A Medieval Life,* p. 195. On the relationship between this jealousy and Abelard's castration, see Kauffman, *Discourses of Desire,* p. 81.
31. *Ep.* 6, ed. Muckle 245, Hicks 93–94 ll. 189–93 (Radice 165).
32. *Ep.* 6, ed. Muckle 252, Hicks 104–105 ll. 561–66 (Radice 177).
33. Yves Ferroul, "Abelard's Blissful Castration," pp. 129–49, at 133.
34. *Ep.* 5, ed. Muckle 83–84, Hicks 71 ll. 56–59 (Radice 138): "habitus bonarum viduarum . . . vere viduas et desolates ostendit, stipendiis Ecclesiae sustentandas."
35. *Ep.* 6, ed. Muckle 252, Hicks 105 ll. 567–69 (Radice 177): "Unde et Dominus ipse matri suae procuratorem apostolum potius quam virum eius praevidit."

36. *Ep.* 7, ed. Muckle 261, Hicks 119 ll. 434–41. *Ep.* 7, ed. Muckle 270, Hicks 132–33 ll. 883–902.
37. *Ep.* 7, ed. Muckle 269, Hicks 131 ll. 839–43 (Morton). Translations of Abelard's *Ep.* 7 are quoted with kind permission from *Heavenly Brides and Holy Mothers: Texts from Twelfth-Century Convents in England and France,* trans. and intro. Vera Morton. I would like to thank both Vera Morton for allowing me to publish two short passages from this translation, including the phrase *Quae maternae immemor naturae* [Forgetful of her natural maternal love] used in translation of the title of the paper, and Jocelyn Wogan-Browne for bringing this translation to my attention and making it available to me. For further bibliographic information on the text and translation see below n. 41. See Newman, "'Crueel Corage,'" pp. 79–80, on similar medieval usages of the mother of the Maccabees and Jephthah's daughter. For a more detailed discussion of Abelard's use of the daughter of Jephthah, see below, the section on *Planctus* 3.
38. *Ep.* 7, ed. Muckle 263–6, Hicks 122–27 ll. 539–712.
39. *Ep.* 7, ed. Muckle 266, Hicks 127 ll. 687–94 (Morton; emphasis added).
40. Latin text and translation quoted from *Peter Abelard's* Ethics, ed. and trans. by D. E. Luscombe, pp. 38–39.
41. *Peter Abelard*'s Ethics, ed. and trans. by D. E. Luscombe, pp. 40–41; emphasis added: "quarumlibet intentionum ex affectione animae uel infirmitate seu delectatione carnis prouenientium."
42. *Ep.* 8, ed. McLaughlin 243 (Radice 185).
43. *Ep.* 8, ed. McLaughlin 244 (Radice 185). See Newman, "'Crueel Corage,'" p. 81; the verse is Matt. 10.37.
44. *Ep.* 8, ed. McLaughlin 258 (Radice 209–10).
45. Damien van den Eynde and Mary Martin McLaughlin have argued that *Ep.* 2 through 9 form a coherent group with the *Problemata:* see van den Eynde, "Chronologie des écrits d'Abélard à Héloïse," pp. 340–42; and McLaughlin, "Peter Abelard and the Dignity of Women: Twelfth-Century 'Feminism' in Theory and Practice," pp. 287–334, at 330, n. 142. Accordingly, I have dealt with the *Problemata* as following the *Letters* and the *Planctus* as following the *Problemata.* See PL 178.714D-717B. All translations of the *Problemata Heloissae* are quoted from Elizabeth Mary McNamer, *The Education of Heloise: Methods, Content, and Purpose of Learning in the Twelfth-Century* [*sic*].
46. PL 178.715B (McNamer, *Education of Heloise,* p. 163): "virgines Christi . . . spiritali ac longe meliori fructui student."
47. *HC,* ed. Muckle 184, Monfrin 74 ll. 391–93, Hicks 13 ll. 348–49 (Radice 69): "Non multo autem post, puella se concepisse comperit, et cum summa exultatione mihi super hoc illico scripsit" [Soon afterwards the girl found that she was pregnant, and immediately wrote me a letter full of rejoicing]. PL 178.716B (McNamer, *Education of Heloise,* p. 164).
48. PL 178.724D (McNamer, *Education of Heloise,* p. 176).
49. The chronology of Abelard's writings is not sufficiently determined for it to be known when the *Planctus* were written with regard to the later correspondence (*Ep.* 7 to 9) and *Problemata.* Consensus puts them at best after the early correspondence (*Ep.* 1 to 4); see Giuseppe Vecchi, ed. *Pietro Abelardo: I 'Planctus': Introduzione, testo critico, trascrizioni musicali,* No. 35, p. 13; Wolfram von den Steinen, "Die Planctus Abaelards-Jephthas Tochter," pp. 122–23; and Paul Zumthor, trans. *Pierre Abélard. Lamentations. Histoire de mes malheurs. Correspondance avec Héloïse,* p. 20. Given the contiguity of the *Letters* and *Problemata,* I have listed the *Planctus* as following these two sets of texts. I think this chronology will be confirmed by my readings of *Planctus* 2 and 3, which show that they resolve rhetorical positions still contentious in these other texts. On the personal nature of the *Planctus,* see Frederic James Edward Raby who noted this reading in Charles de Rémusat's 1845 biography of Abelard in *A History of Christian-Latin Poetry From the Be-*

ginnings to the Close of the Middle Ages, p. 326. See also Vecchi, *Pietro Abelardo,* p. 14; von den Steinen, "Abaelards-Jephthas Tochter," p. 128; Peter Dronke, "Medieval Poetry—I: Abélard," p. 845 and his *Poetic Individuality in the Middle Ages: New Departures in Poetry 1000–1150* (2nd ed., 1986), pp. 116–18; and W. G. East, "*This Body of Death:* Abelard, Heloise and the Religious Life," pp. 43–59, at 52.

50. Vecchi, *Pietro Abelardo,* pp. 15–16. Dronke describes the association as "tenuous and far-fetched," in *Poetic Individuality,* p. 119, n. 1. Nevertheless, it was repeated as recently as 1992 by Zumthor, *Pierre Abélard,* p. 22.
51. All quotations from the *Planctus* are from the edition by Vecchi, *Pietro Abelardo.* (The more recent edition by Zumthor [*Pierre Abélard*] is not a critical one and does not contain line numbers).
52. Von den Steinen draws the Benjamin/Astrolabe association although he also retains the Jacob/Berengar association, "Abaelards—Jephthas Tochter," p. 128. Régine Pernoud appears otherwise unique in reading Jacob as representing the voice of Abelard: *Heloise and Abelard,* pp. 78–79.
53. Gen. 29.15–30.
54. Abelard, *Peter Abelard's* Hymnarius Paraclitensis: *An Annotated Edition with Introduction,* Vol. II: *The* Hymnarius Paraclitensis: *Text and Notes,* ed. Joseph Szövérffy, p. 216. For a translation, see Sister Jane Patricia [Freeland], *The Hymns of Abelard in English Verse,* p. 116.
55. Nancy A. Jones, "By Woman's Tears Redeemed: Female Lament in St. Augustine's *Confessions* and the Correspondence of Abelard and Heloise," pp. 15–39, at 15. W. M. Temple, "The Weeping Rachel," p. 86.
56. Translations from the *Planctus* are mine. John O. Ward and I are currently preparing a translation of and commentary on Abelard's *Planctus* and *Carmen ad Astralabium.*
57. *Ep.* 3, ed. Monfrin 76 ll. 471–75, Hicks 15 ll. 418–20, Muckle 186 (Radice 71); emphasis added.
58. Gen. 35.16–20.
59. This biblical figure's name is variously spelt "Jephthah" and "Jephtha." I have chosen the former spelling as it appears the more common in current scriptural and theological works. All quotations, however, retain the spelling used by their author.
60. Judg. 11.34.
61. See Dronke, "Medieval Poetry," pp. 842, 845; Margaret Alexiou and Peter Dronke, "The Lament of Jephtha's Daughter: Themes, Traditions, Originality," p. 858, (repr. in *Intellectuals and Poets in Medieval Europe,* ed. Peter Dronke, pp. 345–88 [Chapter 12], especially 383–84; Dronke, *Poetic Individuality,* pp. 117–18; East, "*This Body of Death,*" p. 55.
62. So noted by Mary Martin McLaughlin, "Peter Abelard and the Dignity of Women," p. 312, and East, "*This Body of Death,*" p. 55.
63. For the reference in *Ep.* 3 see: ed. Muckle 74, Hicks 55–56 ll. 58–59 (Radice 121). For a commentary on this usage, see East, "*This Body of Death,*" p. 54. For the reference in *Ep.* 7, see Muckle, 270, Hicks 132–33 ll. 883–902above n. 46; for the reference in Problem 42 see PL 178.724C.
64. *Ep.* 7, ed. Muckle 270, Hicks 132 ll. 890: "Dimissa per duos menses a patre libera."
65. PL 178.724C (McNamer, *The Education of Heloise,* p. 176).
66. Ruys, "Role-Playing in the *Letters,*" p. 61; Linda Georgianna, chapter 8 herein.
67. Martin Irvine, "Abelard and (Re)Writing the Male Body: Castration, Identity, and Remasculinization" pp. 87–106, at 100.
68. Dronke has argued that the final word should be *diluis* rather than *diluit.* See his *Poetic Individuality,* p. 119, n. 2.
69. For Mews's recuperation of this early correspondence, see *The Lost Letters of Heloise and Abelard: Perceptions of Dialogue in Twelfth-Century France.*

CHAPTER 15

PIERRE BAYLE'S REFLECTIONS ON A MUCH DISCUSSED WOMAN: THE HELOISE ARTICLE IN THE *DICTIONNAIRE HISTORIQUE ET CRITIQUE*

Deborah Fraioli

Pierre Bayle's commentary on the Abelard–Heloise correspondence has never been translated into English. The article HELOISE *merits our consideration both for its inherent interest and its relevance to the authenticity question surrounding this correspondence.*

Several kinds of difficulties arise in finding one's way to the invaluable and entertaining article on Heloise by Pierre Bayle, contained in the vast encyclopedia compiled by this seventeenth-century *érudit.* Although Bayle's *Dictionnaire historique et critique* is cited in the bibliography of Charlotte Charrier, *Héloïse dans l'histoire et dans la légende,* 1933, at no. 429, it is translated neither by Richard H. Popkin in the *Historical and Critical Dictionary: Selections* from the *Dictionnaire* nor in the earlier four-volume selections titled *An Historical and Critical Dictionary, Selected and Abridged from the Great Work of Pierre Bayle.* For readers of French, the original four folio volumes of the *Dictionnaire* are cumbersome and relatively rare, meaning that in most cases they are available only in rare book libraries. The best modern access to Bayle's article on Heloise remains the nineteenth-century, sixteen-volume edition, titled *Dictionnaire historique et critique de Pierre Bayle,* edited by Beuchot.

Bayle's *Dictionnaire* article on Heloise is an important source from an early moment for the reception of Abelard and Heloise, but the reader confronts the same question that has plagued readers of the *Historia calamitatum* and correspondence: how do we read and interpret Bayle? Pierre Bayle (1647–1706), a French rationalistic philosopher, forerunner of the *philosophes* of the Enlightenment, champion of religious toleration and tireless polemicist for freedom of conscience, was also such a skilled ironist that sometimes even the victims of his mordant mockery failed to grasp veiled satire of his writing. Beyond the problem posed by Bayle's sophisticated humor, the effort to comprehend him is further impeded by his refusal (many believe as a protection against censure) to treat all aspects of a question in the same article, forcing the reader to pursue a daunting labyrinth of cross-references. Moreover, Bayle cites numerous now-obscure authors, such as Louis Moréri, Papire Masson, François d'Amboise, and André Duchesne, each reference presenting additional interpretive challenges. It is at least clear, however, from Bayle's verbal antics and mocking comments, that his objective in this article is the humorous disparagement of Heloise.

It is unlikely that scholars will agree on the meaning of Bayle's denigration of Heloise. One could argue that Bayle simply exaggerates the most vulnerable aspects of the letters to achieve his satire and that his seventeenth-century ridicule has no bearing at all on how one should interpret the correspondence, which the majority of modern readers, but not the present translator, take to be serious and authentic, although they sometimes concede the self-deprecating humor of Abelard's *Historia calamitatum*. Yet Bayle may be using his humor to prod us to be more critical readers of the correspondence, for his mockery is generally not directed *at* the letters but instead originates from within them. He merely tweaks the texts to show their inherent humor more plainly. Bayle draws attention, for instance, to undertones in the text that cast Fulbert in the role of the stock character of the cuckolded husband, to Heloise's implausible insistence on flaunting her destroyed reputation, and to the absurdity of Abelard's obsessive concern with the loss of his book, whereby the impact of his castration and indictment for heresy are curiously diminished. Here the question we should ask is why Abelard and Heloise would ridicule themselves.

One of the most fascinating issues raised by Bayle's discussion is the challenge he mounts in dispassionate prose ("People wrote Abelard very curious letters of consolation"), to the authenticity of the so-called letter of consolation by Fulco of Deuil. As Peter Dronke reminds us, following the lead of Georg Misch, this letter parodies the consolation letter rather than offering an authentic consolation.* Since Bayle employs this pretense of a letter of consolation to confirm certain points in his article on Heloise (see note F), fundamental questions arise as to what Bayle wishes us to infer from the fictional context framing his remarks on Heloise. Elsewhere in this article, Bayle similarly invokes the authority of the *Lettres portugaises,* a text now commonly judged to be a literary fiction, further amplifying the fictional context.** Moreover, the allusion in both the Abelard–Heloise correspondence and Bayle to St. Jerome's letter 147 "To Sabinian" may signal a pedagogical model crucial for understanding the correspondence between Abelard and Heloise. According to classicist David Wiesen, this letter "reads like the plot of a romance,"*** although he nonetheless takes the circumstances of the letter to be authentic. However, I believe that the letter's dramatic excesses also make it plausible to read it as an outright fiction, as has already been argued for Jerome's letter 117 "To a Mother and Daughter Living in Gaul" and letter 106 "To Sunnia and Fretela," in which case the Abelard–Heloise correspondence would be a fiction in the Jeromian manner, whose purpose and method are to publicize the author's moral indignation through fictional letters.**** In fact, Jerome's consternation at his chance encounter with Sabinian's love correspondence might even be viewed as a blueprint for the medieval composition of the Abelard–Heloise correspondence. Jerome curses the day "on which with utter consternation I read your letters, the contents of which I am forced to remember still! What obscenities they contained! What blandishments! What exultant triumph in the prospect of the virgin's dishonour."*****

The translator of articles from Bayle's *Dictionnaire* faces a number of problems related to the format of the work itself. Even one of Bayle's short articles, such as that on Heloise, contains not only notes designated by capital letters (A through Z) but also a different set designated by lowercase letters (a through l). Distributed among notes A through Z is an additional series of seventy-eight numbered footnotes. Many of these numbered notes refer to Bayle's own sources, references to editions now difficult to procure. In the following translation, all numbered footnotes are by Bayle. Although I have standardized these notes somewhat, all seventy-eight have been maintained for the sake of completeness. Where I deemed an explanatory note necessary, I added in brackets to the appropriate numbered footnote (with my initials, D. F., where further clarification seemed warranted) in order to preserve the numbering of Bayle's footnotes. Finally, since it is Bayle's practice to summarize his Latin excerpts in French before citing the Latin, occasional redundancies occur in the English translation. In such cases, I have provided both translations. Editorial intervention has been confined to such minor changes as the capitalization and italicization of book titles and the standardization of Bayle's abbreviations. Where pertinent, footnotes include reference to Betty Radice's translation, *The Letters of Abelard and Heloise*. The complete translation of Bayle's article HELOISE follows.

Heloise, concubine and then wife of Peter Abelard, nun and then prioress of Argenteuil, finally abbess of the Paraclete, caused too much to be said about her not to merit a rather extensive article in this work. She had a maternal uncle named Fulbert (A), a canon in Paris, who loved her tenderly and diligently saw to her proper upbringing. She quickly became so able, that her talent for learning flew through the entire kingdom (B). Furthermore, she was relatively beautiful (C). There was, at that time in Paris, a famous doctor who gave public lessons of surprising fame. This was Peter Abelard, the most subtle dialectician of his century and he who first made scholastic philosophy and theology the vogue. He enjoyed all the glamour a man of his profession could wish for: he had an infinite number of disciples, was thought of as [*passait pour*] a very great master, and earned a sizable amount of money: but he never made love; he felt this to be a considerable breach in his fortune. So that his happiness would lack for nothing, he thus concluded that he would fall in love, and he chose Heloise for his mistress. We have given elsewhere[(a)] the reasons that led him to make this choice, and how he ended up in the canon's house as domestic preceptor. Old Fulbert had hoped that under a teacher like this, Heloise would advance in academics with marvelous rapidity; but it turned out that she only learned how to make love. Her docility on this score was incomparable; she was made to come so far in so short a period that her teacher soon passed from the highest favor to the lowest; and that happened without anyone's taking it into his head to ask for a promise of marriage. In this way, Abelard had the time of his life (D), which resulted in his neglecting his lessons. He confesses himself that he overstepped the mark, and that he plunged into these pleasures without regard for time or place (E), considering neither holidays nor workdays, sacred places or profane, such that he no longer thought up anything in philosophy and the whole production of his mind was reduced to composing love lyrics (F). His pupils soon went straight to the point in searching the cause of the slackening in his lessons. Malicious gossip promptly ran through the town, finally reaching the uncle's ears (G), and he found it at first unbelievable, so greatly had he counted on the wisdom [*sagesse*] of Abelard and Heloise.

However, by dint of returning to the attack, they dispelled his disbelief. The so-called preceptor left the canon's house. He had Heloise leave too when he learned of her pregnancy; and disguising her as a nun,[b] he sent her to Brittany to the home of one of his sisters, where she gave birth to a son. Fulbert threw a fit of rage at Abelard, who kept his guard up; not without hoping that they would not dare kill him or cut off one of his members, when there remained the fear of reprisals against Heloise. To put an end to his predicament once and for all, he promised the uncle to marry the woman whom he had debauched, provided that the marriage remain secret. He had all the trouble in the world obtaining Heloise's consent, who put forward a thousand reasons to fill him with disgust at [the prospect of] conjugal union (H). She had conceived such a frantic burning love, that it stifled all thoughts of honor from her soul (I); and it sowed its roots so deeply, and so demonstrated its spirit, that she was never cured of it (K). It was useless to have mutilated poor Abelard (L); it was useless for her to have taken the veil; she kept the seeds of this folly forever (M): and it is not through the *Lettres portugaises* that one awakens to the realization that it is only the job of nuns to speak about love. The letters of Heloise had long since been proof of this truth. Be that as it may, this amorous creature enlisted all her intellect and all her eloquence to dissuade Abelard from marriage, but in vain. They were married in secret; but she always swore that she was not his wife.[c] This conduct resulted in her uncle mistreating her, who, to hide the dishonor brought upon the family, had the marriage announced everywhere, despite having promised Abelard that he would say nothing. The abuse to which Heloise was subjected at canon Fulbert's made her husband resolve to take her from these lodgings, and send her to the nuns at Argenteuil, where she had been brought up. This second abduction made the woman's relatives lose all patience: they conceived an exquisite act of vengeance, and executed it by winning over Peter Abelard's servant. This villainous fellow let those who were to administer the blow into his master's room at night. They caught him while asleep, and cut off those parts which no one names.[d] This action caused a great commotion (N): the next morning people practically made a procession to Abelard's chambers. His pupils outdid everyone else with their lamentations. Women too were noteworthy in the very bitterness of their lamentations (O). People wrote him very curious letters of consolation (P). This action was severely punished by the hand of justice (Q): but none of this kept Abelard, inconsolable and overwhelmed with shame, from shutting himself up in the monastery of Saint-Denis, after having given the order that Heloise become a nun at Argenteuil. We have told elsewhere what happened to him after he became a monk, and how he was condemned to throw, himself, into the fire a book that he had written, etc. The loss of that work grieved him even more than the loss of his virility (R); and yet when one loses a book another can take its place, which never happens in the other case (S). As for Heloise, she became prioress of the nuns at Argenteuil: but since self-conduct was very poor in that convent (T), the abbot of Saint-Denis, who claimed to have jurisdiction, chased out the nuns, and this really placed Heloise in need of her husband. He had built a small chapel near Troyes, to which he gave the name of Paraclete,[e] and then he had accepted [to preside over] an abbey in Brittany. Learning that his Heloise had neither hearth nor home since she had been expelled from Argenteuil, he gave her this oratory with all its dependencies, a donation that was confirmed by Pope Innocent II. There she is then, first abbess of the Paraclete. She found such favor with everyone, that she was quickly showered with good fortune. Bishops loved her as their daughter, abbots as their sister, and the people as their mother.[f] Nevertheless, she was very dissatisfied with divine providence,[g] and moaned a lot more than Job. She kept up correspondence with Abelard (U), and asked him for a rule for her nuns, and the solution to various problems. He satisfied her in these matters. I do not find at all that the hope of seeing him raised to the prelacy was the cause of her desire not to marry him (X). When he died a monk at Cluny, she asked the abbey for his body, and when she got it, had him buried at the Paraclete, and wanted to be buried in the same tomb.[(h)] A most surprising miracle is told, which happened when the sepulcher was opened in order to place Heloise's body inside; it is that Abelard held out his arms to receive her, and kissed her firmly (Y). This despite his having been dead a good twenty years; but that should not astonish us: people claim there are other examples of similar things (Z). She died on 17 May 1163. The letters which she had written to her husband are in the edition of the works of Abelard. But what Mr. Moréri affirms is not true, that André Duchesne wrote a commentary on these letters and on Abelard's replies. He only wrote one on the letter in which Abelard tells the story of his calamity to a friend. Jean de Meun translated the letters that Abelard and Heloise had written to one another into French.[(i)] A little book[(k)] has been out for a while titled: *Histoire d'Héloïse et d'Abélard, avec la lettre passionnée qu'elle lui écrivit, traduite du latin*. This so-called translation is nothing more than a few arbitrary selections taken from the letters of that woman, given whatever form was deemed appropriate, suppressing what did not fit, and adding what seemed more appropriate.

The count of Bussy-Rabutin [Roger de Rabutin, Count of Bussy (1618–1693)] translated some of Abelard and Heloise's letters into French. This translation was inserted into volume 2 of his letters, published after his death. "I have never seen more beautiful Latin," he said,[(l)] "especially that of the nun, nor more love and intellect than she had." If he was as knowledgeable about Latin style as he was about French, he would not have commended Heloise's latinity.

(A) *She had a maternal uncle named Fulbert.*] That is all I found really certain regarding Heloise's genealogy; thus I have not said that she belonged legitimately to the ancient house of Montmorency. I definitely read it in the *Apologetical Preface* of François d'Amboise[1]: but as he gives no reference, and André Duchesne[2] makes no mention I hold that to be suspect of error; and all the more inasmuch as Heloise acknowledges in her letters, that her family had received a great honor by her marriage to Abelard, and that he had married well beneath his station.[3] Papire Masson[4] claims that Heloise was the daughter [*fille naturelle*] of a certain John, canon of Paris. André Duchesne is right not to be satisfied with that, since it is not said where that curious circumstance was drawn from; but he is not right to oppose the Calendar of the Paraclete to the annalist [Masson], where one finds these words: *VII Cal. January the canon Hubert died, uncle of the lady Heloise*[5]; for what could be easier than to reconcile Papire Masson and that calendar? Can one and the same girl not be the bastard of one canon and the niece of another? But once again, if a person says that Heloise was the daughter of a canon named John, as long as he refrains from citing anybody, he does not deserve to be believed. If we had to suspect some canon of this, it ought to be Fulbert rather than anyone else; because the tenderness that Abelard attributes to him regarding Heloise is so infrequent in uncles,[6] and resembles in its innocence the affection of the best fathers, that there would be some grounds for imagining that Fulbert acted as an infinite number of others had, who cannot be fathers according to canon law: they hide that relationship under that of uncle, and they raise their children with the label of nephew. That is what one might suspect; but that ought not to dictate style, nor prevent one from giving people the characteristics by which the public knew them. Fulbert in a book need never be anything but an uncle. Note that, according to Papire Masson, the canon who raised Heloise and had Peter Abelard castrated, was named John. That historian therefore does not claim that this girl was the niece of a canon, and natural daughter of a different canon. He claims that the canon whom all the other authors call Fulbert, and whom they consider Heloise's uncle, was the father of Heloise, and was named John.[7]

(B) *She became so able, that her talent for learning y flew through the entire kingdom.*] Let us listen to Master Abelard: "Who [Fulbert] loved her so much that he had done everything in his power to advance her education in letters [*scientiam literarum*]. In looks she did not rank lowest, while in the extent of her learning she stood supreme. A gift for letters [*literatoriae*], that is to say science [*scientiae*], is so rare in women that it added greatly to her charm and had won her renown throughout the realm."[8] In that century, a young girl could pass for a miracle with a very mediocre erudition. We must be attentive to this, if we do not want to exaggerate the ideas made about our Heloise: and yet it must be held as certain that she deserves a glorious place among *very learned* [*bien savantes*] women. She knew not only the Latin language, but also Greek and Hebrew; once again it is Abelard who attests this in a letter he wrote to the nuns of the Paraclete: "You have in your Mother a teaching authority which can suffice for you for all things, that is to say as an example of the virtues, and for the learning of letters. She is skilled not only in Latin, but also in Hebrew and Greek literature. She appears to be the only one at this time who has attained skill in those three languages, which is hailed by all in the Blessed Jerome as a remarkable ornament."[9] Mr. François d'Amboise relates that Heloise subtlety satisfied St. Bernard,[10] who asked her why they did not say in the Convent of the Paraclete, when reciting the Lord's prayer, *panem nostrum quotidianum* instead of *panem nostrum supersubstantialem.* She gave him an answer based on the original texts, and told him that one had to follow the Greek version of the gospel, which St. Matthew had written in Hebrew. I do not know if such an answer would have pleased St. Bernard; but I don't doubt that she could have disoriented him, and made him give up the fight [*quitter la partie*]: and I would willingly have this tale be true; it would teach us that a woman had really embarrassed a great author on a point of controversy, by referring to the Greek text. Therefore I confess to being quite upset, when, having consulted the letter cited by François d'Amboise,[11] I found that Heloise is not involved, and that the whole remark is Abelard's, who wrote about this to St. Bernard after he learned from Heloise what had been found objectionable in *panem supersubstantialem.* This is not said to detract from the erudition of this abbess. If anyone adopted the notion that she only became learned after being cloistered, I would send him to a letter from Peter the Venerable, abbot of Cluny, which attests that before that time she had acquired great erudition; "I had yet not quite," he said to her, "passed the bounds of youth and reached early manhood when I knew of your name and your reputation, not yet for religion but for your virtuous and praiseworthy studies. I used to hear at that time of the woman who, although still caught up in the obligations of the world, devoted all her application to knowledge of letters . . . and to the pursuit of secular learning, and that [. . .] you have surpassed all women in carrying out your purpose, and have gone further than almost every man."[12] The monk of Auxerre assures us that she knew Latin and Hebrew well, and here is what the calendar of the Paraclete says about her: "Heloise, mother and first Abbess here, in doctrine and religion most resplendent."[13]

(C) *She was relatively beautiful.*] I see a great many authors who attribute a ravishing beauty to her, but are they more worthy of belief than Abelard, who, having a greater interest in making things grow bigger [*grossir les choses*] than in making them smaller, is content to say that she was not the last of her sex in beauty, but that she was the first in erudition: "in looks she did not rank lowest, while in the extent of her learning she stood supreme" [Radice 66]. Is this the way one speaks of a perfectly beautiful girl? Does a lover, with an interest in justifying his choice and the strength of his passion, use this kind of figure of rhetoric? Some note that Heloise was eighteen when Abelard debauched her[14]: I have not found that detail in any ancient author. It is true that the term *adolescentula,* which Abelard used,[15] is very compatible with the age of eighteen. That of *juvencula,* which she uses, [16] also agrees with the same age; but nothing can be concluded from such a proof. It is an idle fancy to say that Abelard, in his *Romance of the Rose,* portrayed Heloise in the character of *Beauty.*[17] That romance came into the world only after their death.

(D) *Abelard had the time of his life.*] He has to speak for himself, in order to lose none of the impact of his own expressions: "Our desires left no stage of love-making untried, and if love could devise something new, we welcomed it. We entered on each joy the more eagerly for our previous inexperience, and were the less easily sated."[18] He compares himself to those who have suffered a long hunger, and who then find themselves a way to eat their fill. It is a man who has exercised good morals [*qui a été sage*], rather than a debauchee, who is more apt to abandon himself to excesses with his wife.

(E)[*without regard for time or place.*] Let him again speak for himself, in a letter he wrote to Heloise long after their declaration of the monastic life. He has her recall for a moment their past conduct, and how, finding no other suitable place, he caressed her in a corner of the nuns' refectory at Argenteuil, without respect for the Holy Virgin to whom that place was consecrated: "After our marriage, when you were living in the cloister with the nuns at Argenteuil and I came one day to visit you privately, you know what my uncontrollable desire did with you there, actually in a corner of the refectory, since we had nowhere else to go. I repeat, you know how shamelessly we behaved on that occasion in so hallowed a place, dedicated to the most holy Virgin . . . Need I recall our previous fornication and the wanton impurities which preceded our marriage?"[19] A little later he tells her that she knows well that neither the most solemn holidays, nor even the very day of Christ's passion, turned him away from plunging into the mire, and that when she introduced some scruple or other, he used threats and the whip to impel her to consent.[20] Now here is a man who is far removed from the superstitions of those who observe special days and feast days, new moons and sabbats.[21]

(F) *The whole production of his mind was reduced to composing love lyrics.*] It is he himself who informs us of this: "As my interest and concentration flagged, my lectures lacked all inspiration and were merely repetitive; I could do no more than repeat what had been said long ago, and when inspiration did come to me, it was for writing love songs, not the secrets of philosophy."[22] He adds that these verses were still being sung in several provinces, principally among those people who made love: "A lot of these songs, as you know, are still popular and sung in many places, particularly by those who enjoy the kind of life I led" [Radice, p. 68]. We learn more from Heloise. She says that her Abelard had two things that other philosophers did not, which enabled him to quickly win the hearts of all the women, that is, he wrote well and he sang well; he composed such pretty love lyrics, and such pleasant songs—in terms of their words as well as the music—that everyone was charmed, and talked about nothing but their author. Women were not content to be charmed by Abelard's verses and songs, they were also [charmed] by his person, and they loved him passionately: and since most of his poetry spoke only of his love for Heloise, the name of this mistress soon sailed through the provinces, and prompted jealousy of her happiness from an infinite number of women. I am considerably toning down Heloise's own wording, and I do not think it must be taken literally. Since she loved Abelard madly, she imagined that no woman could see him without falling passionately in love; and that is what made her say that there was not a single woman, wife or girl, who in Abelard's absence was not stirred by desire for him, and who in his presence was not inflamed by love; and that even queens and highborn women envied her the pleasures she enjoyed with such a man. Here is the Latin which says more than my French: "Every wife, every young girl desired you in absence and was on fire in your presence; queens and great ladies envied me my joys and my bed. You had besides, I admit, two things [Radice translates: "two special gifts"] whereby to win at once the heart of any woman—your gifts for composing verse and song, in which we know other philosophers have rarely been successful. This was for you no more than a diversion, a recreation from the labors of your philosophic work, but you left many love-songs and verses which won wide popularity for the charm of their words and tunes and kept your name continually on everyone's lips. The beauty of the airs ensured that even the unlettered did not forget you; more than anything this made women sigh for love of you. And as most of these songs told of our love, they soon made me widely known,[23] and roused the envy of many women against me."[24] Had the *Roman de la Rose* been the work of Abelard, and had he depicted his Heloise under the name of *Beauty*, she would not have kept silent about it, and this was the place to say so: thus even if we did not know that this book was composed one hundred years after Abelard, we could deduce from Heloise's silence that in the little book that I have cited several times, it was wrong to attribute this book to Abelard.[25] That author was even less justified to have Heloise utter this in his translation of her letter. But let us return to our subject. One would not believe, if one judged without the benefit of experience, that poetry, letters and songs would have the benefit of advancing a lover's affairs that much;[26] but here is one witness on the topic worth a thousand. Today eloquent bards complain that their drugs no longer have the same effect as in the time of our ancestors. Times have changed, I admit, but not entirely. See Maimbourg's *New Letters against Calvinism*.[27] Moreover, what Heloise relates concerning the weakness of members of her sex toward Abelard is confirmed by a certain prior named Fulco, whose article needs to be read.

(G) *Malicious gossip . . . finally . . . reaching the uncle's ears.*] That *finally* seems a little strange at first; but those who are knowledgeable in the ways of the world are not ignorant of the fact that those most affected by a piece of news are the last to learn it. Abelard cites a good passage on the subject from a letter by St. Jerome to Sabinian: Everyone in the neighborhood is humming about the disorderly life of our wives and children, when we still know nothing of these improprieties; but we learn of it eventually, and it is not possible for one person to remain ignorant of what everyone else knows:[28] "But what is last to be learned is somehow learned eventually, and common knowledge cannot easily be hidden from one individual."[29] Elsewhere St. Jerome confirmed his maxim through two major examples: the first is that of Sulla, and the second of Pompey. Athens was abuzz with the love affairs of Metella, Sulla's wife, before the husband learned anything about her licentiousness [*ces désordres*]. He first got wind of it through the insults of the Athenians with whom he was at war. The intrigues of Mucia, Pompey's wife, were so open, that no one imagined he could not know about them. Yet at the time that a man serving in his army spoke to him about it he knew nothing: "Metella, consort of L. Sulla (the Fortunate except in the matter of his wife) was openly unchaste. It was the common talk of Athens, as I learnt quickly in my youthful years when we soon pick up what is bad, and yet Sulla was in the dark, and first got to know the secrets of his household through the abuse of his enemies. Cn. Pompey had an impure wife Mucia, who was surrounded by eunuchs from Pontus and troops of the countrymen of Mithridates. Others thought that he knew all and submitted to it; but a comrade told him during the campaign, and the conqueror of the whole world was dismayed at the sad intelligence."[30] Emperor Claudius could be added as a third example who knew nothing of the infamies of Messalina,[31] when everyone knew that she had prostituted herself in public places, and that she had led several ladies there, and that, as the height of imprudence, she had married another man. This century has furnished us with one of these examples in the person of the *Marshal of . . .* We are assured (I still have some difficulty believing it), that he had no idea of his wife's dealings with the *Count of . . .* when the son who had resulted from this union had already been naturalized right in Parliament. People of more modest condition are not exempt from this irregularity. How many people do we see who always know all the gossip of the city, except that which is injurious to their servant? They are like the man Martial mocks so amusingly,[32] and they draw little profit from the ancient proverb: "The corrupt things and the upright things done in our house."[33] Scholars—and I am speaking of those who lock themselves up too much in their studies with their heads always full of something they are writing—sometimes find themselves in the situation occupying us at present. Versed in the subject of the domestic woes of Sulla and Pompey (now long dead) as much as one can be, they do not know that the same trick is being played on them quite close to their studies. So goes the world.

A sixteenth-century writer uses a famous example to confirm the maxim that he had propounded, that those with the greatest stake in being informed of a domestic misadventure are the last to learn of it, while they are the first to learn that gossip to which they must be totally indifferent. "It commonly happens," he says, "that those people who have the most at stake in not being unaware of them are the last to learn of their own domestic misfortunes; and that the same people are the first to learn of others' misfortunes which have nothing at all to do with them."[34] After having advanced a few reasons for this peculiarity, he reports that it was not long ago that a very powerful king had those who had dishonored his nuptial bed punished with the ultimate punishment, and that the haste with which the correction took place was such that not an hour elapsed between the accusation of the guilty parties and their deaths. This proves that the prince had certainly not heard about this disorder any sooner, word of which, nonetheless, had traveled far and wide into foreign countries: "It happened, when I was a boy, in a great and distinguished European court (so that the matter could not remain unknown for long), that in the case of the queen, the tale of her damaged chastity traveled and spread far and wide among foreign peoples before the man, whose majesty was damaged in that matter, could wash away the stain placed upon the royal name, by the blood of those by whose criminal behavior it had been violated. This could be clear proof that he was the last of all to find out, and that he punished the guilty in such a way that he did not allow even one hour to come between his learning the names of the guilty and their punishments."[35]

(H) *She put forward a thousand reasons to fill him with disgust at [the prospect of] conjugal union.*] These reasons came down to two counts of indictment [*deux chefs*]: the peril and dishonor to which marriage would expose Abelard. I know my uncle, she told him: Nothing will appease his resentment; and besides, what glory will I derive by being your wife, since I will ruin your reputation? Are there any curses that I need not fear, if I steal so great a light as you are, from the world? What wrong will I not be committing to the Church? What regrets will I not cause philosophers? What a pity and a shame it will be, if you, whom nature created for the good of all, consecrate your whole being to a woman? Think of these words from St. Paul: "Are you delivered of a wife, do not seek one." [I Cor. 7.27] And if neither the advice of that great apostle, nor the exhortations of the holy Fathers provokes your disgust with that heavy burden, consider at least what the philosophers have said: a Theophrastus, who proved by so many reasons that the wise man never marries; a Cicero, who having repudiated Terentia, replied to Hirtius who was offering him his sister in marriage, that he could not accept that offer, because he could not divide his attention between philosophy and a wife. Moreover, what harmony can there be between servants and scholars, between writing desks and cradles, between books and distaffs, quills and spindles. How can one endure, in the middle of philosophical and theological meditations, the crying of children, nursemaids' singing, and the vexations of a household? I say nothing of the continual filth and stench of small children.[36] Wealthy people can find respite from these inconveniences in their houses with many rooms; everyday expenditures and customary worries cannot upset them: but it is not the same for philosophers; and whoever wishes to accumulate wealth and entangle himself in worldly pursuits renders himself incapable of the functions of theologians and philosophers. Take a lesson from the conduct of ancient wise men, during the ascendancy of paganism as well as among the Jews; and if there were pagans and laymen who preferred celibacy to marriage, what shame would it not be to you, a cleric and canon, to prefer sensual pleasures to the divine office? If you do not bother about the authority of your clerical position, at least uphold the character and dignity of a philosopher. The conclusion of her speech was that there would be more honor for him, and more appeal for her, in the title of lover than in that of husband: that she wanted to remain attached to him, not by the necessity of conjugal bonds, but by her tenderness of heart alone; and that their pleasures would be infinitely heightened, if they only saw each other from time to time. We will talk about the latter reason in remark (U). In the meantime, here are Pasquier's thoughts about Heloise's speech: "I will not produce for you," he said, "all the reasons with which she sought to win him over, but I will tell you that I have never read an orator with so many well-turned phrases and persuasive maxims to accomplish her ends, as those she brought to bear."[37] I am warning my reader that I significantly abridged the girl's remonstrance, and that I was surprised that she did not draw argument from her lover's being in the orders.[38] Does that not seem to prove that people did not yet believe the law of celibacy to be obligatory for ecclesiastics?

(I) *Her love . . . stifled all thoughts of honor from her soul.*] It very often happens that amorous passion suppresses or overcomes feelings of conscience; but it very seldom happens that it destroys sensitivity to [one's] honor. And except for a small number of people of low birth, who most of the time have not even had an ordinary education, all the girls who succumb place one or another of these four strings in their bow: they hope either to avoid conceiving, to expel their fruit by some drug, to give birth without the world knowing, or to get the suitor to marry them. This shows that if love is sometimes the tyrant holding the greatest sway over them, it is a tyrant that leaves honor in possession of its privileges. See the well-known sonnet called the *Abortion,* where the compulsion of honor is so well depicted, and the power of love, by turns, conquered or victorious. Our Heloise loved so passionately that she no longer cared either for honor or reputation. For, in the first place she was elated to find herself pregnant,[39] and in the second place, she did everything she could not to be married to the one who had created the child; two things, which are not only rarer than the most hideous monsters when they are joined together, but even the first alone is never seen, except in cases in which love has little to do with it, and where the aim is to turn something to good account that could not come about if the uproar of a pregnancy was not involved. How many girls are there who would rather be given a husband not to their liking by a parliamentary decree than remain stigmatized? They strongly believe that it will avenge them with interest, and that the decree will prove costly to them, but no matter, provided that the title of spouse mend the rift affecting their honor. Our Heloise was lacking in that kind of fastidiousness. See the following remark and especially remark (U).

(K) . . . *that she was never cured of it.*] Is it being cured, when one says several years after one has renounced the world by embracing the monastic life, *that one would rather be Peter Abelard's whore, than the legitimate wife of the emperor of the whole world?* Now that is what our Heloise said when she was abbess of the Paraclete; it is regarding this that she wanted to take God as her witness: "God is my witness that if Augustus, Emperor of the whole world, thought fit to honour me with marriage and conferred all the earth on me to possess forever, it would be dearer and more honourable to me to be CALLED not his Empress but YOUR WHORE."[40] How can one say her passion disappeared at the abbey of the Paraclete, since it was there that she wrote a frank confession of the wretched state of her soul, which shows that the flame of love was gnawing her to the bone? I would not dare to say in French everything of which she accuses herself. She confesses that the pleasures she tasted in Abelard's arms had seemed so sweet to her, that she dreamed of them night and day, awake as asleep, and even during the celebration of Mass. She would mourn their loss forever, and for lack of something better, she recited them in her mind over and over again. Those who understand Latin will see the high degree of eloquence with which she knew how to express what she felt: "In my case, the pleasures of lovers which we shared have been too sweet—they can never displease me, and can scarcely be banished from my thoughts. Wherever I turn they are always there before my eyes, bringing with them awakened longings and fantasies which will not even let me sleep. Even during the celebration of the Mass, when our prayers should be purer, lewd visions of those pleasures take such a hold upon my unhappy soul that my thoughts are on their wantonness instead of on prayers. I should be groaning over the sins I have committed, but I can only sigh for what I have lost. Everything we did and also the times and places are stamped on my heart along with your image, so that I live through it all again with you. Even in sleep I know no respite. Sometimes my thoughts are betrayed in a movement of my body, or they break out in an unguarded word."[41] That compelled her to cry out with St. Paul: "Miserable creature that I am, who is there to rescue me out of the body doomed to this death?"[42] I wish to God, she continued, that I could truly add "the grace of God through Jesus Christ our Lord!" This grace, she says to her Abelard, warned you, my dear, by delivering you from all the goads of sensuality, by that single cut of the knife that made you a eunuch. . . . But my youth and the experience of past pleasure ignites those fires exceedingly in my soul, and the more infirm my nature, the more I succumb to these violent attacks: "This grace, my dearest, came upon you unsought—a single wound of the body by freeing you from these torments has healed many wounds in your soul. . . . But for me, youth and passion and experience of pleasures which were so delightful intensify the torments of the flesh and longings of desire, and the assault is the more overwhelming as the nature they attack is the weaker."[43] Finally she commends herself to his prayers, all the more carefully inasmuch as it is the only remedy her incontinence can find in him: "I beg you, be fearful for me always, instead of feeling confidence in me, so that I may always find help in your solicitude. Now particularly you should fear, now when I no longer have in you an outlet for my incontinence."[44] Those who found Abelard's frequent trips to the Paraclete to be a target for scandal mongering,[45] were undoubtedly rash, because they did not know the inner disposition of Heloise: but if they had known it, they should rightly have sought the prohibition of these visits; for they should have feared it inevitable, humanly speaking, that this woman would commit acts of impurity with that man. The holy Fathers did not place trust in mutilation: they compared a eunuch to a steer whose horns are cut off, who does not stop banging with his head. See on this subject a wonderful passage by Saint Basil [c. 329–379] in our remarks on the article COMBABUS.[46] But as appearances are sometimes deceiving, I would not approve of those who, knowing what Heloise had in her heart, imagine that her behavior went beyond the rules when she found herself with her husband, and that she sometimes had cause to write to him: "If I were a passionate woman, I should feel betrayed and hurt: as it is I can be thankful even for your coldness."[47]

(L) *It was useless to have mutilated poor Abelard.*] It was, if we can believe certain verses of Cyrano de Bergerac, a remedy for love that was very capable of working.[48] The lines are addressed to a man whom he had called out to in this manner:

> I understand that the diminutive
> that, truly, was made too excessive
> On your flaccid genitive
> Prohibits conjunction.

Then he adds:

> O countenance! o naive resemblance!
> O sovereign haste
> For healing all lascivious members
> From nascent or effective love!
> Neutered gender, hybrid gender,
> Which is man only in the abstract,
> Thanks to your copulative,
> Which the cruel slicing of a knife
> Rendered most imperfect.

But since there is no rule so generally applicable that it does not allow some exception, Heloise's love contradicted the effectiveness of this violent remedy. She shared this with Queen Stratonice, of whom I have spoken above.[49]

(M) *She kept the seeds of this folly forever.*] This derives from the passages that I cited in remark (K). They prove, not only that carnal love dominated poor Heloise, but also that she was a bit deranged; for a person of exemplary conduct [*bien sage*] would never have spoken of the sort. It is apparent that studying had begun to unbalance her, and that love added substantially to the disorder. One sees in her writing lots of signs of a disturbed imagination, something so exaggerated and so ill-assorted, that she is a proof of the maxim of Seneca: "There is no great genius without an admixture of madness."[50]

(N) *This action caused a great commotion.*] Let us look at what Abelard tells us: "Next morning the whole city gathered before my house, and the scene of horror and amazement, mingled with lamentations, cries and groans which exasperated and distressed me, is difficult, no, impossible to describe. In particular, the clerks and, most of all, my pupils tormented me with their unbearable weeping and wailing."[51] See the article to which I refer in the next remark.

(O) *Women too were noteworthy in the very bitterness of their lamentations.*] This is what Abelard fails to mention; but we learn it from one of his friends who wrote him a letter of consolation. See the article FOULQUES ["Fulco"].[52]

(P) *People wrote Abelard very curious letters of consolation.*] Fulco, prior of Deuil, wrote him one which has been inserted in the edition of Abelard's works. We talk about it in the article on this prior, and we transfer there several things [*plusieurs choses*] which belong to Heloise and her husband that would make their articles too long, if they were not detached to be placed elsewhere. Those who say that they would rather find everything in one place, have not thought about it very carefully.

(Q) *This action was severely punished by the hand of justice.*] See the article on FOULQUES,[53] to which I refer for the two preceding remarks.

(R) *The loss of that work grieved him even more than the loss of his virility.*] Authors have been extensively mocked for the excessive tenderness that they conceive for their works, and among other examples, that of the bishop Heliodorus has been cited, who preferred to renounce his bishopric rather than condemn his novel about Theagenes [*The Aethiopica*].[54] The words Sarasin attributed to Voiture have been cited.[55] But I am not aware that Abelard had been cited on such a matter: however, in his case there is something more compelling; for eventually Job recovered his healthy state and fathered sons and daughters, and it is certain that Voiture would have preferred, for a period of time, to be like Job, than, until he died, to be like Abelard, and that he would have thrown all his books and all his muses in the dump, if it had been necessary, to preserve his little love-maker [*son fond d'amourettes*]. Where are the prelates who could not be made to sign away their bishoprics, if they were threatened, razor in hand, to . . . in case they didn't sign. Undoubtedly, the condemnation of Heliodorus's novel could have been obtained, if he had been confronted with that awkward alternative. But here is a man who declares that he counts for little the loss of his natural parts, in comparison with the loss of a work that he was forced to throw on the fire. In order to be perfectly fair, we must not attribute all Abelard's grief to the paternalistic feelings that his position as author inspired in him for his book. There was another thing there that distressed him even more: it is that in requiring him to throw his book on the fire, they issued a charge of heresy, a punishment that is equivalent to the mark of a branding iron. His grumbling against divine providence is another sign of his tenderness. Here are his words; I must relate them, so that I am not suspected of exaggerating things [*de grossir les choses*] just to amuse my readers. "God who judges equity, with what bitterness of spirit and anguish of mind did I reproach you in my madness and accuse you in my fury, constantly repeating the lament of St. Antony[56]—'Good Jesus, where were you?' All the grief and indignation, the blushes for shame, the agony of despair I suffered then I cannot put into words. I compared my present plight with my physical suffering in the past, and judged myself the unhappiest of men. My former betrayal seemed SMALL in COMPARISON with the wrongs I now had to endure, and I wept much more for the injury done to my reputation than for the damage to my body."[57]

(S) *Which never happens in the other case.*] See again the article FOULQUES, remark (F).

(T) *Self-conduct was very poor in that convent.*] Suger, the abbot of Saint-Denis, took advantage of the disordered life of the nuns of Argenteuil to regain possession of that convent. He sent his petition to Rome and received a favorable response. Let us listen to what he says in the story of his life for the year 1127: "We sent our messengers, and ancient charters of the foundation and donation, and the privileges of confirmation to Rome, to Pope Honorius of blessed memory; asking that he would with canonical scrutiny investigate and restore justice to us. Being a protector of good counsel and justice, in accordance with our just cause, as well as the wickedness of the nuns living there, he restored to us that place with its dependencies, so that the religious order should be reformed there." He states the same thing in the *Life of Louis the Fat.*[58] Those who are inclined to think ill of their neighbor will not read this part without entering into violent suspicions about Heloise's life. She confesses that she felt the flames of incontinence keenly[59]; and it is quite normal that the mother superior of a convent not be able to rule over her own passions well when the religious community is ravaged by debauchery.[60] The following consequence can easily be drawn from these two principles, if one derives pleasure from calumny: that the prioress of Argenteuil was no better than her nuns. But as for me, who did not read that she was referred to by name in the scandal furnished by her convent, I will carefully refrain from pointing the slightest finger. We must follow the Lord, and apply his maxim[61]: *Hath no man condemned thee* or accused thee? *I do not condemn thee,* nor do I accuse thee *either.* And it is certainly true that subordinates imitate the bad ways of their superiors, but not their virtuous conduct. The French court of Louis XIII was not more chaste than that of Henry IV.

(U) *She kept up correspondence with Abelard.*] This correspondence only began belatedly, and a chance encounter provided its commencement. Abelard had written an extended account of his misfortunes to a friend, which fell into the hands of Heloise, already the abbess of the Paraclete. Having read it, she wrote straightaway to Abelard the thoughts she had had about it, and supplicated him most ardently to write to her, so that she would no longer be deprived of the consolation that his letters could provide her in his absence. She depicted for him the disinterested nature of her love, and how she had sought neither the honor of marriage, the advantages of a dowry, nor her own pleasure; but his, Abelard's, satisfaction alone. She told him that even though the name of wife seemed more saintly and of greater weight, she had always found sweeter that of his mistress or his concubine or his whore: "The name of wife may seem more sacred or more binding, but sweeter for me will always be the word mistress, or, if you will permit me, that of concubine or whore."[62] She adds that he had reported only part of the reasons she had pointed out to dissuade him from marriage; but that he had eliminated almost all those that were conceived out of the preference she gave both to love outside conjugal bonds, and freedom over restraint.[63] I do not know how that girl meant it, but one of the most mysterious refinements of love is involved. For several centuries it has been thought that marriage makes that certain spiciness lose its principal flavor, and that the moment one does a thing out of commitment, duty or necessity, like a task or chore, the natural appeal is no longer there; so that as the real connoisseurs tell it, one takes a wife *ad honores,* and not *ad delicias:* "Marriage has for its share utility, justice, honor, and constancy: a flat pleasure, but more universal. Love is founded on pleasure alone, and in truth its pleasure is more stimulating, lively, and keen: a pleasure inflamed by difficulty. There must be a sting and a smart in it. It is no longer love if it is without arrows and without fire. The liberality of the ladies is too profuse in marriage, and blunts the point of affection and desire."[64] "Allow me," said a Roman Emperor to his wife,[65] "to exercise my lust with other women; for 'wife' is a name of dignity, not pleasure."[66] So one could give a very bad twist to Heloise's plan never to become the wife of Peter Abelard, but forever his dear mistress; one could suspect her of having feared lest marriage spell the demise of love, and prevent her from tasting her friend's caresses as deliciously as was her wont. The author who paraphrased some selections from the letters of our Heloise attributes essentially this attitude and outlook to her,[67] although the terms are treated tactfully. She is made to say "that she found nothing but insipidity in all those public commitments which form ties that only death can break, and which turn life and love into a sorry necessity[68]; that to wish to find benefit and dignity in the tepid hugs of an apathetic husband is not to love[69]; that she will never believe that the tender pleasures of a sweet union are enjoyed in that way; nor that one feels the secret and charming emotions of two hearts which have long sought each other for purposes of union; and that she is persuaded that if there is some semblance of happiness here on earth, one finds it only in the union of two people who love one another freely which a secret fondness has joined together, and which reciprocal merit has sanctioned."[70] We are going to see that the plan Heloise had to not marry Abelard was thought to have another cause.

(X) *I do not find at all that the hope of seeing him raised to the prelacy was the cause of her desire not to marry him.*] Mr. Amboise[71] mentions a French poet from the past, who, after exhorting men to never subject themselves to the servitude of marriage, confirms his feeling with that of our Heloise, who, he says, employed the most ardent prayers with her lover, in order to prevent him from marrying her; she found herself better served being loved by a man in whose hands she would one day see a good bishopric: "Saying that it was sufficient if she, preserving mutual love deep in her heart, could see him adorned with a bishop's mitre and lappets, of which he was worthy." Mr. Amboise remarks: 1) that this poet casts things in a different light, that is, that Heloise let it be known that the embraces of married people are not accompanied by as delightful a pleasure as unlawful embraces.[72] 2) that one must not think that Heloise preferred the license of concubinage to the state of wife, but that her love and respect for her suitor led her to favor becoming a nun instead of preventing that Abelard, through his marriage, receive the rewards that his mind and erudition earned him, as you would say 'the cardinal's hat.'[73] I did not notice any trace of that in the letters of Heloise: that is why I made it the sixth error of Mr. Moréri in the article on ABELARD. What creates this kind of falsehood is that an author takes the liberty of attributing to others the thoughts that seem to him to conform to their interests. There is often more to be gained for a woman by letting her young man chase after honors in the church, than to block the way by marrying him. But is it permissible because of that to suppose that Heloise held similar views? Here is a rather well-known tale: a man who had a prebend left it in order to marry; the day after the wedding he said to his wife: "See, my friend, how much I love you to have left my prebend so that I might have you."

"You did something really foolish," she replied to him, "you should have kept your prebend, you would not have had to give me up."[74]

(Y) *One tells . . . how Abelard held out his arms and kissed her firmly.*] A manuscript chronicle from Tours reports this beautiful miracle: "This woman [Heloise], as it is told, in her final illness gave instructions that on her death she should be laid in the tomb of her husband. And so, when she died, she was carried to the opened tomb. Her husband, who had died many days before her, raised his arms and received her, and thus he embraced her tightly in his arms."[75] But how does it happen that they are not in the same tomb? François d'Amboise, who tells us that he has seen the tomb at the Paraclete of both the founders, one next to the other[. . .]should have resolved this little difficulty.

(Z) . . . *there are other examples of similar things.*] See what Gregory of Tours reports of two married people who remained forever virgins,[76] and whom the inhabitants of the land[77] named *the two lovers.* The wife died first; the husband upon burying her summoned this prayer: "I thank you, O my Lord and God for being able to return this treasure to you in the same state of purity with which it pleased you to confer it on me." The woman began to smile. "And why," she said to him, "do you speak of a thing no one asks of you?" The husband died shortly thereafter, and they buried him beside his spouse. But the next day the two bodies were found together in the same tomb. This blunt question could make a layman think that the virgin wife did not want the world to know that her husband had been so cold. She contented herself with the merit of her continence, without wanting to be exposed to the opinions one might formulate at the expense of her charms. That is not the way to preserve this trust: to return it exactly the way you received it is not to return it in the best way; God did not institute marriage for that [reason]: " . . . a gift sought not for these purposes" [Vergil]. It is possible, therefore, not to be very happy that the public could think she had not pleased enough him to whom she was entrusted. But the historian will remedy that drawback, if you consult chapter 32 of the *Glory of the Confessors,* where the words of the deceased woman are a little better phrased. Ten chapters later [Gregory of Tours] tells of a senator from Dijon named Hilary lying in his sepulcher for a year,[78] [who] lifted his hand, in order to clasp his wife around the neck, when she was placed in the same grave.

Notes

I wish to thank Peter Marshall for translating a number of Latin passages in Bayle's text. His translations are indicated by the notation [trans. P. Marshall]. I would also like to extend my thanks to Nadia Margolis for making valuable suggestions for improving my introduction and translation. Neither, of course, is responsible for any remaining errors.

*See Peter Dronke, *Abelard and Heloise in Medieval Testimonies* (1976) [repr. *Intellectuals and Poets in Medieval Europe,* pp. 272–73], and Georg Misch, *Geschichte der Autobiographie* 3.1, p. 568.

**After F. C. Green reopened the authenticity controversy to argue against the authenticity of the *Lettres portugaises* with his article "Who Was the Author of the *Lettres portugaises?*" Leo Spitzer followed in 1954 with a confirmation and expansion of the argument against authenticity. See "Les *Lettres portugaises.*" According to translator and editor David Bellos, in *Leo Spitzer: Essays on Seventeenth-Century French Literature,* p. 254, Spitzer's pioneering article "resulted in definitive proof that the author [of the *Lettres* *portugaises*] was indeed Guilleragues, as guessed by Spitzer." Modern criticism seems to concur with Spitzer. Interestingly, Spitzer argued against the authenticity of the Abelard-Heloise correspondence as he did against the *Lettres portugaises,* unconvinced by the arguments of Etienne Gilson in favor of authenticity, calling Heloise's attitude one of "promethean defiance of Jesus" (Bellos, *Leo Spitzer,* p. 267). Bellos, however, is at pains to label Spitzer's viewpoint a minority opinion.

***David Wiesen, *St. Jerome as a Satirist: A Study in Christian Latin Thought and Letters,* p. 93.

****D. de Bruyne, "La Lettre de Jérôme à Sunnia et Fretela sur le Psautier," and in the same volume "Lettres fictives de S. Jérôme," pp. 229–34.

****St. Jerome, *The Principal Works of St. Jerome,* trans. H. W. Fremantle, vol. 6, p. 292 [repr. 1983]. It might be noted here that Bayle includes the correspondence of Abelard and Heloise in his discussion of literary obscenity. See the *Dictionnaire* article SUR LES OBSCENITES, also published separately in Belgium, pp. 20 and 60. [I have retained Bayle's practice of capitalizing all references to articles in the *Dictionnaire.*]

(a) In the article ABELARD, vol. 1, p. 49.

(b) "You know too how when you were pregnant and I took you to my own country you disguised yourself in the sacred habit of a nun, a pretence which was an irreverent mockery of the religion you now profess," Abelard, *Letter to Heloise,* p. 70. [See Radice 146.]

(c) "But Fulbert and his servants, seeking satisfaction for the dishonour done to him, began to spread the news of the marriage and break the promise of secrecy they had given me. Heloise cursed them and swore that there was no truth in this," Abelard, *Historia Calamitatum,* p. 17. [Radice 74]

(d) "They . . . took cruel vengeance on me of such appalling barbarity as to shock the whole world; they cut off the parts of my body whereby I had committed the wrong of which they complained," Abelard, *Historia Calamitatum,* p. 17 [Radice 75.]

(e) See the article PARACLETE, vol. 11.

(f) All this is taken from Abelard's letter titled *Historia Calamitatum,* except for a small number of things, whose evidence I cite separately.

(g) See the article FOULQUES, remark (K), vol. VI, p. 535.

(h) See remark (Y) in the article ABELARD, vol. I, p. 63.

(i) See President Fauchet, in ch. 126 of *Ancient French Poets.*

(k) Published in The Hague, by Jean Alberts, 1693.

(l) Bussy, vol. 2, letter 15, p. 49, Holland edition, 1697.

1. [Preface to] Abelard's *Opera.*
2. Notes to *Historia Calamitatum* of Abelard.
3. "You had made more than necessary reparation by humbling yourself on my account and had raised me and all my kind to your own level—so much less then, in the eyes of God and of your betrayers, should you have been thought deserving of such punishment," p. 57. [see Radice 130.]
4. *Annals,* Book 3.
5. Read "Fulbert."
6. See the evidence cited by Lambin on these words from *Ode XII,* Book 3 of Horace: "Fearing the lash [*verbera*] of an uncle's tongue." [Horace, *The Odes and Epodes,* trans. C. E. Bennett, p. 223.]
7. "John, as canon of Paris, had a natural daughter Heloise of outstanding intelligence and beauty," Papire Masson, *Annales,* Bk. 3, page m. 256. [Trans. P. Marshall.]
8. Abelard, *Opera,* p. 10. [see Radice 66, whose translation I have modified slightly.]
9. Abelard, *Opera,* p. 260. [Trans. P. Marshall.]
10. [François d'Amboise], *Apologetical Preface.*
11. It is the fifth of Book II.

12. See Abelard, *Opera,* p. 337. [Radice 277–78 (Peter the Venerable: Letter 115 to Heloise).]
13. See the *Notes* of André Duchesne on Abelard's Letter in the *Historia Calamitatum,* p. 1187.
14. *L'histoire abrégée d'Eloïse & d'Abelard,* The Hague, 1693.
15. *Operum,* p. 10.
16. Ibidem, p. 47.
17. This is said in *L'histoire abrégée* just cited.
18. p. 11. [Radice 67–68.]
19. p. 69. [Radice 146.]
20. "You know the depths of shame to which my unbridled lust had consigned our bodies, until no reverence for decency or for God even during the days of Our Lord's Passion, or of the greater sacraments could keep me from wallowing in this mire. Even when you were unwilling, resisted to the utmost of your power and tried to dissuade me, as yours was the weaker nature I often forced you to consent with threats and blows." [Radice 147.]
21. See St. Paul's *Epistle to the Colossians* 2.16.
22. p. 12. [Radice 68.]
23. Abelard, *Opera,* p. 46. [Radice 115.]
24. Here is what she says on page 48: "When in the past you sought me out for sinful pleasures your letters came to me thick and fast, and your many songs put your Heloise on everyone's lips, so that every street and house echoed with my name." [Radice 117–18.]
25. *L'histoire d'Eloïse & Abelard,* The Hague, 1693.
26. See Ovid, *De Arte Amandi,* Book 3, p. 205.
27. p. 590 ff and p. 746 ff. [In French: *Les nouvelles lettres contre le Calvinisme de Maimbourg.*
28. From vol. I, letter 48. [Bayle's French translation is preceded in his text by the Latin of Jerome's letter to Sabinian. D. F.]
29. These words are cited in the edition of Abelard's works as the continuation of what I have already cited from St. Jerome's *Letter to Sabinian,* but they are not to be found in that letter.
30. Jerome, *Adversus Jovinianum.* [See Jerome, *Principal Works,* trans. Fremantle, p. 384].
31. Dio Cassius, Book 60. Juvenal, *Satire X,* verse 342, said about this: "He will be the last to know the disgrace of his house." [Trans. P. Marshall.]
32. *Epigram IX,* Book VII. [The reference may be in error, since this epigram has no apparent relationship to Bayle's topic, D. F.]
33. Homer, *Odyssey.* Book 4, line 392: "What evil and what good has been done in your house." [Bayle offers the Greek in this footnote but gives a Latin version in the text where the Latin "nostris" clearly means "our" house, not "your" as implied by the Greek. I wish to thank P. Marshall for the translations and this observation.]
34. Johannes Michael Brutus, in *Praeceptis conjugalibus,* p. 798, edit. 1698. [Trans. P. Marshall.]
35. Brutus, *Praeceptis,* p. 798. [Trans. P. Marshall.]
36. Abelard, *Opera,* p. 14: "Who can concentrate on thoughts of Scripture or philosophy and be able to endure babies crying, nurses soothing them with lullabies, and all the noisy coming and going of men and women about the house? Will he put up with the constant muddle and squalor which small children bring into the home? [Radice 71.] [Bayle paraphrases in French the Latin in this note, hence the redundancy.]
37. [Etienne Pasquier], *Recherches sur la France,* Bk 6, ch. 17.
38. I mean that she did not argue that marriage is prohibited to those who have taken vows.
39. Abelard, *Opera,* p. 13: "Soon afterwards the girl found that she was pregnant, and immediately wrote me a letter full of rejoicing to ask what I thought she should do." [Radice 69.]
40. Abelard, *Opera,* p. 45. [Radice 114; Bayle's capitalization.]

41. Abelard, *Opera,* p. 59. [Radice 133.]
42. Rom. 7.24. [Radice 133.]
43. Abelard, *Opera,* p. 60. [Radice 133.]
44. Abelard, *Opera,* p. 61. [Radice 135.]
45. See the article ABELARD, remark (T), vol. 1, p. 62.
46. Vol. V, p. 256, note 6 [in the article COMBABUS].
47. *Circe greets Polyaenus,* by Petronius. [Petronius, *Satyricon,* trans. W. H. D. Rouse, p. 339. Bayle did not include the lines that follow: "But I should like to know how you are, and whether your feet carry you safely home; the doctors say that people who have lost their sinews (*sine nervis*) cannot walk."
48. See the comedy of the *Tricked Pedant.* [Reference is to Cyrano de Bergerac's *Pédant joué,* where the final word of each line quoted above ends in the suffix "if." D. F.]
49. In the article COMBABUS, vol. V, p. 253.
50. See vol. IV, p. 448, note (78) of the article CARDAN. [Trans. P. Marshall.]
51. Abelard, *Opera,* p. 17. [Radice 75.]
52. At remark (I), vol. VI, p. 533.
53. Remark (M), v. VI, p. 537.
54. See in this vol. remark (B) of the article HELIDORE what we should think about it.
55. "An author who, like me, is dealt a blow in his writing, endures more than Job, although the latter experienced acute suffering," Sarasin, *Poésies,* page m. 37. [I have not attempted a verse translation. D. F.]
56. In Saint Jerome in his *Vita.*
57. Abelard, *Opera,* p. 25. [Radice 84.] [In Victor Cousin's edition of the *Historia Calamitatum,* instead of "verbis non exprimere" he gives "*proferre* non possum" (emphasis D. F.).]
58. "Pope Honorius, a serious and severe man [recognized] the justice of [our claim] concerning the convent of Argenteuil, which was disgraced by the wretched behavior of the girls, etc." [Both trans. from Abbot Suger by P. Marshall.]
59. See above remark (K), notes (41) and (43).
60. It is popular to cite regarding this: "The whole world is arranged according to the king's example" and: "The daughter lightly follows the path of her mother." [Trans. P. Marshall.]
61. Gospel of Saint John 8.10.
62. Abelard, *Opera,* p. 45. [Radice 113.]
63. "There you thought fit to set out some of the reasons I gave in trying to dissuade you from binding us together in an ill-starred marriage. But you kept silent about most of my arguments for preferring love to wedlock and freedom to chains." [Radice 114.]
64. Montaigne, *Essais,* Bk 3, ch. 5, page m. 120. [*The Complete Essays of Montaigne,* trans. Donald M. Frame, p. 649.]
65. Spartianus, *Life of Aelius Varius,* page m. 235. [The reference and translation, for which I wish to thank Peter Marshall, is to chapter 5, section 11, of the *Life,* contained in *Scriptores Historiae Augustae,* a collection of lives of Roman emperors beginning with Hadrian.]
66. See several remarks of this nature in Letter 9 of the *Criticism of Calvinism by Maimbourg* and in Letters 21 and 22 of the continuation of this *Criticism.*
67. See the book titled: *L'histoire d'Héloise et d'Abélard,* The Hague, 1693.
68. p. 51.
69. p. 53.
70. p. 54.
71. [François d'Amboise], *Apologetical Preface* to *Opera* of Abelard.
72. "But the poet twists this into a different meaning, as if she meant to say that the embraces of lovers are sweeter than those of people joined by the laws of marriage" [*Apologetical Preface*]. [Citations here and in text above translated by P. Marshall.]

73. " . . . rather than by the obstacle of his marriage, it prevented Abelard, as overly fond of his wife, from being deprived of the reward of his outstanding intellect and amazing learning, namely the purple and the miter" [*Apologetical Preface*]. [Trans. P. Marshall.]
74. See the book entitled *Le moyen de parvenir,* composed by a canon of Tours, according to what the *Ménagiana* says, p. 366 of the second Holland edition.
75. In André Duchesne, *Notes to the Historia Calamitatum of Abelard* and François d'Amboise, *Apologetical Preface.* [Trans. P. Marshall.]
76. *Histoire des Français* 1.42.
77. Clermont in Auvergne.
78. See Abbot Marolles's *Notes* on Gregory of Tours, vol. 2, p. 283. [Citation from Vergil above, identified and translated by P. Marshall.]

CONTRIBUTORS

ALCUIN BLAMIRES is Reader in the Department of English at Goldsmith College, The University of London. His work on medieval Latin has developed in relation to the debate about women in the Middle Ages, on which he has published an anthology (*Woman Defamed and Woman Defended*) and a monograph *(The Case for Women in Medieval Culture)*. Currently completing a study of iconography and gender in *The Romance of the Rose,* he is also investigating interactions of gender and ethics in Chaucer's writing.

PHYLLIS R. BROWN is Associate Professor in the English Department and Director of Medieval and Renaissance Studies at Santa Clara University, where she has taught since 1982. She has published articles on Louise Labé, Guillaume de Machaut, and Anglo-Saxon poetry. Brown also edits *Chronica* for the Medieval Association of the Pacific.

DONNA ALFANO BUSSELL joined the doctoral program in English and Comparative Literature at Columbia University after a career in nursing and speech-language pathology. She holds M.A.'s in English from San Francisco State University and Columbia University and an M.A. in Communicative Disorders from California State University Fullerton. Her work in progress includes an article on Marie de France's "Equitan." She is a contributor to "An Age of Crisis and Renewal, 1300–1500," edited by Clay Drees.

JANE CHANCE is Professor of English at Rice University. She has published thirteen books, including *The Genius Figure in Antiquity and the Middle Ages, Woman as Hero in Old English Literature, Christine de Pizan's 'Letter of Othea to Hector,' Medieval Mythography: From Roman North Africa to the School of Chartres, Chaucer's Mythography: The Fabulation of Sexual Politics,* and *Gender and Text in the Later Middle Ages.* She also edits the Library of Medieval Women.

NEVILLE CHIAVAROLI is a graduate of the Universities of Melbourne and Cambridge and is currently working toward a doctoral degree at Monash University, Australia, on the works of the major Italian *dictatores* Boncompagno da Signa and Guido Fava.

DEBORAH FRAIOLI is Associate Professor of French at Simmons College. Author of *Joan of Arc: the Early Debate.* She has written about the authenticity controversy in the Abelard–Heloise correspondence in *Falschungen im Mittelalter* (*Monumenta Germanie Historica*) (Hanover, 1988).

LINDA GEORGIANNA is Professor of English at the University of California at Irvine, where she has taught since 1976. She is the author of *The Solitary Self: Individuality in the 'Ancrene Wisse'* and essays on subjects ranging from Beowulf to Chaucer. She is currently writing, with Katherine O'Brien O'Keeffe, *The Literary Cultures of Early England,* the first volume of the New Oxford History of English Literature.

PEGGY MCCRACKEN is Associate Professor of French at the University of Michigan. She is coeditor of *Constructing Medieval Sexuality* and the author of *The Romance of Adultery: Queenship and Sexual Transgression in Old French Literature.*

BRIAN PATRICK MCGUIRE is Professor of Medieval History in a new chair at Roskilde University, Denmark. He holds a B.A. from the University of California at Berkeley (1968), where Robert Brentano introduced him to the Middle Ages. He did his D.Phil. (1971) under Sir Richard Southern at Balliol College, Oxford. Since 1976 he has published eight books and about a hundred articles on various aspects of medieval monastic life and spirituality, including *Friendship and Community: The Monastic Experience* and *Brother and Lover: Aelred of Rievaulx.* His latest book is an introduction and translation of the early writings of the late medieval Paris theologian and church reformer, Jean Gerson.

MARY MARTIN MCLAUGHLIN's forthcoming book, *Heloise and the Paraclete: A Twelfth Century Quest* (New Middle Ages, St. Martin's Press) will join several studies pertaining to Heloise and Abelard, their Paraclete, and its twelfth-century contexts. Another continuing interest is the much larger history of medieval women's religious life and communities, leading to several articles, a book in progress, and a large-scale research project now called *Matrix.* Other interests and publications range from medieval children to the University of Paris in the thirteenth and fourteenth centuries.

GLENDA MCLEOD, Associate Professor of English at Gainesville College, has published several books and articles on early medieval women writers, most notably Christine de Pizan.

JOHN MARENBON is a fellow of Trinity College, Cambridge, where he teaches the History of Philosophy. His publications include *The Philosophy of Peter Abelard.*

CONSTANT MEWS is Senior Lecturer in the Department of History, Monash University, Australia. He has published the critical edition of two versions of Abelard's *Theologia* for the series Corpus Christianorum Continuatio Mediaeualis, vol. 13 and *Peter Abelard,* Authors of the Middle Ages, vol. 2, no. 5, as well as numerous articles on twelfth-century intellectual and religious culture. Most recently he has published *The Lost Love Letters of Heloise and Abelard: Perceptions of Dialogue in Twelfth-Century France.*

JOHN C. PEIFFER II graduated from Santa Clara University with honors in June of 1998. After teaching for a year in the English Department at Bellarmine College Preparatory, he began graduate study in Medieval Religion and Literature at the University of Chicago Divinity School.

MORGAN POWELL teaches at Franklin College, an American international college in Lugano, Switzerland. His current research explores the relationships between monastic models of reading, particularly as developed for women, and the early development of French and German vernacular literature.

JUANITA FEROS RUYS has recently completed her doctoral dissertation entitled *Genre, Gender and Authenticity: Readings of Heloise in the Twentieth Century* at the University of Sydney, Australia. She is currently collaborating with John O. Ward on a translation of and commentary on Abelard's *Planctus* and *Carmen ad Astralabium*.

JOHN O. WARD is a Senior Lecturer in History at the University of Sydney. His special interest and publications in the main concern the history of the study of rhetoric in medieval and Renaissance times. He has also published a number of studies on the history of medieval witchcraft and on medieval historiography.

BONNIE WHEELER is Director of the Medieval Studies Program at Southern Methodist University. She writes about late medieval literature and culture, and is the editor of the quarterly *Arthuriana*. She is the editor of *The New Middle Ages* series for which she has recently co-edited *Fresh Verdicts on Joan of Arc* and *Medieval Mothering*.

KATHARINA WILSON, Professor of Comparative Literature at the University of Georgia, has written and edited numerous volumes on medieval women writers, most recently *Hrotsvit of Gandersheim: A Florilegium of Her Works*.

BIBLIOGRAPHY

Primary Sources

I. Works by Heloise and Abelard.

Abelard, Peter. "Abelard's Letter of Consolation to a Friend, (*Historia calamitatum*)." Ed. J. T. Muckle, C. S. B. *Mediaeval Studies* 12 (1950): 163–213.

———. "Abelard's Rule for Religious Women." Ed. T. P. McLaughlin, C. S. B. *Mediaeval Studies* 18 (1956): 241–92.

———. "'Confessio fidei ad Heloissam': Abelard's Last Letter to Heloise? A Discussion and Critical Edition of the Latin and Medieval French Version." Ed. Charles S. F. Burnett. *Mittellateinisches Jahrbuch* 21 (1986): 147–55.

———. *Dialectica; First Complete Edition of the Parisian Manuscript.* [Or: *Petrus Abaelardus. Dialectica; First Complete Edition of the Parisian Manuscript*]. 2nd. Ed. L[ambertus] M. de Rijk. Wijsgerige Teksten en Studies 1. Assen: Van Gorcum, 1956, 1970.

———. *Historia calamitatum, texte critique avec une introduction.* Ed. J. Monfrin. Bibliothèque des Textes Philosophiques: Textes et Commentaires. Paris: J. Vrin, 1959, 1962 [2nd], 1967 [3rd], 1978.

———. Hymnarius Paraclitensis: *sive hymnorum libelli tres, ad fidem codicum Bruxellensis et Calmontani.* Ed. Guido Maria Dreves. Paris: P. Lethielleux, 1891. Rep. in: Medium aevum: B. Scriptores 5 (2). Bologna: Forni, 1970.

———. *The Hymns of Abelard in English Verse.* Trans. Sister Jane Patricia [Freeland]. Lanham, MD: University Press of America, 1986.

———. *Lamentations; Histoire de mes malheurs; Correspondance avec Héloïse.* Trans. Paul Zumthor. Babel 52. Arles: Actes Sud, 1992.

———. *Peter Abelard, 'Carmen ad Astralabium': A Critical Edition.* Ed. Josepha Marie Annaïs Rubingh-Bosscher. Diss.: Rijkuniversiteit te Groningen, 1987. Groningen: Krips Repro Meppel, 1987.

———. *Peter Abelard, Letters IX-XIV: An Edition with an Introduction.* Ed. Edmé Renno Smits. Groningen: Rijksuniversiteit [te Groningen], 1983.

———. *Peter Abelard's* Ethics. [Or: Ethics]. Ed. and trans. D. E. Luscombe. Oxford Medieval Texts. Oxford: Clarendon Press, 1971.

———. *Peter Abelard's* Hymnarius Paraclitensis: *An Annotated Edition with Introduction.* 2 vols. I: *Introduction to Peter Abelard's Hymns.* II: *The* Hymnarius Paraclitensis: *Text and Notes.* Ed. Joseph Szövérffy. Medieval Classics: Texts and Studies 2–3. Albany, NY: Classical Folia Editions, 1975.

———. *Peter Abaelards Philosophische Schriften.* I: *Die Logica "Ingredientibus."* II: *Die Logica "Nostrorum petitione sociorum."* Ed. Bernhard Geyer. Beiträge zur Geschichte der Philosophie und Theologie des Mittelalters 21. Munster: Aschendorff, 1919–27 [in 4 parts]; 1933 [4 parts in 1 vol.], 1979 [2nd]. Microfilm: Notre Dame, IN: University Libraries, University of Notre Dame, Nov. 1993—1 reel: 35mm.

———. *Petri Abaelardi Opera theologica.* [Or: *Opera theologica*]. 3 vols. I: *Commentaria in Epistolam Pauli ad Romanos. Apologia contra Bernardum.* II: *Theologia Christiana. Theologia scholarium accedunt capitula haeresum Petri Abaelardi.* Ed. Eligius-M. Buytaert. CCCM 11–12. Turnhout:

Brepols, 1969. III: *Theologia 'summi boni'. Theologia 'scholarium'.* Eds. Eligius-M. Buytaert and Constant J. Mews. CCCM 13. Turnhout: Brepols, 1987.

———. *I 'Planctus': Introduzione, testo critico, trascrizioni musicali.* Ed. Giuseppe Vecchi. Testi e manuali. Istituto di filologia romanza della Università di Roma 35. Modena: Società tipografica modenese, 1951, 1967.

[Anonymous]. *Epistolae duorum amantium: Briefe Abaelards und Heloises?* Ed. Ewald Könsgen. Mittellateinische Studien und Texte 8. Leiden: E. J. Brill, 1974.

———. *The Lost Love Letters of Heloise and Abelard: Perceptions of Dialogue in Twelfth-Century France.* Eds. and trans. Constant J. Mews and Neville Chiavaroli. The New Middle Ages. New York: St. Martin's Press, 1999; Basingstoke: Macmillan, 1999.

———. "Manuscrit de Troyes, *Lettres de deux amants* (Héloïse et Abélard?)." In *La Lettre d'amour au Moyen Âge: Boncompagno da Signa,* La roue de Vénus; *Baudri de Bourgueil,* Poésies; *Manuscrit de Tegernsee,* Lettres d'amour; *Manuscrit de Troyes,* Lettres de deux amants *(Héloïse et Abélard?).* Trans. Étienne Wolff and Marie-Claude Char. Le Cabinet de curiosités 1257–9440. Paris: NiL Editions, 1996. pp. 117–51.

———. *Un epistolario d'amore del XII secolo: (Abelardo e Eloisa?).* Ed. and trans. Graziella Ballanti. Saggi/Edizioni Anicia 1. Rome: Edizioni Anicia, 1988.

Heloise and Peter Abelard. *Abélard et Héloïse: Correspondance.* Ed. and trans. Paul Zumthor. Collection 10/18: Série Bibliothèque du Moyen Âge 1309. Paris: Union Générale d'Éditions, 1979. [Title page has only subtitle]. Originally: *Lettres de Héloïse et Abélard.* [Paris]: Mermod, 1950.

———. *The Letters of Abelard and Heloise.* Trans. C. K. Scott-Moncrieff. London: G. Chapman, 1925 [ltd. edn.]. In: Blue Jade Library. New York: A. A. Knopf, 1926, 1929, 1933. In: Alblabooks. New York: A. A. Knopf, 1942 [Alblabook edn.]; Rep. as: A Marandell Book. New York: Cooper Square Publishers, 1974.

———. *The Letters of Abelard and Heloise.* Trans. Betty Radice. Penguin Classics. [Baltimore, MD]: Penguin, 1974.

———. "The Letter of Heloise on the Religious Life and Abelard's First Reply." Ed. J. T. Muckle, C. S. B. *Mediaeval Studies* 17 (1955): 240–81.

———. "The Personal Letters Between Abelard and Heloise." Ed. J. T. Muckle, C. S. B. *Mediaeval Studies* 15 (1953): 47–94.

———. *La vie et les epistres, Pierres Abaelart et Heloys sa fame, Traduction du XIIIe siècle attribuée à Jean de Meun, avec une nouvelle édition des textes latins d'aprés le ms. Troyes Bibl. mun. 802.* [Only one vol. has been pub.]. I: *Introduction, textes.* Ed. Eric Hicks. Nouvelle Bibliothèque du Moyen Âge 16. Paris: Champion, 1991; Paris and Geneva: Champion-Slatkine, 1991. [Old French text from MS BN fr. 920].

[Various authors—Heloise, Abelard, Roscelin, etc.]. PL 178. Vol. 178 of: *Patrologiae cursus completus, series Latina.* 221 vols. Ed. J. P. Migne. Paris: Garnier, 1844–64.

II. Documents Related to the Paraclete.

Boutillier du Retail, A. and P. Piétresson de Saint-Aubin, eds. *Diocèses de Meaux et de Troyes.* Vol. 4 of: *Obituaries de la province de Sens.* 4 vols. Dir. Auguste Longnon. I: *Diocèses de Sens et de Paris* (1902). II: *Diocèse de Chartres* (1906). Ed. A. Molinier [vols. 1 and 2]. III: *Diocèses d'Orléans, d'Auxerre et de Nevers* (1909). Eds. A. Vidier and L. Mirot. IV: *Diocèses de Meaux et de Troyes* (1923). Eds. A. Boutillier du Retail and P. Piétresson de Saint-Aubin. Recueil des historiens de la France, Obituaries 1–4. Paris: Imprimerie nationale: Librairie C. Klincksieck ["Publié par l'Académie des inscriptions et belles-lettres"], 1902–1923. Microfilm: Notre Dame, IN: University Libraries, University of Notre Dame, Jan. 1993—3 reels: 35mm.

Cartulaire de l'abbaye du Paraclet. Vol. 2 of: *Collections des principaux cartulaires du diocèse de Troyes.* 7 vols. I: *Catulaire de l'abbaye de Saint-Loup de Troyes* (1875). II: *Cartulaire de l'abbaye du Paraclet* (1878). III: *Cartulaire de l'abbaye de Basse-Fontaine* (1878). IV: *Cartulaire de l'abbayed de la*

Chapelle-aux-Planches. V: Cartulaire de Saint-Pierre de Troyes (1880). VI: *Cartulaire de Montier-la-Celle* (1882). VII: *Cartulaire de l'abbaye de Montiéramey* (1890). Ed. Charles Lalore. Paris: E. Thorin: 1875–1890.

Cartulaire générale de l'Yonne recueil de documents authentiques pour servir à l'histoire des pays qui forment ce départment. 2 vols. Ed. Maximilien Quantin. Société des sciences historiques et naturelles de l'Yonne, Auxerre. Auxerre: Perriquet, 1854–1860. Microfilm: New Haven, CT: Yale University Library, 1992—1 reel: 35mm. [The imprint of Vol. 2 reads: "Perriquet et Rouillé"].

Delisle, Léopold, ed. *Rouleaux des morts du IXe au XVe siècle.* Société de l'histoire de France 135. Paris: Ve. J. Renouard, 1866; New York: Johnson Reprint, 1968. Microfilm: New York: Columbia University Libraries, 1992—1 reel: 35mm. [A suppl. to this work: "Supplément à la liste des rouleaux mortuaires puliés ou cités dans le recueil imprimé en 1866 pur la Société de l'histoire de France" is contained in Delisle's *Rouleau mortuaire du b. Vital, abbé de Savigni contenant 207 titres écrits en 1122–1123 dans différentes églises de France et d'Angleterre; édition phototypique.* Paris: Photoypie Berthaud frères; Philippe Renouard [et] Librairie Honoré Champion, 1909. Microfilm: Notre Dame, IN: University Libraries, University of Notre Dame, March 1993—1 reel: 35mm. pp. [25]–37. Also in the same vol.: "Résponses d'un grand nombre d'abbayes à la notification qui leur avait été faite de la mort du bienheureux Vital" No. 41 of which, the response of the abbey of Argenteuil, is attributed by the editor to Heloise.]

Hymn Collections from the Paraclete. I: *Introduction and Commentary.* II: *Edition of Texts.* Ed. Chrysogonus Waddell. Cistercian Liturgy Series 8–9. 2 vols. Trappist, KY: Gethsemani Abbey, 1987, 1989.

Merlet, René and [Jules] A[lexandre] Clerval, eds. *Un manuscrit chartrain du XIe siècle Fulbert, évêque de Chartres: martyrologe a l'usage de l'église de Chartres: Fulbert et sa cathédrale nécrologe du chapitre Notre-Dame de Chartres: chartes et pièces liturgiques.* [At head of title: "Société archéologique d'Eure-et-Loir"]. Chartres: Garnier, 1893. Microfilm: Chapel Hill, NC: Library Photographic Services, University of North Carolina at Chapel Hill, 1995—1 reel: 35mm.

The Paraclete Statutes, Institutiones Nostrae: *Troyes, Bibliothèque municipale, MS. 802, ff. 89r–90v. Introduction, Edition, Commentary.* Ed. Chrysogonus Waddell. Cistercian Liturgy Series 20. Trappist, KY: Gethsemani Abbey, 1987.

The Old French Paraclete Ordinary: Paris, Bibliothèque nationale, MS français 14410 and the Paraclete Breviary: Chaumont, Bibliothèque municipale, MS 31. 5 parts. I: *Introduction and Commentary.* II: *The Old French Paraclete Ordinary: Edition.* IIIA: *The Paraclete Breviary: Edition* (Kalendar and Temporal Cycle). IIIB: *The Paraclete Breviary: Edition* (Sanctoral Cycle). IIIC: *The Paraclete Breviary: Edition* (Common of Saints, Varia, Indices). Ed. Chrysogonus Waddell. Cistercian Liturgy Series 3–7. Trappist, KY: Gethsemani Abbey, 1983–85.

III. Other Primary Sources.

Adalabertus Samaritanus. *Praecepta dictaminum.* Ed. Franz-Josef Schmale. MGH Quellen zur Geistesgeschichte des Mittelalters 3. Weimar: H. Böhlaus Nachfolger, 1961.

Aelred of Rievaulx. *De institutione inclusarum.* In *Aelredi Rievallensis opera omnia.* Eds. Anselm Hoste and C[harles] H. Talbot. CCCM 1. Turnhout: Brepols, 1971, 1977, 1989.

———. *La vie de recluse* [et] *La prière pastorale.* [*De institutione inclusarum* in French and Latin]. Ed. and trans. Charles Dumont. Série des textes monastiques d'Occident 6. Sources Chrétiennes 76. Paris: Éditions du Cerf, 1961.

———. *Treatises; The Pastoral Prayer.* Vol. 1 of: *The Works of Aelred of Rievaulx.* Ed. David Knowles. Contents of Vol. 1: *Jesus at the Age of Twelve: The Historical Sense, the Allegorical Sense, the Moral Sense.* Trans. Theodore Berkeley. *A Rule of Life for a Recluse: The Outer Man, the Inner Man, a Threefold Meditation.* Trans. Mary Paul Macpherson. *The Pastoral Prayer.* Trans. R. Penelope

Lawson. Cistercian Fathers Series 2. Spencer, MA: Cistercian Publications, 1971. Kalamazoo, MI: Cistercian Publications, 1971, 1982.

Ancrene Wisse: The English Text of the Ancrene riwle, Edited from MS. Corpus Christi College, Cambridge 402. Ed. J. R. R. Tolkien. EETS 249 [Original Series]. London: Oxford University Press [for EETS], 1962.

Anselm of Canterbury. *The Letters of Saint Anselm of Canterbury.* Trans. Walter Fröhlich. Cistercian Studies Series 96–97, 142. 3 vols. Kalamazoo, MI: Cistercian Publications, 1990–1994.

———. *S. Anselmi cantuariensis archiepiscopi opera omnia.* Ed. Franciscus Salesius Schmitt. 6 vols. Seckau: F. Frommann, 1938; "Destroyed by the Nazis, 1942"; Edinburgh: Thomas Nelson and Sons ["Photoprinted"], 1946, 1961; Rep. [6 vols. in 2]: Stuttgart-Bad-Cannstatt: F. Frommann, 1968, 1984. Microfilm: Notre Dame, IN: University Libraries, University of Notre Dame, Feb. 1992—1 reel: 35 mm [vols 1–4 only]. [Includes the *De veritate*].

Augustine of Hippo [Aurelius Augustinus]. *The* Confessions *and* Letters *of St. Augustin* [*sic*]: *With a Sketch of His Life and Work.* Ed. Philip Schaff ["Prolegomena: St. Augustin's (*sic*) Life and Work"]. Trans. J. G. Pilkington ["The *Confessions* of St. Augustin (*sic*)"]. Trans. J. G. Cunningham ["The *Letters* of St. Augustin (*sic*)"]. A Select Library of Nicene and Post-Nicene Fathers of the Christian Church 1 [1st Series]. Buffalo, NY: Christian Literature Company, 1886, 1892 [New York]; Rep.: Grand Rapids, MI: W. B. Eerdmans, 1954, 1974, 1988; Edinburgh: T & T Clark, 1988.

Bayle, Pierre. *s.v.* "Sur les Obscenités." In *Dictionnaire.* Brussels: Gay and Doucé, 1879.

———. *An Historical and Critical Dictionary, Selected and Abridged from the Great Work of Pierre Bayle.* London: Hunt and Clarke, 1826.

———. *Historical and critical dictionary: selections from the* Dictionnaire. Ed. and trans. Richard H. Popkin. Indianapolis, IN: Hackett, 1991.

———. *Dictionnaire historique et critique de Pierre Bayle.* 16 vols. Ed. Adrien Jean Quentin Beuchot. Paris: Desoer, 1820, 1824.

———. *Dictionnaire historique et critique.* Rotterdam: Reinier Leers, 1697.

Bene da Firenze [Bonus Florentinus]. *Bene Florentini Candelabrum.* [Or: *Candelabrum*]. Ed. Gian Carlo Alessio. Thesaurus Mundi: Bibliotheca scriptorum latinorum mediae et recentioris aetatis 23. Padua: Antenore, 1983.

Benedict [of Nursia]. *The Rule of St. Benedict: In Latin and English with Notes* [*and Thematic Index*]. Ed. Timothy Fry. Collegeville, MN: Liturgical Press, 1981 [full edn.]; 1981 [abr. edn.—no "Thematic Index," etc.]. Now: *The Rule of St. Benedict in English.* 1st. Vintage Spiritual Classics. New York: Vintage Books, 1998.

———. *St. Benedict's Rule for Monasteries.* [Or: *Rule for Monasteries*]. Trans. Leonard J. Doyle. Collegeville, MN: The Liturgical Press, 1948; Collegeville, MN: St. John's Abbey Press, 1948, 1949.

Bernard of Clairvaux. *Treatises I.* Vol. 1 of: *The Works of Bernard of Clairvaux.* Ed. M. Basil Pennington. Trans. Michael Casey. Cistercian Fathers Series 1. Spencer, MA: Cistercian Publications, 1970.

Bernard of Cluny. *Scorn for the World: Bernard of Cluny's 'De contemptu mundi': The Latin Text with English Translation and an Introduction.* Ed. Ronald E. Pepin. Medieval Texts and Studies 8. East Lansing, MI: Colleagues Press, 1991.

Blamires, Alcuin, ed. and trans. *Woman Defamed and Woman Defended: An Anthology of Medieval Texts.* Oxford: Clarendon Press, 1992.

Boethius, [Anicius Manlius Severinus]. *De consolatio Philosophiae.* In *The Theological Tractates* [of] *Boethius, with an English Translation by H. F. Stewart and E. K. Rand;* [and] *The Consolation of Philosophy* [by] *Boethius, with an English Translation by S. J. Tester.* Ed. and trans. H. F. Stewart, E. K. Rand, and S. J. Tester. Loeb Classical Library. Cambridge, MA: Harvard University Press, 1918, 1926, 1936, 1946, 1953, 1962, 1973 [new rev.], 1978, 1990.

Boncompagno da Signa. *Aus Leben und Schriften des Magisters Boncompagno ein Beitrag zur Italienischen Kulturgeschichte im dreizehnten Jahrhundert.* Ed. Carl Sutter. Freiburg im Breisgau and

Leipzig: Akademische Verlagsbuchhandlung von J. C. B. Mohr, 1894, 1980. Microfilm: Cambridge, MA: Harvard University Library Microreproduction Service, 1989—1 reel: 35mm.

———. *Rota Veneris*. Ed. Paolo Garbini. Minima [Rome, Italy] 53. Rome: Salerno Editrice, 1996.

———. *Corona*. Ed. Franco-Lucio Schiavetto. In: "Un'opera sconosciuta di Boncompagno." *Studi Medievali* 34 (1993): 366–80.

Carmina Burana, mit benutzung der vorarbeiten Wilhelm Meyers. [Or: *Carmina Burana*]. 4 parts. [I]: *Text*. [IA]: *Die moralisch-satirischen Dichtungen*. [IB]: *Die liebeslieder*. [IC]: *Die Trink-und Spielerlieder, Die geistlichen Dramen*. [II]: *Kommentar*. [IIA]: *Einleitung (Die Handschrift der Carmina Burana) Die moralische-satirischen dichtungen*. Eds. Otto Schumann, Alfons Hilka, and Wilhelm Meyer. Heidelberg: C[arl] Winter, 1930, [2nd]: 1961, 1969 [II only], 1970, 1978. Microfilm: University Libraries, University of Notre Dame, Apr. 1995—1 reel: 35mm [1930 printing]. [Often catalogued without subtitle].

———. *Love Lyrics from the Carmina Burana*. Ed. and trans. P. G. Walsh. Chapel Hill, NC: University of North Carolina Press, 1993.

Catullus, C[aius/Gaius] Valerius. *Carmina*. [Or: *C. Valerii Catulli carmina*]. Ed. Sir R. A. B. Mynors. Scriptorum Classicorum Bibliotheca Oxoniensis [Script. lat.]. Oxford: Clarendon Press, 1958; [Rep. from corr. sheets of 1st]: 1960, 1972.

Cereta, Laura. *Collected Letters of a Renaissance Feminist*. Trans. Diana Maury Robin. The Other Voice in Early Modern Europe. Chicago, IL: University of Chicago Press, 1997.

Charles, R. H., et al., eds. *The Apocrypha and Pseudepigrapha of the Old Testament in English, with Introduction and Critical and Explanatory Notes to the Several Books Edited, in Conjunction with Many Scholars, by R. H. Charles*. 2 vols. Oxford: Clarendon Press, 1913.

Chartularium Universitatis Parisiensis. 4 vols. I: *Ab anno 1200 usque ad annum 1286*. II: *Ab anno 1286 usque ad annum 1350*. III: *Ab anno 1350 usque ad annum 1394*. IV: *Ab anno 1394 usque ad annum 1452*. Eds. Heinrich Denifle and Émile Châtelain. Paris: Brother Delalain, 1889–97; [Rep.]: 1946, 1964. Microfilm: Notre Dame, IN: University Libraries, University of Notre Dame, Nov. 1994—1 reel: 35mm. Microfiche: Zug, Switzerland: Inter-Documentation Company, 1965—104 fiches.

Cicero, Marcus Tullius. *De inventione; De optimo genere oratorum; Topica*. Ed. and trans. H. M. Hubbell. Loeb Classical Library. Cambridge, MA: Harvard University Press, 1949, 1960, 1976, 1993.

———. *On the Good Life; [selected writings of] Cicero*. [Or: *On the Good Life*]. Trans. with intro. Michael Grant. Penguin Classics. Harmondsworth: Penguin Books, 1971, 1982.

———. *Laelius* [*De amicitia*]. Pub. as: *L'amitié*. Ed. and trans. L. Laurand. Collection des universités de France. Paris: Belles Lettres, 1928, 1942 [2nd], 1952 [3rd], 1957 [3rd rev. and corr.], 1961 [4th], 1965, 1968.

Cicero [Pseudo-Cicero]. *Ad C. Herennium, De ratione dicendi (Rhetorica ad Herennium) with an English Translation by Harry Caplan*. Ed. and trans. Harry Caplan. Loeb Classical Library. Cambridge, MA: Harvard University Press, 1953, 1954, 1964, 1968, 1977, 1981, 1989.

Damian, Peter. *The Letters of Peter Damian*. 4 vols. I: *Letters 1–30*. II: *Letters 31–60*. III: *Letters 61–90*. IV: *Letters 91–120*. Trans. Owen J. Blum. The Fathers of the Church, Mediaeval Continuation 1–3, 5. Washington DC: The Catholic University of America Press, 1989–92.

Dante Alighieri. *Dantis Alagherii epistolae: The Letters of Dante; Emended Text with Introduction, Translation, Notes and Indices, and Appendix on the* Cursus. Ed. and trans. Paget Jackson Toynbee. Oxford: Clarendon Press, 1920; [2nd]: 1966, 1967.

Evergates, Theodore, ed. and trans. *Feudal Society in the Bailliage of Troyes Under the Counts of Champagne, 1152–1284*. Baltimore, MD: Johns Hopkins University Press, 1975, 1976, 1990.

———. *Feudal Society in Medieval France: Documents from the County of Champagne*. The Middle Ages. Philadelphia, PA: University of Pennsylvania Press, 1993.

Fava, Guido. *Summa dictaminis*. Ed. Augusto Gaudenzi. In *Il Propugnatore* 23.3 [New Series] (1890): 287–338.

Fulgentius, Fabius Planciades. *Expositio Virgilianae Continentiae.* In Fabii Planciadir Fulgentii v. c. *Opera accedunt Fabii Claudii Gordiani Fulgentii v. c. De aetatibus mundi et hominis et S. Fulgentii episcopi Super Thebaiden.* [Or: *Opera accedunt Fabii Claudii Gordiani Fulgentii v. c. De aetatibus mundi et hominis et S. Fulgentii episcopi Super Thebaiden*]. Ed. Rudolf Helm. Biblioteca Scriptorum Graecorum et Romanorum Teubneriana [Scriptores Romani]. Leipzig: B. G. Teubner, 1898; Rep.: Stuttgart: B. G. Teubner, 1970. Microfilm: New York: Columbia University—1 reel: 35mm.

———. *Fulgentius the Mythographer.* Trans. Leslie George Whitbread. Columbus, OH: Ohio State University Press, 1971.

Gregory VII [Hildebrand]. *The* Epistolae vagantes *of Pope Gregory VII.* Ed. and trans. H. E. J. Cowdrey. Oxford Medieval Texts. Oxford: Clarendon Press, 1972.

Guibert of Nogent. *De Vita Sua.* [In English translation]: *A Monk's Confession: The Memoirs of Guibert of Nogent.* Ed. and trans. Paul J. Archambault. University Park, PA: Pennsylvania State University Press, 1996. [Also trans. as]: *Self and Society in Medieval France: The Memoirs of Abbot Guibert of Nogent (1064?–c. 1125).* Ed. John F. Benton. Trans. C. C. Swinton Bland. Harper Torchbooks. New York: Harper & Row, 1970; And in: Medieval Academy Reprints for Teaching 15. Toronto: University of Toronto Press [for: Medieval Academy of America], 1984. [Bland translation appeared originally as]: *The Autobiography of Guibert, Abbot of Nogent-sous-Coucy.* Broadway Translations, Medieval Section. London: Routledge; New York: E. P. Dutton, 1925, 1926. [In French translation]: *Autobiographie.* Ed. and trans. Edmonde René Labande. Les Classiques de l'histoire de France au Moyen Âge 34. Paris: Belles Lettres, 1981.

Guillaume de Lorris, and Jean de Meun. *The Romance of the Rose.* Trans. Charles Dahlberg. Princeton, NJ: Princeton University Press, 1971, 1995 [3rd]; Hanover, NH: University Press of New England, 1983.

———. *The Romance of the Rose.* Trans. Frances Horgan. The World's Classics. Oxford: Oxford University Press, 1994.

Hagenmeyer, Heinrich, ed. *Epistulæ et chartæ ad historiam primi belli sacri spectantes quæ svpersvnt ævo æquales ac genvinæ. Die Kreuzzugsbriefe aus den Jahren 1088–1100. Eine quellensammlung zur geschichte des ersten kreuzzuges.* Innsbruck: Wagner'sche universitäts-buchhandlung, 1901. Microfilm: New Haven, CT: Yale University Library, 1988—1 reel: 35mm. Under the title: *Epistulae et chartae ad historiam primi belli sacri spectantes. Die Kreuzzugsbriefe aus den Jahren 1088–1100.* Hildesheim and New York: Georg Olms, 1973. [Note: the 1901 edition is often catalogued under the German subtitle only].

Hildegard of Bingen. *The Letters of Hildegard of Bingen.* 2 vols. to date. Trans. Joseph L. Baird and Radd K. Ehrman. New York: Oxford University Press, 1994–99.

Horace [Q. Horatius Flaccus]. *The Odes and Epodes with an English Translation.* Trans. Charles E. Bennett. Loeb Classical Library. Cambridge, MA: Harvard University Press, 1914, 1918, 1919, 1921, 1924, 1925; [rev.]: 1927, 1929, 1930, 1934, 1939, 1946, 1947, 1952, 1960, 1964, 1968, 1978, 1988. [Translation has appeared in numerous other contexts].

———. *Satires* [*Satirae*]. In Satires, Epistles *and* Ars poetica *with an English Translation.* Ed. and trans. H. Rushton Fairclough. Loeb Classical Library. Cambridge, MA: Harvard University Press, 1920, 1926; [rev.]: 1926, 1929, 1932, 1936, 1939, 1942, 1947, 1955, 1961, 1966, 1970, 1978, 1991. [Imp. varies somewhat].

Hugutio of Pisa. *Magnae derivationes.* Oxford, Bodleian Library MS 376.

Huygens, R. B. C., ed. *Accessus ad auctores.* [*Commentum in Theodulum*]. Collection Latomus 15. Berchem-Brussels: Latomus, 1954. [Detached from ser. and pub.]: Leiden: E. J. Brill, 1970.

Jerome. *The Principal Works of St Jerome.* Trans. W. H. Fremantle. A Select Library of Nicene and Post-Nicene Fathers 6 [2nd series]. Oxford: James Parker; New York: Christian Literature Company, 1893. Grand Rapids, MI: W. B. Eerdmans, 1954, 1983.

———. *Select Letters of St Jerome.* Trans. F. A. Wright. Loeb Classical Library. Cambridge, MA: Harvard University Press, 1933, 1954, 1963, 1975, 1980, 1991. rep. [not in Loeb]: Grand Rapids, MI: W. B. Eerdmans, 1983.

John of Salisbury. *Ioannis Saresberiensis episcopi carnotensis, Metalogicon libri IIII; recognovit et prolegomenis apparatv critico.* Ed. Clement Charles Julian Webb. Oxford: Clarendon Press, 1909, 1929. Microfiche: Maastricht, Holland: Micro Library Canisianum, [1909 printing]. Microfilm: Notre Dame, IN: University Libraries, University of Notre Dame, April 1992—1 reel: 35mm [1929 printing]. [Often catalogued without subtitle].

———. *Metalogicon.* Ed. J. B. Hall. In *Ioannis Saresberiensis Metalogicon.* Eds. Daniel D. McGarry, J. B. Hall, and K. S. B. Keats-Rohan. CCCM 98. Turnhout: Brepols, 1991.

———. *The Metalogicon of John of Salisbury: A Twelfth-Century Defense of the Verbal and Logical Arts of the* Trivium. Trans. Daniel D. McGarry. Berkeley, CA: University of California Press, 1955, 1962; [s.l.]: Cambridge University Press, 1962; Gloucester, MA: Peter Smith, 1971; Westport, CT: Greenwood Press, 1982.

The Life of Christina of Markyate: A Twelfth Century Recluse. Ed. and trans. C[harles] H. Talbot. Oxford Medieval Texts. Oxford: Clarendon Press, 1959, 1987 [new enl. edn.]. Now in: Medieval Academy Reprints for Teaching 39. Toronto: University of Toronto Press [for: Medieval Academy of America], 1998.

Macrobius, [Ambrosius Aurelius Theodosius]. *The Saturnalia.* Trans. Percival Vaughan Davies. Record of Civilization, Sources and Studies 79. New York: Columbia University Press, 1969. Microfilm: Ann Arbor, MI: University of Michigan, University Library, Preservation Office Microfilming Unit, 1997—1 reel: 35mm.

Marbod of Rennes. *Carmina.* Ed. Walther Bulst. As: "Liebesbriefgedichte Marbods." In Walther Bulst. *Lateinisches Mittelalter: Gesammelte Beiträge.* Ed. Walter Berschin. Supplemente zu den Sitzungsberichten der Heidelberger Akademie der Wissenschaften, Philosophisch-Historische Klasse 3. Heidelberg: [Carl] Winter, 1984. pp. 182–96.

Martène, Edmond and Ursin Durand, eds. *Veterum scriptorum et monumentorum historicorum, dogmaticorum, moralium, amplissima collectio.* 9 vols. Paris: apud Montalant, 1724–33. Microfilm: Maastricht, Holland: Micro Library Canisianum—1 reel: 35mm; Vatican City, Vatican City: Biblioteca Apostolica Vaticana—35mm; St. Louis, MO: Pius XII Memorial Library, Saint Louis University, 1962—3 reels: 35mm (Manuscripta, Microfilms of Rare and Out-of-Print Books, 41.25). Microfiche: Zug, Switzerland: Inter Documentation Company; Englewood, CO: Microcard Editions, 1972—260 sheets.

Menander [of Laodicea]. *Menander Rhetor.* Eds. and trans. D. A. Russell and Nigel Guy Wilson. Oxford: Clarendon Press; New York: Oxford University Press, 1981.

Metellus, Hugo. *Epistolae.* In *Sacrae Antiquitatis Monumenta.* 2 vols. Ed. Charles-Louis Hugo. Saint-Die: Joseph Charlot, 1731.

Minio-Paluello, L., ed. *Twelfth Century Logic. Texts and Studies.* I: *Adam Balsamiensis Parvipontani. Ars disserendi (dialectica Alexandri).* II: *Abaelardiana Inedita:* 1. *Super periermenias XII-XIV.* 2. *Sententie secundum M. Petrum.* 2 vols. Rome: Edizioni di Storia e letteratura, 1956.

de Montaigne, Michel. *The Complete Essays of Montaigne.* Trans. Donald Murdoch Frame. Stanford, CA: Stanford University Press, 1958, 1965, 1966, 1976. [Translations have appeared in multiple other contexts].

Morton, Vera, trans. and intro. *Heavenly Brides and Holy Mothers: Texts from Twelfth-Century Convents in England and France.* Medieval Women Series. Cambridge: Boydell and Brewer, forthcoming.

Ovid [P. Ovidius Naso]. *Ars amatoria, Book I.* Ed. A. S. Hollis. Oxford: Oxford University Press, 1977, 1989.

———. *The Art of Love.* In *The Erotic Poems.* Ed. Peter Green. Penguin Classics. London: Penguin Books, 1982, 1988. pp. 166–238.

———. *Heroides.* Trans. Harold Isbell. Penguin Classics. London: Penguin Books, 1990.

———. *Metamorphoses.* 2 vols. Trans. Frank Justus Miller. Rev. G. P. Goold. Loeb Classical Library. Cambridge, MA: Harvard University Press, 1916, 1921, 1922, 1925, 1928, 1929, 1933, 1936, 1944, 1946, 1951, 1956, 1957, 1958, 1960, 1964, 1966, 1968, 1971, 1976, 1977, 1984, 1986. [Multiple rev. edn.; translation has appeared in other contexts].

———. *Ovid:* Heroides *and* Amores *with an English Translation by Grant Showerman.* Ed. and trans. Grant Showerman. Loeb Classical Library. Cambridge, MA: Harvard University Press, 1914, 1921, 1925, 1930, 1931, 1947, 1955, 1958, 1963, 1971; [2nd]: 1977, 1978, 1986, 1996. [2nd revised by G. P. Goold].

Peter the Venerable, *The Letters of Peter the Venerable.* Ed. Giles Constable. Harvard Historical Studies 78. 2 vols. Cambridge, MA: Harvard University Press, 1967.

Petronius Arbiter, [Claudius]. *Circe greets Polyaenus.* From *Satyricon.* In *Petronius, with an English Translation by Michael Heseltine [and] Seneca, Apocolocyntosis, with an English Translation by W. H. D. Rouse.* Eds. and trans. Michael Heseltine and W. H. D. Rouse. Loeb Classical Library. Cambridge, MA: Harvard University Press, 1913, 1916, 1919, 1922, 1925, 1930 [rev.], 1939, 1951, 1956, 1961 [rev.], 1969, 1975, 1987 [rev. E. H. Warmington].

Propertius, Sextus. *Carmina.* Ed. Eric Arthur Barber. Scriptorum Classicorum Bibliotheca Oxoniensis. Oxford: Clarendon Press, 1953, 1957, 1957 [corr.]; [2nd]: 1960, 1967, 1974.

Prudentius, [Aurelius Prudentius Clemens]. *Apotheosis [On the Divinity of Christ].* In Vol. 1 of *Prudentius.* 2 vols. Ed. and trans. H. J. Thomson. Loeb Classical Library. Cambridge, MA: Harvard University Press, 1949, 1961, 1969.

———. "The Battle for the Soul of Man. Hymns for the Various Hours and Days. Epilogue." In: *The Last Poets of Imperial Rome.* Comp. and trans. Harold Isbell. Penguin Classics. New York: Penguin Books, 1971.

Pseudo-Boèce [Pseudo-Boethius]. *De disciplina scolarium.* Ed. Olga Weijers. Studien und Texte zur Geistesgeschichte de Mittelalters 12. Leiden: E. J. Brill, 1976.

Roscelin of Compiègne. *De trinitate* 1. *Epistola ad Abaelardum.* Ed. Josef Reiners. In *Der Nominalismus in der Frühscholastik. Ein Beitrag zur Geschichte der Universalienfrage im Mittelalter. Nebst einer neuen Textausgabe des Briefes Roscelins an Abälard.* Beiträge zur Geschichte der Philosophie des Mittelalters 8.5. Munster: Aschendorff Buchhandlung, 1910.

Seneca, Lucius Annaeus. *Ad Lucilium epistulae morales with an English Translation by Richard M. Gummere.* 3 vols. Ed. and trans. Richard M. Gummere. Loeb Classical Library. Cambridge, MA: Harvard University Press, 1917, 1918, 1920, 1925, 1943, 1953, 1961, 1962, 1967, 1970, 1989, 1991.

Seyfarth, Jutta, ed. *Speculum virginum.* CCCM 5. Turnhout: Brepols, 1990.

Shipley, Frederick W., ed and trans. *Res Gestae Divi Augusti.* In *Velleius Paterculus,* Compendium of Roman History *[and]* Res Gestae Divi Augusti *with an English Translation by Frederick W. Shipley.* Loeb Classical Library. Cambridge, MA: Harvard University Press, 1924, 1955, 1961, 1967, 1979, 1992. pp. 331–405.

Statius, P[ublius] Papinius. *Statius with an English Translation.* [Or: *Statius*]. 2 vols. Ed. and trans. J. H. Mozley. Loeb Classical Library. Cambridge, MA: Harvard University Press, 1928, 1938; [rev.]: 1955, 1957, 1961, 1967, 1982, 1989.

Terence, [P. Terentius Afer]. *Hauton Timorumenos.* In *P. Terenti Afri Comoediae.* [Or: *Comoediae*]. Ed. Alfred Fleckeisen. Bibliotheca Scriptorum Graecorum et Romanorum Teubneriana. Leipzig: B. G. Teubner, 1856, 1857, 1861, 1862, 1868, 1871, 1874, 1881, 1884, 1894, 1895, 1898, 1901, 1905, 1910, 1916.

———. *The Comedies.* 2 vols. I: *The Brothers and Other plays* (1965). II: *Phormio and Other Plays* (1967). Trans. Betty Radice. Penguin Classics. New York: Penguin, 1965, 1967; 1976 [rev. and comb. edn.—in 1 vol.].

Thierry of Chartres. *The Latin Rhetorical Commentaries by Thierry of Chartres.* Ed. Karin Margareta Fredborg. Studies and Texts 84. Toronto: Pontifical Institute of Mediaeval Studies, 1988.

Thomson, Ian, and Louis Perraud, eds. and trans. *Ten Latin Schooltexts of the Later Middle Ages: Translated Selections.* Mediaeval Studies [Lewiston, NY] 6. Lewiston, NY: E. Mellen Press, 1990.

Vergil [P. Vergilius Maro]. *Aeneidos liber quartus.* Ed. R. G. Austin. Oxford: Clarendon Press, 1955, 1963 [corr.], 1966, 1973, 1982.

William of Champeaux. *Sententiae.* In Vol. 5 of: *Problèmes d'histoire littéraire* of: *Psychologie et Morale aux XIIe et XIIIe siècles.* 6 vols. I: *Problèmes de psychologie.* II-IV: *Problèmes de morale.* V-VI: *Problèmes d'histoire littéraire.* Ed. Odon Lottin. I-IV: Louvain: Abbaye du Mont César; V-VI: Gembloux, Duculot, 1942. II-VI: Louvain: Abbaye du Mont César, 1948. I-VI: Gembloux: J. Duculot, 1948, 1960. I [2nd]: Gembloux: Duculot, 1957.

Yves de Chartres. *Correspondance* [Or: *Yves de Chartres: Correspondance*]. Ed. and trans. Jean Leclercq. Les classiques de l'histoire de France du Moyen Âge 22. Paris: Belles Lettres, 1949.

Secondary

Adams, Henry. *Mont Saint Michel and Chartres.* Washington: [s.n.], 1904, 1912; New York: Heritage, 1957. In: Penguin Classics. New York: Penguin, 1986. In: Library of America 14. New York: Dist. Viking Press, 1983, 1986.

Adams, J. N. *The Latin Sexual Vocabulary.* Baltimore, MD: Johns Hopkins University Press, 1982, 1990 [pbk.]; London: Duckworth, 1982.

Albert, Bat-Sheva, Yvonne Friedman, and Simon Schwarzfuchs, eds. *Medieval Studies in Honour of Avrom Saltman.* Bar-Ilan Studies in History (Bar-Ilan Departmental Researches) 4. Ramat-Gan: Bar-Ilan University Press, 1995.

Alexiou, Margaret, and Peter Dronke. "The Lament of Jephtha's Daughter: Themes, Traditions, Originality." *Studi medievali* 12 (1971): 819–63. Rep. in Dronke's *Intellectuals and Poets in Medieval Europe.*

Anderson, W. S. "The *Heroides.*" In *Ovid.* Ed. Binns. pp. 49–83.

Anson, John. "The Female Transvestite in Early Monasticism: The Origin and Development of a Motif." *Viator* 5 (1974): 3–32.

Archambault, Paul [J]. "The Silencing of Cornelia: Heloïse, Abelard, and Their Classics." Papers on Language & Literature 6.1 (Winter 1970): 3–17.

Arenberg, Nancy May. "Epistolary Transvestism: (Re)Visions of Heloise (Seventeenth-Eighteenth Centuries)." Diss.: University of Arizona, 1996.

Astell, Ann W. *The Song of Songs in the Middle Ages.* Ithaca, NY: Cornell University Press, 1990, 1995.

Atkinson, Clarissa W. *The Oldest Vocation: Christian Motherhood in the Middle Ages.* Ithaca, NY: Cornell University Press, 1991.

Baker, Derek, ed. *Medieval Women.* Dedicated and Presented to Professor Rosalind M.T. Hill on the Occasion of Her Seventieth Birthday. Studies in Church History, Subsidia 1. Oxford: Blackwell [for the Ecclesiastical History Society], 1978, 1985, 1989.

Baldwin, Charles Sears. *Medieval Rhetoric and Poetic (to 1400) Interpreted from Representative Works.* New York: The Macmillan Company, 1928; Gloucester, MA: Peter Smith, 1959; St. Clair Shores, MI: Scholarly Press, 1972, 1976.

Ballanti, Graziella. *Pietro Abelardo : la rinascita scolastica del XII secolo.* 1st. Biblioteca di Cultura [Nuova Italia Editrice] 194. Scandicci (Firenze): La nuova Italia, 1995.

Barrow, Julia, Charles Burnett, and David [E] Luscombe. "A Checklist of the Manuscripts Containing the Writings of Peter Abelard and Heloise and Other Works Closely Associated with Abelard and His School." *Revue d'Histoire des Textes* 14–15 (1984–85): 183–301.

Bartlett, Robert. *The Making of Europe: Conquest, Colonization and Cultural Change, 950–1350.* London: Allen Lane, 1993; London: Penguin, 1994.

Benoît, Paul and Denis Cailleaux, eds. *Moines et métallurgie dans la France médiévale.* Colloque Moines et métallurgie dans la France médiévale (1987: Paris, France). Paris: Picard [AEDEH: Association pour l'édition et la diffusion de études historiques], 1991.

Benson, Robert L. and Giles Constable, eds. *Renaissance and Renewal in the Twelfth Century.* Cambridge, MA: Harvard University Press, 1982; Oxford: Clarendon Press, 1982, 1985; Oxford: Oxford University Press, 1985. In: Medieval Academy Reprints for Teaching 26. Toronto: University of Toronto Press [for: Medieval Academy of America], 1991.

Benton, John F. "Consciousness of Self and Perceptions of Individuality." In *Renaissance and Renewal.* Eds. Benson and Constable. pp. 263–95.

———. *Culture, Power and Personality in Medieval France.* Ed. Thomas N. Bisson. London: Hambledon Press, 1990, 1991.

———. "Fraud, Fiction, and Borrowing in the Correspondence of Abelard and Heloise." In *Pierre Abélard–Pierre le Vénérable.* Eds. Louis, Jolivet, and Châtillon. pp. 469–512.

———. "A Reconsideration of the Authenticity of the Correspondence of Abelard and Heloise." In *Petrus Abaelardus, (1079–1142): Person, Werk und Wirkung.* Eds. Thomas, Jolivet, Luscombe, and de Rijk. pp. 41–52.

Berger, Elie. *Notice sur divers manuscrits de la Bibliothèque Vaticane. Richard le Poitevin, moine de Cluny, historien et poëte.* Bibliothèque des Écoles Françaises d'Athènes et de Rome 6. Paris: E. Thorin, 1879.

Berman, Constance H. *Medieval Agriculture, the Southern French Countryside, and the Early Cistercians: A Study of Forty-Three Monasteries.* Transactions of the American Philosophical Society 76.5. Philadelphia, PA: American Philosophical Society, 1986.

Bernards, Matthäus. *Speculum virginum: Geistigkeit und Seelenleben der Frau im Hochmittelalter.* Forschungen zur Volkskunde 36/38. Cologne: Böhlau, 1955; [2nd]: Beihefte zum Archiv für Kulturgeschichte 16. Cologne: Böhlau, 1982. [Note: the 1955 edn. is often catalogued under the German subtitle only].

Bienvenu, Jean-Marc. "Le conflit entre Ulger, évêque d'Angers et Petronille de Chemillé, abbesse de Fontevrault." *Revue Mabillon* 58 (1972): 113–32.

Biller, Peter, and Anne Hudson, eds. *Heresy and Literacy, 1000–1530.* Cambridge Studies in Medieval Literature 23. Cambridge: Cambridge University Press, 1994, 1996 [pbk.].

Biller, Peter, and A. J. Minnis, eds. *Medieval Theology and the Natural Body.* York Studies in Medieval Theology 1. Rochester, NY: York Medieval Press, 1997.

Blamires, Alcuin. "*Caput a femina, membra a viris:* Gender Polemic in Abelard's Letter 'On the Authority and Dignity of the Nun's Profession.'" In *The Tongue of the Fathers.* Eds. Townsend and Taylor. pp. 55–79.

———. *The Case for Women in Medieval Culture.* Oxford: Clarendon Press; New York: Oxford University Press, 1997, 1998 [pbk.].

Bloch, R. Howard. *Medieval Misogyny and the Invention of Western Romantic Love.* Chicago, IL: University of Chicago Press, 1991.

Blomme, Robert. *La doctrine du péché dans les écoles théologiques de la première moitié du XIIe siècle.* Diss. published in series: Universitas Catholica Lovaniensis. Dissertationes ad gradum magistri in Facultate Theologica vel in Facultate Iuris Canonici consequendum conscriptae 3.6. Louvain: Publications universitaires de Louvain, 1958.

Bolton, Brenda. *The Medieval Reformation.* Foundations of Medieval History. London: Edward Arnold, 1983; New York: Holmes & Meier, 1983.

Bond, Gerald A. "Composing Yourself: Ovid's *Heroides,* Baudri of Bourgueil and the Problem of Persona." *Mediaevalia* 13 (1989 [for 1987]): 83–117.

———. "*Iocus amoris:* The Poetry of Baudri of Bourgueil and the Formation of the Ovidian Subculture." *Traditio* 42 (1986): 143–93.

———. *The Loving Subject: Desire, Eloquence, and Power in Romanesque France.* The Middle Ages. Philadelphia, PA: University of Pennsylvania Press, 1995.

Bos, Egbert. "Patterns of Male-Female Religious Friendships and Their Influence on the Construction of the Literary Identities of Medieval Women." In *Worshipping Women.* Eds. Ward and Bussey. pp. 326–36.

Boswell, John. *The Kindness of Strangers: The Abandonment of Children in Western Europe from Late Antiquity to the Renaissance.* New York: Pantheon Books, 1988; [1st Vintage Books edn.]: New York: Vintage Books, 1990; [University of Chicago Press edn.]: Chicago, IL: University of Chicago Press, 1998.

Bouchard, Constance B. "Cistercian Ideals Versus Reality: 1134 Reconsidered." *Cîteaux* 39 (1988): 217–31.

———. *Holy Entrepreneurs: Cistercians, Knights, and Economic Exchange in Twelfth-Century Burgundy.* Ithaca, NY: Cornell University Press 1991.

Boyle, A. J., ed. *Roman Epic.* London: Routledge, 1993, 1996.

Bredero, Adriaan H. "Cluny et Cîteaux au XIIe siècle: les origines de la controverse." *Studi medievali* 12 (1971 [3rd series]): 135–75.

Breisach, Ernst, ed. *Classical Rhetoric and Medieval Historiography.* Studies in Medieval Culture 19. Kalamazoo, MI: Medieval Institute Publications, Western Michigan University, 1985.

Brooke, Christopher. *The Medieval Idea of Marriage.* Oxford: Clarendon Press, 1989, 1994.

Brown, Catherine. "*Muliebriter:* Doing Gender in the Letters of Heloise." In *Gender and Text in the Later Middle Ages.* Ed. Chance. pp. 25–51.

Brown, Peter. *The Body and Society: Men, Women, and Sexual Renunciation in Early Christianity.* Lectures on the History of Religion 13 [New Series]. BOMC edn.: New York: Columbia University Press, 1988; New York: Faber, 1989, 1991 [pbk.].

de Bruyne, D. "La Lettre de Jérôme à Sunnia et Fretela sur le Psautier." *Zeitschrift für die neutestamentliche Wissenschaft* 28 (1929): 1–13.

———. "Lettres fictives de S. Jérôme." *Zeitschrift für die neutestamentliche Wissenschaft* 28 (1929): 229–34.

Burgess, Glyn S., and Robert A. Taylor, et al., eds. *The Spirit of the Court: Selected Proceedings of the Fourth Congress of the International Courtly Literature Society (Toronto 1983).* Woodbridge, Suffolk: D. S. Brewer, 1985.

Bynum, Caroline Walker. *Fragmentation and Redemption: Essays on Gender and the Human Body in Medieval Religion.* New York: Zone Books, 1991, 1992.

———. *Holy Feast and Holy Fast: The Religious Significance of Food to Medieval Women.* The New Historicism: Studies in Cultural Poetics. Berkeley, CA: University of California Press, 1987, 1988.

———. *Jesus As Mother: Studies in the Spirituality of the High Middle Ages.* Publications of the Center for Medieval and Renaissance Studies [UCLA] 16. Berkeley, CA: University of California Press, 1982, 1984 [pbk.].

Cailleaux, Denis. "Les religieux et le travail de fer en Pays d'Othe." In *Moines et métallurgie.* Eds. Benoît and Cailleaux.

Calabrese, Michael. "Ovid and the Female Voice in the *De Amore* and the *Letters* of Abelard and Heloise." *Modern Philology* 95 (1997): 1–26.

Camargo, Martin. *Ars Dictaminis, Ars Dictandi.* Typologie des sources du Moyen Âge occidental 60. Turnhout: Brepols, 1991.

Carruthers, Mary [J]. *The Book of Memory: A Study of Memory in Medieval Culture.* Cambridge Studies in Medieval Literature 10. Cambridge: Cambridge University Press, 1990, 1992 [pbk.], 1998.

Cartlidge, Neil. *Medieval Marriage: Literary Approaches, 1100–1300.* Cambridge: D. S. Brewer, 1997.

Chance, Jane. *Medieval Mythography: From Roman North Africa to the School of Chartres, A.D. 433–1170.* Gainesville, FL: University Press of Florida, 1994.

———. "The Medieval Sources of Cristoforo Landino's Allegorization of the Judgment of Paris." *Studies in Philology* 81 (1984): 145–160.

———. *The Mythographic Chaucer: The Fabulization of Sexual Politics.* Minneapolis, MN: University of Minneapolis Press, 1995.

———., ed. *Gender and Text in the Later Middle Ages.* Gainesville, FL: University Press of Florida, 1996.

Charrier, Charlotte. *Héloïse dans l'histoire et dans la légende.* [Half-title, Errata sheet laid in]: *Sources et critique des sources.* Bibliothéque de la Revue de littérature comparée 102. Paris: Librairie ancienne Honoré Champion, 1933; Rep.: Geneva: Slatkine Reprints, 1977. Microfilm [orig. edn.]: Ann Arbor, MI: University Microfilms—1 reel: 35mm; Notre Dame, IN: University Libraries, University of Notre Dame, Apr. 19095—1 reel: 35mm.

Chenu, Marie-Dominique. *Nature, Man, and Society in the Twelfth Century: Essays on New Theological Perspectives in the Latin West.* Selected, ed., and trans. Jerome Taylor and Lester K. Little.

With preface by Étienne Gilson. Chicago, IL: University of Chicago Press, 1957, 1968, 1979 [Phoenix edn.]. In: Midway Reprints. Chicago, IL: University of Chicago Press, 1983. Now in: Medieval Academy Reprints for Teaching 37. Toronto: University of Toronto Press [for: Medieval Academy of America], 1997. Selections are from the author's: *La théologie au douzième siècle. Préf. d'Etienne Gilson.* Études de philosophie médiévale 45. Paris: J.Vrin, 1957, 1966 [2nd].

Cherewatuk, Karen, and Ulrike Wiethaus, eds. *Dear Sister: Medieval Women and the Epistolary Genre.* The Middle Ages. Philadelphia, PA: University of Pennsylvania Press, 1993.

Cipollone, Maria. "In margine ai *Problemata* Heloissae." *Medium Ævum* 64 (1990): 227–44.

Cizewski, Wanda. "*In Saeculo Quondam Cara Nunc in Christo Carissima:* Heloise and Spiritual Formation at the Convent of the Paraclete." *Proceedings of the PMR Conference: Annual Publication of the International Patristic, Mediaeval & Renaissance Conference* 9 (1984): 69–75.

Clanchy, M.T. *Abelard: A Medieval Life.* Oxford: Blackwell, 1997, 1999.

Cohen, Jeffrey Jerome, and Bonnie Wheeler, eds. *Becoming Male in the Middle Ages.* The New Middle Ages 4. Garland Reference Library of the Humanities 2066. New York: Garland, 1997, 1999 [pbk.].

Cohn, Samuel K., and Steven A. Epstein, eds. *Portraits of Medieval and Renaissance Living: Essays in Memory of David Herlihy.* Ann Arbor, MI: University of Michigan Press, 1996.

Conley, Thomas M. *Rhetoric in the European Tradition.* New York: Longman, 1990; Rep.: Chicago, IL: University of Chicago Press, 1994.

Constable, Giles. *Letters and Letter-Collections.* Typologie des sources du Moyen Âge occidental 17. Turnhout: Brepols, 1976.

———. *Monastic Tithes: From Their Origins to the Twelfth Century.* Cambridge Studies in Medieval Life and Thought 10 [New Series]. Cambridge: Cambridge University Press, 1964.

———. *The Reformation of the Twelfth Century.* Cambridge: Cambridge University Press, 1996, 1998 [pbk.].

———. "Renewal and Reform in Religious Life: Concepts and Realities." In *Renaissance and Renewal.* Eds. Benson and Constable. pp. 37–67.

———. *Three Studies in Medieval Religious and Social Thought: The Interpretation of Mary and Martha, the Ideal of the Imitation of Christ, and the Orders of Society.* Cambridge: Cambridge University Press, 1995; New York: Cambridge University Press, 1998 [pbk.]. [Usually catalogued without subtitle].

Copeland, Rita, ed. *Criticism and Dissent in the Middle Ages.* Cambridge: Cambridge University Press, 1996.

Corino, Karl, ed. *Gefälscht!: Betrug in Politik, Literatur, Wissenschaft, Kunst und Musik.* [1st]: Nördlingen: Greno, 1988; [rev.]: Frankfurt: Eichborn, 1990.

Cremaschi, Giovanni. *Guida allo studio del latino medievale.* Biblioteca di cultura. Padua: Liviana editrice, 1959.

Curtius, Ernst Robert. *European Literature and the Latin Middle Ages.* Trans. Willard R. Trask. London: Routledge & Kegan Paul, 1953, 1979. [New York]: Pantheon Books, 1953. In: Harper Torchbooks. The Bollingen Library, TB 2015. New York: Harper & Row, 1963 [1st Harper Torchbooks edn.]. Also in: Bollingen Series 36. Princeton, NJ: Princeton University Press, 1953 [s.l.], 1967; 1973, 1990 [pbk.; rep. with new epilogue of Pantheon 1952 edn.]. [Originally in German]: *Europäische Literatur und lateinisches Mittelalter.* Bern: Francke [A. Francke], 1948 [1st]; 1954 [2nd rev.], 1969; 1961 [3rd]; 1963 [4th]; 1965 [5th]; 1967 [6th]; 1969 [s.l.; 7th]; 1973 [8th]; 1978 [9th]; 1984 [10th]; 1993 [11th].

Dalarun, Jacques. *L'impossible sainteté: la vie retrouvée de Robert d'Arbrissel (v. 1045–1116), fondateur de Fontevraud.* Cerf-histoire. Paris: Éditions du Cerf, 1985.

———. "Robert D'Arbrissel et les femmes." *Annales: Économies Sociétés Civilizations* 39.6 (Nov.-Dec. 1984): 1140–1160.

Degler-Spengler, Brigitte. "The Incorporation of Cistercian Nuns into the Order in the Twelfth and Thirteenth Century." In *Hidden Springs.* Eds. Nichols and Shank. pp. 85–134.

Denholm-Young, N. *Collected Papers on Mediaeval Subjects.* Oxford: Blackwell, 1946. Also in: *Collected Papers of N. Denholm-Young.* Cardiff: University of Wales Press, 1969.

Desmond, Marilynn. *Reading Dido: Gender, Textuality, and the Medieval* Aeneid. Medieval Cultures 8. Minneapolis, MN: University of Minnesota Press, 1994.

Dickinson, J. C. *The Origins of the Austin Canons and Their Introduction into England.* London: SPCK—Society for the Promotion of Christian Knowledge [for: Church Historical Society], 1950. Microfilm: Ann Arbor, MI: University Microfilms International—1 reel: 35mm.

Douglas, Mary. *Purity and Danger: An Analysis of the Concepts of Pollution and Taboo.* London: Routledge & Kegan Paul, 1966, 1969 [2nd imp. with corr.], 1970, [Rep. of 1969 edn.]: 1976, 1978 and 1980; New York: Praeger, 1966, 1970 [Books That Matter]; London: Routledge, 1991 [Rep. of Ark edn.], 1994, 1996; Binghamton, NY: Vail-Ballou Press, 1980 [Rep. of 1969 edn.]; London: Ark, 1984. In: Pelican Anthropology Library. Harmondsworth: Penguin, 1970.

Dronke, Peter. *Abelard and Heloise in Medieval Testimonies.* W. P. Ker Memorial Lecture 26. [Glasgow]: University of Glasgow Press, 1976; Rep. in his *Intellectuals and Poets in Medieval Europe.* Storia e letteratura 183. Rome: Edizioni di Storia e Letteratura, 1992. pp. 247–94.

———. "Heloise and Marianne: Some Reconsiderations." *Romanische Forschungen* 72 (1960): 236–43.

———. "Heloise's *Problemata* and *Letters:* Some Questions of Form and Content." In *Petrus Abaelardus, (1079–1142): Person, Werk und Wirkung.* Eds. Thomas, Jolivet, Luscombe, and de Rijk. pp. 53–73.

———. *Intellectuals and Poets in Medieval Europe.* Storia e letteratura 183. Rome: Edizioni di Storia e Letteratura, 1992.

———. *Medieval Latin and the Rise of the European Love-Lyric.* 2 vols. I: *Problems and Interpretations.* II: *Medieval Latin Love-Poetry.* Oxford: Clarendon Press, 1965, 1968 [2nd].

———. "Medieval Poetry—I: Abélard." *The Listener* (October 25, 1965): 841–45.

———. *Poetic Individuality in the Middle Ages: New Departures in Poetry, 1000–1150.* Oxford: Clarendon Press, 1970 [1st]. In: Westfield Publications in Medieval Studies 1. London: Westfield College, University of London—Committee for Medieval Studies, 1986 [2nd].

———. *Women Writers of the Middle Ages. A Critical Study of Texts from Perpetua (†203) to Marguerite Porete (†1310).* Cambridge: Cambridge University Press, 1984, 1985.

Duby, Georges. *Love and Marriage in the Middle Ages.* Trans. Jane Dunnett. Cambridge: Polity Press, 1994. Chicago, IL: University of Chicago Press, 1994, 1996 [pbk.]. [Collection of articles previously pub. between 1967 and 1986]. [Originally in French]: *Mâle Moyen Âge: de l'amour et autres essais.* Nouvelle bibliothèque scientifique. [Paris]: Flammarion, 1988.

———. *Que sait-on de l'amour en France au XIIe siècle?* The Zaharoff Lecture for 1982–83. Oxford: Clarendon Press, 1983.

———. *Women of the Twelfth Century.* As 2 vols.: I: *Eleanor of Aquitaine and Six Others.* II: *Remembering the Dead.* Trans. Jean Birrell. Cambridge: Polity Press, 1997. As 3 vols.: I: *Eleanor of Aquitaine and Six Others.* II: *Remembering the Dead.* III: *Eve and the Church.* [Chicago, IL]: University of Chicago Press, 1997. As 1 vol.: *Women of the Twelfth Century.* [s.l.]: [s.n.] "Published in association with Blackwell Publishers Ltd [. . .] with the assistance of the French Ministry of Culture," 1998 [separate ISBN numbers for 1998, 1 vol. printings; most likely abr. edn.]. [Originally in French]: *Dames du XIIe siècle.* [Or: *Dames du douzième siècle*]. 3 vols. I: *Héloise, Aliénor, Iseut et quelques autres.* [Or: *Héloïse, Aliénor, Iseut et quelques autres*]. Collection Folio/histoire 84. [Paris]: Gallimard, 1995, 1997. In: Bibliothèque des histoires. [Paris]: Gallimard, 1995. II: *Le souvenir des aïeules.* Collection Folio/histoire 84. Paris: Gallimard, 1998. III: *Ève et les prêtres.* [Or sometimes: *Eve et les prêtres*]. Bibliothèque des histoires. Paris: Gallimard, 1996. All 3 vols. in: Bibliothèque des histoires. Paris: Gallimard, 1995.

Duval, Yves-Marie, ed. *Jérôme entre l'Occident et l'Orient: XVIe centenaire du départ de saint Jérôme de Rome et de son installation à Bethléem: actes du colloque de Chantilly, septembre 1986.* Paris: Études Augustiniennes, 1988.

East, W. G. "*This Body of Death:* Abelard, Heloise and the Religious Life." In *Medieval Theology and the Natural Body.* Eds. Biller and Minnis. pp. 43–59.

Ehrhart, Margaret J. *The Judgment of the Trojan Prince Paris in Medieval Literature.* The Middle Ages. Philadelphia, PA: University of Pennsylvania Press, 1987.

Ennen, Edith. *The Medieval Woman.* Trans. E. Jephcott. Oxford and Cambridge, MA: Blackwell, 1989. [Originally in German]: *Frauen im Mittelalter.* Munich: C. H. Beck, 1984, 1986, 1985 [2nd], 1987 [3rd rev.], 1991 [4th rev. and enl.]. In: Becks historische Bibliothek. Munich: C. H. Beck, 1994 [5th rev. and enl.].

Enos, Richard Leo, ed. *Oral and Written Communication: Historical Approaches.* Written Communication Annual: An International Survey of Research and Theory 4. Newbury Park, CA: Sage Publications, 1990.

Evans, J. Martin. *Paradise Lost and the Genesis Tradition.* Oxford: Clarendon Press, 1968.

van den Eynde, Damien. "Chronologie des écrits d'Abélard a Héloïse." *Antonianum* 37 (1962): 337–49.

Ferguson, Chris D. "Autobiography as Therapy: Guibert de Nogent, Peter Abelard, and the Making of Medieval Autobiography." *Journal of Medieval and Renaissance Studies* 13 (1983): 187–212.

Ferrante, Joan M. "The Education of Women in the Middle Ages in Theory, Fact, and Fantasy." In *Beyond Their Sex.* Ed. Labalme. pp. 9–42.

———. *To the Glory of Her Sex: Women's Roles in the Composition of Medieval Texts.* Women of Letters [Bloomington, IN]. Bloomington, IN: Indiana University Press, 1997.

Ferroul, Yves. "Abelard's Blissful Castration." In *Becoming Male.* Eds. Cohen and Wheeler. pp. 129–49.

Foster, Hal, ed. *The Anti-Aesthetic: Essays on Postmodern Culture.* [Or: *The Anti-aesthetic*]. Port Townsend, WA: Bay Press, 1983; Rep.: New York: New Press/W. W. Norton, 1998. Also published as: *Postmodern Culture.* London: Pluto, 1985, 1987.

Fraioli, Deborah. "The Importance of Satire in Jerome's *Adversus Jovinianum* as an Argument against the Authenticity of the *Historia calamitatum.*" In Teil 5 of: *Fälschungen im Mittelalter,* MGH 55, pp. 167–99.

Frank, D. K. "Abelard as Imitator of Christ." *Viator* 1 (1970): 107–13.

Frymire, John. "*Petrus Imperfectus:* Abelard and the *Sermo de Eunuchis* Late in the Early High Middle Ages." [Unpublished manuscript].

Garner, Helen. *The First Stone: Some Questions About Sex and Power.* Picador. Sydney: Pan Macmillan Australia, 1995; New York: Free Press, 1997; London: Bloomsbury, 1997.

Georgianna, Linda. "Any Corner of Heaven: Heloise's Critique of Monastic Life." *Mediaeval Studies* 49 (1987): 221–53; Rep. in rev. form in the present volume.

———. *The Solitary Self: Individuality in the Ancrene Wisse.* Cambridge, MA: Harvard University Press, 1981.

Gilson, Étienne. *Héloïse and Abélard.* Trans. L. K. Shook. Chicago, IL: H. Regnery Co., 1951 [2nd French]. London: Hollis & Carter, 1953. In: Ann Arbor Paperbacks 38. [Ann Arbor, MI]: University of Michigan Press, [pbk.]: 1960, 1963, 1968, 1972. [Originally in French]: *Héloïse et Abélard.* Essais d'art et de philosophie. Paris: J. Vrin, 1938; 1948 [2nd]; 1964 [3rd rev.], 1978 [s.l.; 3rd rev., 2nd print.], 1984 [3rd rev., 3rd print.]. In: Bibliothèque des textes philosophiques. Paris: J. Vrin, 1997 [3rd rev., 4th print.].

———. *The Mystical Theology of Saint Bernard.* Trans. Alfred Howard Campbell Downes. London: Sheed & Ward, 1940, 1955, 1982. Now in: Cistercian Studies Series 120. Kalamazoo, MI: Cistercian Publications, 1990. [Originally in French]: *Le théologie mystique de Saint Bernard.* Études de philosophie médiévale 20. Paris: J. Vrin, 1934, 1947 [2nd], 1969 [3rd], 1980 [4th], 1986 [5th].

Gold, Barbara K., Paul Allen Miller, and Charles Platter, eds. *Sex and Gender in Medieval and Renaissance Texts: The Latin Tradition.* SUNY Series in Medieval Studies. Albany, NY: State University of New York Press, 1997.

Gold, Penny Schine. *The Lady & the Virgin: Image, Attitude, and Experience in Twelfth-Century France.* Women in Culture and Society. Chicago, IL: University of Chicago Press, 1985, 1987.

Grant, Lindy. *Abbot Suger of St. Denis: Church and State in Early Twelfth-Century France.* The Medieval World. London: Longman, 1998.

Green, F. C. "Who Was the Author of the *Lettres portugaises?*" *Modern Language Review* 21 (1926): 159–67.

Greer, Germaine. *The Obstacle Race: The Fortunes of Women Painters and Their Work.* London: Secker and Warburg, 1979; New York: Farrar, Straus, and Giroux, 1979; London: Book Club Associates, 1980. In: Picador. London: Pan [in assoc. with Secker & Warburg], 1981.

Grimal, Pierre. *A Concise Dictionary of Classical Mythology.* [Or: *The Dictionary of Classical Mythology*]. Trans. Stephen Kershaw. Oxford: Blackwell, 1986, 1987 [rep. with corr.], 1988, 1990, 1996 [abr. pbk.]. And as: *The Penguin Dictionary of Classical Mythology.* Penguin Reference Books. London: Penguin, 1990, 1991 [abr. edn.]. [Originally in French]: *Dictionnaire de la mythologie grecque et romaine.* Paris: Presses universitaires de France, 1951, 1958 [2nd corr.], 1963 [3rd corr.], 1969 [4th rev.], 1976 [5th rev.], 1979 [6th], 1982 [7th], 1986 [8th], 1988 [9th], 1990 [10th], 1991 [11th], 1994 [12th], 1996 [13th].

Grundmann, Herbert. *Religious Movements in the Middle Ages: The Historical Links Between Heresy, the Mendicant Order, and the Women's Religious Movement in the Twelfth and Thirteenth Century, with the Historical Foundations of German Mysticism.* Trans. S. Rowan. 1935; Notre Dame, IN: University of Notre Dame Press, 1995. [Original in French]: *Religiöse Bewegungen im Mittelalter Untersuchungen über die geschictlichen zusammenhänge Zwischen der Ketzerei, den bettelorden und der religiösen Frauenbewegung um 12. und 13. Jahrhundert und über die geschichtlichen Grundlagen der deutschen Mystik.* Historische Studien 267. Berlin: Verlag Dr. Emil Ebering, 1935. Under the title: *Religiöse Bewegungen im Mittelalter: Unterscuchungen über die geschichtlichen Zusammenänge zwischen der Ketzerei, den Bettelorden und der religiösen Frauenbewegung im 12. und 13. Jahrhundert und über die geschichtlichen Grundlagen der deutschen Mystik: Anhang, Neue Beiträge zur Geschichte der religiösen Bewegungen im Mittelalter.* Darmstadt: Wissenschaftliche Buchgesellschaft and Hildesheim: Olms Verlagsbuchhandlung, 1961 [2nd rev.], 1977 [4th rev. and enl.].

Hall, Kim F. *Things of Darkness: Economies of Race and Gender in Early Modern England.* Ithaca, NY: Cornell University Press, 1995.

Hamilton, Elizabeth. *Héloïse.* London: Hodder & Stoughton, 1966; [1st US edn.]: Garden City, NY: Doubleday, 1967.

Harding, Wendy. "Medieval Women's Unwritten Discourse on Motherhood: A Reading of Two Fifteenth-Century Texts." *Women's Studies* 21 (1992): 197–209.

Haseldine, Julian, ed. *Friendship in Medieval Europe.* Stroud, Glos.: Sutton, 1999.

Hexter, Ralph J. *Ovid and Medieval Schooling: Studies in Medieval School Commentaries on Ovid's* Ars amatoria, Epistulae ex Ponto, *and* Epistulae heroidum. Münchener Beiträge zur Mediävistik und Renaissance-Forschung 38. Munich: Arbeo-Gesellschaft, 1986.

Huchet, Jean-Charles. "La voix d'Héloïse." *Romance Notes* 25 (1984–85): 271–87.

Hunt, Richard William, W. A. Pantin, and R. W. Southern, eds. *Studies in Medieval History Presented to Frederick Maurice Powicke.* Oxford: Clarendon Press, 1948; Rep.: Westport, CT: Greenwood Press, 1979.

Irvine, Martin. "Abelard and (Re)Writing the Male Body: Castration, Identity, and Remasculinization." In *Becoming Male.* Eds. Cohen and Wheeler. pp. 87–106.

———. "Heloise and the Gendering of the Literate Subject." In *Criticism and Dissent.* Ed. Copeland. pp. 87–114.

Jacobson, Howard. *Ovid's* Heroides. Princeton, NJ: Princeton University Press, 1974.

Jaeger, C. Stephen. *Ennobling Love: In Search of a Lost Sensibility.* The Middle Ages. Philadelphia, PA: University of Pennsylvania Press, 1999.

———. *The Envy of Angels: Cathedral Schools and Social Ideals in Medieval Europe, 950–1200.* The Middle Ages. Philadelphia, PA: University of Pennsylvania Press, 1994.

———. *The Origins of Courtliness: Civilizing Trends and the Formation of Courtly Ideals, 939–1210.* The Middle Ages. Philadelphia, PA: University of Pennsylvania Press, 1985, 1989.

———. "The Prologue to the *Historia calamitatum* and the 'Authenticity Question.'" *Euphorion: Zeitschrift für Literaturgeschichte* 74 (1980): 1–15.

Janson, Tore. *Prose Rhythm in Medieval Latin from the 9th to the 13th Century.* Studia Latina Stockholmiensia 20. Acta Universitatis Stockholmiensis. Stockholm: Almqvist & Wisksell International, 1975.

———. "Schools of Cursus in the Twelfth Century and the *Letters* of Heloise and Abelard." In *Retorica e poetica.* Eds. C. Leonardi and E. Menestò (Florence: Scandicci, 1989). pp. 171–200.

Jeudy, Colette. "Un Nouveau Manuscrit de la Correspondance d'Abélard et Héloïse." *Latomus* 50 (1991): 872–81.

Jianu, Ionel and C. Goldscheider. *Rodin.* The Great Sculptors. Paris: Arted, 1967, 1969, 1970, 1979. [Jianu appears as "Jianou" on title page]. [Originally in French]: *Rodin.* Collection Les Grandes sculpteurs. Paris: Arted, 1967, 1970; Paris: Arted—Éditions d'Art, 1971; [s.l.]: Branden Press, 1970.

Johnson, Penelope D. *Equal in Monastic Profession: Religious Women in Medieval France.* Women in Culture and Society. Chicago, IL: University of Chicago Press, 1991, 1993 [pbk.].

Jolivet, Jean, ed. *Abélard en son temps.* Actes du colloques international organisé à l'occasion du 9e centenaire de la naissance de Pierre Abélard, 14–19 mai 1979. Paris: Belles Lettres, 1981.

Jones, Nancy A. "By Woman's Tears Redeemed: Female Lament in St. Augustine's *Confessions* and the Correspondence of Abelard and Heloise." In *Sex and Gender in Medieval and Renaissance Text.* Eds. Gold, Miller, and Platter. pp. 15–39.

Kamuf, Peggy. *Fictions of Feminine Desire: Disclosures of Heloise.* Lincoln, NE: University of Nebraska Press, 1982.

Kauffman, Linda S. *Discourses of Desire: Gender, Genre, and Epistolary Fictions.* Ithaca, NY: Cornell University Press, 1986, 1988.

Kay, Sarah, and Miri Rubin, eds. *Framing Medieval Bodies.* Manchester, Lancs.: Manchester University Press, 1994, 1996; New York: St. Martin's Press, 1994.

Kearney, Eileen "Heloise: Inquiry and the *Sacra Pagina.*" In *Ambiguous Realities.* Eds. Levin and Watson. pp. 66–81.

King, Margaret L., and Albert Rabil, eds. and trans. *Her Immaculate Hand: Selected Works By and About the Women Humanists of Quattrocento Italy.* Medieval & Renaissance Texts & Studies 20. Binghamton, NY: Center for Medieval & Early Renaissance Studies, 1983; Binghamton, NY: Medieval & Renaissance Texts and Studies, 1992; Asheville, NC: Pegasus Press, 1997.

Kneepkens, C. H. "'Mulier Quae Damnavit, Salvavit': A Note on the Early Development of the *relatio simplex.*" *Vivarium* 14 (1976): 1–25.

Knowles, David. "Cistercians and Cluniacs: The Controversy Between St. Bernard and Peter the Venerable." In *The Historian and Character: And Other Essays by David Knowles.* Cambridge: Cambridge University Press, 1963, 1964. pp. 50–75.

Kristeva, Julia. *Powers of Horror: An Essay on Abjection.* Trans. Leon S. Roudiez. European Perspectives. New York: Columbia University Press, 1982. [Originally in French]: *Pouvoirs de l'horreur: essai sur l'abjection.* Collection Tel quel. Paris: Éditions de Seuil, 1980. In: Points 152. Paris: Éditions de Seuil, 1983.

Labalme, Patricia H., ed. *Beyond Their Sex: Learned Women of the European Past.* New York: New York University Press, 1980, 1984 [1st pbk.].

Lalanne, Ludovic. "Quelques doutes sur l'authenticité de la correspondance amoureuse d'Héloïse et Abélard." *La correspondance littéraire* 1 (1856): 27–33.

Landes, Richard Allen, and Thomas [F.] Head, eds. *The Peace of God: Social Violence and Religious Response in France Around the Year 1000.* Ithaca, NY: Cornell University Press, 1992.

Lanham, Carol Dana. "Freshman Composition in the Early Middle Ages: Epistolography and Rhetoric Before the *Ars Dictaminis.*" *Viator* 23 (1992): 115–34.

———. Salutatio *Formulas in Latin Letters to 1200: Syntax, Style, and Theory.* Münchener Beiträge zur Mediävistik und Renaissance-Forschung 22. Munich: Arbeo-Gesellschaft, 1975.

Lanham, Richard A. *A Handlist of Rhetorical Terms; A Guide for Students of English Literature.* Berkeley, CA: University of California Press, 1968, 1969 [pbk.], 1991 [2nd—no sub-title].

Latham, R. E. *Revised Medieval Latin Word-list from British and Irish Sources.* London: Oxford University Press [for the British Academy], 1965, 1973; [rep. with suppl.]: 1980, 1994. [Based on: *Medieval Latin Word-List from British and Irish Sources.* Eds. J. H. Baxter and C. Johnson. First pub. 1934.]

Latzke, Therese. "Die Carmina erotica der Ripollsammlung." *Mittellateinisches Jahrbuch* 10 (1975): 138–201.

———. "Zum 'Iudicium de calumnia molendini Brisesarte' und zu den vier Nonnenepisteln des Hilarius." *Mittellateinisches Jahrbuch* 16 (1981): 73–96.

Laurie, Helen C. R. "Cligès and the Legend of Abelard and Heloise." *Zeitschrift für Romanische Philologie* 107 (1991): 324–42.

———. "The 'Letters' of Abelard and Heloise: A Source for Chrétien de Troyes?" *Studi Medievali* 27 (1986): 123–46.

Lawrence, C. H. *Medieval Monasticism: Forms of Religious Life in Western Europe in the Middle Ages.* London: Longman Press, 1984, 1989 [2nd].

Leclercq, Jean. "'Ad ipsam sophiam Christum': Le témoignage monastique d'Abélard." *Revue d'ascétique et de mystique* 46 (1970): 161–81.

———. *The Love of Learning and the Desire for God: A Study of Monastic Culture.* Trans. Catharine Misrahi. New York: Fordham University Press, 1961; 1974 [2nd rev.]; 1982 [3rd]. London: SPCK—Society for the Promotion of Christian Knowledge, 1978 [2nd rev.]. [Originally in French]: *L'amour des lettres et le désir de Dieu: Initiation aux auteurs monastiques du Moyen Âge.* Paris, Éditions du Cerf, 1957; 1990 [3rd corr.]. Under the title: *Initiation aux auteurs monastiques du moyen age: l'amour des lettres & le désir de Dieu.* Paris: Les éditions du Cerf, 1963 [2nd corr.].

———. "Modern Psychology and the Interpretation of Medieval Texts." *Speculum* 48 (1973): 476–90.

———. "Profession according to the Rule of St Benedict." In *Rule and Life.* Ed. Pennington. pp. 117–49.

Leclercq, Jean, François Vandenbroucke, and Louis Bouyer. *The Spirituality of the Middle Ages.* Vol. 2 of: *A History of Christian Spirituality.* 3 vols. I: *The Spirituality of the New Testament and the Fathers* (1960). II: *The Spirituality of the Middle Ages* (1968). III: *Orthodox Spirituality and Protestant and Anglican Spirituality* (1969). London: Burns and Oates; New York: Seabury Press, 1960, 1963, 1968, 1969, 1977, 1982; New York: Desclee Co., 1963, 1968, 1969. [Originally in French]: *Histoire de la spiritualité chrétienne.* 3 vols. I: *La spiritualité du Nouveau Testament et des Pères.* II: *La spiritualité du Moyen Âge.* III: *La spiritualité orthodoxe et la spiritualité protestante et anglicane.* Paris: Aubier, 1960, 1961. Paris: Aubier-Montaigne, 1966 [rev. and aug.]

Le Goff, Jacques. *Les intellectuels au Moyen Âge.* Collections microcosme: Le Temps qui court 3. [Paris]: Éditions du Seuil, 1955, 1957, 1960, 1962, 1965, 1969, 1972, 1976, 1985 [detached from ser.].

Lekai, Louis Julius. *The Cistercians: Ideals and Reality.* [Kent, OH]: Kent State University Press, 1977.

Lemprière, John. *Lemprière's Classical Dictionary.* London: Bracken, 1994. [Numerous edn. and versions in several languages under various imprints and titles. This edn. is a rev. version of that first pub.: *Bibliotheca classica; or, A Classical Dictionary, Containing a Full Account of All the Proper Names Mentioned in Antient Authors: With Tables of Coins, Weights, and Measures, in Use Among the Greeks and Romans.* T. Cadell, 1788].

Levin, Carole, and Jeanie Watson, eds. *Ambiguous Realities: Women in the Middle Ages and Renaissance.* Detroit, MI: Wayne State University Press, 1987.

Lewis, C. T., and C. Short, eds. *A Latin Dictionary.* Oxford: Clarendon Press, 1933. [Numerous edn. and versions under various titles and imprints, most recently rev. and enlarged: Oxford: Clarendon Press, 1996. Founded on E. A. Andrews' edn. of William Freund's Latin-German lexicon].

Leyser, Henrietta. *Medieval Women: A Social History of Women in England, 450–1500.* London: Weidenfeld and Nicolson, 1995; New York: St. Martin's Press, 1995, 1998 [pbk. with new suppl. biblio.]; London: Phoenix Giant, 1996.

Little, Lester K. "Intellectual Training and Attitudes toward Reform, 1075–1150." In *Pierre Abélard–Pierre le Vénérable.* Eds. Louis, Jolivet, and Châtillon.

Little, Lester K., and Barbara H. Rosenwein, eds. *Debating the Middle Ages: Issues and Readings.* Oxford: Blackwell, 1998.

Loades, Judith, ed. *Monastic Studies: The Continuity of Tradition.* Bangor, Gwynedd: Headstart History, 1990.

Lobrichon, Guy. "The Chiaroscuro of Heresy: Early Eleventh-Century Aquitaine as Seen from Auxerre." In *The Peace of God.* Eds. Allen and Head. pp. 80–103.

Lochrie, Karma. *Margery Kempe and Translations of the Flesh.* New Cultural Studies. Philadelphia, PA: University of Pennsylvania Press, 1991.

Louis, René, Jean Jolivet, and Jean Châtillon, eds. *Pierre Abélard–Pierre le Vénérable: les courants philosophiques, littéraires et artistiques en occident au milieu du XIIe siècle. Abbaye de Cluny, 2 au 9 juillet 1972.* Proceedings of the International Collquium held at Cluny, 2–9 July 1972. Colloques internationaux du Centre national de la recherche scientifique 546. Paris: Éditions du Centre national de la recherche scientifique, 1975.

Louth, Andrew. "The Image of Heloise in English Literature." *Downside Review* 111 (1993): 45–64.

Luscombe, D[avid] E. "From Paris to the Paraclete: The Correspondence of Abelard and Heloise." *Proceedings of the British Academy* 74 (1988): 247–83.

———. "The Letters of Heloise and Abelard Since 'Cluny 1972.'" In *Petrus Abaelardus, (1079–1142): Person, Werk und Wirkung.* Eds. Thomas, Jolivet, Luscombe, and de Rijk. pp. 23–31.

———. "Monasticism in the Lives and Writings of Heloise and Abelard." In *Monastic Studies: The Continuity of Tradition.* Ed. Loades. pp. 1–11.

McCourt, Frank. *Angela's Ashes: A Memoir of Childhood.* London: HarperCollins, 1996 London: Flamingo, 1997, 1999. Under the title: *Angela's Ashes: A Memoir.* New York: Scribner, 1996; Rockland, MA: Wheeler Publishing, 1997 [large print]; New York: Simon & Schuster (A Touchstone Book), 1996, 1999. In: Bower Hill Braillists Foundation (Pittsburgh, PA) 5. New York: Scribner, 1996 [Braille].

McDonnell, Ernest W. *The Beguines and Beghards in Medieval Culture, with Special Emphasis on the Belgian Scene.* New Brunswick, NJ: Rutgers University Press, 1954. New York: Octagon Books, 1969 [rep. with author's middle name given in full].

McGregor, James H. "Ovid at School: From the Ninth to the Fifteenth Century." *Classical Folia* 32 (1978): 29.

McGuire, Brian Patrick. "The Cistercians and Friendship: An Opening to Women." In *Hidden Springs.* Eds. Nichols and Shank. pp. 171–200.

———. "The Cistercians and the Transformation of Monastic Friendships." *Analecta Cisterciensia* 37 (1981): 1–63.

———. *Friendship & Community: The Monastic Experience, 350–1250.* Cistercian Studies Series 95. Kalamazoo, MI: Cistercian Publications, 1988.

McLaughlin, Mary Martin. "Abelard as Autobiographer: The Motives and Meaning of His 'Story of Calamities.'" *Speculum* 42 (1967): 463–88.

———. "Peter Abelard and the Dignity of Women: Twelfth-Century 'Feminism' in Theory and Practice." In *Pierre Abélard–Pierre le Vénérable.* Eds. Louis, Jolivet, and Châtillon. pp. 287–334.

———. "Survivors and Surrogates: Children and Parents from the Ninth to the Thirteenth Centuries." In *The History of Childhood.* Ed. DeMause. pp. 101–81.

McLeod, Enid. *Héloïse: A Biography.* London: Chatto & Windus, 1938, 1971 [2nd].

McLeod, Glenda. "'Wholly guilty, wholly innocent': Self-Definition in Héloïse's Letters to Abélard." In *Dear Sister.* Eds. Cherewatuk and Wiethaus. pp. 64–86.

McNamer, Elizabeth Mary. *The Education of Heloise: Methods, Content, and Purpose of Learning in the Twelfth-Century* [*sic*]. Mediaeval Studies [Lewiston, NY] 8. Lewiston, NY: The Edwin Mellen Press, 1991; [s.l.]: Edwin Mellen Press, Canada, 1992.

Manitius, Max, and Paul Joachim Georg Lehman. *Von Ausbruch des Kirchestreites bis zum Ende des zwslften Jahrhunderts.* Vol. 3 of: *Geschichte der lateinischen Literatur des Mittelalter.* 3 vols. I: *Von Justinian bis zur Mitte des zehnten Jahrhunderts.* II: *Von der Mitte der zehnten Jahrhunderts bis zum Ausbruch des Kampfes zwischen Kirche und Staat.* III: *Von Ausbruch des Kirchestreites bis zum Ende des zwslften Jahrhunderts.* Handbuch der Altertumswissenschaft 9.2. Munich: C. H. Beck, 1911, 1923, 1931, 1964, 1965, 1973, 1974, 1976.

Mantello, F. A. C., and A. G. Rigg, eds. *Medieval Latin: An Introduction and Bibliographical Guide.* Washington, DC: Catholic University of America Press, 1996.

Marenbon, John. *The Philosophy of Peter Abelard.* Cambridge: Cambridge University Press, 1997, 1999.

Matter, E. Ann. *The Voice of My Beloved: The Song of Songs in Western Medieval Christianity.* The Middle Ages. Philadelphia, PA: University of Pennsylvania Press, 1990, 1992 [pbk.].

DeMause, Lloyd, ed. *The History of Childhood.* New York: Psychohistory Press, 1974; London: Souvenir Press, 1976; New York: P. Bedrick Books, 1988; London: Bellew, 1991. In: The Master Work Series. Northvale, NJ: J. Aronson, 1995 [pbk.]. And in: Harper Torchbooks. New York: Harper & Row, 1975.

Merlet, L. "Lettres d'Ives de Chartres et d'autres personnages de son temps." *Bibliothèque de l'École des Chartes* [Paris] 4.1 (1855): 443–71.

Mews, Constant J. "On Dating the Works of Peter Abelard." *Archives d'histoire doctrinale et littéraire du Moyen Âge* 52 (1985): 73–134.

———. "Orality, Literacy, and Authority in the Twelfth-Century Schools." *Exemplaria* 2.2 (Fall 1990): 475–500.

———. *Peter Abelard.* Authors of the Middle Ages 2.5: Historical and Religious Writers of the Latin West. [Printed together with 2.6]. Aldershot, Hants.: Variorum [Ashgate Publishing], 1995.

———. "Un lecteur de Jérôme au douzième siècle." In *Jérôme entre l'Occident et l'Orient.* Ed. Duval. pp. 31–44.

Minnis, A. J. *Medieval Theory of Authorship: Scholastic Literary Attitudes in the Later Middle Ages.* London: Scolar Press, 1984. [2nd]: Aldershot, Hants.: Wildwood, 1988; Aldershot, Hants.: Scolar, 1988; [2nd also in]: The Middle Ages. Philadelphia, PA: University of Pennsylvania Press, 1988.

Misch, Georg. *Geschichte der Autobiographie.* 4 vols. I: *Das Altertum* (1907). II: *Das Mittelalter. Die Frühzeit* (1955). III: *Das Mittelalter. Das Hochmittelalter im Anfang* (1955). IV: *Das Hochmittelalter in der Vollendung. Von der Renaissance bis zu den autobiographischen Hauptwerken des 18. und 19. Jahrhunderts* (1969). [Vol. 1]: Leipzig: B. G. Teubner, 1907, 1931 [2nd rev.]. [Vol. 2 and 3]: Frankfort: G. Schulte-Bulmke, 1955; Frankfort: Frankfort: Vittorio Klostermann, [3rd]: 1976, 1986, 1988; Bern: A. Francke, 1949. [Vols. 1–4]: Frankfort: G. Schulte-Bulmke, [3rd]: 1949; [4th]: 1967, 1974.

Monfrin, Jacques. "Le problème de l'authenticité de la correspondance d'Abélard et d'Héloïse." In *Pierre Abélard–Pierre le Vénérable.* Eds. Louis, Jolivet, and Châtillon. pp. 419–21.

Moore, R. I. "Literacy and the Making of Heresy 1000–1150." In *Heresy and Literacy, 1000–1530.* Eds. Biller and Hudson, pp. 19–37. Also in: *Debating the Middle Ages.* Eds. Little and Rosenwein. pp. 363–75.

———. *The Origins of European Dissent.* Oxford: Allen Lane, 1977; New York: St. Martin's Press, 1977; [rei. with corr.]: Oxford: Blackwell, 1985; New York: Blackwell, 1985. Now in:

Medieval Academy Reprints for Teaching 30. Toronto: University of Toronto Press [for: Medieval Academy of America], 1994.

Moore, R. I., trans. *The Birth of Popular Heresy.* Documents of Medieval History [London] 1. London: Edward Arnold, 1975; New York: St. Martin's Press, 1976. Now in: Medieval Academy Reprints for Teaching 33. Toronto: University of Toronto Press [for: Medieval Academy of America], 1995.

von Moos, Peter. *Consolatio: Studien zur mittellateinischen Trostliteratur über den Tod und zum Problem der christlichen Trauer.* I: *Darstellungsband.* II: *Anmerkungsband.* III: *Testimonienband.* IV: *Indexband.* 4 parts. Münstersche Mittelalter-Schriften 3.1–4. Munich: W. Fink, 1971–72.

———. "Heloise und Abaelard." In *Gefälscht!: Betrug in Politik, Literatur, Wissenschaft, Kunst und Musik.* Ed. Corino. pp. 150–61.

———. *Mittelalterforschung und Ideologiekritik: Der Gelehrtenstreit um Héloise.* Kritische Information 15. Munich: W. Fink, 1974.

———. "Palatini quaestio quasi peregrini: Ein gestiger Streitpunkt aus der Abelard-Heloise-Kontroverse nochmals überprüft." *Mittellateinisches Jahrbuch* 9 (1973): 124–58.

———. "*Post festum:* Was kommt nach der Authentizitätsdebatte über die Briefe Abaelards und Heloises?" In *Petrus Abaelardus, (1079–1142): Person, Werk und Wirkung.* Eds. Thomas, Jolivet, Luscombe, and de Rijk. pp. 75–100.

———. "Le Silence d'Héloïse et les idéologies modernes." In *Pierre Abélard–Pierre le Vénérable.* Eds. Louis, Jolivet, and Châtillon. pp. 425–68. In rev. form: "Die Bekehrung Heloises." *Mittelateinisches Jahrbuch* 11 (1976): 95–125.

Morris, Colin. *The Papal Monarchy: The Western Church from 1050 to 1250.* Oxford History of the Christian Church. Oxford: Clarendon Press, 1989; New York: Oxford University Press, 1989; Oxford: Clarendon Press, 1991.

Morrison, Karl. *Conversion and Text: The Cases of Augustine of Hippo, Herman-Judah, and Constantine Tsatsos.* Charlottesville, VA: University of Virginia Press, 1992. [Companion vol. to the author's *Understanding Conversion*].

———. *Understanding Conversion.* The Page-Barbour Lectures for 1990. Charlottesville, VA: University of Virginia Press, 1992. [Companion vol. to the author's *Conversion and Text: The Cases of Augustine of Hippo, Herman-Judah, and Constantine Tsatsos*].

Muldoon, James, ed. *Varieties of Religious Conversion in the Middle Ages.* Gainesville, FL: University of Florida Press, 1997.

Murphy, James Jerome. *Rhetoric in the Middle Ages: A History of Rhetorical Theory from Saint Augustine to the Renaissance.* Berkeley, CA: University of California Press, 1974, 1981 [pbk.].

Newman, Barbara. "Authority, Authenticity, and the Repression of Heloise." *Journal of Medieval and Renaissance Studies* 22 (1992): 121–57. Reprinted in her: *From Virile Woman to WomanChrist.* pp. 46–75.

———. "Flaws in the Golden Bowl: Gender and Spiritual Formation in the Twelfth Century." *Traditio* 45 (1989/90): 111–46. Reprinted in her: *From Virile Woman to WomanChrist.* pp. 19–45.

———. *From Virile Woman to WomanChrist: Studies in Medieval Religion and Literature.* The Middle Ages. Philadelphia, PA: University of Pennsylvania Press, 1995.

Newman, Martha G. *The Boundaries of Charity: Cistercian Culture and Ecclesiastical Reform, 1098–1180.* Figurae [Stanford, CA]. Stanford, CA: Stanford University Press, 1996.

Nichols, John A., and Lillian Thomas Shank, eds. *Medieval Religious Women.* 4 parts. I: *Distant Echoes.* II: *Peaceweavers.* IIIA and IIIB: *Hidden Springs: Cistercian Monastic Women.* Cistercian Studies Series 71–72, 113. The third part is also in: Medieval Religious Women 3. Kalamazoo, MI: Cistercian Publications, 1984, 1995.

Niermeyer, J. F. *Mediae Latintatis Lexicon Minus. A Medieval Latin-French/English Dictionary.* 2 vols. Leiden: E. J. Brill, 1954, 1959, 1960, 1961, 1967, 1976, 1984, 1993, 1997.

Norden, E. *Die Antike Kunstprosa vom VI. Jahrhundert v. Chr. bis in die Zeit der Renaissance.* 2 vols. Leipzig: B. G. Teubner, 1898, 1909, 1915, 1923, 1958, 1981, 1983. Stuttgart: B. G. Teubner, 1971, 1974. Darmstadt: Wissensch Buchgesellsch, 1974.

Nouvet, Claire. "La castration d'Abélard: impasse et substitution." *Poétique* 83 (1990): 259–80.

———. "The 'Discourse of the Whore': An Economy of Sacrifice." *Modern Language Notes* 105 (1990): 750–73.

The Oxford Classical Dictionary. [1st]: Ed. M[ax] Cary. Oxford: Clarendon Press, 1949, 1950, 1953, 1957, 1961, 1966, 1968. [2nd]: Eds. N. G. L. Hammond and H. H. Scullard. Oxford: Clarendon Press, 1970, 1972, 1977, 1984, 1991. [3rd]: Eds. Simon Hornblower and Antony Spawforth. Oxford: Clarendon Press, 1996.

Oxford Latin Dictionary. 8 vols. Ed. P. G. W. Glare. Oxford: Clarendon Press, 1968–92 [issued in parts, those pub. after 1973 ed. Glare]; [comb. edn.]: 1 vol. Oxford: Clarendon Press, 1983, 1990, 1996 [with corr.].

Parisse, Michel. *Les nonnes au Moyen Âge.* Des Français ensemble. Le Puy: C. Bonneton, 1983.

Parsons, John Carmi, and Bonnie Wheeler, eds. *Medieval Mothering.* The New Middle Ages 3. Garland Reference Library of the Humanities 1979. New York: Garland, 1996, 1999 [pbk.].

Partner, Nancy F. "No Sex, No Gender." *Speculum* 68 (1993): 419–43.

Payen, Jean-Charles. *Le Moyen Âge.* Paris: Arthaud, 1990 [2nd]. [New rev. in]: Histoire de la littérature française, GF Flammarion 957. Paris: GF Flammarion, 1997.

———. *Le motif du repentir dans la littérature français médiévale (des origines à 1230).* Publications romanes et françaises 98. Geneva: Droz, 1967.

Pennington, M. Basil, ed. *Rule and Life: An Interdisciplinary Symposium.* Cistercian Studies Series 12. Spencer, MA: Cistercian Publications, 1971; Shannon, Ire.: Irish University Press, 1971.

Pernoud, Régine. *Heloise and Abelard.* Trans. Peter Wiles. New York: Stein and Day; London: Collins, 1973. [Originally in French]: *Héloïse et Abélard.* Paris: A. Michel, 1970; [new edn.]: Paris: A. Michel, 1987. In: Bibliothèque de culture historique. [s.l.]: [s.n.], 1970 [1979?]; In: Le Livre de poche 5459. [Paris]: A. Michel, 1980.

Peters, Edward. *The Magician, the Witch, and the Law.* Sussex: The Harvester Press, 1978. In: The Middle Ages. Philadelphia, PA: University of Pennsylvania Press, 1978, 1992.

Philippides, Katerina. "Canace Misunderstood: Ovid's *Heroides* XI." *Mnemosyne: A Journal of Classical Studies* 49.4 [Series 4] (Sept. 1996): 426–39.

Polak, Emil J. *Medieval and Renaissance Letter Treatises and Form Letters.* I: *A Census of Manuscripts Found in Eastern Europe and the Former U.S.S.R.* II: *A Census of Manuscripts Found in Part of Western Europe, Japan, and the United States of America.* 2 vols. Davis Medieval Texts and Studies 8–9. Leiden: E. J. Brill, 1993–94.

Polheim, Karl. *Die lateinische Reimprosa.* Berlin: Weidmann, 1925; Rep.: 1963. Microfilm: Notre Dame, IN: University Libraries, University of Notre Dame, Apr. 1995—1 reel: 35mm.

Pontenay de Fontette, Micheline. *Les religieuses à l'âge classique de droit canonique: recherches sur les structures juridiques des branches féminines des Ordres.* Bibliothèque de la Société d'histoire ecclésiastique de la France. Paris: J. Vrin, 1967.

Porter, J. M. B. "Preacher of the First Crusade? Robert of Arbrissel After the Council of Clermont." In *From Clermont to Jerusalem.* Ed. Murray. pp. 43–53.

Powell, Morgan. *The Mirror and the Woman: Instruction for Religious Women and the Emergence of Vernacular Poetics 1120–1250.* 2 vols. Diss.: Princeton, NJ: Princeton University, 1997.

Power, Eileen Edna. *Medieval Women.* Ed. M. M. Postan. Cambridge: Cambridge University Press, 1975, 1997 [Canto edn.].

Quinn, Kenneth. *The Catullan Revolution.* Melbourne: Melbourne University Press, 1959; London: Cambridge University Press, 1959. [Rev. imp.]: Cambridge: Heffer, 1969; Ann Arbor Paperbacks. [Ann Arbor, MI]: University of Michigan Press, 1971. [2nd]: BCP Paperback Series. Bristol: Bristol Classical, 1999.

———. *Latin Explorations: Critical Studies in Roman Literature.* New York: Humanities Press; London: Routledge and Paul, 1963. London: Routledge and Kegan Paul, 1969 [2nd imp. with corr.].

Rabil, Albert, Jr. *Laura Cereta, Quattrocento Humanist.* Medieval & Renaissance Texts and Studies 3. Binghamton, NY: Center for Medieval & Renaissance Studies, 1981.

Raby, F. J. E. *A History of Christian-Latin Poetry From the Beginnings to the Close of the Middle Ages.* Oxford: Clarendon Press, 1927; [2nd]: 1953, 1966. Microfilm: [Cambridge, MA]: Harvard University Library Microreproduction Dept., [198-]—1 reel: 35 mm [1927 edn.]; New Haven, CT: filmed by Micrographic Systems of Conn. for New York University Libraries, Preservation Dept., New York, NY, 1988—1 reel: 35mm [1953, 2nd].

Racinet, Philippe. "L'implantation monastique dans la basse vallée de l'Oise au Moyen Âge." *Moyen Age* 95 (1989): 5–35.

Radice, Betty. "The French Scholar-Lover: Heloise." In *Medieval Women Writers.* Ed. Wilson. pp. 90–108.

Reed, Thomas L., Jr. *Middle English Debate Poetry and the Aesthetics of Irresolution.* Columbia, MO: University of Missouri Press, 1990.

de Ridder-Symoens, Hilde, ed. *Universities in the Middle Ages.* Vol. 1 of: *A History of the University in Europe.* 4 vols. Dir. Walter Rüegg. I: *Universities in the Middle Ages.* Ed. Hilde de Ridder-Symoens. (1992). II: *Universities in Early Modern Europe (1500–1800).* Ed. Hilde de Ridder-Symoens. (1996). III: *Universities in the Nineteenth and Early Twentieth Centuries (1800–1945).* Ed. Walter Rüegg. (In prepartion). IV: *Universities from 1945 to the Present.* Ed. Asa Briggs. (In prepartion). Cambridge: Cambridge University Press, 1992 [Vol. 1], 1996 [Vol. 2]. [Pub. simultaneaously in German as]: *Geschichte der Universität in Europa.* 4 vols. I: *Mittelalter.* (1993). II: *Von der Reformation zur Französischen Revolution (1500–1800).* (1993). III: *Vom 19. Jahrhundert zum Zweiten Weltkrieg (1800–1945).* (In prep.). IV: *Die Nachkriegzeit.* (In prep.). Munich: C. H. Beck, 1993.

Riessner, Claus. *Die "Magnae derivationes" des Uguccione da Pisa und ihre Bedeutung für die romanische Philologie.* Temi e testi 11. Rome: Edizioni di storia e letteratura, 1965.

Robertson, D. W., Jr. *Abelard and Heloise.* London: Purnell Book Services [in arrangement with Millington], 1972 [Book Club edn.]; [London]: Millington, 1974. In: Crosscurrents in World History. New York: Dial Press, 1972.

Robinson, I. S. "The *colores rhetorici* in the Investiture Contest." *Traditio* 32 (1976): 210–38.

Roserot, Alphonse. *Dictionnaire historique de la Champagne méridonale (Aube) des origines à 1790 avec des illustrations, des cartes et des tableaux généalogiques précédé d'une introduction sur l'histoire générale de cette région.* 3 vols. [Vols. 1–2]: Langres: Champenois, 1942 [500 copies]. [Vol. 3]: Troyes: Paton, 1948 [500 copies]; Angers: Éditions de l'Ouest, 1948 [500 copies]. Microfilm: Notre Dame, IN: University Libraries, University of Notre Dame, Feb. 1994—1 reel: 35mm. Rep. as: *Dictionnaire historique de la Champagne meridionale (Aube) des origines à 1790.* 3 vols. Marseille: Laffitte Reprints, 1983.

Rousselle, Aline. *Porneia: On Desire and the Body in Antiquity.* Trans. Felicia Pheasant. Family, Sexuality, and Social Relations in Past Times. Oxford: Blackwell, 1988; Cambridge, MA: Blackwell, 1993. [Detached from ser.]: New York: Barnes & Noble Books, 1996. [Originally in French]: *Porneia: de la maîstrise du corps à la privation sensorielle, Iie-IVe siècles de l'ère chrétienne.* Les Chemins de l'histoire. Paris: Presses universitaires de France, 1983.

Le Roy Ladurie, Emmanuel. *Montaillou: Cathars and Catholics in a French Village, 1294–1324.* London: Scolar, 1978. Harmondsworth: Penguin, 1980, 1981. As: A Peregrine Book. Harmondsworth: Penguin, 1984. [In the United States, under the title]: *Montaillou, the Promised Land of Error.* New York: G. Braziller, 1978. New York: Vintage Books, 1979. [Originally in French]: *Montaillou, village occitan de 1294 à 1324.* Bibliothèque des histoires. Paris: Gallimard, 1975. Now [rev. and corr.] in: Collection Folio/Histoire 9. Paris: Gallimard, 1982, 1985, 1991, 1998.

Rubner, Heinrich. *Untersuchungen zur Forstverfassung des mittelalterlichen Frankreichs.* Vierteljahrschrift für Sozial- und Wirtschaftsgeschichte, Beihefte 49. Wiesbaden: F. Steiner, 1965.

Ruys, Juanita Feros. *Genre, Gender and Authenticity: Reading Heloise in the Twentieth Century.* Diss.: Sydney, Australia: Department of English, University of Sydney, 1999.

———. "Role-Playing in the Letters of Heloise and Abelard." *Parergon* 11 (1993 [New Series]): 53–78.

Sanford, Eva Matthews. "The Use of Classical Latin Authors in the *Libri Manuales.*" *Transactions of the American Philological Association* 55 (1924): 190–248.

Schmeidler, Bernhard. "Abaelard und Heloise: eine geschichtlich-psychologische Studie." *Die Welt als Geschichte* 6 (1940): 93–123.

———. "Der Briefwechsel zwischen Abaelard und Heloise dennoch eine literarische Fiktion Abaelards." *Revue Bénédictine* 52 (1940): 85–95.

———. "Der Briefwechsel zwischen Abälard und Heloise als eine literarische Fiktion Abälards." *Zeitschrifte für Kirchengeschichte* 54 (1935): 323–38.

———. "Der Briefwechsel zwischen Abälard und Heloise eine Fälschung?" *Archivum für Kulturgeschichte* 11 (1913): 1–30.

Shahar, Shulamith. *Childhood in the Middle Ages.* London: Routledge, 1990, 1992 [new edn.]. [In Hebrew]: *Yaldut bi-Yeme-ha-benayim.* Tel-Aviv: Devir, 1990. [Title page verso: "Medieval Childhood"]. [In German]: *Kindheit im Mittelalter.* Munich: Artemis und Winkler, 1993.

———. *The Fourth Estate: A History of Women in the Middle Ages.* Trans. Chaya Galai. London: Methuen, 1983; Cambridge: Cambridge University Press, 1983; Rep.: London: Routledge, 1990. [In Hebrew]: *ha-Ma'amad ha-re'i: ha-ishah be-hevrat Yeme-ha-benayim.* Tel-Aviv: Devir, Bet ha-sefer le-historyah 'ash. ZalmAran, Universitat Tel-Aviv, 1982, 1990 [2nd]. [Title page verso: "The fourth order"]. [In German]: *Die Frau im Mittelalter.* Athenäum Faschenbücher 115. Frankfurt: Athenäum, 1988.

Silvestre, Hubert. "Héloïse et le témoignage du 'Carmen ad Astralabium'." *Revue d'histoire ecclésiastique* 83.3–4 (July–Dec. 1988): 635–60.

———. "Die Liebesgeschichte zwischen Abaelard und Heloise: der Anteil des Romans." In Teil 5 of: *Fälschungen im Mittelalter*, MGH 55, pp. 121–65.

Skinner, Mary. "Benedictine Life for Women in Central France, 850–1100: A Feminist Revival." In *Distant Echoes.* Eds. Nichols and Shank. pp. 87–113.

Smith, Jacqueline. "Robert of Arbrissel: *Procurator Mulierum.*" In *Medieval Women.* Ed. Baker. pp. 175–84. [Table of Contents lists as: "Robert of Arbrissel's relations with women"].

Souter, Alexander. *A Glossary of Later Latin to 600 A.D.* Oxford: Clarendon Press, 1949, [Rep. from corr. sheets of 1st]: 1957, 1959, 1964. New York: Oxford University Press, 1996 [special edn. for Sandpiper Books, Ltd.].

Southern, R. W. "Lanfranc of Bec and Berengar of Tours." In *Studies in Medieval History Presented to Frederick Maurice Powicke.* Eds. Hunt, Pantin, and Southern. pp. 27–483.

———. *Medieval Humanism and Other Studies.* Oxford: Blackwell, 1970; 1984 [pbk.]. As: A Torchbook Library Edition. New York: Harper & Row, 1970. pp. 86–104.

———. *Scholastic Humanism and the Unification of Europe.* Oxford: Blackwell, 1995, 1997 [pbk.]. [Vol. 1: *Foundations,* of a multi. vol. work, only vol. 1 has been pub.].

———. *Western Society and the Church in the Middle Ages.* The Pelican History of the Church 2. Harmondsworth: Penguin Books, 1970, 1972, 1978, 1979, 1981, 1985, 1990; London: Hodder and Stoughton, 1970, 1971; Grand Rapids, MI: W. B. Eerdmans, 1970.

Spitzer, Leo. *Leo Spitzer: Essays on Seventeenth-Century French Literature.* Ed. David Bellos. Cambridge Studies in French. Cambridge: Cambridge University Press, 1983.

———. "Les *Lettres portugaises.*" *Romanische Forschungen* 65 (1954): 94–135.

Staley, Lynn. *Margery Kempe's Dissenting Fictions.* University Park, PA: Pennsylvania State University Press, 1994.

von den Steinen, Wolfram. "Die Planctus Abaelards–Jephthas Tochter." *Mittellateinisches Jahrbuch* 4 (1967): 122–44.

Stelten, Leo F. *Dictionary of Ecclesiastical Latin: With an Appendix of Latin Expressions Defined and Clarified.* Peabody, MA: Hendrickson, 1995.

Sticca, Sandro. *Il Planctus Mariae nella tradizione drammatica del Medio Evo.* Sulmona: Teatro Club, 1984. [In English]: *The Planctus Mariae in the Dramatic Tradition of the Middle Ages.* Athens: University of Georgia Press, 1988.

Stock, Brian. *The Implications of Literacy: Written Language and Models of Interpretation in the Eleventh and Twelfth Centuries.* Princeton, NJ: Princeton University Press, 1983.

———. *Listening for the Text: On the Uses of the Past.* Parallax: Re-Visions of Culture and Society. Baltimore, MD: Johns Hopkins University Press, 1990. In: The Middle Ages. Philadelphia, PA: University of Pennsylvania Press, 1996 [pbk.].

———. "Literacy and Society in the Twelfth Century." In *The Spirit of the Court.* Eds. Burgess and Taylor, et al. pp. 1–4.

———. "Medieval Literacy, Linguistic Theory, and Social Organization." *New Literary History* 16 (1984): 13–29.

Stone, D. M. "Heloise: *la très sage abbesse* of the Paraclete." *Tjurunga* 37 (1989): 20–31.

Stowers, Stanley Kent. *Letter Writing in Greco-Roman Antiquity.* Library of Early Christianity 5. Philadelphia, PA: Westminister Press, 1986, 1989 [pbk.].

Sutherland, Christine Mason, and Rebecca J. Sutcliffe, eds. *The Changing Tradition: Women in the History of Rhetoric.* Calgary: University of Calgary Press, 1999.

Teetaert, Amédée. *La confession aux laïques dans l'église latine depuis le VIIIe jusqu'au XIVe siècle étude de théologie positive.* Universitas catholica lovaniensis. Dissertationes ad gradum magistri in Facultate theologica consequendum conscripté 17 [2nd Series]. Paris: J. Gabalda, 1926; Wetteren: J. de Meester et fils, 1926.

Temple, W. M. "The Weeping Rachel." *Medium Ævum* 28.2 (1959): 81–86.

Thomas, Rudolf, Jean Jolivet, David E. Luscombe, and Lambertus M. de Rijk, eds. *Petrus Abaelardus, (1079–1142): Person, Werk und Wirkung.* Proceedings of the International Colloquium held at Trier, 17–19 April 1979. Trierer Theologische Studien 38. Trier: Paulines-Verlag, 1980.

Thompson, Sally. "The Problem of the Cistercian Nuns in the Twelfth and Early Thirteenth Centuries." In *Medieval Women.* Ed. Baker. pp. 227–52.

———. *Women Religious: The Founding of English Nunneries After the Norman Conquest.* Oxford: Clarendon Press, 1991; New York: Oxford University Press, 1991.

Tinkler, John F. "Renaissance Humanism and the *genera eloquentiae.*" *Rhetorica* 5.3 (1987): 279–309.

Townsend, David and Andrew Taylor, eds. *The Tongue of the Fathers: Gender and Ideology in the Twelfth-Century Latin.* The Middle Ages. Philadelphia, PA: University of Pennsylvania Press, 1998.

Tunberg, Terence O. "Prose Styles and *cursus.*" In *Medieval Latin.* Eds. Mantello and Rigg. pp. 111–21.

Ulmer, Gregory L. "The Object of Post-Criticism." In *The Anti-Aesthetic.* Ed. Foster. pp. 83–110.

Venarde, Bruce L. "*Praesidentes Negotiis:* Abbesses as Managers in Twelfth-Century France." In *Portraits of Medieval and Renaissance Living.* Eds. Cohn and Epstein. pp. 189–205.

———. *Women's Monasticism and Medieval Society: Nunneries in France and England, 890–1215.* Ithaca, NY: Cornell University Press, 1997.

Verger, Jacques. "Abélard et les milieux sociaux de son temps." In *Abélard en son temps.* Ed. Jolivet. pp. 125–28.

Vickers, Brian. *In Defence of Rhetoric.* Oxford: Clarendon Press, 1988, 1989, 1997 [rep. with corr.].

———. "Leisure and Idleness in the Renaissance: The Ambivalence of *otium.*" *Renaissance Studies* 4.1 (1990): 1–37 and 4.2 (1990): 107–154.

Waddell, Chrysogonus. "Peter Abelard as Creator of Liturgical Texts." In *Petrus Abaelardus, (1079–1142): Person, Werk und Wirkung.* Eds. Thomas, Jolivet, Luscombe, and de Rijk. pp: 267–86.

———. "St. Bernard and the Cistercian Office at the Abbey of the Paraclete." *Studies in Medieval Cistercian History* 5 (1980): 76–121.

Waithe, Mary Ellen. "Heloise." In *Medieval, Renaissance and Enlightenment Women Philosophers, A.D. 500–1600.* Ed. Waithe.

Waithe, Mary Ellen, ed. *Medieval, Renaissance and Enlightenment Women Philosophers, A.D. 500–1600.* Vol. 2 of: *A History of Women Philosophers.* 4 vols. I: *Ancient Women Philosophers, 600 B.C.–500 A.D.* (1987). II: *Medieval, Renaissance and Enlightenment Women Philosophers, A.D. 500–1600* (1987). III: *Modern Women Philosophers, 1600–1900* (1989). IV: *Contemporary Women Philosophers, 1900–today* (1995). Boston, MA: Kluwer Academic Press, 1987, 1989, 1995.

Wakerley, Véronique. "Heloys: André or Andreas? A Problem of Authorship in MS Royal 16F II in the British Museum Library." *Nottingham French Studies* 35 (1996): 18–26.

Waldman, T. "Abbot Suger and the Nuns of Argenteuil." *Traditio* 41 (1985): 239–72.

Ward, John O. "After Rome: Medieval Epic." In *Roman Epic.* Ed. Boyle. pp. 261–93.

———. "The *Catena* Commentaries on the Rhetoric of Cicero and Their Implications for the Development of a Teaching Tradition in Rhetoric." *Studies in Medieval and Renaissance Teaching* 6.2 (1998): 79–95.

———. *Ciceronian Rhetoric in Treatise, Scholion, and Commentary.* Typologie des Sources du Moyen Âge Occidental 58. Turnhout: Brepols, 1995.

———. "Some Principles of Rhetorical Historiography in the Twelfth Century." In *Classical Rhetoric and Medieval Historiography.* Ed. Breisach. pp. 103–165.

———. "The First Crusade as Disaster: Apocalypticism and the Genesis of the Crusading Movement." In *Medieval Studies in Honour of Avrom Saltman.* Eds. Albert, Friedman, and Schwarzfuchs. pp. 253–92.

———. "From Marginal Gloss to *catena* Commentary: The Eleventh-Century Origins of a Rhetorical Teaching Tradition in the Medieval West." *Parergon* 13.2 (1996): 109–20.

———. "Magic and Rhetoric from Antiquity to the Renaissance: Some Ruminations." *Rhetorica* 6.1 (1988): 57–118.

———. "Quintilian and the Rhetorical Revolution of the Middle Ages." *Rhetorica* 13.3 (1995): 231–84.

———. "Rhetoric in the Faculty of Arts at the Universities of Paris and Oxford in the Middle Ages: A Summary of the Evidence." *Archivum Latinitatis Medii Aevi* [Union Académique Internationale: Bulletin du Cange] 54 (1996): 159–232.

———. "Rhetoric, Truth, and Literacy in the Renaissance of the Twelfth Century." In *Oral and Written Communication.* Ed. Enos. pp. 126–57.

———. "Women and Latin Rhetoric from Hrotsvit to Hildegard." In *The Changing Tradition.* Eds. Sutherland and Sutcliffe. pp. 121–32.

Ward, J[ohn] O., and Francesca C. Bussey, eds. *Worshipping Women: Misogyny and Mysticism in the Middle Ages: Six Essays with an Introduction and a Note on the Ruthwell Cross.* Sydney Studies in History 7. Sydney: Department of History, Sydney University [University Printing Services], 1997.

Weingart, Richard E. *The Logic of Divine Love: A Critical Analysis of the Soteriology of Peter Abailard.* Oxford: Clarendon Press, 1970.

Werner, Jakob. *Beiträge zur Kunde der lateinischen Literatur des Mittelalters.* 2nd ed. with an enl. app. Aarau: H. H. Sauerländer, 1905; Rep.: Hildesheim & New York: G. Olms, 1979.

Wetherbee, Winthrop. *Platonism and Poetry in the Twelfth Century: The Literary Influence of the School of Chartres.* Princeton, NJ: Princeton University Press, 1972.

Wheeler, Bonnie. "Origenary Fantasies: Abelard's Castration and Confession." In *Becoming Male.* Eds. Cohen and Wheeler. pp. 107–28.

Wiesen, David S. *St. Jerome as a Satirist: A Study in Christian Latin Thought and Letters.* Cornell Studies in Classical Philology 34. Ithaca, NY: Cornell University Press, 1964.

Williams, Paul L. *The Moral Philosophy of Peter Abelard.* Lanham, MD: University Press of America, 1980.

Wilson, Katharina M., ed. *Medieval Women Writers.* Manchester, Lancs.: Manchester University Press, 1984; Athens, GA: University of Georgia Press, 1984.

Wogan-Browne, Jocelyn. "Chaste Bodies: Frames and Experiences." In *Framing Medieval Bodies.* Eds. Kay and Rubin. pp. 24–42.

Wood, Charles T. "The Doctors' Dilemma: Sin, Salvation, and the Menstrual Cycle in Medieval Thought." *Speculum* 56 (1981): 710–27.

Worstbrock, Franz Josef, Monika Klaes, and Jutta Lütten. *Repertorium der Artes dictandi des Mittelalters.* Münstersche Mittelalter-Schriften 66. Munich: W. Fink, 1992.

Worthington, Marjorie Muir. *The Immortal Lovers: Héloise and Abélard.* Garden City, NY: Doubleday, 1960; London: R. Hale, 1962.

Zumthor, Paul. "Héloïse et Abélard." *Revue des sciences humaines* 91 (1958): 313–32.

INDEX OF PROPER NAMES APPEARING IN TEXT